Logical Foundations
of
Functional Programming

EDITED BY

Gérard Huet
INRIA Rocquencourt

Addison-Wesley Publishing Company
Reading, Massachusetts • Menlo Park, California • New York
Don Mills, Ontario • Wokingham, England • Amsterdam • Bonn
Sydney • Singapore • Tokyo • Madrid • San Juan

This book is in the University of Texas at Austin Year of Programming Series.

Library of Congress Cataloging-in-Publication Data

Logical foundations of functional programming / edited by Gérard Huet.
p. cm. -- (The UT year of programming series)
Includes bibliographical references.
ISBN 0-201-17234-8
1. Functional programming (Computer science) I. Huet, Gérard.
II. Series.
QA76.62.L64 1990
005.1'1--dc20 89-17772
CIP

Reproduced by Addison-Wesley from camera-ready copy supplied by the series editor.

ABCDEFGHIJ-MA-943210

The UT Year of Programming Series

Series editor: HAMILTON RICHARDS JR. The University of Texas at Austin

Developments in Concurrency and Communication
Editor: C. A. R. HOARE Oxford University

Logical Foundations of Functional Programming
Editor: GERARD HUET INRIA Rocquencourt

Research Topics in Functional Programming
Editor: DAVID TURNER University of Kent

Formal Development of Programs and Proofs
Editor: EDSGER W. DIJKSTRA The University of Texas at Austin

The UT Year of Programming Series

The design for the books was commissioned by the publisher, Addison-Wesley. The designer was Jean Hammond, and the design was transformed into a LaTeX style specification by William H. Miner Jr. of TeX*niques* in Austin, Texas. The book was composed in LaTeX, primarily by the UT Year of Programming staff —Suzanne Kain Rhoads, Ana M. Hernandez, and Hamilton Richards Jr.— using Macintosh[1] SE personal computers, but also by several authors who supplied their manuscripts as TeX[2] or LaTeX source files. The Macintosh implementation of TeX —TeXTURES— is a product of Blue Sky Research of Portland, Oregon. Illustrations were redrawn for the book using Cricket Draw.[3] Draft versions of the manuscript were printed on an Apple[4] LaserWriter II NTX printer, and the final copy was produced on a Linotronic 100[5] by Publishing Experts of Austin.

The typeface in which the book is set is Lucida,[6] a product of Adobe Systems Incorporated, whose permission to use a beta version of the Lucida Math fonts is gratefully acknowledged; a few additional PostScript characters were created using Fontographer.[7] Lucida was installed in LaTeX and TeXTURES by Buff Miner and by David Mallis of Publishing Experts; the value of their dedication and expertise is beyond calculation.

The publisher's vital assistance and patient encouragement were personified by Peter S. Gordon (Publishing Partner for Computer Science), Helen M. Goldstein (Assistant Editor), Helen M. Wythe (Production Supervisor), Mona Zeftel (Electronic Production Consultant), and Lorraine Ferrier (Copy Editor).

---

1. Macintosh is a trademark of Apple Computer, Inc.
2. TeX is a trademark of the American Mathematical Society.
3. Cricket Draw is a trademark of Cricket Software, Inc.
4. Apple and LaserWriter are registered trademarks of Apple Computer, Inc.
5. Linotronic 100 is a trademark of Allied Corporation.
6. Lucida is a registered trademark of Bigelow & Holmes.
7. Fontographer is a registered trademark of Altsys Corporation.

Contents

PART II. Polymorphic lambda-calculus

PART III. Topics in constructive type theory

Foreword

This volume is a product of the 1987 University of Texas Year of Programming ("YoP"), an initiative of UT-Austin's Department of Computer Sciences underwritten by grants from Lockheed/Austin, an anonymous donor, and —principally— the U. S. Office of Naval Research.[1]

The Year of Programming's general objectives were

> to advance the art and science of programming by bringing together leading computing scientists for discussions and collaboration, and
>
> to disseminate among leading practitioners the best of what is known — and being discovered— about the theory and practice of programming.

These objectives grew out of the original proposal's statement of purpose:

> Programming includes all aspects of creating an executable representation of a problem [solution]... from mathematical formulation to representation of an algorithm [for a] specific architecture.... The Year of

1. under Contract N00014–86–K–0763

> Programming will... address... the conversion of programming into a mathematical... discipline.

Almost from the outset, it was agreed that the Year of Programming would make its greatest contribution by steering away from topics and formats already well addressed by industrial concerns, government agencies, and the technical societies. Hence it was decided to leave such topics as programming psychology, sociology, and management to entities better qualified to deal with them, and to concentrate on those aspects of programming most amenable to scientific treatment.

As planning progressed, the YoP developed mainly into a series of Programming Institutes. Although each institute focused on a different sector of computing's scientific frontier, all proceeded from a conviction that good programming is the art and science of keeping things simple, and that the conversion of programming from a craft into a mathematical discipline requires an unorthodox type of mathematics in which the traditional distinction between "pure" and "applied" need not appear.

Each institute was organized by a scientific director recruited for his contributions to the art and science of programming or to the mathematics that it requires. Each director in turn enlisted a few colleagues —between four and a dozen or so— to assist him in discussing, refining, and presenting their school of thought. Over a period of one or two weeks, each institute team presented tutorials, research papers, and public lectures, and engaged in panel discussions and workshops. The institutes' audiences numbered from 30 to over 100, and converged on Austin from many parts of North America and Europe.

The selection criterion was wide enough to admit a broad variety of approaches, and many institute topics were considered. From a welter of conflicting schedules and commitments finally emerged six Programming Institutes, whose scientific directors and topics were as follows:

1. C. A. R. Hoare, Oxford University (visiting UT Austin for the academic year 1986–87). *Concurrent Programming*, February 23–March 6.

2. David Gries, Cornell University. *Encapsulation, Modularization, and Reusability*, April 1–10.

3. Gérard Huet, INRIA. *Logical Foundations of Functional Programming*, June 8–12.

4. Michael J. C. Gordon, Cambridge University, and Warren A. Hunt Jr., University of Texas, Austin (co-directors). *Formal Specification and Verification of Hardware*, July 8–17.

5. David A. Turner, University of Kent, Canterbury, UK. *Declarative Programming*, August 24–29.
6. Edsger W. Dijkstra, University of Texas, Austin. *Formal Development of Programs and Proofs*, October 26–30.

The volume you hold in your hands is a product of the third Programming Institute. It is not a proceedings in the usual sense, for it is not a mere collection of materials brought to the Institute by its participants. Instead, it attempts to capture the essence of the institute as seen after the fact —and after some reflection— by its principal participants. Some of the articles do indeed closely resemble their authors' presentations in Austin; others were not presented at all, but are included here as indispensable background material. Still others represent work that was carried out either at the institute or as a result of it.

Several of the chapters in this volume have been published, or will soon be published, elsewhere. The authors and editors of this volume express their appreciation to their publishers —Academic Press,Inc., Springer-Verlag, Elsevier Science Publishers B. V., and ACM— for permission to include these chapters (individual acknowledgments appear on the chapters' opening pages).

Whatever success YoP has achieved reflects primarily the caliber and dedication to excellence of the many computing scientists who contributed as scientific directors, lecturers, workshop participants, and authors. Enlisting such dedicated colleagues to serve as scientific directors was mainly the achievement of the YoP executive subcommittee's three leaders —James C. Browne, Edsger W. Dijkstra, and C. A. R. Hoare. Their task was greatly eased by the resources put at YoP's disposal by its sponsors, which made it possible for YoP to attract the very best scientific talent in the field; personifying the sponsors' support and encouragement were Charles Holland and Andre van Tilborg at the Office of Naval Research, and Stephen Sherman at Lockheed. Finally, the YoP Management Committee deserves great credit for its guidance, and for much sage advice and wise counsel, from YoP's earliest days.

Hamilton Richards Jr.

Preface

The YoP Institute on Logical Foundations originated in the Fall of 1986 at the suggestion by Tony Hoare to present during the University of Texas Year of Programming the current research developments in "Type, Domain, and Category Theories in Programming". I gratefully accepted this opportunity to present recent research results in a fast developing area of theoretical computer science. I decided to shift the emphasis slightly by omitting domain theory, a more well-established area for which a substantial amount of tutorial material already exists, and by toning down category theory, at least in the title, in order not to discourage practically minded computer scientists with too much abstract intellectual terrorism. I replaced "Type" by "Logical Foundation", since one of the dominant themes of this research is the isomorphism between logical propositions and types, and I emphasized the potential application of the theory to the design and implementation of functional programming languages, a topic which we are pursuing eagerly in our group at INRIA.

Knowing from experience that it is hard to sustain continued interest in lengthy seminars, and that people in our profession tend to be generally busy, I decided to have the whole seminar concentrated in one week. Considering the amount of material presented during the Institute this was considered slightly crazy, but both the speakers and the attendants of the Institute survived the experience, and seem to have kept rather pleasant memories of the happening over all.

The hard thing was to give food to the thoughts of the advanced researchers of the domain, by inviting research leaders to present their latest developments, without hopelessly losing the beginners. Accordingly, the week was partitioned between a three-day tutorial on functional programming and type theory, and a two-day more advanced research seminar, for which the tutorial was preparation.

The research seminar was centered on two topics. The first one, linear logic, is a fine-grained logic which is proposed by J. Y. Girard as a foundation for parallel computation. This is a promising research topic for computer science, since it gives new insights on the formalization of parallelism. It seemed a good idea to invite Girard to give an extensive seminar on the present state of development of the theory, together with material on his previous work on qualitative domains and coherent spaces, which are general semantic tools.

The other topic of the seminar could be called "constructive semantics". The idea is to relate closely semantic modeling and computability, in order to understand how to use semantic tools in the design of correct programs. The general methodology is to design inference systems for type theories. Semantic models (often inspired from category theory) are used to show the consistency of the rules and to give guidelines on how to build such inference systems. The development of proofs in the type theory should be amenable to program extraction. The program is thus seen as the information contents in a development which mixes constructive and abstract reasoning. The lecturers of the seminar were Susumu Hayashi from Kyoto University, Albert Meyer from MIT, John Mitchell, then from AT&T Bell Laboratories and now at Stanford University, John Reynolds from Carnegie Mellon University, and André Scedrov from the University of Pennsylvania.

The tutorial was taught by Guy Cousineau, from Laboratoire d'Informatique at Ecole Normale Supérieure and University Paris 7, and myself. We surveyed category theory, λ-calculus, natural deduction, the propositions-as-types principle, and type theory. These topics were motivated by applying them to the design and implementation of polymorphic, statically scoped and typed, functional programming languages, exemplified by ML. This course was illustrated by our implementation CAML, i.e., ML implemented on the Categorical Abstract Machine. The CAML implementation was available for participants in the Institute to experiment with.

This volume is not a faithful proceedings from the YoP Institute. First of all, the documents pertaining to linear logic are not included. This was done partly because otherwise it would not have been possible to make a single volume, partly because articles that had already appeared in journal form would have had to be typeset again, and partly because this is a self-contained topic which merits a comprehensive treatment of its own. We refer the reader to Girard's article in *Theoretical Computer Science* (special issue 50-1) for the state of the art at the end of 1986.

The volume is organized in three parts. The first part concerns CAML: the theory linking categorical combinators and λ-calculus, its application to the design of the Categorical Abstract Machine, and finally an article by A. Suárez, the chief implementor of CAML, concerning the compilation of ML on the CAM.

The second part concerns the topic of polymorphic λ-calculus, an extension of the polymorphism present in ML to full type quantification. This formalism was first proposed and studied by J. Y. Girard in the context of proof theory, and independently proposed by J. Reynolds as a framework for parametric polymorphism in programming languages. This topic emerged at the Institute as one of the most active research areas, and the nine chapters appearing in this part are a selection of recent research papers.

The third part contains a survey of type theory evolved from my lecture notes in the tutorial, together with four research papers on the general area I call "constructive semantics". This part does not have as strong a uniting theme as the first two, but it represents state-of-the-art research on type theory and its application to the synthesis of verified programs.

We do not pretend to cover the area completely in this volume. The most notable omissions are, concerning functional programming languages, lazy languages executed on graph machines, such as MIRANDA, and, concerning type theory, the predicative calculi such as Martin-Löf's intuitionistic type theory. The first topic should be adequately covered by the proceedings of the YoP Institute on Declarative Programming, edited by D. A. Turner, which is to appear in the same series as this volume. For the second topic, we refer the reader to the monograph by P. Martin-Löf "Intuitionistic Type Theory" (*Studies in Proof Theory,* Bibliopolis, 1984), and to the book by Constable et al., *Implementing Mathematics with the NUPRL system,* (Prentice Hall, 1986). A survey by the Göteborg research group is also in preparation.

I would like to thank all the people who helped in the creation and organization of this Institute, as well as in the preparation of this volume. First Tony Hoare, who was not only our godfather, but also one of the most active participants. Ham Richards was the real organizer of the happening, and it is a pleasure to acknowledge his extreme efficiency and personal commitment. He was able to solve any problem that arose, no matter how late or seemingly entangled the situation was. Thanks to the University of Texas, who sponsored the whole YoP and provided workstations and system help on University facilities for the practically minded participants. Thanks to Randy Pollack, who helped the people brave enough to try CAML programming. Thanks to the Driskill Hotel, who provided superb facilities, and especially their grandiose ballroom. Thanks to all the speakers, who delivered their lectures under the added pressure of video recording. Thanks to A. Suárez and T. Coquand, who wrote papers specially for this volume. Thanks to John Gray, Walter Hill, Richard Kieburtz and John Lipton, who wrote helpful reviews for this volume. Thanks finally to all the participants who interacted in this memorable gathering.

Gérard Huet

Part I

CAML: The Theory, the Machine, and the Language

Introduction to Part I

1

Guy Cousineau
Ecole Normale Supérieure

This part of the book describes in some detail how it is possible to specify and realize a functional programming language implementation using the translation from λ-calculus to cartesian closed categories as a compilation paradigm. It is therefore far from being an exhaustive presentation of implementation techniques for functional languages, and the reader might refer to [1, 3] to know more about this subject.

The categorical approach given here furnishes a theoretical foundation for environment-based implementations, and its interest lies in the fact that it describes implementations down to the level of machine instructions in a single unifying framework. Moreover, it is an effective way of implementing functional languages and is used, exactly as it is described here, in the implementation of the CAML language [2].

1 Functional Programming Languages

We should first say what we mean by "functional" when we talk about programming languages since there is no general agreement on this point. We consider here that a language can be termed functional if functions are *first-class values,* i.e., that there are expressions in the language to denote these values, that variables are bound to these values in just the same way as they are bound to basic values, and that these values can be taken as arguments or obtained as results of other functions without restrictions. In fact, this amounts to saying that there exists in the language some construct *fun* $x \rightarrow e$ denoting the function yielding e as result for argument x and some general application construct by which a functional value can be applied to some argument. In other words, functional languages are those that contain λ-calculus as a sublanguage.

1.1 History

The ancestor of all functional programming languages seems to be ISWIM (If you See What I Mean) proposed more than twenty years ago by J. Landin. ISWIM, which consisted basically of λ-calculus augmented with conditionals and recursive definitions, constitutes the kernel of today's well known functional languages such as Standard ML and Miranda. The main additions since ISWIM have been polymorphic type systems (ML) and also data types with constructors and function invocation by pattern-matching (Hope and Standard ML).

There are in fact two schools in functional programming language design, one more pragmatic and the second more purist. To the first one belongs the ML family of functional languages which has been initiated by R. Milner in view of a specific application, the LCF proof assistant. Here the emphasis was not on pure language design but on the possibility to effectively use a functional programming language for describing mathematical theories and programming complex proof strategies. To achieve this goal, it has seemed necessary to adopt features such as call-by-value evaluation, exceptions, and even updatable values, which are certainly shocking from the purist's point of view.

The purist school is represented by D. Turner and the SASL-KRC-Miranda family of functional languages. Here the emphasis is on promoting a totally new style of programming that insists on referential transparency and prohibits in the programming activity any reference to notions of state or sequencing. This purist point of view, though more difficult to put into use on present-day computers, is supposed to be better adapted for execution on the massively parallel computers of tomorrow.

1.2 *Implementation Techniques*

The basic problem for functional-language implementations is how to represent functional values. A function text (or a function code obtained by standard compiling techniques) is not sufficient since functions can refer in their text to free variables that may no longer exist in the current environment when the function is applied to an argument. A possible answer to the problem is to represent functional values as a function code plus an environment that contains the values of free variables. This is the approach proposed by Landin with the SECD machine, and we shall see that it corresponds theoretically to a categorical point of view. This environment approach with various optimizations is used in implementations of ML and also in Lisp-like functional languages such as Scheme and T.

A different approach is to abandon completely the traditional way of compiling functions and to replace it with an execution model based on rewriting. Here the problem of free variables also occurs, but it can be solved by a technique called *λ-lifting* that replaces arbitrary functional expressions with combinator definitions that are first-order rewrite rules. In this approach, functional values are just formal terms waiting to be inserted into an application context in order to be rewritten. This technique is used in most pure functional-language implementations and is described in [3].

2 *The Development of CAML*

The development of CAML has taken place in the Formel Project, created and animated at INRIA by Gérard Huet, now a joint project between INRIA and ENS (Ecole Normale Supérieure). The long-range goals of this project concern automatic theorem proving and advanced programming environments in which programs could be developed consistently with their proofs. The research activity of the project, which is reflected in the content of the present volume, is divided between the calculus of constructions, which is a powerful formalism for developing mathematical theories in a constructive way, and the functional programming language CAML, which is used in all the programming activities of the project.

The Formel Project was strongly influenced by the experience of the LCF Project, for which R. Milner had designed the ML language to be used both as a meta-language and as an implementation language for the LCF proof assistant. When the project started (around 1981), we had no intention to develop our own functional language implementation; our plan was to use some existing implementation of ML with some adaptation to our needs. Two facts motivated us to change this plan and start a new implementation. The first one was that some of us had proposed a new implementation scheme for functional languages based on the so-called Categorical Abstract Machine (CAM) that we wanted to try in a full-scale implementation. The second motivation was that at the same time, Robin Milner made his proposal for Standard ML, which improved original ML on many points. The desire to have an ML incorporating the new features brought an extra motivation for a new implementation based on the CAM, and that is how CAML was born, reflecting in its name the reasons for its existence.

The ideas underlying the design of the categorical abstract machine came from Pierre-Louis Curien, who had worked for a long time on cartesian closed categories as models of functional programming languages and who had used concrete equational presentations of cartesian closed categories to describe the evaluation of the language CDS. The idea to use the intertranslation between λ-calculus and cartesian closed categories (known since the work of Lambek) as a compiling paradigm for functional languages evolved into the design of the categorical abstract machine when it was realized (by G. Cousineau and P-L. Curien) that the categorical combinators were not merely abstract objects that could be executed through rewriting but that they could be considered as real machine instructions.

The development of CAML was originally the work of Ascánder Suárez, with decisive contributions from Michel Mauny and Pierre Weis. Other important contributors are Maria-Virginia Aponte, Francis Dupont, Alain Laville, and Didier Remy.

References

[1] Cardelli, L. "The Amber Machine." In *Combinators and Functional Programming Languages* (Proceedings, 1985), G. Cousineau, P.-L. Curien, and B. Robinet, eds. Lecture Notes in Computer Science, vol. 242. Springer-Verlag, Berlin, 1986.

[2] Cousineau, G. and Huet, G. "The CAML Primer." Technical report, Projet Formel, INRIA-ENS. Version 2.5, Dec. 1987.

[3] Peyton-Jones, S. L. *The Implementation of Functional Languages.* Prentice-Hall, Hemel Hempstead, U.K., 1987.

Cartesian Closed Categories and Lambda-Calculus

2

Gérard Huet
INRIA Roquencourt

The purpose of these notes is to propose an equational framework for the formalization, and ultimately the mechanization, of categorical reasoning. This framework is explained by way of example in the axiomatization of cartesian closed categories. The relationship with intuitionistic sequent calculus and lambda calculus is explained.

1 *The Equational Nature of Category Theory*

Category theory reasoning proves equality of arrow compositions, as determined by diagrams. The corresponding equality is given in the model, i.e., in the category under consideration. But the proofs do not appeal to any particular property of the equality relation, such as extensionality. All we assume is that equality is a congruence with respect to the arrow operators.

However, we are dealing not with simple homogeneous equational theories but with typed theories. For instance, every arrow is equipped with its type $f : A \to B$. Here A and B are expressions denoting objects. These expressions are formed in turn by functorial operations and constants representing distinguished objects. The object terms can be considered untyped only within the context of one category. As soon as several categories are concerned, we must type the objects as well, with sorts representing categories. We thus have implicitly two levels of type structure.

The main difference between typed theories and untyped ones is that in untyped (homogeneous) theories one usually assumes the domain of discourse to be nonempty. For instance, a first-order model has a nonempty carrier. Thus a variable always denotes something. In typed theories one does not usually make this restriction. Thus we do not want to impose the Hom-set $A \to B$ to be always nonempty for every A and B in the category, in the same way that we want to consider partial orderings.

This has an unfortunate consequence: The law of substitution of equals for equals does not hold whenever one replaces an expression containing a variable universally quantified over an empty domain with an expression not containing this variable, since we replace something which does not denote with something which may denote. For instance, consider the signature $H : A \to B$, $T : B$, $F : B$, and the equations $H(x) = T$ and $H(x) = F$. These equations are valid in the model where A is the empty set, H is the empty function, and B is a set of two elements $\{0, 1\}$, with T interpreted as 1 and F interpreted as 0. In this model we *do not* have $T = F$. We shall have to keep this problem in mind in the following.

1.1 *The General Formalism*

We have thus a formalism with four levels. At the first level, we have the alphabet of categories $\mathbf{Cat} = \{\mathbf{A}, \ldots, \mathbf{Z}\}$. At the second level, we have the alphabet of object operators. Every category is defined over an object alphabet Φ of operators given with an arity. Φ is where the (internal) functors live. We then form *sequents* by pairs of terms $M \to N$, with $M, N \in \mathbf{T}(\Phi, V)$. V is a set of variables denoting arbitrary objects of the category. At the third level we have the alphabet Σ of arrow operators. An operator from Σ is given as an *inference rule* of the form:

$$S_1, \ldots, S_n \vdash S \ ,$$

where the S_i's and S are sequents. Such an operator is *polymorphic* over the free variables of the S_i's and S, which are supposed to be universally quantified over the inference rule. Such operators are familiar from logic, either as schematic inference rules, or as (definite) Horn clauses. Of course the arrows with domain M and codomain N are represented as terms over $\mathbf{T}(\Sigma, F)$ of type $M \to N$. Here F is a set of arrow variables, indexed by sequents $A \to B$. Finally, at the fourth level we have the *proofs* of arrow equalities. The alphabet consists of a set $\mathcal{R}$ of conditional rules of the form:

$$f_1 =_{S_1} g_1, \ldots, f_n =_{S_n} g_n \models f =_S g \ .$$

Here the f's and g are arrow expressions of type S, and similarly for the f_i's and g_i's. All object and arrow variables appearing in the rule are supposed to be universally quantified in front of the rule.

1.2 A *Simplified Formalism*

From now on, we shall assume that we are in one category of discourse which is left implicit. We shall therefore deal only with the last three levels. Furthermore, we shall assume that the only proof rules are:

$$\mathit{Refl}: \ f =_{A \to B} f \ ,$$

$$\mathit{Trans}: \ f =_{A \to B} g \ , \ g =_{A \to B} h \models f =_{A \to B} h \ ,$$

$$\mathit{Sym}: \ f =_{A \to B} g \models f =_{A \to B} g \ ,$$

together with the rules stating that = is a congruence with respect to the operators in Σ, all other rules being given by simple identities, i.e., by rules with an empty set of premises (n=0).

The further simplification comes from the realization that we are not really obliged to specify the types of all variable arrows and equalities completely, since there is a lot of redundancy. This fact exploits unification, and the following meta-theorem.

Meta-theorem

Let Σ be an arbitrary arrow signature, and let E be an arbitrary term formed by operators from Σ and untyped variables. If there is an assignment of types to the variables of E that makes E well-typed with respect to Σ, there is a most general such assignment, independent in each variable, and furthermore the resulting type of E is most general. Here "more general" means "has as substitution instance". We call this assignment, together with the resulting type of E, the *principal* typing of E. More generally, for every type sequent S, if there is an assignment of types which makes E of a type some instance of S, there is a principal such assignment.

The meta-theorem above is most useful. It permits us to omit most of the types. When we write an equation $E = E'$, we shall implicitly refer to the principal typing giving E and E' the same type $A \to B$. So from now on, all equations in $\mathcal{R}$ are written without type, the types being implicit from the principality assumption.

1.3 *The Initial Theory* Categ

We are now ready to start category theory. The initial theory **Categ** has $\Phi = \emptyset$, and $\Sigma = \{Id, \_;\_\}$, given with respective signatures:

$$Id \ : \ A \to A \ ,$$

$$\_;\_ \ : A \to B \ , \ B \to C \ \vdash A \to C \ .$$

The notation $\_;\_$ means that we use the infix notation $f;g$ for the composition of arrows f and g. We can read *f then g* and follow arrow composition along diagrams with semicolon as concatenation of the labels. But since more people are accustomed to the standard set-theoretic composition notation, we shall below use $f \circ g$ as an abbreviation for $g;f$.

The equations $\mathcal{R}$ of **Categ** are simply the laws of a monoïd:

$$Ass \ : \ (f \circ g) \circ h \ = \ f \circ (g \circ h) \ ,$$

$$Idl \ : \ Id \circ f \ = \ f \ ,$$

$$Idr \ : \ f \circ Id \ = \ f \ .$$

It is to be noted that the identification of the Hom-set symbol $\to$ with the sequent entailment arrow is not fortuitious. Actually *Id* and ; are well-known inference rules of intuitionistic propositional calculus. However, the logic is quite poor at this stage: We have no propositional connective whatsoever, just the basic mechanism for sequent composition, stating that entailment is reflexive and transitive. The rules of $\mathcal{R}$, considered as a left-to-right rewriting system, define a normal form on the sequent calculus proofs, i.e., on the arrow expressions.

Before we embark on more complicated theories, let us give a recipe on how to cook an equational presentation from a categorical statement.

1.4 *What the Category Theorists Don't Say*

Open a standard book on category theory, and consider a typical categorical definition. It usually reads: "Mumble, such that the following diagram commutes". Similarly, a typical categorical result states: "If $diagram_1$ and ... and *diagram*$_n$ commute, then *diagram* commutes". The first step in understanding such statements is to determine exactly their universality: What is exactly quantified, universally or existentially; what depends on what; what are exactly the parameters of the (frequent) unicity condition. The next step is to realize that the diagram states conditional equalities on arrows, and that it is enough to state the equalities of the inside diagrams in order to get all equalities.

A uniform compilation of such statements as an equational theory proceeds as follows. First write completely explicitly the quantification prefix of the statement, in two lines: one for the objects and one for the arrows. Then Skolemize the statement independently in the first and the second line. That is, for every existentially quantified variable x following the universally quantified $y_1, \ldots, y_n$, introduce a new n-ary operator X and replace every x by $X(y_1, \ldots, y_n)$. The Skolemization of the object variables determines Φ. The Skolemization of the second line, together with the types implicit from the diagram, determines Σ. Finally, following arrows around the inner diagrams determines $\mathcal{R}$. This concerns the *existential* part. For the *unicity* part, proceed as follows. Let f be the arrow whose unicity is asserted. The existence part provides, by Skolemization, an $F(g_1, \ldots, g_k)$ in place of f. Write a supplementary arrow h on the diagram parallel to f, and use the commutation conditions to eliminate all the g_i's as $G_i(h)$. Add an extra equation $F(G_1(h), \ldots, G_k(h)) = h$.

Once we have convinced ourselves that the category theoretic statements and proofs are of an equational nature, we may ask: Why do the category theorists use diagrams at all? The reason is that diagram chasing is a sophisticated way of doing complex equality reasoning, using several equations simultaneously, on a shared data structure (the graph underlying the diagram). So diagrammatic reasoning may be considered a good tool for high level equational reasoning. On the other hand, equality reasoning techniques such as rewrite-rule analysis are good for mechanical implementation, and this is why we stress here the equational theories hidden behind the diagrams.

Remark Let us finally remark that more general categorical concepts than the simple universal statements that we shall now consider may force us to generalize the basic formalism. For instance, more complicated limit constructions such as pullbacks force the dependence of objects on arrows. The Skolemization cannot be effected separately on the object and the arrow variables, and we shall have to place ourselves in a more complicated type theory with dependent types.

2 Products

2.1 *The Theory* Prod

We shall apply the recipe above to the definition of *product* in a category. We recall that a category possesses a product if for all objects A, B there exists an object C and there exist arrows *fst*, *snd* such that for every object D and every arrows f, g there exists a unique arrow h such that the following diagram commutes:

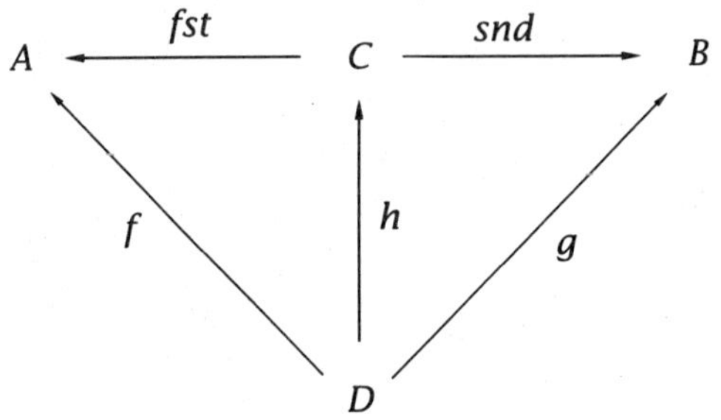

We now get the theory **Prod** by enriching **Categ** as follows. The Skolemization of C gives the binary functor $\times$, and we write with the infix notation $A \times B$ in place of C. So now $\Phi = \{\times\}$. Similarly, we add to Σ the following operators, issued respectively from *fst*, *snd* and h:

$$Fst : A \times B \to A \ ,$$

$$Snd : A \times B \to B \ ,$$

$$< \_ , \_ > : D \to A \ , \ D \to B \vdash D \to A \times B \ ,$$

and we now have the usual diagram:

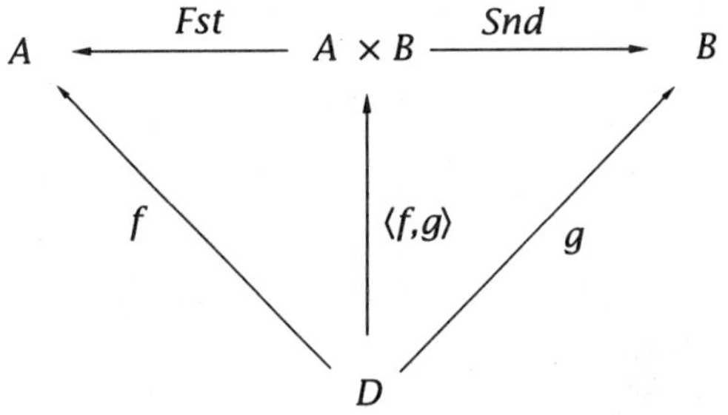

The existence of h, that is the commutation of the two triangles, gives two new equations in $\mathcal{R}$:

$$\pi_1 \ : \ Fst \circ <f,g> = f \ ,$$

$$\pi_2 \ : \ Snd \circ <f,g> = g \ .$$

Unicity of h gives one last equation:

$$UniPair \ : <Fst \circ h,\ Snd \circ h> = h \ .$$

The arrow part of the functor × may be defined as a derived operator as follows:

$$\_\times\_ \ : \ A \to B \ , \ C \to D \ \vdash \ A \times C \to B \times D \ ,$$

$$Def\times \ : \ f \times g \ = <f \circ Fst,\ g \circ Snd> \ .$$

Remark There is a possible source of confusion in our terminology. We talked about the elements of Φ as functors. Actually these are just function symbols denoting object constructors. Skolemization of a diagram will determine certain such function symbols, but there is no guarantee that there will be a corresponding functor. For instance, for product, we had to define the arrow part of × above, and we had to verify that indeed it obeys the functoriality laws.

2.2 *The Logical Point of View*

From the logical point of view, specifying a product amounts to defining conjunction. Read $A \times B$ as $A \wedge B$, and recognize *Fst*, *Snd*, and $<\_,\_>$ as $\wedge$-elim-left, $\wedge$-elim-right, and $\wedge$-intro, respectively [8, 17, 26].

The rules of $\mathcal{R}$ have a computational meaning: They specify how to reduce a proof to its normal form. Here we may apply known results from the theory of term rewriting systems, in order to complete $\mathcal{R}$ to a *canonical* system [19, 11].

The Knuth-Bendix completion procedure, when applied to theory **Prod**, generates two additional rewrite rules:

$$IdPair \ : <Fst, Snd> = Id \ ,$$

$$DistrPair \ : <f,g> \circ h \ = <f \circ h,\ g \circ h> \ .$$

The resulting system $\mathcal{R}$ is canonical and can be used to decide the equality of arrows in the theory **Prod**. Of course, the equations above do not modify the theory, since they have been obtained by equational reasoning.

Finally, let us note that other presentations of the same theory are possible. For instance, we could have obtained product as the right adjoint of the diagonal functor. The unit of this adjunction is the *duplicator*, which can be defined here as:

$$D = <Id, Id> \quad .$$

Note that type-checking imposes that the two identities are the same, so that $D_A : A \rightarrow A \times A$. As its name suggests, the duplicator duplicates, in the sense that we can prove $D \circ f = <f, f>$. The co-unit of the adjunction is the pair of projections (Fst, Snd).

2.3 *Finite Products*

We say that a category admits all finite products if it admits products and a terminal object. Equationally, this amounts to enrich the theory **Prod** to a theory **Prods** by adding a constant 1 to Φ, a polymorphic constant $Nil : A \rightarrow 1$ to Σ, and a unicity equation $Uni1$ to $\mathcal{R}$:

$$Uni1 \ : \ h = Nil \ .$$

Note that this does not make the equational theory inconsistent: Variable h above is principally typed to $A \rightarrow 1$. However, this equation brings up two problems. The first one is the one mentioned in the beginning of these notes, since variable h appears on the left but not on the right of $Uni1$. The second problem is that $Uni1$ cannot be considered as a term rewriting rule in the usual sense, since it would rewrite Nil to itself and therefore does not satisfy the finite termination criterion. Note that $Uni1$ entails with the other equations two consequences:

$$Zero \ : \ f \circ Nil = Nil \ ,$$

$$Id1 \ : \ Id = Nil \ .$$

Again, $Id1$ does not identify every Id with every Nil, but only (restoring explicit types) Id_1 with Nil_1. Now it can be checked that $Uni1$ is actually a consequence of $Zero$ and $Id1$. The rule $Zero$ is a bona fide rewrite rule, which leaves the special equality $Id1$ to be dealt with in an ad hoc fashion.

Using operators $\times$ and 1, we can now construct n-tuples of objects, which we shall call *contexts*. 1 is the empty context, and if E is a context of length n and A an object term, $E \times A$ is a context of length $n+1$. We write $|E|$ for the length of a context. If C is the current set of (representable) objects, i.e., $\mathbf{T}(\Phi, V)$, we denote by C^* be the set of contexts.

If $1 \leq i \leq |E|$, we define the ith component E_i of E recursively, as

$$\begin{aligned} (E \times A)_i &= A \quad \text{if } i = 1 \\ &= E_{i-1} \quad \text{if } i > 1 \ . \end{aligned}$$

If E and E' are contexts, we define their concatenation $E@E'$ as a context recursively:

$$E@1 = E ,$$

$$E@(E' \times A) = (E@E') \times A .$$

Similarly, using operators $< \_, \_ >$ and *Nil* we can construct lists, or n-tuples of arrows of same domain D. The empty arrow list is *Nil*, of length 0; and if $L : D \to E$ is an arrow list of length n, then $< L, f >: D \to E \times A$ is an arrow list of length $n+1$, for every $f : D \to A$. Finally, for every object list and every n, with $1 \leq n \leq |E|$ we define recursively the projection arrow $\pi_E(n) \ : \ E \to E_n$, as:

$$\begin{aligned} \pi_E(n) &= Snd && \text{if } n = 1 \\ &= \pi_{E'}(n-1) \circ Fst && \text{if } n > 1 \text{ and } E = E' \times A . \end{aligned}$$

3 *CCC*

3.1 *The Theory* Exp

We obtain the theory **Exp** by enriching the theory **Prods** as follows. First, we add a binary operator $\Rightarrow$ to Φ. Next we add two operators to Σ, the constant *App* (application) and the unary operator **[ ]** (abstraction):

$$App \ : \ (B \Rightarrow C) \times B \ \to \ C ,$$

$$[\,] \ : A \times B \to C \ \vdash \ A \to (B \Rightarrow C) .$$

Finally, we add the following equations to $\mathcal{R}$:

$$ExAbs \ : \ App \circ ([\,]f \times Id) = f ,$$

$$UniAbs \ : \ [\,](App \circ (f \times Id)) = f .$$

As before, this equational theory can be generated mechanically from the following diagram:

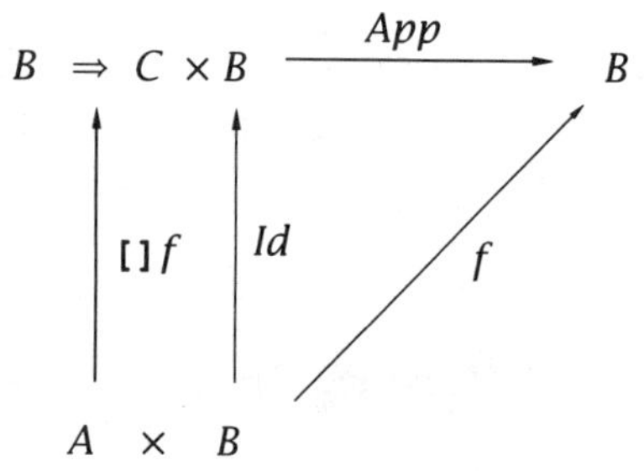

The logical point of view here is that $\Rightarrow$ is the (intuitionistic) implication. The operator *App* is $\Rightarrow$-introduction. It plays the role of the Modus Ponens inference rule (although here it is a constant, and not a binary operator). Abstraction is $\Rightarrow$-elimination, and plays somewhat the role of the deduction theorem.

Let us give a few equational consequences of the theory **Exp**:

$$IdExp : [\,]App = Id \ ,$$

$$Red_1 : App \circ <[\,]f \circ y, x> = f \circ <y, x> \ ,$$

$$Red : App \circ <[\,]f, x> = f \circ <Id, x> \ ,$$

$$DistrAbs : [\,]f \circ g = [\,](f \circ (g \times Id)) \ .$$

We can also show that abstraction is a bijection between the arrows of $A \times B \rightarrow C$ and those of $A \rightarrow B \Rightarrow C$, with inverse:

$$[\,]^{-1}f = App \circ <f \times Id> \ .$$

Thus we could have presented **Exp** in terms of $[\,]$ and $[\,]^{-1}$, and we could have defined *App* as $[\,]^{-1}Id$. This corresponds to the fact that we could have rather axiomatized exponentiation by an adjunction to the product, whose co-unit is *App* (the unit being $[\,]\,Id$).

Finally, we define the arrow part of the functor $\Rightarrow$ (which is contravariant in its first argument) as:

$$f \Rightarrow g = [\,](g \circ App \circ (Id \times f)) \ .$$

4 *Lambda-Calculus*

Sometimes $[\,]$ is called Curryfication, in honor of Curry. In fact there is an important relation between combinatory logic and CCC's, which we shall exhibit on λ-calculus.

4.1 *The λ-Terms*

We assume that the current theory is an extension of **Exp**. We define recursively a relation $E \vdash M : A$, read "*M* is a *term* of *type A* in *context E*", where $A \in C$ and $E \in C^*$, as follows:

Variable : If $1 \leq n \leq |E|$ then $E \vdash n : E_n$.

Abstraction : If $E \times A \vdash M : B$ then $E \vdash [A]M : A \Rightarrow B$.

Application : If $E \vdash M : A \Rightarrow B$ and $E \vdash N : A$ then $E \vdash (M\ N) : B$.

Thus a term may be a natural number, or may be of the form $[A]M$ with A an object and M a term, or may be of the form $(M\ N)$ with M, N two terms.

We thus obtain λ-terms typed with objects of the CCC currently axiomatized. Variables are coded as de Bruijn's indexes [2], i.e., as integers denoting their reference depth (distance in the tree to their binder). This representation avoids all the renaming problems associated with actual names (α conversion), but we shall use such names whenever we give examples of terms. For instance, the term $[A](1\ [B](1\ 2))$ shall be presented under a concrete representation such as $[x : A](x\ [y : B](y\ x))$. In Church's original notation, the left bracket was a λ and the right bracket a dot, typing being indicated by superscripting, like: $\lambda x^A \cdot (x\ \lambda y^B \cdot (y\ x))$.

Note that the relation $E \vdash M : A$ is functional, in that A is uniquely determined from E and M. Thus the definition above can be interpreted as the recursive definition of a function $A = \tau_E(M)$.

4.2 *A Translation from λ-Terms to CCC Arrows*

We shall now show how to translate λ-terms to CCC arrows. More precisely, to every term M such that $E \vdash M : A$ we associate an arrow $F_E(M) : E \to A$ as follows:

$$F_E(n) = \pi_E(n)$$

$$F_E([A]M) = [\,]F_{E\times A}(M)$$

$$F_E((M\ N)) = App \circ < F_E(M), F_E(N) >$$

It can be easily proved by induction that $F_E(M)$ is a well-typed arrow expression.

Example The closed term $M = [f : nat \Rightarrow nat]\ [x : nat](f\ (f\ x))$ of type $A = (nat \Rightarrow nat) \Rightarrow (nat \Rightarrow nat)$ in the empty context $E = 1$, gets translated to:

$$F_E(M) = [\,]\,[\,](App \circ < Snd \circ Fst, App \circ < Snd \circ Fst, Snd >>) : 1 \to A\ .$$

4.3 *The Syntactic Theory of Terms*

The advantage of the name-free terms is that we have no name conflict. The disadvantage is that we have to explicitate relocation operations for terms containing free variables. For instance, let us define for every term M the term M^{+n} obtained in incrementing its free variables by n. Let $M^{+n} = R_n^0(M)$, with:

$$R^i_n(k) = k \quad \text{if } k \leq i$$
$$= k+n \quad \text{if } k > i$$

$$R^i_n([A]M) = [A]R^{i+1}_n(M) ,$$

$$R^i_n((M\ N)) = (R^i_n(M)\ R^i_n(N)) .$$

The reader will check that $E \vdash M : A$ if and only if $E@E' \vdash M^{+n} : A$, where E' is an arbitrary context of length n.

We now define *substitution* to free variables. Let $E{\times}A \vdash M : B$, and $E \vdash N : A$. We shall define a term $M\{N\}$, and show that $E \vdash M\{N\} : B$. First we define recursively:

$$\Sigma^n_N(k+1) = k+1 \quad \text{if } k < n$$
$$= N^{+n} \quad \text{if } k = n$$
$$= k \quad \text{if } k > n ,$$

$$\Sigma^n_N([A]M) = [A]\Sigma^{n+1}_N(M) ,$$

$$\Sigma^n_N((M\ M')) = (\Sigma^n_N(M)\ \Sigma^n_N(M')) .$$

It is easy to show that substitution preserves the types, in the sense that $(E \times A)@E' \vdash M : B$ and $E \vdash N : A$ implies $E@E' \vdash \Sigma^n_N(M) : B$, with $n = |E'|$.

Now we define $M\{N\} = \Sigma^0_N(M)$, and we get that $\tau_E(M\{N\}) = \tau_{E \times A}(M)$, with $A = \tau_E(N)$.

We are now ready to define the *computation* relation $\triangleright$ as follows:

$$([A]M\ N) \triangleright M\{N\} , \tag{β}$$

$$M \triangleright M' \Longrightarrow [A]M \triangleright [A]M' , \tag{ξ}$$

$$M \triangleright M' \Longrightarrow (M\ N) \triangleright (M'\ N) ,$$

$$M \triangleright M' \Longrightarrow (N\ M) \triangleright (N\ M') .$$

It is clear that computation preserves the types of terms. But it also preserves their values, in the sense of the translation to CCC arrows: If $E \vdash M : A$ and $M \triangleright N$, then $F_E(M) = F_E(N)$ in the theory **Exp**, as we shall show.

The computation relation presented above is traditionally called (strong) β-reduction. It is confluent and nœtherian (because of the types!), and thus every term possesses a canonical form, obtainable by iterating computation nondeterministically. Another valid conversion rule is η-conversion:

$$[x:A](M\,x) = M \qquad (\eta)$$

whenever x does not appear in M. Let us show that it corresponds to *UniAbs*, using our translation above.

First we define the *relocation* combinators $\rho(i)$ as follows:

$$\rho(0) = Fst\ ,$$
$$\rho(i+1) = \rho(i) \times Id\ .$$

It is easy to show that (with appropriate types)

$$\pi(k) \circ \rho(i) = \pi(k) \quad \text{if } k \leq i$$
$$= \pi(k+1) \quad \text{if } k > i\,,$$

and thus that $R^i_1(M) = M \circ \rho(i)$. As a particular case we get $M^{+1} = M \circ Fst$ and thus we can read the law *UniAbs* as $[x](M^{+1}\ x) = M$. Whenever x does not occur in M the expressions M and M^{+1} are concretely identical, and we obtain the η-conversion rule. Note however that *UniAbs* is an algebraic law, whereas η makes sense only relatively to concrete representations.

We are now going to show that *Red* validates the β-reduction rule. First we define the *substitution* combinators as follows:

$$\sigma_N(0) = \ <Id, N>\ ,$$
$$\sigma_N(n+1) = \sigma_N(n) \times Id\ .$$

Next we check that for every λ-terms M,N and every integer n the following equation is provable in **Exp** (confusing M with $F(M)$, and assuming types are correct):

$$\Sigma^n_N(M) = M \circ \sigma_N(n)\ .$$

This suggests defining in **Exp** the derived operator

$$\_\{\_\} : A \times B \rightarrow C\,,\ A \rightarrow B \vdash A \rightarrow C$$

with defining equation

$$Subst : f\{x\} = f \circ <Id, x>\ ,$$

and now the rule *Red* reads:

$$App \circ <[\,]f, x> = f\{x\}\ ,$$

which clearly validates the computation relation $\triangleright$.

CCC arrows are richer than λ-terms. This suggests enriching λ-calculus with further operators *fst, snd, pair, nil* with appropriate supplementary reduction rules, and to allow "varstruct" binding in order to have variables correspond to arbitrary sequences of *Fst* and *Snd*, as opposed to just integers coded up in unary notation. For instance, ML (without recursion) can be translated into CCC arrows by a simple extension of the translation F above. Actually, such a translation is the basis for an efficient implementation of the language [3, 4].

4.4 *The CCC Word Problem, and Related Subsystems*

The **Exp** theory above is decidable [29]. Unfortunately, no canonical system is known for the full theory. We remark that the usual theory of term rewriting systems can be used, since any typed system such as **Exp** can be considered an (untyped) equational theory in the ordinary sense, by mixing the arrow structure and the object structure as follows: Every arrow subterm M of type $A \to B$ is represented as $:(M, A, B)$, where $:$ is a special ternary function symbol. Note that variables in the type subparts get instantiated by matching and unification, in the same way as the variables in the arrow subparts. This supports our view of the polymorphic nature of the categorical combinators.

The study of categorical combinators and their relation to various λ-calculi was initiated by Pierre-Louis Curien, in the extensive monography [7] issued from his Thèse d'Etat. The state of the art in the study of subsystems of CCC axiomatizations, at the end of 1987, is the Thèse of Thérèse Hardin-Accart [10]. We list here a few of her results. The presentation of **Exp** given by the rules:

$$\begin{aligned} CCL\beta\eta SP \;=\; & \{Ass, Idl, Idr, \pi_1, \pi_2, DistrPair, IdPair, UniPair, Red, \\ & DistrAbs, IdExp, UniAbs\}\;, \end{aligned}$$

or *strong categorical combinatory logic*, is not canonical, since it is not even locally confluent. The subsystem

$$CCL\beta SP \;=\; \{Ass, Idl, Idr, \pi_1, \pi_2, DistrPair, IdPair, UniPair, Red, DistrAbs\}$$

is locally confluent, but not confluent. However, this system is confluent when restricted to the terms that are translations from λ-calculus terms. The system

$$Subst \;=\; \{Ass, Idl, Idr, \pi_1, \pi_2, DistrPair, IdPair, UniPair, DistrAbs\}$$

is canonical. This system is especially important, since it simulates substitution in λ-calculus.

4.5 *Possible Extensions*

It is also possible to enrich the type structure with sums, corresponding to categorical coproduct. The **Exp** theory is enriched with injections and a conditional operator. The corresponding models are the bicartesian closed categories.

Finally, we can postulate the existence of a universal object U and build the full untyped λ-calculus in the manner of Scott, as described in [27]. That is, we postulate a retract pair between U and $U \Rightarrow U$:

$$Quote : (U \Rightarrow U) \rightarrow U \ ,$$

$$Eval : U \rightarrow (U \Rightarrow U) \ ,$$

verifying:

$$Retract : Eval \circ Quote = Id \ .$$

Let us call **Univ** the theory obtained by the corresponding enrichment of **Exp**.

We can now translate any $M \in \lambda_n$ as an arrow $A_n(M) : U^n \rightarrow U$ as follows:

$$A_n(k) = \pi_{U^n}(k) \ ,$$

$$A_n([\,]M) = Quote \circ [\,]A_{n+1}(M) \ ,$$

$$A_n((M\ N)) = App \circ < Eval \circ A_n(M), A_n(N) > \ .$$

We leave it to the reader to check that the β rule is still an equational consequence of **Univ**. However, note that the η rule is not valid anymore, since it would entail that *Eval* and *Quote* define an isomorphism between U and $U \Rightarrow U$.

Caution Some combinations of the above extensions can be incompatible, in that they can lead to an inconsistency, in the sense that the only model of the extended theory is the trivial category **1**. For instance, Lawvere showed that the theory of bicartesian closed categories with fixpoints is inconsistent [22, 15].

Acknowledgments

The general formalization was developed in 1983, after the author listened to a talk by P. L. Curien in Sophia-Antipolis on categorical combinators. The translation from Section 4.2 was derived after the author noticed the close connection between the categorical operators of Lambek [20] and de Bruijn's nameless notation for λ-calculus [2]. Instrumental to this was a close study of the ML compiler developed by Lockwood Morris for the LCF project [9]. The syntactic theory from Section 4.3 is similar to the formalization of Automath by Jutting [16], except that the absence of dependent types makes things a little simpler. This treatment of λ-calculus computation was the basis of the author's implementation in ML of the calculus of constructions [5]. The author acknowledges numerous discussions on categorical combinators with P. L. Curien, T. Hardin, A. Poigné, and D. Scott.

References

[1] Barendregt, H. *The Lambda-Calculus: Its Syntax and Semantics.* North-Holland, Amsterdam, 1980.

[2] de Bruijn, N. G. "Lambda-calculus notation with nameless dummies, a tool for automatic formula manipulation, with application to the Church-Rosser theorem". *Indag. Math. 34,* 5 (1972), pp. 381–392.

[3] Cousineau, G., Curien, P.L., and Mauny, M. "The Categorical Abstract Machine". *Functional Programming Languages and Computer Architecture,* J. P. Jouannaud, ed., pp. 50–64. Lecture Notes in Computer Science, vol. 201. Springer-Verlag, Berlin, 1985.

[4] Cousineau, G. "The Categorical Abstract Machine". This volume, Chapter 3.

[5] Coquand,Th. and Huet, G. "Constructions: A higher order proof system for mechanizing mathematics". In *Proceedings of EUROCAL '85* (Linz). Lecture Notes in Computer Science, vol. 203. Springer-Verlag, Berlin, 1985.

[6] Curien, P. L. "Categorical combinatory logic". In *Automata, Languages, and Programming* (Proceedings, Nafplion, 1985), W. Brauer, ed. Lecture Notes in Computer Science, vol. 194. Springer-Verlag, Berlin, 1985.

[7] Curien, P. L. *Categorical Combinators, Sequential Algorithms and Functional Programming.* Monograph to appear, Pitman (1985).

[8] Gentzen, G. *The Collected Papers of Gerhard Gentzen.* E. Szabo,ed. North-Holland, Amsterdam, 1969.

[9] Gordon, M. J., Milner, R., and Wadsworth, C. P. *Edinburgh LCF.* Lecture Notes in Computer Science, vol. 78. Springer-Verlag, Berlin, 1979.

[10] Hardin-Accart, T. "Résultats de confluence pour les règles fortes de la logique combinatoire catégorique et liens avec les lambda-calculs". Thèse de Doctorat, Université Paris VII, October 1987.

[11] Huet, G. "Confluent reductions: Abstract properties and applications to term rewriting systems". *J. ACM 27,* 4 (1980), pp. 797–821.

[12] Huet, G. "Initiation à la Théorie des Catégories". Polycopié de cours de DEA, Uni-

versité Paris VII, November 1985.

[13] Huet, G. "Deduction and computation". *Fundamentals of Artificial Intelligence,* W. Bibel and Ph. Jorrand, eds., pp. 39–74. Lecture Notes in Computer Science, vol. 232. Springer-Verlag, Berlin, 1986.

[14] Huet, G. "Formal structures for computation and deduction". Course Notes, Carnegie-Mellon University, May 1986.

[15] Huwig, H. and Poigné, A. "A note on inconsistencies caused by fixpoints in a cartesian closed category". Personal communication, April 1986.

[16] Jutting, L. S. van Benthem. "The language theory of Λ_∞, a typed λ-calculus where terms are types". Personal communication, 1984.

[17] Kleene, S. C. *Introduction to Meta-mathematics.* North Holland, Amsterdam, 1952.

[18] Klop, J. W. "Combinatory reduction systems". Ph. D. Thesis, Mathematisch Centrum Amsterdam, 1980.

[19] Knuth, D. and Bendix, P. "Simple word problems in universal algebras". *Computational Problems in Abstract Algebra,* J. Leech, ed., pp. 263–297. Pergamon, Oxford, 1970.

[20] Lambek, J. "From lambda-calculus to Cartesian closed categories". In *To H. B. Curry: Essays on Combinatory Logic, Lambda-calculus and Formalism,* J. P. Seldin and J. R. Hindley, eds. Academic Press, New York, 1980.

[21] Lambek, J. and Scott, P. J. "Aspects of higher order categorical logic". *Contemporary Mathematics 30* (1984), pp. 145–174.

[22] Lawvere, F. W. "Diagonal arguments and Cartesian closed categories". In *Category Theory, Homology Theory and their Applications II.* Lecture Notes in Mathematics, vol. 92. Springer-Verlag, Berlin, 1969.

[23] Mac Lane, S. *Categories for the Working Mathematician.* Springer-Verlag, Berlin, 1971.

[24] Mann, C. "The connection between equivalence of proofs and Cartesian closed categories". *Proc. London Math. Soc. 31* (1975), pp 289–310.

[25] Poigné, A. "On semantic algebras ". Universitat Dortmund, March 1983.

[26] Prawitz, D. *Natural Deduction.* Almqist and Wiskell, Stockolm, 1965.

[27] Scott, D. "Relating theories of the lambda-calculus". In *To H. B. Curry: Essays on Combinatory Logic, Lambda-calculus and Formalism,* J. P. Seldin and J. R. Hindley, eds. Academic Press, New York, 1980.

[28] Stenlund, S. *Combinators, λ-terms, and Proof Theory.* Reidel, Dordrecht, Netherlands, 1972.

[29] Szabo, M. E. *Algebra of Proofs.* North-Holland, Amsterdam, 1978.

The Categorical Abstract Machine

3

Guy Cousineau
Ecole Normale Supérieure

We explain in this chapter how categorical combinators as described in the preceding chapter and by P-L. Curien in [9] can be evaluated, and how this evaluation leads to a compiling technique for lambda-calculus and, more generally, for functional programming languages. In contrast to other implementation techniques based on combinators [13, 18, 19, 22], the one described here relies not on rewriting but rather on direct execution of combinators considered as machine instructions for a Von Neumann-like machine that we call the Categorical Abstract Machine (or in abbreviation, CAM). This Machine is reminiscent of the SECD machine introduced by Landin in [15], since it uses a similar notion of closure for representing functional values, but the CAM can be introduced in a much more natural way since its structure is induced by categorical combinators' properties. Morever, the CAM approach leads to implementations that are very different from implementations based on traditional optimizations of the SECD machine such as the FAM machine of L. Cardelli [1, 4]. The point is that the CAM approach tends to optimize closure building and environment sharing instead of optimizing access to values, and thus becomes more efficient on highly functional programs and also allows for lazy evaluation [16]. The CAM approach has been used to implement the CAML language [11], which is a variant of Standard ML [17]. A description of the CAML compiler is also given in the next chapter. The *CAM* machine was first described in [5].

1 *Evaluating Categorical Combinators*

We first recall the equations for cartesian closed categories as presented in the previous chapter under the name *Exp*. We use the notation $\_;\_$ for composition, rather than $\_\circ\_$, since this will make more explicit the identification of some combinators with machine instructions and of composition with instruction sequencing. The abstraction is denoted by Cur(_).

$$Ass : (f;g);h = f;(g;h) ,$$

$$Idl : Id;f = f ,$$

$$Idr : f;Id = f ,$$

$$\pi_1 : <f,g>;Fst = f ,$$

$$\pi_2 : <f,g>;Snd = g ,$$

$$UniPair : <h;Fst, h;Snd> = h .$$

$$Cur : <Fst;Cur(f), Snd>;App = f ,$$

$$UniCur : Cur(<Fst;f, Snd>;App) = f .$$

In the following, categorical terms will be considered as machine code, and therefore the above equivalence rules will be used for performing code transformations that preserve equivalence. This will enable us to give formal justifications for code optimizations in the CAML compiler.[1]

The above equations have many interesting equational consequences. We list below a few of them together with their proofs. The first one is distribu-

1. Note, however, that some of these rules are not correct for call-by-value execution.

tion of composition over pair.

$$Dpair \; : \; f; <g, h> = <f; g, f; h> \; ,$$

$$
\begin{array}{rcl}
 & & f; <g, h> \\
(Unipair) & = & <(f; <g, h>); Fst, (f; <g, h>); Snd> \; , \\
(Ass) & = & <f; (<g, h>; Fst), f; (<g, h>; Snd)> \; , \\
(Fst, Snd) & = & <f; g, f; h> \; .
\end{array}
$$

The next two reduction rules enable some function applications to be performed at compile time rather than at execution time. *Red*1 is easily obtained from *Red*2 by letting y be *Id*. We therefore give a proof only of *Red*2.

$$Red1 \; : <Cur(f), x>; App \; = <Id, x>; f \; ,$$

$$Red2 \; : <y; Cur(f), x> = <y, x>; f \; ,$$

$$
\begin{array}{rcl}
 & & <y, x>; f \; , \\
(Cur) & = & <y, x>; \; <Fst; Cur(f), Snd>; App \; , \\
(Dpair) & = & <<y, x>; \; (Fst; Cur(f)), <y, x>; Snd>; App \; , \\
(Ass, Fst, Snd) & = & <y; Cur(f), x>; App \; .
\end{array}
$$

The last one is some kind of distribution of composition over currying.

$$DCur \; : \; x; Cur(f) \; = \; Cur(<Fst; x, Snd>; f) \; ,$$

$$
\begin{array}{rcl}
 & & Cur(<Fst; x, Snd>; f) \; , \\
(Cur) & = & Cur(<Fst; x, Snd>; \; <Fst; Cur(f), Snd>; App) \; , \\
(Dpair, Fst, Snd) & = & Cur(<Fst; x; Cur(f), Snd>; App) \; , \\
(UniCur) & = & x; Cur(f) \; .
\end{array}
$$

1.1 *Evaluation by Rewriting*

In order to give a computational meaning to our combinators, we have to introduce value domains and interpret combinators as operations that can be applied to values to produce new values. The very minimum we shall assume is that we have a domain called *Unit* with a single element denoted by (), and that for any two domains D_1 and D_2, we have a domain $D_1 \times D_2$ containing all the couples (d_1, d_2) with $d_1 \in D_1$ and $d_2 \in D_2$. To deal with a realistic programming language, we shall assume later on that we also have basic domains like booleans, numbers, strings, etc.

We shall denote by $x \bullet C$ the result of sending a value x to combinator term C (or in other words applying C to x). The intended behavior of our combinators is given by the following term rewriting system:

$$
\begin{array}{ll}
(id) & x \bullet Id \to x \ , \\
(ass) & x \bullet (M;N) \to (x \bullet M) \bullet N \ , \\
(dpair) & x \bullet <M,N> \to (x \bullet M, x \bullet N) \ , \\
(fst) & (x,y) \bullet Fst \to x \ , \\
(snd) & (x,y) \bullet Snd \to y \ , \\
(cur) & x \bullet (y \bullet Cur(M)) \to (y,x) \bullet M \ , \\
(app) & (x,y) \bullet App \to y \bullet x. \ .
\end{array}
$$

This system is clearly confluent since it has no critical pair. We give below a rewriting for term

$$<Cur(<Snd,Snd>;App),Cur(Snd)>;App \ ,$$

which is the translation of the λ-term $(\lambda x.x)(\lambda x.x)$. The combinator term operates on the value (), which plays the role of the empty environment.

$$
\begin{array}{lcl}
 & & ()\bullet <Cur(Snd),Cur(Snd)>;App \ , \\
(ass) & = & (()\bullet <Cur(<Snd),Cur(Snd)>) \bullet App \ , \\
(dpair) & = & (() \bullet Cur(<Snd), () \bullet Cur(Snd)) \bullet App \ , \\
(app) & = & (() \bullet Cur(Snd)) \bullet (() \bullet Cur(<Snd)) \ , \\
(cur) & = & ((), () \bullet Cur(Snd)) \bullet Snd \ , \\
(snd) & = & () \bullet Cur(Snd) \ .
\end{array}
$$

We remark that $Cur(Snd)$ is the categorical translation of $\lambda x.x$, which is the normal form of the λ-term we have considered.

We now give a second example involving a numerical computation. We consider the λ-term $(\lambda fx.f(fx))(\lambda x.x * x)3$. We must first explain how we translate numerical constants and numerical operations into combinators. For any constant c, we just take

$$[\![c]\!] = {}'c$$

and the extra rewriting rules

$$(quote) \quad x \bullet\ 'c \rightarrow c\ .$$

This corresponds to the traditional way of functionalizing a constant. For a basic operation f of type $A \rightarrow B$ (e.g., $+ : Num \times Num \rightarrow Num$), we shall take

$$[\![f]\!] = Cur(Snd; f)\ .$$

When the functional constant is applied to some argument, we can in fact improve this translation using categorical rules:

$$\begin{aligned} [\![fe]\!] &= \ <Cur(Snd; f), [\![e]\!] >; App\ , \\ (Red1) &= \ <Id, [\![e]\!] >; (Snd; f)\ , \\ (Ass, \pi_2) &= [\![e]\!] ; f\ . \end{aligned}$$

For our numerical example, we thus have

$$\begin{aligned} & [\![(\lambda fx.f(fx))(\lambda x.x * x)3]\!] \\ = & << Cur(Cur(A)), Cur(B) >; App,\ '3 >; App \end{aligned}$$

with

$$\begin{aligned} A &= \ <Fst; Snd, <Fst; Snd, Snd >; App >; App\ , \\ B &= \ <Snd, Snd >; *\ . \end{aligned}$$

The computation is the following:

$$\begin{aligned} & () \bullet << Cur(Cur(A)), Cur(B) >; App,\ '3 >; App\ , \\ (ass, dpair) &= (() \bullet < Cur(Cur(A)), Cur(B) >; App, () \bullet\ '3) \bullet App\ , \\ (ass, dpair, quote) &= ((() \bullet Cur(Cur(A)), () \bullet Cur(B)) \bullet App, 3) \bullet App\ , \\ (ac) &= (((), () \bullet Cur(B)) \bullet Cur(A), 3) \bullet App\ , \\ (ac) &= (((), () \bullet Cur(B)), 3) \bullet \\ & \quad < Fst; Snd < Fst; Snd, Snd >; App >; App\ , \\ (ass, dpair, fst, snd) &= (() \bullet Cur(B), (() \bullet Cur(B), 3) \bullet App) \bullet App\ , \\ (ac) &= (() \bullet Cur(B), ((), 3) \bullet < Snd, Snd >; *) \bullet App\ , \\ (ass, dpair, snd) &= (() \bullet Cur(B), (3, 3) \bullet *) \bullet App\ , \\ (multiplication) &= (() \bullet Cur(B), 9) \bullet App, \\ (ac) &= ((), 9) \bullet < Snd, Snd >; *\ , \\ (ass, dpair, snd) &= (9, 9) \bullet *\ , \\ (multiplication) &= 81\ . \end{aligned}$$

1.2 *Direct Execution*

We will now restrict our execution mechanism to innermost reduction (call-by-value) and modify it in such a way that it can appear as an evaluation relation noted

$$u \bullet C \triangleright v \ ,$$

where u and v are values belonging to suitable domains of values that we shall define below, and C is a combinatory term that operates on the start value u to give a result value v. Note that the rewriting mechanism we have considered so far does not satisfy these requirements since, for instance, $() \bullet Cur(Snd)$ does not reduce to any value.

The values we consider are typed, and the evaluation relation will respect types in that $u \bullet C \triangleright v$ will be meaningful only if C has some type $A \rightarrow B$, u has type A, and v has type B.

Given basic computational domains $D_1, \ldots, D_n$, their elements are values and so are elements of all cartesian products built with these domains. So we have

$$\frac{x \in D_i}{x : D_i} \ ,$$

$$\frac{x : U \quad y : V}{(x, y) : U \times V} \ .$$

Except for *Cur* and *App*, all the other combinators manipulate values of this kind, and the previous evaluation rules, interpreted as call-by-value rules, satisfy our purposes.

$$\frac{x : U}{x \bullet Id \triangleright x} \ ,$$

$$\frac{C_1 : U \rightarrow V \quad C_2 : V \rightarrow W \quad x \bullet C_1 \triangleright y \quad y \bullet C_2 \triangleright z}{x \bullet C_1 ; C_2 \triangleright z} \ ,$$

$$\frac{x : U \quad y : V}{(x, y) \bullet Fst \triangleright x} \ ,$$

$$\frac{x : U \quad y : V}{(x, y) \bullet Snd \triangleright y} \ ,$$

$$\frac{C_1 : U \rightarrow V \quad C_2 : U \rightarrow W \quad x \bullet C_1 \triangleright y \quad x \bullet C_2 \triangleright z}{x \bullet < C_1, C_2 > \triangleright (y, z)} \ .$$

On the other hand, rule *Cur* is a problem. When a term $Cur(C) : U \rightarrow (V \Rightarrow W)$ is applied to some value $x : U$, it should produce some kind of (functional) value or—in computer science terms—it should be frozen into some data structure waiting to be applied to some argument later on. Such a data structure is traditionally called a *closure*, and we shall denote it by $[x : C]$. So we add one more clause to our definition of values:

$$\frac{C : U \times V \rightarrow W \quad x : U}{[x : C] : V \Rightarrow W},$$

and we introduce an evaluation rule that builds closures:

$$\frac{C : U \times V \rightarrow W \quad x : U}{x \bullet Cur(C) \triangleright [x : C]},$$

and an evaluation rule that applies closures:

$$\frac{C : U \times V \rightarrow C \quad x : U \quad y : V \quad (x, y) \bullet C \triangleright z}{([x : C], y) \bullet App \triangleright z}.$$

1.3 *Correctness of the Evaluation Mechanism*

We must now establish the correctness of this evaluation mechanism with respect to the categorical framework. The first problem is to ensure that the embedding of basic computation domains in a cartesian closed category can indeed be done. Given a category C it is possible to build the cartesian closed category $\hat{C}$ freely generated by C, and the canonical functor $\hat{ } : C \rightarrow \hat{C}$. The following theorem is stated and proved by Lafont in [14].

Theorem

For any category C, the canonical functor $\hat{ } : C \rightarrow \hat{C}$ is full and faithful; i.e., it establishes a bijection between $\mathbf{Hom}_C(A, B)$ and $\mathbf{Hom}_{\hat{C}}(A, B)$ for any pair (A, B) of objects in C.

This means that the construction does not add any arrow between objects of C, nor any equation between arrows of C. The proof given in [14] is completely general and does not assume that objects of C are sets. For our purposes, this result means that any predefined computation domain can be safely embedded in a cartesian closed category. This result can be extended a bit further. Given a category C that already contains products, it is possible to extend it to a CCC while preserving C. This means, for example, that we can start with an integer domain *Num* and binary operations on this domain such as $+ : Num \times Num \rightarrow Num$.

This of course is not enough. We must relate the values we manipulate in the evaluation relation to arrows of $\hat{C}$, and we must establish the coherence of the evaluation mechanism with respect to the the composition of arrows in $\hat{C}$. We shall assume for the moment that the only basic computation domain is the one-element domain *Unit* with element (). To every value $x : U$, we associate an arrow $'x : Unit \to U$:

$$\frac{}{() : Unit \qquad '() = Id : Unit \to Unit}\ ,$$

$$\frac{x : U \qquad y : V}{(x,y) : U \times V \qquad '(x,y) = <\ 'x,\ \ 'y >: Unit \to U \times V}\ ,$$

$$\frac{C : U \times V \to W \qquad x : U}{[x : C] : V \Rightarrow W \qquad '[x : C] =\ \ 'x; Cur(C) : Unit \to V \Rightarrow W}\ .$$

The correctness of the evaluation process is given by the following proposition.

Proposition
If $u \bullet C \rhd v$ then $'u; C\ =\ 'v$.

Proof The proposition is proved by induction on the length of the proof that $u \bullet C \rhd v$, examining each possible construction for C and using categorical rules. For example, if $C = App$, then u must be of the form $([x : C], y)$, and we must have $(x, y) \bullet C \rhd v$. We have

$$\begin{array}{rcl} & & '([x : C], y)\,; App\ , \\ (def) & = & <\ '[x : C],\ \ 'y >; App\ , \\ (def) & = & <\ 'x; Cur(C),\ \ 'y >; App\ , \\ (Red2) & = & <\ 'x,\ \ 'y >; C\ , \\ (def) & = & '(x, y)\,; C\ , \\ (ind) & = & 'v\ .\ \square \end{array}$$

2 *The Categorical Abstract Machine*

The evaluation relation $u \bullet C \rhd v$ suggests that C is some code operating on some data u to produce some result v. The categorical composition corresponds to code sequentiality. *Id* is the "skip" instruction and *Fst* and *Snd* are functions that access the components of a pair. This suggests a very simple machine with a register which contains a pointer to some value and a program counter which contains a pointer to some code.

Now we must find an operational meaning for the remaining combinators $<\_,\_>$, *Cur*(_), and *App*. The evaluation rule for the categorical pair $< C_1, C_2 >$,

$$\frac{C_1 : U \to V \quad C_2 : U \to W \quad x \bullet C_1 \triangleright y \quad x \bullet C_2 \triangleright z}{x \bullet < C_1, C_2 > \triangleright (y, z)} ,$$

can be interpreted as a parallel execution of codes C_1 and C_2 on some common argument u. If we want to use a sequential machine, then we have to sequentialize these executions into

1. save u ,
2. execute C_1 on u getting some result v_1 ,
3. save v_1 and restore u ,
4. execute C_2 on u getting some result v_2 ,
5. build the pair (v_1, v_2) .

If we use a stack for saving and restoring values, this can be translated to

1. push content u of the register on the stack ,
2. execute C_1 on u getting some result v_1 ,
3. swap v_1 with top of the stack u ,
4. execute C_2 on u getting some result v_2 ,
5. build a pair with top of the stackv_1 and v_2 .

This suggests that each of the three symbols "<", ",", and ">" be interpreted as three instructions *Push*, *Swap*, and *Cons*.

The instruction *Cur*(*C*) operating on some value u just builds the closure $[u : C]$.

The instruction *App* operates on a pair $([u : C], v)$ and must build the pair (u, v) and run C on it and then proceed with the code following this *App* instruction. We shall use the stack to save the return address, which will be popped when the execution of C is completed. For that purpose, we will end code C with a "return" instruction.

Finally, the quote combinator can be interpreted as a "load immediate" instruction that just loads a constant in the register, and basic operations correspond to basic machine instructions. Of course, it is not very realistic to consider that an instruction such as "add" takes a linked pair of numbers as its argument, but this can be easily optimized in real implementations by letting one argument be in the register and the second at the top of the stack.

Table 1. The Categorical Abstract Machine.

configuration			configuration		
value	stack	code	value	stack	code
s	S	$id; C$	s	S	C
(s, t)	S	$fst; C$	s	S	C
(s, t)	S	$snd; C$	t	S	C
s	S	$push; C$	s	$s.S$	C
t	$s.S$	$swap; C$	s	$t.S$	C
t	$s.S$	$cons; C$	(s, t)	S	C
s	S	$Cur(C); C1$	$[s : C]$	S	$C1$
$([s : C], t)$	S	$app; C1$	(s, t)	$C1.S$	C
s	S	$(quote\ c); C$	c	S	C
(m, n)	S	$add; C$	$m + n$	S	C
s	$C.S$	$return; C$	s	S	C

The machine is summarized in Table 1.

We now run our example on the machine:

$$\llbracket\ (\lambda fx.f(fx))(\lambda x.x * x)3\ \rrbracket$$

$$= Push; Push; Cur(Cur(U)); Swap; Cur(V);$$

$$Cons; App; Swap; Quote3; Cons; App\ ,$$

with

$$U = Push; Fst; Snd; Swap; Push; Fst; Snd; Swap; Snd; Cons;$$

$$App; Cons; App\ ,$$

$$V = Push; Snd; Swap; Snd; Cons; Mult\ .$$

The computation is described in Table 2, in which the code is displayed as a vertical array and code addresses have form *Cnn*. These addresses are used in closures and on the stack to remember return addresses.

Table 2. Execution example for the CAM.

CAM states				Code
()	[]	C00		
()	[()]	C01	C00	*Push*
()	[();()]	C02	C01	*Push*
[():C12]	[();()]	C03	C02	*Cur*(C12)
()	[[():C12)];()]	C04	C03	*Swap*
[():C28]	[[():C12)];()]	C05	C04	*Cur*(C28)
([():C12],[():C28])	[()]	C06	C05	*Cons*
((),[():C28])	[C07;()]	C12	C06	*App*
[((),[():C28]):C14]	[C07;()]	C13	C07	*Swap*
[((),[():C28]):C14]	[()]	C07	C08	*Quote*3
()	[[((),[():C28]):C14]]	C08	C09	*Cons*
3	[[((),[():C28]):C14]]	C09	C10	*App*
([((),[():C28]):C14],3)	[]	C10	C11	*Return*
(((),[():C28]),3)	[C11]	C14		
(((),[():C28]),3)	[((),[():C28]),3);C11]	C15		
((),[():C28])	[((),[():C28]),3);C11]	C16	C12	*Cur*(C14)
[():C28]	[((),[():C28]),3);C11]	C17	C13	*Return*
[():C28])	[(((),[():C28]),3);[():C28];C11]	C18		
(((),[():C28]),3)	[[():C28];[():C28];C11]	C19		
((),[():C28])	[[():C28];[():C28];C11]	C20	C14	*Push*
3	[[():C28];[():C28];C11]	C21	C15	*Fst*
[():C28]	[3,[():C28];C11]	C22	C16	*Snd*
3	[[():C28];C11]	C23	C17	*Swap*
([():C28],3)	[[():C28];C11]	C24	C18	*Push*
((),3)	[C25;[():C28];C11]	C28	C19	*Fst*
((),3)	[((),3);C25;[():C28];C11]	C29	C20	*Snd*
3	[((),3);C25;[():C28];C11]	C30	C21	*Swap*
((),3)	[3;C25;[():C28];C11]	C31	C22	*Snd*
3	[3;C25;[():C28];C11]	C32	C23	*Cons*
(3,3)	[C25;[():C28];C11]	C33	C24	*App*
9	[C25;[():C28];C11]	C34	C25	*Cons*
9	[[():C28];C11]	C25	C26	*App*
([():C28],9)	[C11]	C26	C27	*Return*
((),9)	[C27;C11]	C28		
((),9)	[((),9);C27;C11]	C29		
9	[((),9);C27;C11]	C30	C28	*Push*
((),9)	[9;C27;C11]	C31	C29	*Snd*
9	[9;C27;C11]	C32	C30	*Swap*
(9,9)	[C27;C11]	C33	C31	*Snd*
81	[C27;C11]	C34	C32	*Cons*
81	[C11]	C27	C33	*Mult*
81	[]	C11	C34	*Return*

3 Compiling a Functional Language

In order to be concrete, we shall consider the problem of compiling the following small language.

$e ::=$	ce	constant
	$\mid var$	variable
	$\mid e1\ e2$	application
	$\mid e1\ op\ e2$	binary operation
	$\mid (e1, e2)$	couple
	$\mid$ if $e1$ then $e2$ else $e3$	conditional
	$\mid fun\ p \rightarrow e$	abstraction
	$\mid$ let { rec } $p = e1$ in $e2$	local definition
$p ::=$	var	variable pattern
	$\mid ()$	empty pattern
	$\mid (p1, p2)$	paired pattern

This language contains the λ-calculus as a sublanguage. The extensions are the use of patterns instead of simple variables, the conditionals, the local definitions, and recursion. These extensions bring out various kinds of problems. Adding patterns requires no modification of the machine but only a slight extension of the compiling process. Conditionals require the introduction of a new "branch" instruction. Local definitions that are not recursive can be considered as mere abbreviations that lead to compiling optimizations. We shall show that when they are recursive, they can be taken into account in a natural way by the production of infinite (looping) code.

3.1 *Patterns*

Introducing patterns creates environments that are not mere lists but full binary trees. But the categorical combinators *Fst* and *Snd* are precisely access functions into binary trees, so there is no problem. The compiling process uses a pattern that is the formal image of the environment.

$$[\![M]\!] = [\![M]\!]_{()} \ ,$$

$$[\![x]\!]_{(p,x)} = Snd \ ,$$

$$[\![x]\!]_{(x,p)} = Fst \ ,$$

$$[\![x]\!]_{(p_1,p_2)} = (Snd;[\![x]\!]_{p_2})?(Fst;[\![x]\!]_{p_1}) \ ,$$

$$[\![(MN)]\!]_{P} = <[\![M]\!]_{P},[\![N]\!]_{P}>;App \ ,$$

$$[\![(M,N)]\!]_P = \langle [\![M]\!]_P, [\![N]\!]_P \rangle \ ,$$

$$[\![\lambda p.M]\!]_P = Cur([\![M]\!]_{(P,p)}) \ .$$

3.2 *Conditionals*

We shall consider booleans as a basic type *Bool* with values "true" and "false" and the combinator *Branch*:

$$\frac{C_1 : U \to V \qquad C_2 : U \to V}{Branch(C_1, C_2) : U \times Bool \to V} \ ,$$

$$\frac{C_1 : U \to V \qquad C_2 : U \to V}{\langle Id, \ 'true \rangle; Branch(C_1, C_2) = C_1} \ ,$$

$$\frac{C_1 : U \to V \qquad C_2 : U \to V}{\langle Id, \ 'false \rangle; Branch(C_1, C_2) = C_2} \ .$$

This gives the following evaluation rules:

$$\frac{x \bullet C_1 \triangleright y}{(x, true) \bullet Branch(C_1, C_2) \triangleright y} \ ,$$

$$\frac{x \bullet C_2 \triangleright y}{(x, false) \bullet Branch(C_1, C_2) \triangleright y} \ ,$$

and the following machine rules:

configuration			configuration		
value	stack	code	value	stack	code
(x,true)	S	*branch*($C1, C2$)	x	S	$C1$
(x,false)	S	*branch*($C1, C2$)	x	S	$C2$

The compilation rule for the conditional is

$$[\![\textit{if } e_1 \textit{ then } e_2 \textit{ else } e_3]\!]_P = \langle Id, [\![e_1]\!]_P \rangle; Branch([\![e_1]\!]_P, [\![e_2]\!]_P) \ .$$

If we express this as code, it becomes

$$= Push; Id; Swap; [\![e_1]\!]_P; Cons; Branch([\![e_1]\!]_P, [\![e_2]\!]_P) \ ,$$

and since *Push*; *Id*; *Swap* is clearly equivalent to *Push*, this becomes

$$= Push; [\![e_1]\!]_P; Cons; Branch([\![e_1]\!]_P, [\![e_2]\!]_P) \ .$$

In a real implementation, we could optimize *Branch* exactly as we did the binary primitive; i.e., we could let *Branch* take its boolean argument in the register and the other one on the stack. This would eliminate the *Cons* instruction.

3.3 *Local Definitions*

The construction *let* $p = e_1$ *in* e_2 is traditionally considered equivalent to $(fun\ p \rightarrow e_2)e_1$. Therefore, we can take the following translation:

$$[\![\ let\ p = e_1\ in\ e_2\ ]\!]_P = <Cur([\![\ e_2\ ]\!]_{(P,p)}),[\![\ e_1\ ]\!]_P>; App\ .$$

It is possible, however, to improve this translation using rule (*Red*1) as we already did the translation of functional constants application:

$$\begin{aligned} & <Cur([\![\ e_2\ ]\!]_{(P,p)}),[\![\ e_1\ ]\!]_P>; App\ , \\ (Red1) = \ & <Id,[\![\ e_1\ ]\!]_P>;[\![\ e_2\ ]\!]_{(P,p)}\ . \end{aligned}$$

If we express this as machine code, we have

$$Push; Id; Swap;[\![\ e_1\ ]\!]_P; Cons;[\![\ e_2\ ]\!]_{(P,p)}\ ,$$

and once again we can simplify *Push*; *Id*; *Swap* to *Push*:

$$[\![\ let\ p = e_1\ in\ e_2\ ]\!]_P = Push;[\![\ e_1\ ]\!]_P; Cons;[\![\ e_2\ ]\!]_{(P,p)}\ .$$

We shall describe another optimization for the *let* construct in the case where *let* is used to define a function. This optimization is also the key to compiling recursive function definitions.

We shall use annotations in patterns to relate functional variables to their code without building a closure for these variables. In $P\{f = C\}$, the annotation $\{f = C\}$ means that code C is associated to variable f. The new compiling rules are the following:

$$[\![\ let\ f\ x = e_1\ in\ e_2\ ]\!]_P = [\![\ e_2\ ]\!]_{P'}\ where\ \ P' = P\{f = [\![\ (fun\ x \rightarrow e_1)\ ]\!]_P\}\ ,$$

$$[\![\ f\ ]\!]_{P\{f=C\}} = C\ .$$

When f appears in the operator position, i.e., in some expression $f\ e$, we have:

$$[\![\ fe\ ]\!]_P = Push; Fst^i; Cur(C); Swap;[\![\ e\ ]\!]_P; Cons; App\ ,$$

where

$$P = (\ldots(P'\{f = Cur(C)\}, x_{i-1}).\ldots, x_0)\ ,$$

which we can optimize into

$$[\![\ fe\ ]\!]_P = Push; Fst^i; Swap;[\![\ e\ ]\!]_P; Cons; C$$

using rule (*Red*2).

This optimization is particularly useful in conjunction with combinator optimizations as explained in the CAML compiler description.

3.4 *Recursion*

There are two ways to take recursion into account. We can add instructions to the CAM that build recursive closures, or we can leave the machine as it is and let the compilation process produce infinite (looping) code. We choose to present the latter method here because it seems more consistent with the categorical point of view. Moreover, it leads in fact to efficient compilation, and it is perfectly realistic if we bear in mind that loops are transformed to jump instructions when CAM code is expanded to real machine code for execution.

The compilation rule is the following:

$$[\![\; let\ rec\ f\,x = e_1\ in\ e_2 \;]\!]_P = [\![\; e_2 \;]\!]_{P'}$$

$$\text{where } P' = P\{f = [\![\; (fun\ x \to e_1) \;]\!]_{P'}\} \; .$$

Now the "where" in the definition is actually a "where rec" in the ML convention. This definition assumes that the compiler is written in a lazy language, or at least in a language lazy enough to accept this kind of definition.

The rest of the compiling process is not modified.

4 *Comparison with the SECD Machine*

The SECD machine was introduced by Landin [15] in 1966 for implementing λ-calculus in a manner correct with respect to variable scoping (in contrast to Lisp-like implementations). It has a closure mechanism which is very similar to the one we have here, and an *apply* instruction which corresponds to our *App*. But Landin's *apply* also entails saving mechanisms, which in our setting are carried out by *push* and *swap*.

We try to make the similarity clear, starting from the classical description of the SECD machine as found in the original paper [15], or in tutorial presentations such as [12], with the difference that, for consistency with the CAM compiler, we assume evaluation from left to right in applications. So the code for λ-calculus application *MN* is the code of *M* followed by the code of *N* followed by *apply*. The code for accessing the *n*th value in the environment is *access n*, and the code for constants and abstractions is as in the CAM. Products are avoided by currying * and +. The rules of the machine, which has a stack of values, an environment component, a code component, and a stack where environments are saved (the *dump* in the SECD terminology), are shown in Table 3.

At this stage, nothing is said about how environments are represented. The notation is not only vague, but even rather contradictory: *access n* suggests

Table 3. Rules of the SECD machine.

configuration				configuration			
stack	env	code	dump	stack	env	code	dump
S	E	$(access\ n).C$	D	$v.S$	E	C	D
S	E	$(quote\ c).C$	D	$c.S$	E	C	D
S	E	$(cur\ C).C1$	D	$[E : C].S$	E	$C1$	D
$v.[E1 : C].S$	E	$apply.C1$	D	S	$v.E1$	$C; C1$	$E.D$
$n.m.S$	E	$plus.C$	D	$m + n.S$	E	C	D
S	$E1$	$return.C$	$E.D$	S	E	C	D

a vector, but the operation $v.E1$ is practically unfeasible as such. Thus we are free to interpret the SECD machine in a context where environments are represented as in the CAM. Then *access n* has to be changed into a sequence *access*; *fst*; ... ; *fst*; *snd*, where the role of *access* is to copy the top of the environment stack to the value stack. We reformulate the machine as shown in Table 4, also simplifying it by considering the E component as being the top of the D component. This does not look very different from the CAM. To stress the similarity even more, we present in Table 5 a two-component version of the CAM, where the value component is now the top of the stack.

It should now be clear that the difference between Tables 4 and 5 lies only in how environments are saved. The CAM is conceptually simpler (this is reflected by the simplicity of the correctness proof [5], as compared with the proof of correctness of the SECD machine [20]). The other approach seems to save some stack manipulations (think of expressions $MN_1N_2 \ldots N_n$, or $< \ldots < M_1, M_2 >, \ldots, M_n >$), but some optimizations of the CAM tend to minimize the number of stack manipulations by recognizing when expressions really need their environments [21].

There exists another interpretation of the abstract description of the SECD machine, adopted for example in L. Cardelli's Functional Abstract Machine [1]. He keeps the environment-as-vector point of view; his solution in the *apply* rule is to keep v in the stack and to create environments-as-vectors only when closures have to be built. This entails a distinction between *local* and *global* variables, which are accessed in the stack and in the vector, respectively. The efficiency of his method as compared with ours is clear for access times and

Table 4. Rules of the reformulated SECD machine.

configuration			configuration		
stack	code	dump	stack	code	dump
S	$access; C$	$s.D$	$s.S$	C	$s.D$
$(s, t).S$	$fst; C$	D	$s.S$	C	D
$(s, t).S$	$snd; C$	D	$t.S$	C	D
S	$(quote\ c); C$	D	$c.S$	C	D
S	$(cur\ C); C1$	$s.D$	$[s : C].S$	$C1$	$s.D$
$t.[s : C].S$	$apply; C1$	D	S	$C; C1$	$(s, t).D$
$n.m.S$	$add; C$	D	$m + n.S$	C	D
S	$return; C$	$t.D$	S	C	D

Table 5. Rules of the reformulated CAM.

stack	code	stack	code
$(s, t).S$	$fst; C$	$s.S$	C
$(s, t).S$	$snd; C$	$t.S$	C
$s.S$	$(quote\ c); C$	$c.S$	C
$s.S$	$(cur\ C); C1$	$[s : C].S$	$C1$
$s.S$	$push; C$	$s.s.S$	C
$t.s.S$	$swap; C$	$s.t.S$	C
$t.s.S$	$cons; C$	$(s, t).S$	C
$t.[s : C].S$	$app; C1$	$(s, t).C1.S$	C
$s.C.S$	$return; C1$	$s.S$	C
$n.m.S$	$add; C$	$m + n.S$	C

function application, while closure building is his most expensive operation. This cost becomes really apparent when running highly functional programs or implementing laziness. On the other hand, an actual implementation for a functional language will represent the top-level environment with a symbol table, so that the access-time problem concerns only the local environments, which in practice are of small size.

5 *Lazy Evaluation*

The CAM can be considered as a true machine, and it is a nice outcome of the categorical approach that it enables us to establish a correspondence between machine instructions and the building blocks of category theory. The counterpart is that CAM is a call-by-value machine, as machines usually are. If we want to have lazy evaluation, then we have to build it on top of call-by-value.

We add to the CAM a "freeze" instruction (noted *fre*), which takes a code C as argument and, when applied to some value s, freezes the evaluation of C on s into a new form of closure $(s \bullet C)$. We also add the converse instruction "unfreeze" (noted *unf*) which resumes a frozen execution $(s \bullet C)$.

value	stack	code	value	stack	code
x	S	$fre(C); C1$	$(x \bullet C)$	S	C
$(x \bullet C)$	S	$unf; C1$	x	$C1.S$	C
x	S	$unf; C1$	x	S	$C1$

Of course, the second case for the definition of *unf* applies only when the first does not, i.e., when the value in the register is not frozen. Note that in instruction *fre*(C) the code C must end with a ***return*** instruction for the machine to behave correctly.

For the moment we have achieved delayed evaluation but not lazy evaluation, since we have no way of preventing a frozen value from being evaluated (i.e., computed) several times. To do so, we must be able to replace a frozen value by its computed value after this value has been computed. This is done with the "update" (*upd*) instruction, which replaces the closure, which has been kept on the stack by the *unf* instruction, with its value. Here are the transitions:

value	stack	code	value	stack	code
x	S	$fre(C); C1$	$(x \bullet C)$	S	C
$(x \bullet C)$	S	$unf;; C1$	x	$(x \bullet C).C1.S$	C
x	S	$unf; C1$	x	S	$C1$
y	$(x \bullet C).S$	$upd; C1$	$(x \bullet C)[(x \bullet C) \leftarrow y]$	S	$C1$

We now describe a compiler for lazy evaluation. We decide to freeze components of pairs in order to have lazy data structures and arguments of applications (including those introduced with the "let" construct) in order to have normal-order evaluation.

It is necessary to modify the compilation of primitive operations by including the code necessary to unfreeze the strict part of their argument. We denote by $insl_f$ the instruction list associated with primitive operation f.

We compile here a language which does not use patterns. Including them would only complicate somewhat the compilation of variables, since we would have to distinguish between access in the environment, where no "unfreeze" is necessary, and access in patterns, where it can be necessary at each level.

$$\llbracket f \rrbracket_P = Cur(snd; unf; insl_f)$$

$$\llbracket c \rrbracket_P = {}'c$$

$$\llbracket (f\ e) \rrbracket_P = \llbracket e \rrbracket_P; insl_f$$

$$\llbracket x \rrbracket_{(P,x)} = snd; unf$$

$$\llbracket x \rrbracket_{(P,y)} = fst; \llbracket x \rrbracket_P \quad if\ x \neq y$$

$$\llbracket (e_1, e_2) \rrbracket_P = push; fre(\llbracket e_1 \rrbracket_P; upd; return); swap; fre(\llbracket e_2 \rrbracket_P; upd; return); cons$$

$$\llbracket (fun\ x \rightarrow e) \rrbracket_P = Cur(\llbracket e \rrbracket_{(P,x)})$$

$$\llbracket (e_1\ e_2) \rrbracket_P = push; \llbracket e_1 \rrbracket_P; swap; fre(\llbracket e_2 \rrbracket_P; upd; return); cons; app$$

$$\llbracket (let\ x = e_1\ in\ e_2) \rrbracket_P = push; fre(\llbracket e_1 \rrbracket_P; upd; return); cons; \llbracket e_2 \rrbracket_{(P,x)}$$

$$\llbracket if\ e\ then\ e_1\ else\ e_2 \rrbracket_P = push; \llbracket e \rrbracket_P; branch(\llbracket e_1 \rrbracket_P, \llbracket e_2 \rrbracket_P)$$

References

[1] Cardelli, L. "ML under Unix". *Polymorphism I,* 3 (Dec. 1983).

[2] Cardelli, L. "Compiling a functional language". In *Proceedings of the ACM Symposium on Lisp and Functional Programming* (Austin, Texas, 1984). ACM, New York, 1984.

[3] Cardelli, L. "Basic polymorphic typechecking". *Polymorphism II,*1 (Jan. 1985).

[4] Cardelli, L. "The Amber machine". In *Combinators and Functional Programming Languages* (Proceedings, 1985). G. Cousineau, P.-L. Curien, and B. Robinet, eds. Lecture Notes in Computer Science, vol. 242. Springer-Verlag, Berlin, 1986.

[5] Cousineau, G., Curien, P.-L., and Mauny, M. "The Categorical Abstract Machine". *Functional Programming Languages and Computer Architecture* (Nancy, France, 1985), J.-P. Jouannaud, ed., pp. 50–64. Lecture Notes in Computer Science, vol. 201. Springer-Verlag, Berlin, 1986. (Full version in *Science of Computer Programming 8* (1987), pp. 173–202.)

[6] Cousineau, G., Curien, P.-L., Mauny, M., and Suarez, A. "Combinateurs catégoriques et implémentation des langages fonctionnels". In *Combinators and Functional Programming Languages* (Proceedings, 1985), G. Cousineau, P.-L. Curien, and B. Robinet, eds. Lecture Notes in Computer Science, vol. 242. Springer-Verlag, Berlin, 1986.

[7] Chailloux, J. "La machine virtuelle LLM3". Technical Report 55, INRIA, June 1985.

[8] Chailloux, J. "Le_Lisp 15.2, manuel de reference". Tech. report, 2nd edition, INRIA, May 1986.

[9] Cousineau, G. and Huet, G. "The CAML primer". Technical report, Version 2.5. Projet Formel, INRIA-ENS, December 1987.

[10] Curien, P.-L. *Categorical Combinators, Sequential Algorithms and Functional Programming.* Pitman monographs in Computer Science.

[11] Gordon, M., Milner, R., and Wadsworth, C. *Edinburgh LCF.* Lecture Notes in Computer Science, vol. 78. Springer-Verlag, Berlin, 1979.

[12] Henderson, P. *Functional Programming: Application and Implementation.* Prentice-Hall International, Englewood Cliffs, N.J., 1980.

[13] Johnsson, T. "Efficient compilation of lazy evaluation". In *Proceedings of the 1984 ACM SIGPLAN Conference on Compiler Construction* (June). ACM, New York, 1984.

[14] Lafont, Y. "Logiques, catégories et machines". Thesis, University Paris VII, Jan. 1988

[15] Landin, P. J. "The mechanical evaluation of expressions". *Computer Journal 6* (1964), pp. 308–320.

[16] Mauny, M. and Suárez, A. "Implementing functional languages in the Categorical Abstract Machine". In *Proceedings of the 1986 Symposium on Lisp and Functional Programming* (Boston, August). ACM, New York, 1986.

[17] Milner, R. "A proposal for Standard ML". In *Proceedings of the ACM Symposium on Lisp and Functional Programming* (Austin, Texas, 1984). ACM, New York, 1984.

[18] Peyton Jones, S. L. "An introduction to fully-lazy supercombinators". In *Combinators and Functional Programming Languages* (Proceedings, 1985). G. Cousineau, P.-L. Curien, and B. Robinet, eds. Lecture Notes in Computer Science, vol. 242. Springer-Verlag, Berlin, 1986.

[19] Peyton Jones, S. L. *The Implementation of Functional Programming Languages.* Prentice-Hall International, Englewood Cliffs, N.J., 1987.

[20] Plotkin, G.D. "Call-by-name, call-by-value and the λ-calculus". *Theoretical Computer Science 1* (1975), pp. 125–159 .

[21] Suárez, A. Thesis, University Paris VII, to appear.

[22] Turner, D.A. "A new implementation technique for applicative programming languages". *Software Practice and Experience 9* (1979), pp. 31–49.

Compiling ML into CAM

4

Ascánder Suárez[1]
INRIA

The Categorical Abstract Machine (CAM) has been used for the implementation of the *CAML* language, a variant of Standard ML developed at INRIA and LIENS [1]. The implementation is written in CAML itself. We present here a description of the CAML compiler that produces efficient code for this language.

Compared to the rudimentary compiler presented in the CAM paper, this one contains several optimizations which concern access to local variables and function applications. The detection of closed expressions (expressions with no free variables) leads to important optimizations in the treatment of closed functions or combinators. An analysis of the use of local variables in expressions enables the detection of local variables that are never used in

1. Now at Paris Research Laboratory, Digital Equipment Corporation.

closures. These variables, which we call "ephemeral", are put on the stack and not in the environment. This gives constant-time access to them and speeds up access to other variables in the environment. Other optimizations concern curried function applications. Finally the combinator optimization is improved using other optimizations to reduce the number of free variables.

1 *The Syntax*

We represent CAML programs using CAML concrete types. Types **MLexpr**, **MLdecl** and **MLpat** correspond respectively to CAML expressions, declarations, and patterns.

Program 1.1 Syntax of expressions.

type MLexp =	
MLconst **of** MLconst	*Constant*
| MLvar **of** string	*Variable*
| MLcond **of** MLexp & MLexp & MLexp	*Conditional*
| MLpair **of** MLexp & MLexp	*Pair*
| MLin **of** bool ref & MLdecl & MLexp	*Local Declaration*
| MLmatch **of** MLpat & MLexp	*Abstraction*
| MLapp **of** MLexp & MLexp	*Application*
and MLdecl =	
MLlet **of** MLpat & MLexp	*Value Declaration*
and MLpat =	
MLconspat **of** MLconst	*Constant Pattern*
| MLvarpat **of** string	*Variable Pattern*
| MLpairpat **of** MLpat & MLpat	*Paired Pattern*
and MLconst = mlconst **of** obj	

We have made no syntactic distinction here between nonrecursive and recursive definitions. We consider that a declaration "**let** *pat* = *exp*" is recursive if and only if expression *exp* contains occurrences of variables that appear in pattern *pat*.

In the following, we use $[\![exp]\!]_\rho$ to denote the compilation of expression *exp* in the formal environment ρ. Type **fenv** is used for the representation of formal environments during compilation.

Program 1.2 Formal environments.

```
type fenv =
      nullenv                       empty environment
    | fenv of fenv & MLpat          environment constructor
    | senv of MLpat                 simplified environment
    | annotenv of                   annotations
      fenv & bool & (string & code) list
```

Simplified environments will be used in Section 3 and annotations in Section 4.1.

The compilation of access to values in a formal environment ρ is denoted by $\mathcal{A}(\,\mathbf{v}\,)_\rho$.

2 *The Basic Compiler*

The basic compiler, which we denote here by C_0, is defined by case analysis on the language syntax constructors. Constants are compiled using instruction **Quote**.

Compilation Rule 2.1 Constants.

$[\![c]\!]_\rho =$ **(Quote** c**)**

Predefined operators, such as those for arithmetic or string processing, are compiled by instruction **Prim(n,nom)**, which takes the number of arguments (0, 1, or 2) and the name of the operator and produces the result of the operation applied to its arguments. We denote by $\hat{g}$ the operation associated to name **g** .

The CAM					
value	stack	code	value	stack	code
t	S	**Prim(0,g)**;C	$\hat{g}$ ()	S	C
t	S	**Prim(1,g)**;C	$\hat{g}$ t	S	C
t	s.S	**Prim(2,g)**;C	$\hat{g}$ (s t)	S	C

Normally, the distinction between variables and basic operators is done at type-checking time, but it can also be done when compiling access to variables. A primitive operation can have one or two arguments (if we need more, we can use structure arguments). The binary primitive operations use the register and the top of the stack for their arguments. When a primitive operation occurs in a position where it is not applied to its arguments (for instance as a parameter of a higher order function) the translation is more complicated.

Program 2.1 Primitive functions.

```
let CompilePrimitive name =
    Cur(Acc 0;
        match primitiveArgNumber name
        with 2 → Push;Car;Swap;Cdr;Prim(2,name)
        |    n → Prim(n,name)
        )
```

Access to local variables is performed in two steps. The access in the environment is compiled to the instruction **(Acc n)**, where **n** is the depth in the environment of the variable block in question (corresponding to some pattern). Then the access within this block is compiled to a sequence of instructions **Car** and **Cdr**.

Program 2.2 Access to variables.

$[\![v]\!]_\rho = \mathcal{A}(v)_\rho$

```
let 𝒜( v )ρ = (accessEnv 0 ρ ? compilePrimitive v)
              where rec accessEnv n =
              fun (ρ , pat) → (Acc n) ;accessPat pat ?
                              accessEnv(n+1)ρ
              and accessPat =
              fun (MLvarpat w) → if v=w then [] else fail
              |   (MLpairpat(pat1 , pat2)) →
                              accessPat pat2 ;Cdr ?
                              accessPat pat1 ;Car
```

Pairs, conditionals, abstractions, applications, and nonrecursive “lets” are compiled as in the preceding chapter.

Compilation Rule 2.2 Pairs.

$$[\![(exp_1\,,\ exp_2)]\!]_\rho \;=\; \mathtt{\textbf{Push}};[\![exp_1]\!]_\rho;\mathtt{\textbf{Swap}};[\![exp_2]\!]_\rho;\mathtt{\textbf{Cons}}$$

Compilation Rule 2.3 Conditionals.

$$[\![\textbf{if}\ exp_1\ \textbf{then}\ exp_2\ \textbf{else}\ exp_3]\!]_\rho \;=$$
$$\mathtt{\textbf{Push}};[\![exp_1]\!]_\rho;\mathtt{\textbf{Branch}}([\![exp_2]\!]_\rho,[\![exp_3]\!]_\rho)$$

Compilation Rule 2.4 Abstractions.

$$[\![\textbf{fun}\ pat \rightarrow exp]\!]_\rho \;=\; \mathtt{\textbf{Cur}}\ \ [\![exp]\!]_{(\rho,\,pat)}$$

Compilation Rule 2.5 Applications.

$$[\![(exp_1\ exp_2)]\!]_\rho \;=\; \mathtt{\textbf{Push}};[\![exp_1]\!]_\rho;\mathtt{\textbf{Swap}};[\![exp_2]\!]_\rho;\mathtt{\textbf{App}}$$

Compilation Rule 2.6 Local declarations.

$$[\![\textbf{let}\ pat{=}exp\ \textbf{in}\ exp_1]\!]_\rho = \mathtt{\textbf{Push}};[\![exp]\!]_\rho;\text{Cons};[\![exp_1]\!]_{(\rho,\,pat)}$$

For recursive definitions, we present here two techniques. We first use the λ-calculus fixpoint combinator defined by "**`Y M = M(Y M)`**". We can consider **`Y`** as a primitive functional constant and rewrite expressions such as

"**let rec** *pat* = *exp* **in** exp_1"

into

"**let** *pat* = **`Y`**(**fun** *pat* → *exp*) **in** exp_1".

It is possible to simulate the behavior of combinator **`Y`** in the CAM, by building a schema of the value exp_1 using information given by pattern *pat* in which variables are replaced by dummy values, and then updating it after the expression has been evaluated.

Example 2.1 For the expression "**let rec** x=1::y **and** y=2::x **in** x", the schema contains two values corresponding to "x" and "y".

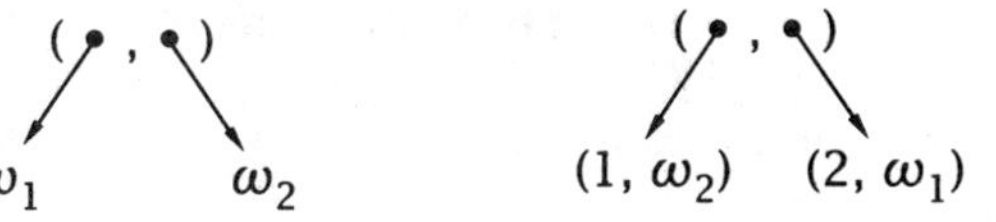

schema computed value

The computation ends by updating the components of the schema, producing the following result:

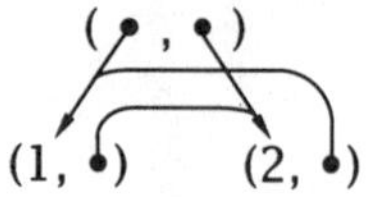

result

The **CompileScheme** function produces the code for building the schema corresponding to a given pattern.

Program 2.3 Creating schemas for recursive values.

```
let rec CompileScheme =
    fun (MLvarpat _) → (Quote ()) ;Push;Cons
    |  (MLpairpat(pat₁ , pat₂)) → Push;(CompileScheme pat₁);Swap
                                   (CompileScheme pat₂);Cons
```

The next step is to evaluate the expression in an environment extended with the schema. This produces a result containing closures with pointers to the schema. Then the schema's variables are replaced by the actual values. Using CAM's **Upd** instruction, the following function generates code to update the schema.

The CAM					
value	stack	code	value	stack	code
t	s.S	Upd;C	s[s ← t]	S	C

The basic case is for patterns that are just variables:

Program 2.4 Updating schemas.

```
let UpdateScheme =
  fun (MLvarpat _) → Upd
 |pat → Cons;Push;(Update [] pat);Pop;Car
    where rec Update code =
    fun (MLvarpat _) → Push;Car;code;Swap;Cdr;code;Upd
    |   (MLpairpat(pat₁ , pat₂)) → Push;(Update (code;Car) pat₁);
                                   Pop;(Update (code;Cdr) pat₂)
```

Compilation Rule 2.7 Recursive declarations.

$[\![$ **let rec** *pat=exp* **in** $exp_1]\!]_\rho$=

Push; CompileScheme *pat*; **Cons;Push;Push;Cdr;Swap;**

$[\![exp]\!]_{(\rho, pat)}$; UpdateScheme *pat*; **Pop;** $[\![exp_1]\!]_{(\rho, pat)}$

3 *Closed Expressions*

The compiler produces code containing instructions that are necessary to save and restore environments, as in the compilation of pairs:

$$[\![(exp_1\ ,\ exp_2)]\!]_\rho \;=\; \texttt{Push};\ ([\![exp_1]\!]_\rho)\ ;\texttt{Swap};\ ([\![exp_2]\!]_\rho)\ ;\texttt{Cons}\ .$$

Some of these environment manipulations can be avoided because an environment is needed only in the case where a computed expression has free variables. In the other case it is possible to use a more compact code.

Moreover, for closed abstractions (i.e., combinators), one can use this idea to factorize access to the argument and to optimize applications of these combinators.

The detection of closed expressions is performed in a traversal of the expressions' syntax trees, during which the list of free variables is computed. A closed expression is characterized by an empty list.

Program 3.1 Free variables in expressions.

```
let rec freeVars =
fun "c" → []  where c is a constant
|   "v" → [v] where v is a variable
|   "if x then y else z" →
          union (freeVars x)
           (union (freeVars y) (freeVars z))
|   "(x , y)" →
          union (freeVars x) (freeVars y)
|   "(x y)" →
          union (freeVars x) (freeVars y)
|   "let pat=exp in exp1" →
          union (subtract (freeVars exp) vars)
                (subtract (freeVars exp1) vars)
          where vars = (varsInPat pat [])
|   "fun pat → exp" →
          subtract (freeVars exp) (varsInPat pat [])

and varsInPat =
fun "v" l →   where v is a variable
          if mem v l then l else v::l
|   "(p1 , p2)" → varsInPat p1 o varsInPat p2

let isClosed = null o freeVars
```

We define a new version of the compiler named C_1 to take into account closed expressions.

To compile conditionals involving closed expressions, we introduce a new CAM instruction **`Branchi(code,code)`**, in which there is no environment restoration. This instruction is also useful when compiling call-by-pattern.

The CAM					
value	stack	code	value	stack	code
true	S	(**Branchi**(C1,C2));C	true	S	C1;C
false	S	(**Branchi**(C1,C2));C	true	S	C2;C

Compilation Rule 3.1 Compilation for conditionals.

$[\![$ **if** exp_1 **then** exp_2 **else** exp_3 $]\!]_\rho$ =
  if isClosed exp_2 & isClosed exp_3
    then $[\![exp_1]\!]_\rho$;**Branchi**($[\![exp_2]\!]_{()}$,$[\![exp_3]\!]_{()}$)
    else Push; $[\![exp_1]\!]_\rho$;**Branch**($[\![exp_2]\!]_\rho$,$[\![exp_3]\!]_\rho$)

An application can be compiled more efficiently when its argument is closed. The same holds for a pair whose right part is closed.

Program 3.2 "CompilePair" produces code associated with binary constructions.

let CompilePair (exp_1, exp_2)ρ = **if** isClosed ρ exp_2
  then $[\![exp_1]\!]_\rho$; **Push**; $[\![exp_2]\!]_{()}$
  else Push; $[\![exp_1]\!]_\rho$; **Swap**; $[\![exp_2]\!]_\rho$

Compilation Rule 3.2 Application and pairs.

$[\![(exp_1\ exp_2)]\!]_\rho$ = CompilePair (exp_1,exp_2); **App**

$[\![(exp_1\ ,\ exp_2)]\!]_\rho$ = CompilePair (exp_1,exp_2); **Cons**

When an expression "**fun** *pat* → *exp*" is a combinator, applying it to an argument exp_1 results in executing code for *exp* in an environment (ρ, exp_1) where only exp_1 is used. We can therefore factorize the code that gives access to exp_1. The code for a combinator "**fun** *pat* → *exp*" then takes the form

Cur((Acc 0);$[\![exp]\!]_{pat}$**)**, where **Acc 0** leaves in the machine register the value of the argument. This reduces the access path and makes the code smaller. The main interest of this optimization lies elsewhere, however, as will be explained in the sequel.

To express the fact that combinators involve special access to their arguments, we use a new formal environment constructor "senv" (simplified environment).

We introduce a new instruction in the CAM to access the argument of a combinator. This new instruction **(Rest n)** is equivalent to Fst^n; it yields an environment and not a component.

The CAM					
value	stack	code	value	stack	code
t	S	(**Rest** 0);C	t	S	C
(t , s)	S	(**Rest** n);C	t	S	(**Rest** (n-1));C

This instruction is used for compiling access to the argument of a combinator.

Program 3.3 Access to environments.

$[\![v]\!]_\rho = \mathcal{A}(v)_\rho$

```
let A( v )ρ = (accessEnv 0 ρ ? compilePrimitive v)
        where rec accessEnv n =
        fun (ρ , pat) → (Acc n) ; accessPat pat ?
                          accessEnv(n+1)ρ
        |   pat → (Rest n) ; accessPat pat
        and accessPat =
        fun (MLvarpat w) → if v=w then [] else fail
        |   (MLpairpat(pat1 , pat2)) →
                          accessPat pat2 ; Cdr ?
                          accessPat pat1 ; Car
```

Compilation Rule 3.3 Abstractions.

$[\![$ **fun** *pat* → *exp* $]\!]_\rho$ = **if** isClosed "**fun** *pat* → *exp*"
then Cur (Acc 0 ; $[\![exp]\!]_{pat}$**) else Cur (**$[\![exp]\!]_{(\rho, pat)}$**)**

In the construction "**let** *pat* = *exp* **in** exp_1" it is possible to produce better code if one of the two expressions (or, even better, both of them) is closed with respect to *pat*. If we take into account the fact that the declaration can be recursive, there are six different cases.

Compilation Rule 3.4 Local declarations.

$[\![$ **let** $pat = exp$ **in** $exp_1]\!]_\rho =$
  if isClosed "**fun** $pat \rightarrow exp_1$"
    then $[\![exp]\!]_\rho$;$[\![exp_1]\!]_{pat}$
    else `Push`; $[\![exp]\!]_\rho$; `Cons`; $[\![exp_1]\!]_{(\rho, pat)}$
$[\![$ **let rec** $pat = exp$ **in** $exp_1]\!]_\rho =$
  if isClosed "**fun** $pat \rightarrow exp_1$"
    then if isClosed "**fun** $pat \rightarrow exp$"
      then CompileScheme *pat*; `Push`; $[\![exp]\!]_{pat}$;
        UpdateScheme *pat* ; $[\![exp_1]\!]_{pat}$
      else `Push`; CompileScheme *pat*;
        `Cons`; `Push`; `Acc 0`; `Swap`; $[\![exp]\!]_{(\rho, pat)}$;
        UpdateScheme *pat*; $[\![exp_1]\!]_{pat}$
    else if isClosed "**fun** $pat \rightarrow exp$"
      then `Push`; CompileScheme *pat*; `Push`; $[\![exp]\!]_{pat}$;
        UpdateScheme *pat*; `Cons`; $[\![exp_1]\!]_{(rho, pat)}$
      else `Push`; CompileScheme *pat*; `Cons`;
        `Push`; `Push`; `Acc 0`; `Swap`; $[\![exp]\!]_{(\rho, pat)}$;
        UpdateScheme *pat*; `Pop`; $[\![exp_1]\!]_{pat}$

4 *Local Functions*

It is often useful to define local functions, as in

let map f = maprec **where** maprec l =
  if null l **then** [] **else** (f (hd l)::maprec (tl l)) **in** map

When executing the code for "maprec", the execution environment contains function "f", function "maprec", and the argument. Inside the closure for function "maprec", one can find closures for "f" and "maprec" as well. This information is redundant since the environment is duplicated, and the code, which is known at compile time, could be used more directly. So we apply the idea of annotating the environments with associations between functions and code.

Example 4.1 Function "map" will serve as an illustration of what we want to do.

$[\![$ **let** map f = e **in** map $]\!]_{()}$
where e = **let** maprec = exp_1 **in** maprec
and exp_1 = **fun** [] → [] | (x::l) → (f x::maprec l)

⇒$[\![$ map $]\!]_{()}$\{map = Code\}
where Code = $[\![$ **fun** f → e $]\!]_{()}$

⇒(Cur (Acc 0;$[\![$ maprec $]\!]_{\rho\prime}$))
where $\rho\prime$ = f\{maprec = $[\![$ exp_1 $]\!]_{\rho\prime}$\}

The formal environment used for compiling exp_1 is recursive, and this permits us to obtain code represented by a cyclic graph. Thus loops in the execution environment are replaced by loops in the code.

Moreover, more expressions become closed since functional variables introduced by "let" can be withdrawn from the list of free variables of expressions.

Management of annotations in the recursive case requires lazy evaluation.

4.1 *Annotations*

Since annotations concern only functions, it is necessary to partition simultaneous declarations into function declarations and other declarations. This is the purpose of the following function.

Program 4.1 The function *pickUp* partitions patterns and expressions, and the function *flat* rebuilds patterns and expressions with pieces that will not be part of the annotation.

```
flatAndPickUp :
(MLpat & MLexp) → (MLpat & MLexp) & (string & MLexp) list
let flatAndPickUp =

 functions in the right part
 let rec pickUp =
  fun (MLpairpat (pat1 , pat2) , MLpair (exp1 , exp2)) →
        let pat1 , f1) = pickUp (pat1 , exp1)
        and pat2 , f2) = pickUp (pat2 , exp2) in
        (pat1@pat2),(f1@f2)
 |    (MLvarpat v,(MLmatch _ as e)) → [],[v,e]
 |    pE → [pE],[]

 Rebuilds patterns and expressions
 and flat =
```

```
fun [pE] → pE
|   ((pat, exp)::l) → MLpairpat(pat, pat₁), MLpair(exp, exp₁)
     where pat₁ , exp₁ = flat l in
```

First pickUp, *then* flat

```
fun (pat, exp as pE) → let pl,fl=pickUp pE in
      (if null fl then (pat, exp)
      if null pl then nullPE else
      flat pl),fl;;
```

We shall use the notation: $\rho\{f_1 = code_1, \ldots, f_n = code_n\}$ for formal environment ρ decorated with annotations $\{f_1 = code_1, \ldots, f_n = code_n\}$.

We have to take into account annotated environments as a new kind of environment. The boolean flag indicates whether or not functions are closed.

Program 4.2 The function "decorate" builds a new environment from an environment ρ and a list of annotating functions (this initial version of "decorate" will be augmented in Section 4.2).

```
let decorate ρ fl =
  let rec annot =
  map (fun (v,e) → v,⟦ e ⟧ρ{annot}) fl in
 (fun ρ → ρ{annot})
```

4.2 *r-Closed Expressions*

We replace the notion of closed expression with the more technical notion of *r*-closed. These are expressions all of whose free variables are functional variables whose code is defined in annotations and which does not itself contain access to the environment. In the following, we shall denote closed annotations with a star ($\rho\{\cdots\}^*$) when this information is important.

Program 4.3 The function "rCloseVar" tests whether a variable which is free in an expression is *r*-closed with respect to some given environment ρ. This test is extended to expressions by function "isRClosed".

```
rCloseVar : string → fenv → bool
let rCloseVar v =rClose
 where rec rClose =
 fun (ρ,pat) →
       if isVarInPat v pat then false else rClose ρ
 |   (ρ{annot}*) →
```

```
      (assoc v annot;true) ? rClose ρ
  |  (ρ{annot}) →
      (assoc v annot;false) ? rClose ρ
  |  pat → if isVarInPat v pat then false else
      isGlobal v or (failwith 'rCloseVar')
  |  () → isGlobal v or (failwith 'rCloseVar');;

let isRClosed ρ e =
  let vl = freeVars e in null vl or
           (forAll (C rCloseVar env) vl)
```

An annotation is *r*-closed if all annotating functions are *r*-closed. This property is easy to check in the nonrecursive case: An annotation is closed if each expression defining the annotating functions is *r*-closed. In the recursive case, one can find an approximation by assuming that annotating functions are closed while performing the verification on the corresponding expressions. Here is a new version of "decorate" which incorporates computation of the *r*-closure indicator.

Program 4.4 One can now augment function "decorate" (defined in the preceding section) to introduce the computation of the *r*-closure indicator.

```
let decorate ρ fl =
  let rec close =
   forAll (isRClosed ρ{annot}* o snd) fl
  and annot =
   map (fun (v,e) → v,⟦ e ⟧ρ{annot}^close) fl in
 (fun ρ → ρ{annot}^close)
```

A more precise method would be to associate an *r*-closure indicator with every annotating function $f_1, \ldots, f_n$. In that case, the non-*r*-closed functions are the smallest set such that

If e_i is non-*r*-closed without taking into account the annotating functions, then f_i belongs to the set.

If e_i has a member of the set as a free variable, then f_i also belongs to the set.

Example 4.2 This example shows the difference between the two methods.

"**let** u=1 **in let** f x = u,g x **and** g x = x,x **in** f (g 3)"

With the first method, the two functions are considered as non-r-closed. With the second, "g" is considered as r-closed.

4.3 *Inheritance of Annotations*

In compiler C_1, the formal environment is not kept available when compiling closed subexpressions. This can cause a problem for r-closed expressions since they can use r-closed annotations defined above them. For that, we need a mechanism to "inherit" r-closed annotations.

Program 4.5 Constructing annotated environments.

```
let inhAnnot,inhNull =
 let rec inherit (names,annots) =
 fun (ρ,p) → inherit (varsInPat p names,annots) ρ
 |   (ρ{As}*) → Annotation r-close
        inherit(names,annots') env
        where annots' =
         listIt (fun (v,code as arg) l →
                   if mem v names then l else arg::l)
         As annots
 |   (ρ{As}) →
        inherit(union (map fst As) names,annots) env
 |   p → annots
 |   () → annots in

 (fun ρι → let annots = inherit ([],[]) ρι in
    fun ρ → annotenv(ρ,true,annots)),
 (fun ρι → let annots = inherit ([],[]) ρι in
    annotenv((),true,annots))
```

4.4 *The Compiler C_2*

To compile a variable we have to find it in the formal environment. If the variable corresponds to an annotation, and if the annotation is closed, we just have to take the corresponding code. If the annotation is not closed, we have to find the right environment. The variables that cannot be found in the environment are considered as primitives, since undeclared variables would have been trapped by the type-checker.

Compilation Rule 4.1 Access to variables.

```
⟦ v ⟧ρ = 𝒜( v )ρ
let 𝒜( v )ρ =
(accessEnv 0 ρ ? CompilePrimitive v)
where rec accessEnv n =
fun (ρ,pat) → (Acc n);accessPat pat ?
                  accessEnv (n+1) ρ
|   pat →         (Rest n);(accessPat pat)
|   ρ{annot}^close →
                  (let code = assoc v annot in
                   if close or n=0 then code else (Rest n);code) ?
                  accessEnv n ρ
and accessPat =
fun (MLvarpat w) → if v=w then [] else fail
|   (MLpairpat(pat1 , pat2)) → accessPat pat2 ; Cdr ?
                               accessPat pat1 ; Car
```

Program 4.6 "CompilePair" redefined to use the tests on *r*-closed expressions.

```
let CompilePair (exp1, exp2) ρ = if isRClosed ρ exp2
   then ⟦ exp1 ⟧ρ ; Push; ⟦ exp2 ⟧inhNullρ
   else Push; ⟦ exp1 ⟧ρ ; Swap; ⟦ exp2 ⟧ρ
```

Compilation Rule 4.2 Abstractions, conditionals, and pairs.

```
⟦ fun pat → exp ⟧ρ = if isRClosed ρ "fun pat → exp"
  then Cur (Acc 0 ; ⟦ exp ⟧inh_annotρ pat)
  else Cur (⟦ exp ⟧(ρ, pat))

⟦ if exp1 then exp2 else exp3 ⟧ρ =
  if isRClosed ρ exp2 & isRClosed ρ exp3
     then ⟦ exp1 ⟧ρ;Branchi(⟦ exp2 ⟧inhNullρ,⟦ exp3 ⟧inhNullρ)
     else Push; ⟦ exp1 ⟧ρ;Branch (⟦ exp2 ⟧ρ,⟦ exp3 ⟧ρ)

⟦ exp1 , exp2 ⟧ρ = (CompilePair (exp1, exp2) ρ); Cons
```

The CAM					
value	stack	code	value	stack	code
t	S	**Cycle**(C0);C	t	C.S	C0

Compiling applications requires some care.

Compilation Rule 4.3 Applications.

$[\![$ (v exp_2) $]\!]_\rho$ =
match ($\mathcal{A}$(v)$_\rho$,exp_2)
with ((**Cur(Acc 0**; *code*)),exp_2) → $[\![$ exp_2 $]\!]_\rho$; **Cycle** (*code*)
| (**Restn**; **Cur** (*code*), exp_2) →
if isRClosed ρ exp_2
then Rest n; **Push**; $[\![$ exp_2 $]\!]_\rho$; **Cons**; **Cycle** (*code*)
else Push; **Rest n**; **Swap**; $[\![$ exp_2 $]\!]_\rho$; **Cons**; **Cycle** (*code*)
| (**Cur** (*code*) , exp_2) →**Push**; $[\![$ exp_2 $]\!]_\rho$; **Cons**; **Cycle** (*code*)
| (**Cur(Acc 0**; **Push**; **Car**; **Swap**; **Cdr**; *code*),(exp_{21}, exp_{22})) →
CompilePair (exp_{21}, exp_{22}) ρ; *code*
| (*code* , exp_2) → **if** isRClosed ρ exp_2
then *code*; **Push**; $[\![$ exp_2 $]\!]_{\text{inhNull}\rho}$; **App**
else Push; *code*; **Swap**; $[\![$ exp_2 $]\!]_\rho$; **App**

$[\![$ (exp_1 exp_2) $]\!]_\rho$ = CompilePair (exp_1, exp_2) ρ; **App**

Compilation Rule 4.4 Local declarations.

$[\![$ **let** *pat* = *exp* **in** exp_1 $]\!]_\rho$ =
let (*pat′* , *exp′*),fl = flatAndPickUp (*pat* , *exp*) **in**
let decor = decorate ρ fl **in**
let ρ' = decor (inhAnnot(ρ, *pat′*) *pat′*) **in**
if isEmptyPat *pat′* *only abstractions*
then $[\![$ exp_1 $]\!]_{\text{decor}\rho}$
if isRClosed (decor ρ) "**fun** *pat′* → exp_1"
then $[\![$ *exp′* $]\!]_\rho$; $[\![$ exp_1 $]\!]_{\rho'}$
else Push; $[\![$ *exp′* $]\!]_\rho$; **Cons**; $[\![$ exp_1 $]\!]_{\text{decor}(\rho,\, pat')}$

$[\![$ **let rec** *pat* = *exp* **in** exp_1 $]\!]_\rho$ =
let (*pat′* , *exp′*),fl = flatAndPickUp (*pat* , *exp*) **in**
let decor = decorate ρ fl **in**

```
let ρ′ = decor (inhAnnot(ρ, pat′) pat′) in
if isEmptyPat pat′   only abstractions
  then ⟦ exp₁ ⟧decorρ
if isRClosed (decor ρ) "fun pat′ → exp₁"
  then if isRClosed (decor ρ) "fun pat′ → exp"
         then CompileScheme pat′; Push; ⟦ exp′ ⟧ρ′;
              UpdateScheme pat′; ⟦ exp₁ ⟧ρ′
         else Push; CompileScheme pat′;
              Cons; Push; Acc 0; Swap; ⟦ exp′ ⟧decor(ρ, pat′);
              UpdateScheme pat′; ⟦ exp₁ ⟧ρ′
  else if isRClosed (decor ρ) "fun pat′ → exp"
         then Push; CompileScheme pat′; Push; ⟦ exp ⟧ρ′;
              UpdateScheme pat′; Cons; ⟦ exp₁ ⟧decor(rho, pat′)
         else Push; CompileScheme pat′; Cons;
              Push; Push; Acc 0; Swap; ⟦ exp ⟧decorate(ρ, pat′);
              UpdateScheme pat′; Pop; ⟦ exp₁ ⟧decor(ρ, pat′)
```

Example 4.3 Here is the code for the Fibonacci function.

```
⟦ let fib n = if n=1 then 1
              if n=2 then 2
              else fib(pred n)+fib(n-2)
   in fib 20 ⟧()

⇒ (Quote 20 ;code) where code =
    (Push ;Push ;Quote 1 ;=
     ;(Branch (Quote 1 ,
               Push ;Push ;Quote 2 ;=
               ;(Branch (Quote 2 ,
                         Push ;pred ;code ;Swap ;Push
                         ;Quote 2 ;- ;code ;+)))))
```

Example 4.4 An example of mutually recursive functions.

```
⟦ let pair x = if x=0 then true else impair(pred x)
  and impair x = if x=0 then false else pair(pred x)
  in impair 5 ⟧()

⇒ (Quote 5 ;code₁)
   where code₁ = (Push ;Push ;Quote 0 ;=
                  ;(Branch (Quote false , pred ;code₂)))
```

```
and code₂ = (Push ;Push ;Quote 0 ;=
              ;(Branch (Quote true , pred ;code₁)))
```

Example 4.5 Here function "f" is not *r*-closed and the execution environment must be saved and restored.

$[\![$ **let** x=1 **in let** f y = x+y **in let** g z =f z,f z **in** g 3 $]\!]_{()}$

```
⇒ (Quote 1 ;Push ;Quote 3 ;Cons ;code₁)
  where code₁ = (Push ;Push ;Rest 1 ;Swap
                 ;Acc 0 ;Cons ;code₂ ;Swap ;Push ;Rest 1
                 ;Swap ;Acc 0 ;Cons ;code₂ ;Cons)
  and code₂ = (Push ;Rest 1 ;Swap ;Acc 0 ;+)
```

5 *Local Variables*

Now we try to optimize access to variables without losing the property that closure building costs only one "cons". When a local variable has no occurrence in an abstraction, it need not be put in the environment but can be put on the stack instead. Then environments are reduced to minimum.

5.1 *Local Variables Classification*

Local variables will be classified as ephemeral or persistent. The lifetime of an ephemeral variable is that of the expression in which it is used. For instance, in the expression "**let** x=3 **in let** y=x–3 **in** x,y,x", variables "x"and "y" are used during the execution of the expression "x,y,x", and then can be thrown away. On the contrary, persistent variables remain accessible through closures as for instance "u" in the expression "**let** u =3 **in fun** x → x+u".

A local declaration is persistent if one of its declared variables is persistent; otherwise it is ephemeral. This classification can be done with a single traversal of the program tree. This must be done before compilation in order to take into account this classification when computing the *r*-closedness property. In the CAML implementation, this is done together with type-checking.

We use a modifiable data structure to record the persistency property.

Program 5.1 The type "localLevel" defines data structure we use.

```
type localLevel
     = ownLevel of (MLpat & bool ref) list
     | funLevel of MLpat & (MLpat & bool ref) list
```

Program 5.2 When going down in the tree a new functional level is created with each function ("newFunLevel"). For each local declaration, a pair formed with the pattern and a nonpositioned persistence indicator is entered ("newDeclLevel").

```
newFunLevel: MLpat → localLevel list → localLevel list
let newFunLevel pat levels = (funLevel(pat,[])::levels)

newDeclLevel: (MLpat & bool ref) → localLevel list → localLevel list
and newDeclLevel patFlag =
    fun [ownLevel l] → [ownLevel(patFlag::l)]
    |   (funLevel(pat,l)::levels) →
          (funLevel(pat,(patFlag::l))::levels);;
```

Program 5.3 Marking patterns.

```
setPersVar: string → localLevel list → void
let setPersVar v = spv false where rec spv b =
 fun [ownLevel pats] →
        (let r = snd (find (isVarInPat v o fst) pats) in
        r:=!r or b;()) ? () Local variables
 |   (funLevel(pat,pats)::levels) →
        (let r = snd (find (isVarInPat v o fst) pats) in
        r:=!r or b;()) ?
        (if isVarInPat v pat then ()
         else spv true levels);;
```

Program 5.4 Introducing information on variable classification.

```
let rec classifyLocalVariables levels = clv where rec clv =
   fun "fun pat → exp" → classifyLocalVariables
            (newFunLevel pat levels) exp
   |  "let pat = exp in exp1^rb" → doList
            (classifyLocalVariables
            (newDeclLevel (pat, rb) levels))
            [exp ; exp1]
   |  "v" →    A variable
            setPersVar s levels
   |  "if exp1 then exp2 else exp3" →
            doList clv [exp1 ; exp2 ; exp3]
   |  "(exp1 , exp2)" → doList clv [exp1 ; exp2]
   |  "(exp1 exp2)" → doList clv [exp1 ; exp2]
   |  E → ()
```

5.2 *Compiling Abstractions with Local Variables*

We will use a new instruction `(Elem n)`, that gives access to the *n*th element in the stack.

The CAM					
value	stack	code	value	stack	code
t	S	(**Elem** *n*);C	*S*[*n*]	S	C

Access to ephemeral variables must take into account the exact state of the stack. For that purpose, we extend formal environments with new constructions.

```
type fenv =
| PersEnv of fenv & MLpat   persistent values
| EphEnv of fenv & MLpat   ephemeral values
| Unknown of fenv   unknowns
```

The code to access local values is decomposed into access in the environment or in the stack, in order to get to the pattern, followed by an access inside the pattern.

```
let Access s = acc (0,0)
    where rec acc (n,m) =
    fun (Unknown::imgl) → acc (succ n,m) imgl
    |   ((EphEnv pat)::imgl) →
            accPat [Local n] pat ? acc (succ n,m) imgl
    |   ((PersEnv pat)::imgl) →
            accPat [Acc m] pat ? acc (n,succ m) imgl

and accPat code =
fun (MLvarpat s1) → if s=s1 then rev code else fail
|   (MLpairpat(pat1,pat2)) →
        accPat (Cdr;code) pat2 ? accPat (Car;code) pat1

let CompileExpr imgl Expr =
    let CompilePush = CompileExpr (Unknown;imgl)
    in match Expr
    with (MLephLet(Pat,e1,e)) →
                Push;CompilePush e1;Swap;
                CompileExpr (EphEnv Pat::imgl) e;Swap;Pop
    |   (MLpersLet(Pat,e1,e)) →
```

```
                Push;CompilePush e1;Cons;
                CompileExpr (PersEnv Pat::imgl) e
    |   (MLvar s) → Access s imgl
    |   (MLmatch(_,Pat,e)) →
                [Cur(CompileExpr (PersEnv Pat::imgl) e)]
    |   (MLapp(e1,e2)) →
                Push;CompilePush e1;
                Swap;CompilePush e2;App
    |   (MLconst c) → [Quote(CompileConst c)]
    |   (MLpair(e1,e2)) →
                Push;CompilePush e1;
                Swap;CompilePush e2;Cons
    |   (MLcond(e1,e2,e3)) →
                Push;CompilePush e1;
                Branch(CompilePush e2,
                       CompilePush e3)
```

Example 5.1 For the expression

let x=1 **in let** y=2 **in** x,y;;

the compiled code is

```
[Push; (Quote "1"); Swap;
  Push; (Quote "2"); Swap;
   Push; (Loc 2); Swap; (Loc 1); Cons;
  Swap; Pop;
Swap; Pop] : code
```

If we add optimizations on closed expressions, the code becomes:

```
[(Quote "1"); Push; (Quote "2"); Cons] : code
```

Example 5.2 Note that access to persistent variables is also improved, since access paths are shortened:

fun x → **let** y=2 **in let** z=x,y **in** z,z,(**fun** t→ x,t)

The code is:

```
[Cur [Push; (Quote 2); Swap;
      Push; Push; (Acc 0); Swap; (Loc 2); Cons; Swap;
      Push; (Loc 1); Swap; Push; (Loc 2); Swap;
      Cur[Push; (Acc 1); Swap; (Acc 0); Cons];
          Cons; Cons; Swap; Pop; Swap; Pop]]
```

This technique, however, complicates the computation of access code too much to be used in the actual implementation. We propose an alternative below.

In the case of embedded ephemeral values, the code has the following shape:

let $P_1 = E_1$ **in**	**Push** $[\![E_1]\!]$ **Swap**
...	...
let $P_n = E_n$ **in**	**push** $[\![E_n]\!]$ **Swap**
E	$[\![E]\!]$
	Swap Pop
	...
	Swap Pop

At the end, ephemeral values are dropped from the stack. It seems reasonable to introduce a notion of "block" in order to manage these values globally. We introduce a new instruction, **Block** (*n*, *Code*), which executes instructions *Code* in an environment in which *n* local variables are used. We use instruction **NewLocal** *n* to store the value of the *n*th local variable and **Local** *n* to retrieve it.

Here is a new version of the compiler.

```
let Access s (imgl,n) = acc (pred n,0) imgl
    where rec acc (n,m) =
    fun (EphEnv pat::imgl) →
            accPat [Local n] pat ? acc (pred n,m) imgl
    |   (PersEnv pat::imgl) →
            accPat [Acc m] pat ? acc (n,succ m) imgl

and accPat code =
    fun (MLvarpat s') → if s=s' then rev code else fail
    |   (MLpairpat(pat1,pat2)) →
            accPat (Cdr;code) pat2 ? accPat (Car;code) pat1
```

The function "CompileBlock" introduces instruction **Block** for ephemeral variables.

```
let rec CompileExpr (imgl,n as env) =
(Compil where rec Compil =
     fun (MLephLet(Pat,e1,e)) →
            Push; Compil e1;NewLocal n;Pop;
```

```
        CompileExpr (EphEnv Pat::imgl,succ n) e
  |  (MLpersLet(Pat,e1,e)) →
        Push; Compil e1; Cons;
        CompileExpr (PersEnv Pat::imgl,n) e
  |  (MLvar s) → Acces s env
  |  (MLmatch(ephN,Pat,e)) →
        [Cur(CompileBlock (PersEnv Pat::imgl,ephN) e)]
  |  (MLapp(e1,e2)) →
        Push; Compil e1; Swap; Compil e2; App
  |  (MLconst c) → (Quote(CompileConst c))
  |  (MLpair(e1,e2)) →
        Push; Compil e1; Swap; Compil e2; Cons
  |  (MLcond(e1,e2,e3)) →
        Push; Compil e1; Branch(Compil e2,Compil e3))
and CompileBlock =
    fun (imgl,0 as env) → CompileExpr env
  |  (imgl,n) e → [Block(n,CompileExpr (imgl,0) e)]
```

Example 5.3 Application of the new compiler.

let x=1 **in let** y=2 **in** x,y

```
[Block (2,
 [Push; (Quote 1); (NewLocal 0);
  Pop; Push; (Quote 2); (NewLocal 1);
  Pop; Push; (Local 0); Swap; (Local 1); Cons])]
```

With optimizations of closed expressions, we get:

```
[Block (2,
 [(Quote 1); (NewLocal 0); (Quote 2); (NewLocal 1);
  (Local 0); Push; (Local 1); Cons])]
```

6 *Curried Functions*

Writing a function in a curried form is often more pleasant, but it can be costly because it causes the construction of intermediate closures.

Example 6.1 The code for

$[\![$ **let** f x y z = x*y+z **in** f $]\!]_\rho$

has the shape

$$[\texttt{Cur[Acc 0;}\quad \texttt{Cur[Cur}\ [\![\text{x*y+z}]\!]_{(((\rho,\mathbf{x}),\mathbf{y}),\mathbf{z})}\texttt{]]]} == $$

```
[Cur[Acc 0;
      Cur[Cur[Push; Push; Rest 2; Swap;
                  Acc 1; *; Swap; Acc 0; +]]]]  ,
```

and an application of this function in a context where all its arguments are given is compiled as follows:

$[\![\textbf{let}\ \text{f x y z} = \text{x*y+z}\ \textbf{in}\ \text{f 3 4 5}]\!]_\rho ==$

$[\![\text{f 3 4 5}]\!]_{\rho\{\text{f} \equiv \textbf{fun}\ \text{xyz} \rightarrow \text{x} * \text{y} + \text{z}\}} ==$

```
[Cur[Acc 0;
      Cur[Cur[Push; Push; Rest 2; Swap;
                  Acc 1; *; Swap; Acc 0; +]]]]
[Push; '3; App; Push;'4; App; Push; '5; App]  .
```

Figure 1 shows how the first two "Cur" instructions are used in the execution. The execution of the third "**Cur**" instruction starts when an environment formed with the three arguments has been constructed. It seems possible to produce code that just builds this environment and calls the internal code directly. This is the first optimization we describe below. The second one concerns access to local variables inside the most internal function, and aims at using the stack instead of building the environment when possible.

6.1 *Optimizing Applications of Curried Functions*

The idea is essentially to execute intermediate applications at compile time. The code produced for the immediate application of a match is in the general case

$[\![(\textbf{fun}\ p \rightarrow e)\ e_1]\!]_\rho =$

$\quad \texttt{Push;}[\![\textbf{fun}\ p \rightarrow e]\!]_\rho\texttt{; Swap; }[\![e_1]\!]_\rho\texttt{; App} =$

$\quad \texttt{Push; Cur[}[\![e]\!]_{(\rho,p)}\texttt{]; Swap; }[\![e_1]\!]_\rho\texttt{; App}$

This is very similar to the "**let**" situation, and we can apply the same optimization.

Compilation Rule 6.1 Compilation for application.

$[\![(e_1\ e_2)]\!]_\rho =$

let $c_1 = [\![e_1]\!]_\rho$ **in**

let empty,aCode =applyOpt c_1 **in**

```
(match (last c1,e2)
with (Cur (Acc 0;Push;Car;Swap;Cdr;Code),
 (MLpair pair)) →
  if empty or isRClosed env e2
  then aCode(CompilPair pair ;Code)
  else Push;aCode(Pop;CompilPair pair;Code)
 | (Cur (Acc 0;Code) ,e2) →
  if empty or isRClosed env e2
  then aCode (⟦ e2 ⟧ρ ; Code)
  else Push;aCode (Pop;⟦ e2 ⟧ρ;Code)
```

Figure 1. Execution of **let** f x y z = x*y+z **in** f 3 4 5 .

value	code	stack	
()	Cur[Acc 0;Cur[· · ·]];· · ·	empty	⇒
(().Acc 0;· · ·)	Push;'3; · · ·	empty	⇒
(().Acc 0;· · ·)	'3; App;· · ·	(().Acc 0;· · ·)	⇒
3	App;Push;· · ·	(().Acc 0;· · ·)	⇒
(().3)	Acc 0;Cur[· · ·]	Push;'4· · ·	⇒
3	Cur[Cur[· · ·]]	Push;'4· · ·	⇒
(3.Cur[· · ·])	Push;'4; · · ·	empty	⇒
(3.Cur[· · ·])	'4; App;· · ·	(3.Cur[· · ·])	⇒
'4	App;Push;'5;App	(3.Cur[· · ·])	⇒
(3.4)	Cur[· · ·]	Push;'5;App	⇒
((3.4).Push;· · ·)	Push;'5;App	empty	⇒
((3.4).Push;· · ·)	'5;App	((3.4).Push;· · ·)	⇒
'5	App	((3.4).Push;Push;· · ·)	⇒
((3.4).5)	Push; Push;· · ·	empty	⇒
	· · ·		⇒
17			

| (**Cur**(Code),e_2) →
  if empty **or** isRClosed env e_2
  then aCode(**Push**; $[\![e_2]\!]_\rho$;**Cons**; Code)
  else Push; aCode(**Swap**; $[\![e_2]\!]_\rho$;**Cons**; Code)
| (_,e_2) → **if** isRClosed env e_2
  then c_1;**Push**; $[\![e_2]\!]_{(\mathbf{inhNull}\ \rho)}$;**App**
  else Push c_1 **Swap**@ $[\![e_2]\!]_\rho$ @**App**)

Example 6.2 The code produced for Example 6.2 is reduced significantly.

$[\![$ **let** f x y z = x*y+z **in** f 3 4 5 $]\!]_\rho$ =
  (**'3;Push;'4;Cons;Push;'5;Cons;**C_1) *where*
  C_1 = (**Push;Push;Rest 2;Swap;Acc 1;*;Swap;Acc 0;+**)

This is very similar to the code produced for the corresponding uncurried function.

$[\![$ **let** f (x,y,z) = x*y+z **in** f (3,4,5) $]\!]_\rho$ =
  (**'3;Push;'4;Push;'5;Cons;Cons;**C_1) *where*
  C_1 = (**Push;Push;Car;Swap;Cdr;Car;*;Swap;Cdr;Cdr;+**)

6.2 *Access to Local Environments*

Now, in case the arguments of the curried function are ephemeral, we can allocate a block to contain them.

Compilation Rule 6.2 The function "CompileBlock" takes a formal environment, an expression to be compiled, and a list of variables to be put in the block.

let CompileBlock ρ *exp* =
  let vars = ephVars *exp* **in**
  let n = length vars **in**
  if n=0 **then** $[\![exp]\!]_\rho$ **else**
    [**Block(n,** listIt lookUp vars (1,$[\![exp]\!]_{\rho'}$))]
  where lookUp v (code,n) =
    (**Push;** $\mathcal{A}(v)_\rho$; **(NewLocal n); Pop;**) code,n+1
  and ρ' = listIt (**fun** v ρ → ephEnv(ρ,v)) vars ρ

We introduce a pseudo-instruction, **Curry(*n*,*b*,code)**, which will be interpreted as a sequence of *n* instructions **Cur** followed by a block then by putting the *n* arguments into the block and finally the code of the internal expression. The boolean value *b* indicates whether or not the function is closed.

We put blocks at the entry to functions having more than a certain number of arguments.

Example 6.3 The code for function "f" of Example 6.1 becomes

```
Curry(3,true,[Local 1;Push;Local 2;*;Push;Local 3;+])
```

or in the expanded form:

```
Cur[Acc0;Cur[Cur[Block(3,[ Push; Rest 2;NewLocal 1;
    Pop;Push;Acc 1;NewLocal 2;
    Pop;Push;Acc 0;NewLocal 3;Pop;
    Local 1;Push;Local 2;*;Push;Local 3;+]) ]]]  .
```

References

[1] Cousineau, G. and Huet, G. "The CAML Primer". Technical report, Projet Formel, INRIA-ENS. Version 2.5, December 1987.

[2] Formel Group. "The CAML Reference Manual". January 1989. Available through INRIA, Domaine de Voluceau, Rocquencourt BP105, 78153 Le Chesnay Cedex, France.

Part II

Polymorphic Lambda Calculus

Introduction to Part II

5

John C. Reynolds
Carnegie Mellon University

The polymorphic (or second-order) typed lambda calculus was invented by Jean-Yves Girard in 1971 [10, 11], and independently reinvented by myself in 1974 [22]. It is extraordinary that essentially the same programming language was formulated independently by the two of us, especially since we were led to the language by entirely different motivations.

In my own case, I was seeking to extend conventional typed programming languages to permit the definition of "polymorphic" procedures that could accept arguments of a variety of types. I started with the ordinary typed lambda calculus and added the ability to pass types as parameters (an idea that was "in the air" at the time, e.g. [4]).

For example, as in the ordinary typed lambda calculus one can write

$$\lambda f_{\mathbf{int} \to \mathbf{int}}.\ \lambda x_{\mathbf{int}}.\ f(f(x))$$

to denote the "doubling" function for the type **int**, which accepts a function from integers to integers and yields the composition of this function with itself. Similarly, using a type variable t, one can write

$$\lambda f_{t \to t}.\ \lambda x_t.\ f(f(x))$$

to denote the doubling function for t. Then, by abstracting on the type variable, one can define a polymorphic doubling function,

$$\Lambda t.\ \lambda f_{t \to t}.\ \lambda x_t.\ f(f(x)),$$

that can be applied to any type to obtain the doubling function for that type, e.g.,

$$(\Lambda t.\ \lambda f_{t \to t}.\ \lambda x_t.\ f(f(x)))[\mathbf{int}]$$

$$\Rightarrow \lambda f_{\mathbf{int} \to \mathbf{int}}.\ \lambda x_{\mathbf{int}}.\ f(f(x))$$

or

$$(\Lambda t.\ \lambda f_{t \to t}.\ \lambda x_t.\ f(f(x)))[\mathbf{real} \to \mathbf{real}]$$

$$\Rightarrow \lambda f_{(\mathbf{real} \to \mathbf{real}) \to (\mathbf{real} \to \mathbf{real})}.\ \lambda x_{\mathbf{real} \to \mathbf{real}}.\ f(f(x)).$$

Notice that an upper case Λ and square brackets are used to indicate abstraction and application of types, and that $\Rightarrow$ denotes a kind of beta reduction for types, in which type expressions are substituted for occurrences of type variables within ordinary expressions.

To accommodate this kind of abstraction and application of types, it is necessary to expand the variety of type expressions to provide types for the polymorphic functions. Somewhat surprisingly, this can be done in such a way that (if the type of every variable binding is given explicitly) type correctness can be determined syntactically (i.e., at compile time). One writes $\Delta t.\ \omega$ (where Δ is a binding operator) to denote the type of polymorphic function that, when applied to a type t, yields a result of type ω. For example, the polymorphic doubling function has type

$$\Delta t.\ (t \to t) \to (t \to t),$$

and the polymorphic identity function,

$$\Lambda t.\ \lambda x_t.\ x,$$

has type

$$\Delta t.\ t \to t.$$

If an expression e has type ω then $\Lambda t.\ e$ has type $\Delta t.\ \omega$, and if an expression e has type $\Delta t.\ \omega$ then $e[\omega']$ has the type obtained from ω by substituting ω' for t. Thus it is straightforward to decide the type of any expression.

The movitation that led Girard to essentially the same language was entirely different; he was seeking to extend an analogy between types and propositions that was originally found by Curry [8, Section 9E] and Howard [12]. Types can be viewed as propositions by regarding the type constructor $\rightarrow$ as the logical connective **implies**. (Similarly, one can regard the Cartesian product constructor $\times$ as the connective **and** and the disjoint union constructor + as the connective **or**.) Then an expression e of type ω becomes an encoding of a proof of the proposition ω in intuitionistic logic.

For example, the doubling function for t encodes the following, rather roundabout proof that (t **implies** t) **implies** (t **implies** t), in which t is some arbitrary proposition and e: indicates that the proof step is encoded by the expression e.

Assume f: t **implies** t.

Assume x: t.

Since f: t **implies** t and x: t, we have $f(x)$: t.

Since f: t **implies** t and $f(x)$: t, we have $f(f(x))$: t.

Discharging the assumption x, we have $\lambda x.\ f(f(x))$: t **implies** t.

Discharging the assumption f, we have
$\lambda f.\ \lambda x.\ f(f(x))$: ($t$ **implies** t) **implies** (t **implies** t).

Girard extended the Curry-Howard analogy by regarding the binding operator $\Delta t.$ as a universal quantifier of a propositional variable, i.e., as "For all propositions t". (He also introduced an analogous existential quantifier.) Thus the polymorphic doubling function encodes a proof that

($\forall t$) (t **implies** t) **implies** (t **implies** t).

Notice that there is a circularity or "impredicativity" here, since such a quantified proposition belongs to the set of propositions being quantified over. (This circularity is also present in the Coquand-Huet Calculus of Constructions, which includes the polymorphic calculus as a sublanguage, but not in the types-as-propositions formalisms of Martin-Löf [17] or Constable [5].)

Despite this circularity, Girard showed that every expression of the polymorphic typed lambda calculus possesses a normal form, i.e., that every expression can be reduced by some finite sequence of beta reductions to a form that cannot be reduced further. (This result was strengthened by Prawitz [21, p. 256] to show that every expression is strongly normalizable, i.e., that no expression is amenable to any infinite sequence of beta reductions.) Proof-theoretically, this means that every proof can be transformed into a "cut-free" proof. Computationally, it means that every expression describes a terminating computation.

This is extraordinary. For any language in which every expression describes a terminating computation, there must be computable functions that cannot be expressed; indeed we are used to taking this fact as evidence that such languages are uninteresting for practical computation. Yet the polymorphic typed lambda calculus is just such a language, in which one can express "almost everything" that one might actually want to compute. Indeed, Girard has shown that every function from natural numbers to natural numbers that can be proved total by using second order arithmetic can be expressed in the calculus. This includes not only primitive recursive functions, but also Ackermann's function as well as far more esoteric (and rapidly growing) functions.

This result depends upon a particular way of encoding the natural numbers called "Church numerals". In his early work on the untyped lambda calculus, Church used the encoding

$$0:\quad \lambda f.\, \lambda x.\, x\,,$$

$$1:\quad \lambda f.\, \lambda x.\, f(x)\,,$$

$$2:\quad \lambda f.\, \lambda x.\, f(f(x))\,,$$

$$\ldots$$

The obvious analogue for the polymorphic calculus is

$$0:\quad \Lambda t.\, \lambda f_{t\to t}.\, \lambda x_t.\, x\,,$$

$$1:\quad \Lambda t.\, \lambda f_{t\to t}.\, \lambda x_t.\, f(x)\,,$$

$$2:\quad \Lambda t.\, \lambda f_{t\to t}.\, \lambda x_t.\, f(f(x))\,,$$

$$\ldots$$

In both cases, n is encoded by a higher-order function mapping f into f^n, reflecting the idea that the fundamental use of a natural number n is to iterate something n times. (For example, 2 is encoded by the doubling function.) But in the polymorphic typed case, there is a particular type

$$\mathbf{nat} \stackrel{\text{def}}{=} \Delta t.\, (t \to t) \to (t \to t)$$

that is possessed by every encoding of a natural number. Moreover, every closed (and constant-free) expression of this type is equivalent (via beta and eta reduction) to such an encoding. Thus it is reasonable to regard **nat** as the type of natural numbers.

Using this encoding, one can program arithmetic functions such as

$$succ \stackrel{\text{def}}{=} \lambda n_{\mathbf{nat}}.\, \Lambda t.\, \lambda f_{t\to t}.\, \lambda x_t.\, f(n[t](f)(x)),$$

$$add \stackrel{\text{def}}{=} \lambda m_{\mathbf{nat}}.\, \lambda n_{\mathbf{nat}}.\, \Lambda t.\, \lambda f_{t\to t}.\, \lambda x_t.\, m[t](f)(n[t](f)(x)).$$

Notice that these are functions that accept and produce polymorphic functions. (Such functions go beyond the kind of implicit polymorphism provided by ML.)

Other fundamental sets can be encoded in a similar spirit. For example, the type

$$\mathbf{bool} \stackrel{\text{def}}{=} \Delta t.\, t \to (t \to t)$$

is possessed by the two "choice" functions

$$\Lambda t.\, \lambda x_t.\, \lambda y_t.\, x \quad \text{and} \quad \Lambda t.\, \lambda x_t.\, \lambda y_t.\, y,$$

and every closed expression of this type beta-reduces to one of these functions. Thus it is reasonable to regard **bool** as the type of Boolean values, reflecting the idea that the fundamental use of a Boolean is to make binary choices.

Less trivially, the closed expressions of type

$$\mathbf{list}(s) \stackrel{\text{def}}{=} \Delta t.\, (s \to (t \to t)) \to (t \to t)$$

have normal forms of the form

$$\Lambda t.\, \lambda f_{s\to(t\to t)}.\, \lambda x_t.\, f(e_1)(\ldots(f(e_n)(x))\ldots),$$

where $e_1, \ldots, e_n$ are subexpressions of type s. Thus **list**(s) can be regarded as the type of lists with elements of type s, reflecting the idea that the fundamental use of a list is to reduce the list (in the sense of APL).

These encodings are all special cases of a general result, discovered independently by Böhm [2] and Leivant [15], and anticipated in the work of Takeuti [28, Proposition 3.15.18]. For any many-sorted algebraic signature without laws, there is a set of polymorphic types (one for each sort) whose closed normal forms constitute an initial algebra. Moreover, the operations of this algebra can be expressed as functions among these types. Thus the polymorphic calculus encompasses algebraic data types as well as number-theoretic computations. Several examples of the kind of programming that is entailed are given in [25].

In summary, the polymorphic typed lambda calculus is far more than an extension of the simply typed lambda calculus that permits polymorphism. It is a language that guarantees the termination of all programs, while providing a surprising degree of expressiveness for computations over a rich variety of data types. In "Computable Values Can Be Classical" (in this volume), Val Breazu-Tannen and Albert Meyer argue that the guarantee of termination substantially simplifies reasoning about programs by permitting the conservation of classical data type specifications. In "Polymorphism Is Conservative over Simple Types" (also in this volume), the same authors further substantiate this argument by showing that polymorphism can be superimposed on familiar programming language features without changing their behavior.

However, the practicality of this language is far from proven. To say that any reasonable function can be expressed by some program is not to say that it can be expressed by the most reasonable program. It is clear that the language requires a novel programming style. Moreover, it is likely that certain important functions cannot be expressed by their most efficient algorithms. Also, the guarantee of termination precludes interesting computations that never terminate, such as those involving lazy computation with infinite data structures. (These reservations apply to the pure polymorphic calculus; if a fixed-point operator is added to provide general recursion, the language expands to include conventional functional programming, including lazy computation, but the guarantee of termination is lost.)

The known semantic models of the polymorphic typed lambda calculus can be divided into two species. In the first, the meaning of a type is (the set of equivalence classes of) a partial equivalence relation on a model of the untyped lambda calculus. This view characterizes the earliest models [11, 29], as well as recent work [16, 20, 9, 14, 3, and in this volume, John Mitchell's "A Type-Inference Approach to Reduction Properties and Semantics of Polymorphic Expressions"] that embeds such models in the natural setting of the "effective topos" [13]. (The connection between this kind of model and the effective topos, or equivalently, the "realizability universe", seems to have been first noted by Moggi.)

In the second kind of model, the meaning of a type is a Scott domain. In the earliest of these models [19], these domains were sets of fixed points of closures of a universal domain, where a closure of a domain is an idempotent continuous function from the domain to itself that extends the identity function. Two facts permit this concept to serve as a model of the polymorphic calculus:

> There is a universal domain U such that $U \to U$, the domain of continuous functions from U to U, is isomorphic to the set of fixed points of a

closure of U.

The set of closures of U, which can be regarded as meanings of types, is isomorphic to the set of fixed points of a closure of $U \to U$.

Similar models have been developed in which the concept of closure is replaced by that of finitary retraction [18] or of finitary projection [1]. More recently, Girard has devised a model based on the use of qualitative domains and stable functions, which is described in his paper "The System F of Variable Types, Fifteen Years Later" (in this volume). Other models of this kind are described in [7, 6].

The domain-based models describe not only the pure calculus but also the extension obtained by adding fixed-point operators. Thus they fail to capture the fact that all expressions denote terminating programs and represent proofs of their type interpreted as a proposition. A vivid consequence of this failure is that the type $\Delta t.\ t$, which is clearly false when interpreted as a proposition (and which is not the type of any expression in the pure language), denotes a nonempty domain. Whether such types have empty denotations is a pivotal question about semantic models, whose implications are described in "Empty Types in Polymorphic λ-Calculus" (in this volume), by Meyer, Mitchell, Moggi, and Statman.

Another shortcoming of the domain-based models is their failure to capture the notion of "parametricity". When Christopher Strachey first coined the word "polymorphism" [27], he distinguished between ad hoc polymorphic functions, which can have arbitrarily different meanings for different types, and parametric polymorphic functions, which must behave similarly for different types. Intuitively, only parametric polymorphic functions can be defined in the polymorphic calculus, but the domains denoted by polymorphic types in the domain-based models also contain ad hoc functions.

It is not known whether any of the partial-equivalence-relation models enforce parametricity (except, in a trival sense, the collapsed term model of [3]). Indeed, at present there is no general agreement on how to define parametricity precisely and generally, although a first attempt in this direction was given in [23], and a more recent approach appears in this volume in "Functional Polymorphism" by Bainbridge, Freyd, Scedrov, and Scott.

The fact that all expressions are strongly normalizable, and that certain types correspond to initial algebras, make it plausible that there should be a model extending the naive set-theoretic model of the simply typed lambda calculus, in which types denote sets and $S \to S'$ denotes the set of all functions from S to S'. Indeed, I made such a conjecture in 1983 [23]. Then in the following year —to my embarassment— I proved the conjecture false [24]. (This proof uses a cardinality argument that can be made in classical, but not constructive, logic. Indeed, as shown in [20] and [16], set-theoretic models can be found in a constructive metatheory.) Soon thereafter, Gordon Plotkin generalized my proof, showing that it is based upon a general property of functors (on the Cartesian closed category underlying an arbitrary model) that can be expressed in the calculus. This generalization is described in this volume in "On Functors Expressible in the Polymorphic Typed Lambda Calculus."

Beneath all these specific models lies the question of what, in general, constitutes a model of the language, which is discussed by Kim Bruce, Albert Meyer, and John Mitchell in "The Semantics of Second-Order Lambda Calculus" (in this volume). A more abstract answer to this question, using category-theoretic concepts, has been given by Seely [26].

The polymorphic lambda calculus also raises the problem of type inference. Although type checking is straightforward for the explicitly typed form of the calculus, the explicit statement of types whenever a variable is bound is a serious burden for the programmer. Ideally, one would like an algorithm that could examine an expression of the untyped lambda calculus and decide whether there is any assignment of types to variables that makes the expression well-typed. However, despite considerable efforts, the existence of such an algorithm for the polymorphic calculus remains an open question.

Current research on this question is described in this volume in "Polymorphic Type Inference and Containment" by John Mitchell. In "A Type-Inference Approach to Reduction Properties and Semantics of Polymorphic Expressions", also in this volume, the same author applies type inference to the study of the calculus itself, obtaining a simplified proof of the strong normalization property and a proof of completeness for a class of partial-equivalence-relation models.

The author wishes to thank Val Breazu-Tannen, Kim Bruce, Carl Gunter, Giuseppe Longo, Albert Meyer, John Mitchell, Eugenio Moggi, Gordon Plotkin, Andre Scedrov, and Rick Statman, all of whom have contributed comments that have improved the accuracy and generality of this introduction.

References

[1] Amadio, R., Bruce, K. B., and Longo, G. "The finitary projection model for second order lambda calculus and solutions to higher order domain equations". In *Proceedings Symposium on Logic in Computer Science*, pp. 122–130, 1986.

[2] Böhm, C. and Berarducci, A. "Automatic synthesis of typed Λ-programs on term algebras". *Theoretical Computer Science 39* (1985), pp. 135–154.

[3] Breazu-Tannen, V. and Coquand, T. "Extensional models for polymorphism". *Theoretical Computer Science 59* 1–2 (July 1988), pp. 85–114.

[4] Cheatham, T. E. Jr., Fischer, A., and Jorrand, P. "On the basis for ELF — an extensible language facility". *Proceedings AFIPS 1968 Fall Joint Computer Conference*, vol. 33, part 2, pp. 937–948. Thompson Book Company, Washington, D. C., 1968.

[5] Constable, R. L. et al. *Implementing Mathematics with the Nuprl Proof Development System*. Prentice-Hall, Englewood Cliffs, N.J., 1986.

[6] Coquand, T., Gunter, C. A., and Winskel. G. "Domain theoretic models of polymorphism". *Information and Computation 81*, 2 (May 1989), pp. 123–167.

[7] Coquand, T., Gunter, C. A, and Winskel, G. "DI-domains as a model of polymorphism". *Mathematical Foundations of Programming Language Semantics* (Proceedings, 1987), M. Main, A. Melton, M. Mislove, and D. Schmidt, eds., pp. 344–363. Lecture Notes in Computer Science, vol. 298. Springer-Verlag, Berlin, 1987.

[8] Curry, H. B. and Feys, R. *Combinatory Logic, Volume I* (second edition). North-Holland, Amsterdam, 1968.

[9] Freyd, P. and Scedrov, A. "Some semantic aspects of polymorphic lambda calculus". *Proceedings Symposium on Logic in Computer Science*, pp. 315–319, 1987.

[10] Girard, J.-Y. "Une extension de l'interpretation de Gödel à l'analyse, et son application a l'elimination des coupures dans l'analyse et la théorie des types". *Proceedings of the Second Scandinavian Logic Symposium*, J. E. Fenstad, ed., pp. 63–92. North-Holland, Amsterdam, 1971.

[11] Girard, J.-Y. *Interprétation Fonctionnelle et Elimination des Coupures dans l'Arithmétique d'Ordre Supérieur*. Thèse de doctorat d'état, Université Paris VII, 1972.

[12] Howard, W. A. "The formulae-as-types notion of construction". *To H. B. Curry: Essays on Combinatory Logic, Lambda Calculus and Formalism*, J. P. Seldin and J. R. Hindley, eds., pp. 479–490. Academic Press, London, 1980.

[13] Hyland, J. M. E. "The effective topos". *The L. E. J. Brouwer Centenary Symposium*, A. S. Troelstra and D. Van Dalen, eds., pp. 165–216. North-Holland, Amsterdam, 1982.

[14] Hyland, J. M. E. "A small complete category". *Annals of Pure and Applied Logic 40*, 2 (November 1988), pp. 135–165.

[15] Leivant, D. "Reasoning about functional programs and complexity classes associated with type disciplines". *24th Annual Symposium on Foundations of Computer Science*, pp. 460–469, 1983.

[16] Longo, G. and Moggi, E. "Constructive natural deduction and its 'modest' interpretation". To appear in *Semantics of Natural and Computer Languages*, J. Meseguer, ed. MIT Press, Cambridge, Mass.

[17] Martin-Löf, P. *Intuitionistic Type Theory*. Bibliopolis, Naples, 1984.

[18] McCracken, N. J. "A finitary retract model for the polymorphic lambda-calculus". To appear in *Information and Control*.

[19] McCracken, N. J. *An Investigation of a Programming Language with a Polymorphic*

Type Structure. Ph. D. dissertation, Syracuse University, June 1979.

[20] Pitts, A. M. "Polymorphism is set theoretic, constructively". *Category Theory and Computer Science*, D. H. Pitt, A. Poigné, and D. E. Rydeheard, eds., pp. 12–39. Lecture Notes in Computer Science, vol. 283. Springer-Verlag, Berlin, 1987.

[21] Prawitz, D. "Ideas and results in proof theory". *Proceedings of the Second Scandinavian Logic Symposium*, J. E. Fenstad, ed., pp. 235–307. North-Holland, Amsterdam, 1971.

[22] Reynolds, J. C. "Towards a theory of type structure". *Proceedings, Colloque sur la Programmation*, pp. 408–425. Lecture Notes in Computer Science, vol. 19. Springer-Verlag, Berlin, 1974.

[23] Reynolds, J. C. "Types, abstraction and parametric polymorphism". *Information Processing 83*, R. E. A. Mason, ed., pp. 513–523, Elsevier Science Publishers B. V. (North-Holland), Amsterdam, 1983.

[24] Reynolds, J. C. "Polymorphism is not set-theoretic". *Semantics of Data Types*, G. Kahn, D. B. MacQueen, and G. D. Plotkin, eds., pp. 145–156. Lecture Notes in Computer Science, vol. 173. Springer-Verlag, Berlin, 1984.

[25] Reynolds, J. C. "Three approaches to type structure". *Mathematical Foundations of Software Development*, H. Ehrig, C. Floyd, M. Nivat, and J. Thatcher, eds., pp. 97–138. Lecture Notes in Computer Science, vol. 185. Springer-Verlag, Berlin, 1985.

[26] Seely, R. A. G. "Categorical semantics for higher order polymorphic lambda calculus". *Journal of Symbolic Logic 52,* 4 (December 1987), pp. 969–989.

[27] Strachey, C. "Fundamental concepts in programming languages". August 1967.

[28] Takeuti, G. *Proof Theory.* North-Holland, Amsterdam, 1975.

[29] Troelstra, A. S. (editor). *Metamathematical Investigation of Intuitionistic Arithmetic and Analysis. Lecture Notes in Mathematics*, vol. 344. Springer-Verlag, Berlin, 1973.

The System F of Variable Types, Fifteen Years Later[1]

6

Jean-Yves Girard
Équipe de Logique Mathématique

per te Serena

Abstract

The semantic study of system *F* stumbles on the problem of *variable types* for which there was no convincing interpretation; we develop here a semantics based on the category-theoretic idea of *direct limit*, so that the behavior of a variable type on *any* domain is determined by its behavior on *finite* ones, thus getting rid of the circularity of variable types. To do so, one has to simplify somehow the extant semantic ideas, replacing Scott domains by the simpler and more finitary *qualitative domains*. The interpretation obtained is extremely compact, as shown on simple examples. The paper also contains the definitions of a very small "universal model" of lambda-calculus, and investigates the concept of totality.

1. This chapter was originally published in *Theoretical Computer Science 45* (1980), pp. 159–192. It is reprinted here with permission of Elsevier Science Publishers B. V.

Introduction

In 1970, the present author [3] introduced the idea of *variable type*, i.e., of a schema of abstraction with respect to types. A typical example was, for instance, to abstract the identity function of any type σ, i.e., $\lambda x^{\sigma}.x^{\sigma}$ from the type σ, thus getting the "universal identity" $\Lambda\alpha.\lambda x^{\alpha}.x^{\alpha}$. This universal identity has in turn the type $\Lambda\alpha.\alpha \Rightarrow \alpha$, which is the type of functions (if one can call them that way) associating to each type σ an object of type $\sigma \Rightarrow \sigma$. In fact, the formalism was quite general, since the formation of type abstraction was not limited at all. What was of course problematic was the schema of evaluation of a function of universal type $\Lambda\alpha.\sigma[\alpha]$, because it was possible to apply an object t of this type to *any* type τ, yielding $t\{\tau\}$ of type $\sigma[\tau/\alpha]$: This obviously gave circularity problems.

However, in [3] it was shown that the obvious rules of conversion for this system, called F by chance, were converging. The proof used a predicate of "hereditary calculability", not expressible in second-order arithmetic PA_2. To do this, we were helped by Gödel's second incompleteness theorem, since we had already shown, using functional interpretation, that if the computations in F were to converge, then every provably total recursive function of PA_2 would be representable in F.

At that time, the results on F did not attract too much attention: People were more interested in the proof of the syntactic form of Takeuti's conjecture, which was contained in the same paper and was practically the same result, from the point of view of the Curry-Howard-De Bruijn isomorphism between typed systems and natural deduction. However, F was one of the first sources of inspiration of Martin-Løf for his famous system; but, in order to handle it, he had to use the axiom "$V \in V$", which later turned out to be inconsistent, and F disappeared from the ulterior background of Martin-Løf's system. One should also mention the semantics for F of Troelstra [9], "hereditarily recursive operations of order 2" (HRO_2), which was a way of interpreting F via indices of partial recursive functions.

Later on, the system was found again by Reynolds [7], and the subject moved in the direction of computer science. The interest for computer science, according to Krivine, lies in the fact that F provides a way of computing in which recursion (in the sense of a program calling itself) is absent, and in which one must program as one makes mathematical proofs; in fact, all kinds of current computer science data—lists, trees, pairs—have a nice description in F. So there has been a lot of progress in the direction of how to use the system F.

Mathematically, the progress has been more limited; the papers written by Leivant, Statman, et al. on the subject just reprove the original results. In fact, there has not been any mathematical progress with respect to the syntax of F. For the semantics, a little more has been done, namely, the work of Reynolds [7] showing the impossibility of a model of F with the set-theoretic interpretation of the implicative types. Also, attempts have been made to give models by means of some kinds of Scott domains, but this kind of approach suffers from the same type of defect as the one by Troelstra already mentioned: They are inspired by analogies with untyped lambda calculi (construction of rather artificial fixpoints, etc.).

This paper uses new semantic ideas (see [6]) to develop a model for F. In [6], the present author introduced two category-theoretic semantics for λ-calculus: one quantitative and the other qualitative. F can be modelized in both, but since [6] was mainly concerned with the quantitative case, here we have chosen to develop the qualitative framework only.

The main problem is of course the interpretation of terms of variable type; i.e., what does it mean that we have $t\{\sigma\}$ for all types σ? As mentioned above, there is an obvious circularity problem. Category theory provides an elegant way of getting rid of this circularity: We interpret a type as a qualitative domain ("qD" for short), and we want to make sense for the concept of a function associating, for any qD X, an object $t\{X\}$ of type $\sigma[X]$. Then we observe that, perhaps, t is a functor from qualitative domains to something not specified, with nice preservation properties, namely, direct limits and pull-backs. Then, using a *normal form theorem* for such functors, it is possible to show that their behavior is determined by what they do on *finite* qD's, and then we get rid of the circularity. Moreover, the term of variable type can in turn be encoded by its *trace*, which is nothing but the set of possible kinds of normal forms, and so a universal type has the good taste to form a qualitative domain. The interpretations thus obtained are very small (because combinations coming from the same normal form are counted only once), and for instance, the universal identity we started with has an interpretation consisting of one point.

The interpretation of F also has an interesting by-product for λ-calculus: It is well known that λ-calculus can be modelized as soon as one can solve an equation

$$X \Rightarrow X \sim X$$

among some kind of domains, in particular qualitative ones. Unfortunately, all solutions of such an equation are more or less arbitrary, i.e., no model of λ-calculus built in this way can claim to be *the* model. In order to get only one model, one simply has to remark that the interpretation t^*_D of t in the model depends functorially on the data (X, H, K) defining D (H and K being the isomorphism and its converse, respectively). Then it suffices to prove that the functor has nice preservation properties, and to compute its invariants (its trace), and we get a very small interpretation t^* from which we can compute t^*_D in any D.

However, the situation is a bit more complex, since an isomorphism is not a direct limit of finite isomorphisms, and we have to somehow liberalize the requirements on H and K. The current requirement is that both $H \circ K$ and $K \circ H$ should be projectors, i.e., subobjects of the identity. For such models, the interpretation increases with respect to β- and η-reduction. It is even simpler to drop any requirement about H and K, and then we discover that we are just interpreting the term of F

$$\Lambda X.\lambda H^{X\Rightarrow(X\Rightarrow X)}.\lambda K^{(X\Rightarrow X)\Rightarrow X}.t^*_{X,H,K}$$

of type

$$\Lambda X.(X\Rightarrow(X\Rightarrow X))\Rightarrow(((X\Rightarrow X)\Rightarrow X)\Rightarrow X).$$

This interpretation, which encodes any possible model of the λ-calculus by means of small sets of invariants, is called $\mathbf{\Lambda}_0$. $\mathbf{\Lambda}_0$ has no property with respect to conversion. But it is possible to define a subset $|\mathbf{\Lambda}_1|$ or $|\mathbf{\Lambda}_0|$, which corresponds exactly to those models for which $H \circ K$ and $K \circ H$ are projectors. Restricted to $|\mathbf{\Lambda}_1|$, the interpretation increases during the reduction process, and this restricted interpretation is enough to get the interpretation of t in any model where, for instance, H and K are reciprocal isomorphisms. Since there is no feedback from $|\mathbf{\Lambda}_0| - |\mathbf{\Lambda}_1|$ on $|\mathbf{\Lambda}_1|$, we have not tried to eliminate the nonincreasing part, which may be of some interest.

This model has been called the intrinsic model for obvious reasons. However, it is intrinsic only within a specified kind of interpretation: here, qualitative domains. If one changes the kind of interpretation, for example, quantitative domains, then the same kind of interpretation will lead to an intrinsic model of that kind.

This work is, to the author's knowledge, perfectly original. It is essentially the transposition of methods already used by the present author in the theory of dilators, to the context of semantics of λ-calculi. However, two important notions used here have already been considered in the literature by Berry [1], namely, "stability" (i.e., the analogue for Scott domains of our Condition (ST3)), and "order" (see our Definition 1.3). Elegant ideas in this domain are not so common, and we therefore decided to use the name "stable" for the functions used here, and to call "order" the *Berry order*. A version of Theorem 1.2 (for Scott domains) can be found in [10].

However, the notion of a qualitative domain, basically a clean refinement of Scott domains, seems to be original.

1 Qualitative Domains and λ-Structures

Let us first recall the basic definitions and results concerning qualitative domains.

Definition 1.1 A *qualitative domain* (qD) is a set X such that

$\varnothing \in X$, (qD1)

X is closed under direct unions,[2] and (qD2)

if $a \in X$ and $b \subset a$, then $b \in X$. (qD3)

We use the notation $|X|$ to denote $\{z; \{z\} \in X\}$; by (qD3), this set is also equal to $\bigcup X$; a qD X therefore appears as a subset of $\mathcal{P}(|X|)$. The basic operation that is problematic is the union of two elements of X; in general, this union need not belong to X. We say that a, b are *compatible* when their union belongs to X; by (qD3) this is equivalent to the existence of a $c \in X$ such that $a, b \subset c$.

Definition 1.2 Let X and X' be two qualitative domains; a function F from X to X' is said to be *stable* when the following conditions are true:

$a \subset b \in X \Rightarrow F(a) \subset F(b)$. (ST1)

F commutes with directed unions: $F(\bigcup_i a_i) = \bigcup_i F(a_i)$; the directed index set I must be nonvoid, since we do not require $F(\varnothing) = \varnothing$. (ST2)

if $a \cup b \in X$ (i.e., if a and b are not compatible), then $F(a \cap b) = F(a) \cap F(b)$.[3] (ST3)

Conditions (ST1) and (ST2) are the analogues for qD's of familiar requirements in the context of Scott domains; (ST3) is the analogue for qD's of Berry's stability condition, and this is why we call our functions "stable". These three conditions are very natural if we view X, X' as categories, because then F appears as a functor (condition (ST1)) preserving direct limits (condition (ST2)) and pull-backs (condition (ST3)).

Theorem 1.1 (Normal Form Theorem)
If F is a stable function from X to X', if $a \in X$ and $z \in F(a)$, then

(i) it is possible to find $a' \subset a$, a' finite such that $z \in F(a')$, and

---

2. In other words, $a \in X$ if and only if all its finite subsets belong to X (using (qD3)). In fact, the only infinite points which interest us in a qD are those that are recursively enumerable.
3. It is enough to state the condition for a, b finite.

(ii) if a' is chosen minimal such that (i) holds, then a' is unique.

Proof

(i) This follows because a is the direct union of its finite subsets: Simply apply (ST2).

(ii) If a' is minimal and $b \subset a$ is such that $z \in F(b)$, then a' and b are compatible. So, by (ST3), $F(a' \cap b) = F(a') \cap F(b)$, thus $z \in F(a' \cap b)$, which forces $a' \subset b$; so a' is minimum. □

Theorem 1.2 (Representation Theorem)

(i) If F is a stable function from X to X', we can define the set

$$\mathrm{Tr}(F) = \{(a, z); a \in X,\ a \text{ finite},\ z \in |x'|,\ z \in F(a), \text{ and } z \notin F(a') \text{ for all } a' \subsetneq a\}.$$

Then F is completely determined by $\mathrm{Tr}(F)$, by means of the equation

$$F(b) = \{z \in |X'|;\ \exists a \subset b, (a, z) \in \mathrm{Tr}(F)\}.$$

(ii) The set of all $\mathrm{Tr}(F)$, when F varies through stable functions from X to X', is a qD, denoted $X \Rightarrow X'$.

Proof

(i) This is just the Normal Form Theorem 1.1.

(ii) Define $X \Rightarrow X'$ to consist of all sets A such that:

$$x \in A \Rightarrow x \text{ is a pair } (a, z) \text{ with } a \text{ finite in } X \text{ and } z \in |X'| \qquad \text{(FS1)}$$

$$\text{given any finite } b \subset X, \text{ then } \{z \in |X'|;\ \exists a \in X, (a, z) \in A\} \in X' \qquad \text{(FS2)}$$

$$\text{if } (a, z), (a', z) \in A \text{ and } a, a' \text{ are compatible, then } a = a'. \qquad \text{(FS3)}$$

It is plain that $X \Rightarrow X'$ is a qualitative domain. Moreover, every set $\mathrm{Tr}(F)$ fulfills (FS1)–(FS3). It remains to show that any $A \in X \Rightarrow X'$ is of the form $\mathrm{Tr}(F)$ for a suitable F: Given $A \in X \Rightarrow X'$, define F by

$$F(b) = \{z \in |X'|;\ \exists a \subset b, (a, z) \in A\}.$$

If b is finite, then $F(b)$ belongs to X' by (FS2). Moreover, for an arbitrary b in X,

$$F(b) = \bigcup \{F(b'); b' \subset b,\ b' \text{ finite}\},$$

which follows from (FS1). Since F is clearly increasing, the directed union of the $F(b')$'s belongs to X': Hence, F maps X into X', and fulfills (ST1) and (ST2).

It remains to prove (ST3). But, if b and b' are compatible and $z \in F(b) \cap F(b')$, then we get $(a, z), (a', z) \in A$ such that $a \subset b$, $a' \subset b'$; but a and a' must be compatible, so $a = a'$ by (FS3), and $a = a' \subset b \cap b'$. Thus, we get $z \in F(b \cap b')$, i.e., $F(b) \cap F(b') \subset F(b \cap b')$, which is the nontrivial half of (ST3). Hence, F is stable.

It now remains to compute the trace of F. It is immediate that $\mathrm{Tr}(F) = A$ so we are done. □

Remarks

(i) $|X \Rightarrow X'| = X_{\text{fin}} \times |X'|$. It can be convenient to use a sequential notation for elements of $|X \Rightarrow X'|$: Instead of the pair (a, z) one can use $a \vdash z$, or even $x_1, \ldots, x_n \vdash z$, with $a = \{x_1, \ldots, x_n\}$; if one uses the latter notation (which should be viewed as the intuitionistic sequent "if $x_1, \ldots, x_n$, then z"), remember that there is no order between $x_1, \ldots, x_n$, so that, for instance, $x_1, x_2 \vdash z$ is the same as $x_2, x_1 \vdash z$.

(ii) It should be clear that condition (ST3) has to be verified for infinite a's and b's only.

Example 1.1

(i) Let 1 be the qualitative domain consisting of $\varnothing$ and $\{0\}$; then there are three stable functions from 1 to itself, namely:

$$F_1(\varnothing) = F_1(\{0\}) = \varnothing, \qquad F_2(\varnothing) = \varnothing, \ \ F_2(\{0\} = \{0\},$$
$$F_3(\varnothing) = F_3(\{0\}) = \{0\}.$$

Their respective traces are $\mathrm{Tr}(F_1) = \varnothing$, $\mathrm{Tr}(F_2) = \{0 \vdash 0\}$, and $\mathrm{Tr}(F_3) = \{\vdash 0\}$.

(ii) If X is a qD, then the identity map from X to itself is clearly stable; the Normal Form Theorem 1.1 for Id^X is as follows: If $z \in \mathrm{Id}^X(a) = a$, then z already belongs to $\mathrm{Id}^X(\{z\}) = \{z\}$, i.e., $\mathrm{Tr}(\mathrm{Id}^x) = \{z \vdash z; z \in |X|\}$.

(iii) If X and Y are qD's, one can define a map f_b from $X \Rightarrow Y$ into Y by $f_b(A) = \{z;\ \exists a \subset b, (a, z) \in A\}$, for any $b \in X$. This map is stable, and its trace consists of all pairs $(\{(a, z)\}, z)$ such that $a \in X$, a is a finite subset of b, and $z \in |Y|$. Hence, f_b can be viewed as an element of $(X \Rightarrow Y) \Rightarrow Y$; the map that associates f_b to b is stable itself: Its trace consists of all tuples $(a, (\{(a, z)\}, z))$ with $a \in X$ finite, and $z \in Y$.

Definition 1.3 The *order of Berry* is defined as follows. Let F, G be stable functions from X to X'; $F \subset G$ means that

$$\forall a, b \in X\ (a \subset b \Rightarrow F(a) = F(b) \cap G(a)).[4]$$

Another equivalent formulation is

$$\forall a, b \in X\ (a, b \text{ compatible } \Rightarrow F(a \cap b) = F(a) \cap G(b)).$$

Note that $F \subset G$ implies $F(a) \subset G(a)$ for all a (in the above definition, take $a = b$). But the reverse is false; typically, the inclusion $F_2 \subset F_3$ fails (see Example 1.1 (i)) while $F_2(a) \subset F_3(a)$ for all a : $F_2(\varnothing) = \varnothing$, but $F_2(\{0\}) \cap F_3(\varnothing) = \{0\}$. In terms of categories, $F \subset G$ means that there is a cartesian natural transformation from F to G.

Proposition 1.1

$$F \subset G \text{ iff } \mathrm{Tr}(F) \subset \mathrm{Tr}(G).$$

Proof

(i) Assume that $F \subset G$, and let $(a, z) \in \mathrm{Tr}(F)$. Then $z \in F(a) \subset G(a)$. In order to show that $(a, z) \in \mathrm{Tr}(G)$, we assume that $z \in G(a')$ for $a' \subset a$. Then $F(a') = F(a) \cap G(a')$, so $z \in F(a')$ and thus $a' = a$.

(ii) Assume conversely that $\mathrm{Tr}(F) \subset Tr(G)$, and that $b' \subset b \in X$. If $z \in F(b) \cap G(b')$, this proves that $(a', z) \in \mathrm{Tr}(G)$ and $(a, z) \in \mathrm{Tr}(F)$ for some $a' \subset b'$, $a \subset b$; but then (a', z) and (a, z) belong to $\mathrm{Tr}(G)$, and since a and a' are compatible, $a = a'$; so $z \in F(b')$. The reversed inclusion is immediate. □

Remarks

(i) If F and G are stable functions from X to X', then one can define a stable function $F \cap G$ from X to X' by $(F \cap G)(a) = F(a) \cap G(a)$; it is immediate that $\mathrm{Tr}(F \cap G) \supset \mathrm{Tr}(F) \cap \mathrm{Tr}(G)$.

(ii) If (F_i) is a family of stable functions from X to X', indexed by a nonvoid directed set I, such that $i \leq j \Rightarrow F_i \subset F_j$, then it is possible to define another stable function $F = \bigcup_i F_i$, by means of the equation $F(a) = \bigcup_i F_i(a)$. It is immediate that $\mathrm{Tr}(F) = \bigcup_i \mathrm{Tr}(F_i)$.

(iii) Stable functions of n arguments: If $X_1, \ldots, X_n$ are qD's, then it makes sense to speak of an n-ary stable function from $X_1, \ldots, X_n$ to Y. One has just to

4. It suffices to consider the particular case where a and b are finite.

adapt the definition, for instance, (ST3) becomes: If a_1, b_1 are compatible, ..., and if a_n, b_n, are compatible, then

$$F(a_1 \cap b_1, \ldots, a_n \cap b_n) = F(a_1, \ldots, a_n) \cap F(b_1, \ldots, b_n).$$

Stable functions of n variables have exactly the same kind of behavior as usual stable functions; there are two equivalent ways of handling them.

1. One can define a trace for such functions: Tr(F) is the set of all tuples $(a_1, \ldots, a_n, z)$ such that $a_1 \in X_1, \ldots, a_n \in X_n$, $z \in |Y|$, $z \in F(a_1, \ldots, a_n)$ and $z \in F(a'_1, \ldots, a'_n)$ for $a'_1 \subset a_1, \ldots, a'_n \subset a_n \rightarrow a'_1 = a_1, \ldots, a'_n = a_n$. Then we define the qD $(X_1, \ldots, X_n \Rightarrow Y)$ to be the set of all sets Tr(F), etc. and prove the analogues of our results for the unary case.
2. One can also define the product $X_1 \times \cdots \times X_n$ to consist of all sets $a_1 \times \{1\} \cup \cdots \cup a_n \times \{n\}$ for $a_1 \in X_1, \ldots, a_n \in X_n$: This is a qD, and to any n-ary stable function F from $X_1, \ldots, X_n$ to Y we can associate F' from $X_1 \times \cdots \times X_n$ to Y by

$$F'(a_1 \times \{1\} \cup \cdots \cup a_n \times \{n\}) = F(a_1, \ldots, a_n) \qquad (*)$$

and, conversely, any stable function from $X_1 \times \cdots \times X_n$ to Y induces an n-ary stable function from $X_1, \ldots, X_n$ to Y by means of (*). In fact, the respective traces of F and F' are related by the formula

$$\mathrm{Tr}(F') = \{(a_1 \times \{1\} \cup \cdots \cup a_n \times \{n\}, z); (a_1, \ldots, a_n, z) \in \mathrm{Tr}(F)\},$$

which defines an isomorphism between $(X_1 \times \cdots \times X_n \Rightarrow Y)$ and $(X_1, \ldots, X_n \Rightarrow Y)$.

In order to handle λ-calculus, we have to take care of n-ary stable functions; the crucial tool is the following.

Notation

(i) When F is a stable function from X to Y, we use the notation $\lambda a.F(a)$ for Tr(F). The λ-notation is used for n-ary stable functions; for example one can use $\lambda a.F(a, a_1, \ldots, a_n)$ to denote the trace of the function $a \rightsquigarrow F(a, a_1, \ldots, a_n)$, $a_1, \ldots, a_n$ being fixed.

(ii) When $A \in X \Rightarrow Y$ and $a \in X$, then Ap(A, a) denotes the result of the stable function encoded by A, at the argument a:

$$\mathrm{Ap}(A, a) = \{z \in |Y|;\ \exists b \subset a, (b, z) \in A\}.$$

Observe that λ and Ap are reciprocal:

$$\mathrm{Ap}(\lambda a.F(a), b) = F(b), \qquad \text{"beta conversion"},$$

$$\lambda a.\mathrm{Ap}(A, a) = A, \qquad \text{"eta conversion"}.$$

Theorem 1.3

(i) The transformation consisting in associating to any $(n+1)$-ary function from $X, X_1, \ldots, X_n$ to Y, the n-ary function

$$G(a_1, \ldots, a_n) = \lambda a.F(a, a_1, \ldots, a_n)$$

is stable: This means that the induced map on traces $(X, X_1, \ldots, X_n \Rightarrow Y)$ to $(X_1, \ldots, X_n \Rightarrow (X \Rightarrow Y))$ is stable.

(ii) If F and G are n-ary stable functions from $X_1, \ldots, X_n$ to $X \Rightarrow Y$ and X respectively, then

$$H(a_1, \ldots, a_n) = \mathrm{Ap}(F(a_1, \ldots, a_n), G(a_1, \ldots, a_n))$$

is a stable function from $X_1, \ldots, X_n$ to Y; moreover, the transformation constructing H from F and G is stable.

Proof This theorem is more or less immediate. Both points contain two distinct results: First, the result of the transformation is stable, and second, the transformation in turn is stable. We shall content ourselves with the expression of the action of these two operations on traces, without justification:

(i) $\mathrm{Tr}(G) = \{(a_1, \ldots, a_n, (a, z)); (a, a_1, \ldots, a_n, z) \in \mathrm{Tr}(F)\}$,

(ii) $\mathrm{Tr}(H) = \{(a_1, \ldots, a_n, z)$ such that one can find $(a'_1, \ldots, a'_n, (a, z)) \in \mathrm{Tr}(F)$ and $(a^1_1, \ldots, a^1_n, x^1), \ldots, (a^p_1, \ldots, a^p_n, x^p) \in \mathrm{Tr}(G)$, such that $a = \{x^1, \ldots, x^p\}$ and $a_i = a'_i \cup a^1_i \cup \cdots \cup a^p_i$ for $i = 1, 2, \ldots, n\}$. □

Definition 1.4 A *λ-structure* $D = (X, H, K)$ consists of:

(i) a qualitative domain X,

(ii) a stable function H from X to $X \Rightarrow X$, and

(iii) a stable function K from $X \Rightarrow X$ to X.

If $t = t[x_1, \ldots, x_n]$ is a term of λ-calculus ($x_1, \ldots, x_n$ include all free variables of t), then one defines an n-ary stable function t^*_D from x^n to $X : a_1, \ldots, a_n \rightsquigarrow t^*_D[x_1, \ldots, x_n]$ by the following inductive clauses:

if t is x_i, then $t^*_D[a_1, \ldots, a_n] = a_i$,

if t is $\lambda x.u[x, x_1, \ldots, x_n]$, then $t^*_D[a_1, \ldots, a_n] = K(\lambda a.u^*_D[a, a_1, \ldots, a_n])$,

if t is $u[x_1, \ldots, x_n](v[x_1, \ldots, x_n])$,
then $t^*_D[a_1, \ldots, a_n] = \mathrm{Ap}(H(u^*_D[a_1, \ldots, a_n]), v^*_D[a_1, \ldots, a_n])$.

Proposition 1.2

(i) Let $t[x, x_1, \ldots, x_n]$ and $u[x_1, \ldots, x_n]$ be λ-terms; then $(t[u/x]^*_D = t^*_D[u^*_D/a]$ with obvious notations for the substitution of a term for a variable, or of a function for an argument.

(ii) Assume that $t^*_D \subset t'^*_D$, and $u^*_D \subset u'^*_D$; then

$$(\lambda x.t)^*_D \subset (\lambda x.t')^*_D, \qquad (t(u))^*_D \subset (t'(u'))^*_D.$$

The proof of this proposition is more or less immediate.

Proposition 1.3

(i) If $H \circ K \subset \mathrm{Id}^{X \Rightarrow X}$, then $((\lambda x.t)(u))^*_D \subset t[u/x]^*_D$.

(ii) If $K \circ H \subset \mathrm{Id}^X$, then $(\lambda x.t(x))^*_D \subset t^*_D$ (x not free in t).

Proof Both (i) and (ii) are practically immediate; for instance, assume that $H \circ K \subset \mathrm{Id}^{X \Rightarrow X}$, which is by far the most interesting hypothesis: Then, given $a_1 \subset b_1, \ldots, a_n \subset b_n$, all in X, we get, with $v = (\lambda x.t)(u)$,

$$\begin{aligned} v^*_D[a_1, \ldots, a_n] &= \mathrm{Ap}(H(K(\lambda a.t^*_D[a, a_1, \ldots, a_n])), u^*_D[a_1, \ldots, a_n]) \\ &= \mathrm{Ap}(\lambda a.t^*_D[a, a_1, \ldots, a_n] \\ &\qquad \cap H(K(\lambda a.t^*_D[a, b_1, \ldots, b_n])), u^*_D[a_1, \ldots, a_n]) \\ &= \mathrm{Ap}(\lambda a.t^*_D[a, a_1, \ldots, a_n], u^*_D[a_1, \ldots, a_n]) \cap v^*_D[b_1, \ldots, b_n] \\ &= (t[u/x])^*_D[a_1, \ldots, a_n] \cap v^*_D[b_1, \ldots, b_n]. \quad \square \end{aligned}$$

Example 1.2 (λ-structures)

(i) The most straightforward example consists of λ-structures (X, H, K) for which H and K are reciprocal isomorphisms: $H \circ K = \mathrm{Id}^{X \Rightarrow X}$ and $K \circ H = \mathrm{Id}^X$. In such structures, two terms which are interconvertible by means of beta- and eta-conversions must have the same interpretation.

(ii) The models mentioned in (i) are extensional, i.e., they interpret η-conversion by the identity. There are reasons to consider nonextensional models, and if we drop the assumption $K \circ H = \mathrm{Id}^X$ in (i), we get nonextensional models, which interpret β-conversion by the identity. Moreover, by choosing a model in which $K \circ H \subset \mathrm{Id}^X$, we can make η-conversion increasing: $t^*_D \supset (\lambda x.t(x))^*_D$ when x is not free in t.

(iii) The next step is to liberalize the requirement $H \circ K = \mathrm{Id}$. The obvious choice is $H \circ K \subset \mathrm{Id}^{X \Rightarrow X}$, which has a lot of finite solutions.

In particular, the β-conversion is increasing:

$$(\lambda x.t[x])(u)^*_D \subset t[u/x]^*_D.$$

In practice, the class of λ-structures corresponding to

$$H \circ K \subset \mathrm{Id}, \quad K \circ H \subset \mathrm{Id}$$

has nice features, because it can be shown (see point (ii) of Section 4.1) that such λ-structures can be approximated by finite λ-structures of the same class.

Also observe that it makes sense to speak of the interpretation

$$t^\beta_D = \bigcup\{u^*_D ; t =/ u\}^5$$

of the Böhm tree of t in such structures, because, by the Church-Rosser property, $\{u : t =/ u\}$ is directed, so t^β_D is a direct union in X.

(iv) The absolute liberalization, no questions asked on (X, H, K), is harder to advocate. However, observe that if we consider the reduction procedure as the execution of a program, then it is important that t^* and u^* should be different when $t =/ u$; but in an increasing interpretation as considered in (iii), a cyclic λ-term would get a constant interpretation as the reduction goes on.

We close this section with a trivial remark. It is possible to choose D such that $t^*_D = u^*_D$ implies that t and u are syntactically equal (i.e., are the same, up to the names of bound variables): Choose D, H and K, a, $b \in |D|$, $a \neq b$ such that

H viewed as a binary function from X, X to X is injective, and $a \in H(\emptyset, \emptyset)$,

K is injective and $b \in K(\emptyset)$.

By the way, observe that this ensures a similar property for the intrinsic interpretation t^* of Section 4:

if $t^* = u^*$, then $t = u$.

5. We use the symbol =/ to denote reduction.

2 *Semantics of Variable Types*

Definition 2.1 Let X, Y be qualitative domains; a morphism from X to Y is an injective function f from $|X|$ to $|Y|$ such that, for all $x_1, \ldots, x_n \in |X|$, $\{x_1, \ldots, x_n\} \in X$ iff $\{f(x_1), \ldots, f(x_n)\} \in |Y|$.

We have therefore defined a category qD whose objects are qualitative domains; the set of all morphisms from X to Y is denoted $\mathrm{qD}(X, Y)$.

If $f \in \mathrm{qD}(X, Y)$, then it is possible to define two associated stable functions:

(i) f^+ from X to Y: $f^+(b) = \{f(z); z \in b\}$,

(ii) f^- from Y to X: $f^-(b) = \{z; f(z) \in b\}$.

Proposition 2.1

(i) $f^- \circ f^+ = \mathrm{Id}^X$.

(ii) $f^+ \circ f^- \subset \mathrm{Id}^Y$.

(*Terminology*: A stable function from qD Z to itself such that $F \subset \mathrm{Id}^Z$ is called a *projector*; hence, $f^+ \circ f^-$ is a projector of Y. The trace of a projector is a set of pairs $(\{z\}, z)$, so the square of a projector is the projector itself.)

The proof of Proposition 2.1 is immediate.

Proposition 2.2

If $f \in \mathrm{qD}(X, X')$ and $g \in \mathrm{qD}(Y, Y')$, then one can define $f \Rightarrow g \in \mathrm{qD}(X \Rightarrow X', Y \Rightarrow Y')$ by $(f \Rightarrow g)(a, z) = (f^+(a), g(z))$.

With obvious abuses of notations (we do not distinguish between a function and its trace), we have

$$(f \Rightarrow g)^+(F) = g^+ \circ F \circ f^- \qquad \text{for } F \in X \Rightarrow Y,$$

$$(f \Rightarrow g)^-(G) = g^- \circ G \circ f^+ \qquad \text{for } G \in X' \Rightarrow Y'.$$

Proof The proof is more or less immediate. Let us for instance compute $(f \Rightarrow g)^+(F)$. Its trace consists of all pairs $(f^+(a), g(z))$, when (a, z) varies through $\mathrm{Tr}(F)$; so,

$$\begin{aligned}(f \Rightarrow g)^+(F)(b) &= \{g(z);\ \exists a, (a, z) \in \mathrm{Tr}(F) \text{ and } f^+(a) \subset b\} \\ &= \{g(z);\ \exists a, (a, z) \subset \mathrm{Tr}(F) \text{ and } a \subset f^-(b)\} \\ &= g^+(F(f^-(b))). \quad \square\end{aligned}$$

Theorem 2.1

"$\Rightarrow$" is a functor from $\mathrm{qD} \times \mathrm{qD}$ to qD preserving direct limits and pull-backs.

Proof X is a *subdomain* of Y when $|X| \subset |Y|$ and $X = Y \cap \mathcal{P}(|X|)$. In other words, X is a subdomain of Y when $|X| \subset |Y|$ and the inclusion map from $|X|$ into $|Y|$ is a morphism. It is convenient to translate questions of limits in the category of domains in terms of the subdomain relation:

(i) Assume that $(X_i)_{i \in I}$ is a family of qualitative domains, indexed by a non-void directed set I, and such that $i \leq j \Rightarrow X_i$ subdomain of X_j. Then it is possible to define a qD $\bar{\bigcup} X_i$ as follows: $|\bar{\bigcup} X_i| = \bigcup |X_i|$; $a \subset |\bar{\bigcup} X_i|$ is an element of $\bar{\bigcup} X_i$ iff, given any *finite* $b \subset a$, $b \in \bigcup X_i$.

It is easy to see that $\bar{\bigcup} X_i$ is a qD, that all X_i's are subdomains of $\bar{\bigcup} X_i$, and that $\bar{\bigcup} X_i$ is the smallest (with respect to the subdomain relation) Y such that all X_i's are subdomains of Y.

For those with some experience of categories it should be clear that preservation of direct limits just means commutation with the operator $\bar{\bigcup}$:

$$(\bar{\bigcup} X_i) \Rightarrow (\bar{\bigcup} Y_i) = \bar{\bigcup} (X_i \Rightarrow Y_i).$$

The verification is left to the reader, but observe that the directedness of I is essential.

(ii) Assume that X, Y are two subdomains of Z; then $X \cap Y$ is again a subdomain of Z. Once more, the reader with some experience of categories will guess that preservation of pull-backs is just the property

$$(X \cap X') \Rightarrow (Y \cap Y') = (X \Rightarrow Y) \cap (X' \Rightarrow Y')$$

where X, X' are subdomians of X'', and Y, Y' are subdomains of Y''. Once more, the verification is quite obvious. □

Theorem 2.2 (Normal Form Theorem for Variable Types)
Let I be a functor from qD to itself preserving direct limits and pull-backs. Let X be a qD and let $x \in |I(X)|$; then there is a finite qD X_0 and a morphism $f \in$ qD(X_0, X) and $x_0 \in |I(X_0)|$ such that:

(i) $x = I(f)(x_0)$ (the **normal form of** x, with respect to I and X_0), and

(ii) given any qD Y, any $f' \in$ qD(Y, X) and any $y \in |I(Y)|$ such that $x = I(f')(y)$, there is a unique $h \in$ qD(X_0, Y) such that

$$y = I(h)(x_0) \quad \text{and} \quad f = f'h.$$

Proof Any qD is the direct union of its finite subdomains. Hence, equation (i) has a solution, taking X_0 to be a finite subdomain of X and f to be the inclusion map from $|X_0|$ to $|X|$. Moreover, we can assume that X_0 has been chosen minimal with respect to the subdomain relation. Then we prove that (ii) holds: Choose Y, f', and y such that $x = I(f')(y)$. Let X_1 be a qD and let $g \in \mathrm{qD}(X_1, X_0)$ and $g' \in \mathrm{qD}(X_1, Y)$ be such that the diagram

$$\begin{array}{ccc} X_1 & \xrightarrow{\;g\;} & X_0 \\ {\scriptstyle g'}\downarrow & & \downarrow{\scriptstyle f} \\ Y & \xrightarrow[\;f'\;]{} & X \end{array}$$

is cartesian, i.e., is a pull-back diagram. Without loss of generality, we can assume that X_1 is a subdomain of X_0, i.e., that g is the inclusion map between $|X_1|$ and $|X_0|$. To say that the diagram is cartesian means that $fg = f'g'$ and $\mathrm{rg}(fg) = \mathrm{rg}(f) \cap \mathrm{rg}(f')$. By preservation of pull-backs, the diagram

$$\begin{array}{ccc} I(X_1) & \xrightarrow{\;I(g)\;} & I(X_0) \\ {\scriptstyle I(g')}\downarrow & & \downarrow{\scriptstyle I(f)} \\ I(Y) & \xrightarrow[\;I(f')\;]{} & I(X) \end{array}$$

is in turn cartesian, i.e., $\mathrm{rg}(I(gf)) = \mathrm{rg}(I(f)) \cap \mathrm{rg}(I(f'))$, and since $x \in \mathrm{rg}(I(f)) \cap \mathrm{rg}(I(f'))$, it turns out that $x \in \mathrm{rg}(I(fg))$, so, since X_0 has been chosen minimal, this forces $X_1 = X_0$, and g to be the identity. But then, $y = I(g')(x_0)$. The condition $f = f'g'$ has only one solution in g'. □

Remark

(i) Theorem 2.2 is the adaptation to the category qD of various normal form theorems obtained by the present author, for example for dilators, but also for normal functors [6]. Theorem 2.2 is much simpler than the corresponding result for normal functors, but more complex than the ultimate simplification of Theorem 1.2: What makes the difference between Theorems 1.2 and 2.2 is that in the former case (stability), the only morphisms are inclusions. Of course, if we have more morphisms, we get more expressions of the form $x = I(f)(y)$, which makes unicity requirements more difficult to fulfill, but in turn the functor is defined by means of a smaller set of data, i.e., a smaller trace.

(ii) A typical example to which we can apply the Normal Form Theorem 1.1 is the functor $I(X) = X \Rightarrow X$, $I(f) = f \Rightarrow f$. For instance, if $0, 1, 2 \in |X|$ and $\mathcal{P}(\{0, 1, 2\}) \subset X$, then $(\{0, 1\}, 2) \in I(X)$, and we can therefore write the normal form $(\{0, 1\}, 2) = I(f)(\{0, 1\}, 2)$ where f is the inclusion map between $3 = \{0, 1, 2\}$ and $|X|$. But consider $f' \in \mathrm{qD}(\mathcal{P}(3), X)$ defined by $f'(0) = 1$, $f'(1) =$

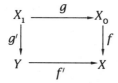

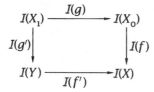

0, $f'(2) = 2$; it is easy to see that

$$(\{0,1\},2) = (\{1,0\},2) = \mathcal{I}(f')(\{0,1\},2),$$

i.e., in the Normal Form Theorem, the function f is not uniquely determined. This corresponds to nonpreservation of kernels.

Definition 2.2

(i) A *variable type* T is (as expected) a functor from qD to qD preserving direct limits and pull-backs

(ii) If T is a variable type, an *object of variable type* T is a family $t = (t(X))$ indexed by all qualitative domains X, such that $t(X) \in T(X)$ for all X, and enjoying the mutilation property: For all X, Y and $f \in \mathrm{qD}(X, Y)$, $t(X) = T(f)^{-}(t(Y))$.

This definition, which is simple transposition of the author's concept of *mutilation* in proofs (see, e.g., *Proceedings Warsaw ICM 1983*) can also be rewritten using $T(f)^{+}$, but the formulation is less manageable:

$$T(f)^{+}(t(X)) = t(Y) \cap \mathrm{rg}(T(f)).$$

Variable objects and types are the obvious candidates to interpret quantification on types; to prove the adequacy of this idea, we have to represent a variable type T by a qD $\mathrm{Tr}(T)$ (the *trace* of T, obtained through the Normal Form Theorem) in such a way that the objects of variable type T will correspond to the elements of $\mathrm{Tr}(T)$.

Definition 2.3 Let T be a variable type; a *trace* of T is any set A formed of pairs (X, x) such that:

(i) X is a finite qD and $x \in |T(X)|$,

(ii) given any qD Y and any $y \in |T(Y)|$, there is a unique (X, x) in A and a morphism f (in general nonunique) such that y has the normal form $y = T(f)(x)$.

We shall use the notation $A = \|\mathrm{Tr}(T)\|$ which may seem ambiguous since there are many possible choices for A. In fact, $\|\mathrm{Tr}(T)\|$ is the set of all equivalence classes of normal forms, and we have preferred to pick up an element in each equivalence class. The way we use the trace will show that our abuse of notations is harmless.

The qD $\mathrm{Tr}(T)$ is defined as a subset of $\mathcal{P}(\|\mathrm{Tr}(T)\|)$. A subset a of $\|\mathrm{Tr}(T)\|$ belongs to $\mathrm{Tr}(T)$ exactly when the following holds: Take $(X_0, x_0), \ldots, (X_n, x_n)$ in a, take a finite qD X and morphisms $f_0 \in \mathrm{qD}(X_0, X), \ldots, f_n \in \mathrm{qD}(X_n, X)$; then $F(f_0)(x_0), \ldots, F(f_n)(x_n) \in F(X)$.

In this definition, $(X_0, x_0), \ldots, (X_n, x_n)$ are not necessarily distinct; so even when a is a singleton, the condition is not always fulfilled (i.e., there are phenomena of "self-incompatibility"), and so in general $|\mathrm{Tr}(T)|$ is strictly included in $\|\mathrm{Tr}(T)\|$ (see, for instance, Theorems 3.3, 3.4, and 3.5).

Theorem 2.3

There is a canonical bijection between $\mathrm{Tr}(T)$ (where T is a variable type) and the set of all objects of variable type T; the bijection is as follows:

(i) to t of variable type T, associate

$$\mathrm{Tr}(t) = \{(X, x) \in \|\mathrm{Tr}(T)\|; x \in t(X)\};$$

(ii) to $a \in \mathrm{Tr}(T)$, associate the function

$$a\{Y\} = \{T(f)(x); (X, x) \in a, f \in \mathrm{qD}(X, Y)\}.$$

Proof If t is of variable type T, then $\mathrm{Tr}(t)$ is a subset of $\|\mathrm{Tr}(T)\|$. Now, if $(X_0, x_0), \ldots, (X_n, x_n) \in \mathrm{Tr}(t)$, if $f_0 \in \mathrm{qD}(X_0, X), \ldots, f_n \in \mathrm{qD}(X_n, X)$, then $T(f_0)(x_0), \ldots, T(f_n)(x_n) \in t(X)$, because $T(f_i)^+$ maps $t(X_i)$ into $t(X)$; so, $\{T(f_0)(x_0), \ldots, T(f_n)(x_n)\} \subset t(X) \in T(X)$. Hence, $\mathrm{Tr}(t) \in \mathrm{Tr}(T)$.

Conversely, let $a \in \mathrm{Tr}(T)$, and define in general $a\{Y\}$ as explained above. The definition of $\mathrm{Tr}(T)$ implies that $a\{Y\} \in T(Y)$ when Y is finite, and, by a direct limit argument, $a\{Y\} \in T(Y)$ for all Y.

Now take Y, Z and $g \in \mathrm{qD}(Y, Z)$; then,

$$T(g)^-(a\{Z\}) = \{T(g)^{-1}T(f)(x);\ (X, x) \in a, f \in \mathrm{qD}(X, Z)\}.$$

Now, among all points of the form $T(g)^{-1}T(f)(x)$, we have of course the points $T(h)(x)$ (with $h \in \mathrm{qD}(X, Y)$): Take $f = gh$. But, conversely, all points of the form $T(g)^{-1}T(f)(x)$ can be written as $T(h)(x)$ for some $h \in \mathrm{qD}(X, Y)$. Write the normal form of $T(g)^{-1}T(f)(x)$: $T(k)(x')$ for some X', some $x' \in T(X')$ and some $k \in \mathrm{qD}(X', Y)$. But then, $T(f)(x) = T(g)T(k)(x') = T(gk)(x')$. If the pair (X', x') has been chosen in $\|\mathrm{Tr}(T)\|$, as is always possible, then necessarily $X' = X, x' = x$, and one can take $h = k$. Summing up, we have just established that $T(g)^-(a\{Z\}) = a\{Y\}$, i.e., the family $(a\{Y\})$ defines an object of variable type T. The fact that the processes (i) and (ii) are inverse is more or less immediate. □

Example 2.1 Let T be the variable type of the preceding Remark; then, if one defines $t(X) = \mathrm{Tr}(Id^X) = \{(\{x\}, x); x \in |X|\}$, it is immediate that t is an object of variable type T. Moreover, $\mathrm{Tr}(t) = \{(1, (\{0\}, 0))\}$ where 1 denotes the qD $\{\varnothing, \{0\}\}$. This example shows that the uniform identity of system F has a finite interpretation!

Remark The inclusion $\mathrm{Tr}(t) \subset \mathrm{Tr}(t')$ between objects of the same variable type T corresponds to the relation

$$t \subset t' \text{ iff for all (finite) qD } X,\ t(X) \subset t'(X).$$

Similarly, the object t'' defined by $\mathrm{Tr}(t'') = \mathrm{Tr}(t) \cap \mathrm{Tr}(t')$, where t and t' are two objects of the same variable type T, satisfies

$$t''(X) = t(X) \cap t'(X).$$

The union of a directed family (t_i) (with respect to inclusion) of objects of variable type T can be defined by $t(X) = \bigcup_i t_i(X)$ and $\mathrm{Tr}(t) = \bigcup_i \mathrm{Tr}(t_i)$.

Example 2.2 Let $T(X) = (X \Rightarrow X) \Rightarrow X$, and let $t_n(X)$ be the following objects of variable T: If $F \in X \Rightarrow X$, then $t_n(X)(F) = F(F(\ldots(F(\emptyset))\ldots))$($n$ times F). We leave the following verifications to the reader:

(i) t_n is a variable object of type T,

(ii) $t_n \subset t_{n+1}$ for all n.

(These can be obtained from our interpretation for system F: Add a constant $\emptyset^\sigma$ of any type σ, and interpret it by $\emptyset$, as expected; then t_n is

$$\Lambda\alpha\lambda x^{\alpha\Rightarrow\alpha}.x(x(\ldots(x(\emptyset))\ldots)).$$

Clearly, $t_0^* \subset t_1^*$, from which we get $t_n^* \subset t_{n+1}^*$ for all n, etc.)

One can define the variable object fp of variable type T by $\mathrm{fp} = \bigcup_n t_n$, and it is clear that $F(\mathrm{fp}(X)(F)) = \mathrm{fp}(X)(F)$ for any X and $F \in X \Rightarrow X$.

Notation

(i) It is necessary to consider variable types in n arguments, i.e., functors from qD^n to qD preserving direct limits and pull-backs. A family $(t(X_1,\ldots,X_n))$ indexed by all n-tuples of qD's $X_1,\ldots,X_n$, and such that $t(X_1,\ldots,X_n) \in T(X_1,\ldots,X_n)$ for all $X_1,\ldots,X_n$ is said to be an object of variable type T when the following holds:

$$\text{given } f_1 \in \mathrm{qD}(X_1,Y_1),\ldots,f_n \in \mathrm{qD}(X_n,Y_n),$$
$$T(f_1,\ldots,f_n)^-(t(Y_1,\ldots,Y_n)) = t(X_1,\ldots,X_n).$$

The ordering between objects of variable type T is, as expected:

$$t \subset t' \text{ iff for all } X_1,\ldots,X_n\text{: } t(X_1,\ldots,X_n) \subset t'(X_1,\ldots,X_n).$$

As usual, it is enough to restrict ourselves to finite $X_1, \dots, X_n$. Intersections and unions are defined in analogy with the preceding Remark.

It could be of some interest to introduce the concept of trace of an n-ary variable type; for instance, $\|\mathrm{Tr}(T)\|$ consists of tuples $(X_1, \dots, X_n; z)$ with $z \in T(X_1, \dots, X_n)$, etc. The details are left to the reader.

(ii) When T is a unary variable type, one can define $\Lambda X.T(X)$ as $\mathrm{Tr}(T)$; when t is an object of variable type T, one can define $\Lambda X.t(X)$ as $\mathrm{Tr}(t) \in \Lambda X.T(X)$. The notation is used to denote the action of abstracting from one argument in the $(n+1)$-ary case: From $T(X, X_1, \dots, X_n)$ or from $t(X, X_1, \dots, X_n)$, construct

$$\Lambda X.T(X, T_1, \dots, X_n) \text{ and } \Lambda X.t(X, X_1, \dots, X_n),$$

which denote the respective traces of the unary variable type and object obtained by fixing the values $X_1, \dots, X_n$.

In fact, $\Lambda X.T(X, X_1, \dots, X_n)$ is a variable type in the n arguments $X_1, \dots, X_n$: If $f_1 \in \mathrm{qD}(X_1, Y_1), \dots, f_n \in \mathrm{qD}(X_n, Y_n)$, consider $(X, x) \in \|\mathrm{Tr}(T(\cdot, X_1, \dots, X_n))\|$; then $T(X, f_1, \dots, f_n)(x) \in T(X, Y_1, \dots, Y_n)$. Now, $T(X, f_1, \dots, f_n)(x)$ has a normal form $T(g, Y_1, \dots, Y_n)(y)$ with $g \in \mathrm{qD}(Y, X)$ and $(Y, y) \in \|\mathrm{Tr}(T(\cdot, Y_1, \dots, Y_n))\|$. We set

$$\Lambda X.T(X, f_1, \dots, f_n)(X, x) = (Y, y).$$

It is easy to prove the existence of an isomorphism $h \in \mathrm{qD}(X, Y)$ such that $y = T(h, f_1, \dots, f_n)(x)$, and from this it easily follows that $\Lambda X.T(X, \cdot, \dots, \cdot)$ is a variable type. Now, if t is of variable type T, then $\Lambda X.t(X, \cdot, \dots, \cdot)$ is easily seen to be of variable type $\Lambda X.T(X, \cdot, \dots, \cdot)$.

(iii) When T is a unary variable type and $t \in \Lambda X.T(X)$ and Y is a qD, then $\mathrm{Ext}(t, Y)$ denotes the element of $T(Y)$ defined by

$$\mathrm{Ext}(t, Y) = \{T(f)(x); (X, x) \in t, f \in \mathrm{qD}(X, Y)\}.$$

It is easy to see that if t is of variable type $\Lambda X.T(X, \cdot, \dots, \cdot)$ and U is an n-ary variable type, then $\mathrm{Ext}(t(X_1, \dots, X_n), U(X_1, \dots, X_n))$ is of variable type V, with $V(X_1, \dots, X_n) = T(U(X_1, \dots, X_n), X_1, \dots, X_n)$, etc.

Finally, observe that Ext and $\lambda.X$ are reciprocal:

$$\mathrm{Ext}(\Lambda X.t(X), Y) = t(Y), \qquad \Lambda X.\mathrm{Ext}(t, X) = t.$$

3 *The System F*

The system F is based on the idea of variable types, and is defined as follows (we have reduced the formalism to the schemes corresponding to $\Rightarrow$

and Λ, and we have also slightly changed the symbols used, to conform to more current traditions).

Definition 3.1 The *types* of F are those that can be generated by the following clauses:

(i) the *type variables* α, β, γ, etc., are types,

(ii) if σ and τ are types, then $\sigma \Rightarrow \tau$ is a type,

(iii) if σ is a type, and α is a type variable, then $\Lambda\alpha.\sigma$ is a type. The variable α is bound in $\Lambda\alpha.\sigma$.[6]

Examples of types are $\Lambda\alpha.(\alpha \Rightarrow \alpha)$ and $\Lambda\alpha.(\alpha \Rightarrow ((\alpha \Rightarrow \alpha) \Rightarrow \alpha))$.

Definition 3.2 We inductively define the concept of a *term of type* σ, where σ is a type of F: A term is anything that can be obtained by the following clauses:

(i) For any type σ the *variables of type* σ, x^σ, y^σ, z^σ, etc., are terms of type σ.

(ii) If t is a term of type τ and x^σ is a variable of type σ, then $\lambda x.t$ is a term of type $\sigma \Rightarrow \tau$; the variable x is bound in $\lambda x.t$

(iii) If t and u are terms of respective types $\sigma \Rightarrow \tau$ and σ, then $\mathrm{Ap}(t, u)$ (often abbreviated as $t(u)$) is a term of type τ.

(iv) If t is a term of type σ and α is a type variable, then $\Lambda\alpha.t$ is a term of type $\Lambda\alpha.\sigma$. The construction is subject to the obvious restriction that, if a variable x of type τ occurs freely in t, then α does not occur freely in τ. The variable α is bound in $\Lambda\alpha.t$.

(v) If t is a term of type $\Lambda\alpha.\sigma$ and τ is a type, then $\mathrm{Ext}(t, \tau)$ (often abbreviated as $t\{\tau\}$) is a term of type $\sigma[\tau/\alpha]$.

Example 3.1

(i) $\Lambda\alpha\lambda x^\alpha.x^\alpha$ is a term of type $\Lambda\alpha.\alpha \Rightarrow \alpha$.

(ii) $\Lambda\alpha.\lambda x^\alpha.\lambda y^{\alpha\Rightarrow\alpha}.y(y(\ldots y(x)\ldots))$ is a term of type $\Lambda\alpha.\alpha \Rightarrow ((\alpha \Rightarrow \alpha) \Rightarrow \alpha)$. This term denotes the integer n, where n is the number of occurrences of y after the $\lambda y.$; hence, we have terms $\bar{n}$ of type $\mathrm{int} = \Lambda\alpha.\alpha \Rightarrow ((\alpha \Rightarrow \alpha) \Rightarrow \alpha)$, and it is easy to check that the only normal (see below) closed terms of type int are the $\bar{n}$'s.

6. Let us advocate the choice of the symbol "Λ": It denotes both a sort of λ-abstraction (capital λ) and also a universal quantifier (although the symbol "$\forall$" is far more common).

Definition 3.3 We define immediate reduction by

$$(\lambda x.t[x])(u) =/_i t[u/x], \quad (\Lambda\alpha.t[\alpha])\{\tau\} =/_i t[\tau/\alpha].$$

Then we define reduction to be the smallest transitive relation containing immediate reduction, and compatible with the formation of terms, for example, if $t =/ u$, then $t\{\tau\} =/ u\{\tau\}$. The proof of the Church-Rosser property for usual λ-calculus can be adapted without problems to F.

Example 3.2

(i) $((\Lambda\alpha.(\lambda x^{\alpha}.x^{\alpha}))\{\tau\})(t) =/ t$ when t is of type τ.

(ii) If t and u are of respective types $\tau \Rightarrow \tau$ and τ, then $\bar{n}\{\tau\}(t)(u) =/ t(t(\ldots t(u)\ldots))(n$ times $t)$.

Definition 3.4

(i) A term is said to be *normal* if no immediate reduction can be done on any of its subterms. The terms $\bar{n}$ are normal, and they are the only normal terms of type int which are closed: This is left as an easy exercise to the reader.

(ii) Let t be a closed term of type int $\Rightarrow$ int; then t induces a partial recursive function from $\mathbb{N}$ to $\mathbb{N}$, defined as follows:

$$|t|(n) \simeq m \text{ iff } t(\bar{n}) =/ \bar{m}.$$

By the Church-Rosser property, if $t(\bar{n})$ has the *normal form* $\bar{m}$, then $\bar{m}$ is unique; the question is, of course, the existence of m.

Theorem 3.1 (Girard [3])

(i) In F, all terms have a normal form. In particular, the functions $|t|$ of Defintion 3.4 (ii) are total recursive functions.

(ii) The class of all functions from $\mathbb{N}$ to $\mathbb{N}$ which are of the form $|t|$ is exactly the class of graphs of all provably total recursive functions of second-order arithmetic PA_2.

Proof It would be a waste of time to reproduce the original proofs here. (For the reader who does not read French, let us mention that the proofs of these results have often been redone in the current literature of the subject, by Leivant, Statman, etc.; see [7] for a bibliography). By a diagonalization argument, (ii) implies that (i) is not provable in PA_2; in fact, the method used to prove (i), "candidats de réductibilité", uses a notion of "calculability" which is not expressible in PA_2. However, if one restricts the schema of Defintion 3.2(v) to finitely many types τ_1 (and the types obtained from them by substitution), then the theorem is provable in PA_2, and this is why the functions $|t|$ are provably total in PA_2; this gives one half of (ii), by far the most difficult part. The strength of the system essentially lies in the schema of Definition 3.2(v), and we get stronger systems as we allow more types τ in this schema. (The proof that this schema preserves "calculability" uses a comprehension axiom to define the set of all computable terms of type τ.) There is little hope of finding a direct combinatorial argument, because the method cannot be formalizable in PA_2. Up to now, the original proof (or its straightforward variants, e.g., to ensure strong normalization) is the only method to prove (i). The remaining part of (ii) can be proved by various means: The original proof used an extension of Gödel's functional interpretation to Heyting's second-order arithmetic HA_2. Soon afterward, in an unpublished manuscript, Per Martin-Løf gave a simpler argument involving a notion of realizability by means of terms of *F*. □

Remark For the readers familiar with natural deduction, the Curry-Howard-De Bruijn isomorphism can be done for *F*: The types are the formulas of (intuitionistic) second-order propositional calculus, and the terms denote deductions of their types, under hypotheses which are the types of their free variables. For instance, the schemes of Defintion 3.2 (iv), (v) respectively correspond to

$$\frac{\begin{matrix}\vdots\\ \sigma[\alpha]\end{matrix}}{\Lambda\alpha.\sigma[\alpha]} \quad\text{and}\quad \frac{\begin{matrix}\vdots\\ \Lambda\alpha.\sigma[\alpha]\end{matrix}}{\sigma[\tau]},$$

which are the obvious quantifier rules for second-order propositional calculus. The reduction in *F* corresponds to the obvious normalization procedure for second-order propositional calculus.

Second-order logic à la Takeuti is practically the same system, except that variables of propositions are replaced by variables for *n*-ary predicates, and that a "first-order part" is added. The first-order part adds absolutely no difficulty, and this is why [3] also contains a proof of the syntactic form of Takeuti's conjecture, which is just a normalization for second-order intuitionistic logic.

3.1 *The Semantics of F: Discussion*

The difficulty is to interpret the universal types $\Lambda\alpha.\sigma$. For the implication, we can bear in mind the naive image of a function from σ to τ, but for the universal type the idea of a function assigning to any type τ an object of type $\sigma[\tau]$ is not satisfactory, because $\sigma[\tau]$ is often more complicated than $\Lambda\alpha.\sigma$. In particular, the idea of interpreting F in standard set-theoretical terms fails; this has been shown quite recently by Reynolds [7].

Up to now, there is only one standard way of interpreting F,[7] namely, to refuse to consider the schemes of Definition 3.2(iv), (v). More precisely, to any term of F, say t, associate a λ-term t^-, as follows:

$$(x^\sigma)^- = x, \qquad (\lambda x^\sigma.t) = \lambda x.t^-, \qquad (t(u))^- = t^-(u^-),$$

$$(\Lambda\alpha.t)^- = t^-, \qquad (t\{\tau\})^- = t^-.$$

It is clear that $t =/ u$ implies $t^- =/ u^-$. Since there are many models for λ-calculus, one can define the interpretation of t in such a model M as the interpretation $M(t^-)$ of t^- in M. If one defines the notion of type of M as being a subset of M enjoying ad hoc closure properties, then it is easy to interpret F:

(i) If σ and τ are interpreted by A and $B \subset M$, then $\sigma \Rightarrow \tau$ is interpreted by $A \Rightarrow B$, which is the set of all $m \in M$ that apply A into B.

(ii) If, for all A, A is interpreted by $F(A)$, then the interpretation of $\Lambda\alpha.\sigma$ is just $\bigcap\{F(A); A \text{ type of } M\}$.

Then it is easy to see that $M(t^-)$ belongs to the interpretation of the type of t.

We consider this interpretation unsatisfactory, because:

(i) it does not interpret the types but simply ignores them; this is just an interpretation of the underlying λ-calculus; and

(ii) the interpretation depends on something rather artificial, namely, a model M for λ-calulus. We would like to have an absolute interpretation and not to be forced to restrict ourselves to a fixed list of types; for instance, the uniform identity can be evaluated on any structure of a given kind, etc.

The reader has understood that this refusal of the straightforward interpretation of F is just a way of introducing our new interpretation, which has of course all possible virtues, etc.

If we want to interpret a variable type $\Lambda\alpha.\sigma$, we stumble on the difficulty that we must consider functions which are defined on all types, including those we have not considered yet. The method already criticized was simply

7. See also McCracken after Scott, Bruce, Meyer, Mitchell, and Longo. These models are based on solutions of fixed-point equations like models of untyped lambda calculus, and therefore hardly catch the naturality of second-order abstraction.

to make these functions constant. But in reality, if we consider the uniform identity $\Lambda\alpha.\lambda x^{\alpha}.x^{\alpha}$, this defines a function $\alpha \rightsquigarrow \lambda x^{\alpha}.x^{\alpha}$ which is not exactly constant in α. Now the method of Section 2 enables us to say that this function is determined by its behavior on finite qualitative domains, i.e., on "finite types", if we identify types with qD's in our interpretation. Then there is no longer any circularity, and the interpretation can be done. We already computed it in the case of the universal identity (Example 2.1) and we just found a structure with one point. Compare with the monster that would interpret the same thing in a model forgetting the types!

Now we give the precise definition of the interpretation; all elements have been given in Sections 1 and 2, and we have just to put things together.

Definition 3.5 By $t[\boldsymbol{\alpha}, \boldsymbol{x}]$ we mean the following:

(i) $\boldsymbol{\alpha}$ is a sequence $\alpha_1, \ldots, \alpha_n$ of type variables.

(ii) $\boldsymbol{x}$ is a sequence $x_1, \ldots, x_m$ of variables of respective types $\sigma_1, \ldots, \sigma_m$; all free variables of the σ_i's are among $\alpha_1, \ldots, \alpha_n$. We use the shorthand notation $\boldsymbol{\sigma}$ for $\sigma_1, \ldots, \sigma_n$.

(iii) t is a term of type τ. The only free type variables of t (and τ) are among $\boldsymbol{\alpha}$, and the only free type variables of t are among $\boldsymbol{x}$.

It will be convenient to individualize one of the variables; for instance, we can write $t[\alpha, \boldsymbol{\alpha}, \boldsymbol{x}]$ or $t[\boldsymbol{\alpha}, y, \boldsymbol{x}]$, etc. In order to interpret $t[\boldsymbol{\alpha}, \boldsymbol{x}]$ (of type τ), we have first to take a sequence $\boldsymbol{X} = X_1, \ldots, X_n$ of qualitative domains; we can then define (see below) qD's $\tau^*[\boldsymbol{X}]$ and $\sigma_i^*[\boldsymbol{X}]$; we use $\boldsymbol{\sigma}^*[\boldsymbol{X}]$ for the sequence $\sigma_1[\boldsymbol{X}], \ldots, \sigma_m[\boldsymbol{X}]$. In fact, $\tau^*[\boldsymbol{X}]$ and the $\boldsymbol{\sigma}^*[\boldsymbol{X}]$'s will be variable types.

Then, given objects $a_1 \in \sigma_1^*[\boldsymbol{X}], \ldots, a_m \in \sigma_m^*[\boldsymbol{X}]$ (notation: $\boldsymbol{a} \in \boldsymbol{\sigma}^*[\boldsymbol{X}]$) we define the interpretation

$$t^*[\boldsymbol{X}, \boldsymbol{a}] \in \sigma^*[\boldsymbol{X}].$$

Interpretation of a type $\tau[\alpha_1, \ldots \alpha_n] = \tau[\boldsymbol{\alpha}]$

(i) If $\tau[\boldsymbol{\alpha}] = \alpha_i$, then $\tau^*[\boldsymbol{X}] = X_i$; if $f_1 \in \mathrm{qD}(X_1, Y_1), \ldots, f_n \in \mathrm{qD}(X_n, Y_n)$ (notation: $\boldsymbol{f} \in \mathrm{qD}(\boldsymbol{X}, \boldsymbol{Y})$), then we define $\tau^*[\boldsymbol{f}] = f_i$.

(ii) If $\tau[\boldsymbol{\alpha}] = \sigma[\boldsymbol{\alpha}] \Rightarrow \rho[\boldsymbol{\alpha}]$, then $\tau^*[\boldsymbol{X}] = \sigma^*[\boldsymbol{X}] \Rightarrow \rho^*[\boldsymbol{X}]$; if $\boldsymbol{f} \in \mathrm{qD}(\boldsymbol{X}, \boldsymbol{Y})$, then $\tau^*[\boldsymbol{f}] = \sigma^*[\boldsymbol{f}] \Rightarrow \rho^*[\boldsymbol{f}]$.

(iii) If $\tau[\boldsymbol{\alpha}] = \Lambda\alpha.\sigma[\alpha, \boldsymbol{\alpha}]$, then $\tau^*[\boldsymbol{X}] = \Lambda X.\sigma^*[X, \boldsymbol{X}] = \mathrm{Tr}(\sigma^*[\cdot, \boldsymbol{X}])$; if $\boldsymbol{f} \in \mathrm{qD}(\boldsymbol{X}, \boldsymbol{Y})$, then $\tau^*[\boldsymbol{f}] = \Lambda X.\sigma^*[X, \boldsymbol{f}] = \mathrm{Tr}(\sigma^*[\cdot, \boldsymbol{f}])$.

The general results of Section 2 show that τ^* is a variable type in n arguments.

Interpretation of a term $t[\boldsymbol{\alpha},\boldsymbol{X}]$ of type $\tau[\boldsymbol{\alpha}]$

(i) If $t[\boldsymbol{\alpha}, \boldsymbol{X}] = x_i$, then let $t^*[\boldsymbol{X}, \boldsymbol{a}] = a_i$.

(ii) If $t[\boldsymbol{\alpha}, \boldsymbol{X}] = \lambda y.u[\boldsymbol{\alpha}, y, \boldsymbol{X}]$, then let $t^*[\boldsymbol{X}, \boldsymbol{a}] = \lambda b.t^*[\boldsymbol{\alpha}, b, \boldsymbol{a}]$.

(iii) If $t[\boldsymbol{\alpha},\boldsymbol{X}] = u[\boldsymbol{\alpha}, \boldsymbol{X}](v[\boldsymbol{\alpha}, \boldsymbol{X}])$, then let $t^*[\boldsymbol{X}, \boldsymbol{a}] = \mathrm{Ap}(u^*[\boldsymbol{X}, \boldsymbol{a}], v^*[\boldsymbol{X}, \boldsymbol{a}])$.

(iv) If $t[\boldsymbol{\alpha}, \boldsymbol{X}] = \Lambda\beta.u[\beta,\boldsymbol{\alpha}, \boldsymbol{X}]$, then let $t^*[\boldsymbol{X}, \boldsymbol{a}] = \Lambda Y.u^*[Y,\boldsymbol{X}, \boldsymbol{a}]$; this makes sense, because $\boldsymbol{\sigma}$ does not depend on β.

(v) If $t[\boldsymbol{\alpha}, \boldsymbol{X}] = u[\boldsymbol{\alpha}, \boldsymbol{X}]\{\sigma[\boldsymbol{\alpha}]\}$, then let $t^*[\boldsymbol{X}, \boldsymbol{a}] = \mathrm{Ext}(u^*[\boldsymbol{X}, \boldsymbol{a}], \sigma^*[\boldsymbol{X}])$.

Verification One has to verify that Definition 3.5 makes sense. We only indicate the main steps, and leave the details:

(i) One has somewhere to verify that the clauses (i)–(v) above (provided they make sense) lead to variable terms of the expected types. This is immediate except for clause (v), for which one needs the straightforward property

$$\tau^*[\sigma^*[\boldsymbol{X}], \boldsymbol{X}] = (\tau[\sigma/\alpha])^*[\boldsymbol{X}].].$$

(ii) More seriously, one has to verify some "stability" requirements for the interpretation; there are two such properties:

1. When $\boldsymbol{X}$ is fixed, then $t^*[\boldsymbol{X}, \cdot]$ is a stable function of m arguments of types $\boldsymbol{\sigma}[\boldsymbol{X}]$.
2. Let $\boldsymbol{f} \in \mathrm{qD}(\boldsymbol{X}, \boldsymbol{Y})$; then for all $\boldsymbol{b} \in \boldsymbol{\sigma}^*[\boldsymbol{X}]$,

$$\tau^*[\boldsymbol{f}]^-(t^*[\boldsymbol{Y}, \boldsymbol{\sigma}[\boldsymbol{f}]^+(\boldsymbol{b})]) = t^*[\boldsymbol{X}, \boldsymbol{b}].$$

The verification of (1) and (2) is an uninteresting exercise.

Theorem 3.2

The interpretation has the following properties:

(i) The interpretation of the schemes of Definition 3.2(i)–(v) preserves inclusions: To say that $t^* \subset u^*$, when t and u are of the same form $t[\boldsymbol{\alpha}, \boldsymbol{X}]$, $u[\boldsymbol{\alpha}, \boldsymbol{X}]$ means that $\boldsymbol{a} \subset \boldsymbol{b} \in \boldsymbol{\sigma}[\boldsymbol{X}]$ implies $t^*[\boldsymbol{X}, \boldsymbol{a}] = t^*[\boldsymbol{X}, \boldsymbol{b}] \cap u^*[\boldsymbol{X}, \boldsymbol{a}]$ (as usual, finite $\boldsymbol{X}$, $\boldsymbol{a}$, $\boldsymbol{b}$ suffice for our purposes). For instance, from $t^* \subset u^*$, one can deduce $(t\{\sigma\})^* \subset (u\{\sigma\})^*$.

(ii) The interpretation of the schemes of Definition 3.2(i)–(v) preserves equality; this is a straightforward consequence of (i).

(iii)

$$((\lambda x.t[x])(u))^* = t[u/x]^*,$$

$$(\lambda x.t(x))^* = t^* \text{ when } x \text{ is not free in } t,$$

$$((\Lambda\alpha.t[\alpha])\{\sigma\})^* = t[\sigma/\alpha]^*,$$

$$(\Lambda\alpha.t\{\alpha\}^* = t^* \text{ when } \alpha \text{ is not free in } t.$$

In other words, two terms which are (β, η)-interconvertible have by (ii) and (iii) the same interpretation.

The proof is left to the reader, but not that easy!

Remark Our interpretation, although it uses a very pretentious formalism, is extremely effective and constructive. In particular, it can be carried out in primitive recursive arithmetic without any problem: qD can be encoded by means of its finite elements, so we can speak of a recursive qD. Moreover, the operations used to construct qD's are primitive recursive.[8] As to elements of a qD, the good taste consists in encoding them by means of a primitive recursive enumerating function, and once more, all our operations are primitive recursive in this encoding.

It is not astonishing that our interpretation is elementary: Note that it extends to a system containing the universal fixed point operator fp of type $\Lambda\alpha.(\alpha \Rightarrow \alpha) \Rightarrow \alpha$, which does not quite lead to normal forms!

Let us end this section with the computation of the traces of simple types.

Theorem 3.3

$(\Lambda\alpha.\alpha)^* = \varnothing$.

Proof $\|\mathrm{Tr}(\Lambda\alpha.\alpha)\|$ consists of only one point: (1, 0), where 1 is the qD $\{\varnothing, \{0\}\}$. We show that this point is incompatible with itself. Consider the qD $A = \{\varnothing, \{u\}, \{v\}\}$ with $u \neq v$; there are two morphisms f_u and f_v from 1 to X; the compatibility condition for $(1, 0)$ alone requires in particular that $\{f_u(0), f_v(0)\} \in A$, but this set is $\{u, v\} \notin A$. □

Theorem 3.4

$(\Lambda\alpha.\alpha \Rightarrow \alpha)^* = \{\varnothing, \{(1, (\{0\}, 0))\}\}$.

Proof As usual, 1 denotes the qD $\{\varnothing, \{0\}\}$. $\|\mathrm{Tr}(\Lambda\alpha.\alpha \Rightarrow \alpha)\|$ consists of all tuples $(X, (a, z))$, where X is a finite qD, $a \in X$, and $X = a \cup \{z\}$. Take such a tuple $(X, (a, z))$, and assume that $|X|$ has at least two points. Consider the set $|Y|$ obtained by duplicating all points of $|X|$ but z: We have two functions $x \rightsquigarrow x'$ and $x \rightsquigarrow x''$ from $|X|$ to $|Y|$ which disagree everywhere but for z: $z' = z'' = z$. We extend our functions to subsets by using the same notation: $'$ and $''$. Observe that $a' \neq a''$. A subset of Y can be written as $d = b' \cup c''$, with $b' = d \cap |X|\,'$ and $c'' = d \cap |X|\,''$, and we declare d to be a member of Y exactly when $b \in X$ and $c \in X$. Then $'$ and $''$ are morphisms from X to Y. Moreover, $a' \cup a'' \in Y$; i.e., a' and a''

8. This is an exaggeration; for the precise statement, see Appendix C.

are compatible. Now the compatibility of $(X, (a, z))$ itself means in particular that $\{(a', z), (a'', z)\} \in Y \Rightarrow Y$; but this is impossible since a', a'' are comparable but distinct.

So the only self-compatible elements of $\|\mathrm{Tr}(\Lambda\alpha.\alpha \Rightarrow \alpha)\|$ are of the form $(X, (a, z))$, with $|X| = \{z\}$ and $a \in X$. Now $a = \varnothing$ is impossible, simply by sending X into A by f_u and f_v (as in Theorem 3.3), which would lead to the inconsistent combination $\{(\varnothing, u), (\varnothing, v)\}$ in $A \Rightarrow A$.

Then $a = \{z\}$, and, up to isomorphism, we are reduced to the solution $(1, (\{0\}, 0))$. □

Theorem 3.5

$\Lambda\alpha.(\alpha \Rightarrow (\alpha \Rightarrow \alpha))$ (boolean type) contains exactly four objects: $\varnothing$ and the singletons of $(1, (\{0\}, (\varnothing, 0)))$ (TRUE), of $(1, (\varnothing, (\{0\}, 0)))$ (FALSE) and of $(1, (\{0\}, (\{0\}, 0)))$ (INTER).

Proof First observe that these three singletons are pairwise incompatible: For instance, if one puts together in the domain 1, FALSE and INTER, then one gets the set $(\varnothing, (\{0\}, 0), (\{0\}, (\{0\}, 0)))$, which is not the trace of any binary stable function from 1^2 to 1.

The general form of an object of $\|\Lambda\alpha.\alpha \Rightarrow (\alpha \Rightarrow \alpha)\|$ is $(X, (a, (b, z)))$, with X a finite qD, $a, b \in X$, and $X = a \cup b \cup \{z\}$. By an imitation of the proof of Theorem 3.4 one easily shows that one can reduce to the case $X = 1$, $z = 0$, and $a \neq \varnothing$ or $b \neq \varnothing$. Then the only possibilities are TRUE, FALSE, INTER.

Now we have to show that these three points are themselves self-consistent. They obviously correspond to the following functions:

$$\mathrm{TRUE}(Y)(a)(b) = a, \qquad \mathrm{FALSE}(Y)(a)(b) = b,$$
$$\mathrm{INTER}(Y)(a)(b) = a \cap b,$$

which fulfill all possible stability requirements. □

Remark Here we see the possible role of semantics: to suggest improvements of the syntax. For instance, F has only two closed normal terms of boolean type, namely $\Lambda\alpha.\lambda x^\alpha.\lambda y^\alpha.x^\alpha$ and $\Lambda\alpha.\lambda x^\alpha.\lambda y^\alpha.y^\alpha$. These two terms are respectively interpreted by TRUE and FALSE. But there are two other objects, $\varnothing$ and INTER. There is little to say about $\varnothing$: The possibility of adding a void object of each type could be seen even before starting the interpretation. But the object INTER is unexpected: This third truth value plays the role of the undetermined value; its adjunction to the syntax could be considered.

Let us recall that the definition by cases of IF THEN ELSE is defined in F by: $\lambda x^{\mathrm{bool}}.\Lambda\alpha.\lambda y^\alpha.\lambda z^\alpha.x\{\sigma\}(y)(z)$, i.e., IF t THEN a ELSE b, where t is of boolean type and a, b of type σ, is $t\{\sigma\}(a)(b)$. In fact, semantically, we get for the four possible values:

$$\begin{aligned}\text{IF TRUE THEN } a \text{ ELSE } b &= a,\\ \text{IF FALSE THEN } a \text{ ELSE } b &= b,\\ \text{IF VOID THEN } a \text{ ELSE } b &= \emptyset,\\ \text{IF INTER THEN } a \text{ ELSE } b &= a \cap b.\end{aligned}$$

If one defines NOT $= \lambda z^{\mathrm{bool}}.\Lambda\alpha.\lambda x^{\alpha}.\lambda y^{\alpha}.z\{\alpha\}(y)(x)$, then

$$\begin{aligned}\text{NOT(TRUE)} &= \text{False},\\ \text{NOT(FALSE)} &= \text{True, and}\\ \text{NOT(INTER)} &= \text{Inter}.\end{aligned}$$

If one similarly defines the connective OR by

$$\text{OR} = \lambda z^{\mathrm{bool}}.\lambda z'^{\mathrm{bool}}.\Lambda\alpha.\lambda x^{\alpha}.\lambda y^{\alpha}.z\{\alpha\}(x)(z'\{\alpha\}(x)(y)),$$

then

$$\begin{aligned}\text{TRUE OR TRUE} &= \text{True},\\ \text{TRUE OR FALSE} &= \text{False Or True} = \text{True},\\ \text{FALSE OR FALSE} &= \text{False},\\ \text{TRUE OR INTER} &= \text{Inter Or True} = \text{True},\\ \text{FALSE OR INTER} &= \text{Inter Or False} = \text{Inter, and}\\ \text{INTER OR INTER} &= \text{Inter}.\end{aligned}$$

This shows that the natural three-valued connectives can be defined in *F*. Of course, syntactically they appear as binary connectives,[9] but semantically they can be seen as three-valued ones. The importance of three-valued logic with respect to questions of normalization is extreme.

3.2 *Case of* int

The type int is already more complicated. $\|\mathrm{int}\|$ is made of tuples $(X, (a, (f, z))$ (denoted $(X, a, f; z)$ for reasons of readability) made of a finite qD X, of $a \in X$, of $f \in X \Rightarrow X$, and of $z \in |X|$ such that $|X|$ is the union of $a, \{z\}$, and of the sets $b \cup \{x\}$, when $(b, x) \in f$. It is possible to characterize $|\mathrm{int}|$, but the result obtained is not very exciting, so we prefer to look at some specific elements of $|\mathrm{int}|$,

9. "Binary" in the sense of "manichean"!

namely those belonging to the interpretation of some integer $\bar{k}$: $\bar{k}^*$ consists of all tuples $(X, a, f; z)$ in |int| such that

(i) $z \in f^k(a)$,

(ii) if $a' \subset a$, $f' \subset f$, and $z \in f^k(a)$, then $a = a'$ and $f = f'$.

Let us give some examples: If $|X| = \{0, \ldots, k\}$, $a = \{0\}$, $f = \{(\{i\}, i+1); i < k\}$, and $z = k$, then $f^k(a) = \{z\}$, and it is easy to see that this point belongs to $\bar{k}^*$; it does not belong to any other $\bar{k}'^*$.

Another example is the following: If $|X| = \{0, 1\}$, $a = \{0\}$, and $f = \{((\{0\}, s), (\{1\}, 1)\}$ (hence $\{0, 1\} \notin X$), then $1 \in f^k(a)$ for all $k > 0$. This point belongs to all $\overline{k+1}^*$'s, but not to $\bar{0}^*$.

Finally, take the example of $|X| = \{0, 1, \ldots, p\}$, of $a = \{0\}$, $f = \{(\{i\}, i+1); i < p\} \cup \{(\{p\}, 0)\}$, and $z = q \leq p$. Then it is easy to see that $z \in f^k(a)$ exactly for $k = q, q+p+1, q+2p+2$, etc.; in fact, it belongs to $\bar{k}^*$ for $k = q+p+1, q+2p+2, q+3p+3$, etc., but not for $k = q$: This is because $z \in f'^q(a)$ for $f' = \{(\{i\}, i+1); i < q\}$.

In fact, it is not difficult to see that the set of all integers k such that a given point $(X, a, f; z)$ of |int| belongs to $\bar{k}^*$ is eventually periodic; for instance, if $N =$ card$(X)!$, then $g^n(b) = g^{n+N}(b)$ for any $n > N$ and any $b \in X$ and $g \in Y \Rightarrow Y$. Hence, if we know which one among the integers $N+1, N+2, \ldots, 2N$ is such that $(X, a, f; z)$ belongs to their interpretation, then we can find all greater solutions by shift.

4 The Intrinsic Model of λ-Calculus

What we have done for the system F enables us to go back to the interpretation of λ-calculus: It is more or less immediate that the interpretation t_D^* of Definition 1.4 is a functor of the λ-structure D; more precisely, t_D^* will appear as an object of an appropriate variable type. Hence, the general results of Sections 2 and 3 will enable us to define t^* as the interpretation of the abstraction term of F (abstracted with respect to X, H, and K) corresponding to t_D^*. Since t^* encodes the value of t_D^* in any D, any fact about the interpretation of t in any qD can be viewed from t^*; since t^* is a universal interpretation, one can expect a deeper understanding of t from the study of t^* than from the study of any t_D^*. One can object that t^* also encodes interpretation with very bad properties; admitting that some of these interpretations have no interest at all, let us recall that t^* is a set of invariants, and that it is possible to restrict our attention to those invariants which are thought to be noble: In t^* it is always possible to separate the wheat from the tares, which we refused to do, since the notions of wheat and tares may depend on personal taste and particular applications.

Definition 4.1 Let α be a type variable, and let w and z be two variables of respective types $\alpha \Rightarrow (\alpha \Rightarrow \alpha)$ and $(\alpha \Rightarrow \alpha) \Rightarrow \alpha$. Then to any λ-term t we associate t° of type α, as follows:

(i) x° is the variable x^α,

(ii) $(\lambda x.t)^\circ$ is $z(\lambda x^\alpha.t^\circ)$,

(iii) $(t(u))^\circ$ is $w(t^\circ)(u)$.

Definition 4.2 Let t be a closed λ-term. Then we define t^* as the interpretation of the closed term of F

$$\Lambda\alpha.\lambda w^{\alpha\Rightarrow(\alpha\Rightarrow\alpha)}.\lambda z^{(\alpha\Rightarrow\alpha)\Rightarrow\alpha}.t^\circ[\alpha, w, z].$$

t^* is an element of the qualitative domain

$$(\Lambda\alpha.(\alpha\Rightarrow(\alpha\Rightarrow\alpha))) \Rightarrow (((\alpha\Rightarrow\alpha)\Rightarrow\alpha) \Rightarrow \alpha)^*.$$

We shall use the notation $\mathbf{\Lambda}_0$ for this qualitative domain.

Theorem 4.1
t^* encodes the value of t^*_D in any λ-structure (X, H, K), by

$$t^*_D = \mathrm{Ap}(\mathrm{Ap}(\mathrm{Ext}(t^*, X), H), K), \quad \text{i.e.,} \quad t^*_D = t^*\{X\}(H)(K).$$

The proof of this theorem is immediate.

4.1 *Discussion about t**

(i) The first thing we want from t^* is that it should encode information about the most obvious λ-structures, namely those for which H and K are reciprocal isomorphisms. First observe that there are nontrivial ex amples of such a situation: Start with a nontrivial X_0 (i.e., $X_0 \neq \varnothing$) and form $X_1 = X_0 \Rightarrow X_0$; we can define $f_0 \in \mathrm{qD}(X_0, X_1)$ by $f_0(x_0) = (\varnothing, x_0)$. Define in general $X_{n+1} = X_n \Rightarrow X_n$, and $f_{n+1} \in \mathrm{qD}(X_{n+1}, X_{n+2})$ by $f_{n+1} = f_n \Rightarrow f_n$. Then (X_n, f_{nm}) is a direct system of qD's, indexed by $\mathbb{N}$ with $f_{nm} = f_{m-1}f_{m-2}\ldots f_n$. Let $(X, g_n) = \lim_{\rightarrow}(X_n, f_{nm})$. Then

$$\begin{aligned}(X\Rightarrow X,\ g_n\Rightarrow g_n) &\simeq \lim_{\rightarrow}(X_n \Rightarrow X_n, f_{nm}\Rightarrow f_{nm})\\ &= \lim_{\rightarrow}(X_{n+1}, f_{n+1m+1}) = (X, g_{n+1}).\end{aligned}$$

So there are unique isomorphisms k from $X\Rightarrow X$ to X and h from X to $X\Rightarrow X$ such that $g_n \Rightarrow g_n = hg_{n+1}$ and $g_{n+1} = k(g_n \Rightarrow g_n)$. Obviously, h and k are reciprocal, and we are done, with $H = h^+, K = k^+$.

(ii) If (X, H, K) is a λ-structure with X nontrivial and H, K reciprocal isomorphisms, then it is not true that (X, H, K) can be approximated by means of similar λ-structures (X_n, H_n, K_n), with X_n finite. So it is more interesting to consider those λ-structures $D = (X, H, K)$ for which

$$H \circ K \subset \mathrm{Id}^{X \Rightarrow X} \quad \text{and} \quad K \circ H \subset \mathrm{Id}^{X}. \tag{**}$$

These λ-structures are increasing with respect to β- and η-conversion. Moreover, let X_i be any finite subset of X, and let g_i be the inclusion map from X_i to X; define

$$K_i = ((g_i \Rightarrow g_i) \Rightarrow g_i)^{-}(K) \quad \text{and} \quad H_i = (g_i \Rightarrow (g_i \Rightarrow g_i))^{-}(H);$$

it is immediate that

$$H_i \circ K_i \subset \mathrm{Id}^{X_i \Rightarrow X_i} \quad \text{and} \quad K_i \circ H_i \subset \mathrm{Id}^{X_i}$$

and (X, H, K) can be approximated by means of finite λ-structures still enjoying $(**)$.

Definition 4.3 Remember that an object of $|\mathbf{\Lambda}_0|$ consists of a tuple $((X, H, K), z)$ where X is a finite qD, (X, H, K) is a λ-structure, and $z \in |X|$. We shall prefer the notation $(X, H, K; z)$. We define the subset $|\mathbf{\Lambda}_1|$ of $|\mathbf{\Lambda}_0|$ to consist of those tuples $(X, H, K; z)$ such that (X, H, K) fulfills condition $(**)$ above.

Theorem 4.2

The interpretation is increasing with respect to β- and η-conversion on $|\mathbf{\Lambda}_1|$; namely, if $t =/ u$ by means of β- and η-conversions, then

$$t^* \cap |\mathbf{\Lambda}_1| \subset u^* \cap |\mathbf{\Lambda}_1|.$$

Proof Let D be a λ-structure enjoying $(**)$; then the interpretation $\cdot^*_D$ is increasing with respect to β- and η-conversion. In particular, if $t =/ u$ and $(X, H, K; z) \in t^* \cap |\mathbf{\Lambda}_1|$, then $z \in t^*_{X,H,K} \cap u^*_{X,H,K}$, so $(X, H, K; z) \in u^*$. □

4.2 *Final Remarks*

(i) In order to separate the wheat from the tares, the restriction to $|\mathbf{\Lambda}_1|$ is the obvious choice: $t^* \cap |\mathbf{\Lambda}_1|$ determines the behavior of t^*_D on a very wide class of λ-structures, namely all those satisfying $(**)$. Moreover, the fact that the interpretation is increasing, namely, that the reduction relation is not interpreted "flatly", is a nice feature. Of course, this was already possible with the traditional approach, i.e., to choose a particular D satisfying $(**)$; but any such D is particularly artificial, while the class of all such D's is a very nice one.

(ii) Of course, if we compute

$$t^\beta = \cup\{u^*; t =/ u\} \cap |\mathbf{\Lambda}_1|,$$

then t^β is an element of $|\mathbf{\Lambda}_0|$ which interprets the Böhm tree of t.

The open question is the relation between the equalities $t^\beta = u^\beta$ and the equality between the Böhm trees of t and u. We have not looked seriously at this question. We simply observe that $t^\beta = u^\beta$ implies t and u having the same interpretation in every λ-structure fulfilling $D \Rightarrow D \sim D$. So the basic problem is to see whether the results relating equality of Böhm trees with the model P_ω can be adapted to qualitative domains.

Appendix A: *F and Related Systems*

Here we consider some other systems, in particular possible strengthenings of F (for which we still get termination of the conversions). As to *strength*, there is a very crude way of measuring it, namely by the class of all number-theoretic functions representable in the system. For instance, systems like Gödel's functional of finite type T, Martin-Løf's system with universes, the language ML without recursion, etc., have normalization proofs which can be carried out in rather small subsystems of second-order arithmetic, and, in particular, the function associating to a term of any of these systems its normal form is (under a suitable coding) provably total in PA_2, i.e., representable in F. So F is definitely stronger than all these systems, which does not mean that F really contains these systems; for instance, Martin-Løf's type theory contains type schemes that are not nicely do-able in F.

A.1 *The Systems F_n*

If we allow formation of types by allowing quantification over *connectives* of type n, then we get a system F_n, which is considerably stronger than F. F_0 is just F, so let us explain F_1: Besides the type variables, we add variables $\Omega_p, \Omega'_p, \Omega''_p$, etc., for p-ary connectives. To the type schemes of F, we add:

if Ω_p is a connective variable and $\tau_1, \ldots, \tau_p$ are types, then $\Omega_p(\tau_1, \ldots, \tau_p)$ is a type,

if σ is a type, then $\Lambda\Omega_p.\sigma$ is a type.

The terms are formed as in F, except that we must now give rules for quantification over connectives:

(i) If t is of type σ and Ω_p is a variable of connective which does not occur freely in the type of a variable occurring freely in t, then $\Lambda\Omega_p.t$ is a term of type $\Lambda\Omega_p.\sigma$.

(ii) If t is of type $\Lambda\Omega_p.\sigma$ and T is an abstraction connective $\lambda\alpha_1 \dots \lambda\alpha_p.\tau$, then $t\{T\}$ is a term of type $\sigma[T/\Omega_p]$.

(Abstraction connectives are defined as follows: If τ is a type and $\alpha_1, \dots, \alpha_p$ are type variables which are pairwise distinct, then $\lambda\alpha_1 \dots \lambda\alpha_p.\tau$ is an abstraction connective. In order to substitute an abstraction connective $T = \lambda\alpha_1 \dots \lambda\alpha_p.\tau$ for a connective variable Ω_p in an expression (term or variable) E, we proceed as follows:

we first make a formal substitution: Replace all Ω_p's by T,

then we replace all expressions $T(\sigma_1, \dots, \sigma_p)$ by $\tau[\sigma_1/\alpha_1, \dots, \sigma_p/\alpha_p]$, and then we get a legal expression of F_1.)

The additional conversion rule of F_1 is as follows:

$$\Lambda\Omega_p.t\{T\} =/ t[T/\Omega_p].$$

In [5], it was proved that

(i) the conversion process terminates, and

(ii) the class of functions from $\mathbb{N}$ to $\mathbb{N}$ representable in F_n is the class of all provably total functions of arithmetic of order $n+2$, namely PA_{n+2}.

This shows of course that the improvement is genuine, even if the ideas are just a straightforward adaptation of those of F.

A.2 *Toward Inconsistency*

Since it was possible to generalize F by using typed connectives, the idea was to look for a more powerful typing than the finite types. So why not type the connectives as in system F? We do not give the details here but it was soon discovered that the system was inconsistent: A form of the Burali-Forti paradox could be derived in it. (In fact, this system—let us call it U, as in [4] where these things are explained—was nothing more than a natural deduction system corresponding to arithmetic, not of finite type, but with type levels as in F, comprehension axioms and quantification over types.)

Simultaneously, Martin-Løf (1971) proposed the first version of his type theory; the system took part of its inspiration in Heyting's semantics of proofs, in the Curry-Howard-De Bruijn isomorphism, and in F. F was translated in such a way in the first version that U could be translated as well, so the system was inconsistent too. Martin-Løf later dropped his axiom "$V \in V$", and since that time, his systems have all been strictly "below" F.

Recently, Coquand and Huet [2] worked out a *Theory of Constructions* which may seem a bit mysterious:

(i) The system roughly speaking embodies features coming from De Bruijn's AUTOMATH, Martin-Løf's sytems, and F (more precisely, the F_n's).

(ii) The syntax is a liberal version of AUTOMATH, in which one can form dependent products as in Martin Løf's. There are three levels for expressions, one corresponding to what we call terms, one corresponding to what we call types, and one corresponding to what we call connectives in F_n. There is no fourth level, because one would meet inconsistency. The somewhat obscure restrictions on the syntax all come from the need to "stick" to the systems F_n, even if their system is much more flexible than the F_n's. The system is clearly stronger than all F_n's.

Up to now, this system is the strongest one ever proposed; moreover, it takes into account ideas coming from other sources of inspiration, so, in some sense, this is the "universal functional system".

All attempts to strengthen this system, in particular to tamper with the fourth level, should be considered very cautiously: The Tarpeian Rock is close to the Capitol.

Appendix B *Scott Domains and Qualitative Domains*

Scott has investigated, in a lot of papers, all possible equivalent ways of looking at his semantics, so-called Scott domains. In one of these papers [8], he presents his domains in a formalism which is close enough to qualitative domains so that we can see the links between the two notions.

(i) A qualitative domain can be seen as a set of atomic propositions (the points of $|X|$), together with a "consistency" relation: $p_1, \ldots, p_n$ are consistent exactly when $\{p_1, \ldots, p_n\} \in X$. We can, for instance, form a theory $T(X)$ by taking as axioms all intuitionistic sequents $p_1, \ldots, p_n \vdash$, where $p_1, \ldots, p_n$ is a subset of $|X|$ not in X (and, for instance, minimal with respect to this property). Then $A \in X$ exactly when $A + T(X)$ is a consistent theory.

(ii) A Scott domain can be seen as a set of atomic propositions, together with a set of axioms of the form $p_1, \ldots, p_n \vdash$ or $p_1, \ldots, p_n \vdash q$. For technical reasons, there is a fixed bottommost point b_0, together with the axiom $\vdash b_0$. A set A of atomic statements belongs to the Scott domain defined by the set S of axioms when

$A + S$ is consistent,

if $A + S \vdash q$, then $q \in A$.

In particular, Scott domains fulfill the analogue of (qD1) (under the form that a Scott domain is nonvoid) and (qD2). But (qD3) is essentially false: In current Scott domains, finite sets will not be closed under consequence.

If one forgets the purely technical b_0, then a qualitative domain is a Scott domain (take no axiom of the form $p_1, \ldots, p_n \vdash q$). The question is therefore: "Do we really need all these sequents $p_1, \ldots, p_n \vdash q$, which complicate the interpretation?"

1. It is possible that some of these sequents are needed to interpret some atomic data structures; these data structures must be slightly uneven, however, since all current ones (trees, lists, etc.) can be done in F, and hence within qualitative domains.
2. In Scott's interpretation, the sequents essentially come from the interpretation of the implicative types. Of course, it is perhaps because Scott wants to take into account nonstable algorithms, such as the well-known "parallel or"; observe that for stable maps only our definition can yield a qD. Now if a binary function f is stable only in its first argument, then for $a \subset b$, $f(.,a)$ is not Berry-smaller than $f(.,b)$, i.e., there is no inclusion between the traces. The only way to obtain a phenomenon of inclusion between some kind of traces is to encode f by means of all pairs (a, z), a finite, $z \in f(a)$. But the set of "traces" thus obtained is not closed under subset, since whenever (a, z) belongs to a trace, all its weakenings (a', z), with $a \subset a'$, belong to this "trace". This is where consequence relations come from. The problem with this consequence relation is that its maintenance will generate new consequence relations..., and that true finiteness has to be dropped for a more liberal notion of "finitely generated", i.e., the closure under consequences of finitely many axioms.... The price is a bit heavy if we keep in mind that nonstable algos never occur in typed or untyped lambda calculi. Moreover, the quantitative semantics developed in [6] handles nonstable algos in a natural way by introducing multiplicities.
3. A type formation scheme where there is a more serious reason to introduce complications is the sum of types. In [6], we have shown how all possible schemes for this type could be interpreted by qualitative domains. However, it is true that one would like to interpret, if possible, the sum of types by something like a sum. This is impossible in qD's: If X and Y are qD's (suppose for simplicity that $|X| \cap |Y| = \emptyset$), and 0 and 1 are two elements not in $|X| \cup |Y|$, then one can consider $X + Y$,

which consists of:

the void set $\varnothing$,

the sets $a \cup \{0\}$ for $a \in X$,

the sets $b \cup \{1\}$ for $b \in Y$.

Condition (qD3) is violated, because, when $a \neq \varnothing$, the subset a of $a \cup \{0\}$ does not belong to $X+Y$. Then one has to add the axioms $z \vdash 0$ for $z \in |X|$ and $z' \vdash 1$ for $z' \in |Y|$. So the usual interpretation of the sum introduces some typical features of Scott domains. However, it is easily seen that the Scott domains that are needed are those for which the closure of a finite consistent set with respect to consequence is finite, and so we do not introduce too much rubbish.

So, in the case of the disjunctive type, there is a clear dilemma:

either we stay within the simple concept of qD, and the price to pay is a slight complication of the interpretation of such types;

or we interpret it as a sum, but then we have to weaken our class of domains so as to accept some reasonable classes of Scott domains.

The interpretation of the sum developed in [6] is compatible (in case of a primitive connective sum added to *F*) with the interpretation given here.

Appendix C *Binary Qualitative Domains*

In qualitative domains not all subsets are accepted. Of course, it is important to understand at which moment one actually needs some kind of incompatibility, because this could simplify the interpretation. So let us start with qD's of the form $\mathcal{P}(|X|)$, where everything is compatible. If we form the function space $X \Rightarrow Y$; then (FS2) introduces no incompatibility, but (FS3) introduces an incompatibility between pairs. (The same would be true in the nonstable case (F$\not{S}$3) sketched in Appendix B, so this has nothing to do with stability.) So incompatible pairs exist by nature! But no scheme introduces incompatible 3-tuples, for instance. This explains the defintions below. In case somebody would later find a reason of incompatibility for 3-tuples, one can obviously replace the integer 2 by any $N \geq 2$, and get a similar concept of N-ary qD.

Definition C.1 A qD X is *binary* when the following holds: If $a \subset |X|$ and $a \notin X$, there are $x, y \in a$ such that $\{x, y\} \notin X$.

Theorem C.1
Everything done so far can be done within the category 2qD of binary qualitative domains.

Proof Essentially we have to prove that:

(i) If X and Y are binary qD's, then $X \Rightarrow Y$ is a binary qD. (FS3) is a binary condition. (FS2) is also a binary condition: If $F(b) \notin Y$, then $\{z, z'\} \notin Y$ for some $z, z' \in F(b)$, so for some $(a, z), (a', z') \in \mathrm{Tr}(F) = A$ we already have incompatibility: $\{(a, z), (a', z')\} \notin X \Rightarrow Y$.

(ii) If F is a variable type, mapping 2qD into 2qD, then we define $\mathrm{Tr}(F)$ as in Definition 2.2 (but we consider only binary qD's). It is obvious that, in the compatibility condition, it suffices to make $n = 1$, i.e., to look at pairs. □

Remark There is a problem with general qD's regarding the effectivity of Definition 2.2, because when a is finite, we cannot give any bound on n (recall that $(X_0, x_0), \ldots, (X_n, n)$ are not necessarily distinct), a problem that would make $\mathrm{Tr}(F)$ uncomputable in some cases. But, if we restrict to binary (or N-ary) qD's, then we can give the bound 2 on the number of points. Now let us remark that there are only finitely many ways to define maps $f_0 \in \mathrm{qD}(X_0, Y)$ and $f_1 \in \mathrm{qD}(X, Y)$, when Y is fixed. Also observe that one can restrict to the case where $|Y| = \mathrm{rg}(f_0) \cup \mathrm{rg}(f_1)$ and then, up to isomorphism, there are only finitely many possible Y's; this shows that the computation of $\mathrm{Tr}(F)$ is decidable in the binary case.[10]

Appendix D *Total Objects*

The interpretation of F has so far been very elementary; we would like to say something that could have some relation with the fact that the conversion process eventually ends, and hence something about the functions the objects involved, being "total". A first superficial impression would be to identify "totality" semantically with maximality, as was done for instance by Scott [8]. This is wrong; moreover, there is not even an inclusion relation between the two notions. For instance, INTER is maximal but can hardly be claimed to be total, since IF INTER THEN TRUE ELSE FALSE = VOID. The void element of type bool is certainly not total, while IF... THEN... ELSE, TRUE, and FALSE *are*, since they belong to F, and we are looking for a concept of "totality" for which the definable objects of F are total and closed under the operations of F. So INTER cannot be total.

10. In later works on linear logic, binary qD's have been renamed "coherence spaces".

On the other hand, the function associating to x of type $\Lambda\alpha.(\alpha \Rightarrow \alpha) \Rightarrow \alpha$ the point $x\{\text{bool}\}\ (\lambda y^{\text{bool}}.y)$, which is definable in F, must be total, but its interpretation is void, so it is included in the interpretation of λx^{bool}. TRUE, whose interpretation is nonvoid.

In order to solve this question of "totality", we simply adopt the method we already used in [3], namely, to quantify over arbitrary definitions.

Definition D.1 A *total* qD is a pair (X, X_t), where X_t is a subset of X. The elements of X_t are said to be total (with respect to X_t).

Definition D.2 If $\tau[\boldsymbol{\alpha}]$ is a type of F, where $\boldsymbol{\alpha}$ lists all variables of type occurring freely in τ, and if $(\boldsymbol{X}, \boldsymbol{X}_t)$ is a sequence of total qD's of the same length as $\boldsymbol{\alpha}$, then we define a total qD $(\tau[\boldsymbol{X}, \boldsymbol{X}_t], \tau[\boldsymbol{X}, \boldsymbol{X}_t]_t)$ as follows:

(i) $\tau[\boldsymbol{X}, \boldsymbol{X}_t] = \tau * [\boldsymbol{X}]$, already defined,

(ii) if $\tau[\boldsymbol{\alpha}]$ is α^i, then $\tau[\boldsymbol{X}, \boldsymbol{X}_t]_t$ is $\boldsymbol{X}_t^i$,

(iii) if $\tau[\boldsymbol{\alpha}]$ is $\sigma[\boldsymbol{\alpha}] \Rightarrow \rho[\boldsymbol{\alpha}]$, then $a \in \tau[\boldsymbol{X}, \boldsymbol{X}_t]_t$ if and only if, for any $b \in \sigma[\boldsymbol{X}, \boldsymbol{X}_t]_t$, we have $a(b) \in \rho[\boldsymbol{X}, \boldsymbol{X}_t]_t$,

(iv) if τ is $\Lambda\alpha.\sigma[\alpha, \boldsymbol{\alpha}]$, then $a \in \tau[\boldsymbol{X}, \boldsymbol{X}_t]$ if and only if, for any total qD (Y, Y_t), $a\{Y\}$ belongs to $\sigma[Y, \boldsymbol{X}, Y_t, \boldsymbol{X}_t]_t$.

Theorem D.1
Let $t[\boldsymbol{\alpha}, \boldsymbol{x}^{\boldsymbol{\sigma}}]$ be a term of type τ; let $(\boldsymbol{X}, \boldsymbol{X}_t)$ be a sequence of total qD's of the same length as $\boldsymbol{\alpha}$, and let $\boldsymbol{a}$ be a sequence of objects in $\boldsymbol{\sigma}[\boldsymbol{X}, \boldsymbol{X}_t]_t$; then $t^*[\boldsymbol{X}, \boldsymbol{a}] \in \tau[\boldsymbol{X}, \boldsymbol{X}_t]_t$.

Proof The proof is practically immediate; the case of EXT requires the following lemma.

Lemma D.1 (Substitution Lemma)

$$\tau[\sigma[\boldsymbol{X}, \boldsymbol{X}_t], \boldsymbol{X}, \sigma[\boldsymbol{X}, \boldsymbol{X}_t]_t, \boldsymbol{X}_t]_t = \tau[\sigma/\alpha, \boldsymbol{X}, \boldsymbol{X}_t]_t.$$

The proof of this lemma is straightforward, but it contains a hidden use of the comprehension axiom of second-order arithmetic, namely to say that $\sigma[\boldsymbol{X}, \boldsymbol{X}_t]_t$ is a set. □

Remark Although we start with arbitrary definitions, when σ is closed, σ_t is well defined, and we therefore have an *intrinsic* concept of a total object of type σ. For instance, the only total objects of type bool are TRUE and FALSE. However, the interpretation is not extensional, in the sense that two total functions may agree on all total arguments, but be different.

Theorem D.2

The only total objects of type int are the integers.

Proof Let A be a total object of type int; if X is a qD, $a \in X$, and $f \in X \Rightarrow X$, then define $X_t = \{f^n(a); n \in \mathbb{N}\}$. Then (X, X_t) is a total qD, and, moreover, the object a and the map f are total (with respect to X_t). So $A\{X\}(a, f) = f^k(a)$ for some k. We show that the integer k can be chosen independently of X, a, and f. First, consider $X_0 = \{\varnothing, \{0\}, \{1\}, \{2\}, \ldots, \}$, $a_0 = \{0\}$, and $f_0 = \{(i, i+1); i \in \mathbb{N}\}$; we obtain $A\{X_0\}(a_0, f_0) = \{k_0\}$. Given (X, a, f), we form a new qD Y by putting together X and two disjoint isomorphic copies X'_0 and X''_0 of X_0; the elements of Y will all be (disjoint) unions $b \cup c' \cup d''$ with $b \in X$, $c, d \in X_0$. Form $b_0 = a \cup a'_0$, $g_0 = f \cup f'_0$; then $b_0 \in Y$ and $g_0 \in Y \Rightarrow Y$, and $A\{Y\}(b_0, g_0) = g_0^l(b_0)$ for an appropriate l. Now considering the morphism $'$ from X_0 to Y, it is easy to show that $(A\{X\}(a_0, f_0))' \subset A\{Y\}(a'_0, f'_0) \subset A\{Y\}(b_0, g_0)$, and this forces $l = k_0$. For similar reasons, if $b_1 = a \cup a''_0$, $g_1 = f \cup f''_0$, then $A\{Y\}(b_1, g_1) = g_1^{k_0}(b_1)$. From this we conclude that $A\{Y\}(b_0 \cap b_1, g_0 \cap g_1) = (g_0 \cap g_i)^{k_0}(b_0 \cap b_1)$. Now if h is the canonical morphism from X to Y, then $h^+(a) = b_0 \cap b_1$ and $(h \Rightarrow h)^+(f) = g_0 \cap g_1$, so

$$A\{Y\}(h^+(a), (h \Rightarrow h)^+(f)) = h^+(f^{k_0}(a)),$$

and hence

$$A\{X\}(a, f) = h^-(A\{Y\}(h^+(a), (h \Rightarrow h)^+(f)) = h^- h^+(f^{k_0}(a)) = f^{k_0}(a).$$

Since $k = k_0$ for all X, a, f, it is clear that A is the intepretation of the integer k_0. ☐

Remarks

(i) Theorem D.1 is not provable in PA_2. Simply observe that Theorem D.2 is provable in PA_2; hence, from Theorem D.1, one can define, for any closed t of type int $\Rightarrow$ int of F, a function t' from $\mathbb{N}$ to $\mathbb{N}$, by $t'(n) = m$ iff $t(\bar{n})^* = \bar{m}^*$. This function is (as we know from the normalization theorem) equal to $|t|$ of Definition 3.4 (ii). But then t' can be extensionally equal to any given provably total recursive function PA_2, etc.

(ii) Theorem D.1 does not immediately imply the normalization theorem, because it is not excluded a priori that $t(\bar{n})^* = \bar{m}^*$ as a result of the interpretation, without having $t(\bar{n}) =/\ \bar{m}$. But the techniques of [3] (functional interpretation) would content themselves with $t(\bar{n})^* = \bar{m}^*$, and from this we obtain that Theorem D.1 implies the 1-consistency of PA_2, which in turn implies normalization.

(iii) A priori, the notion of totality needs third-order arithmetic because $X_t \in \mathcal{P}(\mathcal{P}(|X|))$; this can be lowered to second-order, however, simply by restricting to recursively enumerable total objects, etc.

(iv) An open question remains: If τ is a purely universal type, i.e., if τ consists of quantifiers $\Lambda\alpha_1 \ldots \Lambda\alpha_n$ followed by a quantifier-free part, does the analogue of Theorem D.2 hold? In other words, are there total points of τ^* which are not of the form t^*?

References

[1] Berry, G. "Modèles complètement adéquats et stables des λ-calculs typés". Thèse de Doctorat d'Etat, Université Paris VII, 1979.

[2] Coquand, T. and Huet, G. "Une théorie des constructions". In *Proceedings ASL Congress* (Orsay). North-Holland, Amsterdam, 1986.

[3] Girard, J.-Y. "Une extension de l'interpretation fonctionnelle de Gödel à l'analyse et son application à l'élimination des coupures dans l'analyse et la théorie des types". *Proceedings of the 2nd Scandinavian Logic Symposium*, J. F. Fenstad, ed., pp. 63–92 North-Holland, Amsterdam, 1971.

[4] Girard, J.-Y. "Interprétation fonctionnelle et élimination des coupures de l'arithmétique d'ordre supérieur". Thèse d'Etat, Université Paris VII, 1972.

[5] Girard, J.-Y. "Quelques résultats sur les interprétations fonctionnelles". *Cambridge Summer School in Mathematical Logic*, Mathias and Rogers, eds., pp. 232–252. Lecture Notes in Mathematics, vol. 337. Springer-Verlag, Berlin, 1973.

[6] Girard, J.-Y. "Normal functors, power series and lambda-calculus". *Ann. Pure Appl. Logic 37* (1988), pp. 129–177.

[7] Reynolds, J. C. "Polymorphism is not set-theoretic". *International Symposium on Semantics of Data Types*, pp. 145–156. Lecture Notes in Computer Science, vol. 173. Springer-Verlag, Berlin, 1984.

[8] Scott D. "Domains for denotational semantics". In *Proceedings ICALP '82* (Aarhus). Lecture Notes in Computer Science, vol. 140. Springer-Verlag, Berlin, 1982.

[9] Troelstra, A. S. "Notes on intuitionistic second order arithmetic". *Cambridge Summer School in Mathematical Logic*, Mathias and Rogers, eds., pp. 171–205. Lecture Notes in Mathematics, vol. 337. Springer-Verlag, Berlin, 1973.

[10] Winskel, G. "Events in computation". Ph.D. Thesis, Edinburgh, 1981.

On Functors Expressible in the Polymorphic Typed Lambda Calculus[1]

7

John C. Reynolds
Carnegie Mellon University

Gordon D. Plotkin
University of Edinburgh

Abstract

Given a model of the polymorphic typed lambda calculus based upon a Cartesian closed category $\mathcal{K}$, there will be functors from $\mathcal{K}$ to $\mathcal{K}$ whose action on objects can be expressed by type expressions and whose action on morphisms can be expressed by ordinary expressions. We show that if T is such a functor then there is a weak initial T-algebra and if, in addition, $\mathcal{K}$ possesses equalizers of all subsets of its morphism sets, then there is an initial T-algebra. It follows that there is no model of the polymorphic typed lambda calculus in which types denote sets and $S \to S'$ denotes the set of all functions from S to S'.

1. This chapter has been accepted for publication in *Information and Computation*, and appears here by permission.

The polymorphic, or second-order, typed lambda calculus [5, 6, 18] is an extension of the typed lambda calculus in which polymorphic functions can be defined by abstraction on type variables, and such functions can be applied to type expressions. It is known that all expressions of this language are normalizable [5, 6]; indeed, they are strongly normalizable [17]. It is also known that the elements of any free many-sorted anarchic algebra are isomorphic to the closed normal expressions of a type that is determined by the signature of the algebra [10, 3]. (This result was anticipated in [22, Proposition 3.15.18].) These facts led to the conjecture in [19] that the polymorphic typed lambda calculus should possess a set-theoretic model, in which types denote sets and $S \rightarrow S'$ denotes the set of all functions from S to S'.

However, Reynolds [20] later showed that no such model exists. Shortly thereafter, Plotkin [16] generalized this proof by considering, for models based upon arbitrary Cartesian closed categories, the behavior of functors that can be expressed in the calculus. In this joint paper, we give an exposition of this generalization, and show why it precludes the existence of a set-theoretic model.

1 *Mathematical Preliminaries*

When f is a function, we write $\mathrm{dom}\, f$ for the domain of f, $f \upharpoonright S$ for the restriction of f to $S \subseteq \mathrm{dom}\, f$, and fx (often without parentheses) for the application of f to an argument x. We assume that application is left-associative, so that $fx\,y = (fx)y$.

We write $[\, f \mid x{:}\, x' \,]$ to denote the function with domain $\mathrm{dom}\, f \cup \{x\}$ such that $[\, f \mid x{:}\, x' \,]y =$ **if** $y = x$ **then** x' **else** fy, and also $[\, x_1{:}\, y_1 \mid \dots \mid x_n{:}\, y_n \,]$ (where the x_i's are distinct) to denote the function with domain $\{x_1, \dots, x_n\}$ that maps each x_i into y_i. As a special case, $[\,]$ denotes the empty function. We also write $\langle y_1, y_2 \rangle$ for the pair $[\, 1{:}\, y_1 \mid 2{:}\, y_2 \,]$.

When $\mathcal{K}$ is a category, we write $|\mathcal{K}|$ for the collection of objects of $\mathcal{K}$, $k \xrightarrow[\mathcal{K}]{} k'$ for the set of morphisms from $k \in |\mathcal{K}|$ to $k' \in |\mathcal{K}|$, $\alpha \,;_{\mathcal{K}}\, \alpha'$ for the composition (in diagrammatic order) of $\alpha \in k \xrightarrow[\mathcal{K}]{} k'$ with $\alpha' \in k' \xrightarrow[\mathcal{K}]{} k''$, and $I_k^{\mathcal{K}}$ for the identity morphism in $k \xrightarrow[\mathcal{K}]{} k$. (In these and later notations, we will frequently elide subscripts or superscripts denoting categories or other entities that are evident from context.) We also write $\mathcal{K}^{\mathrm{op}}$ for the dual of $\mathcal{K}$.

Let F be a function from some (finite) set $\mathrm{dom}\, F$ to $|\mathcal{K}|$. Then a (*finite*) *product* of F in $\mathcal{K}$ consists of an object $\prod^{\mathcal{K}} F$ and, for each $v \in \mathrm{dom}\, F$, a morphism $\mathrm{p}^{\mathcal{K}}[F, v] \in \prod^{\mathcal{K}} F \rightarrow Fv$, such that, if $k \in |\mathcal{K}|$ and Γ is a function with the same domain as F that maps each $v \in \mathrm{dom}\, F$ into a morphism in $k \rightarrow Fv$, then there is a unique morphism, denoted by $\langle \Gamma \rangle^{\mathcal{K}}$, in $k \to \prod^{\mathcal{K}} F$ such that

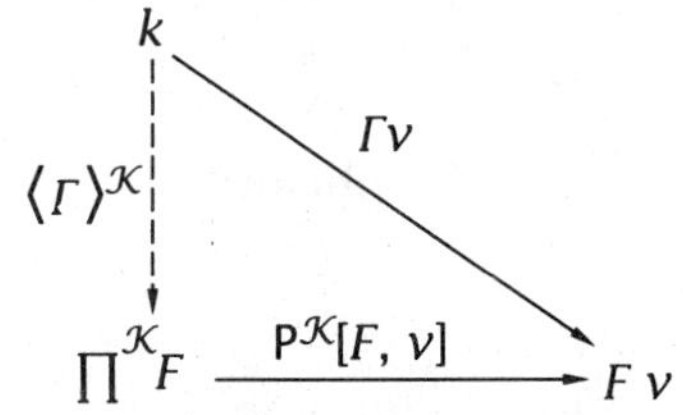

(1)

commutes in $\mathcal{K}$ for all $v \in \operatorname{dom} F$.

It is easily shown that, when $\Gamma v = \mathrm{P}^{\mathcal{K}}[F, v]$ for all $v \in \operatorname{dom} F$,

$$\langle \Gamma \rangle^{\mathcal{K}} = I_{\Pi^{\mathcal{K}} F} \tag{2}$$

and, when $\beta \in k_0 \to k$,

$$\beta \,;\, \langle \Gamma \rangle^{\mathcal{K}} = \langle \Gamma' \rangle^{\mathcal{K}}, \tag{3}$$

where Γ' is the function with the same domain as Γ such that $\Gamma' v = \beta \,;\, \Gamma v$ for all $v \in \operatorname{dom} \Gamma$.

We will frequently use the abbreviations

$$\langle \Gamma \mid v\colon \varphi \rangle^{\mathcal{K}} \stackrel{\text{def}}{=} \langle [\, \Gamma \mid v\colon \varphi \,] \rangle^{\mathcal{K}}$$

and

$$\langle v_1\colon \varphi_1 \mid \dots \mid v_n\colon \varphi_n \rangle^{\mathcal{K}} \stackrel{\text{def}}{=} \langle [\, v_1\colon \varphi_1 \mid \dots \mid v_n\colon \varphi_n \,] \rangle^{\mathcal{K}}.$$

Thus Equation 3 implies

$$\beta \,;\, \langle v_1\colon \varphi_1 \mid \dots \mid v_n\colon \varphi_n \rangle^{\mathcal{K}} = \langle v_1\colon \beta \,;\, \varphi_1 \mid \dots \mid v_n\colon \beta \,;\, \varphi_n \rangle^{\mathcal{K}}. \tag{4}$$

An important special case of the product occurs when F is the empty function. Then its product in $\mathcal{K}$ is an object $\prod^{\mathcal{K}}[\,]$, called a *terminal object*, which we will denote more succinctly by $\mathrm{T}^{\mathcal{K}}$. It has the property that, for each $k \in |\mathcal{K}|$, the set $k \to \mathrm{T}^{\mathcal{K}}$ contains exactly one member, namely $\langle\rangle^{\mathcal{K}}$. (Note that k is determined by context.) The corresponding special case of Equation 4 is that, for $\beta \in k_0 \to k$,

$$\beta \,;\, \langle\rangle^{\mathcal{K}} = \langle\rangle^{\mathcal{K}}. \tag{5}$$

Another important special case occurs when $\operatorname{dom} F = \{1, 2\}$. Here we write $k_1 \times_{\mathcal{K}} k_2$ for $\prod^{\mathcal{K}}[\, 1\colon k_1 \mid 2\colon k_2 \,]$, $\mathrm{p}^{i,\mathcal{K}}_{k_1 \times k_2}$ for $\mathrm{P}^{\mathcal{K}}[[\, 1\colon k_1 \mid 2\colon k_2 \,], i]$, and, when $\alpha_1 \in k \to k_1$ and $\alpha_2 \in k \to k_2$, $\langle \alpha_1, \alpha_2 \rangle^{\mathcal{K}}$ for $\langle\, 1\colon \alpha_1 \mid 2\colon \alpha_2 \,\rangle^{\mathcal{K}}$. The corresponding special cases of Equations 1, 2, and 4 are that, for $\alpha_1 \in k \to k_1$, $\alpha_2 \in k \to k_2$, and $\beta \in k_0 \to k$,

$$\langle \alpha_1, \alpha_2 \rangle \,;\, \mathrm{p}^{i}_{k_1 \times k_2} = \alpha_i, \tag{6}$$

$$\langle \mathrm{p}^{1}_{k_1\times k_2}, \mathrm{p}^{2}_{k_1\times k_2} \rangle = I_{k_1\times k_2}\,, \tag{7}$$

$$\beta\,;\langle \alpha_1, \alpha_2\rangle = \langle \beta\,;\alpha_1, \beta\,;\alpha_2\rangle\,. \tag{8}$$

For $\gamma_1 \in k_1 \to k'_1$, and $\gamma_2 \in k_2 \to k'_2$, we define the morphism

$$\gamma_1 \times_{\mathcal{K}} \gamma_2 \stackrel{\text{def}}{=} \langle (\mathrm{p}^{1,\mathcal{K}}_{k_1\times k_2}\,;\gamma_1), (\mathrm{p}^{2,\mathcal{K}}_{k_1\times k_2}\,;\gamma_2)\rangle^{\mathcal{K}}$$

in $k_1 \times k_2 \to k'_1 \times k'_2$. (The use of $\times$ as an operation on both objects and morphisms reflects the fact that $\times$ is actually a bifunctor.) From Equations 8 and 6 it follows that, for $\alpha_1 \in k \to k_1$, $\alpha_2 \in k \to k_2$, $\gamma_1 \in k_1 \to k'_1$, and $\gamma_2 \in k_2 \to k'_2$,

$$\langle \alpha_1, \alpha_2\rangle\,;(\gamma_1 \times \gamma_2) = \langle \alpha_1\,;\gamma_1, \alpha_2\,;\gamma_2\rangle\,. \tag{9}$$

Let $\mathcal{K}$ be a category with finite products, and k', $k'' \in |\mathcal{K}|$. Then an *exponentiation* of k'' by k' consists of an object $k' \underset{\mathcal{K}}{\Longrightarrow} k''$ and a morphism $\mathrm{ap}^{\mathcal{K}}_{k'k''} \in (k' \underset{\mathcal{K}}{\Longrightarrow} k'')\times k' \to k''$ such that, for each $k \in |\mathcal{K}|$ and $\rho \in k\times k' \to k''$, there is a unique morphism, denoted by $\mathrm{ab}^{\mathcal{K}}\rho$, in $k \to (k' \underset{\mathcal{K}}{\Longrightarrow} k'')$ such that

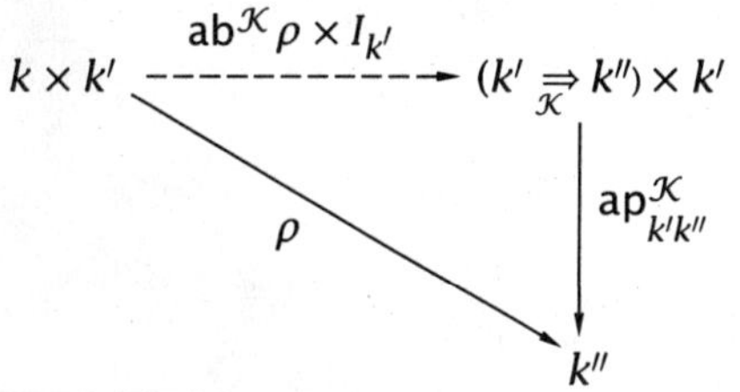

(10)

commutes in $\mathcal{K}$.

A category is said to be *Cartesian closed* if it possesses all finite products (including a terminal element) and all exponentiations. (For a given category, there may be several definitions of $\prod$, $\Rightarrow$, and their associated morphisms that meet the definitions given above. However, when we speak of a category as Cartesian closed, we will assume that these entities have unambiguous meanings, i.e., that a Cartesian closed category is a category with *distinguished* finite products and exponentiations.)

For $\alpha \in k_0 \to (k' \Rightarrow k'')$ and $\alpha' \in k_0 \to k'$ we define

$$\alpha \rhd_{\mathcal{K}} \alpha' \stackrel{\text{def}}{=} \langle \alpha, \alpha'\rangle^{\mathcal{K}}\,;\mathrm{ap}^{\mathcal{K}}_{k'k''}\,.$$

From Equation 8, it follows that, for $\beta \in k_1 \to k_0$,

$$\beta\,;(\alpha \rhd \alpha') = \beta\,;\alpha \rhd \beta\,;\alpha'\,. \tag{11}$$

For $\rho \in k\times k' \to k''$, $\delta \in k_0 \to k$, and $\theta \in k_0 \to k'$, the definition of $\rhd$ and Equation 9 give

$$\delta\,;\mathrm{ab}\,\rho \rhd \theta = \langle \delta, \theta\rangle\,;(\mathrm{ab}\,\rho \times I_{k'})\,;\mathrm{ap}_{k'k''}\,,$$

so that Diagram 10 gives

$$\delta \,;\, \mathrm{ab}\,\rho \triangleright \theta = \langle \delta, \theta \rangle \,;\, \rho\,. \tag{12}$$

On the other hand, suppose Equation 12 holds for all $\rho \in k \times k' \to k''$, $\delta \in k_0 \to k$, and $\theta \in k_0 \to k'$. Taking $k_0 = k \times k'$, $\delta = \mathrm{p}^1_{k \times k'}$, and $\theta = \mathrm{p}^2_{k \times k'}$, the definition of $\triangleright$ and Equation 9 give

$$\langle \mathrm{p}^1_{k\times k'}, \mathrm{p}^2_{k\times k'} \rangle \,;\, (\mathrm{ab}\,\rho \times I_{k'}) \,;\, \mathrm{ap}_{k'k''} = \langle \mathrm{p}^1_{k\times k'}, \mathrm{p}^2_{k\times k'} \rangle \,;\, \rho\,,$$

so that Equation 7 gives Diagram 10. Thus, for $\rho \in k \times k' \to k''$, $\mathrm{ab}\,\rho$ is the unique morphism in $k \to (k' \Rightarrow k'')$ such that Equation 12 holds for all $k_0 \in |\mathcal{K}|$, $\delta \in k_0 \to k$, and $\theta \in k_0 \to k'$.

In a category with a distinguished terminal element, a morphism in $\mathrm{T} \to k$ is called an *element* of k. When the category is Cartesian closed, there is an isomorphism between the elements of $k' \Rightarrow k''$ and the morphisms in $k' \to k''$. To see this, suppose $\alpha \in k' \to k''$ and take $k = \mathrm{T}$, $k_0 = k'$, $\delta = \langle\rangle$, $\theta = I_{k'}$, and $\rho = \mathrm{p}^2_{\mathrm{T}\times k'} \,;\, \alpha$ in Equation 12. Then, by Equation 6, $\mathrm{ab}(\mathrm{p}^2_{\mathrm{T}\times k'} \,;\, \alpha)$ is the unique solution of

$$\langle\rangle \,;\, \mathrm{ab}(\mathrm{p}^2_{\mathrm{T}\times k'} \,;\, \alpha) \triangleright I_{k'} = \alpha\,.$$

Thus, if we define the functions $\phi^{\mathcal{K}}_{k'k''}$ from $\mathrm{T} \to (k' \Rightarrow k'')$ to $k' \to k''$ and $\psi^{\mathcal{K}}_{k'k''}$ from $k' \to k''$ to $\mathrm{T} \to (k' \Rightarrow k'')$ by

$$\phi^{\mathcal{K}}_{k'k''}\gamma \stackrel{\mathrm{def}}{=} \langle\rangle \,;\, \gamma \triangleright I_{k'}\,, \tag{13}$$

and

$$\psi^{\mathcal{K}}_{k'k''}\alpha \stackrel{\mathrm{def}}{=} \mathrm{ab}(\mathrm{p}^2_{\mathrm{T}\times k'} \,;\, \alpha)\,,$$

then

$$\phi_{k'k''}(\psi_{k'k''}\alpha) = \alpha\,, \tag{14}$$

and

$$\psi_{k'k''}(\phi_{k'k''}\gamma) = \gamma\,.$$

For any object B of a Cartesian closed category $\mathcal{K}$, there is a functor $Q^{\mathcal{K}}_B$ from $\mathcal{K}$ to $\mathcal{K}^{\mathrm{op}}$ such that $Q^{\mathcal{K}}_B(k) = k \underset{\mathcal{K}}{\Rightarrow} B$ for all $k \in |\mathcal{K}|$. A characterization of the action of $Q^{\mathcal{K}}_B$ on morphisms can be obtained from Equation 12 by replacing k by $k' \Rightarrow B$, k' by k, and k'' by B, to find that, for $\rho \in (k' \Rightarrow B) \times k \to B$, $\mathrm{ab}\,\rho$ is the unique morphism in $(k' \Rightarrow B) \to (k \Rightarrow B)$ such that 12 holds for all $k_0 \in |\mathcal{K}|$, $\delta \in k_0 \to (k' \Rightarrow B)$, and $\theta \in k_0 \to k$. Next, for any $\alpha \in k \to k'$, take $\rho = (I_{k' \Rightarrow B} \times \alpha) \,;\, \mathrm{ap}_{k'B}$, so that $\langle \delta, \theta \rangle \,;\, \rho = \delta \triangleright \theta \,;\, \alpha$ by Equation 9 and the definition of $\triangleright$, and define $Q_B\alpha$ to be $\mathrm{ab}\,\rho$. Then $Q_B\alpha$ is the unique morphism in

$(k' \Rightarrow B) \rightarrow (k \Rightarrow B)$ such that

$$\delta\,;Q_B\alpha \triangleright \theta = \delta \triangleright \theta\,;\alpha \tag{15}$$

holds for all $k_0 \in |\mathcal{K}|$, $\delta \in k_0 \rightarrow (k' \Rightarrow B)$, and $\theta \in k_0 \rightarrow k$.

It is immediately evident that $Q_B I_k = I_{k \Rightarrow B}$. To see that Q_B satisfies the composition law for functors, suppose $\alpha \in k \rightarrow k'$, $\alpha' \in k' \rightarrow k''$, $\delta' \in k_0 \rightarrow (k'' \Rightarrow B)$, and $\theta \in k_0 \rightarrow k$. Substituting $\delta'\,;Q_B\alpha'$ for δ in Equation 15 and $\theta\,;\alpha$ for θ' in the analogous equation with primed variables gives

$$\delta'\,;Q_B\alpha'\,;Q_B\alpha \triangleright \theta = \delta'\,;Q_B\alpha' \triangleright \theta\,;\alpha = \delta' \triangleright \theta\,;\alpha\,;\alpha',$$

which establishes that $Q_B(\alpha\,;\alpha') = Q_B\alpha'\,;Q_B\alpha$.

2 The Polymorphic Typed Lambda Calculus

The following syntactic description is somewhat unusual, since we wish to avoid assumptions that are stronger than necessary to obtain our results. In particular, we wish to encompass extensions of the polymorphic typed lambda calculus involving, for example, additional type and expression constructors.

We assume that the language is built from infinite sets $\mathcal{T}$ of *type variables* and $\mathcal{V}$ of *ordinary variables*. For each finite set N of type variables, there is a set Ω_N of *type expressions* over the type variables in N. These sets must satisfy:

1. If $\tau \in N$ then $\tau \in \Omega_N$,
2. if $\omega, \omega' \in \Omega_N$ then $\omega \rightarrow \omega' \in \Omega_N$,
3. if $\tau \in \mathcal{T}$ and $\omega \in \Omega_{N \cup \{\tau\}}$ then $\Delta\tau.\,\omega \in \Omega_N$,
4. if $N \subseteq N'$ then $\Omega_N \subseteq \Omega_{N'}$.

For example,

$$\mathbf{s} \in \Omega_{\{\mathbf{s}\}} \subseteq \Omega_{\{\mathbf{s},\mathbf{t}\}},$$

$$\mathbf{s} \rightarrow \mathbf{t} \in \Omega_{\{\mathbf{s},\mathbf{t}\}},$$

$$\Delta\mathbf{s}.\,\mathbf{s} \rightarrow \mathbf{t} \in \Omega_{\{\mathbf{t}\}} \subseteq \Omega_{\{\mathbf{s},\mathbf{t}\}}.$$

We will not need to make any assumptions about equality of type expressions (although it is usual to regard as equal type expressions that are alpha variants with respect to the binding structure induced by Δ).

A *type assignment* π over N is a function from some finite set dom π of ordinary variables to Ω_N; we write Ω_N^* for the set of type assignments over N.

For example,

$$[\mathbf{x}{:}\,\mathbf{s} \mid \mathbf{f}{:}\,\mathbf{s} \to \mathbf{t} \mid \mathbf{p}{:}\,\Delta\mathbf{s}.\,\mathbf{s} \to \mathbf{t}] \in \Omega^*_{\{\mathbf{s},\mathbf{t}\}}.$$

From Condition 4, we have

5. if $N \subseteq N'$ then $\Omega^*_N \subseteq \Omega^*_{N'}$.

Finally, we must define ordinary expressions. For each finite set N of type variables and finite set V of ordinary variables, there is a set E^N_V of *ordinary expressions* over the variables in N and V. These sets must satisfy:

6. If $v \in V$ then $v \in E^N_V$,

7. if $e_1, e_2 \in E^N_V$ then $e_1 e_2 \in E^N_V$,

8. if $v \in \mathcal{V}$, $\omega \in \Omega_N$, and $e \in E^N_{V \cup \{v\}}$ then $\lambda v_\omega.\, e \in E^N_V$,

9. if $e \in E^N_V$ and $\omega \in \Omega_N$ then $e[\omega] \in E^N_V$,

10. if $\tau \in \mathcal{T}$ and $e \in E^{N \cup \{\tau\}}_V$ then $\Lambda\tau.\, e \in E^N_V$,

11. if $N \subseteq N'$ and $V \subseteq V'$ then $E^N_V \subseteq E^{N'}_{V'}$.

The relationship between ordinary and type expressions is expressed by formulas called *typings*. If $\pi \in \Omega^*_N$, $\omega \in \Omega_N$, and e is an ordinary expression then $\pi \vdash_N e{:}\,\omega$ is a typing that asserts that e belongs to $E^N_{\mathrm{dom}\,\pi}$ and takes on type ω when its free ordinary variables are assigned types by π. We assume that the following inference rules for typings are valid:

12. For $\pi \in \Omega^*_N$ and $v \in \mathrm{dom}\,\pi$:

$$\frac{}{\pi \vdash_N v{:}\,\pi v,}$$

13. for $\pi \in \Omega^*_N$ and $\omega, \omega' \in \Omega_N$:

$$\frac{\pi \vdash_N e_1{:}\,\omega \to \omega' \qquad \pi \vdash_N e_2{:}\,\omega}{\pi \vdash_N e_1 e_2{:}\,\omega',}$$

14. for $\pi \in \Omega^*_N$ and $\omega, \omega' \in \Omega_N$:

$$\frac{[\pi \mid v{:}\,\omega] \vdash_N e{:}\,\omega'}{\pi \vdash_N \lambda v_\omega.\, e{:}\,\omega \to \omega',}$$

15. for $\pi \in \Omega^*_N$, $\omega \in \Omega_N$, and $\tau \in N$:

$$\frac{\pi \vdash_N e{:}\,\Delta\tau.\,\omega}{\pi \vdash_N e[\tau]{:}\,\omega,}$$

16. for $\pi \in \Omega^*_{N-\{\tau\}}$ and $\omega \in \Omega_{N\cup\{\tau\}}$:

$$\frac{\pi \vdash_{N\cup\{\tau\}} e:\omega}{\pi \vdash_N \Lambda\tau.\, e:\Delta\tau.\,\omega\,,}$$

17. for $N \subseteq N'$, $\pi \in \Omega^*_N$, and $\omega \in \Omega_N$:

$$\frac{\pi \vdash_N e:\omega}{\pi \vdash_{N'} e:\omega\,,}$$

18. for $\pi, \pi' \in \Omega^*_N$ such that $\pi = \pi' \upharpoonright \operatorname{dom}\pi$, and $\omega \in \Omega_N$:

$$\frac{\pi \vdash_N e:\omega}{\pi' \vdash_N e:\omega\,.}$$

For example, the following are valid typings:

$[\mathbf{f}:\mathbf{t}\to\mathbf{t} \mid \mathbf{x}:\mathbf{t}] \vdash_{\{\mathbf{t}\}} \mathbf{f}:\mathbf{t}\to\mathbf{t}$,	by 12
$[\mathbf{f}:\mathbf{t}\to\mathbf{t} \mid \mathbf{x}:\mathbf{t}] \vdash_{\{\mathbf{t}\}} \mathbf{x}:\mathbf{t}$,	by 12
$[\mathbf{f}:\mathbf{t}\to\mathbf{t} \mid \mathbf{x}:\mathbf{t}] \vdash_{\{\mathbf{t}\}} \mathbf{f}\mathbf{x}:\mathbf{t}$,	by 13
$[\mathbf{f}:\mathbf{t}\to\mathbf{t} \mid \mathbf{x}:\mathbf{t}] \vdash_{\{\mathbf{t}\}} \mathbf{f}(\mathbf{f}\mathbf{x}):\mathbf{t}$,	by 13
$[\mathbf{f}:\mathbf{t}\to\mathbf{t}] \vdash_{\{\mathbf{t}\}} \lambda\mathbf{x}_\mathbf{t}.\, \mathbf{f}(\mathbf{f}\mathbf{x}):\mathbf{t}\to\mathbf{t}$,	by 14
$[\,] \vdash_{\{\mathbf{t}\}} \lambda\mathbf{f}_{\mathbf{t}\to\mathbf{t}}.\, \lambda\mathbf{x}_\mathbf{t}.\, \mathbf{f}(\mathbf{f}\mathbf{x}):(\mathbf{t}\to\mathbf{t})\to(\mathbf{t}\to\mathbf{t})$,	by 14
$[\,] \vdash_{\{\}} \Lambda\mathbf{t}.\, \lambda\mathbf{f}_{\mathbf{t}\to\mathbf{t}}.\, \lambda\mathbf{x}_\mathbf{t}.\, \mathbf{f}(\mathbf{f}\mathbf{x}):\Delta\mathbf{t}.\,(\mathbf{t}\to\mathbf{t})\to(\mathbf{t}\to\mathbf{t})$,	by 16
$[\,] \vdash_{\{\mathbf{t}\}} \Lambda\mathbf{t}.\, \lambda\mathbf{f}_{\mathbf{t}\to\mathbf{t}}.\, \lambda\mathbf{x}_\mathbf{t}.\, \mathbf{f}(\mathbf{f}\mathbf{x}):\Delta\mathbf{t}.\,(\mathbf{t}\to\mathbf{t})\to(\mathbf{t}\to\mathbf{t})$,	by 17
$[\,] \vdash_{\{\mathbf{t}\}} (\Lambda\mathbf{t}.\, \lambda\mathbf{f}_{\mathbf{t}\to\mathbf{t}}.\, \lambda\mathbf{x}_\mathbf{t}.\, \mathbf{f}(\mathbf{f}\mathbf{x}))[\mathbf{t}]:(\mathbf{t}\to\mathbf{t})\to(\mathbf{t}\to\mathbf{t})$,	by 15
$[\mathbf{g}:\mathbf{t}\to\mathbf{t}] \vdash_{\{\mathbf{t}\}} (\Lambda\mathbf{t}.\, \lambda\mathbf{f}_{\mathbf{t}\to\mathbf{t}}.\, \lambda\mathbf{x}_\mathbf{t}.\, \mathbf{f}(\mathbf{f}\mathbf{x}))[\mathbf{t}]:(\mathbf{t}\to\mathbf{t})\to(\mathbf{t}\to\mathbf{t})$.	by 18

Actually, for the ordinary polymorphic typed lambda calculus, Inference Rule 15 is subsumed by the more general rule

15′. For $\pi \in \Omega^*_N$, $\omega \in \Omega_{N\cup\{\tau\}}$, and $\omega' \in \Omega_N$:

$$\frac{\pi \vdash_N e:\Delta\tau.\,\omega}{\pi \vdash_N e[\omega']:(\omega/\tau \to \omega')\,,}$$

where $(\omega/\tau \to \omega')$ denotes the result of substituting ω' for τ in ω. However, Rule 15 is sufficient for our needs, and we wish to avoid the difficulty of defining substitution (with renaming) in a way that would not circumscribe possible extensions of the language.

The notion of typing is prerequisite to any semantics of the polymorphic typed lambda calculus; ordinary expressions will possess meanings only when they satisfy typings, which will determine the kind of meanings they will possess. Specifically, for each $\pi \in \Omega_N^*$ and $\omega \in \Omega_N$, the set

$$E^N_{\pi\omega} \stackrel{\text{def}}{=} \{ e \mid e \in E^N_{\operatorname{dom}\pi} \text{ and } \pi \vdash_N e{:}\,\omega \},$$

of expressions that take on type ω under the type assignment π, must be mapped into meanings appropriate to π and ω.

3 $\mathcal{K}$-Models

It is well known that Cartesian closed categories provide models of the ordinary typed lambda calculus. In this section, we formalize the idea of extending such models to the polymorphic case. As with syntax, the properties that we postulate for such extensions are weaker than those one would normally require of a model; our intent is to assume only those properties needed to obtain the results of this paper.

(We believe that these properties hold for any general category-theoretic definition of the concept of a model. For example, given a PL category $(\mathbf{G}, \mathbf{S})$ in the sense of Seely [21], one can take $\mathcal{K}$ to be the Cartesian closed category $\mathbf{G}(1)$, where 1 is the terminal object of $\mathbf{S}$.)

Given a category $\mathcal{K}$, a function from a finite set of type variables to $|\mathcal{K}|$ is called an *object assignment*. Then, a *$\mathcal{K}$-model* of the polymorphic typed lambda calculus consists of:

1. A Cartesian closed category $\mathcal{K}$.

2. For each object assignment O with domain N, a semantic function $\mathcal{M}O$ from Ω_N to $|\mathcal{K}|$. These functions must satisfy:

   (a) If $\tau \in N$ then

$$\mathcal{M}O\tau = O\tau, \tag{16}$$

   (b) if $\omega, \omega' \in \Omega_N$ then

$$\mathcal{M}O(\omega \rightarrow \omega') = \mathcal{M}O\omega \underset{\mathcal{K}}{\Longrightarrow} \mathcal{M}O\omega', \tag{17}$$

   (c) if $O = O' \upharpoonright N$ and $\omega \in \Omega_N$ then

$$\mathcal{M}O'\omega = \mathcal{M}O\omega. \tag{18}$$

3. For each object assignment O with domain N, $\pi \in \Omega_N^*$, and $\omega \in \Omega_N$, a semantic function $\mu^O_{\pi\omega}$ from $E^N_{\pi\omega}$ to $\prod^{\mathcal{K}}(\mathcal{M}O \cdot \pi) \underset{\mathcal{K}}{\rightarrow} \mathcal{M}O\omega$, where $\mathcal{M}O \cdot \pi$ denotes the function from $\operatorname{dom}\pi$ to $|\mathcal{K}|$ such that $(\mathcal{M}O \cdot \pi)\nu = \mathcal{M}O(\pi\nu)$ for all $\nu \in \operatorname{dom}\pi$. These functions must satisfy:

(a) If $\pi \in \Omega_N^*$ and $v \in \operatorname{dom} \pi$ then

$$\mu^O_{\pi,\pi v}[\![v]\!] = \mathrm{P}[\mathcal{M}O \cdot \pi, v] \in \prod(\mathcal{M}O \cdot \pi) \underset{\mathcal{K}}{\to} \mathcal{M}O(\pi v),$$

(b) if $\pi \in \Omega_N^*$, $\omega, \omega' \in \Omega_N$, $\pi \vdash_N e_1 : \omega \to \omega'$, and $\pi \vdash_N e_2 : \omega$ then

$$\mu^O_{\pi\omega'}[\![e_1 e_2]\!] = \mu^O_{\pi,\omega\to\omega'}[\![e_1]\!] \triangleright \mu^O_{\pi\omega}[\![e_2]\!] \in \prod(\mathcal{M}O \cdot \pi) \underset{\mathcal{K}}{\to} \mathcal{M}O\omega',$$

(c) if $\pi \in \Omega_N^*$, $\omega, \omega' \in \Omega_N$, and $[\pi \mid v : \omega] \vdash_N e : \omega'$ then

$$\mu^O_{\pi,\omega\to\omega'}[\![\lambda v_\omega .\ e]\!] = \mathrm{ab}(\langle \Xi \mid v : \mathrm{p}^2_{\Pi(\mathcal{M}O\cdot\pi)\times\mathcal{M}O\omega} \rangle ; \mu^O_{[\pi|v:\omega],\omega'}[\![e]\!]),$$

where Ξ is the function with the same domain as π such that

$$\Xi v' = \mathrm{p}^1_{\Pi(\mathcal{M}O\cdot\pi)\times\mathcal{M}O\omega} ; \mathrm{P}[\mathcal{M}O \cdot \pi, v']$$

for all $v' \in \operatorname{dom} \pi$; in other words, $\mu^O_{\pi,\omega\to\omega'}[\![\lambda v_\omega .\ e]\!]$ is the unique morphism in $\prod(\mathcal{M}O \cdot \pi) \underset{\mathcal{K}}{\to} (\mathcal{M}O\omega \Rightarrow \mathcal{M}O\omega')$ such that

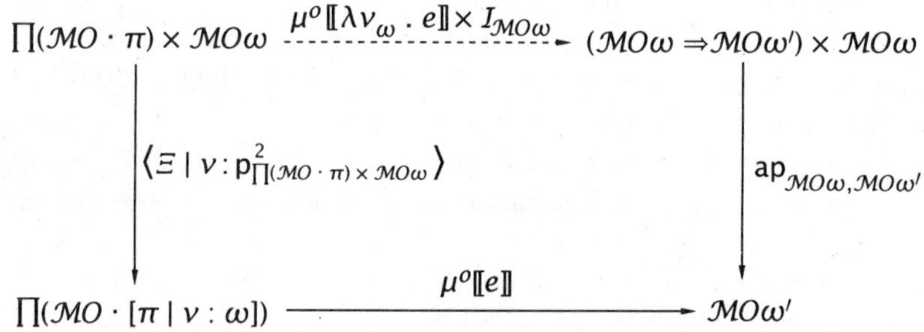

commutes in $\mathcal{K}$, where

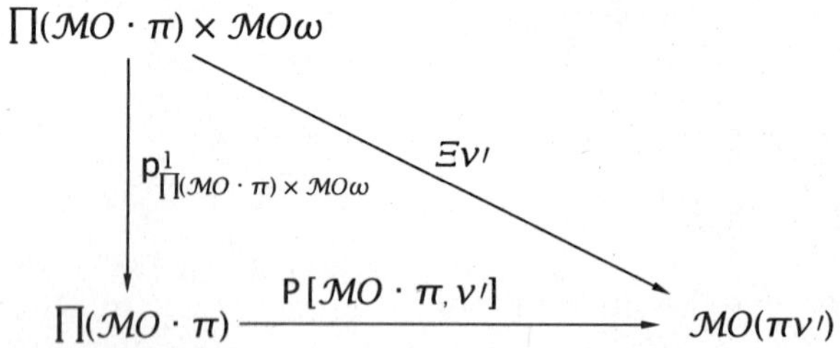

commutes for all $v' \in \operatorname{dom} \pi$.

(d) If $O = O' \upharpoonright N$, $\pi \in \Omega_N^*$, $\omega \in \Omega_N$, and $\pi \vdash_N e : \omega$ then

$$\mu^{O'}_{\pi\omega}[\![e]\!] = \mu^O_{\pi\omega}[\![e]\!], \tag{19}$$

(e) if $\pi, \pi' \in \Omega_N^*$, $\pi = \pi' \upharpoonright \operatorname{dom} \pi$, $\omega \in \Omega_N$, and $\pi \vdash_N e : \omega$ then

$$\mu^O_{\pi'\omega}[\![e]\!] = \langle \Upsilon \upharpoonright \operatorname{dom} \pi \rangle ; \mu^O_{\pi\omega}[\![e]\!],$$

where Υ is the function with the same domain as π' such that

$$\Upsilon v' = \mathrm{P}[\mathcal{M}O \cdot \pi', v']$$

for all $v' \in \operatorname{dom} \pi'$,

(f) if $\pi \in \Omega^*_{N-\{\tau\}}$, $\omega \in \Omega_N$, $\tau \in N$, and $\pi \vdash_N e\colon \omega$ then

$$\mu^O_{\pi\omega}[\![(\lambda v_{\Delta\tau.\,\omega}.\ v[\tau])(\Lambda\tau.\ e)]\!] = \mu^O_{\pi\omega}[\![e]\!]. \tag{20}$$

Conditions 2a, 2b, 3a, 3b, and 3c stipulate that the semantics of the ordinary typed lambda calculus, which is a sublanguage of the polymorphic typed lambda calculus, is the standard semantics given by the Cartesian closed category $\mathcal{K}$. Conditions 2c and 3d stipulate that the meanings of type and ordinary expressions are independent of irrelevant type variables, while Condition 3e stipulates that the meanings of ordinary expressions are independent of irrelevant ordinary variables. Condition 3f stipulates the soundness of the following combination of an ordinary and type beta-reduction:

$$(\lambda v_{\Delta\tau.\,\omega}.\ v[\tau])(\Lambda\tau.\ e) \Longrightarrow (\Lambda\tau.\ e)[\tau] \Longrightarrow e.$$

Conditions 3a, 3b, 3c, and 3e can be recast in forms more suitable for analyzing the meanings of specific expressions. In the following, suppose Γ is a function with the same domain as π such that $\Gamma v \in k_0 \to \mathcal{M}O(\pi v)$ for all $v \in \operatorname{dom} \pi$, Γ' bears a similar relation to π', and $\varphi \in k_0 \to \mathcal{M}O\omega$. If $\pi \in \Omega^*_N$ and $v \in \operatorname{dom} \pi$ then Condition 3a and Equation 1 give

$$\langle \Gamma \rangle \,;\, \mu^O_{\pi,\pi v}[\![v]\!] = \Gamma v. \tag{21}$$

If $\pi \in \Omega^*_N$, ω, $\omega' \in \Omega_N$, $\pi \vdash_N e_1\colon \omega \to \omega'$, and $\pi \vdash_N e_2\colon \omega$ then 3b and 11 give

$$\langle \Gamma \rangle \,;\, \mu^O_{\pi\omega'}[\![e_1 e_2]\!] = \langle \Gamma \rangle \,;\, \mu^O_{\pi,\omega\to\omega'}[\![e_1]\!] \triangleright \langle \Gamma \rangle \,;\, \mu^O_{\pi\omega}[\![e_2]\!]. \tag{22}$$

If $\pi \in \Omega^*_N$, ω, $\omega' \in \Omega_N$, and $[\,\pi \mid v\colon \omega\,] \vdash_N e\colon \omega'$ then 3c, 12, 3, 6, and 1 give

$$\langle \Gamma \rangle \,;\, \mu^O_{\pi,\omega\to\omega'}[\![\lambda v_\omega.\ e]\!] \triangleright \varphi = \langle \Gamma \mid v\colon \varphi \rangle \,;\, \mu^O_{[\pi|v:\omega],\omega'}[\![e]\!]. \tag{23}$$

If π, $\pi' \in \Omega^*_N$, $\pi = \pi' \restriction \operatorname{dom} \pi$, $\omega \in \Omega_N$, and $\pi \vdash_N e\colon \omega$ then 3e, 3, and 1 give

$$\langle \Gamma' \rangle \,;\, \mu^O_{\pi'\omega}[\![e]\!] = \langle \Gamma' \restriction \operatorname{dom} \pi \rangle \,;\, \mu^O_{\pi\omega}[\![e]\!]. \tag{24}$$

The use of these equations is illustrated by the following proposition, which shows that a nontrivial $\mathcal{K}$ leads to a nontrivial $\mathcal{K}$-model.

Proposition 1

Let $\mathbf{B} \overset{\text{def}}{=} \Delta\mathbf{k}.\ \mathbf{k} \to (\mathbf{k} \to \mathbf{k}) \in \Omega_{\{\}}$ and, in some $\mathcal{K}$-model, $B \overset{\text{def}}{=} \mathcal{M}[\,]\mathbf{B} \in |\mathcal{K}|$. If any morphism set of $\mathcal{K}$ has more than one member, then B has more than one element.

Proof It suffices to show that if the elements of B are all equal then any pair of members of any morphism set are equal. Consider the ordinary expressions

$$\Lambda\mathbf{k}.\,\lambda\mathbf{x_k}.\,\lambda\mathbf{y_k}.\,\mathbf{x},\quad \Lambda\mathbf{k}.\,\lambda\mathbf{x_k}.\,\lambda\mathbf{y_k}.\,\mathbf{y} \in E^{\{\}}_{[\,],\mathbf{B}},$$

which are mapped by $\mu^{[\,]}$ into elements of B. If these elements are equal then, for any k_0, $k \in |\mathcal{K}|$ and $\alpha, \beta \in k_0 \to k$,

$$\begin{aligned} &((\langle\rangle\,;\mu^{[\mathbf{k}:k]}[\![\lambda\mathbf{b_B}.\,\mathbf{b}[\mathbf{k}]]\!] \triangleright \langle\rangle\,;\mu^{[\,]}[\![\Lambda\mathbf{k}.\,\lambda\mathbf{x_k}.\,\lambda\mathbf{y_k}.\,\mathbf{x}]\!]) \triangleright \alpha) \triangleright \beta \\ = {} &((\langle\rangle\,;\mu^{[\mathbf{k}:k]}[\![\lambda\mathbf{b_B}.\,\mathbf{b}[\mathbf{k}]]\!] \triangleright \langle\rangle\,;\mu^{[\,]}[\![\Lambda\mathbf{k}.\,\lambda\mathbf{x_k}.\,\lambda\mathbf{y_k}.\,\mathbf{y}]\!]) \triangleright \alpha) \triangleright \beta. \end{aligned}$$

But the left side of this equation equals

$$\begin{aligned} &(\langle\rangle\,;\mu^{[\mathbf{k}:k]}[\![(\lambda\mathbf{b_B}.\,\mathbf{b}[\mathbf{k}])(\Lambda\mathbf{k}.\,\lambda\mathbf{x_k}.\,\lambda\mathbf{y_k}.\,\mathbf{x})]\!] \triangleright \alpha) \triangleright \beta, && \text{by 19, 22} \\ &= (\langle\rangle\,;\mu^{[\mathbf{k}:k]}[\![\lambda\mathbf{x_k}.\,\lambda\mathbf{y_k}.\,\mathbf{x}]\!] \triangleright \alpha) \triangleright \beta, && \text{by 20} \\ &= \langle\mathbf{x}{:}\,\alpha\rangle\,;\mu^{[\mathbf{k}:k]}[\![\lambda\mathbf{y_k}.\,\mathbf{x}]\!] \triangleright \beta, && \text{by 23} \\ &= \langle\mathbf{x}{:}\,\alpha \mid \mathbf{y}{:}\,\beta\rangle\,;\mu^{[\mathbf{k}:k]}[\![\mathbf{x}]\!], && \text{by 23} \\ &= \alpha, && \text{by 21} \end{aligned}$$

and by a similar argument the right side equals β. □

4 SET-*Models*

An important special case of a $\mathcal{K}$-model arises when $\mathcal{K}$ is the Cartesian closed category SET, for which:

1. |SET| is the class of sets, and

(a) $k \xrightarrow[\text{SET}]{} k'$ is the set of all functions from k to k',

(b) composition is functional composition,

(c) I^{SET}_k is the identity function on k.

2. $\prod^{\text{SET}}$ is the general Cartesian product, and

(a) if $v \in \operatorname{dom} F$ then $\mathrm{P}[F, v] \in \prod F \to Fv$ is the function such that

$$\mathrm{P}[F, v]\eta = \eta v$$

for all $\eta \in \prod F$,

(b) if, for all $v \in \text{dom} F$, $\Gamma v \in k \to Fv$, then $\langle \Gamma \rangle \in k \to \prod F$ is the function such that

$$\langle \Gamma \rangle x\, v = \Gamma v x$$

for all $x \in k$ and $v \in \text{dom} F$.

3. $\times_{\text{SET}}$ is the binary Cartesian product, and

(a) $\mathsf{p}^i_{k_1 \times k_2} \in k_1 \times k_2 \to k_i$ is the function such that

$$\mathsf{p}^i_{k_1 \times k_2} \langle x_1, x_2 \rangle = x_i$$

for all $x_1 \in k_1$ and $x_2 \in k_2$,

(b) if $\alpha_1 \in k \to k_1$ and $\alpha_2 \in k \to k_2$ then $\langle \alpha_1, \alpha_2 \rangle^{\text{SET}} \in k \to k_1 \times k_2$ is the function such that

$$\langle \alpha_1, \alpha_2 \rangle^{\text{SET}} x = \langle \alpha_1 x, \alpha_2 x \rangle$$

for all $x \in k$.

4. $k' \underset{\text{SET}}{\Longrightarrow} k''$ is the set $k' \to k''$, and

(a) $\mathsf{ap}_{k'k''} \in (k' \to k'') \times k' \to k''$ is the function such that

$$\mathsf{ap}_{k'k''} \langle f', x' \rangle = f' x'$$

for all $f' \in k' \to k''$ and $x' \in k'$,

(b) if $\rho \in k \times k' \to k''$ then $\mathsf{ab}\, \rho \in k \to (k' \to k'')$ is the function such that

$$\mathsf{ab}\, \rho\, x\, x' = \rho \langle x, x' \rangle$$

for all $x \in k$ and $x' \in k'$.

By substituting these equations into the general definition of a $\mathcal{K}$-model, we find that a SET-model consists of the following.

1. The Cartesian closed category SET.

2. For each set assignment O with domain N, a semantic function $\mathcal{M}O$ from Ω_N to $|\text{SET}|$, such that:

(a) If $\tau \in N$ then

$$\mathcal{M}O\tau = O\tau\,,$$

(b) if $\omega, \omega' \in \Omega_N$ then

$$\mathcal{M}O(\omega \to \omega') = \mathcal{M}O\omega \to \mathcal{M}O\omega'\,,$$

(c) if $O = O' \upharpoonright N$ and $\omega \in \Omega_N$ then

$$\mathcal{M}O'\omega = \mathcal{M}O\omega\,.$$

3. For each set assignment O with domain N, $\pi \in \Omega_N^*$, and $\omega \in \Omega_N$, a semantic function $\mu_{\pi\omega}^O$ from $E_{\pi\omega}^N$ to $\prod^{\mathrm{SET}}(\mathcal{M}O \cdot \pi) \to \mathcal{M}O\omega$, such that

(a) if $\pi \in \Omega_N^*$ and $v \in \operatorname{dom}\pi$ then, for all $\eta \in \prod(\mathcal{M}O \cdot \pi)$,

$$\mu_{\pi,\pi v}^O[\![v]\!]\eta = \eta v\,,$$

(b) if $\pi \in \Omega_N^*$, ω, $\omega' \in \Omega_N$, $\pi \vdash_N e_1 : \omega \to \omega'$, and $\pi \vdash_N e_2 : \omega$ then, for all $\eta \in \prod(\mathcal{M}O \cdot \pi)$,

$$\mu_{\pi\omega'}^O[\![e_1 e_2]\!]\eta = (\mu_{\pi,\omega\to\omega'}^O[\![e_1]\!]\eta)(\mu_{\pi\omega}^O[\![e_2]\!]\eta)\,,$$

(c) if $\pi \in \Omega_N^*$, ω, $\omega' \in \Omega_N$, and $[\,\pi \mid v{:}\,\omega\,] \vdash_N e : \omega'$ then, for all $\eta \in \prod(\mathcal{M}O \cdot \pi)$ and $a \in \mathcal{M}O\omega$,

$$\mu_{\pi,\omega\to\omega'}^O[\![\lambda v_\omega .\ e]\!]\eta a = \mu_{[\pi|v:\omega],\omega'}^O[\![e]\!][\,\eta \mid v{:}\,a\,]\,,$$

(d) if $O = O' \upharpoonright N$, $\pi \in \Omega_N^*$, $\omega \in \Omega_N$, and $\pi \vdash_N e : \omega$ then

$$\mu_{\pi\omega}^{O'}[\![e]\!] = \mu_{\pi\omega}^O[\![e]\!]\,,$$

(e) if π, $\pi' \in \Omega_N^*$, $\pi = \pi' \upharpoonright \operatorname{dom}\pi$, $\omega \in \Omega_N$, and $\pi \vdash_N e : \omega$ then, for all $\eta' \in \prod(\mathcal{M}O \cdot \pi')$,

$$\mu_{\pi'\omega}^O[\![e]\!]\eta' = \mu_{\pi\omega}^O[\![e]\!](\eta' \upharpoonright \operatorname{dom}\pi)\,,$$

(f) if $\pi \in \Omega_{N-\{\tau\}}^*$, $\omega \in \Omega_N$, $\tau \in N$, and $\pi \vdash_N e : \omega$ then

$$\mu_{\pi\omega}^O[\![(\lambda v_{\Delta\tau.\,\omega}.\ v[\tau])(\Lambda\tau.\ e)]\!] = \mu_{\pi\omega}^O[\![e]\!]\,.$$

Note that 2a, 2b, 3a, 3b, and 3c stipulate the "classical" set-theoretic semantics of the ordinary typed lambda calculus.

5 *Expressible Functors*

Let T be a functor from $\mathcal{K}$ to $\mathcal{K}$. Roughly speaking, we say that T is *expressible* in a $\mathcal{K}$-model when its action on objects can be expressed by type expressions and its action on morphisms can be expressed by ordinary expressions. More precisely, T is *expressible* in a $\mathcal{K}$-model if and only if:

1. For each $\omega \in \Omega_N$, there is a type expression $\mathbf{T}[\omega] \in \Omega_N$ such that, for all object assignments O with domain N,

$$\mathcal{M}O(\mathbf{T}[\omega]) = T(\mathcal{M}O\omega)\,, \tag{25}$$

2. for each $\omega, \omega' \in \Omega_N$, $\pi \in \Omega_N^*$, and e satisfying $\pi \vdash_N e : \omega \to \omega'$, there is an ordinary expression $\mathbf{T}_{\omega\omega'}[e]$ satisfying $\pi \vdash_N \mathbf{T}_{\omega\omega'}[e] : \mathbf{T}[\omega] \to \mathbf{T}[\omega']$ such that, for all object assignments O with domain N and elements η of $\prod(\mathcal{M}O \cdot \pi)$,

$$\phi(\eta\,;\mu^O[\![\mathbf{T}_{\omega\omega'}[e]]\!]) = T(\phi(\eta\,;\mu^O[\![e]\!]))\,, \tag{26}$$

where ϕ is the isomorphism defined by Equation 13.

Trivially, the identity function can be expressed by $\mathbf{T}[\omega] = \omega$ and $\mathbf{T}_{\omega\omega'}[e] = e$. A less trivial family of expressible functors is provided by the following proposition.

Proposition 2

Suppose $\mathbf{B} \in \Omega_{\{\}}$ and, in some $\mathcal{K}$-model, $B = \mathcal{M}[\,]\mathbf{B} \in |\mathcal{K}|$. Then there is an expressible functor T, from $\mathcal{K}$ to $\mathcal{K}$, such that $Tk = (k \Rightarrow B) \Rightarrow B$ for all $k \in |\mathcal{K}|$.

Proof We take T to be the composition of the functor Q_B, from $\mathcal{K}$ to $\mathcal{K}^{\mathrm{op}}$, with itself, so that $Tk = Q_B(Q_B k) = (k \Rightarrow B) \Rightarrow B$.

Our main task is to show that, roughly speaking (since it is a functor from $\mathcal{K}$ to $\mathcal{K}^{\mathrm{op}}$ rather than from $\mathcal{K}$ to $\mathcal{K}$), Q_B is expressible. For $\omega \in \Omega_N$, let

$$\mathbf{Q}[\omega] \stackrel{\text{def}}{=} \omega \to \mathbf{B} \in \Omega_N\,.$$

Then, for any object assignment O with domain N,

$$\mathcal{M}O(\mathbf{Q}[\omega]) = \mathcal{M}O\omega \Rightarrow B = Q_B(\mathcal{M}O\omega)\,. \tag{27}$$

Next, for $\omega, \omega' \in \Omega_N$, $\pi \in \Omega_N^*$, and e satisfying $\pi \vdash_N e : \omega \to \omega'$, let

$$\mathbf{Q}_{\omega\omega'}[e] \stackrel{\text{def}}{=} (\lambda \mathbf{f}_{\omega\to\omega'}.\ \lambda \mathbf{g}_{\omega'\to\mathbf{B}}.\ \lambda \mathbf{x}_{\omega}.\ \mathbf{g}(\mathbf{f}\,\mathbf{x}))e\,,$$

which satisfies $\pi \vdash_N \mathbf{Q}_{\omega\omega'}[e] : \mathbf{Q}[\omega'] \to \mathbf{Q}[\omega]$. Then, for any object assignment O with domain N, element η of $\prod(\mathcal{M}O \cdot \pi)$, object $k_0 \in |\mathcal{K}|$, and morphisms $\delta \in k_0 \to (\mathcal{M}O\omega' \Rightarrow B)$ and $\theta \in k_0 \to \mathcal{M}O\omega$,

$$\begin{aligned}
&\delta\,;\phi(\eta\,;\mu^O[\![\mathbf{Q}_{\omega\omega'}[e]]\!]) \triangleright \theta \\
&= (\langle\rangle\,;\eta\,;\mu^O[\![\mathbf{Q}_{\omega\omega'}[e]]\!] \triangleright \delta) \triangleright \theta && \text{by 13, 11, 5} \\
&= ((\langle\rangle\,;\mu^O[\![\lambda \mathbf{f}_{\omega\to\omega'}.\ \lambda \mathbf{g}_{\omega'\to\mathbf{B}}.\ \lambda \mathbf{x}_{\omega}.\ \mathbf{g}(\mathbf{f}\,\mathbf{x})]\!] \triangleright \langle\rangle\,;\eta\,;\mu^O[\![e]\!]) \\
&\qquad \triangleright \delta) \triangleright \theta && \text{by 22, 24} \\
&= \langle \mathbf{f}\colon \langle\rangle\,;\eta\,;\mu^O[\![e]\!] \mid \mathbf{g}\colon \delta \mid \mathbf{x}\colon \theta \rangle\,;\mu^O[\![\mathbf{g}(\mathbf{f}\,\mathbf{x})]\!] && \text{by 23} \\
&= \delta \triangleright (\langle\rangle\,;\eta\,;\mu^O[\![e]\!] \triangleright \theta) && \text{by 22, 21} \\
&= \delta \triangleright \theta\,;\phi(\eta\,;\mu^O[\![e]\!])\,. && \text{by 5, 11, 13}
\end{aligned}$$

Thus, by the uniqueness property of Equation 15,

$$\phi(\eta\,;\mu^O[\![\mathbf{Q}_{\omega\omega'}[e]]\!]) = Q_B(\phi(\eta\,;\mu^O[\![e]\!]))\,. \tag{28}$$

Finally, for $\omega \in \Omega_N$, let

$$\mathbf{T}[\omega] \stackrel{\text{def}}{=} \mathbf{Q}[\mathbf{Q}[\omega]] \in \Omega_N\,,$$

and, for $\omega, \omega' \in \Omega_N$, $\pi \in \Omega_N^*$, and e satisfying $\pi \vdash_N e\colon \omega \to \omega'$, let

$$\mathbf{T}_{\omega\omega'}[e] \stackrel{\text{def}}{=} \mathbf{Q}_{\mathbf{Q}[\omega'],\mathbf{Q}[\omega]}[\mathbf{Q}_{\omega\omega'}[e]]\,,$$

which satisfies $\pi \vdash_N \mathbf{T}_{\omega\omega'}[e]\colon \mathbf{T}[\omega] \to \mathbf{T}[\omega']$. Then Equations 27 and 28 imply that T is expressed by $\mathbf{T}[\omega]$ and $\mathbf{T}_{\omega\omega'}[e]$. □

We can now establish our main result about expressible functors.

Proposition 3

Suppose T is a functor from $\mathcal{K}$ to $\mathcal{K}$ that is expressible in a $\mathcal{K}$-model. Then there is an object $P \in |\mathcal{K}|$ and a morphism $H \in TP \to P$ such that, for all $k \in |\mathcal{K}|$ and $\alpha \in Tk \to k$, there is a morphism $M \in P \to k$ making the diagram

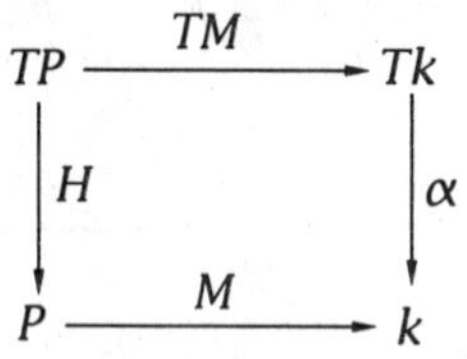

commute in $\mathcal{K}$.

Proof Let

$$\mathbf{P} \stackrel{\text{def}}{=} \Delta\mathbf{k}.\,(\mathbf{T}[\mathbf{k}] \to \mathbf{k}) \to \mathbf{k} \in \Omega_{\{\}}\,,$$

$$\mathbf{M} \stackrel{\text{def}}{=} \lambda\mathbf{p}_\mathbf{P}.\,\mathbf{p}[\mathbf{k}]\mathbf{f}\,,$$

$$\mathbf{H} \stackrel{\text{def}}{=} \lambda\mathbf{q}_{\mathbf{T}[\mathbf{P}]}.\,\Lambda\mathbf{k}.\,\lambda\mathbf{f}_{\mathbf{T}[\mathbf{k}]\to\mathbf{k}}.\,\mathbf{f}(\mathbf{T}_{\mathbf{P}\mathbf{k}}[\mathbf{M}]\mathbf{q})\,,$$

so that

$$[\,\mathbf{f}\colon \mathbf{T}[\mathbf{k}] \to \mathbf{k}\,] \vdash_{\{\mathbf{k}\}} \mathbf{M}\colon \mathbf{P} \to \mathbf{k}\,,$$

$$[\,] \vdash_{\{\}} \mathbf{H}\colon \mathbf{T}[\mathbf{P}] \to \mathbf{P}\,.$$

Intuitively, our proof is based on the fact that the diagram

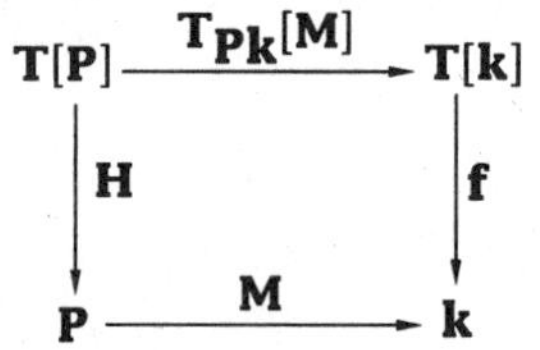

commutes syntactically, i.e., by expressing composition as usual in the lambda calculus, and using beta reduction and type beta reduction. To formalize this intuition, we must work through the semantics of the expressions in this diagram.

Let $P \stackrel{\mathrm{def}}{=} \mathcal{M}[\,]\mathbf{P}$. Since $\mu^{[\,]}[\![\mathbf{H}]\!]$ is an element of $\mathcal{M}[\,](\mathbf{T[P]} \to \mathbf{P})$, and by Equations 17 and 25, $\mathcal{M}[\,](\mathbf{T[P]} \to \mathbf{P}) = TP \Rightarrow P$, we may define

$$H \stackrel{\mathrm{def}}{=} \phi(\mu^{[\,]}[\![\mathbf{H}]\!]) \in TP \to P. \tag{29}$$

Then, for any $k \in |\mathcal{K}|$ and $\alpha \in Tk \to k$, by Equations 17, 25, and 16,

$$\psi\alpha \in \mathrm{T} \to (Tk \Rightarrow k) = \mathrm{T} \to \mathcal{M}[\,\mathbf{k}\colon k\,](\mathbf{T[k]} \to \mathbf{k}),$$

so that

$$\langle \mathbf{f}\colon \psi\alpha \rangle ; \mu^{[\mathbf{k}:k]}[\![\mathbf{M}]\!] \in \mathrm{T} \to \mathcal{M}[\,\mathbf{k}\colon k\,](\mathbf{P} \to \mathbf{k}),$$

and by Equations 17, 18, and 16, $\mathcal{M}[\,\mathbf{k}\colon k\,](\mathbf{P} \to \mathbf{k}) = P \Rightarrow k$, so that we may define

$$M \stackrel{\mathrm{def}}{=} \phi(\langle \mathbf{f}\colon \psi\alpha \rangle ; \mu^{[\mathbf{k}:k]}[\![\mathbf{M}]\!]) \in P \to k. \tag{30}$$

Finally, we must show that the diagram given in the proposition commutes, i.e., that $H ; M = TM ; \alpha$. We have

$$H ; M$$

$$= H ; (\langle\rangle ; \langle \mathbf{f}\colon \psi\alpha \rangle ; \mu^{[\mathbf{k}:k]}[\![M]\!] \rhd I_P) \qquad \text{by 30, 13}$$

$$= \langle \mathbf{f}\colon \langle\rangle ; \psi\alpha \rangle ; \mu^{[\mathbf{k}:k]}[\![M]\!] \rhd H \qquad \text{by 11, 5, 4}$$

$$= \langle \mathbf{f}\colon \langle\rangle ; \psi\alpha \mid \mathbf{p}\colon H \rangle ; \mu^{[\mathbf{k}:k]}[\![\mathbf{p[k]f}]\!] \qquad \text{by 23}$$

$$= \langle \mathbf{p}\colon H \rangle ; \mu^{[\mathbf{k}:k]}[\![\mathbf{p[k]}]\!] \rhd \langle\rangle ; \psi\alpha \qquad \text{by 22, 24, 21}$$

$$= (\langle\rangle ; \mu^{[\mathbf{k}:k]}[\![\lambda\mathbf{p}_\mathbf{P}.\ \mathbf{p[k]}]\!] \rhd H) \rhd \langle\rangle ; \psi\alpha \qquad \text{by 23}$$

$$= (\langle\rangle ; \mu^{[\mathbf{k}:k]}[\![\lambda\mathbf{p}_\mathbf{P}.\ \mathbf{p[k]}]\!] \rhd \langle \mathbf{q}\colon I_{TP} \rangle ; \mu^{[\,]}[\![\Lambda\mathbf{k}.\ \lambda\mathbf{f}_{\mathbf{T[k]}\to\mathbf{k}}.\ \mathbf{f}(\mathbf{T_{Pk}[M]q})]\!])$$

$$\rhd \langle\rangle ; \psi\alpha \qquad \text{by 29, 13, 23}$$

$$= \langle \mathbf{q}: I_{TP} \rangle ; \mu^{[\mathbf{k}:k]}[\![(\lambda \mathbf{p}_\mathbf{P}.\ \mathbf{p}[\mathbf{k}])(\Lambda \mathbf{k}.\ \lambda \mathbf{f}_{\mathbf{T}[\mathbf{k}] \to \mathbf{k}}.\ \mathbf{f}(\mathbf{T}_{\mathbf{P}\mathbf{k}}[\mathbf{M}]\mathbf{q}))]\!]$$

$$\triangleright \langle\rangle ; \psi\alpha \qquad \text{by 24, 19, 22}$$

$$= \langle \mathbf{q}: I_{TP} \rangle ; \mu^{[\mathbf{k}:k]}[\![\lambda \mathbf{f}_{\mathbf{T}[\mathbf{k}] \to \mathbf{k}}.\ \mathbf{f}(\mathbf{T}_{\mathbf{P}\mathbf{k}}[\mathbf{M}]\mathbf{q})]\!] \triangleright \langle\rangle ; \psi\alpha \qquad \text{by 20}$$

$$= \langle\rangle ; \psi\alpha \triangleright \langle \mathbf{q}: I_{TP} \mid \mathbf{f}: \langle\rangle ; \psi\alpha \rangle ; \mu^{[\mathbf{k}:k]}[\![\mathbf{T}_{\mathbf{P}\mathbf{k}}[\mathbf{M}]\mathbf{q}]\!] \qquad \text{by 23, 22, 21}$$

$$= \langle \mathbf{q}: I_{TP} \mid \mathbf{f}: \langle\rangle ; \psi\alpha \rangle ; \mu^{[\mathbf{k}:k]}[\![\mathbf{T}_{\mathbf{P}\mathbf{k}}[\mathbf{M}]\mathbf{q}]\!] ; (\langle\rangle ; \psi\alpha \triangleright I_{Tk}) \qquad \text{by 11, 5}$$

$$= \langle \mathbf{q}: I_{TP} \mid \mathbf{f}: \langle\rangle ; \psi\alpha \rangle ; \mu^{[\mathbf{k}:k]}[\![\mathbf{T}_{\mathbf{P}\mathbf{k}}[\mathbf{M}]\mathbf{q}]\!] ; \alpha \qquad \text{by 13, 14}$$

$$= (\langle \mathbf{f}: \langle\rangle ; \psi\alpha \rangle ; \mu^{[\mathbf{k}:k]}[\![\mathbf{T}_{\mathbf{P}\mathbf{k}}[\mathbf{M}]]\!] \triangleright I_{TP}) ; \alpha \qquad \text{by 22, 24, 21}$$

$$= \phi(\langle \mathbf{f}: \psi\alpha \rangle ; \mu^{[\mathbf{k}:k]}[\![\mathbf{T}_{\mathbf{P}\mathbf{k}}[\mathbf{M}]]\!]) ; \alpha \qquad \text{by 4, 13}$$

$$= T(\phi(\langle \mathbf{f}: \psi\alpha \rangle ; \mu^{[\mathbf{k}:k]}[\![\mathbf{M}]\!])) ; \alpha \qquad \text{by 26}$$

$$= TM ; \alpha . \qquad \text{by 30}$$

□

6 *T-algebras*

Our result about expressible functors can be stated more succinctly by introducing the concepts of T-algebras and weak initiality.

If $\mathcal{K}$ is a category and T is a functor from $\mathcal{K}$ to $\mathcal{K}$, then Talg is the category such that

$$|T\mathrm{alg}| \stackrel{\mathrm{def}}{=} \{\langle k, \alpha\rangle \mid k \in |\mathcal{K}| \text{ and } \alpha \in Tk \xrightarrow[\mathcal{K}]{} k\},$$

$$\langle k, \alpha\rangle \xrightarrow[T\mathrm{alg}]{} \langle k', \alpha'\rangle \stackrel{\mathrm{def}}{=} \{\beta \mid \beta \in k \xrightarrow[\mathcal{K}]{} k' \text{ and } T\beta ;_{\mathcal{K}} \alpha' = \alpha ;_{\mathcal{K}} \beta\},$$

$$\beta ;_{T\mathrm{alg}} \beta' \stackrel{\mathrm{def}}{=} \beta ;_{\mathcal{K}} \beta' ,$$

$$I^{T\mathrm{alg}}_{\langle k,\alpha\rangle} \stackrel{\mathrm{def}}{=} I^{\mathcal{K}}_{k} .$$

The objects of Talg are called *T-algebras*, and the morphisms in $\langle k, \alpha\rangle \xrightarrow[T\mathrm{alg}]{} \langle k', \alpha'\rangle$ are called *homomorphisms* from $\langle k, \alpha\rangle$ to $\langle k', \alpha'\rangle$.

An *initial* (*weak initial*) object of a category $\mathcal{K}$ is an object $v \in |\mathcal{K}|$ such that, for all $k \in |\mathcal{K}|$, the set $v \to k$ contains exactly one (at least one) morphism.

Then Proposition 3 can be restated as follows.

Proposition 4

If a functor T from $\mathcal{K}$ to $\mathcal{K}$ is expressible in a $\mathcal{K}$-model then there is a weak initial T-algebra.

7 Equalizers and Initiality

Our next goal is to sharpen Proposition 4 by finding circumstances in which expressible functors will lead to initial, rather than just weak initial, T-algebras. We will find that a sufficient condition is the existence of enough equalizers in $\mathcal{K}$.

Suppose $\mathcal{K}$ is any category, $k, k' \in |\mathcal{K}|$, and $S \subseteq k \to k'$. If $u \in |\mathcal{K}|$ and $\varepsilon \in u \to k$ are such that

$$u \xrightarrow{\ \varepsilon\ } k \overset{\beta_1}{\underset{\beta_2}{\rightrightarrows}} k'$$

commutes for all $\beta_1, \beta_2 \in S$, then ε is said to be an *equalizing cone* of S. If $\varepsilon \in u \to k$ is an equalizing cone of S and, for all equalizing cones $\varepsilon' \in u' \to k$ of S, there is exactly one morphism $\theta \in u' \to u$ such that

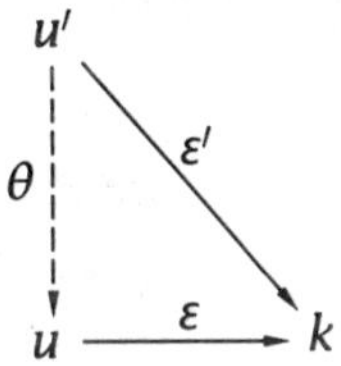

commutes, then ε is said to be an *equalizer* of S.

In the particular case where $\mathcal{K}$ is SET, it is easily seen that an equalizer of S is obtained by taking ε to be the identity injection from u to k, where

$$u = \{x \mid x \in k \text{ and } (\forall \beta_1, \beta_2 \in S)\ \beta_1 x = \beta_2 x\}.$$

Thus SET possesses equalizers of all subsets of its morphism sets.

For any category $\mathcal{K}$, suppose $\varepsilon \in u \to k$ is an equalizer of some $S \subseteq k \to k'$, and $\phi, \psi \in u' \to u$. Then $\phi ; \varepsilon$ and $\psi ; \varepsilon$ are both equalizing cones of S. Thus, if $\phi ; \varepsilon = \psi ; \varepsilon$ then the commutativity of

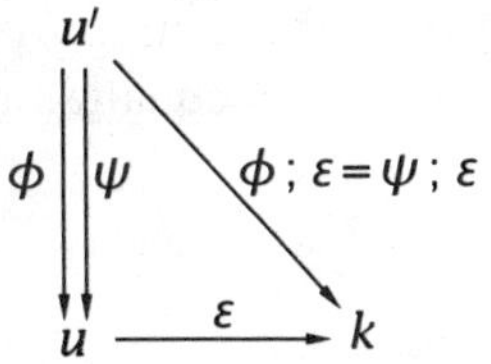

implies $\phi = \psi$. In other words, equalizers are right-cancellable or *monic*.

The connection between equalizers and initiality is established by the following proposition, which is a slight variation of Theorem V.6.1 in [11].

Proposition 5
In a category with a weak initial object w, there is an initial object v if and only if both:

1. $w \to w$ has an equalizer,

2. for all objects k and k', the morphism set $k \to k'$ has an equalizing cone.

Proof Suppose Conditions (1) and (2) hold, and let $\varepsilon \in v \to w$ be the equalizer of $w \to w$. For every object k, since w is weakly initial, there is a morphism $\phi \in w \to k$, so that $\varepsilon \,;\, \phi \in v \to k$; thus v is also weakly initial. To see that it is actually initial, suppose $\beta_1, \beta_2 \in v \to k$. Let $\varepsilon' \in u \to v$ be an equalizing cone of $v \to k$, and let ρ be some morphism in $w \to u$, whose existence is insured by the weak initiality of w. Then

$$v \xrightarrow{\;\varepsilon\;} w \xrightarrow{\;\rho\;} u \xrightarrow{\;\varepsilon'\;} v \underset{\beta_2}{\overset{\beta_1}{\rightrightarrows}} k$$

commutes, since ε' is an equalizing cone. But

$$v \xrightarrow{\;\varepsilon\;} w \underset{I_w}{\overset{\rho\,;\,\varepsilon'\,;\,\varepsilon}{\rightrightarrows}} w$$

also commutes, since ε equalizes $w \to w$. Moreover, since ε is monic, $\varepsilon;\rho;\varepsilon';\varepsilon = \varepsilon$ implies $\varepsilon \,;\, \rho \,;\, \varepsilon' = I_v$. Thus

$$\beta_1 = \varepsilon \,;\, \rho \,;\, \varepsilon' \,;\, \beta_1 = \varepsilon \,;\, \rho \,;\, \varepsilon' \,;\, \beta_2 = \beta_2 \,.$$

On the other hand, suppose v is initial, with unique morphisms $\varepsilon_k \in v \to k$ for each object k. Then, for any morphism set $k \to k'$, ε_k is an equalizing cone of $k \to k'$ since, for $\beta_1, \beta_2 \in k \to k'$, initiality gives $\varepsilon_k \,;\, \beta_1 = \varepsilon_{k'} = \varepsilon_k \,;\, \beta_2$.

Moreover, if w is weakly initial then ε_w is an equalizer of $w \to w$. To see this, suppose $\varepsilon' \in v' \to w$ is an equalizing cone of $w \to w$, and let ρ be some morphism in $w \to v$, whose existence is guaranteed by the weak initiality of w. Then $\rho \,;\, \varepsilon_w \in w \to w$, so that $\varepsilon' \,;\, \rho \,;\, \varepsilon_w = \varepsilon' \,;\, I_w$ since ε' is an equalizing cone. Thus taking $\theta = \varepsilon' \,;\, \rho$ makes

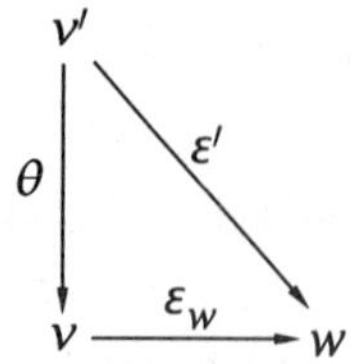

commute. On the other hand, the initiality of v gives $I_v = \varepsilon_w ; \rho$. Thus, if θ is any morphism making the above diagram commute, then $\theta = \theta ; \varepsilon_w ; \rho = \varepsilon' ; \rho$.
□

Next, to apply the above proposition to the existence of initial T-algebras, we must relate equalizers in Talg to equalizers in the underlying category $\mathcal{K}$.

Proposition 6

Suppose T is a functor from $\mathcal{K}$ to $\mathcal{K}$ and, for some T-algebras $\langle k, \alpha \rangle$ and $\langle k', \alpha' \rangle$,

$$S \subseteq \langle k, \alpha \rangle \xrightarrow[\mathrm{Talg}]{} \langle k', \alpha' \rangle \subseteq k \xrightarrow[\mathcal{K}]{} k' .$$

If S has an equalizer in $\mathcal{K}$ then S has an equalizer in Talg.

Proof Let $\varepsilon \in u \to k$ be the equalizer of S in $\mathcal{K}$. For any $\beta_1, \beta_2 \in S$, consider the diagram

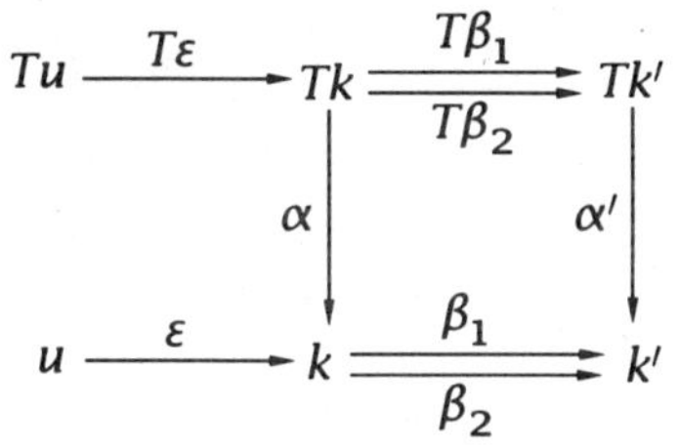

in $\mathcal{K}$. Since ε is an equalizer, $\varepsilon ; \beta_1 = \varepsilon ; \beta_2$, and since T is a functor, $T\varepsilon ; T\beta_1 = T\varepsilon ; T\beta_2$. Then, since β_1 and β_2 are morphisms of T-algebras,

$$T\varepsilon ; \alpha ; \beta_1 = T\varepsilon ; T\beta_1 ; \alpha' = T\varepsilon ; T\beta_2 ; \alpha' = T\varepsilon ; \alpha ; \beta_2 .$$

Thus $T\varepsilon ; \alpha$ is an equalizing cone of S in $\mathcal{K}$, so that there is a unique $\theta \in Tu \to u$ such that

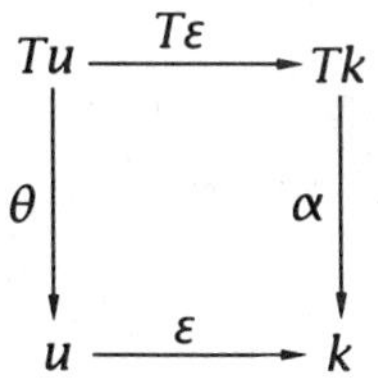

commutes. This implies that $\varepsilon \in \langle u, \theta \rangle \xrightarrow[\mathrm{Talg}]{} \langle k, \alpha \rangle$. Moreover, for any $\beta_1, \beta_2 \in S$, since composition is the same in Talg as in $\mathcal{K}$, we have $\varepsilon ;_{\mathrm{Talg}} \beta_1 = \varepsilon ;_{\mathrm{Talg}} \beta_2$. Thus ε is an equalizing cone of S in Talg.

Now suppose $\varepsilon' \in \langle u', \theta' \rangle \xrightarrow[\mathrm{Talg}]{} \langle k, \alpha \rangle$ is any equalizing cone of S in Talg. Since composition is the same in Talg as in $\mathcal{K}$, ε' is also an equalizing cone of S in

$\mathcal{K}$, so that there is a unique σ such that

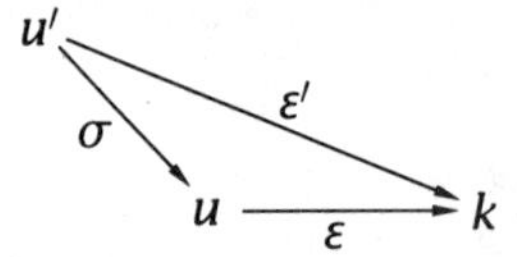

commutes in $\mathcal{K}$. Then σ will also be the unique morphism such that

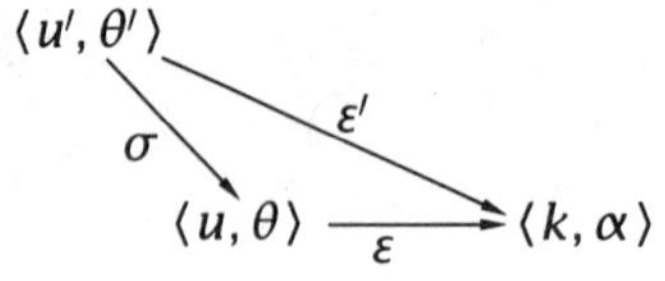

commutes in Talg, providing it is a morphism of T-algebras.

To see that $\sigma \in \langle u', \theta' \rangle \xrightarrow[\text{Talg}]{} \langle u, \theta \rangle$, consider the diagram

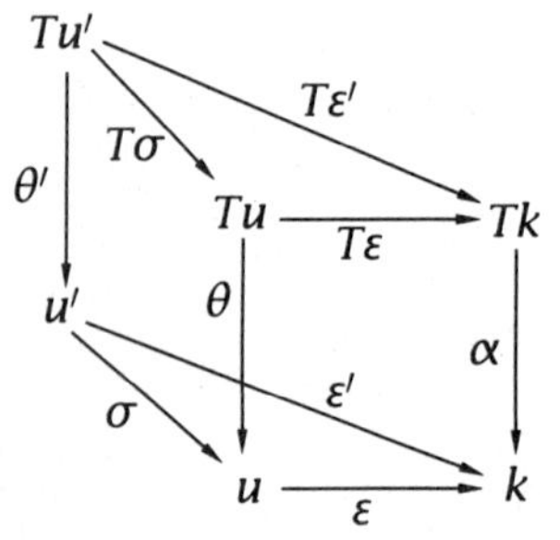

in $\mathcal{K}$. The lower triangle commutes since ε is an equalizer and ε' is an equalizing cone, and the upper triangle then commutes since T is a functor. The square commutes since $\varepsilon \in \langle u, \theta \rangle \xrightarrow[\text{Talg}]{} \langle k, \alpha \rangle$, and the rear parallelogram commutes since $\varepsilon' \in \langle u', \theta' \rangle \xrightarrow[\text{Talg}]{} \langle k, \alpha \rangle$. Thus

$$T\sigma \,;\, \theta \,;\, \varepsilon = T\sigma \,;\, T\varepsilon \,;\, \alpha = T\varepsilon' \,;\, \alpha = \theta' \,;\, \varepsilon' = \theta' \,;\, \sigma \,;\, \varepsilon\,,$$

and since ε is monic, $T\sigma \,;\, \theta = \theta' \,;\, \sigma$. Thus $\sigma \in \langle u', \theta' \rangle \xrightarrow[\text{Talg}]{} \langle u, \theta \rangle$. □

From Propositions 4, 5, and 6 follows Proposition 7.

Proposition 7

If a functor T from $\mathcal{K}$ to $\mathcal{K}$ is expressible in a $\mathcal{K}$-model and all subsets of the morphism sets of $\mathcal{K}$ have equalizers, then there is an initial T-algebra.

8 *Initial* T-*Algebras and Isomorphisms*

To complete our development, we use the fact that the morphism parts of initial T-algebras are isomorphisms. The following proposition is given in [2], where it is attributed to J. Lambek.

Proposition 8

If $\langle u, \theta\rangle$ is an initial T-algebra, then θ is an isomorphism from Tu to u in $\mathcal{K}$.

Proof From the obviously commuting diagram

$$\begin{array}{ccc} T(Tu) & \xrightarrow{T\theta} & Tu \\ \Big\downarrow{\scriptstyle T\theta} & & \Big\downarrow{\scriptstyle \theta} \\ Tu & \xrightarrow{\theta} & u \end{array}$$

it is evident that $\langle Tu, T\theta\rangle$ is a T-algebra and $\theta \in \langle Tu, T\theta\rangle \xrightarrow[\text{Talg}]{} \langle u, \theta\rangle$. Let η be the unique morphism in $\langle u, \theta\rangle \xrightarrow[\text{Talg}]{} \langle Tu, T\theta\rangle$. Then $\eta\,;\theta$ and I_u are both morphisms belonging to $\langle u, \theta\rangle \xrightarrow[\text{Talg}]{} \langle u, \theta\rangle$, so that the initiality of $\langle u, \theta\rangle$ gives $\eta\,;\theta = I_u$. Moreover, since $\eta \in \langle u, \theta\rangle \xrightarrow[\text{Talg}]{} \langle Tu, T\theta\rangle$ and T is a functor,

$$\theta\,;\eta = T\eta\,;T\theta = T(\eta\,;\theta) = T(I_u) = I_{Tu}\,. \quad \square$$

Propositions 7 and 8 imply Proposition 9.

Proposition 9

If a functor T from $\mathcal{K}$ to $\mathcal{K}$ is expressible in a $\mathcal{K}$-model, and all subsets of the morphism sets of $\mathcal{K}$ have equalizers, then there is a $u \in |\mathcal{K}|$ such that Tu is isomorphic to u.

9 *The Impossibility of* SET-*Models*

Suppose that there is a SET-model. Let $B = \mathcal{M}[\,]\mathbf{B}$, where $\mathbf{B} = \Delta\mathbf{k}.\ \mathbf{k} \to (\mathbf{k} \to \mathbf{k})$. Since SET has morphism sets with more than one member, Proposition 1 shows that B has more than one element. Moreover, since the terminal element of SET is (some) singleton set, the elements of B are in one-to-one correspondence with the members of B, so that B has more than one member.

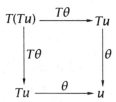

By Proposition 2 there is an expressible functor T from SET to SET such that $Tk = (k \Rightarrow B) \Rightarrow B$, which in SET is the set of functions $(k \to B) \to B$. Thus by Proposition 9, since all subsets of the morphism sets of SET have equalizers, there is a set u such that $(u \to B) \to B$ is isomorphic to u. But it is well known that, when B has more than one member, $(u \to B) \to B$ has higher cardinality than u, and thus cannot be isomorphic to u. From this follows Proposition 10.

Proposition 10
There is no SET-model.

10 *Application to Known Models*

In several models of the polymorphic typed lambda calculus, the meaning of a type is (the set of equivalence classes of) a partial equivalence relation on a model of the untyped lambda calculus [6, 23, 14, 15, 4, 9]. The underlying Cartesian closed categories of such models possess the equalizers needed to apply Propositions 7 and 9. An important open question for these models, however, is whether the equalizer construction is necessary, or whether $\langle P, H \rangle$, as defined in the proof of Proposition 3, is already an initial (rather than just weakly initial) T-algebra.

Other models, such as [13], [12], [1], and [7], have an underlying Cartesian closed category that is a subcategory of the category of complete partial orders (with a least element) and continuous functions. Unfortunately, these subcategories have a paucity of equalizers. For example, if w is the two-point c.p.o.

$$\begin{array}{c} \top \\ | \\ \bot \end{array}$$

and $\beta_1, \beta_2 \in w \to w$ are the constant functions yielding $\bot$ and $\top$, then $\{\beta_1, \beta_2\}$ has no equalizer.

Indeed, there are few T-algebras for the category of complete partial orders and continuous functions; the usual notion of continuous algebra [8] is equivalent to that of a T-algebra for the category of complete partial orders and *strict* continuous functions, which possesses equalizers of all subsets of its morphism sets, but is not Cartesian closed.

There seems to be a connection between the weak T-algebras obtained for these models and continuous algebras based on the category of complete partial orders and strict continuous functions. However, we have been unable to formulate a precise description of this connection.

Acknowledgments

The research by John C. Reynolds reported here was supported by the Institut National de Recherche en Informatique et en Automatique, and by NSF

Grants MCS–8017577 and CCR–8620191. A portion of the research was also sponsored by the Defense Advanced Research Projects Agency (DOD), ARPA Order No. 4976, under contract number F33615–87–C–1499, monitored by the Air Force Wright Aeronautical Laboratories, Wright-Patterson AFB, Ohio. The views and conclusions contained in this document are those of the authors and should not be interpreted as representing the official policies, either expressed or implied, of any agency of the U.S. Government.

The research by Gordon D. Plotkin reported here was supported by the British Petroleum Venture Research Group.

References

[1] Amadio, R., Bruce, K. B., and Longo, G. "The finitary projection model for second order lambda calculus and solutions to higher order domain equations". *Proceedings Symposium on Logic in Computer Science*, pp. 122–130, 1986.

[2] Barr, M. "Coequalizers and free triples". *Mathematische Zeitschrift 116* (1970), pp. 307–322.

[3] Böhm, C. and Berarducci, A. "Automatic synthesis of typed Λ-programs on term algebras". *Theoretical Computer Science 39* (1985), pp. 135–154.

[4] Freyd, P. and Scedrov, A. "Some semantic aspects of polymorphic lambda calculus". *Proceedings Symposium on Logic in Computer Science*, pp. 315–319, 1987.

[5] Girard, J.-Y. "Une extension de l'interpretation de gödel à l'analyse, et son application a l'elimination des coupures dans l'analyse et la théorie des types". *Proceedings of the Second Scandinavian Logic Symposium*, J. E. Fenstad, ed., pp. 63–92. North-Holland, Amsterdam, 1971.

[6] Girard, J.-Y. *Interprétation Fonctionnelle et Elimination des Coupures dans l'Arithmétique d'Ordre Supérieur.* Thèse de doctorat d'état, Université Paris VII, 1972.

[7] Girard, J.-Y. "The system *F* of variable types, fifteen years later". *Theoretical Computer Science 45* (1986), pp. 159–192. Reprinted in this volume (Chapter 6).

[8] Goguen, J. A., Thatcher, J. W., Wagner, E. G., and Wright, J. B. "Initial algebra semantics and continuous algebras". *Journal of the ACM, 24* (January 1977), pp. 68–95.

[9] Hyland, J. M. E. "A small complete category". *Annals of Pure and Applied Logic 40*, 2 (November 1988), pp. 135–165.

[10] Leivant, D. "Reasoning about functional programs and complexity classes associated with type disciplines". In *24th Annual Symposium on Foundations of Computer Science*, pages 460–469, 1983.

[11] Mac Lane, S. *Categories for the Working Mathematician.* Springer-Verlag, New York, 1971.

[12] McCracken, N. J. "A finitary retract model for the polymorphic lambda-calculus".

To appear in *Information and Control.*

[13] McCracken, N. J. *An Investigation of a Programming Language with a Polymorphic Type Structure.* Ph. D. dissertation, Syracuse University, June 1979.

[14] Mitchell, J. C. "A type-inference approach to reduction properties and semantics of polymorphic expressions (summary)". *Proceedings of the 1986 ACM Conference on Lisp and Functional Programming*, pp. 308–319. ACM, New York, 1986. Included, with corrections, in this volume (Chapter 9).

[15] Pitts, A. M. "Polymorphism is set theoretic, constructively". *Category Theory and Computer Science*, D. H. Pitt, A. Poigné, and D. E. Rydeheard, eds., pp. 12–39. Lecture Notes in Computer Science, vol. 283. Springer-Verlag, Berlin, 1987.

[16] Plotkin, G. D. Private communication. July 1984.

[17] Prawitz, D. "Ideas and results in proof theory". *Proceedings of the Second Scandinavian Logic Symposium*, J. E. Fenstad, ed., pp. 235–307. North-Holland, Amsterdam, 1971.

[18] Reynolds, J. C. "Towards a theory of type structure". *Proceedings, Colloque sur la Programmation*, pp. 408–425. Lecture Notes in Computer Science, vol. 19. Springer-Verlag, Berlin, 1974.

[19] Reynolds, J. C. "Types, abstraction and parametric polymorphism". *Information Processing 83*, R. E. A. Mason, ed., pp. 513–523. Elsevier Science Publishers B. V. (North-Holland), Amsterdam, 1983.

[20] Reynolds, J. C. "Polymorphism is not set-theoretic". *Semantics of Data Types*, G. Kahn, D. B. MacQueen, and G. D. Plotkin, eds., pp. 145–156. Lecture Notes in Computer Science, vol. 173. Springer-Verlag, Berlin, 1984.

[21] Seely, R. A. G. "Categorical semantics for higher order polymorphic lambda calculus". *Journal of Symbolic Logic 52,* 4 (December 1987), pp. 969–989.

[22] Takeuti, G. *Proof Theory.* North-Holland, Amsterdam, 1975.

[23] Troelstra, A. S. (ed.). *Metamathematical Investigation of Intuitionistic Arithmetic and Analysis.* Lecture Notes in Mathematics, vol. 344. Springer-Verlag, Berlin, 1973.

Polymorphic Type Inference and Containment[1]

8

John C. Mitchell
Stanford University

Abstract

Type expressions may be used to describe the functional behavior of untyped lambda terms. We present a general semantics of polymorphic type expressions over models of untyped lambda calculus and give complete rules for inferring types for terms. Some simplified typing theories are studied in more detail, and containments between types are investigated.

1 *Introduction*

The use of type expressions to describe the functional behavior of untyped lambda terms originated with Curry's theory of functionality [2, 5, 14, 15, 16].

1. This chapter was originally published in *Information and Computation*, and appears here with permission of the publisher.

Curry's original theory uses types like $t \rightarrow t$, the type of terms which map elements of t to elements of t. This paper will be concerned with an extension to Curry's functionality theory, using additional type expressions like $\forall t.t \rightarrow t$ with universal quantifiers [19, 20, 21]. Intuitively, the type $\forall t.t \rightarrow t$ describes terms which, for all types t, map t to t. We will develop a general semantics of quantified types and present complete inference rules for deducing types of terms. In addition, "pure" typing theories and containments between types will be investigated.

When deriving types for terms, we may use assumptions about the types of other terms and equations between terms. For example, if we assume that M has type $\sigma \rightarrow \tau$ (i.e., M behaves like a function from σ to τ) and N has type σ, then the result MN of applying M to N will have type τ. Similarly, if we assume that $M = N$ and M has type σ, then we may conclude that N has type σ. The completeness theorems in Section 4 show that the inference rules are sound and complete for deducing the semantic consequences of any set of assumptions about the types of terms and any set of equations between terms. Assumptions about the types of terms would be useful if we wanted to assume that the "fixed-point" operator Y had type $\forall t.(t \rightarrow t) \rightarrow t$, for example. Equations between terms would help in studying the typing theories of various lambda models. However, we will not explore either of these directions in this paper.

One interesting set of typings consists of those that are provable using only α-equivalence of terms (renaming of bound variables) and no assumptions about the types of terms. This "pure" typing theory is related to the syntax of second-order lambda calculus [11, 32]: A term M has type σ in the pure theory if and only if there is an essentially similar typed term N of the second-order lambda calculus with the same type σ. When nontrivial equations between terms are involved in typing, it is easy to show that the set of provable typings is undecidable. However, it is not known whether the pure typing theory is decidable. There is practical motivation for finding an efficient decision procedure for this theory, or some reasonable fragment, since it would be useful to enhance the ML type checker with second-order typings (see [12, 19, 22, 25]).

Curry typing has a decision procedure based on *principal* types [6, 14]. The principal Curry typing for a term M has the property that every other Curry typing for M may be derived by substitution. Since every Curry-typable term has a principal typing, a term can be typed by finding principal typings for subterms. With type quantifiers, we do not know how to describe the set of types of an arbitrary term M. One approach to this problem is to examine the containment relation on types. We will think of types as sets of terms (or meanings of terms) and write $\sigma \subseteq \tau$ if the set σ is contained in the set

τ. Since $\sigma \subseteq \tau$ implies that every term with type σ will also have type τ, containments give us some insight into the set of types associated with a term M. We will study the containments that hold in all semantic models using a pure type assignment system based on containment. Although interesting, the valid containments do not seem to characterize the set of types of a term M completely.

In the general study of type inference, we will make very few assumptions about the meaning of $\rightarrow$. A more specialized interpretation of $\rightarrow$ will be studied in Sections 4.2 and 6. In *simple inference models*, the type constructor $\rightarrow$ is interpreted as the set of all elements that map σ into τ (cf. [2, 15]). Simple inference models have much richer containment theories than arbitrary models, and containments in simple models seem to provide more useful information about alternate typings of terms. We characterized the containments that are valid in all simple inference models using inference rules and, alternatively, using terms of second-order lambda calculus. In addition, we show that certain terms have minimal typings over all simple inference models.

2 *Lambda Calculus and Typing*

2.1 *Untyped Lambda Terms*

The terms of untyped lambda calculus are defined by

$$M ::= x \mid MN \mid \lambda x.M\,.$$

We always consider lambda terms modulo α-conversion,

$$(\alpha)\quad \lambda x.M = \lambda y.[y/x]M \ \text{ if } y \text{ is not free in M}\,,$$

so that we can rename bound variables. Some additional axioms are

$$(\beta)\quad (\lambda x.M)N = [N/x]M\,,$$

$$(\eta)\quad \lambda x.Mx = M \ \text{ if } x \text{ is not free in } M\,,$$

where substitution $[N/x]M$ of N for x in M is defined with renaming of bound variables of M to avoid capture, as usual. We may also use (β) and (η) as directed rewrite rules, replacing subterms that match the left-hand sides of either equation with the corresponding right-hand sides. These rewrite operations are β-reduction and η-reduction. See [1] for more information.

A *lambda theory* is a set of equations which contains all instances of (α) and (β), and is closed under the following inference rules:

$$\text{(sym)} \qquad \frac{M = N}{N = M},$$

$$\text{(trans)} \qquad \frac{M = N, N = P}{M = P},$$

$$\text{(cong)} \qquad \frac{M = N, P = Q}{MP = NQ},$$

$$(\xi) \qquad \frac{M = N}{\lambda x.M = \lambda x.N}.$$

A theory is *extensional* if it also contains all instances of (η). A set of equations is a *congruence* if it contains $M = M$ for every term M, all instances of (α), and is closed under inference rules (sym), (trans), (cong) and (ξ). Thus any congruence containing all instances of (β) is a lambda theory.

2.2 *Type Expressions*

Type expressions are built from type variables and constants using the connective $\rightarrow$ and the binding operator $\forall$. These are the type expressions of second-order lambda calculus [11, 32]. We adopt the notational conventions that

$r, s, t, \ldots$ denote type variables,

$\rho, \sigma, \tau, \ldots$ denote type expressions.

The set of type expressions is defined by the grammar

$$\tau ::= t \mid \sigma \rightarrow \tau \mid \forall t.\sigma .$$

We identify type expressions that differ only in the names of bound variables. Thus, assuming s is not free in σ, we have $\forall t.\sigma = \forall s.[s/t]\sigma$, where $[s/t]\sigma$ is the result of substituting s for free occurrences of t in σ. The only equations between type expressions that we will consider are equations that result from renaming bound type variables. In the terminology of [28], we allow only normal form type expressions.

2.3 *Typing Rules*

A *basic typing statement* is an expression $M{:}\sigma$, where M is a lambda term and σ is a type expression. The basic typing statement $M{:}\sigma$ may be read, "the term M has type σ." Since the type of a term depends on the types of its free variables, we will work with typing statements that incorporate an association between types and variables. A *type assignment* A is a finite set of basic typing statements of the form $x{:}\sigma$ with no variable x appearing twice in A. We will write $A,x{:}\sigma$ for the type assignment

$$A,x{:}\sigma = A \cup \{x{:}\sigma\},$$

where in writing this we always assume that x does not occur in A. It is also sometimes convenient to write $A(x)$ for the type σ such that $x{:}\sigma \in A$, if there is one. A *typing statement* is an expression $A \supset M{:}\sigma$. The only axiom for typing statements is

$$(var) \quad \{x{:}\sigma\} \supset x{:}\sigma .$$

The inference rules for functional and polymorphic types are

$$(\rightarrow I) \quad \frac{A,x{:}\sigma \supset M{:}\tau}{A \supset \lambda x.M{:}\sigma \rightarrow \tau},$$

$$(\rightarrow E) \quad \frac{A \supset M{:}\sigma \rightarrow \tau,\ A \supset N{:}\sigma}{A \supset MN{:}\tau},$$

$$(\forall I) \quad \frac{A \supset M{:}\sigma}{A \supset M{:}\forall t.\sigma}, \quad \text{provided } t \text{ does not occur free in } A,$$

$$(\forall E) \quad \frac{A \supset M{:}\forall t.\sigma}{A \supset M{:}[\tau/t]\sigma}.$$

We also have a rule for adding typing hypotheses:

$$(\text{add hyp}) \quad \frac{A \supset M{:}\tau}{A, x{:}\sigma \supset M{:}\tau}, \quad x \text{ does not occur in } A,$$

a type equality inference rule:

$$(\text{type eq}) \quad \frac{A \supset M{:}\sigma,\ \sigma = \tau}{A \supset M{:}\tau},$$

so that we can rename bound variables in the types of terms, and a rule for giving equal terms the same types:

$$(\text{term eq}) \quad \frac{A \supset M{:}\sigma,\ M = N}{A \supset N{:}\sigma}.$$

An implicit parameter of the inference system is the relation = on terms. We will always assume that = includes α-equivalence, but not always (β) or (η).

We will see that when term equality is closed under (β), the above rules are complete for inferring the typing statements that are valid in all models. However, two additional rules are needed to capture semantic implication of sets of typing statements. One is a rule allowing redundant typings to be removed from a type assignment, and the other is a substitution rule. For reasons that will be explained later on, we will generally assume that all types are nonempty. Without empty types, the rule,

$$\text{(remove hyp)} \quad \frac{A, x{:}\sigma \supset M{:}\tau}{A \supset M{:}\tau}, \quad x \text{ not free in } M,$$

is sound, since the value of a variable x not free in M does not affect the meaning of M. (With empty types, the rule is unsound, since the implication $A,x{:}\sigma \supset M{:}\tau$ will hold vacuously if σ is empty, while the typing statement $A \supset M{:}\tau$ may fail.)

A few preliminary definitions make the substitution rule easier to write down. If B is a type assignment,

$$B = \{x_1{:}\sigma_1, \ldots, x_k{:}\sigma_k\},$$

and S is a substitution of terms for ordinary variables and type expressions for type variables, then we write SB for the set of typing statements,

$$SB = \{Sx_1{:}S\sigma_1, \ldots, Sx_k{:}S\sigma_k\},$$

and use $A \supset SB$ as an abbreviation for the list of typing statements,

$$A \supset Sx_1{:}S\sigma_1, \ldots, A \supset Sx_k{:}S\sigma_k .$$

Note that if S substitutes an ordinary variable for each x in B, then SB will be a well-formed type assignment. The substitution rule for typing is

$$(subst) \quad \frac{A \supset SB, B \supset M{:}\sigma}{A \supset SM{:}S\sigma}.$$

If $A \supset M{:}\sigma$ is derivable from a set S of typing assumptions $B \supset N{:}\tau$ and set $\mathcal{E}$ of equations $N = P$ between lambda terms, we write $S, \mathcal{E} \vdash A \supset M{:}\sigma$. It is worth pointing out that although we will not consider proofs from sets of equations between types, there is no loss of generality in not doing so. Specifically, instead of assuming $\sigma = \tau$, we may assume that $\{x{:}\sigma\} \supset x{:}\tau$ and $\{x{:}\tau\} \supset x{:}\sigma$. This has essentially the same effect since rule (subst) may be used to derive $A \supset M{:}\tau$ from $A \supset M{:}\sigma$ and $\{x{:}\sigma\} \supset x{:}\tau$, and conversely.

There are a number of admissible and derived typing rules. A straightforward induction on derivations shows that if we have no typing assumptions, then the set of typings provable from any set of equations between terms is closed under rules (remove hyp) and (subst).

Lemma 1

Suppose $\mathcal{E} \vdash A \supset M{:}\sigma$. Then there is a proof of $A \supset M{:}\sigma$ from $\mathcal{E}$ that does not use rule (remove hyp) or (subst).

Consequently, when we study pure typing (without "nonlogical" typing hypotheses), we will assume that typings are proved without these two rules. A useful special case of (subst) is when the substitution S is the identity substitution. In this case, the rule states that from

$$B \supset x_1{:}\sigma_1, \ldots, B \supset x_k{:}\sigma_k, \text{ and } \{x_1{:}\sigma_1, \ldots, x_k{:}\sigma_k\} \supset M{:}\sigma$$

we may conclude $B \supset M{:}\sigma$. Another derived rule, involving (add hyp) and (remove hyp) is

$$(fv) \quad \frac{A \supset M{:}\sigma}{B \supset M{:}\sigma}, \quad \text{provided } A|_M \subseteq B|_M,$$

where $A|_M$ is the set $\{x{:}\sigma \in A \mid x \in FV(M)\}$ of typing statements from A about free variables of M. The following lemma is proved using lambda abstraction or ($\forall I$), followed by application or ($\forall E$), to effect substitution of terms or types.

Lemma 2
Let S be a substitution of type expressions for type variables and ordinary variables for ordinary variables. Then from $A \supset M{:}\sigma$ we can prove $SA \supset SM{:}S\sigma$.

Using induction on derivations, we may also prove the following lemma.

Lemma 3
If $\mathcal{E} \vdash A, x{:}\sigma \supset M{:}\tau$ and $\mathcal{E} \vdash A \supset N{:}\sigma$, then $\mathcal{E} \vdash A \supset [N/x]M{:}\tau$.

If $\mathcal{E}$ is a congruence relation and no typing statements are taken as assumptions, then it suffices to use rule (term eq) only once.

Lemma 4
(Equality Postponement) Suppose the set $\mathcal{E}$ of equations is a congruence. If $\mathcal{E} \vdash A \supset M{:}\sigma$, then there is some N such that $\vdash A \supset N{:}\sigma$ and $M = N \in \mathcal{E}$.

Lemma 4 is essentially the Equality Postponement Theorem of [5], reformulated for the present set of typing rules (see also [15]).

3 *Semantics of Type Inference*

3.1 *Lambda Models*

Typing statements may be interpreted semantically using a model for untyped lambda terms, an "abstract" interpretation for type expressions, and a mapping *subset* which assigns a subset of the lambda model to each type.

Lambda models are reviewed briefly before discussing the interpretation of types.

A *lambda model* $\langle D, \bullet, \epsilon\rangle$ consists of a set D together with binary operation $\bullet$ and element ϵ of D such that

$$(\epsilon \bullet d) \bullet e = d \bullet e\,,$$

$$\forall e(d_1 \bullet e = d_2 \bullet e) \text{ implies } \epsilon \bullet d_1 = \epsilon \bullet d_2\,,$$

$$\epsilon \bullet \epsilon = \epsilon\,.$$

Furthermore, D must contain elements K and S with the simple algebraic properties

$$(K \bullet x) \bullet y = x\,,$$

$$((S \bullet x) \bullet y) \bullet z = (x \bullet z) \bullet (y \bullet z)\,.$$

This is the combinatory model definition of [23]; see also [1]. It is customary to drop $\bullet$, and to omit parentheses when applications associate to the right. Thus we often write Kxy for $(K \bullet x) \bullet y$.

Given a lambda model $\langle D, \bullet, \epsilon\rangle$ and environment η mapping variables to elements of D, the meaning of a lambda term M is defined inductively by

$$[\![x]\!]\eta = \eta(x)\,,$$

$$[\![MN]\!]\eta = [\![M]\!]\eta \bullet [\![N]\!]\eta\,,$$

$$[\![\lambda x.M]\!]\eta = \epsilon \bullet d, \text{ where } d \bullet e = [\![M]\!]\eta[e/x] \text{ all } e \in D\,.$$

The existence of K and S ensure that there always exists a d as required in the definition of $[\![\lambda x.M]\!]$. The function ϵ makes the meaning of $\lambda x.M$ independent of the specific choice of d. Again, the reader is referred to [1, 23] for more information.

One important model is the term model. Given any lambda theory Th, we let $[M]_{Th}$ be the set of terms N with $M = N \in Th$. The term model $\langle D, \bullet, \epsilon\rangle$ for Th has equivalence classes of terms as elements:

$$D = \{[M]_{Th} | M \text{ an untyped term}\}\,.$$

We generally omit the subscript Th when no confusion is likely to occur. Application, $\bullet$, in term models is defined by

$$[M] \bullet [N] = [MN]\,,$$

and the choice element ϵ is defined by

$$\epsilon = [\lambda x.\lambda y.xy]\,.$$

See [1, 23] for properties of term models.

3.2 Which Sets Are Types?

In studies of type inference without quantifiers, e.g., [2, 15, 16, 25, 27], we may interpret types as arbitrary subsets of lambda models. In this approach, the meaning of a type expression depends on an environment mapping type variables to arbitrary subsets and an interpretation of $\rightarrow$ as an operation on sets. Two reasonable interpretations for $\rightarrow$ are

$$\text{(simple)} \quad A \rightarrow B = \{d \in D \mid d \bullet A \subseteq B\},$$

$$(F) \quad A \rightarrow B = \{d \in D \mid d \bullet A \subseteq B\} \cap \mathcal{F},$$

where $d \bullet A$ is shorthand for the set $\{d \bullet e \mid e \in A\}$ and $\mathcal{F}$ is the range of ϵ.[2] While there is some appeal to considering every subset a type, this raises some difficulties when quantifiers are involved.

Intuitively, the typing statement $M{:}\forall t.\sigma$ means that for all possible values of the type variable t, we have $M{:}\sigma$. Therefore, it makes sense to define the meaning of $\forall t.\sigma$ by intersection. If all sets are considered types, then we are led to the naive definition

$$\text{(naive)} \quad [\![\forall t.\sigma]\!]\eta = \cap_{S\subseteq D} [\![\sigma]\!]\eta[S/t]\,.$$

However, there are some significant problems with this. Using (naive), the meaning of $\forall t.t$ is the empty set in *every* model. This makes any typing statement of the form $A,x{:}\forall t.t \supset M{:}\sigma$ vacuously valid, since the assignment $A,x{:}\forall t.t$ is unsatisfiable. Specifically, no model and environment η can satisfy $x{:}\forall t.t$ since $[\![\forall t.t]\!]_{(\text{naive})}$ is always empty. While it is reasonable for $\forall t.t$ to be empty in some models, we would prefer not to rule out interpretations in which $\forall t.t$ is nonempty.

One relatively natural semantics of type inference which makes $\forall t.t$ nonempty is developed in [20, 21]. If we restrict our attention to models with order structure, then we can single out *ideals*, sets which are *nonempty*, "downward closed", and "closed under limits of chains", as the meanings of types. We can then define

$$\text{(ideal)} \quad [\![\forall t.\sigma]\!]\eta = \cap_{I\subseteq D \text{ an ideal}} [\![\sigma]\!]\eta[I/t]\,.$$

Since every nonempty, downward closed set contains the least element $\bot$, we have $\bot \in \forall t.t$. However, since the ideal model seems to be a commitment to a number of complicated relationships between types, we will use a more general definition which encompasses the ideal model of [20, 21] as an important special case. It is worth remarking that the ideal model provides semantics

2. The significance of $\mathcal{F}$ is that every unary function from D to D that is represented by some element of D (by left application) has a unique representative in $\mathcal{F}$. See [15] for further discussion.

for recursively-defined types, while the models considered in this paper do not.

To simplify the presentation, we will begin by assuming that all types are nonempty in every model. After proving completeness for general models without empty types, and for some specific classes of models, we will discuss the modifications needed to achieve semantic completeness when empty types are allowed.

3.3 *Interpretation of Type Expressions*

At first reading, the structures used to interpret type expressions may seem overly complicated. In addition to requiring a set T of types, models will involve a set $T \Rightarrow T$ of functions from T to T, a set $T \Rightarrow (T \Rightarrow T)$ of functions from T to $T \Rightarrow T$, and so on. There are two reasons for considering sets other than T. The first is that $\forall$ is essentially a mapping from some set of functions $T \Rightarrow T$ into T, so making $T \Rightarrow T$ part of the model makes the domain of $\forall$ explicit. The second reason has to do with whether $T \Rightarrow T$ contains all the functions that enter into the meanings of type expressions. One easy way of ensuring that the domain $T \Rightarrow T$ of $\forall$ is rich enough is to require that T and $T \Rightarrow T$ be part of a model of the ordinary typed lambda calculus. The definition below is in the same spirit as [3].

The set of *kinds* is defined by the grammar

$$\kappa ::= T \mid \kappa_1 \Rightarrow \kappa_2 .$$

A *type structure* $\mathcal{T}$ for a $\rightarrow$, $\forall$ is a tuple

$$\langle \mathcal{U}, \rightarrow^{\mathcal{T}}, \forall^{\mathcal{T}} \rangle ,$$

where $\mathcal{U}$ is a family of sets $\{U_\kappa\}$ indexed by kinds,
$U_{\kappa_1 \Rightarrow \kappa_2}$ is a set of functions from U_{κ_1} to U_{κ_2} ,
$\rightarrow^{\mathcal{T}}$ is an element of $U_{T \Rightarrow (T \Rightarrow T)}$, and
$\forall^{\mathcal{T}}$ is an element of $U_{(T \Rightarrow T) \Rightarrow T}$.

We require that $\mathcal{U}$ be a model of the ordinary typed lambda calculus and define the meaning $[\![\sigma]\!]\eta$ of a type expression σ in environment η by treating $\forall t.\sigma$ as an abbreviation for $\forall(\lambda t.\sigma)$ with constant $\forall$:

$$[\![\forall t.\sigma]\!]\eta = \forall^{\mathcal{T}}([\![\lambda t.\sigma]\!]\eta) ;$$

cf. [1, 10, 13, 35]. We write $T^{\mathcal{T}}$ for $\mathcal{U}_T$, and similarly for other kinds, omitting the superscript when clear from context.

One example of a type structure is the term structure constructed from expressions of all kinds. The *constructor expressions* and their kinds are defined by the following inference rules. We write c^κ to indicate that c is a constant of kind κ and similarly v^κ to indicate that v is a variable of kind κ. We assume we have infinitely many variables of each kind and take $\rightarrow^{T\Rightarrow T\Rightarrow T}$ and $\forall^{(T\Rightarrow T)\Rightarrow T}$ as constructor constants.

$$c^\kappa{:}\kappa,\ v^\kappa{:}\kappa\,,$$

$$\frac{\mu{:}\kappa_1 \Rightarrow \kappa_2,\ \omega{:}\kappa_1}{\mu\omega{:}\kappa_2}\,,$$

$$\frac{\mu{:}\kappa_2}{\lambda v^{\kappa_1}.\mu{:}\kappa_1 \Rightarrow \kappa_2}\,.$$

It is easy to see that every type expression (as defined in Section 2.2) is a constructor expression of kind T. Furthermore, if we extend the typing rules by taking all constructor expressions of kind T as types (and use β, η-conversion in rule (type eq)), the new typing system is a conservative extension over the old one. More specifically, if σ is a type expression with no symbols of higher kinds other than $\rightarrow$ and $\forall$, then $A \supset M{:}\sigma$ is provable in the original system if and only if it is provable in the extended system allowing all constructor expressions of kind T as types.

Since constructor expressions are just typed lambda terms (with types now called kinds to avoid confusion), we can use the usual term model construction for typed lambda calculus to build type structures. The type structure $\mathcal{T} = \langle \mathcal{U}, \rightarrow^{\mathcal{T}}, \forall^{\mathcal{T}} \rangle$ of constructors modulo β,η-conversion is defined as follows. The elements of kind κ are functions defined by (possibly open) constructor expressions over constants $\forall$ and $\rightarrow$. We first define

$$[\sigma] = \{\tau \mid \sigma\ \beta,\eta\text{-converts to } \tau\}$$

for any constructor expression σ of kind T. If μ is an expression of kind $\kappa_1 \rightarrow \kappa_2$, then $[\mu]$ is the function defined by

$$[\mu]([v]) = [\mu v] \text{ all } v \text{ of kind } \kappa_1\,.$$

We then let $\mathcal{U}_\kappa$ be the set of all $[\mu]$ for μ of kind κ, and take $\rightarrow^{\mathcal{T}}$ and $\forall^{\mathcal{T}}$ to be $[\rightarrow]$ and $[\forall]$, respectively. It is not hard to verify that $\mathcal{U} \models \mu = \omega$ if and only if μ and v are β,η-convertible. In particular, for type expressions σ and τ that have no β,η-redexes, $\mathcal{U} \models \sigma = \tau$ iff σ and τ differ only in the names of bound variables (see [3, 10, 13, 35]).

3.4 *Models of Type Inference*

A *model of type inference*, or *inference model* for short, is a triple $\langle \mathcal{T}, \mathcal{D}, subset \rangle$ with

$\mathcal{T} = \langle \mathcal{U}, \rightarrow, \forall \rangle$	a type structure,
$\mathcal{D} = \langle D, \bullet, \epsilon \rangle$	a model of untyped lambda calculus, and
subset	a function from $T^{\mathcal{T}}$ to subsets of D,

satisfying the following conditions. We write D_a for *subset*(a) and require that for all $a, b \in T$ and $f \in T \Rightarrow T$,

(Arrow.1) if $d \in D_{a \rightarrow b}$, then $d \bullet D_a \subseteq D_b$;

(Arrow.2) if $d \bullet D_a \subseteq D_b$, then $\epsilon \bullet d \in D_{a \rightarrow b}$;

(ForAll) $D_{\forall f} = \cap_{a \in T} D_{f(a)}$.

Condition (Arrow.1) "says" that any element of $D_{a \rightarrow b}$ defines a function from D_a to D_b, while (Arrow.2) forces every function from D_a to D_b which is represented by some element in the model to be represented by some element in $D_{a \rightarrow b}$. Condition (ForAll) defines $D_{\forall f}$ by intersection. As mentioned earlier, we will assume, unless specifically stated otherwise, that every subset D_a is nonempty. This assumption simplifies the completeness proof but does not affect the interpretation of typing statements in any model.

We interpret typing statements in inference models using environments that map type variables to elements of T and ordinary variables to elements of D. An environment η for inference model I satisfies a typing $M{:}\sigma$, written $\eta \models M{:}\sigma$, if

$$[\![M]\!]\eta \in D_{[\![\sigma]\!]\eta} ,$$

and satisfies type assignment A, written $\eta \models A$, if

$$[\![x]\!]\eta \in D_{[\![\sigma]\!]\eta} \text{ for all } x{:}\sigma \text{ in } A .$$

A model satisfies a typing statement $A \supset M{:}\sigma$ if every environment satisfying A also satisfies $M{:}\sigma$.

3.5 *Examples of Inference Models*

A number of inference models may be constructed using a fairly general method. Given a model $\mathcal{D} = \langle D, \bullet, \epsilon \rangle$ of the untyped lambda calculus, the method requires a subset $Z \subseteq D$ with some special properties. A *zero set* Z of $\mathcal{D}$ is a subset $Z \subseteq D$ such that

$$\forall z \in Z.\ \forall d \in D.\ z \bullet d \in Z .$$

For any zero set $Z \subseteq D$, we can construct an inference model in which the meaning of $\forall t.t$ is Z. The empty set is always a zero set, giving us one easy model construction, but we will see that there are many other interesting examples of zero sets.

Given a zero set Z for model $\mathcal{D} = \langle D, \bullet, \epsilon \rangle$, we define the inference model

$$\mathcal{D}_Z = \langle\langle \mathcal{U}, \rightarrow, \forall \rangle, \mathcal{D}, subset \rangle$$

as follows. Let the set T of types be the set of subsets of D that contain Z, and define the binary operation $\rightarrow$ on types using the simple semantics.[3] To see that T is closed under the operation

$$A \rightarrow B = \{d \in D \mid d \bullet A \in B\},$$

note that for every $z \in Z$, we have $z \bullet A \subseteq Z \subseteq B$. Thus $Z \subseteq A \rightarrow B \in T$. There is no harm in letting the domain $T \Rightarrow T$ of $\forall$ be all functions from T to T, and similarly for $(T \Rightarrow T) \Rightarrow T$, etc. We define $\forall$ using intersection: For any $f \in T \Rightarrow T$, let

$$\forall f = \cap_{A \in T} f(A) .$$

Since $Z \subseteq f(A)$ for all $A \in T$, we have $\forall f \in T$. The association between elements of T and subsets of D is just the straightforward one. For all $A \in T$, let

$$D_A = subset(A) = A .$$

This completes the definition of the inference model $\mathcal{D}_Z$.

To give some concrete examples of inference models without empty types, several untyped models and nonempty zero sets are listed below.

1. For any $\mathcal{D} = \langle D, \bullet, \epsilon \rangle$, the set D is a zero set. In the zero set model $\mathcal{D}_D$, there is only one type.

2. Let $\mathcal{D} = \langle D, \bullet, \epsilon \rangle$ be any ordered model of the untyped lambda calculus with least element $\bot \in D$ such that $\bot \bullet x = \bot$. The singleton $Z = \{\bot\}$ is a zero set. The model based on this zero set is reminiscent of the ideal model since $\{\bot\}$ is the meaning of $\forall t.t$ in both models.

3. Let $\mathcal{D} = \langle D, \bullet, \epsilon \rangle$ be any untyped model and consider the term YK, where

$$Y = \lambda f.(\lambda x.f(xx))(\lambda x.f(xx)), \quad K = \lambda x \lambda y.x$$

as usual. The term Y has the property that $Yx = x(Yx)$. In particular, $YK = K(YK)$. Consequently,

$$(YK)x = (K(YK))x = (YK) ,$$

---

3. We may also use the F-semantics, provided we choose Z so that $\epsilon \bullet Z = Z$.

and the singleton $Z = \{[\![YK]\!]\}$ is a zero set. Since the term YK has no head normal form, this term is equal to $\perp$ in D_∞, P^ω and related models [1, 17, 37].

4. Let $\mathcal{D} = \langle D, \bullet, \epsilon\rangle$ be a term model. The elements of D are equivalence classes $[M]$ of terms. For any variable x, consider the set

$$Z = \{[xM_1 \ldots M_n] \mid M_1, \ldots, M_n \text{ are terms, } n \geq 0\}.$$

Since $[xM_1 \ldots M_n] \bullet [N] = [xM_1 \ldots M_n N]$, Z is a zero set. In general, this Z is an infinite proper subset of D.

While the entire domain D is a type in any zero-set model, we can generalize the construction slightly to produce models in which every type is a proper subset of D. Specifically, under certain assumptions on subsets Z, $W \subseteq D$, we can use the lattice $\mathcal{L}(Z, W)$ of all sets S with $Z \subseteq S \subseteq W$ as the collection of types. Since every typable term will have a value in W, we no longer need Z to be a zero set for all of D. Instead, we only require that

$$\forall z \in Z.\ \forall d \in W.\ z \bullet d \in Z.$$

It is clear that $\mathcal{L}(Z, W)$ is closed under intersection, but we will need another assumption to guarantee that $\mathcal{L}(Z, W)$ is closed under $\rightarrow$. The second condition on Z and W is

$$\text{If } \forall w \in W.\ d \bullet z \in W, \text{ then } d \in W.$$

It is not hard to show that under these two assumptions about subsets Z, $W \subseteq D$, we can construct an inference model by taking $\mathcal{L}(Z, W)$ as the collection of types in the zero set model construction above. The details are left to the interested reader.

4 Completeness of Type Inference

4.1 Completeness for Inference Models without Empty Types

It is relatively straightforward to show that the inference rules are sound.

Lemma 5
If S, $\mathcal{E} \vdash A \supset M{:}\sigma$, then every model satisfying S and $\mathcal{E}$ also satisfies $A \supset M{:}\sigma$.

Proof The proof is by induction on the derivation of $A \supset M{:}\sigma$. We prove the cases for $(\rightarrow E)$, $(\rightarrow I)$, and $(\forall I)$ to show how conditions (Arrow.1), (Arrow.2), and (ForAll) figure in the proof. Rule (remove hyp) relies on the assumption that all types are nonempty, and the remaining cases are straightforward and left to the reader.

Suppose $A \supset MN{:}\sigma$ follows by $(\rightarrow E)$. If $\eta \models A$, then by the inductive assumption,

$$[\![M]\!]\eta \in D_{[\![\sigma\rightarrow\tau]\!]\eta} \text{ and } [\![N]\!]\eta \in D_{[\![\sigma]\!]\eta}\,.$$

Therefore, by property (Arrow.1) of inference models,

$$[\![MN]\!]\eta \in D_{[\![\tau]\!]\eta}\,.$$

If $A \supset \lambda x.M{:}\sigma \rightarrow \tau$ follows from $A, x{:}\sigma \supset M{:}\tau$, then by the inductive hypothesis the function

$$g = \lambda d \in D_{[\![\sigma]\!]\eta}.[\![M]\!]\eta[d/x]$$

maps $D_{[\![\sigma]\!]\eta}$ into $D_{[\![\tau]\!]\eta}$, and so by property (Arrow.2) we have $[\![\lambda x.M]\!]\eta \in D_{[\![\sigma\rightarrow\tau]\!]\eta}$.

For $(\forall I)$, suppose that

$$\mathcal{S}, \mathcal{E} \vdash A \supset M{:}\forall t.\sigma$$

$(\forall I)$, and assume that $\eta \models A$. Let t be a type variable that does not appear free in A. For any $a \in \mathcal{T}$, the environment $\eta[a/t]$ satisfies A, so by the inductive hypothesis,

$$[\![M]\!]\eta = [\![M]\!]\eta[a/t] \in D_{[\![\sigma]\!]\eta[a/t]}\,.$$

Therefore, by condition (ForAll),

$$[\![M]\!]\eta \in \cap_{a\in\mathcal{T}} D_{[\![\sigma]\!]\eta[a/t]} = D_{[\![\forall t.\sigma]\!]\eta}\,.$$

This finishes the proof of the Lemma. □

We now show that the rules are complete. The proof uses a syntactic model construction that is somewhat similar to the completeness proof of [15].

Theorem 1

Let $\mathcal{S}$ be any set of typing hypotheses of the form $B \supset N{:}\tau$ and let $\mathcal{E}$ be any lambda theory. There is an inference model $\mathcal{I}$ without empty types satisfying precisely the equations in $\mathcal{E}$ and with the property that $\mathcal{S}, \mathcal{E} \vdash B \supset M{:}\sigma$ iff $\mathcal{I}$ satisfies $B \supset M{:}\sigma$.

Note that $\mathcal{S}, \mathcal{E} \vdash B \supset M{:}\sigma$ for every $B \supset M{:}\sigma$ in $\mathcal{S}$, so that the model $\mathcal{I}$ in the statement of the theorem must also satisfy $\mathcal{S}$.

Proof We will construct an inference model $\mathcal{I} = \langle \mathcal{T}, \mathcal{D}, \mathit{subset}\rangle$ with the properties given in the statement of the theorem. Let $\mathcal{D} = \langle D, \bullet, \epsilon\rangle$ be the term model for $\mathcal{E}$, so that

$$D = \{[M]_{\mathcal{E}} \mid M \text{ is an untyped term}\}\,.$$

By construction, $\mathcal{D}$ satisfies $\mathcal{E}$. It remains to define $\mathcal{T} = \langle \mathcal{U}, \rightarrow, \forall \rangle$ and subsets $D_a \subseteq D$. We let $\mathcal{T}$ be the term structure of constructor expressions modulo β,η-conversion described in Section 3.3. Recall that the elements of $T = T^{\mathcal{U}}$ are equivalence classes of constructor expressions

$$[\sigma] = \{\tau \mid \sigma\ \beta,\eta\text{-converts to } \tau\}.$$

Let A be any infinite set of variable statements $x{:}\sigma$ such that no x appears twice in A and for every type expression σ, there are infinitely many variables x with $x{:}\sigma \in A$. We define *subset* by

$$D_{[\sigma]} = \{[M] \mid S, \mathcal{E} \vdash B \supset M{:}\sigma, \text{ some finite } B \subseteq A\}.$$

By rule (type eq), the mapping *subset* is well-defined. Note that by choice of A, every $D_{[\sigma]}$ is nonempty.

We now show that I satisfies every $B \supset M{:}\sigma$ provable from S and $\mathcal{E}$ (which includes all $B \supset M{:}\sigma$ in S). Suppose $S, \mathcal{E} \vdash B \supset M{:}\sigma$, and let η be any environment satisfying B. We must show that $\eta \models M{:}\sigma$. Let S be any substitution such that for any free ordinary variable x in B or M,

$$\eta(x) = [Sx],$$

and for any free type variable t in B or σ,

$$\eta(t) = [St],$$

By the usual properties of term models [1, 23],

$$[\![M]\!]\eta = [SM] \text{ and } [\![\sigma]\!]\eta = [S\sigma],$$

Since $\eta \models B$, we have

$$S, \mathcal{E} \vdash A \supset SB,$$

Therefore, by the substitution typing rule (subst),

$$S, \mathcal{E} \vdash A \supset SM{:}\,S\sigma,$$

Thus $[SM] \in D_{[S\sigma]}$ and $\eta \models M{:}\sigma$. This shows that $I = \langle \mathcal{T}, \mathcal{D}, subset \rangle$ satisfies $B \supset M{:}\sigma$.

For the converse, we must show that if $B \supset M{:}\,\sigma$ holds in I, then $S, \mathcal{E} \vdash B \supset M{:}\sigma$. Given a typing $B \supset M{:}\,\sigma$ that holds in I, let S be a substitution mapping each type variable to itself and mapping each ordinary variable x with $x{:}\tau \in B$ to some y with $y{:}\tau \in A$. Let η_0 be the environment mapping each type variable t to its equivalence class $[t]$ and mapping each ordinary variable x to the equivalence class $[Sx]$ of the ordinary variable Sx. For each $x{:}\tau \in B$, we have

$$\eta_0(x) = [Sx] \in D_{[\tau]} = D_{[\![\tau]\!]\eta_0}\,,$$

and so $\eta_0 \models B$. Since $B \supset M{:}\sigma$ holds in $\mathcal{I}$, it follows that

$$[\![M]\!]\eta_0 = [SM] \in D_{[\sigma]}\,,$$

and so by definition of $\mathcal{I}$ we have

$$S, \mathcal{E} \vdash A_1 \supset SM{:}\sigma$$

for some finite $A_1 \subseteq A$. By choice of S and derived typing rule (fv), we may assume $A_1 = SB$. Since S only renames ordinary variables, M is a substitution instance of SM, and similarly for B and SB. Therefore, by Lemma 2 we conclude that $S, \mathcal{E} \vdash B \supset M{:}\sigma$.

It remains to check that $\mathcal{I}$ satisfies the definition of an inference model. We verify property (Arrow.1) first. Suppose that $[M] \in D_{[\sigma\to\tau]}$. Then $S, \mathcal{E} \vdash B_1 \supset M{:}\sigma \to \tau$ for some finite $B_1 \subseteq A$, and similarly, for any $[N]$ in $D_{[\sigma]}$, we have $S, \mathcal{E} \vdash B_2 \supset N{:}\sigma$ for some finite $B_2 \subseteq A$. Therefore,

$$S, \mathcal{E} \vdash B_1 \cup B_2 \supset MN{:}\tau$$

by rules (add hyp) and $(\to E)$. Consequently $[M] \bullet [N] = [MN] \in D_{[\tau]}$. This shows that (Arrow.1) holds. We now show (Arrow.2); i.e., if $[M] \bullet D_{[\sigma]} \subseteq D_{[\tau]}$ then $\epsilon \bullet [M] \in D_{[\sigma\to\tau]}$. Here we use the fact that A supplies infinitely many variables of each type. If $[M] \bullet D_{[\sigma]} \subseteq D_{[\tau]}$ then there is some variable x not free in M with $x{:}\sigma \in A$. By definition of $D_{[\tau]}$ we have

$$S, \mathcal{E} \vdash B \supset Mx{:}\tau$$

for some finite $B \subseteq A$. In light of rule (fv), we may assume that $x{:}\sigma \in B$. Therefore, by rule $(\to I)$,

$$S, \mathcal{E} \vdash B \supset \lambda x.Mx{:}\sigma \to \tau\,.$$

This shows that $[\lambda x.Mx] = \epsilon \bullet [M] \in D_{[\sigma\to\tau]}$, demonstrating (Arrow.2).

We show (ForAll) by demonstrating both containments. If $[M] \in D_{[\forall t.\sigma]}$, then for any τ, we have $[M] \in D_{[[\tau/t]\sigma]}$ by rule $(\forall E)$. Conversely, if $[M]$ is an element of every $D_{[[\tau/t]\sigma]}$, then for some variable s not free in $A(x)$ for any x free in M, and some finite $B \subseteq A$, we have

$$S, \mathcal{E} \vdash B \supset M{:}[s/t]\sigma\,.$$

Therefore, $S, \mathcal{E} \vdash B \supset M{:}\forall s.[s/t]\sigma$ by $(\forall I)$ and $S, \mathcal{E} \vdash B \supset M{:}\forall t.\sigma$ by (type eq). Thus $[M] \in D_{[\forall t.\sigma]}$. This demonstrates (ForAll) and concludes the proof of the theorem. □

4.2 *Completeness for Simple Semantics*

In this section, we will prove a completeness theorem for a particular class of inference models. A *simple inference model* is an inference model satisfying

$$D_{a \to b} = \{d \in D \mid d \bullet D_a \subseteq D_b\}.$$

Put a different way, $d \in D_{a \to b}$ iff $e \in D_a$ implies $d \bullet e \in D_b$. The typing rule

$$\text{(simple)} \quad \frac{A \supset \lambda x.Mx{:}\sigma \to \tau}{A \supset M{:}\sigma \to \tau}, \quad x \text{ not free in } M,$$

is sound for simple inference models since

$$(\lambda x.Mx)y = My$$

holds in every lambda model (provided x is not free in M). Rule (simple) is a derived rule in Curry's theory of functionality (see [15]), but as we will see in Section 6.1, it is not a derived rule in the system we have considered so far.

If $A \supset M{:}\sigma$ is derivable from a set S of typing assumptions and set $\mathcal{E}$ of equations, using (simple) together with the rules presented in Section 2, we write

$$S, \mathcal{E} \vdash_s A \supset M{:}\sigma.$$

It can be shown that $\vdash_s A \supset M{:}\sigma$ if and only if there is some N that η-reduces to M with $\vdash A \supset N{:}\sigma$. We have the following completeness theorem for simple inference models.

Theorem 2

Let S be any set of typing hypotheses of the form $B \supset N{:}\tau$ and let $\mathcal{E}$ be any lambda theory. There is a simple inference model $\mathcal{I}$ without empty types satisfying precisely the equations in $\mathcal{E}$ and with the property that $S, \mathcal{E} \vdash_s B \supset M{:}\sigma$ iff $\mathcal{I}$ satisfies $B \supset M{:}\sigma$.

Proof The proof of Theorem 2 differs from the proof of Theorem 1 only in the verification of condition (Arrow.2). We show that

$$[M] \bullet D_\sigma \subseteq D_\tau \text{ implies } [\lambda x.Mx] \in D_{\sigma \to \tau},$$

as in the proof of Theorem 1. Then, by (simple) and the definition of $D_{\sigma \to \tau}$, we conclude $[M] \in D_{\sigma \to \tau}$. □

4.3 $\mathcal{F}$ Semantics

We may also consider the $\mathcal{F}$ semantics introduced in [15, 16] and further studied in [7]. An *$\mathcal{F}$ inference model* is an inference model satisfying

$$D_{a \to b} = \{d \in \mathcal{F} \mid d \bullet D_a \subseteq D_b\},$$

where $\mathcal{F}$ is the range of ϵ. As noted in Section 3, the significance of $\mathcal{F}$ is that every function from D to D that is represented by some element of D has a unique representative in $\mathcal{F}$. In [16], the Curry typing rules are shown to be complete for the $\mathcal{F}$ semantics of $\to$. We do not know whether $\vdash$ is complete for $\mathcal{F}$ inference models.

4.4 Completeness for Quotient-Set Semantics

Another semantics of typing is the quotient-set semantics. We will discuss this semantics only briefly, referring the reader to the literature for further information. The quotient-set semantics has its origins in the study of effective functionals [18, 30] and is closely related to Kreisel's structure HEO (see [36]). A second-order version of HEO, called HEO_2, is defined in [11, 36] and was rediscovered independently by Moggi and Plotkin (private communication, 1985). The name "quotient-set" seems to originate with Hindley [15], where the idea of using quotients as a semantics of type inference is credited to Scott [34]. Further work is reported in the more recent papers [4, 28].

The quotient-set interpretation of types differs from the inference models considered so far in that types are associated with quotients of subsets instead of subsets of a lambda model. In the notation we have been using, this means that instead of having a mapping *subset* from T to subsets of D, a quotient-set model has a mapping *relation* from T to equivalence relations on subsets of D. The intuition behind this approach is that different types often have different notions of equality associated with them. For example, two elements d_1 and d_2 of a lambda model may be considered equal elements of type $s \to t$ if $d_1 \bullet e = d_2 \bullet e$ for all $e \in s$, but different elements of type $r \to t$ if they behave differently when applied to some element of r.

We will think of a symmetric and transitive binary relation R on D as giving us both a set $|R| = \{d \mid \langle d, d\rangle \in R\}$ and an equivalence relation R on $|R|$. Thus *relation* will be a mapping from T to symmetric and transitive relations. More specifically, a *quotient-set inference model* is a triple $\langle \mathcal{T}, \mathcal{D}, relation\rangle$ with $\mathcal{T}$ a type structure, $\mathcal{D} = \langle D, \bullet, \epsilon\rangle$ a lambda model, and *relation* a mapping from T to symmetric and transitive relations on D. The mapping *relation* must satisfy three conditions which are similar to the conditions on *subset* in the definition of inference model.

$(\text{Arrow.1})_{rel}$ If $\langle d_1, d_2\rangle \in relation(a \to b)$ and $\langle e_1, e_2\rangle \in relation(a)$, then $\langle d_1 \bullet e_1, d_2 \bullet e_2\rangle \in relation(b)$.

$(\text{Arrow.2})_{model}$ If $\langle d_1 \bullet e_1, d_2 \bullet e_2\rangle \in relation(b)$ for all $\langle e_1, e_2\rangle \in relation(a)$, then $\langle \epsilon \bullet d_1, \epsilon \bullet d_2\rangle \in relation(a \to b)$.

$(\text{ForAll})_{rel}$ $relation(\forall f) = \bigcap_{a\in T} relation(f(a))$.

The definitions of satisfaction and validity of typing statements over quotient-set models are similar to the definitions over ordinary inference models, with

$$\eta \models M{:}\sigma \text{ iff } \langle [\![M]\!]\eta, [\![M]\!]\eta\rangle \in relation([\![\sigma]\!]\eta)\,.$$

A completeness theorem for quotient-set inference models may be proved just by observing that subsets may be regarded as relations. Specifically, given an ordinary inference model $I = \langle \mathcal{T}, \mathcal{D}, subset\rangle$, we can define a quotient-set inference model $I_{rel} = \langle \mathcal{T}, \mathcal{D}, relation\rangle$ with the same typing theory just by taking

$$relation(a) = subset(a) \times subset(a)$$

for every $a \in T$. It is easy to see that a typing statement holds in I if and only if it holds in I_{rel}. Consequently, $\vdash$ is complete for quotient-set inference models. This "encoding" of subsets by relations is also used to prove completeness of Curry typing for the quotient-set semantics in [15], where the idea is credited to Mario Coppo.

We can prove a second completeness theorem for a more specialized class of quotient-set inference models which resemble simple inference models. (This more specialized class of models is actually closer to the spirit of previous work on quotient-set semantics.) A *simple quotient-set model* is a quotient-set inference model $\langle \mathcal{T}, \mathcal{D}, relation\rangle$ satisfying

$(\text{Arrow})_{s\text{-}rel}$ $\langle d_1, d_2\rangle \in relation(a \to b)$ iff $\langle d_1 \bullet e_1, d_2 \bullet e_2\rangle \in relation(b)$ for all $\langle e_1, e_2\rangle \in relation(a)$.

It is worth noting that $(\text{Arrow})_{s\text{-}rel}$ implies both $(\text{Arrow.1})_{rel}$ and $(\text{Arrow.2})_{rel}$. It is also easy to check that if I is a simple inference model, then I_{rel} (defined above) is a simple quotient-set model. Therefore $\vdash_s$ is complete for simple quotient-set models. Further information about quotient-set inference models may be found in [4, 28].

4.5 *Completeness with Empty Types*

The typing rules and soundness and completeness theorems we have seen so far are based on the assumption that all types are nonempty. If we consider models with empty types, then all of the axioms and inference rules remain sound, except (remove hyp). To see why (remove hyp) becomes unsound with empty types, consider the typing statement $\lambda x.k{:}a \rightarrow b$, where k is a term constant (or any term) and a, b are type constants (or any types). If types a and b are empty, then certainly $\lambda x.k{:}a \rightarrow b$ holds, since $\lambda x.k$ denotes an element in the range of ϵ that maps every element of a to some element of b. However, from $\lambda x.k{:}a \rightarrow b$ we can easily prove $\{x{:}a\} \supset k{:}b$, which by rule (remove hyp) allows us to conclude that $k{:}b$. But since we assumed that b was empty, this conclusion is false. In short, (remove hyp) is unsound since $B, x{:}\sigma \supset M{:}\tau$ might hold simply because σ is empty, in which case it would be erroneous to infer that $B \supset M{:}\tau$.

An analysis of equational reasoning for second-order lambda calculus over models which may have empty types is given in [24]. Most of that discussion also applies to typing with empty types. In particular, we may prove completeness by extending the axiom system. However, the form of completeness with empty types is weaker than the form of completeness without empty types. This is because certain typing assumptions express "disjunctive" information, and so it is impossible to construct a single model satisfying only the logical consequences of these assumptions.

The inference system for models that may have empty types is obtained by extending the syntax of type assignments, as in [24], and by adopting two additional rules. In a type assignment, a basic typing statement $x{:}\sigma$ has the effect of assuming that σ is nonempty (since otherwise σ could not have x as a member). To reason about empty types, it is also useful to be able to assume that certain types are empty. An *extended type assignment* is a finite set A of basic typing statements $x{:}\sigma$ about variables and *emptiness statements* of the form $empty(\sigma)$. An environment η satisfies an extended type assignment A, written $\eta \models A$, if $\eta(x) \in D_{[\![\sigma]\!]\eta}$ for every $x{:}\sigma \in A$, and $D_{[\![\sigma]\!]\eta} = \varnothing$ for every $empty(\sigma) \in A$. The definitions of satisfaction and validity of typing statements $A \supset M{:}\sigma$, with A an extended type assignment, are straightforward.

Since it is inconsistent to assume that a type is both empty and not, we have the axiom scheme

$$(empty\,I) \qquad x{:}\sigma, empty(\sigma) \supset M{:}\tau\,.$$

This lets us introduce emptiness hypotheses into typing derivations. The inference rule for discharging emptiness hypotheses is

$$(empty\,E) \qquad \frac{A, x{:}\sigma \supset M{:}\tau, \; A, empty(\sigma) \supset M{:}\tau}{A \supset M{:}\tau}, \quad x \text{ not free in } M\,.$$

Intuitively, this rule says that if $A \supset M{:}\tau$ holds when we assume σ is not empty,[4] and also when we assume σ is empty, then we must have $A \supset M{:}\tau$.

4. Since x does not occur free in M, the only effect of $x{:}\sigma$ is to assume that σ is nonempty.

We write $S, \mathcal{E} \vdash_e A \supset M{:}\sigma$ if the typing statement $A \supset M{:}\sigma$ is provable from S and $\mathcal{E}$ using the typing axioms (var) and (*empty I*), and inference rules ($\rightarrow I$), ($\rightarrow E$), ($\forall I$), ($\forall E$), (add hyp), (type eq), (term eq), (subst), and (*empty E*).

With empty types, we no longer have minimal models for every typing theory. To see this, consider the typing statement $\lambda x.y{:}a \rightarrow b$. This may hold if a is empty, or if every term has type b. In the case that a is empty, we have $\lambda x.y{:}a \rightarrow c$ for any other type c, while if a is not empty, then we must have $y{:}b$. However, neither of the typing statements $\lambda x.y{:}a \rightarrow c$ or $y{:}b$ is logically implied by $\lambda x.y{:}a \rightarrow b$, so any model for $\lambda x.y{:}a \rightarrow b$ must satisfy some statement that is not a logical consequence of this typing statement. For this reason, we have only the weaker form of completeness for typing with empty types.

Theorem 3

Let S be any set of typing hypotheses $B \supset N{:}\tau$, and let $\mathcal{E}$ be any lambda theory. Then $S, \mathcal{E} \vdash_e A \supset M{:}\sigma$ if and only if for every model $\mathcal{I}$ satisfying S and $\mathcal{E}$ and every $\mathcal{I}$ environment $\eta \models A$, we have $\eta \models M{:}\sigma$.

Proof Suppose we are given S and $\mathcal{E}$ and a typing statement $A_0 \supset M_0{:}\sigma_0$ that is not provable from S and $\mathcal{E}$. We will construct a model $\mathcal{I}$ satisfying S and $\mathcal{E}$, but not $A_0 \supset M_0{:}\sigma_0$. The construction differs from the proof of Theorem 1 primarily in the definition of infinite type assignment A. Instead of letting A have infinitely many variables of every type, which would produce an inference model with every type nonempty, we must use S, $\mathcal{E}$, and $A_0 \supset M_0{:}\sigma_0$ to decide which types will be nonempty.

Let $\tau_1, \tau_2, \tau_3, \ldots$ be an enumeration of all type expressions. Beginning with A_0 as given, we will construct a sequence of infinite extended type assignments $A_0 \subseteq A_1 \subseteq A_2 \subseteq \ldots$ with the property that each A_i contains, for all $j < i$, either $empty(\tau_j)$ or $x{:}\tau_j$ for infinitely many variables x. In addition, we will *not* have $S, \mathcal{E} \vdash_e B \supset M_0{:}\sigma_0$ for any finite $B \subseteq A_i$.

Given A_i, we define A_{i+1} as follows. Let y be some fresh variable not in A_i and not free in M_0. If

$$S, \mathcal{E} \nvdash_e B, y{:}\tau_{i+1} \supset M_0{:}\sigma_0$$

for every finite $B \subseteq A_i$, then we let $x_1, x_2, \ldots$ be any infinite sequence of distinct fresh variables, and let

$$A_{i+1} = A_i \cup \{x_1{:}\tau_{i+1}, x_2{:}\tau_{i+1}, \ldots\}.$$

Otherwise, we let $A_{i+1} = A_i \cup \{empty(\tau_{i+1})\}$. In the first case, it is easy to see that

$$S, \mathcal{E} \nvdash_e B \supset M_0{:}\sigma_0$$

for every finite $B \subseteq A_{i+1}$. However, if we have put $empty(\tau_{i+1})$ in A_{i+1}, then we must use (*empty E*) to show that we cannot prove $B \supset M_0{:}\sigma_0$ for any finite $B \subseteq A_{i+1}$.

Suppose, for the sake of deriving a contradiction, that $empty(\tau_{i+1}) \in A_{i+1}$ and that

$$S, \mathcal{E} \vdash_e B \supset M_0{:}\sigma_0$$

for some $B \subseteq A_{i+1}$. Since we could not prove $B \supset M_0{:}\sigma_0$ for $B \subseteq A_i$, by the inductive hypothesis of the construction, it must be that

$$S, \mathcal{E} \vdash_e B, empty(\tau_{i+1}) \supset M_0{:}\sigma_0$$

for some $B \subseteq A_i$. We also know that

$$S, \mathcal{E} \vdash_e B, y{:}\tau_{i+1} \supset M_0{:}\sigma_0$$

for some $B \subseteq A_i$, since otherwise we would have added $x_1{:}\tau_{i+1}, x_2{:}\tau_{i+1}, \ldots$ to A_i. Therefore, using rule (*empty E*), we can prove $B \supset M_0{:}\sigma_0$ for some finite $B \subseteq A_i$, which contradicts the induction hypothesis of the construction. Therefore, in the case that $A_{i+1} = A_i \cup \{empty(\tau_{i+1})\}$, we cannot prove $B \supset M_0{:}\sigma_0$ for any finite $B \subseteq A_{i+1}$.

Using (*empty I*), it is easy to see that we do not have both $empty(\tau)$ and $x{:}\tau$ in any A_i, since otherwise this would allow us to prove $B \supset M_0{:}\sigma_0$ for some $B \subseteq A_i$. Thus, if we let A be the union of the A_i's, then for any type τ, we either have infinitely many variables of type τ, or $empty(\tau) \in A$, but not both.

We now construct an inference model $\mathcal{I}$ using A as in the proof of Theorem 1. If $S, \mathcal{E} \vdash_e B \supset M{:}\sigma$, then we show that $\mathcal{I}$ satisfies $B \supset M{:}\sigma$ as in the proof of Theorem 1, and it is easy to show that $\mathcal{I}$ does not satisfy $A_0 \supset M_0{:}\sigma_0$ by the construction of $\mathcal{I}$. The verification of conditions (Arrow.1) and (ForAll) are as before, but (Arrow.2) is complicated slightly by the presence of empty types.

Assume that $[M] \bullet D_{[\sigma]} \subseteq D_{[\tau]}$. We must show that $\epsilon \bullet [M] \in D_{[\sigma\to\tau]}$. There are two cases, depending on whether or not $D_{[\sigma]}$ is empty. If $D_{[\sigma]}$ is not empty, then we have infinitely many x with $x{:}\sigma \in A$, and we use the argument for (Arrow.2) given in the proof of Theorem 1. If $D_{[\sigma]}$ is empty, then $empty(\sigma) \in A$, and so using axiom (*empty I*) we have

$$S, \mathcal{E} \vdash_e B, x{:}\sigma \supset Mx{:}\tau$$

for fresh x and some finite $B \subseteq A$ with $empty(\sigma) \in B$. By ($\to I$), this gives us

$$S, \mathcal{E} \vdash_e B \supset \lambda x.Mx{:}\tau\,,$$

which shows that

$$[\lambda x.Mx] = \epsilon \bullet [M] \in D_{[\sigma\to\tau]}\,.$$

This proves the theorem. □

The proof of Theorem 3 may also be adapted to prove completeness for typing over simple inference models and quotient-set inference models that may have empty types.

5 *Pure Typing*

5.1 *Second-Order Lambda Calculus*

The second-order lambda calculus, developed in [11, 32], is a typed expression language. The types that appear in this language are the functional types of the form $\sigma \to \tau$ and polymorphic types $\forall t.\sigma$ defined in Section 2. In fact, the typing rules for second-order lambda calculus and the first seven type inference rules presented in Section 2 are essentially identical. As discussed in [8, 9, 29, 32], a number of polymorphic programming languages may be viewed as extensions or syntactic variants of second-order lambda calculus. Since the syntax of second-order lambda calculus is somewhat cluttered with type expressions, it would be useful to develop algorithms for automatically inserting types into partially-typed second-order lambda expressions. This kind of automatic deduction of types is used in the ML programming language [12, 25, 26], but ML typing is much less flexible than typing based on second-order lambda calculus (cf. [19, 22]). In the remaining sections of the paper, we explore some properties of "pure" polymorphic typing based on second-order lambda calculus.

Since we will use terms of second-order lambda calculus to characterize some relationships between types, we review the syntax of second-order terms. We define the syntax using typing rules similar to those used in Section 2:

$$(\mathrm{var})_2 \qquad \{x{:}\,\sigma\} \supset x{:}\,\sigma\,,$$

$$(\to I)_2 \qquad \frac{A, x{:}\sigma \supset M{:}\tau}{A \supset \lambda x \in \sigma.M{:}\sigma \to \tau}\,,$$

$$(\to E)_2 \qquad \frac{A \supset M{:}\sigma \to \tau,\ A \supset N{:}\sigma}{A \supset MN{:}\tau}\,,$$

$$(\forall I)_2 \qquad \frac{A \supset M{:}\sigma}{A \supset \lambda t.M{:}\forall t.\sigma}\,, \quad \text{provided } t \text{ does not occur free in } A\,,$$

$$(\forall E)_2 \qquad \frac{A \supset M{:}\forall t.\sigma}{A \supset M\tau{:}[\tau/t]\sigma}\,,$$

$$\text{(add hyp)} \quad \frac{A \supset M{:}\tau}{A, x{:}\sigma \supset M{:}\tau}, \quad x \text{ does not occur in } A\,,$$

$$\text{(type eq)} \quad \frac{A \supset M{:}\sigma,\ \sigma = \tau}{A \supset M{:}\tau}\,.$$

Note that if a second-order lambda term M has any type with respect to the type assignment A, then this type is unique up to type equality. We write $\vdash_2 A \supset P{:}\sigma$ if $A \supset P{:}\sigma$ can be derived using the rules above.

5.2 *Properties of Pure Typing*

The syntax of second-order lambda calculus is related to the type inference rules of Section 2 in a relatively straightforward way. If P is a second-order lambda term, then we let *erase(P)* be the result of erasing all type information from P. The function erase has a straightforward inductive definition; the nontrivial clauses of the definition are

$$erase(\lambda x \in \sigma.M) = \lambda x.erase(M)\,,$$

$$erase(\lambda t.M) = erase(M), \quad \text{and}$$

$$erase(M\tau) = erase(M)\,.$$

It is not hard to show that for any untyped term M, we have $\vdash A \supset M{:}\sigma$ if and only if there is a second-order lambda term P with $erase(P) = M$ and $\vdash_2 A \supset P{:}\sigma$ (see Theorem 4.1 of [19]). Furthermore, the derivation of $A \supset M{:}\sigma$ corresponds directly to the derivation of $A \supset P{:}\sigma$ (which follows the structure of P). Therefore, given M, the problem of finding P with $erase(P) = M$ is equivalent to the problem of finding a derivation of $A \supset M{:}\sigma$ using only α-equivalence in rule (term eq).

It is not hard to see that β-redexes in an untyped term *erase(P)* correspond exactly to typed β-redexes in the typed term P. Therefore, whenever M β-reduces to N we also know that *erase(M)* β-reduces to *erase(N)*. This observation can be used to prove the following lemma.

Lemma 6
If $\vdash A \supset M{:}\sigma$ and M β-reduces to N, then $\vdash A \supset N{:}\sigma$.

From Lemma 4 and Lemma 6, we have the following corollary of the completeness theorem.

Corollary 1
If M is in β-normal form, and $\models A \supset M{:}\sigma$, then $\vdash A \supset M{:}\sigma$.

It is worth noting that the converse of Lemma 6 is false: $A \supset M{:}\sigma$ may not be provable, even if M β-reduces to N with $\vdash A \supset N{:}\sigma$. Since $\vdash A \supset M{:}\sigma$ implies that M is strongly normalizable [9, 11], there will be many terms equal to $\lambda x.x$, for example, which cannot be typed. One term that cannot be typed is

$$(\lambda w\, \lambda x.x)(\lambda y.yy\, \lambda y.yy)\,.$$

Although this term reduces to $\lambda x.x$ in one step, it is not strongly normalizing since the subterm $(\lambda y.yy\, \lambda y.yy)$ may be reduced infinitely many times.

5.3 *Typing Rules Based on Containment*

We may gain some insight into pure typing derivations by reformulating the inference rules so that proofs correspond more closely to the structure of terms. In the Curry inference system [2, 5, 14, 15, 25] consisting only of $(\rightarrow I)$ and $(\rightarrow E)$, every proof of a statement $A \supset MN$, for example, must end with rule $(\rightarrow E)$. Similarly, any proof of a typing for an abstraction $\lambda x.M$ must end with rule $(\rightarrow I)$. It is this property of the Curry system, coupled with the fact that the inference rules are defined by schemes, that gives Curry typing principal type schemes (cf. [14]). While it seems unlikely that the polymorphic inference rules are equivalent to an inference system consisting only of "syntax-directed" rules, we will be able to replace $(\forall I)$ and $(\forall E)$ by a single "syntax-independent" rule based on containments between types. In order to do so, however, we will need to alter rules $(\rightarrow I)$ and $(\rightarrow E)$ slightly. One benefit of reformulating the inference rules is the characterization of pure typing shown in Fig. 1, which provides a simple bound on the lengths of derivations in the containment-based system to be presented below. In this characterization, it is convenient to write $A[x{:}\sigma]$ for the type assignment $(A-\{x{:}\,A(x)\})\cup\{x{:}\sigma\}$.

The correctness of this characterization follows easily from Theorem 4 be-

Figure 1. Characterization of pure typing.

$\vdash A \supset x{:}\tau$	iff $A(x) \subseteq \tau$
$\vdash A \supset MN{:}\rho$	if and only if there exist $\vec{s}$, σ, τ such that $\vdash A \supset M{:}\forall\vec{s}(\sigma \rightarrow \tau)$, $\vdash A \supset N{:}\forall\vec{s}.\sigma$, and $\forall\vec{s}.\tau \subseteq \rho$.
$\vdash A \supset \lambda x.M{:}\,\rho$	if and only if there exist $\vec{s}$, σ, τ such that $\vdash A[x{:}\sigma] \supset M{:}\tau$, the list $\vec{s}$ only contains type variables not free in A, and $\forall\vec{s}.(\sigma \rightarrow \tau) \subseteq \rho$.

low by a simple induction on containment-based proofs. It is apparent from this characterization that testing $\vdash A \supset M{:}\sigma$ can be reduced to testing containments between types and performing simple operations on sets of the form

$$Types(\vec{x}, N) = \{\vec{\sigma}, \tau \mid \vdash \{x_1{:}\sigma_1, \ldots, x_n{:}\sigma_n\} \supset N{:}\tau\}$$

for terms N simpler than M. Although it will be easy to see that $\subseteq$ is decidable, we do not know how to represent $Types(\vec{x}, N)$ simply, or how to compute intersections of such sets. It would certainly be convenient if $Types(\varnothing, M)$, for example, consisted of the set of types which contain some minimal "principal" type for M, but this does not seem to be the case. However, we may have unique minimal typings if we consider the rules for typing over simple inference models. This will be discussed in Section 6.

We now present a type inference system based on containments between types. The inference system consists of the axiom for typing variables, together with (add hyp) and the following typing rules:

$$(\to I_\forall) \quad \frac{A, x{:}\sigma \supset M{:}\tau}{A \supset \lambda x.M{:}\forall\vec{s}(\sigma \to \tau)}, \quad \vec{s} \text{ lists type variables not free in } A,$$

$$(\to E_\forall) \quad \frac{A \supset M{:}\forall\vec{s}(\sigma \to \tau),\ A \supset N{:}\forall\vec{s}.\sigma}{A \supset MN{:}\forall\vec{s}.\tau},$$

$$(\text{cont}) \quad \frac{A \supset M{:}\sigma,\ \sigma \subseteq \tau}{A \supset N{:}\tau}.$$

Since we will no longer be concerned with sets of typing hypotheses, rules (remove hyp) and (subst) are no longer needed (by Lemma 1 of Section 2).

The single subsidiary rule for deducing containments is the axiom scheme

$$(\text{sub}) \quad \forall\vec{t}.\sigma \subseteq \forall\vec{r}.[\vec{\tau}/\vec{t}]\sigma, \quad \text{where } \vec{r} \text{ are not free in } \forall\vec{t}.\sigma,$$

which includes renaming of bound variables as a special case. The substitution axiom (sub) is similar to to the notion of generic instance considered in [6]. It is easy to see that the instances of (sub) are decidable, using an algorithm similar to unification [31, 33]. One important special case of (sub) is $\forall t.\sigma \subseteq [\tau/t]\sigma$, and another is $\sigma \subseteq \forall t.\sigma$ if t is not free in σ. Some other admissible containment rules are

$$(\text{ref}) \quad \sigma \subseteq \sigma,$$

$$(\text{trans}) \quad \rho \subseteq \sigma,\ \sigma \subseteq \tau \vdash \rho \subseteq \tau,$$

$$(\text{congruence}) \quad \sigma \subseteq \tau \vdash \forall t.\sigma \subseteq \forall t.\tau.$$

We write $\vdash_c A \supset M{:}\sigma$ if $A \supset M{:}\sigma$ can be proved using the rules above, and (term eq) restricted to α-equivalence of terms. The following lemmas are used to show that $\vdash$ and $\vdash_c$ are equivalent for pure typing.

Lemma 7

Let x be an ordinary variable that does not occur free in term M. Then

$$\text{(i)} \quad A \supset M{:}\forall\vec{s}(\sigma \to \tau) \vdash A \supset \lambda x.Mx{:}\forall\vec{s}.\sigma \to \forall\vec{s}.\tau$$

and

$$\text{(ii)} \quad A \supset M{:}\forall\vec{s}(\sigma \to \tau), A \supset N{:}\forall\vec{s}.\sigma \vdash A \supset MN{:}\forall\vec{s}.\tau$$

Proof To simplify notation, let us assume that the type variables in $\vec{s}$ are not free in A. If not, then we just rename bound type variables. For x as in the statement of the Lemma, we can prove $A, x{:}\forall\vec{s}.\sigma \supset Mx{:}\tau$ from the variable-typing axiom using rules ($\forall E$) and ($\to E$). Therefore, using rules ($\forall I$) followed by ($\to I$), we may prove $A \supset \lambda x.Mx{:}\forall\vec{s}.\ \sigma \to \forall\vec{s}.\tau$. The proof of the second part of the Lemma uses rules ($\forall E$), ($\to E$) and ($\forall I$). □

Lemma 8

Suppose $A \supset M{:}\sigma \vdash A \supset M{:}\tau$ using only rules ($\forall I$) and ($\forall E$). Let $\vec{s} = s_1, \ldots, s_n$ contain all free type variables in σ that are not free in A. Then $\forall\vec{s}.\sigma \subseteq \tau$ is an instance of the containment axiom (sub). Conversely, if $\forall\vec{s}.\sigma \subseteq \tau$ is an instance of the containment axiom (sub), then for any term M, we have

$$A \supset M{:}\forall\vec{s}.\sigma \vdash A \supset M{:}\tau$$

using only rules ($\forall I$) and ($\forall E$).

Proof Suppose $A \supset M{:}\sigma \vdash A \supset M{:}\tau$ using only ($\forall I$) and ($\forall E$). Let $\vec{s}$ be a finite list containing all free type variables in σ that are not free in A. Let $\mathcal{V}$ be the set of type variables free in M which do not appear free in A. Note that by choice of $\vec{s}$, no $v \in \mathcal{V}$ occurs free in $\forall\vec{s}.\sigma$. The derivation $A \supset M{:}\sigma \vdash A \supset M{:}\tau$ is a sequence

$$A \supset M{:}\sigma_0 \vdash \ldots \vdash A \supset M{:}\sigma_m$$

with $\sigma_0 = \sigma$ and $\sigma_m = \tau$, and each σ_{i+1} the result of either substituting for a bound variable in σ_i or binding some variable in $\mathcal{V}$. We use induction on i to show that

(*) For any $\vec{v}$ from $\mathcal{V}$, the containment $\forall\vec{s}.\sigma \subseteq \forall\vec{v}.\sigma_i$ is an instance of the axiom scheme (sub).

The case $i = 0$ is trivial.

Assume that each $\forall\vec{s}.\sigma \subseteq \forall\vec{v}.\sigma_i$ is an instance of (sub). If σ_{i+1} is the result of quantifying over some variable from $\mathcal{V}$, then the (*) follows immediately from the inductive hypothesis. Otherwise, note that

$$\sigma_i = \forall u, \vec{v}.[\vec{\rho}/\vec{r}]\sigma$$

for some u, $\vec{v}$, $\vec{r}$, and $\vec{\rho}$. If σ_{i+1} follows by $(\forall E)$, then

$$\sigma_{i+1} = [\mu/u]\forall\vec{v}.[\vec{\rho}/\vec{r}]\sigma\,.$$

We may rename bound variables so that no free variables in μ are among $\vec{v}$. Thus

$$\sigma_{i+1} = \forall\vec{v}.[\mu/u][\vec{\rho}/\vec{r}]\sigma\,,$$

and so

$$\forall\vec{s}.\sigma \subseteq \sigma_{i+1}$$

is an instance of (sub). In addition, since no variable in $\mathcal{V}$ appears free in $\forall\vec{s}.\sigma$, each containment $\forall\vec{s}.\sigma \subseteq \forall\vec{v}.\sigma_{i+1}$ with $\vec{v}$ from $\mathcal{V}$ is an instance of (sub). This proves the first half of the Lemma. The converse is straightforward. □

Theorem 4

$\vdash_c A \supset M{:}\sigma$ iff $\vdash A \supset M{:}\sigma$.

Proof We first show that if $\vdash A \supset M{:}\sigma$, then $\vdash_c A \supset M{:}\sigma$. We argue, by induction on proofs, that if $\vdash A \supset M{:}\sigma$ and $\vec{s}$ is any sequence of type variables not free in A, then $\vdash_c A \supset M{:}\forall\vec{s}.\sigma$. The addition of quantifiers into rules $(\rightarrow I_\forall)$ and $(\rightarrow E_\forall)$ makes these two cases straightforward. Any $(\forall I)$ steps are trivial, and the $(\forall E)$ case uses Lemma 8. This proves half of the theorem.

To prove the converse, suppose that $\vdash_c A \supset M{:}\sigma$. We show that $\vdash A \supset M{:}\sigma$ by showing that each rule for $\vdash_c$ is a derived rule of $\vdash$. It is easy to see that $(\rightarrow I_\forall)$ is a derived rule, and $(\rightarrow E_\forall)$ is a derived rule by Lemma 7. By Lemma 8, (cont) is also a derived rule. □

It follows that the containment rules are semantically complete.

Corollary 2

Every containment that is valid in all inference models is an instance of the axiom scheme (sub).

The corollary is proved by noting that if $\sigma \subseteq \tau$ holds in all models, then $\lambda x.x{:}\sigma \rightarrow \tau$ is valid. By the completeness theorem and Corollary 1, it follows that $\vdash_c \lambda x.x{:}\sigma \rightarrow \tau$. By a straightforward induction on typing derivations using containments, this implies that $\sigma \subseteq \tau$ is an instance of (sub).

6 *Principal Typings and Containments in Simple Inference Models*

6.1 *Toward Minimal Types*

In the characterization of pure typing presented in Section 5.1, we saw that an important subproblem in typing is to compute simple operations on sets of the form

$$Types(\vec{x}, N) = \{\vec{\sigma}, \tau \mid \vdash \{x_1{:}\sigma_1, \ldots, x_n{:}\sigma_n\} \supset N{:}\tau\}.$$

This requires some method of representing these infinite sets efficiently. By analogy with Curry typing, we might hope that for any closed term M, the set $Types(\varnothing, M)$ might have the form $\{\rho | \tau \subseteq \rho\}$ for some "minimal" type τ (providing a similar characterization for open terms). We will see below that this is not the case for $\vdash$ or $\vdash_c$. However, it seems that there may be minimal types if we adopt the additional rule (simple) for simple inference models (see Section 4.1). We motivate the study of containment in simple models with an intuitive discussion of mappings between types.

6.2 *Retyping Functions in Second-Order Lambda Calculus*

An intuitive, syntactic notion of embedding type σ into type τ is that we can write down a second-order term that maps elements from σ to τ solely by "manipulating types." For example, the typed function

$$M = \lambda x \in (\forall t.\sigma).x\tau$$

from $\forall t.\sigma$ to $[\tau/t]\sigma$ seems only to "change the type" of its argument. One way to say precisely that M only "changes types" is to note that *erase*(M) is the identity function $I = \lambda x.x$.

We will define a class of second-order terms that seem to manipulate types without changing the functional behavior of terms. A second example will provide a little more motivation. The combinator

$$S = \lambda x.\lambda y.\lambda z.\,(xz)(yz)$$

has principal Curry type scheme

$$(r \to s \to t) \to (r \to s) \to r \to t.$$

We can prove that S has the quantified type

$$\sigma_1 = \forall r \forall s \forall t.(r \to s \to t) \to (r \to s) \to r \to t$$

using any of the inference systems discussed so far. Alternatively, we can type S so that the term $SIII$ is typable. To type $SIII$, we give S the type

$$\sigma_2 = (\forall t.t \to t) \to (\forall t.t \to t) \to (\forall t.t \to t) \to (\forall t.t \to t)\,.$$

At first glance, there may not seem to be any obvious relationship between σ_1 and σ_2. However, there is a typed term M with type $\sigma_1 \to \sigma_2$ which seems only to "change the type" of its argument, not alter its functionality. The term M is

$$M = \lambda w \in \sigma_1\ \lambda x \in \tau.\ \lambda y \in \tau.(w\tau\tau\tau)(\lambda v \in \tau.x\tau v\tau)(y\tau)\,,$$

where $\tau = \forall t.t \to t$. The erasure of this term is

$$erase(M) = \lambda w.\lambda x.\lambda y.\ w(\lambda v.xv)y\,,$$

which η-reduces to the untyped identity I. It is interesting to see what happens when we apply M to the second-order lambda term

$$S_1 = \lambda r.\ \lambda s.\ \lambda t.\ \lambda x \in r \to s \to t.\ \lambda y \in r \to s.\ \lambda z \in r.\ xz(xy)$$

with type σ_1 and $erase(S_1) = S$. After β-reduction, we obtain the second-order lambda term

$$S_2 = \lambda x \in \tau.\ \lambda y \in \tau.\ \lambda z \in \tau.(x\tau z\tau)(y\tau z)$$

with type σ_2 and $erase(S_2) = S$. Essentially, M "retypes" S_1 to S_2. Note that we cannot η-reduce M to I before erasing type information since type applications prevent M from having any η-redexes.

We adopt the intuitive idea that if $erase(M)$ η-reduces to I, then M "only changes the type" of its argument, and call any closed second-order term M with $erase(M) \to_\eta I$ a *retyping function*. Retyping functions seem to be a useful way of examining relationships between types, and they are related to simple inference models by the following lemma.

Lemma 9

The containment $\sigma \subseteq \tau$ is valid in all simple inference models if and only if there is a retyping function from σ to τ.

Proof The lemma is proved by observing that $\vdash_s \{x{:}\sigma\} \supset x{:}\tau$ if and only if there is some M such that $\vdash \{x{:}\,\sigma\} \supset M{:}\tau$ and M η-reduces to x. Consequently, if $\sigma \subseteq \tau$ is valid in all simple inference models, then $\vdash_s \{x{:}\,\sigma\} \supset x{:}\tau$ and so $\vdash \lambda x.M{:}\sigma \to \tau$ for some retyping function $\lambda x.M$. Conversely, if $\vdash \{x{:}\,\sigma\} \supset M{:}\tau$ for some M which η-reduces to x, then a straightforward induction using (simple) shows that $\vdash_s \{x{:}\sigma\} \supset x{:}\tau$. Therefore, by the soundness of $\vdash_s$, the containment $\sigma \subseteq \tau$ is valid in all simple inference models. □

Retyping functions can also be used to show that (simple) is not a derived rule of $\vdash$, as follows. Any second-order term M in normal form with $erase(M) =$

I must be of the form

$$\lambda\vec{r}\,\lambda x \in (\forall\vec{t}.\tau).\,\lambda\vec{s}.\,x\vec{\sigma}\,.$$

Therefore, the only $\vdash$-provable types for I are those of the form

$$\forall\vec{r}(\forall\vec{t}.\tau \to \forall\vec{s}.\,[\vec{\sigma}/\vec{t}]\tau)\,.$$

Since the retyping function M considered in the discussion of *SIII* has a typing that is not of this form, it follows that (simple) is not a derived rule of $\vdash$.

6.3 *Containment Rules for Simple Semantics*

We now present inference rules for deducing containments that hold in all simple inference models. These rules can be used in conjunction with the containment-based typing rules of Section 5.2 to derive typings that hold in all simple inference models.

Containment Axioms

(sub) $\forall\vec{t}.\sigma \subseteq \forall\vec{r}.[\vec{\tau}/\vec{t}]\sigma$, where $\vec{r}$ are not free in $\forall\vec{t}.\sigma$,

(dist) $\forall\vec{s}.(\tau \to \sigma) \subseteq \forall\vec{s}.\tau \to \forall\vec{s}.\sigma\,.$

Containment Inference Rules

(arrow) $\sigma_1 \subseteq \sigma, \tau \subseteq \tau_1 \vdash \sigma \to \tau \subseteq \sigma_1 \to \tau_1\,,$

(trans) $\rho \subseteq \sigma, \sigma \subseteq \tau \vdash \rho \subseteq \tau\,,$

(congruence) $\sigma \subseteq \tau \vdash \forall t.\sigma \subseteq \forall t.\tau\,.$

Note that rules (dist) and (arrow) are sound for simple inference models but not for arbitrary inference models. We write $\vdash_{sc} A \supset M{:}\sigma$ if $A \supset M{:}\sigma$ may be derived using the typing rules of Section 5.2, together with the containment rules above.

The main difficulty in establishing the equivalence of $\vdash_s$ and $\vdash_{sc}$ lies in proving that (simple) is a derived rule of $\vdash_{sc}$.

Lemma 10

If $\vdash_{sc} A \supset M{:}\sigma$ and $M\eta$-reduces to N, then $\vdash_{sc} A \supset N{:}\sigma$.

Proof It suffices to consider an η-redex $\lambda x.Mx$ since the lemma then follows by an easy induction on terms. Suppose $\vdash_{sc} A \supset \lambda x.Mx{:}\sigma$, with x not free in M. By inspection of the proof system, we know that the derivation of $A \supset \lambda x.Mx{:}\sigma$ ends by proving the following statements:

$$A, x{:}\mu \supset M{:}\forall\vec{s}(\rho \to \tau)\,,$$

$$A,x{:}\mu \supset x{:}\forall \vec{s}.\rho\,,$$

$$A,x{:}\mu \supset Mx{:}\forall \vec{s}.\tau, \quad \forall \vec{s}.\tau \subseteq \nu\,,$$

$$A,x{:}\mu \supset Mx{:}\nu\,,$$

$$A \supset \lambda x.Mx{:}\forall \vec{u}(\mu \to \nu), \quad \forall \vec{u}(\mu \to \nu) \subseteq \sigma\,,$$

$$A \supset \lambda x.Mx{:}\sigma\,.$$

In order to show $\vdash_{sc} A \supset M{:}\sigma$, it suffices to show that $\forall \vec{s}(\rho \to \tau) \subseteq \forall \vec{u}(\mu \to \nu)$. From the second line above, we know $\mu \subseteq \forall \vec{s}.\rho$, and from the third line, $\forall \vec{s}.\tau \subseteq \nu$. Therefore

$$\forall \vec{s}(\rho \to \tau) \subseteq (\forall \vec{s}.\rho) \to \forall \vec{s}.\tau \subseteq \mu \to \nu\,.$$

Since $\vec{u}$ must not occur free in A, we may assume that these variables do not appear free in $\forall \vec{s}(\rho \to \tau)$. Thus we derive the desired inclusion by quantifying over $\vec{u}$. □

Lemma 17

If $\vdash_s A \supset M{:}\sigma$, and $\sigma \subseteq \tau$ follows from the containment inference rules for simple models, then $\vdash_s A \supset M{:}\tau$.

Proof We prove the lemma using induction on the derivation of $\sigma \subseteq \tau$. If the containment is an axiom, then we use Lemma 8 or 7. If the containment follows by (trans), then it is trivial; and if it follows by (cong), then we use ($\forall I$) and ($\forall E$). The remaining case is (arrow). The type σ must be of the form $\sigma_1 \to \sigma_2$ and τ of the form $\tau_1 \to \tau_2$, with $\tau_1 \subseteq \sigma_1$ and $\sigma_2 \subseteq \tau_2$. The inductive hypothesis yields, for all N and P, if $\vdash_s A \supset N{:}\tau_1$ then $\vdash_s A \supset N{:}\sigma_1$ and similarly if $\vdash_s A \supset P{:}\sigma_2$ then $\vdash_s A \supset P{:}\tau_2$. Therefore,

$$A,x{:}\tau_1 \supset x{:}\sigma_1\,,$$

and since $A \supset M{:}\sigma$, we have

$$A,x{:}\tau_1 \supset Mx{:}\sigma_2\,.$$

Applying the inductive hypothesis again, we have

$$A,x{:}\tau_1 \supset Mx{:}\tau_2$$

and so

$$\vdash_s A \supset \lambda x.Mx{:}\tau\,,$$

from which the lemma follows by (simple). □

Theorem 5

$$\vdash_s A \supset M{:}\sigma \text{ iff } \vdash_{sc} A \supset M{:}\sigma \ .$$

Proof The proof is similar to the proof of Theorem 4, but uses Lemmas 10 and 11. □

By an argument similar to the proof of Corollary 2, we have semantic completeness for the simple containment rules.

Corollary 3

The simple containment rules are sound and complete for deducing the containments that are valid in all simple inference models.

The rules for $\vdash_{sc}$ also provide an inductive characterization of $\vdash_s$ typing. The characterization is the same as the one for $\vdash$ described in Section 5, but with $\subseteq$ interpreted as containment over simple models. In the next subsection, this characterization is used to show that certain terms have minimal typings.

6.4 *Principal Typings for a Limited Class of Terms*

Although we do not know how to represent $Types(\vec{x}, M)$ in general, we can show that some terms have a certain kind of principal $\vdash_s$ types. We will work with terms that do not contain any embedded λ's and have a particularly simple form. Specifically, an *elementary applicative term* is a λ-free term M such that if a variable x occurs twice in M, then distinct occurrences of x are in disjoint subterms, and, in all occurrences, x is applied to the same number of arguments. For example, $y(xzz)(xww)$ is an elementary applicative term, but $x(wxx)$ and $y(xz)(xww)$ are not.

We will show that every elementary applicative term has a principal typing, and we will use this to show that the lambda-closure of each elementary applicative term has a minimal typing with respect to $\subseteq$. To be more specific, we make the following definition. A typing statement $B \supset M{:}\sigma$ is a $\subseteq$-*instance* of the typing statement $A \supset M{:}\tau$ if there is some substitution S of types for type variables such that

$$B(x) \subseteq S(A(x)) \text{ for all } x \text{ free in } M, \text{ and } S\tau \subseteq \sigma .$$

We will show that every elementary applicative term M has a typing $A \supset M{:}\sigma$ such that all $\vdash_s$-provable typings for M are $\subseteq$-instances of $A \supset M{:}\sigma$. It will follow that $\lambda\vec{x}.M$ has a $\subseteq$-principal type, i.e., a type σ such that $\lambda\vec{x}.M{:}\tau$ iff $\sigma \subseteq \tau$. We first demonstrate a connection between $\subseteq$-instances and type containment.

Lemma 12
Suppose $\{x_1{:}\rho_1, \ldots, x_n{:}\rho_n\} \supset M{:}\sigma$ is a $\subseteq$-instance of $\{x_1{:}\mu_1, \ldots, x_n{:}\mu_n\} \supset M{:}\tau$. Then

$$\forall\vec{s}(\mu_1 \to \ldots \to \mu_n \to \tau) \subseteq \forall\vec{r}(\rho_1 \to \ldots \to \rho_n \to \sigma)$$

holds in all simple inference models, where we assume that both type expressions are closed by the quantification over $\vec{r}$ and $\vec{s}$.

Proof Since the first typing statement is an instance of the second, there is a substitution S such that

$$\rho_i \subseteq S\mu_i \text{ and } S\tau \subseteq \sigma .$$

Therefore, by repeated application of rule (arrow), we see that

$$(S\mu_1) \to \ldots \to (S\mu_n) \to (S\tau) \subseteq \rho_1 \to \ldots \to \rho_n \to \sigma .$$

Since $\forall\vec{s}(\mu_1 \to \ldots \to \mu_n \to \tau)$ is contained in $(S\mu_1) \to \ldots \to (S\mu_n) \to (S\tau)$, we have

$$\forall\vec{s}(\mu_1 \to \ldots \to \mu_n \to \tau) \subseteq \rho_1 \to \ldots \to \rho_n \to \sigma ,$$

from which we derive the desired containment by quantifying over $\vec{r}$ (which do not appear free in the left hand side as it is closed). □

A typing $A \supset M{:}\tau$ for term M is *$\subseteq$-principal* if $\vdash_s A \supset M{:}\tau$, and whenever $\vdash_s B \supset M{:}\sigma$, the typing $B \supset M{:}\sigma$ is a $\subseteq$-instance of $A \supset M{:}\tau$.

Lemma 13
If M is an elementary applicative term, then M has a $\subseteq$-principal typing $A \supset M{:}\tau$. Furthermore, no type quantifiers appear in A or τ.

Proof Every elementary applicative term M has the form $xM_1 \ldots M_k$, where $M_1, \ldots, M_k$ are elementary applicative terms, $k \geq 0$, and x does not appear in any of the subterms $M_1, \ldots, M_k$. We will show, by induction on k, that M has a quantifier-free $\subseteq$-principal typing of the form

$$\{x{:}s_1 \to \ldots \to s_k \to t\} \cup A_1 \ldots \cup A_k \supset xM_1 \ldots M_k{:}t ,$$

where each $A_i \supset M_i{:}s_i$ is a $\subseteq$-principal typing of the same form, t is different from all the s_i, and t does not appear in any A_i.

The case $k = 0$ is relatively straightforward. To see that $\{x{:}t\} \supset x{:}t$ is $\subseteq$-principal, suppose $\{x{:}\rho\} \supset x{:}\sigma$ is any other provable typing for x. Let S be the substitution $[\sigma/t]$ of σ for t. Since $\rho \subseteq \sigma$, the typing $\{x{:}\,\rho\} \supset x{:}\sigma$ is an instance of $\{x{:}\,t\} \supset x{:}t$ using substitution S.

For $k > 0$, we assume we have $\subseteq$-principal typings

$$\{x{:}s_1 \to \ldots \to s_{k-1} \to r\} \cup A_1 \cup \ldots \cup A_{k-1} \supset xM_1 \ldots M_{k-1}{:}r$$

and

$$A_k \supset M_k{:}s_k\,.$$

Without loss of generality, we may assume that if some variable y appears in both M_k and some M_i with $i < k$, then y is assigned the same type in all of the relevant type assignments. This assumption is possible since we know that y must be applied to the same number of arguments in each subterm, and the type assigned to any variable depends only on the number of arguments to which it is applied (up to renaming of type variables). Therefore, we may assume that the same type has been used for all occurrences of y.

We show that $\{x{:}s_1 \to \ldots \to s_k \to t\} \cup A_1 \cup \ldots \cup A_k \supset xM_1 \ldots M_k{:}t$ is $\subseteq$-principal, where t is fresh. Clearly this typing is $\vdash_s$ provable and involves no type quantification. Let

$$B \supset xM_1 \ldots M_k{:}\forall\vec{s}.\tau$$

be provable, by a proof ending with rule $(\to E)$. By inspection of the $\vdash_{sc}$ proof system, we know that this typing follows from provable typings

$$B \supset xM_1 \ldots M_{k-1}{:}\forall\vec{s}.(\sigma \to \tau) \;\text{ and }\; B \supset M_k{:}\forall\vec{s}.\sigma\,.$$

By the induction hypothesis, there is a substitution S such that

$$B(x) \subseteq S(s_1 \to \ldots \to s_{k-1} \to r),$$

$$B(y) \subseteq S((A_1 \cup \ldots \cup A_k)(y)), \quad \text{all } y \neq x \text{ free in } M,$$

$$Ss_k \subseteq \forall\vec{s}.\sigma, \quad \text{and}$$

$$Sr \subseteq \forall\vec{s}.(\sigma \to \tau)\,.$$

It is easy to see that $B \supset xM_1 \ldots M_k{:}\forall\vec{s}.\tau$ is an instance of $\{x{:}s_1 \to \ldots \to s_k \to t\} \cup A_1 \cup \ldots \cup A_k \supset xM_1 \ldots M_k{:}t$ by the substitution S_1 which differs from S only in that $S_1 t = \forall\vec{s}.\tau$. The only nontrivial part is verifying that $B(x) \subseteq S_1(s_1 \to \ldots \to s_k \to t)$. To see that this containment holds, notice that

$$Sr \subseteq \forall\vec{s}.(\sigma \to \tau) \subseteq (\forall\vec{s}.\sigma) \to \forall\vec{s}.\tau\,,$$

the second containment by the "distributivity" rule (dist). Since

$$S_1 s_k = Ss_k \subseteq \forall\vec{s}.\sigma$$

and $S_1 t = \forall\vec{s}.\tau$, we have

$$Sr \subseteq \forall\vec{s}.\sigma \to \forall\vec{s}.\tau \subseteq S_1(s_k \to t)\,.$$

Thus

$$B(x) \subseteq S(s_1 \to \ldots \to s_{k-1} \to r) \subseteq (Ss_1) \to \ldots \to (Ss_{k-1}) \to (Sr)$$
$$\subseteq S_1(s_1 \to \ldots \to s_k \to t)\,.$$

This proves the lemma. □

Theorem 6

Let M be a closed term of the form $\lambda\vec{x}.N$, where N is an elementary applicative term. Then M has a Curry type scheme σ_0 with universal closure $\sigma = \forall\vec{s}.\sigma_0$. Furthermore, $\vdash_s M{:}\tau$ if and only if the containment $\sigma \subseteq \tau$ holds in all simple inference models.

Proof If M is of the form $\lambda\vec{x}.N$ described in the theorem then, by Lemma, there is a $\subseteq$-principal typing

$$\{x_1{:}\mu_1, \ldots, x_k{:}\mu_k\} \supset N{:}\nu$$

for N. Let σ_0 be the Curry type $\mu_1 \to \ldots \to \mu_k \to \nu$ and let σ be the universal closure of σ_0. By Lemma 12, we know that σ is contained in any other $\vdash_s$ provable typing for M. □

It is worth noting that there may be many $\subseteq$-principal types for a single term. For example, the two types

$$\forall s, t(t \to s \to t) \text{ and } \forall t(t \to \forall s(s \to t))$$

are both similar to the principal Curry type $t \to s \to t$ for $K = \lambda x, y.x$. By the theorem above, the first is a $\subseteq$-principal type for K. In fact, both are principal since they denote the same set in any simple inference model.

Many terms that are not of the form $\lambda\vec{x}.N$ as in the lemma may also be shown to have most general $\vdash_s$ types. For example, the term $\lambda z.z(\lambda x.x)$ has most general type $\forall s.((\forall t.t \to t) \to s) \to s$. Note that this is not the universal closure of the principal type scheme $((t \to t) \to s) \to s$.

The analogous theorem for $\vdash$ (with $\vdash$ replacing $\vdash_s$ and "$\sigma \subseteq \tau$ in all models" replacing $\sigma \subseteq \tau$ over simple models) is false, as shown by the two $\vdash$-provable typings for the untyped combinator S. Thus $\vdash_s$ seems more likely to have principal type schemes than $\vdash$.

7 Conclusions and Open Problems

We have developed a semantics for quantified types over arbitrary models of untyped lambda calculus. Inference models are a generalization of the *ideal* models of [20, 21], and a number of other example of inference models are given in Section 3.5. We have proved completeness theorems for arbitrary inference models without empty types and the more specialized simple inference models. Completeness theorems for the quotient-set semantics of types follow as corollaries, as discussed in Section 4.4. We have also proved a completeness theorem for models that may have empty types, but it remains to prove a completeness theorem for the $\mathcal{F}$-semantics, which was discussed briefly in Section 4.3 and more fully in, e.g., [15].

It is not known whether pure typing assertions $\vdash A \supset M{:}\sigma$, or any significant fragment of pure typing that extends ML, is decidable. The containment-based inference rules provide an inductive characterization of typability and a bound on the lengths of proofs in a modified proof system. In addition, the containment-based rules reduce typability to a number of calculations involving containments and sets of types. Although certain terms have minimal types over all simple inference models, we do not know whether there is a fruitful notion of principal quantified type. The containment rules provide one approach to characterizing the set of types of a term, but it may be useful to investigate other possibilities.

Some other directions for further investigations are to extend the semantics presented here to recursively-defined types (cf. [21]) and to investigate the typing theories of various models, e.g., the continuous model D_∞ and P^ω.

References

[1] Barendregt, H. *The Lambda Calculus: Its Syntax and Semantics.* North Holland, 1984 (revised edition).

[2] Barendregt, H., Coppo, M., and Dezani-Ciancaglini, M. "A filter lambda model and the completeness of type assignment". *J. Symbolic Logic 48*, 4 (1983), pp. 931–940.

[3] Bruce, K. B., Meyer, A. R., and Mitchell, J. C. "The semantics of second-order lambda calculus". *Information and Computation* (to appear, 1990). Reprinted in this volume (Chapter 10).

[4] Coppo, M. and Zacchi, M. "Type inference and logical relations". *Proceedings of the IEEE Symposium on Logic in Computer Science* (June), pp. 218–226. IEEE Press, New York, 1986.

[5] Curry, H. B. and Feys, R. *Combinatory Logic*, vol. 1. North-Holland, Amsterdam, 1958.

[6] Damas, L. and Milner, R. "Principal type schemes for functional programs". *Proceedings of the 9th ACM Symposium on Principles of Programming Languages*, pp. 207–212. ACM, New York, 1982.

[7] Dezani-Ciancaglini, M. and Margaria, I. "*F*-Semantics for intersection type discipline". *Proceedings of the International Symposium on Semantics of Data Types* (Sophia-Antipolis, France), pp. 279–300. Lecture Notes in Computer Science, vol. 173. Springer-Verlag, Berlin, 1984.

[8] Donahue, J. "On the semantics of data type". *SIAM J. Computing 8* (1979), pp. 546–560.

[9] Fortune, S., Leivant, D. and O'Donnell, M. "The expressiveness of simple and second order type structures". *J. ACM 30*, 1 (1983), pp. 151–185.

[10] Friedman, H. "Equality between functionals". *Logic Colloquium*, R. Parikh, ed., pp. 22–37. Springer-Verlag, Berlin, 1975.

[11] Girard, J. Y. "Interpretation fonctionelle et elimination des coupures de l'arithmetique d'ordre superieur". These D'Etat, Universite Paris VII, 1972.

[12] Gordon, M. J., Milner R., and Wadsworth, C. *Edinburgh LCF*. Lecture Notes in Computer Science, vol. 78. Springer-Verlag, Berlin, 1979.

[13] Henkin, L. "Completeness in the theory of types". *J. Symbolic Logic 15*, 2 (June 1950), pp. 81–91.

[14] Hindley, R. "The principal type-scheme of an object in combinatory logic". *Trans. American Mathematical Society 146* (1969), pp. 29–60.

[15] Hindley, R. "The completeness theorem for typing lambda terms". *Theoretical Computer Science 22* (1983), pp. 1–17.

[16] Hindley, R. "Curry's type rules are complete with respect to the *F*-Semantics too". *Theoretical Computer Science 22* (1983), pp. 127–133.

[17] Hyland, J. M. E. "A syntactic characterization of the equality in some models of the Lambda calculus". *J. London Math. Society 2*, 12 (1976), pp. 361–370.

[18] Kreisel, G. "Interpretation of analysis by means of constructive functionals of finite types". *Constructivity in Mathematics*, A. Heyting (ed.), pp. 101–128. North-Holland, Amsterdam, 1959.

[19] Leivant, D. "Polymorphic type inference". *Proceedings of the 10th ACM Symposium on Principles of Programming Languages*, pp. 88–98. ACM, New York, 1983.

[20] MacQueen, D. and Sethi, R. "A semantic model of types for applicative languages". *ACM Symposium on LISP and Functional Programming*, pp. 243–252. ACM, New York, 1982.

[21] MacQueen, D., Plotkin, G., and Sethi, R. "An ideal model for recursive polymorphic types". *Information and Control 71*, 1/2 (1986), pp. 95–130.

[22] McCracken, N. "The typechecking of programs with implicit type structure". *Proceedings of the International Symposium on Semantics of Data Types* (Sophia-Antipolis, France, June), pp. 301–316. Lecture Notes in Computer Science, vol. 173. Springer-Verlag, Berlin, 1984.

[23] Meyer, A. R. "What is a model of the lambda calculus?" *Information and Control 52,* 1 (1982), pp. 87–122.

[24] Meyer, A. R., Mitchell, J. C., Moggi, E., and Statman R. "Empty types in polymorphic lambda calculus". *Proceedings of the 14th ACM Symposium on Principles of Programming Languages* (January), pp. 253–262. ACM, New York, 1987. Included, with corrections, in this volume (Chapter 11).

[25] Milner, R. "A theory of type polymorphism in programming". *J. Computer and System Sciences 17* (1978), pp. 348–375.

[26] Milner, R. "The Standard ML core language". *Polymorphism 2,* 2 (1985). An earlier version appeared in *Proceedings of the 1984 ACM Symposium on LISP and Functional Programming.*

[27] Mitchell, J. C. "Coercion and type inference (Summary)". *Proceedings of the 11th ACM Symposium on Principles of Programming Languages* (January), pp. 175–185. ACM, New York, 1984.

[28] Mitchell, J. C. "A type-inference approach to reduction properties and semantics of polymorphic expressions". *ACM Conference on LISP and Functional Programming* (August), pp. 308–319. ACM, New York, 1986. Included, with corrections, in this volume (Chapter 9).

[29] Mitchell, J. C. and Plotkin, G. D. "Abstract types have existential types". *ACM Trans. on Programming Languages and Systems 10,* 3 (1988), pp. 470–502. Preliminary version appeared in *Proceedings of the 12th ACM Symposium on Principles of Programming Languages,* 1985.

[30] Myhill, J. R. and Shepherdson, J. C. "Effective operations on partial recursive functions". *Zeitschrift für mathematische Logik und Grundlagen der Mathematik 1,* 1955.

[31] Paterson, M. S. and Wegman, M. N. "Linear unification". *J. Computer and System Sciences 16* (1978), pp. 158–167.

[32] Reynolds, J.C. "Towards a theory of type structure". *Paris Colloqium on Programming,* pp. 408–425. Lecture Notes in Computer Science, vol. 19. Springer-Verlag, Berlin, 1974.

[33] Robinson, J. A. "A machine oriented logic based on the resolution principle". *J. ACM 12,* 1 (1965), pp. 23–41.

[34] Scott, D. "Data types as lattices". *SIAM J. Computing 5,* 3 (1976), pp. 522–587.

[35] Statman, R. "Equality between functionals, revisited". *Harvey Friedman's Research on the Foundations of Mathematics,* pp. 331-338. North-Holland, Amsterdam, 1985.

[36] Troelstra, A.S. *Mathematical Investigation of Intuitionistic Arithmetic and Analysis.* Lecture Notes in Mathematics, vol. 344. Springer-Verlag, Berlin, 1973.

[37] Wadsworth, C. "The relation between computational and denotational properties for Scott's D_∞ models". *SIAM J. Computing* 5, 3 (1976).

A Type-Inference Approach to Reduction Properties and Semantics of Polymorphic Expressions (Summary)[1]

9

John C. Mitchell
Stanford University

Abstract

Some insight into both the operational and denotational semantics of polymorphic lambda calculus may be gained by considering types as equivalence relations on subsets of an untyped domain. A general theorem stating that the meaning of any typed term belongs to the appropriate collection of values may be used to prove strong normalization of typed terms. The interpretation of types as equivalence relations also gives rise to the "HEO-like" models of polymorphic lambda calculus. We characterize the equational theories of HEO-like models and prove a completeness theorem for a non-standard set of axioms.

1. An earlier version of this chapter appeared in the proceedings of the 1986 ACM Conference on Lisp and Functional Programming.

1 *Introduction*

There are two different ways of introducing polymorphism into programming languages. These may be distinguished by calling one *implicit* and the other *explicit polymorphism*. In implicit polymorphism, types are thought of as predicates, or subsets of some universal space of values. These subsets may overlap, giving some terms more than one type. For example, the ML identity function $\lambda x.x$ has types **int** → **int**, **bool** → **bool**, and many others. In contrast, polymorphism enters into programming languages like Ada, CLU, and Russell by allowing functions, procedures, and packages (all of which we will call terms) to have type parameters. This style of polymorphism is called explicit because a term acquires a variety of types only by explicitly applying the term to a variety of type arguments. For example, the polymorphic identity function

$$I_{poly} = \lambda t{:}Type\ \lambda x{:}t.x,$$

which might also be written

function *f* [*t*:*Type*](*x*:*t*);
  return *x*
  end,

has a single type $\forall t.t \to t$. We can apply I_{poly} to integers by supplying **int** as the first actual parameter, apply I_{poly} to booleans by supplying **bool** as the first actual parameter, and so on. In explicit polymorphism, types have a status approaching that of other values, and each term has only one type.

Operationally, implicit polymorphism relieves a lot of notational clutter. Since types do not appear explicitly in terms, the computational behavior of terms may be studied without regard to their types and without involving computation rules for types. Denotationally, implicit polymorphism involves typeless value spaces, which are more commonly studied than polymorphically typed families of domains. The main problem in passing from untyped meanings to typed meanings of terms is the extensionality of functions. Extensionality means that two functions are equal if they have identical values for all arguments in their common domain. Thus if M and N are explicitly typed terms, both with functional type $\sigma \to \tau$, and $Mx = Nx$ for all $x{:}\sigma$, then we wish to consider M and N equal. However, distinct implicitly typed terms $U \neq V$ of type $\sigma \to \tau$ may give equal values $Ux = Vx$ for all $x{:}\sigma$ without being equal. Essentially, this is because U and V may have other types, and Ux may be different from Vx for some x not of type σ. Thus implicit and explicit views of typing lead to different notions of equality between terms.

In this paper, we will use implicit polymorphism to study explicit polymorphism. Our model of explicit polymorphism will be the second-order lambda calculus of [8, 24]. The corresponding implicit system is a set of type inference rules for untyped lambda terms. This type inference system has been studied in [13, 15, 16, 17, 21]. The main organizing idea in our study is the definition of *partial equivalence relation interpretation of type inference*, or *PER interpretation* for short. A *partial equivalence relation* is a symmetric and transitive relation; alternatively, a partial equivalence relation over D may be defined as an equivalence relation over some subset of D. Informally, a PER interpretation is a structure which combines a way of interpreting untyped lambda terms as elements of some set D with a way of interpreting types as partial equivalence relations over D. PER interpretations are similar to the "quotient-set inference models" defined in [21], except that the underlying structure D is not required to respect β-conversion of untyped lambda terms. The reason for associating equivalence relations with types is to come to grips with the difference between untyped equality and typed equality; we think of the equivalence relation associated with a type σ as typed equality between terms of type σ. The reason the equivalence relations associated with types must be partial is simply that not all terms have all types. In a PER interpretation, we say a value d has type σ if d is in the domain of the equivalence relation associated with σ, i.e., d is related to d by the σ relation.

The first important theorem about PER interpretations, type soundness, is that whenever we can infer that an untyped term U has type σ, then the interpretation of U has type σ. In other words, the inference rules for deriving types of untyped terms are sound for PER interpretations. One corollary of type soundness is the strong normalization theorem for implicitly typed terms. This theorem says that no matter how we apply β-reduction (the computation rule for lambda calculus) to a lambda term which has a type (implicitly), we arrive at a normal form (a term that can no longer be reduced). From this we can derive a second corollary, strong normalization for explicitly typed terms. This theorem, which implies the consistency of analysis (second-order Peano arithmetic) [6, 8] was originally proved by [8] and has been adapted and refined by a number of others. In particular, [14] also uses implicit typing to simplify Girard's proof, but Leivant introduces a syntactic translation into second-order logic, which we shall see is unnecessary. We can also derive other facts about reduction, like the Church-Rosser theorem for typable terms, from type soundness.

The main reason for considering partial equivalence relations is extensional equality. In the first part of the paper, we allow PER interpretations which do not respect β-conversion of untyped terms and which may have non extensional type relations. This makes the type soundness theorem as general as possible and allows us to study reduction by constructing PER interpretations which give β-equivalent terms different interpretations. In the second part of the paper, when we study the semantics of terms, we will restrict our attention to PER interpretations that respect β-conversion of untyped terms and that give extensional equality at functional types. These PER interpretations are called *PER models.* In a PER model, the relation associated with a functional type $\sigma \to \tau$ equates U and V whenever $Ux = Vx$ for all $x{:}\sigma$. We do not study a possible "intermediate" structure, nonextensional PER models, in which β-conversion is satisfied but equality is nonextensional. While non extensional models of second-order lambda calculus may be of some interest, they do not seem particularly enlightening in this setting.

The main result of the semantic analysis is a characterization of the equational theories of PER models. This characterization comes in three parts. The first is that any PER model I determines a structure $\mathcal{A}_I$ which is a second-order lambda model in the sense of [4, 3, 20]. This implies that the usual axioms and inference rules for deducing equations between typed terms are sound. Next, we show that the meaning of an explicitly-typed term M in $\mathcal{A}_I$ is the equivalence class of the untyped term derived from M by erasing all types. This implies that some unusual-looking equations hold in all second-order models based on partial equivalence relations. Finally, we prove a completeness theorem which shows that the only unexpected equations between typed terms that hold in all $\mathcal{A}_I$ are those that stem from equating terms that look the same when we erase all the types. In summary, we show that second-order models based on partial equivalence relations (1) satisfy the accepted axioms and inference rules for second-order lambda terms, (2) satisfy some additional equations that can be described by erasing types from terms, and (3) do not entail any unexpected equations other than those described by (2).

It should be emphasized that the idea of interpreting types as partial equivalence relations is far from original. The use of partial equivalence relations for first-order function types was introduced in [22] and extended to higher-order functional types $\sigma \to \tau$ in [12]. Kreisel's structure is also described in [28], where it is called HEO, for the *hereditarily effective operations.* The structure HEO is extended to an interpretation of predicative polymorphic types in [2] and an interpretation HEO_2 of impredicative polymorphic functions (polymorphic functions as discussed in the present paper) in [8, 28]. The structure HEO_2 was also discovered independently by Moggi and Plotkin (personal communication, 1985), from whom the author learned of this interpretation. It is closely related to the effective topos [11], as pointed out in [7]. A partial equivalence relation interpretation of functional types (in a somewhat different setting) is also discussed in [26] and taken up in the study of implicit polymorphism in, e.g., [10, 5].

2 Syntax

2.1 Types

Type expressions are built from type variables and type constants using the function-space constructor $\rightarrow$ and the polymorphic-type constructor $\forall$. We adopt the notational conventions that

$r, s, t, \ldots$ are arbitrary type variables,

$\rho, \sigma, \tau, \ldots$ are arbitrary type expressions.

The set of type expressions is defined by the grammar

$$\tau ::= t \mid \sigma \rightarrow \tau \mid \forall t.\sigma\,.$$

We identify type expressions that differ only in the names of bound variables. Thus $\forall t.\sigma = \forall s.[s/t]\sigma$, where $[s/t]\sigma$ is the result of substituting s for free occurrences of t in σ.

2.2 Terms

To keep implicitly typed and explicitly typed terms separate, we will use U, V, ... for untyped terms and M, N, ... for explicitly typed terms. Since some discussion will apply equally well to both classes of terms, it will be convenient to use X, Y, ... to refer to terms which may be either typed or untyped.

The *unchecked typed terms* are defined by

$$M ::= c \mid x \mid MN \mid \lambda x{:}\sigma.M \mid M\sigma \mid \lambda t.M\,,$$

while the *untyped lambda terms* are given by

$$U ::= c \mid x \mid UV \mid \lambda x.U\,.$$

In both definitions, c may be any constant and x any ordinary variable (ordinary variables x, y, z, ...are assumed distinct from type variables r, s, t, ...). Terms are given types using the inference rules presented in the next section.

A useful tool for discussing implicit and explicit typing is the function Erase, which erases types from terms. This function has a straightforward inductive definition; the nontrivial clauses are

$$\text{Erase}(\lambda x{:}\sigma.M) = \lambda x.\text{Erase}(M),$$

$$\text{Erase}(M\sigma) = \text{Erase}(M),$$

$$\text{Erase}(\lambda t.M) = \text{Erase}(M).$$

Clearly Erase of any unchecked typed terms is an untyped lambda term.

2.3 *Typing Rules*

A *typing statement* is an expression $X{:}\sigma$, where X is a term and σ is a type expression. The statement $X{:}\sigma$ may be read, "the term X has type σ". In general, the type of a term depends on the types of its free variables, so we will use a formal system for deducing typing statements from sets assumptions about variables. A *type assignment* A is a finite set of basic typing statements $x{:}\sigma$ about variables, with no x appearing twice. When x does not occur in A, we will write $A,x{:}\sigma$ for the type assignment

$$A,x{:}\sigma = A \cup \{x{:}\sigma\}.$$

It is often useful to think of a type assignment A as a partial function and to write $A(x)$ for the unique type σ with $x{:}\sigma \in A$, if such a type exists.

The only axiom about the entailment relation on typings is

$$\{x{:}\sigma\} \vdash x{:}\sigma.$$

We also have the structural rule

$$\text{(add hyp)} \qquad \frac{A \vdash X{:}\,\tau}{A, x{:}\,\sigma \vdash X{:}\,\tau}, \quad x \text{ not in } A,$$

which allows us to add additional basic typing statements to a type assignment.

The inference rules for explicit typing are

$$(\rightarrow I)_{exp} \qquad \frac{A,x{:}\sigma \vdash M{:}\tau}{A \vdash \lambda x{:}\sigma.M{:}\sigma \rightarrow \tau},$$

$$(\rightarrow E)_{exp} \qquad \frac{A \vdash M{:}\sigma \rightarrow \tau, A \vdash N{:}\sigma}{A \vdash MN{:}\tau},$$

$$(\forall I)_{exp} \qquad \frac{A \vdash M{:}\sigma}{A \vdash \lambda t.M{:}\forall t.\sigma}, \quad t \text{ not free in } A,$$

$$(\forall E)_{exp} \qquad \frac{A \vdash M{:}\forall t.\sigma}{A \vdash M\tau{:}[\tau/t]\sigma}.$$

As in [13, 15, 16, 21], we may also give inference rules for deriving types for untyped terms. However, as we will not be concerned with the structure of typing derivations, we will not describe the implicit rules here. The implicit rules are easily constructed from the explicit rules above by applying Erase to the antecedent and consequent of each rule. For example, the implicit $(\forall E)$ rule is

$$(\forall E)_{imp} \qquad \frac{A \vdash \text{Erase}(M){:}\forall t.\sigma}{A \vdash \text{Erase}(M\tau){:}[\tau/t]\sigma},$$

or, simplifying the applications of Erase,

$$(\forall E)_{imp} \quad \frac{A \vdash U{:}\forall t.\sigma}{A \vdash U{:}[\tau/t]\sigma}.$$

General soundness and completeness theorems for implicit polymorphic typing are proved in [21], where additional rules are also considered. While the additional typing rules are needed to give semantic completeness with respect to arbitrary typing and equational hypotheses, neither the completeness theorem nor the additional typing rules will play any role here. The only property of implicit typing that is relevant to the present investigation is that $A \vdash_{imp} U{:}\sigma$ iff there is some explicitly typed M with $A \vdash_{exp} M{:}\sigma$ and Erase(M) = U.

3 *Partial Equivalence Relation Interpretations*

3.1 *Introduction*

We will use a general kind of "interpretation" of polymorphic type inference, based on [21]. The interpretation is general in that it allows lambda terms to be interpreted over lambda models or weaker structures that may be largely syntactic in nature. For example, one important interpretation uses α-equivalence classes of terms as the "meanings" of lambda expressions. Types are then interpreted as partial equivalence relations over meanings of terms. For the study of reduction properties in Section 4, it would be sufficient to interpret types as predicates. However, to cut down on the number of definitions, we will use partial equivalence relations throughout.

3.2 *Lambda Interpretations*

A *lambda interpretation* is a triple,

$$\mathcal{D} = \langle D, \bullet, [\![\ \ ]\!] \rangle,$$

where D is a set, $\bullet$ is a binary operation on D, and $[\![\ \ ]\!]$ is a mapping from terms and environments η (mapping variables to elements of D) to D such that

(i) $[\![x]\!]\eta = \eta(x)$

(ii) $[\![MN]\!]\eta = [\![M]\!]\eta \bullet [\![N]\!]\eta$

(iii) $[\![\lambda x.M]\!]\eta = [\![\lambda y.[y/x]M]\!]\eta$

(iv) If $[\![M]\!]\eta[d/x] = [\![N]\!]\eta[d/x]$ all $d \in D$, then $[\![\lambda x.M]\!]\eta = [\![\lambda x.N]\!]\eta$, where $\eta[d/x]$ is the environment mapping x to d and y to $\eta(y)$ for variable y different from x,

(v) if $\eta(x) = \eta'(x)$ for all $x \in FV(M)$, then $[\![M]\!]\eta = [\![M]\!]\eta'$.

Hindley and Longo [1, 9] define models of lambda calculus as lambda interpretations that satisfy the additional condition

(vi) $[\![\lambda x.M]\!]\eta \bullet d = [\![M]\!]\eta[d/x]$ all $d \in D$.

It is easy to see that if $\mathcal{D}$ satisfies all instances of the axiom scheme

$$(\beta) \quad (\lambda x.M)N = [N/x]M\,,$$

then (vi) holds and $\mathcal{D}$ is a lambda model. Other definitions of lambda models (cf. [1]) are, of course, essentially equivalent to Hindley and Longo's. For example, it is easy to verify that if a λ-interpretation $\mathcal{D}$ satisfies the model condition (vi), then

$$\mathcal{D}_{env} \;=\; \langle D, \bullet, [\![\lambda x\lambda y.xy]\!]\rangle$$

is a combinatory model, as defined in [18].

We define satisfaction and validity of equations between lambda terms as usual.

Example 1 A simple lambda interpretation $\mathcal{D}_\alpha = \langle D, \bullet, [\![\;\;]\!]\rangle$ may be constructed using α-equivalence classes of lambda terms. For each lambda term M, let $\langle M\rangle$ denote the set of terms N that differ from M only in the names of bound variables. Let D be the set of all $\langle M\rangle$, and define $\langle M\rangle \bullet \langle N\rangle$ to be the set of terms $\langle MN\rangle$. It is not hard to see that $\bullet$ is well defined. We define $[\![\;\;]\!]$ using substitution. An environment η for D is a mapping from terms to equivalence classes of terms. For any environment η, let S_η be any substitution mapping each variable x to an element of the set of terms $\eta(x)$. We define $[\![\;\;]\!]$ by

$$[\![M]\!]\eta \;=\; \langle S_\eta M\rangle.$$

It is not hard to check that $[\![M]\!]\eta$ is a well defined function of M and η and that $[\![\;\;]\!]$ satisfies conditions (i) through (v).

Example 2 Any model of lambda calculus is a lambda interpretation. A straightforward axiom system, essentially comprising the usual rules, but without (β), is easily shown to be sound and complete for λ-interpretations.

3.3 *PER Interpretations*

We will interpret typing statements over PER interpretations. A *PER interpretation* is a triple,

$$I = \langle \mathcal{T}, \mathcal{D}, Rel\rangle\,,$$

with

$\mathcal{T} = \langle \mathcal{U}, \to^I, \forall^I \rangle$ a type structure as in [21]; i.e., $\mathcal{U}$ must be a model of ordinary typed lambda calculus consisting of a hierarchy of sets T, $T \to T$, $T \to (T \to T)$, ... with elements $\to^{\mathcal{T}} \in T \to (T \to T)$ and $\forall^{\mathcal{T}} \in (T \to T) \to T$;

$\mathcal{D} = \langle \mathcal{D}, \bullet, [\![\ ]\!] \rangle$ a lambda interpretation; and

$Rel: T \to 2^{D \times D}$ assigning a symmetric, transitive relation to each type;

such that the following three conditions are satisfied:

(Arrow.1) If $\langle d_1, d_2 \rangle \in Rel(a \to b)$ and $\langle e_1, e_2 \rangle \in Rel(a)$ then $\langle d_1 \bullet e_1,\ d2 \bullet e_2 \rangle \in Rel(b)$;

(Arrow.2) if $\langle [\![M_1]\!]\eta[d_1/x],\ [\![M_2]\!]\eta[d_2/x] \rangle \in Rel(b)$ for all $\langle d_1, d_2 \rangle \in Rel(\text{a})$, then $\langle [\![\lambda x.M_1]\!]\eta,\ [\![\lambda x.M_2]\!]\eta \rangle \in Rel(a \to b)$;

(ForAll) $Rel(\forall f) = \cap_{a \in T}\ Rel(f(a))$.

If $\mathcal{D}$ is a λ-model, then (Arrow.2) may be simplified to

(Arrow.2_{model}) If $\langle d_1 \bullet e_1, d_2 \bullet e_2 \rangle \in Rel(b)$ for all $\langle e_1, e_2 \rangle \in Rel(a)$, then $\langle [\![\lambda x \lambda y.xy]\!] \bullet d_1, [\![\lambda x \lambda y.xy]\!] \bullet d_2 \rangle \in Rel(a \to b)$, where the meaning of the closed term $\lambda x \lambda y.xy$ does not depend on the environment η.

We will later obtain extensional models of explicit typing by imposing an extensionality condition on relations. In the meantime, this more general definition allows us to prove soundness for a wide class of PER interpretations. It is often convenient to write D_a for $\{d \mid \langle d, d \rangle \in Rel(a)\}$.

We will interpret typing statements using environments that map type variables to elements of T and ordinary variables to elements of D. For technical reasons, it will be convenient to consider environments that are not defined on all ordinary variables. The reason for this, which is related to the fact that type assignments only mention finitely many variables, should become evident from the statement of the characterization theorem (Theorem 2) below. Therefore, an *environment* will be a total function from type variables to types, and a partial function from ordinary variables to values. The meaning of a type expression σ in an environment η for interpretation $\langle \mathcal{T}, \mathcal{D}, Rel\rangle$ is defined by induction on σ as follows.

$$[\![t]\!]\eta = \eta(t),$$
$$[\![\sigma \to \tau]\!]\eta = \to^I ([\![\sigma]\!]\eta)([\![\tau]\!]\eta),$$
$$[\![\forall t.\sigma]\!]\eta = \forall^I (\lambda a \in T.[\![\sigma]\!]\eta[a/t]),$$

where $\eta[a/t]$ denotes the environment η modified so that $(\eta[a/t])(t) = a$. Further discussion of type structures $\mathcal{T} = \langle \mathcal{U}, \to^I, \forall^I\rangle$ may be found in [21].

An environment η for interpretation $\langle \mathcal{T}, \mathcal{D}, Rel\rangle$ satisfies a typing $M{:}\sigma$, written $\eta \models M{:}\sigma$, if η is defined on all free variables of M and

$$[\![M]\!]\eta \in D_{[\![\sigma]\!]\eta}.$$

An environment η satisfies type assignment A, written $\eta \models A$, if $\eta \models x{:}\sigma$ for all $x{:}\sigma \in A$. We say η *matches* A if η and A are defined on the same set of ordinary variables, and $\eta \models A$. The soundness of type inference is proved by induction on derivations.

Theorem 1 (Type Soundness)
If $A \vdash M{:}\sigma$ and $\eta \models A$, then $\eta \models M{:}\sigma$.

A general completeness theorem as in [21] can also be proved.

4 *Reduction Properties*

4.1 *Strong Normalization for Pure Terms*

As mentioned in [13, 21], the normalization of implicitly typed terms implies the normalization of explicitly typed terms. Specifically, we have the following lemma.

Lemma 1
If M is an explicitly typed term and M reduces to N by type β-reduction

$$(\lambda t.P)\sigma \to_\beta [\sigma/t]P,$$

then N has one less type abstraction than M.

Lemma 2
Let M, N be any explicitly typed terms. If M β-reduces to N by a sequence of reductions that includes one ordinary β-reduction

$$(\lambda x{:}\sigma.P_1)P_2 \to_\beta [P_2/x]P_1,$$

then Erase(M) β-reduces to Erase(N) by a sequence of at least one untyped β-reduction.

Consequently, if there is an infinite sequence of β-reductions starting from the explicitly typed term M, then there is an infinite sequence of untyped β-reductions starting from Erase(M).

We now show that for every explicitly typed term M with $A \vdash M{:}\sigma$ there is no infinite sequence of β-reductions from Erase(M). This is proved by showing that for any "type-closed" set S of untyped lambda terms, there is a PER interpretation in which every typed value is an element of S. We then observe that the set of strongly normalizing terms is "type-closed" and apply type soundness to conclude that whenever $A \vdash M{:}\sigma$, the term Erase(M) is strongly normalizing. From this we can also conclude that M is strongly normalizing. Since we are primarily concerned with type membership, the proof could be carried out using subsets as types instead of relations.

Let S be a set of untyped lambda terms. A subset $B \subseteq S$ is a *type set relative to S* if

(i) $xM_1 \ldots M_k \in B$ whenever $M_1, \ldots, M_k \in S$,

(ii) $(\lambda x.M)N_0 \ldots N_k \in B$ whenever $([N_0/x]M)N_1 \ldots N_k \in B$ and $N_0 \in S$.

A set S of lambda terms is *type-closed* if S is a type set relative to S and we have $M \in S$ whenever $MN \in S$.

Lemma 3

The set of strongly normalizing untyped lambda terms is type-closed.

If S is type-closed, then the *type structure* $\mathcal{T}_S = \langle \mathcal{U}, \rightarrow^{\mathcal{T}}, \forall^{\mathcal{T}} \rangle$ is defined by taking T to be the set of all type sets relative to S, $\mathcal{U}$ the full hierarchy of set-theoretic function spaces over T (i.e., $T \rightarrow T$ is the set of all functions from T to T, $T \rightarrow (T \rightarrow T)$ the set of all functions from T to $T \rightarrow T$, and so on) and defining $\rightarrow^{\mathcal{T}}$ and $\forall^{\mathcal{T}}$ by

$$B \rightarrow^{\mathcal{T}} C = \{M | N \in B \text{ implies } MN \in C\},$$

$$\forall^{\mathcal{T}} f = \cap_{B \in T}\ f(B).$$

Lemma 4

If S is type-closed, then $\mathcal{T}_S$ is a type structure.

We can combine the lambda interpretation $\mathcal{D}_\alpha$ of α-equivalence classes with any $\mathcal{T}_S$ constructed from a type-closed S to produce a PER interpretation.

Lemma 5
If S is type closed, then the triple $\langle \mathcal{T}_S, \mathcal{D}_\alpha, Rel \rangle$ with Rel mapping each $B \in T_S$ to the relation $B \times B$ is a PER interpretation.

It now follows from type soundness that every typable term belongs to every type-closed set of untyped terms.

Lemma 6
If S is type closed and $A \vdash M{:}\sigma$, then Erase(M) $\in S$.

Since the set of strongly normalizing terms is type-closed, we have the following normalization theorems.

Corollary 1
If $A \vdash M{:}\sigma$, then Erase(M) is a strongly normalizing untyped term.

Using Lemmas 1 and 2, we have

Corollary 2
If $A \vdash M{:}\sigma$, then M is a strongly normalizing typed term.

Some other type-closed sets are the set of terms M from which all reductions are confluent and the set of terms M for which standard reduction reaches a normal form. Thus the theorem above has the Church-Rosser theorem for typable terms and the completeness of standard reduction for typable terms as corollaries. The similarity between strong normalization proofs and proofs of other reduction properties is also pointed out in [27]. It is worth mentioning that it is generally more difficult to derive properties of M from properties of Erase(M) than in the special case of strong normalization.

5 *Models*

A *PER model* $I = \langle \mathcal{T}, \mathcal{D}, Rel \rangle$ is a PER interpretation in which $\mathcal{D}$ is a lambda model and Rel gives extensional relations to $\sigma \to \tau$. Specifically, we replace (Arrow.1) and (Arrow.2) by the single extensionality condition

$$(\text{Arrow})_{ext} \quad \langle d_1, d_2 \rangle \in Rel(a \to b) \text{ iff } \langle d_1 \bullet e_1, d_2 \bullet e_2 \rangle \in Rel(b) \text{ for all } \langle e_1, e_2 \rangle \in Rel(a).$$

Since the equivalence relation associated with polymorphic types $\forall t.\sigma$, defined by intersection, is already extensional, we do not need to strengthen (ForAll).

Every PER model I determines an extensional second-order model $\mathcal{A}_I = \langle Type, Dom, \{\Phi\}\rangle$ satisfying the model definition proposed in [3, 21, 4]. The type structure *Type* of the second-order model is the same as the structure of the inference model. The set Dom^a of elements of type a is the set of equivalence classes

$$\mathrm{Dom}^a = \{[d]_a \mid d \in D_a\}, \text{ where } [d]_a = \{e \mid \langle d, e\rangle \in Rel(a)\}.$$

Ordinary application $\Phi_{a,b}$ of elements of type $a \to b$ to arguments of type a is defined by

$$\Phi_{a,b}[d]_{a\to b}[e]_a = [d \bullet e]_b\,,$$

while type application is defined by

$$\Phi_f[d]_{\forall f}a = [d]_{f(a)}.$$

Note that type application is not vacuous, since in general $Rel(f(a))$ will be a finer relation than $Rel(\forall f)$.

Lemma 7

A structure $\mathcal{A}_I$ constructed from a PER model I is an extensional second-order lambda model. In particular, every typed term has a meaning, and the usual equivalences between terms hold.

There is a correspondence between environments for a PER model I and the second-order model $\mathcal{A}_I$, provided we have a type assignment in mind. Specifically, suppose η is an environment for I which matches a type assignment A. We define the environment η_A for $\mathcal{A}_I$ by

$$\eta_A(t) = \eta(t)$$

for any type variable t, and

$$\eta_A(x) = [\eta(x)]_{[\![A(x)]\!]\eta}$$

for any ordinary variable x in the domain of η and A. Since the domain of A is necessarily finite, the environment η_A will be defined only on finitely many ordinary variables. There is a converse of sorts (i.e., an adjoint situation): given any environment η' for $\mathcal{A}_I$, we can use the axiom of choice to find an environment η for I such that $\eta_A = \eta'$. Using the mapping from η to η_A, we can now describe the relationship between meanings of terms in I and $\mathcal{A}_I$.

Theorem 2 (Characterization)

Let $I = \langle \mathcal{T}, \mathcal{D}, Rel\rangle$ be a PER model and $\mathcal{A}_I$ the second-order model determined by I. Suppose $A \vdash M{:}\sigma$ and η is an environment for I which matches A. Then

$$\mathcal{A}[\![M]\!]\eta_A = [\mathcal{D}[\![\mathrm{Erase}(M)]\!]\eta]_{[\![\sigma]\!]\eta}.$$

In other words, the meaning of M in $\mathcal{A}_I$ is the equivalence class of the untyped meaning of Erase(M).

The characterization theorem shows that if M and N have the same type and Erase(M)=Erase(N), then $\mathcal{A}_I \models M = N$ for every second-order model constructed using partial equivalence relations. For example, the equation

$$\lambda x{:}\forall t.t.\ x = \lambda x{:}\forall t.t.(x\ \forall t.t)$$

holds in every $\mathcal{A}_I$ since both terms have the same type, and the two terms have the same erasure. More generally, if $[\tau_1/s]\sigma_1 = [\tau_2/t]\sigma_2$ and similarly $[\rho_1/s]\sigma_1 = [\rho_2/t]\sigma_2$, then the equation

$$\lambda x{:}\forall s(\sigma_1 \to r).\lambda y{:}\forall t.\sigma_2.(x\tau_1)(y\tau_2) = \lambda x{:}\forall s(\sigma_1 \to r).\lambda y{:}\forall t.\sigma_2.(x\rho_1)(y\rho_2)$$

holds in every second-order model based on PER's. There are, of course, many more examples. However, the following completeness theorem shows that this is the only kind of unexpected equation that holds in all PER models.

Theorem 3 (Completeness)
Let *Th* be any second-order lambda theory such that whenever $A \vdash M{:}\sigma$ and $A \vdash N{:}\sigma$ with Erase(M) syntactically identical to Erase(N), we have $A \vdash M = N{:}\sigma \in Th$. Then there is a second-order model $\mathcal{A}_I$ with $\mathcal{A}_I \models M = N$ *iff* $A \vdash M = N{:}\sigma \in Th$.

6 *Conclusion and Directions for Further Investigation*

We have proved type soundness for PER interpretations. Using PER interpretations which are largely syntactic in nature, we can use this to prove that every polymorphically typed term is strongly normalizing. This normalization proof seems simpler than earlier ones, and the use of PER interpretations helps clarify the structure of the proof. In addition, other reduction properties of terms may be proved as a consequence of type soundness in much the same way.

The second part of the paper focuses on PER models, a special case of PER interpretations. Every PER model may be viewed as an extensional model of second-order typed lambda calculus. The characterization theorem shows that the meaning of any explicitly typed second-order term M is the equivalence class of the untyped meaning of Erase(M). It follows from the characterization theorem that whenever Erase(M) = Erase(N) and M and N have the same type, the typed equation $M = N$ holds in all second-order models based on partial equivalence relations. However, the completeness theorem shows that these equations (and their provable consequences) are the only equations that hold in all PER models that do not follow from the usual axioms and inference rules.

Although we have not checked all the details, it seems that the analysis of reduction properties can be extended to applied versions of second-order lambda calculus with constants and "δ-reductions". By adding an additional clause for "δ-head expansion" to the definition of "type set", we can prove normalization for δ-reductions that satisfy the hypotheses of Mitschke's "δ-reduction theorem" (Theorem 15.3.3 of [1]) and that respect typing in a uniform way. This gives us a method for constructing second-order term models with decidable theories.

Following a suggestion of Eugenio Moggi, we can also drop the normalization requirement and construct models containing arbitrary algebraic structures by this means. Specifically, we may combine untyped lambda calculus with any multi-sorted algebra by adding constants to the lambda terms, one constant for each function or element of the algebra. We then add reduction rules for evaluating variable-free algebraic expressions over these constants. Since the resulting β, δ-reduction may be proved Church-Rosser using Mitschke's δ-reduction theorem (mentioned above), algebraic δ-reduction over expressions without variables and β-reduction of lambda terms combine to characterize an untyped lambda theory. This theory may be used to construct an untyped term model, which may be combined with a type structure to form a PER model. If we use equivalence relations as types of the type structure, by a construction analogous to the "zero set" construction of [21], and include the identity relations on the sorts of the original algebra as types, then we obtain a model with an isomorphic copy of the original multi-sorted algebra. This gives us a full and faithful embedding of any multi-sorted algebra into a second-order lambda model. In particular, we may construct second-order models with the integers, booleans, etc. as base types. However, there is no natural nonempty zero set in general, and so this construction leads to consider models with empty sets as types. Further discussion of the consequences of empty types may be found in [19].

Another generalization of this work is to consider PER models $\langle \mathcal{T}, \mathcal{D}, Rel \rangle$ where $\mathcal{D}$ is a partial combinatory model instead of a (total) lambda model. Further information on partial combinatory algebras may be found in [23, 25]. One example of a partial combinatory algebra is the set of natural numbers, with function application defined via Gödel numbering of partial recursive functions. The PER model based on this partial combinatory algebra is the structure HEO_2 mentioned in the introduction and defined precisely in [8, 28]. All of the results of this paper seem to carry over naturally to PER's over partial combinatory algebras, although one must often argue that a particular untyped application is defined. In particular, the characterization theorem for PER models based on partial combinatory models will still imply that $M = N$ whenever Erase(M)=Erase(N) and M and N have the same type. Since lambda models are a special case of partial combinatory algebras, our completeness theorem implies completeness for the more general class of PER models. However, it would be interesting to characterize the equational theories of specific models, such as HEO_2.

Acknowledgments

Thanks to Kim Bruce and Eugenio Moggi for helpful comments on an earlier version of this paper.

References

[1] Barendregt, H. P. *The Lambda Calculus: Its Syntax and Semantics.* North Holland, Amsterdam, 1984 (revised edition).

[2] Beeson, M. "Recursive models for constructive set theories". *Ann. Mathematical Logic 23* (1982), pp. 127–178.

[3] Bruce, K. B. and Meyer, A. R. "A completeness theorem for second-order polymorphic lambda calculus". *Proceedings of the International Symposium on Semantics of Data Types* (Sophia-Antipolis, France), pp. 131–144. Lecture Notes in Computer Science, vol. 173. Springer-Verlag, Berlin, 1984.

[4] Bruce, K. B., Meyer, A. R., and Mitchell, J. C. "The semantics of second-order lambda calculus". *Information and Computation* (to appear, 1990). Included in this volume (Chapter 10).

[5] Coppo, M. and Zacchi, M. "Type inference and logical relations". *Proceedings of the IEEE Symposium on Logic in Computer Science* (June), pp. 218–226. IEEE Press, New York, 1986.

[6] Fortune, S., Leivant, D., and O'Donnell, M. "The expressiveness of simple and second order type structures". *JACM 30*, 1 (1983), pp. 151–185.

[7] Freyd, P. and Scedrov, A. "Some semantic aspects of polymorphic lambda calculus". *IEEE Symposium on Logic in Computer Science* (June), pp. 315–319. IEEE Press, New York, 1987.

[8] Girard, J. Y. "Interpretation fonctionelle et elimination des coupures de l'arithmetique d'ordre superieur". These D'Etat, Université Paris VII, 1972.

[9] Hindley, R. and Longo, G. "Lambda calculus models and extensionality". *Z. Math. Logik Grundlag Math 26* (1980), pp. 289–310.

[10] Hindley, R. "The completeness theorem for typing lambda terms". *Theoretical Computer Science 22* (1983), pp. 1–17.

[11] Hyland, J. M. E. "The effective topos". *The L.E.J. Brouwer Centenary Symposium*, pp. 165–216. North Holland, Amsterdam, 1982.

[12] Kreisel, G. "Interpretation of analysis by means of constructive functionals of finite types". *Constructivity in Mathematics*, A. Heyting, ed., pp. 101–128. North-Holland, Amsterdam, 1959.

[13] Leivant, D. "Polymorphic type inference". *Proceedings of the 10th ACM Symposium on Principles of Programming Languages*, pp. 88–98. ACM, New York, 1983.

[14] Leivant, D. "Typing and convergence in the lambda calculus". Unpublished manuscript, 1984.

[15] MacQueen, D. and Sethi, R. "A semantic model of types for applicative languages". *ACM Symposium on LISP and Functional Programming*, pp. 243–252. ACM, New York, 1982.

[16] MacQueen, D., Plotkin, G., and Sethi, R. "An ideal model for recursive polymorphic types". *Information and Control 71*, 1/2 (1986), pp. 95–130.

[17] McCracken, N. "The typechecking of programs with implicit type structure". *Proceedings of the International Symposium on Semantics of Data Types* (Sophia-Antipolis, France, June), pp. 301–316. Lecture Notes in Computer Science, vol. 173. Springer-Verlag, Berlin, 1984.

[18] Meyer, A. R. "What is a model of the lambda calculus?" *Information and Control 52*, 1 (1982), pp. 87–122.

[19] Meyer, A. R., Mitchell, J. C., Moggi, E., and Statman R. "Empty types in polymorphic lambda calculus". *Proceedings of the 14th ACM Symposium on Principles of Programming Languages* (January), pp. 253–262. ACM, New York, 1987. Included, with corrections, in this volume (Chapter 10).

[20] Mitchell, J. C. "Semantic models for second-order lambda calculus". *Proceedings of the 25th IEEE Symposium on Foundations of Computer Science*, pp. 289–299. IEEE Press, New York, 1984.

[21] Mitchell, J. C. "Polymorphic type inference and containment". *Information and Computation 76*, 2/3 (1988), pp. 211–249. Included, with corrections, in this volume (Chapter 8).

[22] Myhill, J. R. and Shepherdson, J. C. "Effective operations on partial recursive functions". *Zeitschrift für mathematische Logik und Grundlagen der Mathematik 1*, 1955.

[23] Plotkin, G. "Denotational semantics with partial functions". Lecture notes, C.S.L.I. Summer School, Stanford, 1985.

[24] Reynolds, J. C. "Towards a theory of type structure". *Paris Colloqium on Programming*, pp. 408–425. Lecture Notes in Computer Science, vol. 19. Springer-Verlag, Berlin, 1974.

[25] Rosolini, G. "Continiuity and effectiveness in topoi". Ph.D. thesis, Merton College,

Oxford, 1986.

[26] Scott, D. "Data types as lattices". *SIAM J. Computing 5*, 3 (1976), pp. 522–587.

[27] Statman, R. "Logical relations and the typed lambda calculus". *Information and Control 65* (1985), pp. 85–97.

[28] Troelstra, A. S. *Mathematical Investigation of Intuitionistic Arithmetic and Analysis.* Lecture Notes in Mathematics, vol. 344. Springer-Verlag, Berlin, 1973.

The Semantics of Second-Order Lambda Calculus[1]

10

Kim B. Bruce
Williams College

Albert R. Meyer
MIT

John C. Mitchell
Stanford University

Abstract

In the second-order (polymorphic) typed lambda calculus, lambda abstraction over type variables leads to terms denoting polymorphic functions. Straightforward cardinality considerations show that a naive set-theoretic interpretation of the calculus is impossible. We give two definitions of semantic models for this language and prove them equivalent. Our syntactical "environment model" definition and a more algebraic "combinatory model"

1. This chapter is scheduled for publication in *Information and Computation 84*, 1 (January 1990) and appears here by permission. Copyright ©1990 by Academic Press, Inc.

definition for the polymorphic calculus correspond to analogous model definitions for untyped lambda calculus. Soundness and completeness theorems are proved using the environment model definition. We verify that some specific interpretations of the calculus proposed in the literature indeed yield models in our sense.

---

1 *Introduction*

The second-order lambda calculus, formulated independently by Girard [20] and Reynolds [60], is an extension of the usual typed lambda calculus. Like other kinds of lambda calculus, the ordinary parameter-binding mechanism of this language corresponds closely to parameter binding in many programming languages (cf. [29, 61, 74]). The particular type structure of the second-order system corresponds to the type structures of programming languages with polymorphism and data abstraction [18, 52]. Like Ada *generics* and parameterized modules in CLU [56, 32]), polymorphic functions in the second-order lambda calculus are formed by explicit lambda abstraction over types.[2] Since the calculus is composed of only a few constructs, second-order lambda calculus is a useful tool for studying and giving semantics to programming languages where types appear explicitly as parameters. In this paper, we examine the mathematical semantics of second-order lambda calculus, proving a completeness theorem and providing two characterizations of models.

The syntax of second-order lambda calculus, which is defined precisely in Sections 2 and 3, may be separated into three parts. The first is the set of second-order lambda expressions, or *terms*. Intuitively, terms are the "ordinary expressions" that describe computable functions and results of computation. The second syntactic class contains the type expressions. Expressions of the third class, the *kinds*, are used to describe the functionality of subexpressions of type expressions. For example, if t is any type, then the term

$$\lambda x{:}\, t.x$$

2. An alternative to second-order lambda calculus is to introduce polymorphism "implicitly" by assignment of more than one type to a single expression. The reader is referred to [2, 30, 45, 33, 46, 47] for further discussion of this alternative.

denotes the identity function on type t. The type of this term is $t \to t$, the type of functions from t to t. Given any argument y of type t, the value of the function application $(\lambda x\colon t.x)y = y$ may be computed by substituting y for the bound variable (formal parameter) x in the body of the term. Second-order lambda calculus allows us to lambda abstract over types, which produces polymorphic functions. Since we made no assumptions about the type t in writing $\lambda x\colon t.x$, we may regard t as a free type variable. (We will use $r, s, t, \ldots$ for type variables and $x, y, z, \ldots$ for ordinary variables.) The polymorphic identity function

$$I ::= \lambda t.\lambda x\colon t.x$$

is formed by lambda abstracting the type variable t. We may apply (or "instantiate") the polymorphic identity I to any type σ, coputing the value of the application $I\sigma$ by substituting σ for t in the body $\lambda x\colon t.x$. Thus

$$I\sigma = \lambda x\colon \sigma.x\,.$$

The polymorphic function I has a polymorphic type. Intuitively, the domain of I is the collection of all types, and the range of I is the union of all types of the form $t \to t$. We can express the type of I more specifically using the mapping $\lambda t.t \to t$ from types to types. Given an argument σ, we can compute the type of $I\sigma$ by applying the function $\lambda t.t \to t$ to σ. Thus we expect the type of the polymorphic identity to be derived from the function $\lambda t.t \to t$ in some way. We use the operator $\forall$ to produce a type from any function mapping types to types, and write $\forall(\lambda t.t \to t)$ for the type of the polymorphic identity I. In general, if M has type $\forall(\lambda t.\tau)$ then the type of the application $M\sigma$ is $(\lambda t.\tau)\sigma$. We usually abbreviate $\forall(\lambda t.t \to t)$ to $\forall t.t \to t$. The difference between $\lambda t.t \to t$ and $\forall t.t \to t$ is that $\lambda t.t \to t$ is a function from types to types, while $\forall t.t \to t$ is a type.

In second-order lambda calculus, each term has a type, and types are written using higher-order symbols (type constructors), $\to$ and $\forall$. The function-type constructor $\to$ is an infix binary operator on types. The polymorphic-type constructor $\forall$ takes a function from types to types and produces a type. If we wish to expand the language to allow product types (ordered pairs or records), sum types, and so on, then we will need to add new type constructors. Anticipating these and other extensions to the language, we will define second-order lambda terms with respect to any set of type constructors. Therefore, in addition to terms and type expressions, we will also have a general class of constructor expressions. To keep the syntax of constructor expressions straight, we use "kinds," which were called "orders" in [20]. Kinds were introduced independently in [37] and used subsequently in [34, 33]. Essentially, kinds are the "types" of things that appear in type expressions.

Subexpressions of type expressions may denote types, functions from types to types, functions from type functions to types, and so on. We will use T to denote the *kind* consisting of all types and $\kappa_1 \Rightarrow \kappa_2$ for the kind consisting of functions from kind κ_1 to κ_2. Thus we regard a function like $\lambda t.t \to t$ from types to types as a constructor expression of kind $T \Rightarrow T$. Similarly the constructor expression "$\to$" is of kind $T \Rightarrow (T \Rightarrow T)$ and $\forall$ has kind $(T \Rightarrow T) \Rightarrow T$. In effect, we use the ordinary typed lambda calculus in the syntax of type expressions. However, to reduce confusion between types and kinds, we use $\Rightarrow$ instead of $\to$ and call the types of this language kinds. Thus we have a hierarchy from lambda expressions to constructor expressions (which include the type expressions) to kind expressions. Lambda expressions have types and constructor expressions have kinds. While our main focus is on terms and their types, kinds play an important role in organizing the subexpressions of type expressions.

A number of proof-theoretic properties of second-order lambda calculus have been studied. The class of functions that can be represented in the calculus, the normalization theorem, and other proof theoretic results are described in [20, 71, 18]. However, the semantics of second-order lambda calculus is not entirely straightforward. The reason for this is illustrated by the fact that terms may be applied to their own types. For example, the polymorphic identity I can be applied to its own type $\forall t.t \to t$. If we think of a type as the set of all objects having that type, we are led to a contradiction with classical mathematics: The polymorphic identity I must denote a function whose domain contains the set $\forall t.t \to t$, and, at the same time, the set $\forall t.t \to t$ must contain I. We will see that we can make mathematical sense of second-order lambda calculus, but we must depart from the naive approach of letting λ-terms denote functions and types denote sets of functions.

Although general descriptions of models (essentially based on terms over arbitrary sets of constant symbols) were already given in [20, 35, 73], and a semantic model based on recursive function application was presented in [20], this was not known to many American computer scientists studying the system. Reynolds [60] attempted to construct a domain-theoretic model for the language but ran into difficulties, and he later demonstrated that no model in which the function-space constructor $\to$ behaves set-theoretically is possible [63]. Donahue [16] attempted to construct a model using retracts over complete lattices, but he ran afoul at a rather technical step where a retract of all retracts seemed to be necessary. McCracken [37], building on ideas from [66] and working independently of Donahue, produced the first correct domain-theoretic model of the second-order polymorphic lambda calculus.

This model was constructed from Scott's universal domain $\mathcal{P}\omega$, using closures (a special kind of retract) to represent types. In $\mathcal{P}\omega$, the set of all closures is the range of a closure, so that the problem encountered by Donahue may be avoided. McCracken [39], following a suggestion of Scott [67], has also shown that finitary retracts over certain finitary complete partial orders can be used to represent types. Bruce and Longo [1], again using ideas appearing in several papers by Scott, have also constructed a model using finitary projections over complete partial orders. In a somewhat different vein, Leivant [31] suggested a framework for the "structural semantics" of the second-order polymorphic lambda calculus. Since the types are the closed type expressions, Leivant's general model definition is an amalgam of a mathematical model for the elements and a syntactic model for the types.

We will give two definitions of model, the environment model and the more algebraic combinatory model. Our environment model definition first appeared in [10] and the combinatory model definition in [47]. In support of our definitions, we will prove soundness and completeness theorems and show that the two definitions of model are equivalent. (For simplicity, we assume in the soundness and completeness theorems that no type is empty.) We also indicate how our general notion of semantics relates to known examples of models such as Girard's HEO_2 based on recursive function application and the domain-theoretic models of McCracken and others. As mentioned earlier, Girard, Stenlund, Martin-Löf, and Leivant have also proposed general model definitions [20, 73, 35, 31], and polymorphic combinators were discussed in [73]. Our semantics encompasses the earlier general descriptions of models (which use type expressions and/or terms over arbitrary sets of constants) and was originally formulated without knowledge of the the earlier work of Girard, Stenlund, or Martin-Löf.

In Section 2 we describe the syntax and typing rules, and in Section 3 we present the axiom system for proving equations between terms. The relationship between the particular calculus we have chosen to use and other similar systems presented in the literature is discussed at the end of Section 2. In Section 4, the definition of environment model and the semantics of second-order lambda terms and constructor expressions are presented. We prove soundness and completeness theorems in Section 5. Section 6 introduces combinatory algebras and models and establishes the equivalence of combinatory and environment model definitions. We explain how the models of Girard, McCracken, and others fit our framework in Section 7. In the concluding Section 8, we discuss some extensions of this work as well as some open problems. It is worth repeating that we assume, throughout the paper, that all types are nonempty. Empty types introduce a number of complications, which are considered in [41, 51].

2 Syntax

2.1 Constructors and Kinds

As described in the Introduction, every term has a type, and every subexpression of a type expression has a kind. The subexpressions of type expressions, which may be type expressions or operators like $\rightarrow$ and $\forall$, will be called constructors. We will define the sets of kinds and constructor expressions before introducing the syntax and type checking rules for terms.

We will use the constant T to denote the kind consisting of all types. The set of kind expressions is given by

$$\kappa ::= T \mid \kappa_1 \Rightarrow \kappa_2 \,.$$

Intuitively, the kind $\kappa_1 \Rightarrow \kappa_2$ is the kind of functions from κ_1 to κ_2. For example, functions from types to types have kind $T \Rightarrow T$. We define the set of constructor expressions, beginning with a set of constructor constants. Let C_{cst} be a set of constant symbols c^κ, each with a specified kind (which we write as a superscript when necessary) and let $\mathcal{V}_{\mathrm{cst}}$ be a set of variables v^κ, each with a specified kind. We assume we have infinitely many variables of each kind. The constructor expressions over C_{cst} and $\mathcal{V}_{\mathrm{cst}}$, and their kinds, are defined by the following derivation system:

$$c^\kappa\colon \kappa, \quad v^\kappa\colon \kappa \,,$$

$$\frac{\mu\colon \kappa_1 \Rightarrow \kappa_2, \quad \nu\colon \kappa_1}{\mu\nu\colon \kappa_2} \,,$$

$$\frac{\mu\colon \kappa_2}{\lambda v^{\kappa_1}.\mu\colon \kappa_1 \Rightarrow \kappa_2} \,.$$

For example, $(\lambda v^T.v^T)c^T$ is a constructor expression with kind T. Free and bound variables are defined as usual. Substitution $\{\mu/u\}\nu$ of μ for free occurrences of u in ν has the usual inductive definition, including renaming bound variables in ν to avoid capture of free variables in μ.

A subset of the constructor expressions are the type expressions, the constructor expressions of kind T. Since we will often be concerned with type expressions rather than arbitrary constructor expressions, it will be useful to distinguish them by notational conventions. We adopt the conventions that

$r, s, t, \ldots$ stand for arbitrary type variables,

$\rho, \sigma, \tau, \ldots$ stand for arbitrary type expressions.

As in the definition above, we will generally use μ and ν for constructor expressions. We include the usual second-order types in the language by assuming that C_{cst} contains the function-type constructor constant

$$\rightarrow : T \Rightarrow (T \Rightarrow T)$$

and the polymorphic-type constructor constant

$$\forall : (T \Rightarrow T) \Rightarrow T\,.$$

As usual, we write $\rightarrow$ as an infix operator, as in the type expression $\sigma \rightarrow \tau$, and we write $\forall t.\sigma$ for $\forall(\lambda t.\sigma)$. In extensions of the basic language with direct products or disjoint sums, for example, we would include additional constants $\times, + : T \Rightarrow (T \Rightarrow T)$ in C_{cst}. In this paper, we will be concerned primarily with $\rightarrow$ and $\forall$.

Since we have a "kinded" lambda calculus, there are many nontrivial equations between types and constructors. While it would be more general to allow nonlogical axioms for constructor equality, this would complicate the syntax nontrivially, as discussed briefly in the conclusion of the paper. For simplicity, we will consider only the "pure" constructor equations that follow from the logical axioms below. The axioms and inference rules for constructors are essentially the familiar rules of the ordinary simple typed lambda calculus.

Constructor Axioms

$$\lambda v^{\kappa}.\mu = \lambda u^{\kappa}.\{u^{\kappa}/v^{\kappa}\}\mu, \quad u^{\kappa} \text{ not free in } \mu\,, \qquad (\alpha_{\kappa})$$

$$(\lambda v^{\kappa}.\mu)\nu = \{\nu/v^{\kappa}\}\mu\,, \qquad (\beta_{\kappa})$$

$$\lambda v^{\kappa}.(\mu, v^{\kappa}) = \mu, \quad v^{\kappa} \text{ not free in } \mu\,. \qquad (\eta_{\kappa})$$

The inference rules are the usual congruence rules and are similar to the inference rules (sym), (trans), (cong), and (ξ) given for terms in the next section. If $\mu = \nu$ is provable from the axioms and rules for constructors, we write $\vdash_c \mu = \nu$. The constructor axiom system will be used to assign types to terms, since equal types will be associated with the same set of terms. It is worth mentioning that since we will consider only the pure theory of constructor equality, every constructor is provably equal to a unique normal form constructor with no subexpression matching the left-hand side of axiom (β) or (η). Consequently, we have the following lemma.

Lemma 1

If $\vdash_c \sigma_1 \rightarrow \tau_1 = \sigma_2 \rightarrow \tau_2$, then $\vdash_c \sigma_1 = \sigma_2$ and $\vdash_c \tau_1 = \tau_2$. Similarly, if $\vdash_c \forall\mu = \forall\nu$, then $\vdash_c \mu = \nu$.

2.2 *Terms and Their Types*

We follow Reynolds [60] and write free variables without type labels. However, we will always assign types to free variables using a technical device we call a type assignment. Since a constant must name a specific semantic value, we will require each constant to have a fixed type without free constructor variables.

Let $\mathcal{V}_{\text{term}}$ be an infinite collection of variables, which will remain fixed throughout the paper. Let C_{term} be a set of constants, each with a fixed, closed type. The set $PreTerm(C_{\text{cst}}, C_{term})$, of *preterms* over variables from $\mathcal{V}_{\text{cst}}$ and $\mathcal{V}_{term}$ and the indicated sets of constants, is defined by

$$M ::= c \mid x \mid \lambda x\colon \sigma.M \mid MN \mid \lambda t.M \mid M\sigma\,,$$

where $c \in C_{\text{term}}$, $x \in \mathcal{V}_{\text{term}}$, t is a type variable, and σ is a type expression over C_{cst} and $\mathcal{V}_{\text{cst}}$. We will define the well typed terms below. The usual definitions of free and bound variables in lambda expressions may be stated without reference to typing: λ binds x in $\lambda x\colon \sigma.M$ and t in $\lambda t.M$. Substitutions $\{N/x\}M$ of N for x and $\{\sigma/t\}M$ of σ for t are defined as usual to include renaming of bound variables in M to avoid capture.

As in most typed programming languages, the type of a second-order lambda term will depend on the context in which it occurs. We must know the types of all free variables before assigning a type. A *syntactic type assignment* B is a finite set

$$B = \{x_1\colon \sigma_1, \ldots, x_k\colon \sigma_k\}$$

of associations of types to variables, with no variable x appearing twice in B. If x does not occur in a syntactic type assignment B, then we write $B, x\colon \sigma$ for the type assignment

$$B, x\colon \sigma = B \cup \{x\colon \sigma\}\,.$$

If x occurs in B, then it is sometimes convenient to write $B(x)$ for the unique σ with $x\colon \sigma \in B$.

The typing relation is a three-place relation between type assignments, preterms, and type expressions. Let B be a syntactic type assignment, $M \in PreTerm(C_{\text{cst}}, C_{\text{term}})$, and $\sigma\colon T$ a type expression. We define $B \vdash M\colon \sigma$, which is read "M has type σ with respect to B," by the derivation system below. The axioms about the typing relation are

$$\vdash c^{\tau}\colon \tau \quad \text{and} \quad x\colon \sigma \vdash x\colon \sigma\,.$$

The type derivation rules are

$$\frac{B \vdash M\colon \sigma \to \tau, B \vdash N\colon \sigma}{B \vdash MN\colon \tau}, \qquad (\to E)$$

$$\frac{B, x\colon \sigma \vdash M\colon \tau}{B \vdash \lambda x\colon \sigma \to \tau}, \qquad (\to I)$$

$$\frac{B \vdash M\colon \forall \mu}{B \vdash M\tau\colon \mu\tau}, \qquad (\forall E)$$

$$\frac{B \vdash M\colon \tau}{B \vdash \lambda t.M\colon \forall t.\tau}, \quad t \text{ not free in } B, \qquad (\forall I)$$

and two rules that apply to terms of any form. A few comments are in order before discussing the remaining two typing rules.

In rule $(\forall E)$, we know that μ must have kind $T \Rightarrow T$, since $\forall\mu$ is assumed to be a type, and $\forall$ has kind $(T \Rightarrow T) \Rightarrow T$. Therefore, $\mu\tau$ will be a well-formed type expression. A related point about $(\forall I)$ is that while we can introduce $\forall$-types only of the form $\forall t.\sigma ::= \forall(\lambda t.\sigma)$, we will be able to use the type equality rule below to derive typings of the form $B \vdash \lambda t.M\colon \forall\mu$, where μ is not of the form $(\lambda t.\sigma)$.

The restriction in the rule $(\forall I)$ is basically a matter of scope. In

$$x\colon t \vdash \lambda y\colon t \to t.yx\colon (t \to t) \to t,$$

for example, the type variable t refers to the same type on both sides of the turnstile. Therefore, it would not make sense to bind the occurrences on the right-hand side without binding those on the left at the same time. If we were to allow the variable t to be bound on the right only, giving us

$$x\colon t \vdash \lambda t.\lambda y\colon t \to t.yx\colon \forall t.(t \to t) \to t,$$

then using $(\forall E)$ we could derive $x\colon t \vdash \lambda y\colon s \to s.yx\colon (s \to s) \to s$, which does not make any sense at all. This pathology is also discussed in Section 5.2 of [18].

Since additional hypotheses about the types of variables do not effect the type of a term, we have the rule

$$\frac{B \vdash M\colon \tau}{B, x\colon \sigma \vdash M\colon \tau}, \quad x \text{ not in } B, \qquad \text{(add hyp)}$$

for adding typing hypotheses. In addition, we have the type equality rule

$$\frac{B \vdash M\colon \sigma, \vdash_c \sigma = \tau}{B \vdash M\colon \tau}. \qquad \text{(type eq)}$$

We say M is a *term* if $B \vdash M\colon \sigma$ for some B and σ. However, we will seldom have occasion to write terms without also writing the relevant type assignment and type as well. In writing $B \vdash M\colon \sigma$ in the rest of the paper, we will mean that the typing $B \vdash M\colon \sigma$ is derivable, unless explicitly stated otherwise.

A simple induction on type derivations shows that if a term M has two types σ and τ, then these types are provably equal. Rule (type eq) guarantees the converse, so that for any type assignment B and preterm M, either M has no type with respect to B or else the type of M is unique, up to equality. Furthermore, any derivation of a typing $B \vdash M : \sigma$ uses only the free variables of M, and depends only on $B(x)$ up to type equality. Therefore, we have the following lemma.

Lemma 2

Suppose $B \vdash M : \sigma$ is well typed and let A be any syntactic type assignment such that $\vdash_c A(x) = B(x)$ for all x free in M. Then $A \vdash M : \tau$ if and only if $\vdash_c \sigma = \tau$.

Since we have chosen the pure theory of β, η-conversion between constructor expressions, every equivalence class of constructor expressions has a unique normal form. Therefore, for each syntactic type assignment B and $M \in PreTerm(C_{\text{cst}}, C_{\text{term}})$, if $B \vdash M : \sigma$ and $B \vdash M : \tau$ then σ and τ may be simplified to the same normal form. Assuming that the types given in B are in normal form, it is easy to write an efficient algorithm which computes the normal form type of M with respect to B when it exists, and returns *error* if it does not (cf. [30]).[3] Typings have some natural substitution properties. For example, if $B \vdash N : \rho$ and $B, x : \rho \vdash M : \sigma$, then $B \vdash \{N/x\}M : \sigma$. In addition, if we define $\{\sigma/t\}B$ by substituting σ for t in every type occurring in B, then whenever $B \vdash M : \rho$, we have $\{\sigma/t\}B \vdash \{\sigma/t\}M : \{\sigma/t\}\rho$. In particular if t is not free in B, then $B \vdash \{\gamma/t\}M : \{\gamma/t\}\rho$. Another useful substitution property is summarized by the following lemma.

Lemma 3

Let S be a substitution of constructor expressions for constructor variables and preterms for ordinary variables such that $A \vdash Sx : S\sigma$ is derivable for every $x : \sigma \in B$. If $B \vdash M : \tau$ is derivable, then so is $A \vdash SM : S\tau$.

2.3 *Relationship to Other Systems*

It is best to think of the second-order lambda calculus as a family of related systems, rather than as a single calculus. The particular calculus we have chosen is a compromise between the most basic calculus presented in [60] and the extensions considered in [20, 37]. The types used in the second-order lambda calculus of Reynolds [60], studied in [16, 18, 30, 31, 63], are a subset of ours. Specifically, only normal form type expressions are used, and no constructor symbols besides type variables, type constants, $\rightarrow$, and $\forall$

3. If types in B are not given in normal form, then they may have to be simplified, which cannot necessarily be done efficiently [70].

are allowed. It is possible to show that our typing rules and equational proof rules are conservative over Reynolds', and so we consider the variables of higher kinds an essentially benign extension. However, because of lambda abstraction in type expressions, type equality in our system becomes more complicated.

One straightforward extension of Reynolds' calculus is to add cartesian product types $\sigma \times \tau$. This system may be obtained from ours by adding a type constructor $\times: T \Rightarrow (T \Rightarrow T)$ and constants for pairing and projection functions. Girard also considers a system with existential types, a calculus with type constructor $\exists$ of kind $(T \Rightarrow T) \Rightarrow T$ which is "dual" to $\forall$ and related to existential quantification in logical formulas (see [20, 52] for further discussion). One advantage of the calculus we have chosen is that it is easy to extend the syntax to include additional type constructors of any kind, and it will be quite easy to see how to modify the model definitions accordingly.

A more significant extension of the basic second-order calculus, which Girard called F_2, is obtained by allowing lambda abstaction in terms over variables of higher kinds. For example, if $f^{T \Rightarrow T}$ is a variable of kind $T \Rightarrow T$, then the system we have defined allows the term $\lambda x{:}ft.x{:}ft \rightarrow ft$. It is quite sensible to allow the variable f to be lambda bound, giving us the term $\lambda f^{T \Rightarrow T}.\lambda x{:}\,ft.x$. To type this term, we need a "higher-order" $\forall$ of kind $((T \Rightarrow T) \Rightarrow T) \Rightarrow T$. Adding this constructor constant, and allowing the associated lambda abstraction, leads to Girard's "higher-order" lambda calculus F_3. By adding type quantification over successively higher kinds, we obtain the languages $F_4, F_5, \ldots$; the union of all these languages is F_ω. (See Section I.9 of [20] for further discussion.) We hope that by including variables of higher kinds, we will provide enough information to allow the reader to extend our model definition and completeness proof to any of Girard's higher-order calculi, or the calculus of the theory of species discussed in [73].

In addition to the generality of considering constructor expressions of all kinds, constructors will be used in the discussion of combinatory models to write down the types of polymorphic combinators. Another subtle function of variables of higher kind will be mentioned after the definition of environment models and summarized in Lemma 10.

3 *Equations between Terms*

Since we write terms with type assignments, it is natural to include type assignments in equations as well. By *equation*, we will mean an expression

$$B \vdash M = N{:}\,\sigma\,,$$

where $B \vdash M\colon \sigma$ and $B \vdash N\colon \sigma$. Intuitively, an equation $\{x_1\colon \sigma_1, \ldots, x_k\colon \sigma_k\} \vdash M = N\colon \sigma$ means, "if the variables $x_1, \ldots, x_k$ have types $\sigma_1, \ldots, \sigma_k$ (respectively), then terms M and N denote the same element of type σ." Since $\vdash$ is considered an implication, an equation may hold vacuously if it is impossible to assign the variables meanings of the correct types. This may happen when types are empty, a complication we will avoid by assuming that every type is nonempty. (Empty types are discussed in [41, 51]; see also the discussion following inference rule (remove hyp) below.)

The axioms and inference rules for equations between second-order lambda terms are similar to the axioms and rules of the ordinary typed lambda calculus. The main difference is that we tend to have two versions of each axiom or rule, one for ordinary function abstraction or application, and another for type abstraction or application.

Axioms for Terms

$$B \vdash \lambda x\colon \sigma.M = \lambda y\colon \sigma.\{y/x\}M\colon \sigma \to \tau,\ y \text{ not in } B\,,$$
$$B \vdash \lambda t.M = \lambda s.\{s/t\}M\colon \forall t.\sigma,\ s \text{ not free in } \lambda t.M\,, \qquad (\alpha)$$

$$B \vdash (\lambda x\colon \sigma.M)N = \{N/x\}M\colon \sigma\,,$$
$$B \vdash (\lambda t.M)\tau = \{\tau/t\}M\colon \sigma\,, \qquad (\beta)$$

$$B \vdash \lambda x\colon \sigma.Mx = M\colon \sigma \to \tau,\ x \text{ not free in } M\,,$$
$$B \vdash \lambda t.Mt = M\colon \forall t.\sigma,\ t \text{ not free in } M\,. \qquad (\eta)$$

Although some authors prefer to omit it, we have included the extensionality axiom (η). This axiom is used to prove that if $Mx = Nx$ for a fresh variable x not appearing in M or N, then $M = N$. Models satisfying (η) seem more natural, since (η) (in combination with the other axioms and rules) implies that two elements of functional type $\sigma \to \tau$ are equal whenever they give equal results for all arguments of type σ. In addition, assuming extensionality will simplify much of the discussion of combinatory models in Section 6. Nonextensional models will be discussed briefly in Section 6.5.

It is not necessary to include a reflexivity axiom because $M = M$ follows from (β) by the symmetry and transitivity rules below. In (α) for ordinary variables, the assumption that y is not declared in B may be weakened to y not free in M. However, the axiom as stated is slightly easier to work with (see the soundness proof in Section 5), and the alternative axiom is easily derived using the following inference rules.

Inference Rules for Terms

$$\frac{B \vdash M = N\colon \sigma}{B \vdash N = M\colon \sigma}, \qquad \text{(sym)}$$

$$\frac{B \vdash M = N\colon \sigma, B \vdash N = P\colon \sigma}{B \vdash M = P\colon \sigma}, \qquad \text{(trans)}$$

$$\frac{B \vdash M = N\colon \sigma \to \tau,\ B \vdash P = Q\colon \sigma}{B \vdash MP = NQ\colon \tau}, \qquad \text{(cong)}_1$$

$$\frac{B \vdash M = N\colon \forall \mu,\ \vdash_c \sigma = \tau}{B \vdash M\sigma = N\tau\colon \mu\sigma}, \qquad \text{(cong)}_2$$

$$\frac{B, x\colon \sigma \vdash M = N\colon \rho,\ \vdash_c \sigma = \tau}{B \vdash \lambda x\colon \sigma.M = \lambda x\colon \tau.N\colon \sigma \to \rho}, \qquad (\xi)_1$$

$$\frac{B \vdash M = N\colon \sigma}{B \vdash \lambda t.M = \lambda t.N\colon \forall t.\sigma}, \quad t \text{ not free in } B, \qquad (\xi)_2$$

$$\frac{B \vdash M = N\colon \sigma, \mu\colon \kappa}{B \vdash \{\mu/\nu^{\kappa}\}M = \{\mu/\nu^{\kappa}\}N\colon \{\mu/\nu^{\kappa}\}\sigma}, \quad \nu^{\kappa} \text{ not free in } B \text{ and } \kappa \neq T. \qquad \text{(constr sub)}$$

Since type assignments and types are included in the syntax of equations, we need equational versions of the (add hyp) and (type eq) typing rules:

$$\frac{B \vdash M = N\colon \sigma}{B, x\colon \sigma \vdash M = N\colon \sigma}, \quad x \text{ not in } B, \qquad \text{(add hyp)}$$

$$\frac{B \vdash M = N\colon \sigma,\ \vdash_c \sigma = \tau}{B \vdash M = N\colon \tau}. \qquad \text{(type eq)}$$

In addition, we will adopt an inference rule for removing typing hypotheses:

$$\frac{B, x\colon \sigma \vdash M = N\colon \tau}{B \vdash M = N\colon \tau}, \quad x \text{ not free in } M \text{ or } N. \qquad \text{(remove hyp)}$$

This rule allows us to eliminate assumptions about variables that do not occur free in either term. While the analogous typing rule is an admissible rule of the language (Lemma 2), this equational rule is sound only if we assume that every type is nonempty. For example, the equation

$$z\colon \sigma \vdash \lambda x\colon t.\lambda y\colon t.x = \lambda x\colon t.\lambda y\colon t.y\colon t \to t \to t$$

may hold vacuously in some nontrivial model if σ is an empty type. However, the equation

$$\varnothing \vdash \lambda x\colon t.\lambda y\colon t.x = \lambda x\colon t.\lambda y\colon t.y\colon t \to t \to t,$$

which follows by rule (remove hyp), holds only in trivial models with no more than one element of each type.

It is easy to check that for each of the inference rules, if the antecedents are well typed equations, then the consequent is a well typed equation. The only slightly nontrivial cases are $(\text{cong})_2$ and $(\xi)_1$, in which we must consider type equality. In rule $(\text{cong})_2$, if $B \vdash M = N : \forall\mu$ and $\vdash_c \sigma = \tau$, then $\vdash_c \mu\sigma = \mu\tau$, and so $B \vdash M\sigma : \mu\sigma$ and $B \vdash N\tau : \mu\tau$ have provably equal types. The verification of $(\xi)_1$ is similar, but uses Lemma 2 to show that if $B, x{:}\sigma \vdash M = N : \rho$ is well typed and $\vdash_c \sigma = \tau$, then we have $B, x{:}\tau \vdash N : \rho$, and so $B \vdash \lambda x{:}\sigma.M = \lambda x{:}\tau.N : \sigma \to \rho$ is well typed. The reason for including type equality in these two inference rules is so that term equality respects constructor equality. More precisely, term equality has the following substitution property.

Lemma 4

If $B \vdash M : \sigma$ is well typed, $\vdash_c \mu = \nu$, and N is obtained from M by substituting $\nu : \kappa$ for one or more occurrences of $\mu : \kappa$, then we can prove $B \vdash M = N : \sigma$ from the axioms and inference rules above.

This lemma is easily proved by induction on M, using Lemma 2 to show that the equation $B \vdash M = N : \sigma$ is well typed. Rule (constr sub) is used to show that equality is closed under substitution. Since we have lambda abstraction and application for type variables and ordinary variables, we can prove substitution instances of equations using (β). However, since we cannot lambda-abstract constructor variables of kind κ different from T, we need rule (constr sub) to complete the proof of the following lemma.

Lemma 5

Let S be a substitution of constructor expressions for constructor variables and preterms for ordinary variables such that $A \vdash Sx : S\sigma$ for every $x{:}\sigma \in B$. Then from any well typed equation $B \vdash M = N : \tau$ we can prove $A \vdash SM = SN : S\tau$.

Lemma 3 may be used to show that the equation $A \vdash SM = SN : S\tau$ in the statement of Lemma 5 is well typed.

A *second-order lambda theory* Γ is a set of equations containing all instances of the term axioms and closed under the inference rules. We will not include equations between constructors in theories, since we will always use the same constructor equations.

4 Second-Order Environment Models

4.1 Introduction

Models for second-order lambda calculus will have several parts: We use "kind frames" to interpret kinds and constructors and additional sets indexed by types to interpret terms. All of these parts will be collected together in what we call a frame (after [24]). We define models as frames that satisfy an additional condition involving the meanings of terms. This form of definition is similar to the "environment model" definition for untyped lambda calculus given in [42]. Since the definition of second-order model is fairly complicated, we will try to illustrate some of the underlying ideas using untyped lambda calculus.

Untyped lambda calculus has untyped applications MN and function expressions $\lambda x.M$. If we think of M and N as denoting elements of some "domain" D, then the application MN of M to N makes sense if we have some way of turning M into a function. This is accomplished using an *element-to-function* map Φ. Conversely, we can easily regard $\lambda x.M$ as a function from D to D, since M specifies a single function value for every value of x. But in order to find a meaning for $\lambda x.M$ in D, we need a *function-to-element* map $\Psi = \Phi^{-1}$.[4] An *extensional applicative structure* $\langle D, \Phi \rangle$ consists of a set D together with a mapping Φ such that for some set $[D \to D]$ of functions from D to D,

$$\Phi : D \to [D \to D] \text{ is } \textit{one-to-one} \text{ and } \textit{onto}.$$

In other words, an extensional applicative structure $\langle D, \Phi \rangle$ consists of a set D together with a bijection Φ between D and a set $[D \to D]$ of functions from D to D. In general, we will be a bit informal about Φ and abbreviate $(\Phi(d))(e)$ to de.

If η is an environment mapping untyped variables to D, then the meaning $[\![M]\!]\eta$ of term M in environment η is defined by

$$[\![x]\!]\eta = \eta(x),$$

$$[\![MN]\!]\eta = \Phi([\![M]\!]\eta)([\![N]\!]\eta),$$

$$[\![\lambda x.M]\!]\eta = \Phi^{-1}(f), \text{ where } f: D \to D \text{ satisfies } f(d) = [\![M]\!]\eta[d/x].$$

Although this definition may look fine, there is a serious problem with the meanings of terms. The meaning of a lambda term $\lambda x.M$ is defined by applying Φ^{-1} to some function f. The function f is well defined, but f may not be

4. Since we are only concerned with extensional models (see Section 6.5), we assume that $\Psi = \Phi^{-1}$. In nonextensional models, there may be two elements $d_1, d_2 \in D$ representing the same function $f = \Phi(d_1) = \Phi(d_2)$. In this case, Φ has no inverse and we rely on a second function Ψ to choose a particular $d = \Psi(f)$ representing f. See [4, 42] for further discussion.

in the domain $[D \to D]$ of Φ^{-1}. Consequently, the meaning of $\lambda x.M$ may not be defined. Thus we must distinguish models, structures in which every term has a meaning, from arbitrary applicative structures. One straightforward model definition is the environment model definition. We say an applicative structure is an *environment model* if the meaning of every term M in every environment η is a well defined element of D. Some equivalent model definitions are discussed in [4, 26, 42].

A similar definition can be given for the ordinary typed lambda calculus. With typed application, we need an "element-to-function" map $\Phi_{a,b}$ for each pair of types a and b. The function $\Phi_{a,b}$ maps the domain $\mathrm{Dom}^{a \to b}$ of elements of type $a \to b$ to some set $[\mathrm{Dom}^a \to \mathrm{Dom}^b]$ of functions from Dom^a to Dom^b, and we use $\Phi_{a,b}^{-1}$ to give meaning to typed lambda abstractions $\lambda x{:}\,\sigma.M{:}\,\sigma \to \tau$. Since constructor expressions are a notational variant of simple typed lambda terms, we will interpret constructor expressions in structures like this.

4.2 *Semantics of Constructor Expressions*

Constructor expressions are interpreted using kind frames, which are essentially frames for the simple typed lambda calculus. A *kind frame Kind* for a set C_{cst} of constructor constants is a tuple,

$$\mathit{Kind} = \langle \{\mathrm{Kind}^{\kappa}\} \mid \kappa \text{ a kind}\}, \{\Phi_{\kappa_1,\kappa_2} \mid \kappa_1, \kappa_2 \text{ kinds}\}, \mathcal{I} \rangle \,,$$

where

$$\Phi_{\kappa_1,\kappa_2}\colon \mathrm{Kind}^{\kappa_1 \Rightarrow \kappa_2} \to [\mathrm{Kind}^{\kappa_1} \to \mathrm{Kind}^{\kappa_2}]$$

is a bijection between $\mathrm{Kind}^{\kappa_1 \Rightarrow \kappa_2}$ and some set $[\mathrm{Kind}^{\kappa_1} \to \mathrm{Kind}^{\kappa_2}]$ of functions from Kind^{κ_1} to Kind^{κ_2}, and

$$\mathcal{I}\colon C_{\mathrm{cst}} \to \cup_{\kappa} \mathrm{Kind}^{\kappa}$$

preserves kinds; i.e., $\mathcal{I}(c^{\kappa}) \in \mathrm{Kind}^{\kappa}$. Since constructor expressions include all typed lambda expressions, we will be interested in kind frames that are models of the simple typed lambda calculus.

Let η be an environment mapping constructor variables to $\cup_{\kappa}\mathrm{Kind}^{\kappa}$ such that for each v^{κ}, we have $\eta(v^{\kappa}) \in \mathrm{Kind}^{\kappa}$. The meaning $[\![\mu]\!]\eta$ of a constructor expression μ in environment η is defined as follows (see [4, 19, 24, 72]):

$$[\![v^{\kappa}]\!]\eta = \eta(v^{\kappa}) \,,$$

$$[\![c^{\kappa}]\!]\eta = \mathcal{I}(c^{\kappa}) \,,$$

$$[\![\mu\nu]\!]\eta = (\Phi_{\kappa_1,\kappa_2}[\![\mu]\!]\eta)[\![\nu]\!]\eta \,,$$

$$[\![\lambda v^{\kappa}.\mu]\!]\eta = \Phi^{-1}_{\kappa_1,\kappa_2} f, \text{ where } f(a) = [\![\mu]\!]\eta[a/v^{\kappa}] \text{ for all } a \in \text{Kind}^{\kappa}.$$

We say *Kind* is a *kind environment model* for C_{cst} if every constructor expression over C_{cst} has a meaning in every environment for *Kind*. We will give an equivalent algebraic definition in Section 6.

Note that we have not had to distinguish $\rightarrow$ and $\forall$ from other constructor constants. It is implicit in the definition of kind frame that Kind^T must be closed under $\rightarrow$ (viewed as a binary operation) and that the result of applying $\forall$ to any function in $\text{Kind}^{T\Rightarrow T}$ is also an element of Kind^T. The advantage of working with constructors and kinds is that our definition applies to any set of type constructors. If we also have a "product-type" constructor

$$\times : \text{Kind}^{T\Rightarrow(T\Rightarrow T)}$$

among our constants C_{cst}, then the definition of kind frame also requires that Kind^T be closed under $\times$ (viewed as a binary operation).

Since it is a very convenient way of making definitions more readable, we will often use $\forall, \rightarrow$ and other constants for their denotations in *Kind* when there is no danger of confusion. For example, if $f \in \text{Kind}^{T\Rightarrow T}$, we write $\forall f$ rather than $(\mathcal{I}(\forall))f$. It is worth mentioning that we could dispense with the mappings Φ_{κ_1,κ_2} in kind frames by letting $\text{Kind}^{\kappa_1\Rightarrow\kappa_2}$ be a set of functions from Kind^{κ_1} to Kind^{κ_2}. However, the slightly more involved setting described above provides more motivation for the interpretation of terms below. (In interpreting polymorphic terms, we cannot eliminate the Φ functions.) In addition, the functions Φ_{κ_1,κ_2} and $\Phi^{-1}_{\kappa_1,\kappa_2}$ simplify the completeness proof slightly.

4.3 *Frames and Environment Models*

As in the definition of untyped environment model, we first define a structure, called a frame, and then define models by distinguishing frames that interpret all terms from those that do not. Second-order frames will include typed versions of Φ, plus an additional collection of Φ's for polymorphic types. Intuitively, a polymorphic term $\lambda t.M$ denotes a function from the set of types to elements of types. More precisely, we will be able to regard the meaning of $\lambda t.M$ as an element of the cartesian product $\Pi_{a\in\text{Kind}^T}.\text{Dom}^{f(a)}$ for some function $f\colon \text{Kind}^{T\Rightarrow T}$ determined from the typing of M. Therefore, for every function $f \in \text{Kind}^{T\Rightarrow T}$, a second-order model will have a function Φ_f mapping $\text{Dom}^{\forall f}$ to some subset $[\Pi_{a\in\text{Kind}^T}.\text{Dom}^{f(a)}]$ of $\Pi_{a\in\text{Kind}^T}.\text{Dom}^{f(a)}$.

A *second-order frame* $\mathcal{F}$ for terms over constants from C_{cst} and C_{term} is a tuple

$$\mathcal{F} = \langle \mathit{Kind}, \mathit{Dom}, \{\Phi_{a,b} \mid a, b \in \text{Kind}^T\}, \{\Phi_f \mid f \in \text{Kind}^{T\Rightarrow T}\}\rangle$$

satisfying conditions (i) through (iv) below.

(i) $Kind = \langle\{\mathrm{Kind}^{\kappa}\}, \{\Phi_{\kappa_1,\kappa_2}\}, \mathcal{I}\rangle$ is a kind frame for C_{cst};

(ii) $Dom = \langle\{\mathrm{Dom}^a \mid a \in \mathrm{Kind}^T\}, \mathcal{I}_{Dom}\rangle$ is a family of nonempty sets Dom^a indexed by elements $a \in \mathrm{Kind}^T$, together with a function $\mathcal{I}_{Dom}: C_{term} \to \cup_a \mathrm{Dom}^a$ with $\mathcal{I}_{Dom}(c^\tau) \in \mathrm{Dom}^{[\![\tau]\!]}$ for all c^τ in C_{term};

(iii) for each $a, b \in \mathrm{Kind}^T$, we have a set $[\mathrm{Dom}^a \to \mathrm{Dom}^b]$ of functions from Dom^a to Dom^b with bijection $\Phi_{a,b}: \mathrm{Dom}^{a \to b} \to [\mathrm{Dom}^a \to \mathrm{Dom}^b]$;

(iv) for every $f \in \mathrm{Kind}^{[T \Rightarrow T]}$, we have a subset $[\Pi_{a \in \mathrm{Kind}^T}\mathrm{Dom}^{f(a)}] \subseteq \Pi_{a \in \mathrm{Kind}^T}\mathrm{Dom}^{f(a)}$ with bijection $\Phi_f: \mathrm{Dom}^{\forall f} \to [\Pi_{a \in \mathrm{Kind}^T}\mathrm{Dom}^{f(a)}]$.

Essentially, condition (iii) states that $\mathrm{Dom}^{a \to b}$ must "represent" some set $[\mathrm{Dom}^a \to \mathrm{Dom}^b]$ of functions from Dom^a to Dom^b. Similarly, condition (iv) specifies that $\mathrm{Dom}^{\forall f}$ must represent some subset $[\Pi_{a \in \mathrm{Kind}^T}\mathrm{Dom}^{f(a)}]$ of the product $\Pi_{a \in \mathrm{Kind}^T}\mathrm{Dom}^{f(a)}$.

Terms are interpreted using Φ's for application and Φ^{-1}'s for abstraction. Since different Φ and Φ^{-1} functions are used, depending on the types of terms, the type of a term will be used to define its meaning. If B is a type assignment and η an environment mapping $\mathcal{V}_{cst}$ to elements of the appropriate kinds and $\mathcal{V}_{term}$ to elements of $\cup\, Dom$, we say that η *satisfies* B, written $\eta \models B$, if

$$\eta(x) \in \mathrm{Dom}^{[\![\sigma]\!]\eta}$$

for every $x{:}\sigma \in B$.

Let $\mathcal{F}$ be a second-order frame. For any well typed term $B \vdash M{:}\sigma$ and environment $\eta \models B$, we will define the meaning $[\![B \vdash M{:}\sigma]\!]\eta$ inductively below. Although it may seem unnecessarily complicated, the simplest way to define meanings seems to be by induction on the derivation of typings, rather than the structure of terms. This is simply a technical device. Since any derivation of $B \vdash M{:}\sigma$ must follow the structure of M fairly closely, there is not much difference between the two forms of induction. However, since there is some flexibility in where rules (add hyp) and (type eq) might be used, there is a little more structure in the derivation of a typing of $B \vdash M{:}\sigma$ than in the expression $B \vdash M{:}\sigma$ itself. In particular, a derivation gives specific typings to each of the subterms, while the fact that $B \vdash M{:}\sigma$ is derivable only determines the types of subterms of M up to type equality.

The lambda abstraction case illustrates some of the advantages of induction on typing derivations. If we define the meaning of $B \vdash \lambda x{:}\sigma.M{:}\rho$ using induction on the structure of terms, we must argue that $\vdash_c \rho = \sigma \to \tau$ for some τ, and that it does not matter which τ we pick. We need $\rho = \sigma \to \tau$ so that we know the domain and range types, and we need to show that the choice of τ

is inessential so that it is clear that the meaning of each term is uniquely determined. These arguments are not entirely trivial since rule (type eq) allows the syntactic type of the lambda abstraction to have almost any form. In addition, we need to find some type assignment A with $A \vdash M\colon \tau$ so that we may apply the induction hypothesis, and argue that the choice of A is inessential. However, using induction on typing derivations, the inductive assumption for rule $(\rightarrow I)$ is that $B \vdash \lambda x\colon \sigma.M\colon \sigma \rightarrow \tau$ follows from typing $B, x\colon \sigma \vdash M\colon \tau$, and that the meaning of $B, x\colon \sigma \vdash M\colon \tau$ is defined for any environment satisfying $B, x\colon \sigma$. This gives us a specific domain and range types for the lambda term, and also guarantees that x does not occur in B, so that $B, x\colon \sigma$ is a well-formed type assignment. Some similar points apply in the $(\forall I)$ case and will be mentioned below. Once we have given the definition of meaning, it will be easy to prove that the meaning of a well typed term $B \vdash M\colon \sigma$ does not depend on the way this typing is derived.

The inductive clauses of the meaning function are given in the same order as the typing rules in Section 2.2, with rules $(\rightarrow E), (\rightarrow I), (\forall E)$, and $(\forall I)$ preceding rules (add hyp) and (type eq), which do not rely on the forms of terms:

$$[\![B \vdash x\colon \sigma]\!]\eta = \eta(x)\ ;$$

$$[\![B \vdash c\colon \sigma]\!]\eta = \mathcal{I}_{Dom}(c)\ ;$$

$$[\![B \vdash MN\colon \tau]\!]\eta = (\Phi_{a,b}[\![B \vdash M\colon \sigma \rightarrow \tau]\!]\eta)[\![B \vdash N\colon \sigma]\!]\eta\ ,$$

where $a = [\![\sigma]\!]\eta$ and $b = [\![\tau]\!]\eta$;

$$[\![B \vdash \lambda x\colon \sigma.M\colon \sigma \rightarrow \tau]\!]\eta = \Phi_{a,b}^{-1} g, \text{ where}$$

$g(d) = [\![B, x\colon \sigma \vdash M\colon \tau]\!]\eta[d/x]$ for all $d \in \text{Dom}^a$, and

$a = [\![\sigma]\!]\eta$ and $b = [\![\tau]\!]\eta$;

$$[\![B \vdash M\tau\colon \mu\tau]\!]\eta = (\Phi_f[\![B \vdash M\colon \forall\mu]\!]\eta)[\![\tau]\!]\eta, \text{ where } f = [\![\mu]\!]\eta\ ;$$

$$[\![B \vdash \lambda t.M\colon \forall t.\sigma]\!]\eta = \Phi_f^{-1} g, \text{ where}$$

$g(a) = [\![B \vdash M\colon \sigma]\!]\eta[a/t]$ for all $a \in \text{Kind}^T$, and

$f \in \text{Kind}^{T \Rightarrow T}$ is the function $[\![\lambda t.\sigma]\!]\eta$;

$$[\![B, x\colon \sigma \vdash M\colon \tau]\!]\eta = [\![B \vdash M\colon \tau]\!]\eta,$$

where the left-hand typing follows by rule (add hyp) ;

$$[\![B \vdash M\colon \tau]\!]\eta = [\![B \vdash M\colon \sigma]\!]\eta,$$

where the left-hand typing follows by rule (type eq).

It is relatively easy to see that the environments mentioned on the right-hand sides of these clauses all satisfy the appropriate syntactic type assignments. One nontrivial case is type abstraction by rule ($\forall I$). Since we assume that $B \vdash \lambda t.M\colon \forall t.\sigma$ follows from $B \vdash M\colon \sigma$, we know that t does not occur free in B. Therefore, if $\eta \models B$, then any $\eta[a/t]$ satisfies B as well.

In the inductive definition of meaning, there is no guarantee that $[\![B \vdash M\colon \sigma]\!]\eta$ exists for every well typed term. For example, g in the $\lambda x\colon \sigma.M$ case may not be in the domain of $\Phi_{a,b}^{-1}$, and similarly for g in the $\lambda t.M$ case. Therefore, we make the following definition. A second-order frame,

$$\mathcal{F} = \langle Kind, Dom, \{\Phi_{a,b} \mid a, b \in \text{Kind}^T\}, \{\Phi_f \mid f \in \text{Kind}^{T\Rightarrow T}\}\rangle,$$

is an *environment model* if (i) *Kind* is a kind environment model, and (ii) for every term $B \vdash M\colon \sigma$ and every environment $\eta \models B$, the meaning $[\![B \vdash M\colon \sigma]\!]\eta$ exists as defined above.

It is easy to check that the meanings of terms have the appropriate semantic types.

Lemma 6

Let η be an environment for a model $\langle Kind, Dom, \{\Phi_{a,b}\}, \{\Phi_f\}\rangle$. If $\eta \models B$, then $[\![B \vdash M\colon \sigma]\!]\eta \in \text{Dom}^{[\![\sigma]\!]\eta}$.

In addition, we can show that the meaning of a well typed term $B \vdash M\colon \sigma$ does not depend on the derivation of the typing. This is the intent of the following two lemmas. It will be helpful to name typing derivations and to write, e.g., Δ, Δ_1 for the derivation Δ followed by derivation Δ_1. An easy induction on typing derivations shows that rules (add hyp) and (type eq) do not effect the meanings of terms.

Lemma 7

Suppose Δ is a derivation of $A \vdash M\colon \sigma$ and Δ, Δ_1 is a derivation of $B \vdash M\colon \tau$ such that only rules (add hyp) and (type eq) appear in Δ_1. Then for any $\eta \models B$, we have

$$[\![A \vdash M\colon \sigma]\!]\eta = [\![B \vdash M\colon \tau]\!]\eta,$$

where the meanings are taken with respect to derivations Δ and Δ, Δ_1.

Using induction on the structure of terms, and Lemmas 1, 2, and 7, we can now show that the meanings of "compatible" typings of a term are equal.

Lemma 8
Suppose Δ and Δ_1 are derivations of typings $A \vdash M{:}\,\sigma$ and $B \vdash M{:}\,\tau$, respectively, and that $\vdash_c A(x) = B(x)$ for every x free in M. Then

$$[\![A \vdash M{:}\,\sigma]\!]\eta = [\![B \vdash M{:}\,\tau]\!]\eta\,,$$

where the meanings are defined using Δ and Δ_1, respectively.

It follows that the meaning of any well typed term is independent of the typing derivation.

Corollary 1
Suppose Δ and Δ_1 are derivations of a typing $B \vdash M{:}\,\sigma$. Then for any environment $\eta \models B$, the meaning $[\![B \vdash M{:}\,\sigma]\!]\eta$ defined using induction on Δ is the same as the meaning defined using Δ_1.

This corollary allows us to regard an equation $B \vdash M = N{:}\,\sigma$ as an equation between M and N, rather than derivations of typings $B \vdash M{:}\,\sigma$ and $B \vdash N{:}\,\sigma$. In addition to the corollary, Lemma 8 shows that meaning is a congruence with respect to type equality, which will be useful in showing the soundness of the equational proof rules for terms.

A very useful fact is the following substitution lemma.

Lemma 9 (Substitution)

(i) Suppose $B,\ x{:}\,\sigma \vdash M{:}\,\tau$, and $B \vdash N{:}\,\sigma$. If $\eta \models B$ then

$$[\![B \vdash \{N/x\}M{:}\,\sigma]\!]\eta = [\![B, x{:}\,\sigma \vdash M{:}\,\tau]\!]\eta[[\![B \vdash N{:}\,\sigma]\!]\eta/x]\,.$$

(ii) If $B \vdash M{:}\,\sigma$ and t is not free in B, then

$$[\![B \vdash \{\tau/t\}M{:}\,\{\tau/t\}\sigma]\!]\eta = [\![B \vdash M{:}\,\sigma]\!]\eta[[\![\tau]\!]\eta/t]\,.$$

(iii) If μ, ν are constructor expressions with $\nu{:}\,\kappa$ and $v \in \mathcal{V}_{cst}$ a variable of kind κ, then

$$[\![\{\nu/v\}\mu]\!]\eta = [\![\mu]\!]\eta[[\![\nu]\!]\eta/v]\,.$$

Parts (i) and (ii) of the lemma are easily proved by induction on terms. Part (iii) is a well-known property of simple typed lambda calculus. It is also easy to prove that the meaning $[\![B \vdash M{:}\,\sigma]\!]\eta$ does not depend on $\eta(x)$ or $\eta(t)$ for x or t not free in M.

An important lemma about the environment model condition is that it does not depend on the set of constants of the language.

Lemma 10

Let $\mathcal{F}$ be an environment model for terms over constants C_{cst} and C_{term}. If we expand C_{cst} and C_{term} to C_{cst}' and C_{term}', and interpret the fresh constants as any elements of $\mathcal{F}$ of the appropriate kinds or types, then we obtain an environment model for terms over constants from C_{cst}' and C_{term}'.

This lemma, which will be used in the proof of the combinatory model theorem (Theorem 3), is easily proved using the fact that every constant is equal to some variable in some environment. More specifically, if we want to know that a term $B \vdash M\colon \sigma$ with constants has a meaning in some environment $\eta \models B$ for frame $\mathcal{F}$, then we begin by replacing the constants with fresh variables. Then, we choose some environment η_1 which is identical to η on the free variables of $B \vdash M\colon \sigma$, and which gives the new variables the values of the constants they replace. If $\mathcal{F}$ is an environment model, then the new term must have a meaning in the chosen environment, and so it is easy to show that $B \vdash M\colon \sigma$ must have a meaning in η. However, this argument applies only if we have variables of all kinds; without this, the hypothesis that $\mathcal{F}$ is an environment model for constants C_{cst} and C_{term} is not enough. In particular, the lemma fails if our frames include an arbitrary set of functions in $\mathrm{Kind}^{T \Rightarrow T}$ but do not have variables of kind $T \Rightarrow T$. This was overlooked in [10].

5 *Completeness*

In this section, we show that the axioms and inference rules are sound and complete for deducing equations between terms. We need the usual definitions of satisfaction and semantic implication to state the soundness and completeness theorems. An environment $\eta \models B$ for model $\mathcal{F}$ *satisfies* an equation $B \vdash M = N\colon \sigma$, written

$$\mathcal{F}, \eta \models B \vdash M = N\colon \sigma\,,$$

if $[\![B \vdash M\colon \sigma]\!]\eta = [\![B \vdash N\colon \sigma]\!]\eta$. A model $\mathcal{F}$ *satisfies* an equation $B \vdash M = N\colon \sigma$, written

$$\mathcal{F} \models B \vdash M = N\colon \sigma$$

if $\mathcal{F}$ and η satisfy $B \vdash M = N\colon \sigma$ for all $\eta \models B$. Similarly, a model $\mathcal{F}$ *satisfies* a set Γ of equations if $\mathcal{F}$ satisfies every equation in Γ. A set Γ of equations *semantically implies* an equation $B \vdash M = N\colon \sigma$, written

$$\Gamma \models B \vdash M = N\colon \sigma\,,$$

if $\mathcal{F} \models B \vdash M = N\colon \sigma$ whenever $\mathcal{F} \models \Gamma$.

It is easy to verify that the axioms and inference rules are sound for models without empty types.

Lemma 11 (Soundness)
Let Γ be a set of equations and let $B \vdash M = N\colon \sigma$ be an equation. If Γ proves $B \vdash M = N\colon \sigma$, then $\Gamma \models B \vdash M = N\colon \sigma$.

Proof The proof is entirely straightforward. We will show that two axioms, (α) and (β), are valid, leaving the details for remaining axioms and inference rules to the reader. Suppose $B \vdash \lambda x\colon \sigma.M\colon \sigma \to \tau$ is well typed, and assume the variable y does not occur in B. Let $\eta \models B$. For $a = [\![\sigma]\!]\eta$ and $b = [\![\tau]\!]\eta$, we have

$$\begin{aligned}
&[\![B \vdash \lambda x\colon \sigma.M\colon \sigma \to \tau]\!]\eta \\
&\quad = \Phi^{-1}_{a,b}(\lambda d \in D_a.[\![B, x\colon \sigma \vdash M\colon \tau]\!]\eta[d/x]) \\
&\quad = \Phi^{-1}_{a,b}(\lambda d \in D_a.[\![B, y\colon \sigma \vdash \{y/x\}M\colon \tau]\!]\eta[d/y]) \\
&\quad = [\![B \vdash \lambda y\colon \sigma.\{y/x\}M]\!]\eta.
\end{aligned}$$

The second equation follows from the substitution lemma (Lemma 9)(i). The soundness of (α) for type variables is proved similarly using Lemma 9(ii).

For (β), consider any term $B \vdash (\lambda x\colon \sigma.M)N\colon \tau$ with types $a, b \in \mathrm{Kind}^T$ and the meanings of σ and τ as above. We have

$$\begin{aligned}
&[\![B \vdash (\lambda x\colon \sigma M)N\colon \tau]\!]\eta \\
&\quad = \Phi_{a,b}(\Phi^{-1}_{a,b}(\lambda d \in D_a.[\![B, x\colon \sigma \vdash M\colon \tau]\!]\eta[d/x]))[\![B \vdash N\colon \sigma]\!]\eta \\
&\quad = [\![B, x\colon \sigma \vdash M\colon \tau]\!]\eta[[\![B \vdash N\colon \sigma]\!]\eta/x] \\
&\quad = [\![B \vdash \{N/x\}M\colon \tau]\!]\eta,
\end{aligned}$$

using Lemma 9(i). The soundness of (β) for types is proved similarly. The extensionality axioms (η) depend on the fact that $\Phi_{a,b}$ and Φ_f are bijections. It is easy to prove that semantic equality is an equivalence relation. The only subtlety in the (cong) and (ξ) rules are in (cong)$_2$ and (ξ)$_1$, where we must use Lemma 8 to account for the typing differences. As mentioned earlier, rule (remove hyp) relies on our assumption that no Dom^a is empty. The remaining rules are straightforward. ☐

We now show that the axioms and inference rules are complete for environment models without empty types.

Theorem 1 (Completeness)
Let Γ be a second-order theory over terms with constants from C_{cst} and C_{term}. There is an environment model $\mathcal{F}$ for C_{cst} and C_{term} such that $\mathcal{F} \models (B \vdash M = N\colon \sigma)$ iff $B \vdash M = N\colon \sigma \in \Gamma$.

Proof The proof uses a term model construction as in [4, 19, 42]. We begin by defining a kind frame $Kind = \langle\{\text{Kind}^{\kappa}\}, \{\Phi_{\kappa_1,\kappa_2}\}, \mathcal{I}\rangle$ for C_{cst}. Let *Kind* be the "term model" for C_{cst} built from equivalence classes of constructors as in [19]. Thus Kind^T is the set of equivalence classes of type expressions. We will use $\langle\mu\rangle$ to denote the equivalence class of the constructor μ. As usual, the interpretation of a constant $c \in C_{cst}$ is its equivalence class $\langle c\rangle$. In particular $\mathcal{I}(\forall) = \langle\forall\rangle$ and $\mathcal{I}(\rightarrow) = \langle\rightarrow\rangle$. An inductive argument, sketched in the proof of the *Claim* below, shows that *Kind* is a kind environment model.

We will define *Dom* using equivalence classes of terms. We will start with infinitely many variables of each type, since this will make it possible to prove extensionality of *Dom* quite easily. Let A be an infinite "type assignment" $A = \{x_1 : \sigma_1, \ldots\}$ assigning each variable a single type and providing infinitely many variables of each type. Although the infinite set A is not a syntactic type assignment, we will abuse notation slightly and write $A \vdash M : \sigma$ to mean that $A_1 \vdash M : \sigma$ for some finite subset $A_1 \subseteq A$.

We now define $\text{Dom}^{\langle\sigma\rangle}$ for each equivalence class $\langle\sigma\rangle$, using sets of terms proved equal by Γ. For any $A \vdash M : \sigma$, let $\langle M\rangle$ denote the equivalence class

$$\langle M\rangle = \{N \mid A \vdash M = N : \sigma \in \Gamma\},$$

and for each $\langle\sigma\rangle \in \text{Kind}^T$, let

$$\text{Dom}^{\langle\sigma\rangle} = \{\langle M\rangle \mid A \vdash M : \sigma\}.$$

Note that by choice of A, no $\text{Dom}^{\langle\sigma\rangle}$ is empty. In addition, by Lemma 2, $\text{Dom}^{\langle\sigma\rangle}$ depends only on the equivalence class $\langle\sigma\rangle$, and not on the type expression σ. We define $\mathcal{I}$ by interpreting each constant $c \in C_{term}$ as its equivalence class $\mathcal{I}_{Dom}(c) = \langle c\rangle$. It remains to define the families of functions $\{\Phi_{a,b}\}$ and $\{\Phi_f\}$.

For each $\langle\sigma\rangle, \langle\tau\rangle \in \text{Kind}^T$, define $\Phi_{\langle\sigma\rangle,\langle\tau\rangle}$ by

$$(\Phi_{\langle\sigma\rangle,\langle\tau\rangle}\langle M\rangle)\langle N\rangle = \langle MN\rangle,$$

for all M and N of the appropriate types. Let $[\text{Dom}^{\langle\sigma\rangle} \rightarrow \text{Dom}^{\langle\tau\rangle}]$ be the range of $\Phi_{\langle\sigma\rangle,\langle\tau\rangle}$. The function $\Phi_{\langle\sigma\rangle,\langle\tau\rangle}$ is well defined by (cong), and can be shown to be one to one using $(\xi)_1$ and (η).

For each $\langle\mu\rangle \in \text{Kind}^{T \Rightarrow T}$, define $\Phi_{\langle\mu\rangle}$ by

$$(\Phi_{\langle\mu\rangle}\langle M\rangle)\langle\tau\rangle = \langle M\tau\rangle$$

for every $A \vdash M : \forall\mu$ and $\langle\tau\rangle \in \text{Kind}^T$. We take $[\Pi_{\langle y\rangle \in \text{Kind}^T}\text{Dom}^{\langle\mu g\rangle}] \subseteq \Pi_{\langle y\rangle \in \text{Kind}^T}\text{Dom}^{\langle\mu g\rangle}$ to be the range of $\Phi_{\langle\mu\rangle}$ and note that $\Phi_{\langle\mu\rangle}$ is one to one by $(\xi)_2$ and (η). Thus we have a frame $\mathcal{F} = \langle Kind, Dom, \{\Phi_{a,b}\}, \{\Phi_f\}\rangle$ for terms over constants from C_{cst} and C_{term}.

It remains to show that $\mathcal{F}$ is an environment model and that $\mathcal{F}$ satisfies precisely the equations belonging to Γ. We will show that $\mathcal{F}$ is a model by giving an explicit description of the meaning of every constructor and term. If η is any environment for $\mathcal{F}$, we let η be any substitution of constructor expressions for constructor variables and terms for ordinary variables such that

$$\{\eta\}v \in \eta(v) \text{ and } \{\eta\}x \in \eta(x)$$

for every constructor variable v and ordinary variable x. Although the value of $\{\eta\}x$ is not uniquely determined, the equivalence class $\langle\{\eta\}x\rangle$ is uniquely determined by η. This is sufficient, since we will be concerned with the effect of $\{\eta\}$ only up to provable equivalence from Γ. It is easy to verify that if $\langle M\rangle = \langle N\rangle$, then $\langle\{\eta\}M\rangle = \langle\{\eta\}N\rangle$. The proof that $\mathcal{F}$ is a model satisfying precisely the equations in Γ rests on the following claim.

Claim For any constructor μ, term $B \vdash M\colon\sigma$, and any environment $\eta \models B$, we have

$$[\![\mu]\!]\eta = \langle\{\eta\}\mu\rangle \text{ and } [\![B \vdash M\colon\sigma]\!]\eta = \langle\{\eta\}M\rangle\,.$$

If we can verify the claim, then it is clear that $\mathcal{F}$ is an environment model; i.e., that every constructor and term has a meaning in $\mathcal{F}$. We can also use the claim to show that $\mathcal{F}$ satisfies precisely the equations in Γ, as follows. First, suppose $B \vdash M = N\colon\sigma \in \Gamma$ and $\eta \models B$. Since $\eta \models B$, we have $A \vdash \{\eta\}x\colon\{\eta\}\tau$ for every $x\colon\tau \in B$, and so by Lemma 3, it follows that $A \vdash \{\eta\}M\colon\{\eta\}\sigma$, and similarly for N. By Lemma 5, it follows that

$$A \vdash \{\eta\}M = \{\eta\}N\colon\{\eta\}\sigma \text{ is provable from } B \vdash M = N\colon\sigma \in \Gamma\,.$$

Therefore $[\![B \vdash M\colon\sigma]\!]\eta = \langle\{\eta\}M\rangle = \langle\{\eta\}N\rangle = [\![B \vdash N\colon\sigma]\!]\eta$. Conversely, we must show that if $\mathcal{F} \models B \vdash M = N\colon\sigma$, then $B \vdash M = N\colon\sigma \in \Gamma$. For any B, we can choose an environment $\eta_0 \models B$ which maps every constructor variable v^κ to its equivalence class $\langle v^\kappa\rangle$ and maps every ordinary variable x with $x\colon\tau \in B$ to the equivalence class of some variable y with $y\colon\tau \in A$. If $\mathcal{F} \models B \vdash M = N\colon\sigma$, then we have

$$A \vdash \{\eta_0\}M = \{\eta_0\}N\colon\sigma \in \Gamma\,.$$

Since η_0 just renames ordinary variables, M is a substitution instance of $\{\eta_0\}M$, and similarly for N. Therefore, by Lemma 5, we conclude $B \vdash M = N\colon\sigma \in \Gamma$. This proves the theorem, except for the claim.

We verify the claim using induction on constructor expressions and induction on typing derivations for terms. It is not hard to show $[\![\mu]\!]\eta = \langle\{\eta\}\mu\rangle$ by induction on constructors, using essentially the same steps we use for terms below. In particular, we have $[\![\sigma]\!]\eta = \langle\{\eta\}\sigma\rangle$ for type expressions σ. We now consider terms. For any typing $x{:}\,\sigma \vdash x{:}\,\sigma$ of a variable, we have

$$[\![x{:}\,\sigma \vdash x{:}\,\sigma]\!]\eta = \eta(x) = \langle\{\eta\}x\rangle\,.$$

The application case $(\rightarrow E)$ is also straightforward. For any $B \vdash MN{:}\,\tau$ typed using $(\rightarrow E)$ as the last step, we have

$$\begin{aligned}[\![B \vdash MN{:}\,\tau]\!]\eta &= (\Phi_{a,b}[\![B \vdash M{:}\,\sigma \rightarrow \tau]\!]\eta)[\![B \vdash N{:}\,\sigma]\!]\eta\\ &= (\Phi_{a,b}\langle\{\eta\}M\rangle)\langle\{\eta\}N\rangle\\ &= \langle\{\eta\}M\{\eta\}N\rangle\\ &= \langle\{\eta\}(MN)\rangle,\end{aligned}$$

where $a = [\![\sigma]\!]\eta$ and $b = [\![\tau]\!]\eta$. For λ-abstractions typed by $(\rightarrow I)$, we have

$$[\![B \vdash \lambda x{:}\,\sigma.M{:}\,\sigma \rightarrow \tau]\!]\eta = \Phi_{a,b}^{-1}g\,,$$

where $a = [\![\sigma]\!]\eta$, $b = [\![\tau]\!]\eta$ and g is the function satisfying

$$g(d) = [\![B, x{:}\,\sigma \vdash M{:}\,\tau]\!]\eta[d/x]$$

for all $d \in \mathrm{Dom}^a$. We can see that $g = (\Phi_{a,b}\langle\{\eta\}\lambda x{:}\,\sigma.M\rangle)$ using the inductive hypothesis and the substitution lemma as follows. For any $\langle N\rangle \in \mathrm{Dom}^a$, we have

$$\begin{aligned}g\langle N\rangle &= [\![B, x{:}\,\sigma \vdash M{:}\,\tau]\!]\eta[\langle N\rangle/x]\\ &= \langle\{\eta[\langle N\rangle/x]\}M\rangle\\ &= \langle(\{\eta\}\lambda x{:}\,\sigma.M)N\rangle\\ &= (\Phi_{a,b}\langle\{\eta\}\lambda x{:}\,\sigma.M\rangle)\langle N\rangle.\end{aligned}$$

Since $\Phi_{a,b}^{-1}$ is the inverse of $\Phi_{a,b}$, it follows easily that

$$\begin{aligned}&[\![B \vdash \lambda x{:}\,\sigma.M{:}\,\sigma \rightarrow \tau]\!]\eta\\ &\quad= \Phi_{a,b}^{-1}(\Phi_{a,b}\langle\{\eta\}\lambda x{:}\,\sigma.M\rangle)\\ &\quad= \langle\{\eta\}\lambda x{:}\,\sigma.M\rangle.\end{aligned}$$

Similar arguments demonstrate the claim for the $(\forall E)$ and $(\forall I)$ cases, and rules (add hyp) and (type eq) are trivial. This finishes the proof of the claim and hence the theorem. □

6 *Combinatory Algebras and Models*

6.1 *Introduction*

In this section, we present an alternative to the environment model. The environment model definition has two parts: the definition of a frame, and the stipulation that a frame $\mathcal{F}$ is a model only if every term has a meaning in $\mathcal{F}$. While the definition of frame has the same mathematical flavor as, say, the definition of a group or vector space, the condition distinguishing environment models from frames is largely syntactic since it relies on the inductive definition of the meanings of terms. In this section, we present an equivalent "combinatory model" definition based on algebraic properties of elements. Since second-order combinatory models are analogous to untyped combinatory models, we will illustrate the basic ideas by reviewing the untyped definitions (see [4, 42] for further discussion).

An applicative structure is said to be combinatorially complete if every implicitly definable function is represented in the model. More precisely, an untyped applicative structure $\mathcal{D} = \langle D, \Phi \rangle$ is *combinatorially complete* if, for every expression M with no occurrence of λ, all variables among $x_1, \ldots, x_n$, and possibly containing constants from D, there is a constant $d \in D$ such that

$$\mathcal{D} \models M = d x_1 \ldots x_n .$$

Intuitively, this means that for every implicit "polynomial" description M of a function of n variables, there is an element of D representing this function. For untyped extensional applicative structures, it can be shown that combinatory completeness is equivalent to the environment model condition that every term have a meaning [4, 42].

Combinatory completeness also has a relatively simple definition which is algebraic in nature. An untyped applicative structure $\mathcal{D} = \langle D, \Phi \rangle$ is a *combinatory algebra* if it has elements $K, S \in D$ satisfying

$$K\,x\,y = x\,,$$

$$S\,x\,y\,z = (x\,z)(y\,z)$$

for all $x, y, z \in D$.[5] It can be shown that the combinators K and S are an "algebraic basis" for the implicitly definable functions. Consequently, an applicative structure $\mathcal{D}$ is combinatorially complete if and only if $\mathcal{D}$ is a combinatory algebra [4, 26, 28, 42]. Since both K and S can be defined explicitly by lambda terms, an extensional applicative structure $\mathcal{D}$ is an untyped environment model if and only if $\mathcal{D}$ is an untyped combinatory algebra.

Combinators for ordinary typed lambda calculus are similar to the untyped combinators, as we shall see in the discussion of kind structures below. Instead of using two untyped combinators K and S, typed combinatory algebras

5. Combinatory algebras are often defined as structures interpreting constants K and S such that $K^{\mathcal{D}}$ and $S^{\mathcal{D}}$ satisfy the equations above. If $\mathcal{D}$ is not extensional, then the equations may hold for many $K, S \in D$, and it may be useful to have a structure $\mathcal{D}$ single out specific K and S. Since our structures will be extensional, we will not require combinatory algebras to choose specific combinators.

are characterized using an infinite family of typed K combinators, and a similar family of typed S combinators.

In the discussion of second-order combinatory models, we will define second-order combinatory completeness and second-order combinatory algebras. Instead of infinite collections of typed K and S combinators, second-order combinatory algebras will be characterized using a single polymorphic K, a single polymorphic S, and infinite families of additional combinators. As in the untyped case, each combinator is characterized by an equation. We will see that every second-order lambda-definable function can be viewed as an applicative combination of the combinators, and we will show that an extensional frame $\mathcal{F}$ is a second-order environment model if and only if $\mathcal{F}$ is a second-order combinatory algebra.

It is worth pointing out that the situation becomes more complicated if we do not assume extensionality. The correspondence between combinatory completeness and combinatory algebras holds in general, but nonextensional combinatory models are more complicated than nonextensional combinatory algebras (see [4, 26, 42]). Except for a brief discussion in Section 6.5, we will consider only extensional second-order frames.

6.2 *Constructor Combinators*

Recall that a kind environment model is a kind frame,

$$Kind = \langle \{\mathrm{Kind}^{\kappa} \mid \kappa a \text{ kind}\}, \{\Phi_{\kappa_1,\kappa_2} \mid \kappa_1, \kappa_2 \text{ kinds}\}, I \rangle ,$$

in which every constructor has a meaning. As the first step toward giving a model definition that does not rely on the meanings of terms, we will substitute a condition involving "kinded" combinators K and S.

As described in [4, 19], the requirement that every constructor expression has a meaning in *Kind* is equivalent to stipulating that for all kinds κ_1, κ_2 and κ_3, there must be elements

$$K_{\kappa_1,\kappa_2} \in \mathrm{Kind}^{\kappa_1 \Rightarrow (\kappa_2 \Rightarrow \kappa_1)},$$

$$S_{\kappa_1,\kappa_2,\kappa_3} \in \mathrm{Kind}^{(\kappa_1 \Rightarrow \kappa_2 \Rightarrow \kappa_3) \Rightarrow (\kappa_1 \Rightarrow \kappa_2) \Rightarrow \kappa_1 \Rightarrow \kappa_3}$$

with the familiar properties

$$K_{\kappa_1,\kappa_2} u\, v = u ,$$

$$S_{\kappa_1,\kappa_2,\kappa_3} u\, v\, w = (u\, w)(v\, w)$$

for all u, v, and w of the appropriate kinds. (As usual, we have abbreviated $(\Phi_{\kappa_1,\kappa_2}(\Phi_{\kappa_1,\kappa_2 \Rightarrow \kappa_1} K_{\kappa_1,\kappa_2})u)v$ to $K_{\kappa_1,\kappa_2} uv$, and similarly for $S_{\kappa_1,\kappa_2,\kappa_3}$.) In the following discussion of frames and combinators, we will assume that every kind frame has combinators K_{κ_1,κ_2} and $S_{\kappa_1,\kappa_2,\kappa_3}$ for all kinds κ_1, κ_2, and κ_3. This will allow us to focus on combinators for terms.

6.3 *Second-Order Combinatory Completeness*

Intuitively, a second-order frame is second-order combinatorially complete if it is closed under definition by polynomials over ordinary variables and type variables. We will show that combinatory completeness is equivalent to the existence of a set of combinators, each characterized by an equational axiom. Later, in Section 6.4, we will see how to describe combinators formally without introducing extra constants into the language. However, constants for elements will be convenient for discussing combinatory completeness and for proving the equivalence of combinatory and environment model conditions.

If $\mathcal{F}$ is a second-order frame, then the *$\mathcal{F}$-terms* are the applicative terms (terms without $\lambda x{:}\,\sigma.M$ or $\lambda t.M$) of the language with a constant for each element of $\mathcal{F}$. It is understood that if c is the "constant for d," then $\mathcal{I}(c) = d$. Since the $\mathcal{F}$-terms do not involve any lambda abstraction, every $\mathcal{F}$-term has a meaning in the frame $\mathcal{F}$, regardless of whether $\mathcal{F}$ is an environment model. One minor complication with the $\mathcal{F}$-terms is that the syntactic type of an element is not determined uniquely (since our syntax does not allow arbitrary equations between constructors). For example, if $f, g \in \text{Kind}^{T\Rightarrow T}$ are distinct, but $\forall f = \forall g$ are the same element of Kind^T, then a constant c for $d \in \text{Dom}^{\forall f}$ could be given syntactic type $\forall f$ or $\forall g$. We will take the rather brute-force approach of assuming we have many constants for each element, one for each equivalence class of type expressions over constants from *Kind*. It is important to have each typing included, since the syntactic type of a constant determines the way the constant may be used in terms.

A frame $\mathcal{F} = \langle Kind, Dom, \{\Phi_{a,b}\}, \{\Phi_f\}\rangle$ is *second-order combinatorially complete* if for every $\mathcal{F}$-term $B \vdash M{:}\,\sigma$ without free variables of higher kinds (kinds other than T) there is a constant d from $\mathcal{F}$ such that

$$\mathcal{F} \models B \vdash M = d\,\vec{s}\,\vec{x}{:}\,\sigma\,,$$

where $\vec{x}$ is a list of all ordinary variables in B and $\vec{s}$ lists all type variables of $B \vdash M{:}\,\sigma$. This definition is similar to the usual definition of combinatory completeness for untyped lambda calculus [4, 42], but with the added consideration of types and type variables. We do not consider implicit functions of variables of higher kinds since we cannot λ-bind variables of higher kinds in second-order terms.

We will see that a second-order frame is combinatorially complete if and only if it has elements K, S, A, B, C, and D satisfying certain equational axioms. Since these elements may be defined as the meanings of closed terms (in a language with enough constructor constants to write down their types), they are called combinators. The combinators K and S are similar to the combinators of the same names used in untyped lambda calculus, while A, B, C, and D are related to type application and type abstraction. A useful abbreviation is to write $T^i \Rightarrow T$ for the kind $T \Rightarrow \ldots \Rightarrow T$ with $i+1$ occurrences of T.

A second-order frame $\mathcal{F}$ is a *second-order combinatory algebra* if it contains elements

$$K \in \mathrm{Dom}^{\forall s.\forall t.s \to t \to s},$$

$$S \in \mathrm{Dom}^{\forall r.\forall s.\forall t.(r \to s \to t) \to (r \to s) \to r \to t},$$

and, for all integers $i, j, k \geq 0$ and all $f \in \mathrm{Kind}^{T^{i+1} \Rightarrow T}$, $g \in \mathrm{Kind}^{T^{j+1} \Rightarrow T}$, and $h \in \mathrm{Kind}^{T^{k+2} \Rightarrow T}$, elements

$$A_f \in \mathrm{Dom}^{\forall r.\forall \vec{s}\,[(r \to \forall t.f\vec{s}\,t) \to \forall t.(r \to f\vec{s}\,t)]},$$

$$B \in \mathrm{Dom}^{\forall r[r \to \forall t.r]},$$

$$C_{f,g} \in \mathrm{Dom}^{\forall \vec{r}.\forall \vec{s}\,[\forall t[(f\vec{r}\,t) \to (g\,\vec{s}\,t)] \to \forall t(f\,\vec{r}\,t) \to \forall t(g\vec{s}\,t)]},$$

$$D_{h,f} \in \mathrm{Dom}^{\forall \vec{r}.\forall \vec{s}\,[\forall t.\forall u(h\vec{r}\,t\,u) \to \forall t(h\,\vec{r}\,t(f\,\vec{s}\,t))]},$$

with the properties described below.

The combinators K and S must satisfy

$$K\,s\,t\,x\,y = x,$$
$$S\,r\,s\,t\,x\,y\,z = x\,z\,(y\,z)$$

for all types r, s, t and all elements x, y, and z of the appropriate types. The types of x, y, z, omitted to improve readability, are easily determined from the types of the combinators. For example, to be more specific, K must satisfy

$$K\,s\,t\,x\,y = x \text{ for all } s, t \in \mathrm{Kind}^T \text{ and all } x \in \mathrm{Dom}^s, y \in \mathrm{Dom}^t.$$

The combinator B and every A, C, and D must have the following equational properties, where again the types of x and y may be determined from the types given above:

$$(A_f r\,\vec{s})\,x\,t\,y = (x\,y)\,t,$$

$$(B\,r)\,x\,t = x,$$

$$(C_{f,g}\vec{r}\,\vec{s})\,x\,y\,t = x\,t(y\,t),$$

$$(D_{h,f}\vec{r}\,\vec{s})\,x\,t = x\,t(f\,\vec{s}\,t).$$

It is worth noting that this set of combinators has been chosen for ease in proofs and is not intended to be minimal.

We now introduce a language for describing elements of combinatory algebras. One complicating feature of second-order lambda calculus, mentioned briefly earlier, is that we cannot necessarily write closed expressions for all of the types of any given frame. Similarly, we cannot necessarily define all of the elements of each kind $T^i \Rightarrow T$. Since we need a closed expression μ for $f \in \text{Kind}^{T^i \Rightarrow T}$ to make use of a constant for combinator A_f, the set of constructor constants of a language limits our ability to add combinator constants. Therefore, we will have to pay particularly close attention to the set C_{cst} of constructor constants in the following discussion. To describe the connection between lambda terms and combinators as generally as possible, we will use languages which contain as many combinator constants as the constructor expressions will allow.

For any set C_{cst} of constructor constants and set C_{term} of term constants, the *combinatory terms* $C\mathcal{L}(C_{cst}, C_{term})$ are the applicative second-order terms over constants C_{cst}, C_{term} and additional fresh constants for the combinators K, S, A, B, C, and D. Specifically, in addition to the constructor constants C_{cst} and term constants C_{term}, the language $C\mathcal{L}(C_{cst}, C_{term})$ has fresh constants

$$K\colon \forall s.\forall t.s \to t \to s\,,$$

$$S\colon \forall r.\forall s.\forall t.(r \to s \to t) \to (r \to s) \to r \to t\,,$$

and, for all closed constructor expressions $\mu\colon T^{i+1} \Rightarrow T$, $\nu\colon T^{j+1} \Rightarrow T$, and $\pi\colon T^{k+2} \Rightarrow T$ of $C\mathcal{L}(C_{cst}, C_{term})$, constants A_μ, B, $C_{\mu,\nu}$, and $D_{\pi,\mu}$. Note that, as described above, the set of combinator constants depends on the set of closed constructor expressions. A special case of particular interest are the $C\mathcal{L}(\mathcal{F})$ terms, which are the combinatory terms over the language with a constant for every element of every Kind^κ and Dom^a of $\mathcal{F}$.

A model for combinatory terms will be called a combinatory frame. More precisely, a *second-order combinatory frame for* $C\mathcal{L}(C_{cst}, C_{term})$ is a frame $\mathcal{F}$ for the constants of $C\mathcal{L}(C_{cst}, C_{term})$ such that the combinator equations hold for all of the combinator constants in the language $C\mathcal{L}(C_{cst}, C_{term})$. There are two differences between combinatory algebras and combinatory frames. The first is that a combinatory frame interprets constants of some $C\mathcal{L}(C_{cst}, C_{term})$ with combinator constants, while a combinatory algebra need not interpret any combinator constants. The second difference is that a combinatory frame need only have those $A_f, C_{f,g}$, and $D_{h,f}$ which have f, g, h definable in $C\mathcal{L}(C_{cst}, C_{term})$. If $f \in \text{Kind}^{T^i \Rightarrow T}$ is not the meaning of any closed constructor expression of $C\mathcal{L}(C_{cst}, C_{term})$, then a combinatory frame might not have an element A_f satisfying the associated equation. Essentially, combinatory algebras are frames with a set of semantic properties, while combinatory frames are frames that interpret certain languages in a certain way. The two notions are very similar, however, if we add enough constants to our language. Specifically, if $\mathcal{F}$ is a combinatory frame for $CL(\mathcal{F})$, then every combinator of $\mathcal{F}$ has a constant in $CL(\mathcal{F})$, and so $\mathcal{F}$ must be a combinatory algebra. Conversely, it follows easily from the definitions that any combinatory algebra $\mathcal{F}$ can be extended to a combinatory frame for $CL(\mathcal{F})$ by interpreting the combinator constants of $CL(\mathcal{F})$ appropriately. In the proof of the combinatory model theorem, we will use $CL(\mathcal{F})$. However, we will use more general combinatory terms $CL(C_{\text{cst}}, C_{\text{term}})$ in proving a general equivalence between lambda terms and combinatory terms.

We will now justify the name "combinatory algebra" by showing that every combinatory algebra is combinatorially complete. It is clear that every combinatorially complete frame is a combinatory algebra since each combinator is defined by an equation involving variables and $\mathcal{F}$-terms. To show how combinators allow us to represent functions, we define "pseudo-abstraction" for ordinary variables and type variables. For every combinatory term $B, x{:}\sigma \vdash M{:}\tau$ without free variables of higher kinds, we define the combinatory term $B \vdash \langle x{:}\sigma\rangle M{:}\sigma \to \tau$ using induction on the derivation of typing $B, x{:}\sigma \vdash M{:}\tau$ as follows. We omit the trivial cases for (add hyp) and (type eq). Since B and $\sigma \to \tau$ are clear, we specify only $\langle x{:}\sigma\rangle M$:

$$\langle x{:}\sigma\rangle x = S\,\sigma\,\sigma \to \sigma\,\sigma(K\,\sigma\,\sigma \to \sigma)(K\,\sigma\,\sigma)\;;$$

$\langle x{:}\sigma\rangle y = K\,\tau\,\sigma\,y,$ where τ is the type of y and y is different from x ;

$\langle x{:}\sigma\rangle c = K\,\tau\,\sigma\,c,$ where τ is the type of constant c ;

$\langle x{:}\sigma\rangle(MN) = S\,\sigma\,\rho\,\tau(\langle x{:}\sigma\rangle M)(\langle x{:}\sigma\rangle N),$ where $B, x{:}\sigma \vdash M{:}\rho \to \tau$;

$\langle x{:}\sigma\rangle(M\rho) = (A_f\sigma\vec{s})(\langle x{:}\sigma\rangle M)\rho$,
where $B, x{:}\sigma \vdash M{:}\,\forall\mu$, all free variables of μ are among $\vec{s}$, and f is the closed constructor $\lambda\vec{s}.\lambda t.\tau$.

The definition of $\langle x{:}\sigma\rangle x$ is analogous to the usual untyped translation into combinators $\langle x\rangle x = SKK$. If $B \vdash M{:}\tau$ is well typed and t does not occur free in B, we define $B \vdash \langle t\rangle M{:}\,\forall t.\tau$ by induction on derivation of typing $B \vdash M{:}\tau$ as follows. Again, we omit the trivial cases and specify only $\langle t\rangle M$:

$\langle t\rangle y = B\,\tau\,y,$ where τ is the type of y ;

$\langle t\rangle c = B\,\tau\,c,$ where τ is the type of constant c ;

$\langle t\rangle(MN) = C_{f,g}\vec{r}\vec{s}(\langle\langle t\rangle M)(\langle\langle t\rangle N)$,
where f and g are determined by the typing of MN as follows: If $B \vdash M: \sigma \to \tau$ and $B \vdash N: \sigma$, let $\vec{r}$ and $\vec{s}$ be lists of type variables so that $f \equiv \lambda\vec{r}.\lambda t.\sigma$ and $g \equiv \lambda\vec{s}.\lambda t.\tau$ are closed;

$\langle t\rangle(M\tau) = D_{h,f}\vec{r}\vec{s}(\langle t\rangle M)$,
where f and h are determined from τ and the typing $B \vdash M: \forall u.\sigma$ by taking lists $\vec{r}$ and $\vec{s}$ of type variables so that $f \equiv \lambda\vec{s}.\lambda t.\tau$ and $h \equiv \lambda\vec{r}.\lambda t.\lambda u.\sigma$ are closed constructor expressions.

It is not hard to verify that $B \vdash \langle x: \sigma\rangle M: \sigma \to \tau$ and $B \vdash \langle t\rangle M: \forall t.\tau$ are well typed. The assumption that M has no free variables of higher kinds is needed to show that, for example, f and g in the definition of $\langle t\rangle(MN)$ may be closed. (If this were not possible, we could not give $C_{f,g}$ a closed type, and so $C_{f,g}$ would not really be constant.) The essential properties of pseudo-abstraction are described by the following lemma.

Lemma 12
Let $\mathcal{F}$ be a second-order combinatory frame for $\mathcal{CL}(C\text{cst}, C_{\text{term}})$. For any combinatory terms $B, x: \sigma \vdash M: \tau$ and $B \vdash N: \sigma$ of $\mathcal{CL}_A(C_{\text{cst}}, C_{\text{term}})$ without free variables of higher kinds, we have

$$\mathcal{F} \models B \vdash (\langle x: \sigma\rangle M)N = \{N/x\}M: \tau .$$

Similarly, if $B \vdash M: \tau$ with t not free in B and σ is any type expression without free variables of higher kinds, we have

$$\mathcal{F} \models B \vdash (\langle t\rangle M)\sigma = \{\sigma/t\}M: (\lambda t.\tau)\sigma .$$

The lemma is proved by an easy induction. Using Lemma 12 we can prove the following combinatory completeness theorem.

Theorem 2 (Combinatory Completeness)
A frame $\mathcal{F}$ is second-order combinatorially complete if and only if $\mathcal{F}$ is a second-order combinatory algebra.

Proof If $\mathcal{F} = \langle \mathit{Kind}, \mathit{Dom}, \{\Phi_{a,b}\}, \{\Phi_f\}\rangle$ is second-order combinatorially complete, then $\mathcal{F}$ is a combinatory algebra since each combinator is defined by a polynomial over $\mathcal{F}$. Conversely, suppose $\mathcal{F}$ is a combinatory algebra and let $\{x_1: \sigma_1, \ldots, x_j: \sigma_j\} \vdash M: \sigma$ be any $\mathcal{F}$-term whose free type variables are among $s_1, \ldots, s_i$. Using Lemma 12, it is easy to show that

$$N = \langle s_1\rangle \ldots \langle s_i\rangle \langle x_1: \sigma_1\rangle \ldots \langle x_j: \sigma_j\rangle M$$

is a closed term of $\mathcal{CL}(\mathcal{F})$ with

$$\mathcal{F} \models x_1{:}\sigma_1, \ldots, x_j{:}\sigma_j \vdash M = Ns_1 \ldots s_i\, x_1 \ldots x_j{:}\sigma\,.$$

Thus $\mathcal{F}$ is combinatorially complete. □

6.4 *Combinatory Models*

In this section, we show that an extensional frame $\mathcal{F}$ is an environment model if and only if $\mathcal{F}$ is a combinatory algebra. This will establish that the "algebraic" definition of combinatory algebra is equivalent to the syntactic condition in the environment model definition. We will use translations CL and LAM between lambda terms and combinatory terms over the same sets of constants, which may also be of independent interest.

Let $B \vdash M{:}\,\sigma$ be a second-order lambda term over constants from C_{cst} and C_{term}, without free variables of higher kinds. We define the combinatory term $B \vdash \text{CL}(M){:}\,\sigma$ of $\mathcal{CL}(C_{\text{cst}}, C_{\text{term}})$ by induction on the derivation of $B \vdash M{:}\,\sigma$. As usual, the trivial cases (add hyp) and (type eq) are omitted, and, since B and σ are already determined, we mention only CL(M):

$$\text{CL}(x) = x\,,$$

$$\text{CL}(MN) = \text{CL}(M)\,\text{CL}(N)\,,$$

$$\text{CL}(\lambda x{:}\,\sigma.M) = \langle x{:}\,\sigma\rangle\,\text{CL}(M)\,,$$

$$\text{CL}(M\sigma) = \text{CL}(M)\sigma\,,$$

$$\text{CL}(\lambda t.M) = \langle t\rangle\,\text{CL}(M)\,.$$

We can use Lemma 12 to show the following lemma.

Lemma 13

Suppose $\mathcal{F}$ is an extensional combinatory frame for $\mathcal{CL}(C_{\text{cst}}, C_{\text{term}})$ and $B \vdash M{:}\,\sigma$ is a second-order lambda term over C_{cst} and C_{term} without free variables of higher kinds. If $\eta \models B$, then the meaning of $B \vdash M{:}\,\sigma$ exists in $\mathcal{F}$ and is given by

$$[\![B \vdash M{:}\,\sigma]\!]\eta = [\![B \vdash \text{CL}(M){:}\,\sigma]\!]\eta\,.$$

We will use the lemma later to show that every combinatory model is an environment model. In doing so, we will eliminate the restriction on free variables of higher kinds.

Proof The lemma is proved by induction on the typing of terms. The only nontrivial cases are ($\to I$) and ($\forall I$). Since these two cases are similar, we consider only the first. Recall that the meaning of $B \vdash \lambda x\colon \sigma.M\colon \sigma \to \tau$ typed by ($\to I$) is

$$[\![B \vdash \lambda x\colon \sigma.M\colon \sigma \to \tau]\!]\eta = \Phi_{a,b}^{-1} g, \text{ where}$$

$$g(d) = [\![B, x\colon \sigma \vdash M\colon \tau]\!]\eta[d/x] \text{ for all } d \in \mathit{Dom}^a \text{ and}$$

$$a, b \text{ are the meanings of } \sigma \text{ and } \tau \text{ in } \eta.$$

By the inductive hypothesis,

$$g(d) = [\![B, x\colon \sigma \vdash \text{CL}(M)\colon \tau]\!]\eta[d/x] \text{ for all } d \in \mathit{Dom}^a.$$

By the substitution lemma and Lemma 12,

$$(\Phi_{a,b}[\![B \vdash \langle x\colon \sigma\rangle\, \text{CL}(M)\colon \sigma \to \tau]\!]\eta)d = [\![B, x\colon \sigma \vdash \text{CL}(M)\colon \tau]\!]\eta[d/x] = g(d)$$

for all $d \in \mathit{Dom}^a$. Therefore,

$$[\![B \vdash \langle x\colon \sigma\rangle\, \text{CL}(M)\colon \sigma \to \tau]\!]\eta = \Phi_{a,b}^{-1} g,$$

proving the lemma. □

We now show how to translate combinatory terms into lambda terms. For any combinatory term $B \vdash M\colon \tau$ of $\mathcal{CL}(C_{cst}, C_{term})$, we define the lambda term $B \vdash \text{LAM}(M)\colon \tau$ over C_{cst} and C_{term} as follows:

$$\text{LAM}(x) = x,$$

$$\text{LAM}(c) = c \text{ for } c \in C_{term},$$

$$\text{LAM}(K) = \lambda s\, \lambda t\, \lambda x\colon s\, \lambda y\colon t.x,$$

$$\text{LAM}(S) = \lambda r\, \lambda s\, \lambda t\, \lambda x\colon r \to s \to t\, \lambda y\colon r \to s\, \lambda z\colon r.x\, z(y\, z),$$

$$\text{LAM}(A_f) = \lambda r\, \lambda \vec{s}\, \lambda x\colon r \to \forall t(f\, \vec{s}\, t) \lambda t\, \lambda y\colon r.x\, y\, t,$$

$$\text{LAM}(B) = \lambda r\, \lambda x\colon r\, \lambda t.x,$$

$$\text{LAM}(C_{f,g}) = \lambda \vec{r}\, \lambda \vec{s}\, \lambda x\colon \forall t(f\, \vec{r}\, t) \to (g\, \vec{s}\, t)) \lambda y\colon \forall t(f\, \vec{r}\, t) \lambda t.(x\, t)(y\, t),$$

$$\text{LAM}(D_{h,f}) = \lambda \vec{r}\, \lambda \vec{s}\, \lambda x\colon \forall t \forall u(h\, \vec{r}\, t\, u) \lambda t.xt(f\, \vec{s}\, t),$$

$$\text{LAM}(MN) = \text{LAM}(M)\, \text{LAM}(N),$$

$$\text{LAM}(M\sigma) = \text{LAM}(M)\sigma.$$

Note that for combinators indexed by constructors, such as A_f, we have A_f in $\mathcal{CL}C_{cst}, C_{term})$ only if f is a closed constructor expression. Therefore, for every A_f in $\mathcal{CL}(C_{cst}, C_{term})$, the term LAM($A_f$) will be a closed lambda term over C_{cst} and C_{term}. In the special case that $\mathcal{CL}(C_{cst}, C_{term})$ is $\mathcal{CL}(\mathcal{F})$, then LAM translates every combinator of $\mathcal{F}$ into a closed lambda term over constructor constants from $\mathcal{F}$.

If $\mathcal{F} = \langle Kind, Dom, \{\Phi_{a,b}\}, \{\Phi_f\}\rangle$ is an environment model for terms over C_{cst} and C_{term}, then we define $\mathcal{F}^+$ to be the result of extending I_{Dom} to interpret the fresh combinator constants of $\mathcal{CL}(C_{cst}, C_{term})$ as the lambda terms above. It is easy to prove the following lemma.

Lemma 14

Let $\mathcal{F}$ be an extensional environment model for terms over C_{cst} and C_{term}. Then $\mathcal{F}^+$ is a combinatory frame for $\mathcal{CL}(C_{cst}, C_{term})$ such that for every $B \vdash M{:}\,\sigma$ of $\mathcal{CL}(C_{cst}, C_{term})$, we have $\mathcal{F}^+ \models B \vdash M = \text{LAM}(M){:}\,\sigma$.

Using Lemmas 13 and 14, we can now prove the combinatory model theorem. This theorem is analogous to the combinatory model theorem of [42], but somewhat more simply stated since we have only considered extensional structures.

Theorem 3 (Combinatory Model Theorem)

An extensional second-order frame $\mathcal{F}$ is an environment model if and only if $\mathcal{F}$ is a combinatory algebra.

Proof First, suppose $\mathcal{F}$ is an environment model. By Lemma 10, the environment model condition does not depend on the choice of constants, and so we may assume $\mathcal{F}$ is an environment model for lambda terms over constants from $\mathcal{F}$. Therefore, by Lemma 14, $\mathcal{F}^+$ is a combinatory frame for $\mathcal{CL}(\mathcal{F})$, and so $\mathcal{F}$ must be a combinatory algebra.

We now suppose $\mathcal{F}$ is a combinatory algebra and show that $\mathcal{F}$ must be an environment model. To prove this, we must remove the restriction of Lemma 14 to terms without free variables of higher kinds. This will be done by substituting constants for variables. To this end, we first extend $\mathcal{F}$ to be a combinatory frame for $\mathcal{CL}(\mathcal{F})$ with constants for every element of $\mathcal{F}$.

Let $\mathcal{V}$ be any set of constructor variables, not containing any type variables, let η_0 be any environment for $\mathcal{F}$, and let $\mathcal{E}_{\mathcal{V},\eta_0}$ be the class of all environments for $\mathcal{F}$ which agree with η_0 on all variables from $\mathcal{V}$, i.e.,

$$\eta(v) = \eta_0(v) \quad \text{for all } \eta \in \mathcal{E}_{\mathcal{V},\eta_0} \text{ and } v \in \mathcal{V}.$$

We will say that $B \vdash M{:}\,\sigma$ is a *$\mathcal{V}$-term* if all free variables of $B \vdash M{:}\,\sigma$ are ordinary variables, type variables, or variables from $\mathcal{V}$. If $B \vdash M\colon \sigma$ is a $\mathcal{V}$-term, then let $M_{\mathcal{V},\eta_0}$ be the result of replacing each variable v from $\mathcal{V}$ by the constant for $\eta_0(v)$. By Lemma 13, we know that every $B \vdash M_{\mathcal{V},\eta_0}\colon \sigma$ has a meaning in $\mathcal{F}$. An easy induction shows that for every $\mathcal{V}$-term $B \vdash M\colon \sigma$, and every environment $\eta \in \mathcal{E}_{\mathcal{V},\eta_0}$, we have

$$[\![B \vdash M\colon \sigma]\!]\eta = [\![B \vdash M_{\mathcal{V},\eta_0}\colon \sigma]\!]\eta\ .$$

Thus every $\mathcal{V}$-term has a meaning in $\mathcal{F}$. Since every term is a $\mathcal{V}$-term for some $\mathcal{V}$, it follows that $\mathcal{F}$ is an environment model. □

6.5 *Second-Order Type Theory*

The combinatory characterization of untyped lambda models shows how to reduce untyped lambda calculus to first-order logic. Specifically, when combined with the extensionality axiom,

$$\forall z(xz = yz) \supset x = y\ ,$$

the combinator axioms

$$\forall x, y.Kxy = x,$$

$$\forall x, y, z.S\ x\ y\ z = (x\ z)(y\ z)$$

provide a first-order axiomatization of extensional models for untyped lambda calculus [4, 42]. Second-order combinatory algebras and models may also be defined in first-order logic. However, since the details of interpreting second-order lambda calculus in first-order logic are not very enlightening, we will show how to axiomatize combinatory algebras and models in the logical system $\mathcal{ST}$ of "second-order type theory". This axiomatization is relatively natural since the type structure of $\mathcal{ST}$ matches that of second-order lambda calculus. By a further reduction of $\mathcal{ST}$ to first-order logic, which is entirely routine, one may see that the semantics of second-order lambda calculus is reducible to first-order model theory. However, we will not go into the details of the reduction to first-order logic.

The language $\mathcal{ST}$ is built from applicative second-order terms using equality, the logical connectives, and quantification. To be more precise, an $\mathcal{ST}$ *atomic formula* is an equation $B \vdash M = N\colon \sigma$ without lambda binding of ordinary variables or type variables in M or N. If $B \vdash G_1$ and $B \vdash G_2$ are $\mathcal{ST}$ formulas, then so are

$$B \vdash G_1 \wedge G_2 \text{ and } B \vdash \neg G_1\ .$$

In addition, if v^κ does not appear free in B, then

$$B \vdash \forall v^\kappa.G$$

is an $\mathcal{ST}$ formula. Similarly, if $B, x{:}\,\sigma \vdash G$ is an $\mathcal{ST}$ formula, then

$$B \vdash \forall x{:}\,\sigma.G$$

is an $\mathcal{ST}$ formula as well. Finally, we need an (add hyp) rule for formulas since formulas include type assignments for ordinary variables. We do not need (type eq) for formulas since the types of formulas are not part of the syntax. Formulas of $\mathcal{ST}$ are interpreted by giving the logical connectives $\wedge$ and $\neg$ their usual meanings, and by interpreting quantifiers as ranging over the appropriate sets of the frame. Since only applicative terms appear in formulas of $\mathcal{ST}$, we can interpret logical formulas over any second-order frame for the appropriate set of constants.

It is easy to read through the definition of combinatory algebra and see that all the combinator axioms may be formalized in $\mathcal{ST}$. In axiomatizing combinatory algebras, we may replace constants by existential quantifiers. For example, K is described by the axiom

$$\exists K{:}\,\forall s \forall t(s \to t \to s).\forall s\ \forall t\ \forall x{:}\,s\ \forall y{:}\,t.K\ s\ t\ x\ y = x\,.$$

The axioms for A, C, and D involve variables of higher kinds. In addition, we need infinitely many axioms for each family of combinators. For example, for each $i \geq 0$, we need the A axiom

$$\forall f^{T^{i+1} \Rightarrow T} \exists A_f{:}\,\forall r, \vec{s}\,[(r \to \forall t.f\,\vec{s}\,t) \to \forall t.(r \to f\,\vec{s}\,t)].$$
$$\forall r\ \forall \vec{s}\ \forall x{:}\,(r \to \forall t.f\,\vec{s}\,t) \forall t\ \forall y{:}\,r.(A_f r\,\vec{s})\ x\ t\ y = (x\ y)\ t)\,.$$

It should be clear that an extensional frame $\mathcal{F}$ satisfies the collection of $\mathcal{ST}$ combinator axioms if and only if $\mathcal{F}$ is a combinatory algebra. Therefore, we may axiomatize combinatory algebras without introducing constants into the language.

The language $\mathcal{ST}$ may be reduced to first-order logic using a relatively straightforward method, similar to the reduction of ordinary type theory to first-order logic outlined in [54]. However, in the reduction to first-order logic, we must be careful to specify that frames are extensional. Essentially, this involves introducing axioms

$$\forall \mu^{T \Rightarrow T}\ \forall f{:}\,(\forall \mu)\ \forall g{:}\,(\forall \mu).(\forall t.ft = gt) \supset f = g\,,$$

$$\forall s\ \forall t\ \forall f{:}\,s \to t\ \forall g{:}\,s \to t.(\forall x{:}\,s.fx = gx) \supset f = g$$

to say that elements which have identical functional behavior must be equal. By including typed extensionality axioms and reducing to first-order logic, we can show that second-order lambda calculus is reducible to first-order logic. It is worth emphasizing that, as with other versions of lambda calculus, the first-order axioms are not equational (due here to extensionality), so second-order lambda calculus is not an algebraic theory. One consequence is that the class of second-order lambda models is not closed under homomorphism (cf. [4, 42]).

6.6 *Nonextensional Models*

Throughout this paper, we have emphasized extensional models. Essentially, the extensionality axioms (η) state that if two elements d and e behave the same way as functions (i.e., if $dx = ex$ for all x of the appropriate type or kind), then d and e must be equal. These axioms are quite reasonable, but nonextensional models are occasionally of interest also. Semantically, the extensionality axiom is reflected in the fact that we have assumed a *bijection* $\Phi_{a,b}$ between $\mathrm{Dom}^{a\to b}$ and $[\mathrm{Dom}^a \to \mathrm{Dom}^b]$, and similarly for each Φ_f. Thus every function $g \in [Dom^a \to Dom^b]$ corresponds to precisely one element $\Phi^{-1}(g) \in \mathrm{Dom}^{a\to b}$. In nonextensional models, we let two different elements $d \neq e \in \mathrm{Dom}^{a\to b}$ represent the same function $\Phi_{a,b}(d) = \Phi_{a,b}(e)$. This leads to some complication, since we used Φ^{-1} to find the meanings of lambda abstractions.

In nonextensional models, the main difficulty in interpreting lambda terms becomes the *weak extensionality* property of second-order lambda calculus. Intuitively, weak extensionality states that if M and N both define the same function of $x{:}\,\sigma$, then $\lambda x{:}\,\sigma.M$ must equal $\lambda x{:}\,\sigma.N$; and similarly, if M and N both define the same function of t, then $\lambda t.M$ must equal $\lambda t.N$. This is formalized in the inference rules

$$\frac{B, x{:}\,\sigma \vdash M = N{:}\,\rho, \vdash_c \sigma = \tau}{B \vdash \lambda x{:}\,\sigma.M = \lambda x{:}\,\tau.N{:}\,\sigma \to \rho}, \qquad (\xi)_1$$

$$\frac{B \vdash M = N{:}\,\sigma}{B \vdash \lambda t.M = \lambda t.N{:}\,\forall t.\sigma}, \quad t \text{ not free in } B. \qquad (\xi)_2$$

We satisfy weak extensionality using "choice functions" to determine the meaning of $\lambda x{:}\,\sigma.M$ or $\lambda t.M$. Specifically, we wish to define the meaning of $B \vdash \lambda x{:}\,\sigma.M{:}\,\sigma \to \tau$ from the function

$$g(d) = [\![B, x{:}\,\sigma \vdash M{:}\,\tau]\!]\eta[d/x]\,.$$

In a nonextensional structure, there may be several elements representing g, so we need some extra machinery to choose which one. We need to make sure that if $B, x{:}\,\sigma \vdash M{:}\,\tau$ and $B, x{:}\,\sigma \vdash N{:}\,\tau$ give us the same function g, then we choose the same meaning for $B \vdash \lambda x{:}\sigma.M{:}\sigma \to \tau$ and $B \vdash \lambda x{:}\sigma.N{:}\sigma \to \tau$. The simplest way to do this is to use a choice function $\Psi_{a,b}$ to select the meaning $\Psi_{a,b}(g)$ of a lambda abstraction.

To be more precise, a nonextensional frame is defined in the same way as an extensional frame, except that instead of requiring each $\Phi_{a,b}$ and Φ_f to be bijections, we require additional functions $\Psi_{a,b}$ and Ψ_f such that

$$\Psi_{a,b} \circ \Phi_{a,b} = Id_{[\mathrm{Dom}^a \to \mathrm{Dom}^b]} \text{ and } \Psi_f \circ \Phi_f = Id_{[\pi_{a \in \mathrm{Kind}^T} . \mathrm{Dom}^{fa}]} \,.$$

(We make no assumptions about the reverse compositions $\Phi_{a,b} \circ \Psi_{a,b}$ and $\Phi_f \circ \Psi_f$.) The functions $\Psi_{a,b}$ and Ψ_f then replace $\Phi_{a,b}^{-1}$ and Φ_f^{-1} in defining the meanings of terms of the form $\lambda x{:}\sigma.M$ and $\lambda t.M$. The completeness proof for the nonextensional case is a simple modification of the completeness proof given in Section 5 (see the completeness proof for nonextensional untyped lambda calculus in [42]).

Nonextensional combinatory models are somewhat more complicated than extensional combinatory models. One important feature of the combinatory model definition is that it reduces the definition of model to a set of first-order axioms. It is therefore appropriate to remove the condition $\Psi \circ \Phi = Id$ from the definition of frame and incorporate it into the set of axioms. To do this, we use a family of "choice elements" $\{\varepsilon\}$ corresponding to the family of choice functions $\{\Psi\}$. The basic idea is illustrated in the following discussion of untyped combinatory models.

An *untyped combinatory model* is an untyped combinatory algebra $\mathcal{D} = \langle D, \Phi \rangle$ with element $\varepsilon^{\mathcal{D}} \in D$ satisfying

$$\forall d, e(\varepsilon d)e = de \,, \qquad (\varepsilon.1)$$

$$\forall e(d_1 e = d_2 e) \supset \varepsilon d_1 = \varepsilon d_2 \,, \qquad (\varepsilon.2)$$

$$\varepsilon\varepsilon = \varepsilon \,. \qquad (\varepsilon.3)$$

Untyped lambda abstraction can be interpreted using ε as follows:

$$[\![\lambda x.M]\!]\eta = \varepsilon d, \quad \text{where } de = [\![M]\!]\eta[e/x] \text{ for all } e \in D \,.$$

Since $\mathcal{D}$ is a combinatory algebra, an element $d \in D$ with $de = [\![M]\!]\eta[e/x]$ for all $e \in D$ will exist for any M. Furthermore, weak extensionality (ξ) follows from the properties of ε. Note that

$$\varepsilon = \lambda x \lambda y.xy \,.$$

A comprehensive discussion of the equivalence between the environment and combinatory model definitions for untyped lambda calculus is given in

[42]. Note that since the combinatory algebra axioms are equational, nonextensional combinatory algebras form an algebraic variety [22]. However, the axioms for ε, like the extensionality axioms discussed in the preceding subsection, are not equational.

In the case of second-order lambda calculus, we need a family of typed ε's. At the very least we need an

$$\varepsilon_{a,b} = \lambda x{:}\, a \to b \lambda y{:}\, a.xy$$

for every $a, b \in \mathrm{Kind}^T$ and, for every $f \in \mathrm{Kind}^{T \to T}$,

$$\varepsilon_f = \lambda x{:}\, \forall f.\lambda t.xt$$

to serve the roles of $\Psi_{a,b}$ and Ψ_f. However, these are not quite enough since we have no way of defining, say,

$$\lambda t \lambda x{:}\, t \to t \lambda y{:}\, t.xy$$

from combinators and the above ε's. Essentially, we need to be able to define $\varepsilon_{a,b}$ as a function of a and b.

There seem to be a number of ways of defining nonextensional second-order combinatory models, and we have not made a thorough study of the possibilities. One set of choice elements that yields a combinatory characterization of nonextensional models includes

$$\varepsilon_0 = \lambda s\, \lambda t\, \lambda x{:}\, s \to t\, \lambda y{:}\, s.xy\,,$$

from which we can define any $\varepsilon_{a,b}$ by application, and for each $f{:}\, T^i \Rightarrow T$ an

$$\varepsilon_f = \lambda \vec{s}\, \lambda x{:}\, \forall t(f\vec{s}t)\, \lambda t.x\vec{s}t\,.$$

The types and axioms for these ε's are easily derived from the lambda terms above. The details of this combinatory model definition are cumbersome but essentially straightforward. (The family of choice elements ε_0 and ε_f for all $f{:}\, T^i \Rightarrow T$ repair an oversight in [47].)

7 Examples of Models

7.1 Introduction

We will discuss models of second-order lambda calculus that are constructed from untyped structures. These are the simplest examples of models, and historically the first. The models fall into two groups. In the first class of models, types are represented by elements of a "universal" domain. This allows us to use ordinary untyped lambda calculus to define operations on types. In the second class of models, types are quotients of subsets of an untyped value space. Another class of models, Girard's qualitative domains, are too recent for us to survey here [21]. In addition to describing two kinds of second-order models, we will also see that the ideal model of type inference [34, 33] is not a model, and that there are no nontrivial finite models.

There are several variations on both universal domain and HEO models, but we will not take the time to discuss all of them. Universal domain models may be constructed using closures, finitary retracts, or finitary projections of certain domains. We will discuss the closure model and refer to the literature on finitary retracts and projections. Girard's HEO_2 is a specific model based on recursive function application. The main idea may be used to construct a second-order model over any "partial combinatory algebra," a class of structures which includes all models of untyped lambda calculus [59, 65]. Some variations are discussed in [49], and some connections between retracts and equivalence relations are discussed in Section 7 of [66].

Although it is not very exciting, it is probably worth mentioning a trivial model construction. Any model $\mathcal{D}$ of the untyped λ-calculus may be viewed as a second-order model by taking $\mathcal{D}$ as the sole element of Kind^T.

7.2 *Retract Models*

There are three kinds of models built using retracts of universal domains. A *retraction* is a function f with the property that $f \circ f = f$, and the range of a retraction is called a *retract*. In the retract models, the types are chosen to be some class of retractions of a model of untyped lambda calculus. One of the reasons why retract models are easy to work with is that type operators like $\rightarrow$ and $\forall$ may be represented by lambda-definable functions on retractions (see [66] for further discussion). An important property of the three models below is that in each case, a very rich class of retractions is itself a retract of the untyped value space. Because of the this, each model will have a "type of all types," something which is not generally required of second-order lambda models. The three models will differ primarily in the class of retractions used as the type of types.

The first model construction was based on Scott's $\mathcal{P}\omega$ model of untyped lambda calculus, with types represented by a special class of retracts called closures. This model is due to McCracken [37], drawing on ideas presented in [66]. We assume that the reader is familiar with the $\mathcal{P}\omega$ model of the untyped lambda calculus [66], with

$$\Phi = \textbf{fun}\colon \mathcal{P}\omega \to [\mathcal{P}\omega \to \mathcal{P}\omega]$$

mapping each element of $\mathcal{P}\omega$ to a continuous function on $\mathcal{P}\omega$, and

$$\Psi = \textbf{graph}\colon [\mathcal{P}\omega \to \mathcal{P}\omega] \to \mathcal{P}\omega$$

mapping every continuous function to some element of $\mathcal{P}\omega$. (An important relationship between Φ and Ψ is that $\Phi \circ \Psi$ is the identity function on $[\mathcal{P}\omega \to \mathcal{P}\omega]$.) A certain amount of notational clutter will be eliminated by writing closed lambda terms to describe elements of $\mathcal{P}\omega$, as well as writing

$$de \text{ for } (\Phi d)(e) \text{ when } d, e \in \mathcal{P}\omega\,,$$

$$d \circ e \text{ for } \lambda x.d(ex) \text{ when } d, e \in \mathcal{P}\omega.$$

A *retraction in* $\mathcal{P}\omega$ is an element $\Psi(f) \in \mathcal{P}\omega$ such that the function $f\colon \mathcal{P}\omega \to \mathcal{P}\omega$ is a retraction. This is equivalent to saying that a retraction in $\mathcal{P}\omega$ is an element $a \in \mathcal{P}\omega$ with $a \circ a = a$ in the notation above.

We can build a second-order model from $\mathcal{P}\omega$ by using the closures as types. We say a retraction $a \in \mathcal{P}\omega$ is a *closure* if

$$ad \geq d \text{ for all } d \in \mathcal{P}\omega$$

and let

$$\text{Kind}^T = \{a \in \mathcal{P}\omega \mid a \text{ is a closure}\}$$

be the collection of closures. The elements of type a are the elements fixed by a; i.e., for every $a \in \text{Kind}^T$, we let

$$\text{Dom}^a = \{ad \mid d \in \mathcal{P}\omega\}\,.$$

We may think of the closure a as coercing untyped elements of $\mathcal{P}\omega$ into elements of type a. Since a is a retraction, this coercion leaves elements of type a unchanged. As shown in [66], there is a closure $V \in \text{Kind}^T$ of all closures, so that $\text{Dom}^V = \text{Kind}^T$. This is a particular property of closures of $\mathcal{P}\omega$ which fails for retractions. Specifically, the collection of all retractions in $\mathcal{P}\omega$ is not a retract of $\mathcal{P}\omega$ [66]. If a is a closure, then it will be convenient to write

$$d\colon a \quad \text{for} \quad d = ad\,,$$

which is equivalent to saying $d \in \text{Dom}^a$. In addition, a useful abbreviation is

$$\lambda x\colon a.M \quad \text{for} \quad \lambda y.\{ay/x\}M\,.$$

Intuitively, $\lambda x{:}\, a.M$ is the function $\lambda x.M$, restricted to the range of closure a.

If a and b are closures, then we want $a \rightarrow b$ to be a closure which coerces every element d of $\mathcal{P}\omega$ to a mapping from Dom^a to Dom^b. In addition, we would like to have each function $\Phi(d)$ mapping Dom^a into Dom^b represented exactly once in the range of $a \rightarrow b$, so that $\mathrm{Dom}^{a \rightarrow b}$ is an extensional collection of functions (see [66] for further discussion). Both of these goals can be accomplished by taking

$$a \rightarrow b = \lambda x.b \circ x \circ a\,.$$

Intuitively, $a \rightarrow b$ works by taking any element d and producing the element $b \circ d \circ a$ which, when used as a function, first coerces its argument to an element of type a, then applies d, and then coerces the result to type b. It is easy to see that if $x{:}\, a$, then $((b \circ d \circ a)x){:}\, b$, so $(b \circ d \circ a)$ represents a function from Dom^a to Dom^b. In addition, if d already represents a function from Dom^a to Dom^b, so $dx{:}\, b$ whenever $x{:}\, a$, then $(b \circ d \circ a)x = dx$ for all $x{:}\, a$. What is a little less obvious is that if $(b \circ d_1 \circ a)x = (b \circ d_2 \circ a)x$ for all $x{:}\, a$, then $b \circ d_1 \circ a = b \circ d_2 \circ a$.[6] This means that range of $a \rightarrow b$ contains exactly one representative for each continuous function on $\mathcal{P}\omega$ that maps a into b. Based on this discussion, we define

$$\rightarrow\; = \lambda a{:}\, V.\lambda b{:}\, V.(\lambda x.b \circ x \circ a)$$

and write $\rightarrow$ as an infix operator, as in $a \rightarrow b$. It is easy to verify that for any $a, b \in \mathcal{P}\omega$, the element $a \rightarrow b$ is a closure (see [66]).

Since $\mathrm{Kind}^T = \mathrm{Dom}^V$, we will use the same function space constructor $\rightarrow$ for both types and kinds. For each kind expression κ, we let $\mathrm{TP}(\kappa)$ be the expression obtained by replacing all occurrences of T in κ by V and all occurrences of $\Rightarrow$ by $\rightarrow$. Using the definition of $\rightarrow$ above, we may interpret $\mathrm{TP}(\kappa)$ as a closure, and so we take $\mathrm{Kind}^\kappa = \mathrm{Dom}^{\mathrm{TP}(\kappa)}$. It is now easy to show that $\rightarrow$ is in $\mathrm{Kind}^{T \Rightarrow (T \Rightarrow T)}$. We leave this to the reader.

The intuition behind $\forall$ is quite straightforward. If $f{:}\, V \rightarrow V$ is a function from closures to closures, then every element $x{:}\, \forall f$ should map each closure (type) $t{:}\, V$, to some element xt of type ft. Therefore, $\forall f$ should be a function that coerces any $x \in \mathcal{P}\omega$ to a function which, given any $t{:}\, V$, returns an element $xt{:}\, ft$. Writing this out as a lambda term (including the type assumptions), we are led to the definition

$$\forall = \lambda f{:}\, V \rightarrow V.\lambda x.\lambda t{:}\, V.(ft)(xt)\,.$$

6. This is proved by noticing that the restriction to $x{:}\, a$ is inessential, and so $(b \circ d_1 \circ a)x = (b \circ d_2 \circ a)x$ holds in $\mathcal{P}\omega$. Therefore, by rule (ξ) of untyped lambda calculus, $\lambda x.(b \circ d_1 \circ a)x = \lambda x.(b \circ d_2 \circ a)x$. Working out the definition of $\circ$ gives the desired equation.

Recall that $xt{:}\,ft$ is an abbreviation for $xt = (ft)(xt)$, so we have used $(ft)(xt)$ in the definition of $\forall$. It is easy to verify that if $f \in \text{Kind}^{T \Rightarrow T}$, then $\forall f \in \text{Kind}^{T}$, and that $\forall \in \text{Kind}^{(T \Rightarrow T) \Rightarrow T}$.

To complete the definition of a second-order frame, it remains to define a family of Φ_{κ_1,κ_2} functions that give us a kind structure, and $\Phi_{a,b}$ and Φ_f for every $a, b \in \text{Kind}^T$ and $f \in \text{Kind}^{T \Rightarrow T}$. Surprisingly, all of these may be obtained as restrictions of the untyped Φ mapping $\mathcal{P}\omega$ to $[\mathcal{P}\omega \to \mathcal{P}\omega]$. With Φ_{κ_1,κ_2} defined to be the restriction of Φ to $\text{Kind}^{\kappa_1 \Rightarrow \kappa_2}$ and $\mathcal{I}$ defined as above on $\to$ and $\forall$, it is not hard to verify that $\mathit{Kind}_{\mathcal{P}\omega} = \langle \{\text{Kind}^{\kappa}\}, \{\Phi_{\kappa_1,\kappa_2}\}, \mathcal{I} \rangle$ is a kind structure. Assuming C_{term} is empty, we leave $\mathcal{I}_{Dom}$ empty and take

$$\mathit{Dom}_{\mathcal{P}\omega} = \langle \{\text{Dom}^a \mid a \in \text{Kind}^T\},\ \mathcal{I}_{\text{Dom}} \rangle .$$

For $a, b \in \text{Kind}^T, d \in \text{Dom}^{a \to b}, f \in \text{Kind}^{T \Rightarrow T}$, and $e \in \text{Dom}^{\forall f}$, we let

$$\Phi_{a,b}(d) = \Phi(d)|_{\text{Dom}^a} \text{ and } \Phi_f(e) = \Phi(e)|_{\text{Kind}^T} .$$

These restrictions of the "untyped" Φ have some remarkable properties.

Lemma 15

(i) $\Phi_{a,b}$ is a one-to-one and onto function from $\text{Dom}^{a \to b}$ to $[\text{Dom}^a \to \text{Dom}^b]$, where $[\text{Dom}^a \to \text{Dom}^b]$ is the set of continuous functions from Dom^a to Dom^b.

(ii) Φ_f is a one-to-one and onto function from $\text{Dom}^{\forall(f)}$ to $[\Pi_{a \in \text{Kind}^T} \text{Dom}^{f(a)}]$, where $[\Pi_{a \in \text{Kind}^T} \text{Dom}^{f(a)}]$ is the set of continuous functions from $\Pi_{a \in \text{Kind}^T}$ $\mathit{Dom}^{f(a)}$.

Proof (i) (Sketch) Note that $d \in \text{Dom}^{a \to b}$ implies $d = b \circ d \circ a$. Thus $\Phi(d)(e) = b(d(ae)) \in \text{Dom}^b$. It can also be shown that the range of $\Phi_{a,b}$ is all of $[\text{Dom}^a \to \text{Dom}^b]$. Suppose there are $d_1, d_2 \in \text{Dom}^{a \to b}$ such that $\Phi_{a,b}(d_1) = \Phi_{a,b}(d_2)$. It is then easy to show that $\Phi(d_1) = \Phi(d_2)$. Hence, $\Psi(\Phi(d_1)) = \Psi(\Phi(d_2))$. However $d_1, d_2 \in \text{Dom}^{a \to b}$ implies $d_i = b \circ d_i \circ a$ for $i = 1, 2$, and therefore $\Psi(\Phi(d_i)) = \Psi(\Phi(b \circ d_i \circ a)) = b \circ d_i \circ a = d_i$, where the middle equation holds since $b \circ d_i \circ a$ is of the form $\Psi(g)$ and $\Psi(\Phi(\Psi(g))) = \Psi(g)$. Thus $d_1 = \Psi(\Phi(d_1)) = \Psi(\Phi(d_2)) = d_2$, and it follows that $\Phi_{a,b}$ is one to one. (ii) Similar. $\square$

This shows that $\mathcal{F}_{\mathcal{P}\omega} = \langle \mathit{Kind}_{\mathcal{P}\omega}, \mathit{Dom}_{\mathcal{P}\omega}, \{\Phi_{a,b}, \Phi_f\} \rangle$ is a second-order frame. Since $[\text{Dom}^a \to \text{Dom}^b]$ and $[\Pi_{a \in \text{Kind}^T} \text{Dom}^{f(a)}]$ consist of all continuous functions of the appropriate functionality, it is easy to verify that this is an extensional second-order model.

Theorem 4 [37]
$\mathcal{F}_{P\omega} = \langle Kind_{P\omega}, Dom_{P\omega}, \{\Phi_{a,b}, \Phi_f\}\rangle$, as defined above, is an extensional second-order model.

The model $\mathcal{F}_{P\omega}$ has several interesting features. Perhaps most interesting is that $\text{Kind}^T \in Dom$, giving the set of types a very rich structure. In particular we can solve recursive domain equations in this model. Somewhat surprisingly, given the definition of Kind^T, the correspondence between Kind^T and *Dom* is bijective; i.e., $a = b$ iff $\text{Dom}^a = \text{Dom}^b$.

A similar argument shows that the class of finitary retract models, developed in [38] using ideas of [67], is also an extensional second-order model. We say a cpo is a *domain* if it is ω-algebraic and consistently complete, and a retraction r is *finitary* if the range of r is a domain. The finitary retract model is built from a domain model of untyped lambda calculus by taking finitary retracts as types. While similar to the closure model described above (e.g., in the definitions of $\rightarrow$ and $\forall$), there are some differences. For example, the relation between Kind^T and *Dom* is not bijective. A similar extensional model using finitary projections appears in [1]; the ideas behind this model also appear implicitly in several papers of Scott. The finitary projection model is again bijective in the relationship between Kind^T and *Dom*. In [1] it is shown how to solve higher-order recursive domain equations in this model. The same paper also shows that the type structures of all three models are very similar.

7.3 *The Ideal Model of Polymorphic Type Inference*

The ideal model proposed in [34, 33] was designed to explain polymorphic type inference for untyped lambda calculus. In the programming language ML, for example, the untyped identity function $\lambda x.x$ is given all types of the form $\alpha \rightarrow \alpha$, where α may be any "monotype" without $\forall$ [45]. The assignment of types to untyped terms is formalized as a deductive system for assertions like $\lambda x.x\colon \alpha \rightarrow \alpha$. A natural extension of ML typing is to assign second-order types to untyped lambda terms, giving the untyped identity type $\forall t.t \rightarrow t$, from which all of the ML typings can be obtained. A semantic explanation of the deductive system for polymorphic type assignment involves a structure for interpreting untyped lambda expressions and a way of associating a predicate with each second-order type [47]. The ideal model is an example of such a structure, using ideals over complete partial orders as types [45, 69]. It is sometimes thought that the ideal model is in fact a model of second-order lambda calculus. However, we will see that it is not. The shortcomings of the ideal model (as a second-order model) will be used to motivate the HEO model in the next subsection. We should emphasize that this model was intended to explain only type membership, not equality between typed terms. So it is through no fault of the authors of [34, 33] that the ideal model is not a second-order lambda model.

Although there may be trivial or contrived ways of treating the ideal model as a model of second-order lambda calculus, the most natural way would be to interpret each typed term as the term obtained by erasing all type information. This makes some sense, since the meaning of any typed term ends up belonging to the correct semantic type. The problem with this interpretation of terms is that it is not even weakly extensional, let alone extensional. Every model of second-order lambda calculus (or any other typed lambda calculus) must satisfy the axiom

$$\text{if } M = N \text{ for all } x\colon t, \text{ then } \lambda x\colon t.M = \lambda x\colon t.N\,.$$

We will construct a counterexample to this axiom in the ideal model. For concreteness, the counterexample will use the type $\forall t.t$. However, the argument is quite general.

Let P and Q be any two closed terms of the same type τ which have different meanings in the ideal model. (To be more concrete, we could take $P = \lambda t.\lambda x\colon t.\lambda y\colon t.x$ and $Q = \lambda t.\lambda x\colon t.\lambda y\colon t.y$ of type $\tau = \forall t.t \to t \to t$.) Since $\forall t.t$ has only one element $\bot$, we have

$$x\,\tau\,P = x\,\tau\,Q = \bot$$

for all $x\colon \forall t.t$. Therefore, we would like to obtain equal lambda terms by lambda abstracting $x\colon \forall t.t$ on both sides of the equation. However, we have

$$\lambda x\colon (\forall t.t).x\,\tau\,P \neq \lambda x\colon (\forall t.t).x\,\tau\,Q$$

in the ideal model, since $\lambda x.xP$ and $\lambda x.xQ$ are distinct. Thus weak extensionality fails. For similar reasons, weak extensionality generally fails in interpretations of second-order typed lambda calculus based on the models of type inference discussed in [47].

7.4 *HEO$_2$ and Related Models*

The main reason that ideal model and related structures do not form models of second-order lambda calculus is that equality is untyped, or independent of type. However, we can construct second-order models in much the same spirit if, in addition to a membership predicate, we also associate an equivalence relation with each type. Essentially, the predicates say what the elements of each type are, and the equivalence relations say when two elements are to be regarded as equal with respect to that type. One intuitive explanation for this view of types is is based on computer implementation. In compiling a typed language, we might choose to represent characters or boolean values as single bytes. Any byte would be accepted as a valid representation of either a boolean or a character. However, we are likely to regard any byte with least significant bit 1 as a representation of *true*, and so any two bytes ending with 1 will be regarded as equal booleans. However, all bytes with the same least significant bit will not be considered equal characters. Thus, although characters and booleans may have the same membership predicate on machine-level representations, the equality relations are different.

When we formalize the two-part interpretation of types, it is technically convenient to combine membership predicates and equivalence relations into a single notion. Intuitively, a partial equivalence relation on a set S is intended to be an equivalence relation R on a subset $S_1 \subseteq S$. However, it turns out that the predicate S_1 is superfluous. To begin with $S_1 = \{s \in S | \langle s, s\rangle \in R\}$, so it is easy to see that S_1 is determined by R. In addition, R is an equivalence relation on some subset of S iff R is a symmetric and transitive relation on all of S. Therefore, we will simplify the technical details by working with symmetric, transitive relations instead of predicates and equivalence relations. If S is any set, we say a binary relation R on S is a *partial equivalence relation* if R is symmetric and transitive.

The use of partial equivalence relations has a significant history. Partial equivalence relations for first-order function types were introduced in [55] and extended to higher-order functional types $\sigma \rightarrow \tau$ in [27]. Kreisel's structure is also described in [75], where it is called HEO, for the *hereditarily effective operations.* The structure HEO was extended to an interpretation of predicative polymorphic types in [5] and to a second-order model HEO_2 in [20, 75]. The structure HEO_2 was also discovered independently by Moggi and Plotkin (personal communication, 1985). A partial equivalence relation interpretation of functional types (in a somewhat more general setting) is also discussed in [66] and taken up in the study of polymorphic type inference in, e.g., [25, 12]. Further discussion and some general results about partial equivalence relation models of second-order lambda calculus are given in [49].

We will now concentrate on Girard's model HEO_2, which is a particular model of second-order lambda calculus based on partial equivalence relations. Instead of using partial equivalence relations over untyped lambda models, HEO_2 is based on the integers with partial recursive function application. We assume some enumeration of all partial recursive functions, and we write $\{n\}m$ for the application of the nth recursive function to m. As in [20], we will assume that the recursive functions are numbered so that $\{0\}m = 0$

for every integer m. With this assumption on the coding of recursive functions, we will end up with at least one element of every type (namely, the equivalence class of 0).

The first step in describing HEO_2 is to define the kind frame $Kind_{HEO}$. We let Kind^T be the set of all partial equivalence relations R over the integers, subject to the constraint that $\langle 0, 0\rangle \in R$. The remaining Kind^κ are defined inductively, with $\mathrm{Kind}^{\kappa_1 \Rightarrow \kappa_2}$ the set of all functions from Kind^{κ_1} to Kind^{κ_2}. Since $\mathrm{Kind}^{\kappa_1 \Rightarrow \kappa_2}$ is a set of functions, we let Φ_{κ_1,κ_2} be the identity. For any $R, S \in \mathrm{Kind}^T$, we let $R \to S$ be the relation

$$R \to S = \{\langle n_1, n_2\rangle | \text{ if } \langle m_1, m_2\rangle \in R \text{ then } \langle \{n_1\}m_1, \{n_2\}m_2\rangle \in S\}.$$

It is easy to see that $\langle 0, 0\rangle \in R \to S$, and so $\to \in \mathrm{Kind}^{T \Rightarrow T \Rightarrow T}$. If $f \in \mathrm{Kind}^{T \Rightarrow T}$ is any function from types (partial equivalence relations) to types, then we define $\forall f$ by

$$\forall f = \cap_{R \in \mathrm{Kind}^T} f(R).$$

It is also quite easy to see that $\langle 0, 0\rangle \in \forall f$, and so $\forall$ is a function of the appropriate kind. We let $Kind = \langle \{\mathrm{Kind}^\kappa\}, \{\Phi_{\kappa_1,\kappa_2}\}, \mathcal{I}\rangle$ with $\mathcal{I}(\to)$ and $\mathcal{I}(\forall)$ as above. Since *Kind* is a full function hierarchy, it is clear that every constructor expression has a meaning in *Kind*.

For every $R \in \mathrm{Kind}^T$ and every integer n with $\langle n, n\rangle \in R$, we let $[n]_R$ be the equivalence class

$$[n]_R = \{m \mid \langle n, m\rangle \in R\},$$

and define Dom^R to be the set of all such equivalence classes

$$Dom^R = \{[n]_R \mid \langle n, n\rangle \in R\}.$$

We then take Dom_{HEO} to be the collection of all Dom^R. Note that since $\langle 0, 0\rangle \in R$ for every R, every Dom^R is nonempty. The functions $\Phi_{R,S}$ and Φ_f are defined by

$$\Phi_{R,S}\ [n]_{R\to S}[m]_R = [\{n\}m]_S,$$

$$\Phi_f\ [n]_{\forall f}R = [n]_{f(R)},$$

and the sets $[\mathrm{Dom}^R \to \mathrm{Dom}^S]$ and $[\Pi_{R \in \mathrm{Kind}^T}.\mathrm{Dom}^{f(R)}]$ are defined to be the ranges of functions $\Phi_{R,S}$ and Φ_f, respectively. It is easy to see that both functions are well defined on equivalence classes. Although Φ_f may look trivial, it is not entirely so since $[n]_{f(R)}$ will generally be a larger equivalence class than $[n]_{\forall f}$. At this point, we have a frame

$$HEO_2 = \langle Kind_{HEO}, Dom_{HEO}, \{\Phi_{a,b}, \Phi_f\}\rangle,$$

and it remains to show that every term has a meaning.

The proof that HEO_2 is a model relies on elementary facts from recursive function theory, such as recursive sequencing functions and the s_n^m theorem (see, e.g., [64]). The main idea is to show inductively that for every term $B \vdash M\colon \sigma$, there is a recursive function for the meaning $[\![B \vdash M\colon \sigma]\!]$. This shows not only that every term has a meaning, but also that we can compute the meaning of every term as a function of the environment. Since HEO_2 contains only recursive functions, we use the stronger induction hypothesis to show that lambda abstractions have meaning in the model.

Recall that the meaning of a term depends only on the finite sequence of values given to its free variables, not on the entire environment. Consequently, we may regard $[\![B \vdash M\colon \sigma]\!]$ as a function on finite sequences of values, the types of these values given by B. Since every value in HEO_2 is an equivalence class of integers, we will consider $[\![B \vdash M\colon \sigma]\!]$ recursive if we have a corresponding recursive function on integer representatives (or "codes") for values. More precisely, we say f is *a recursive function for* $[\![\{x_1\colon \sigma_1, \ldots, x_k\colon \sigma_k\} \vdash M\colon \sigma]\!]$ if, for any environment $\eta \models \{x_1\colon \sigma_1, \ldots, x_k\colon \sigma_k\}$ and any sequence $\langle n_1, \ldots, n_k\rangle$ of integers with $n_i \in \eta(x_i)$, the function f computes an integer

$$f(\langle n_1, \ldots, n_k\rangle) \in [\![\{x_1\colon \sigma_1, \ldots, x_k\colon \sigma_k\} \vdash M\colon \sigma]\!]\eta \,.$$

A straightforward induction shows that there is a recursive function for the meaning of every term and that the recursive function for $[\![B \vdash M\colon \sigma]\!]$ has the appropriate type. The only nontrivial case is lambda abstraction, which uses the s_n^m theorem. It follows that HEO_2 is a second-order lambda model.

7.5 *Finite Models*

One distinction between untyped lambda calculus and the ordinary typed lambda calculus is that typed lambda calculus has nontrivial models in which all types are finite, but the untyped lambda calculus has no finite models (see [4], Proposition 5.1.15). A simple argument due to Gordon Plotkin (private communication, 1985) shows that there are no nontrivial models of second-order lambda calculus in which all types are finite. The *numerals* are the terms of the form

$$\lambda t.\lambda f\colon t \to t.\lambda x\colon t.f^n x \,,$$

where $f^n x$ is the term $f(f \ldots (fx) \ldots)$ with n occurrences of f (see [71, 18]). All of the numerals have type $\forall t.(t \to t) \to t \to t$. We write $\bar{n}$ for the numeral $\lambda t.\lambda f\colon t \to t.\lambda x\colon t.f^n x$.

Since every integer function that can be proved total recursive in analysis is definable in second-order lambda calculus [20, 71], there is a term EQ with

$$\vdash EQ\,\bar{m}\bar{n} = \text{ true if } m = n\,,$$

$$\vdash EQ\,\bar{m}\bar{n} = \text{ false if } m \neq n\,,$$

where true and false are the terms

$$\text{true} ::= \lambda t\, \lambda x{:}\, t\, \lambda y{:}\, t.x\,,$$

$$\text{false} ::= \lambda t\, \lambda x{:}\, t\, \lambda y{:}\, t.y\,,$$

with type $\forall t.t \to t \to t$. (The term EQ can also be constructed explicitly using the arithmetic functions given in [18], page 167.) If $\mathcal{F}$ is a finite model, then clearly $\mathcal{F} \models \bar{m} = \bar{n}$ for some $m \neq n$, since there are only finitely many elements of type $\forall t.(t \to t) \to t \to t$. Therefore, in any finite model $\mathcal{F}$, we have

$$\mathcal{F} \models \text{ false } = EQ\,\bar{m}\,\bar{n} = EQ\,\bar{n}\,\bar{n} = true\,.$$

However, it is easy to see that if true = false, then for any type t and $x, y{:}\, t$, we have

$$x = \text{ true } t\,x\,y = \text{ false } t\,x\,y = y\,.$$

It follows that every equation holds in $\mathcal{F}$, and $\mathcal{F}$ is a trivial model. This concludes the proof that the only second-order model with no infinite types is the trivial model.

8 *Summary and Directions for Future Work*

The second-order lambda calculus is a very expressive, explicitly typed extension of the ordinary typed lambda calculus. In this paper, we have examined the semantics of the language. Intuitively, a term $\lambda x{:}\,\sigma.M$ denotes a function from type σ to some type τ, and a term $\lambda t.M$ denotes a function from types to the union of all types. However, since terms like $\lambda t.\lambda x{:}\, t.x$ can be applied to their own types, the naive interpretation of second-order lambda terms contradicts standard set theory. Borrowing an idea from the semantics of untyped lambda calculus [4, 42, 66], we use a set together with an "element-to-function" map Φ in place of a set of functions. We interpret a λ-abstraction with domain a and range b as an element d which we may regard as a function by applying the map $\Phi_{a,b}$ to d. Since the range of $\Phi_{a,b}$ need not be all set-theoretic functions from type a to b, we can associate a set with each type and avoid set-theoretic paradoxes.

A collection of sets, one for each type and kind, together with an appropriate collection of bijective "element-to-function" maps, is called an extensional second-order frame. Second-order frames are analogous to untyped functional domains [42] for untyped lambda calculus and to type frames for ordinary typed lambda calculus [24]. Like their analogs, second-order frames have the right structure for interpreting terms, but they may not contain enough elements to give meanings to all terms.

Environment models are defined as frames in which every well typed term has a meaning. Although it depends on the inductive definition of meanings of terms, this model definition is straightforward and useful. The soundness and completeness theorems suggest that the definition is reasonable and not too restrictive. The soundness theorem shows that every structure that meets our definition has the right equational properties, while completeness demonstrates that every theory has a model. More evidence that our model definition is useful for studying second-order lambda calculus is provided by observing that several models proposed in the literature also meet our definition. However, it is worth mentioning that our soundness and completeness theorems apply only to models without empty types.

After preliminary work on this paper was completed, we became aware of a class of models based on partial equivalence relations, as described in Section 7.4. In some natural variations on these models, there exist empty types. While it is easy to remove the assumption that all types are nonempty from our model definition, the appropriate changes to the proof system are not entirely straightforward. To preserve soundness, the rule (remove hyp) must be discarded. In [41], additional proof rules for reasoning about empty types are given and a completeness theorem is proved.

In showing that certain structures are models in Section 7, we make use of independent characterizations of functions, like continuity or recursiveness. In the absence of such additional structure in the model, it might be more difficult to certify that a second-order frame is actually an environment model. Therefore, we provide an algebraic equivalent of the environment model condition that "everything must work out right." Combinatory models are defined as second-order frames that contain combinators S, K, A, B, C, D, where each combinator is characterized by an equation. We prove that the environment and combinatory model definitions are equivalent and, in the process, show how to translate between lambda terms and equivalent second-order combinatory terms. The combinatory model definition also shows that the model theory of second-order lambda calculus is reducible to the standard model theory of first-order logic.

Product types, sums, and existential types can be added to second-order lambda calculus by adding additional constructor constants and either term constants or additional term formation rules. Although we have not presented the details here, our model definition extends relatively easily. For example, a model of second-order lambda calculus with existential types is a model of the second-order lambda calculus with constructor constant $\exists \in C_{cst}$ of kind $(T \Rightarrow T) \Rightarrow T$ and term formation rules given in [52]. The extra constructor constant produces additional elements of Kind^T, and the additional structure associated with sets $\text{Dom}^{\exists f}$ is easily determined from the operations **rep** and **sum** discussed in [52].

The Automath languages [15] are essentially extensions of the typed lambda calculus formed by allowing the types of terms to be functions of elements of other types. Automath expressions of "first-order dependent type" define elements of $\Pi_{d \in A}\text{Dom}^{f(d)}$ for $A \in Dom$ and $f\colon A \to \text{Kind}^T$. In [3], a model for Classical Automath is constructed using closures, as in the models we discussed in Section 7. A general model definition for Classical Automath, along the lines we have proposed for second-order lambda calculus, seems relatively easy to work out. We are grateful to Robert Harper for extending the semantics of second-order lambda calculus to include first-order dependent types (private communication, 1986). Other extensions of our language, presented in McCracken [37], and the languages $F_3, F_4, \ldots$ of Girard mentioned earlier, allow terms of the form $\lambda v^\kappa.M$, where v^κ is a variable of higher kind. We believe that a straightforward extension of the model definition given here will suffice for this language, but we have not worked out the details. The calculus of constructions developed by Coquand and Huet [14] encompasses some of these extensions, but we have not worked out a precise model definition.

We have not considered second-order theories involving equations between constructors. The language is defined to suggest this possibility, and the term model construction in the completeness proof does not seem to rely on the absence of constructor axioms. However, there are some complications that must be resolved. To begin with, Lemma 1 fails: If we take $\sigma_1 \to \tau_1 = \sigma_2 \to \tau_2$ as a nonlogical axiom, it does not follow that $\sigma_1 = \sigma_2$ or $\tau_1 = \tau_2$. Since Lemma 1 figures crucially in the proof of Lemma 8, it is no longer possible to show that the meaning of every well typed term $B \vdash M\colon \sigma$ is independent of the way in which the typing is derived. Since Lemma 8 is important in our understanding of what an equation means (as discussed in Section 4.3), it would seem best to add more type information to terms so that Lemma 8 can be restored. Essentially, the syntax of terms would have to determine the types of all subterms up to constructor equivalence. For example, applications (MN) would have to be typed in a way that makes the types of M and N unambiguous. Some related discussion of ordinary typed lambda calculus with type equations is given in [7].

Another extension of the second-order lambda calculus involving "bounded quantification" is proposed in [11]. A polymorphic function of the form $\lambda t \le \tau.M$ will take any subtype of τ as a type parameter. In this calculus, we may write functions such as the identity $\lambda t \le \text{int}.\lambda x\colon t.t$ on all subtypes of int. (A related form of polymorphism was developed in [46].) This extension is designed to model the uses of subtypes and inheritance in object-oriented languages. A semantics of this language based on the PER model of Section 7.4 is developed in [9], while a semantics based on interval models is presented in [36]. While bounded quantification seems more expressive in an intuitive sense, there is an interpretation of bounded quantification into pure second-order lambda calculus [6]. This interpretation allows us to use models of second-order lambda calculus as models of bounded quantification.

There are a number of interesting open problems involving the semantics of the second-order lambda calculus. Recent work on a category theoretic approach to second-order lambda calculus [53, 68, 57, 40] seems quite promising in presenting another way of looking at this language. Based on recent work on categorical models of ordinary typed lambda calculus [51], we expect the categorical models of second-order lambda calculus to be intuitionistic versions of our model definition. However, the details of this correspondence have yet to be worked out. Another direction for investigation is the relationship between our model definition and models based on Girard's qualitative domains [21], which were developed after the bulk of this paper was written. Since maps from types to types in Girard's model (and the related model of [13]) are functors rather than functions, extensionality may fail for kind $T \Rightarrow T$. We believe that if our extensionality requirement is dropped, then these models satisfy our definition. However, we have not checked the details. Although there are a growing number of examples of second-order models, we still do not know very much about them. It would be interesting to discover more models and study both the local structure (equational theories) and global structure of models.

One way to study the global structure of models is by examining the isomorphisms or retractions between types. In [63], Reynolds shows that in every "set-theoretic" model, there is some type S which is isomorphic to $(S \to B) \to B$ for some nontrivial B. This conflicts with classical set-theoretic function spaces quite clearly, implying that set-theoretic models (i.e., models in which the function space construction gives the full classical set-theoretic function space) do not exist. In contrast, Bruce and Longo have characterized the class of isomorphisms that must hold in every second-order model [8]. Essentially, these isomorphisms all follow from the "commutativity" of Cartesian product; i.e., $\sigma \times \tau$ is isomorphic to $\tau \times \sigma$. This property of $\times$ applies to the language without $\times$ since $\sigma \times \tau \to \rho$ is isomorphic to both $\sigma \to \tau \to \rho$ and $\tau \to \sigma \to \rho$, and so we expect $\sigma \to \tau \to \rho$ and $\tau \to \sigma \to \rho$ to be isomorphic. Similarly, regarding $\forall t(\sigma \to \tau)$ as a type of functions from types to σ to τ, we expect $\forall t(\sigma \to \tau)$ to be isomorphic to $\sigma \to \forall t.\tau$ when t does not appear free in σ. Since these are all the isomorphisms that hold in all models, Reynolds' problematic isomorphism does not hold in general. This leaves open the possibility of relatively "natural" models which do not satisfy isomorphisms like S isomorphic to $(S \to B) \to B$. We might gain further insight by studying retractions instead of isomorphisms.

In our models, higher-order operations on types are elements of higher kinds. For example pair, sum, list, stack, tree, etc. are all type constructors of kind $T \Rightarrow T$. We can avoid having a separate hierarchy of kinds by making the set of types a domain. Once we have $\text{Kind}^T \in Dom$, it is natural to identify the function-space constructor $\Rightarrow$ on kinds with the function-space constructor $\to$ on types, putting every Kind^K into Dom. All of the retract models in Section 7.2 have this property. In the finitary projection model, with kinds as types and recursion over all types, Amadio, Bruce, and Longo have shown how to solve recursive domain equations [1]. A natural question to ask is whether every second-order model $\mathcal{F}$ can be embedded in a model $\mathcal{G}$ with $\text{Kind}^T_{\mathcal{G}} \in Dom_{\mathcal{G}}$ so that $\mathcal{F}$ and $\mathcal{G}$ satisfy the same equations between second-order terms. Meyer and Reinhold have shown that adding a type of all types to the syntax of a related language has dramatic effects [43], but this does not settle the question for second-order lambda calculus.

Since much of the interest in second-order lambda calculus stems from the similarity between the typing rules of the calculus and typing in programming languages like Ada, CLU, ML, and Russell, we expect the semantics of second-order lambda calculus to be useful for studying semantic properties of modern programming languages. One important property of typed programming languages is "representation independence," which has been studied by Reynolds and others [16, 17, 23, 60, 62]. Roughly speaking, representation independence ensures that the meaning of a program does not depend on whether the boolean value *true* is represented by 1 and *false* by 0, or vice versa. All that matters is that the operations on booleans behave properly. Two of the authors have studied representation independence for second-order lambda calculus using the model theory proposed in the present paper [50, 48], proving general representation independence theorems. Another important topic in programming languages is full abstraction [44, 58]. While it is probably more difficult to construct a fully abstract model for second-order lambda calculus than for ordinary typed lambda calculus (without polymorphism), this topic is well worth investigating.

Acknowledgments

Kim B. Bruce is partially supported by NSF Grants #DCR–8402700 and #DCR–8603890 and by a grant from Williams College. Albert R. Meyer is partially supported by NSF Grant #MCS80–10707. John C. Mitchell is partially supported by an NSF Presidential Young Investigator Award.

The authors would like to thank Giuseppe Longo, Eugenio Moggi, and Richard Statman for many helpful conversations.

References

[1] Amadio, R., Bruce, K., and Longo, G. "The finitary projection model for second order lambda calculus and solutions to higher order domain equations". *IEEE Symposium on Logic in Computer Science*, pp. 122–130. IEEE, New York, 1986.

[2] Barendregt, H., Coppo, M., and Dezani-Ciancaglini, M. "A filter lambda model and the completeness of type assignment". *J. Symbolic Logic 48*, 4 (1983), pp. 931–940.

[3] Barendregt, H. and Rezus, A. "Semantics for classical automath and related systems". *Information and Control 59* (1983), pp. 1–3.

[4] Barendregt, H. P. *The Lambda Calculus: Its Syntax and Semantics*. North-Holland, Amsterdam, 1984.

[5] Beeson, M. "Recursive models for constructive set theories". *Annals on Mathematical Logic 23* (1982), pp. 127–178.

[6] Breazu-Tannen, V., Coquand, T., Gunter, C. A., and Scedrov, A. "Inheritance and explicit coercion". In *Fourth IEEE Symposium on Logic in Computer Science*. IEEE, New York, 1989 (to appear).

[7] Breazu-Tannen, V. and Meyer, A. R. "Lambda calculus with constrained types". *Logics of Programs*, pp. 23–40 (June 1985). Lecture Notes in Computer Science, vol. 193. Springer-Verlag, Berlin, 1985.

[8] Bruce, K. and Longo, G. "Provable isomorphisms and domain equations in models of typed languages". *17th ACM Symposium on Theory of Computing*, pp. 263–272. ACM, New York, 1985.

[9] Bruce, K. and Longo, G. "A modest model of records, inheritance and bounded quantification". *Third IEEE Symposium on Logic in Computer Science*, pp. 38–51. IEEE, New York, 1988.

[10] Bruce, K. and Meyer, A. "A completeness theorem for second-order polymorphic lambda calculus". *Proceedings of the Internatinal Symposium on Semantics of Data Types* (Sophia-Antipolis, France), pp. 131–144. Lecture Notes in Computer Science, vol. 173. Springer-Verlag, Berlin, 1984.

[11] Cardelli, L. and Wegner, P. "On understanding types, data abstraction, and polymorphism". *Computing Surveys 17*, 4 (1985), pp. 471–522.

[12] Coppo, M. and Zacchi, M. "Type inference and logical relations". *Proceedings of the IEEE Symposium on Logic in Computer Science* (June), pp. 218–226. IEEE, New York, 1986.

[13] Coquand, T., Gunter, C. A., and Winskel, G. "Domain-theoretic models of polymorphism". *Information and Computation* (to appear), 1989.

[14] Coquand, T. and Huet, G. "The calculus of constructions". *Information and Computation 76* (1988), 2/3.

[15] De Bruijn, N. G. "A survey of the project automath". *To H. B. Curry: Essays on Combinatory Logic, Lambda Calculus and Formalism*, pp. 579–607. Academic Press, New York, 1980.

[16] Donahue, J. "On the semantics of data type". *SIAM J. Computing 8* (1979), pp. 546–560.

[17] Fokkinga, M. M. "On the notion of strong typing". *Algorithmic Languages*, DeBakker and van Vliet, eds., pp. 305–320. IFIP (North-Holland), Amsterdam, 1981.

[18] Fortune, S., Leivant, D., and O'Donnell, M. "The expressiveness of simple and second order type structures". *JACM 30*, 1 (1983), pp. 151–185.

[19] Friedman, H. "Equality between functionals". *Logic Colloquium*, R. Parikh, ed., pp. 22–37. Springer-Verlag, Berlin, 1975.

[20] Girard, J.-Y. "Interpretation fonctionelle et elimination des coupures de l'arithmetique d'ordre superieur". These D'Etat, Universite Paris VII, 1972.

[21] Girard, J.-Y. "The system *F* of variable types, fifteen years later". *Theoretical Computer Science 45*, 2 (1986), pp. 159–192. Reprinted in this volume (Chapter 6).

[22] Grätzer, G. *Universal Algebra*. Van Nostrand, 1968.

[23] Haynes, C. T. "A theory of data type representation independence". *Proc. Int. Symp. on Semantics of Data Types*, (Sophia-Antipolis, France), pp. 157–176. Lecture Notes in Computer Science, vol. 173. Springer-Verlag, Berlin, 1984.

[24] Henkin, L. "Completeness in the theory of types". *Journal of Symbolic Logic 15*, 2 (June 1950), pp. 81–91.

[25] Hindley, R. "The completeness theorem for typing lambda terms". *Theoretical Computer Science 22* (1983), pp. 1–17.

[26] Koymans, C. P. J. "Models of the lambda calculus". *Information and Control 52*, 3 (1982), pp. 306–323.

[27] Kreisel, G. "Interpretation of analysis by means of constructive functionals of finite types". *Constructivity in Mathematics*, A. Heyting, ed., pp. 101–128. North-Holland, Amsterdam, 1959.

[28] Lambek, J. "From lambda calculus to cartesian closed categories". *To H. B. Curry: Essays on Combinatory Logic, Lambda Calculus and Formalism*, pp. 375–402. Academic Press, New York, 1980.

[29] Landin, P. J. "A correspondence between ALGOL 60 and Church's lambda notation". *CACM 8* (1965), pp. 89–101 and 158–165.

[30] Leivant, D. "Polymorphic type inference". *Proceedings of the 10th ACM Symposium on Principles of Programming Languages*, pp. 88–98. ACM, New York, 1983.

[31] Leivant, D. "Structural semantics for polymorphic types". *Proc. 10th ACM Symp.*

on Principles of Programming Languages, pp. 155–166. ACM, New York, 1983.

[32] Liskov, B. et al. *CLU Reference Manual*. Lecture Notes in Computer Science, vol. 114. Springer-Verlag, Berlin, 1981.

[33] MacQueen, D., Plotkin, G., and Sethi, R. "An ideal model for recursive polymorphic types". *Information and Control 71*, 1/2 (1986), pp. 95–130.

[34] MacQueen, D. and Sethi, R. "A semantic model of types for applicative languages". *ACM Symp. on Lisp and Functional Programming*, pp. 243–252. ACM, New York, 1982.

[35] Martin-Löf, P. "About models for intuitionistic type theories and the notion of definitional equality". *3rd Scandinavian Logic Symposium*, S. Kanger, ed., pp. 81–109. North-Holland, Amsterdam, 1975.

[36] Martini, S. "Bounded quantifiers have interval models". *ACM Conference on LISP and Functional Programming* (August), pp. 164–173. ACM, New York, 1988.

[37] McCracken, N. *An Investigation of a Programming Language with a Polymorphic Type Structure*. PhD thesis, Syracuse Univ., 1979.

[38] McCracken, N. "A finitary retract model for the polymorphic lambda calculus". Manuscript, 1984.

[39] McCracken, N. "The typechecking of programs with implicit type structure". *Proceedings International Symposium on Semantics of Data Types* (Sophia-Antipolis, France, June), pp. 301–316. Lecture Notes in Computer Science, vol. 173. Springer-Verlag, Berlin, 1984.

[40] Meseguer, J. "Relating models of polymorphism". In *Proceedings of the 16th ACM Symp. on Principles of Programming Languages*. ACM, New York, 1989 (to appear).

[41] Meyer, A. R., Mitchell, J. C., Moggi, E., and Statman, R. "Empty types in polymorphic lambda calculus". *Proceedings of the 14th ACM Symposium on Principles of Programming Languages*, pp. 253–262. ACM, New York, 1987. Reprinted in this volume (Chapter 11).

[42] Meyer, A. R. "What is a model of the lambda calculus?" *Information and Control 52*, 1 (1982), pp. 87–122.

[43] Meyer, A. R. and Reinhold, M. B. "Type is not a type". *Proceedings of the 13th ACM Symposium on Principles of Programming Languages*, pp. 287–295. ACM, New York, 1986.

[44] Milner, R. "Fully abstract models of typed lambda calculi". *Theoretical Computer Science 4*, 1 (1977).

[45] Milner, R. "A theory of type polymorphism in programming". *J. Computer and System Sciences 17* (1978), pp. 348–375.

[46] Mitchell, J. C. "Coercion and type inference (summary)". *Proceedings of the 11th ACM Symposium on Principles of Programming Languages*, pp. 175–185. ACM, New York, 1984.

[47] Mitchell, J. C. "Semantic models for second-order lambda calculus". *Proceedings of the 25th IEEE Symposium on Foundations of Computer Science*, pp. 289–299. IEEE, New York, 1984.

[48] Mitchell, J. C. "Representation independence and data abstraction". *Proceedings of the 13th ACM Symposium on Principles of Programming Languages*, pp. 263–276. ACM, New York, 1986.

[49] Mitchell, J. C. "A type-inference approach to reduction properties and semantics of polymorphic expressions". *ACM Conference on LISP and Functional Programming*, pp. 308–319. ACM, New York, 1986. Included, with corrections, in this volume (Chapter 9).

[50] Mitchell, J. C. and Meyer, A. R. "Second-order logical relations". *Logics of Programs*, pp. 225–236. Lecture Notes in Computer Science, vol. 193. Springer-Verlag, Berlin, 1985.

[51] Mitchell, J. C. and Moggi, E. "Kripke-style models for typed lambda calculus". *IEEE Symposium on Logic in Computer Science* (June), pp. 303–314. IEEE, New York, 1987. Revised version to appear in *J. Pure and Applied Logic.*

[52] Mitchell, J. C. and Plotkin, G. D. "Abstract types have existential types". *ACM Trans. on Programming Languages and Systems 10*, 3 (1988), pp. 470–502. Preliminary version appeared in *Proceedings of the 12th ACM Symposium on Principles of Programming Languages*, 1985.

[53] Moggi, E. "Internal category interpretation of second-order lambda calculus". Manuscript, 1984.

[54] Monk, J. D. *Mathematical Logic.* Graduate Texts in Mathematics, vol. 37. Springer-Verlag, Berlin, 1976.

[55] Myhill, J. R. and Shepherdson, J. C. "Effective operations on partial recursive functions". *Zeitschrift für mathematische Logik und Grundlagen der Mathematik 1*, (1955).

[56] US Dept. of Defense. *Reference Manual for the Ada Programming Language.* GPO 008–000–00354–8, 1980.

[57] Pitts, A. M. "Polymorphism is set-theoretic, constructively". In *Proceedings Summer Conference on Category Theory and Computer Science.* Lecture Notes in Computer Science, (to appear). Springer-Verlag, Berlin, 1987.

[58] Plotkin, G. D. "LCF considered as a programming language". *Theoretical Computer Science 5* (1977), pp. 223–255.

[59] Plotkin, G. D. "Denotational semantics with partial functions". Lecture notes, C.S.L.I. Summer School, Stanford, 1985.

[60] Reynolds, J. C. "Towards a theory of type structure". *Paris Colloq. on Programming*, pp. 408–425. Lecture Notes in Computer Science, vol. 19. Springer-Verlag, Berlin, 1974.

[61] Reynolds, J. C. "The essence of ALGOL". *Algorithmic Languages*, de Bakker and van Vliet, eds., pp. 345–372. IFIP (North-Holland, Amsterdam), 1981.

[62] Reynolds, J. C. "Types, abstraction, and parametric polymorphism". *Information Processing '83*, pp. 513–523. North-Holland, Amsterdam, 1983.

[63] Reynolds, J. C. "Polymorphism is not set-theoretic". *Proc. Int. Symp. on Semantics of Data Types* (Sophia-Antipolis, France), pp. 145–156. Lecture Notes in Computer Science, vol. 173. Springer-Verlag, Berlin, 1984.

[64] Rogers, H. *Theory of Recursive Functions and Effective Computability*. McGraw-Hill, 1967.

[65] Rosolini, G. *Continuity and Effectiveness in Topoi*. PhD thesis, Merton College, Oxford, 1986.

[66] Scott, D. S. "Data types as lattices". *SIAM J. Computing 5*, 3 (1976), pp. 522–587.

[67] Scott, D. S. "A space of retracts". Manuscript, Merton College, Oxford, 1980.

[68] Seely, R. A. G. "Categorical semantics for higher-order polymorphic lambda calculus". Manuscript, 1986.

[69] Shamir, A. and Wadge, W. "Data types as objects". *Proceedings of the 4th ICALP Conference*, pp. 465-479. Lecture Notes in Computer Science, vol. 52. Springer-Verlag, Berlin, 1977.

[70] Statman, R. "The typed lambda calculus is not elementary recursive". *Theoretical Computer Science 9* (1979), pp. 73–81.

[71] Statman, R. "Number theoretic functions computable by polymorphic programs". *22nd IEEE Symposium on Foundations of Computer Science*, pp. 279–282. IEEE, New York, 1981.

[72] Statman, R. "Equality between functionals, revisited". *Harvey Friedman's Research on the Foundations of Mathematics*, pp. 331–338. North-Holland, Amsterdam, 1985.

[73] Stenlund, S. *Combinators, λ-terms and Proof Theory*. Reidel, Dordrecht-Holland, 1972.

[74] Trakhtenbrot, B. A., Halpern, J. Y., and Meyer, A. R. "From denotational to operational and axiomatic semantics for ALGOL-like languages: An overview". *Logics of Programs, Proceedings*, E. Clarke and D. Kozen, eds., pp. 474–500. Lecture Notes in Computer Science, vol. 164. Springer-Verlag, Berlin, 1984.

[75] Troelstra, A. S. *Mathematical Investigation of Intuitionistic Arithmetic and Analysis*. Lecture Notes in Mathematics, vol. 344. Springer-Verlag, Berlin, 1973.

Empty Types in Polymorphic Lambda Calculus[1]

Preliminary Report

11

Albert R. Meyer
MIT

John C. Mitchell
Stanford University

Eugenio Moggi
Edinburgh University

Richard Statman
Carnegie-Mellon University

Abstract

The model theory of simply typed and polymorphic (second-order) lambda calculus changes when types are allowed to be empty. For example, the "polymorphic Boolean" type really has *exactly* two elements in a polymorphic model only if the "absurd" type $\forall t.t$ is empty. The standard β-η axioms and equational inference rules, which are complete when all types are nonempty, are *not complete* for models with empty types. Without a little care about variable elimination, the standard rules are not even *sound* for empty types. We extend the standard system to obtain a complete proof system for mod-

1. This is a reprint with corrections of a paper which appeared in *Proc. 14th ACM Symposium on Principles of Programming Languages* (POPL), held in Munich, January, 1987, pp. 253–262.

els with empty types. The completeness proof is complicated by the fact that equational "term models" are not so easily obtained: In contrast to the nonempty case, not every theory with empty types is the theory of a single model.

---

1 *Why Empty Types?*

Functional languages with polymorphic control constructs and polymorphic data types support an attractive programming style which has been examined by several authors [5, 6, 8, 9, 13, 14, 15, 16, 18, 20, 21].

For example, Booleans and conditional operators arise directly from polymorphic concepts. Namely, the type

$$polybool ::= \forall t.\, t \to t \to t$$

is often called the type of *polymorphic Booleans*. One closed term of type *polybool* is

$$True ::= \lambda t.\, \lambda x{:}\, t.\, \lambda y{:}\, t.\, x\,.$$

That is, *True* is the polymorphic projection-on-the-first-argument function, which given any type, t, returns the projection-on-the-first-argument function of type $t \to t \to t$.

Another term of type *polybool* is

$$False ::= \lambda t.\, \lambda x{:}\, t.\, \lambda y{:}\, t.\, y\,,$$

viz., the polymorphic projection-on-the-second-argument function. Indeed, *True* and *False* are the *only* pure, i.e., constant-free, closed terms of type *polybool*. Defining the polymorphic conditional to be simply the identity

$$Cond ::= \lambda b{:}\, polybool.\, b\,,$$

we easily verify that for all $x, y{:}\, t$,

$$Cond\; True\; t\, x\, y = x\,, \tag{1}$$

and likewise,

$$Cond\; False\; t\, x\, y = y\,. \tag{2}$$

Thus it seems that Booleans and conditionals need not be added as a separate feature since they already appear as an intrinsic part of a polymorphic language. However, this appearance is misleading. For example, the equation

$$Cond\; b\; t\, y\, y = y \tag{3}$$

does not follow from the definitions above, even though it *does* follow directly from Equations (1) and (2) when b=*True* and when b=*False*. The problem is that even though *True* and *False* are the only two values of type *polybool* which are *definable* by pure closed terms, there are models with additional polymorphic Boolean elements for which Equation (3) fails, e.g., when $b = \bot_{polybool}$ in the usual cpo-based models [4, 23].

Thus we arrive at the kind of question that led us to the present study: Is it *consistent* to assume Equation (3) as a further axiom of polymorphic calculus? More generally, is it consistent to assume that *True* and *False* are the *only* elements of type *polybool*?

Ingenious model constructions by Moggi [19] and Coquand [7] (see [2, 3]) show that the answer is yes.

Proposition 1.1 (Moggi, Coquand)
There is a model of the polymorphic lambda calculus containing exactly two elements of type *polybool*. Equation (3) is necessarily valid in such a model.

The models satisfying Proposition 1.1 contain types with no elements. It turns out that this is inevitable. To see this, consider the "absurd" type $\forall t.t$. Any element, f, of this type chooses, for any type σ, an element $(f\sigma)$ of type σ. Thus, if *any* type is empty, then the absurd type must be empty as well. The proof of Proposition 1.2 shows that if there is such a choice function, f, which there trivially will be in any model without empty types, then Equation (3) is inconsistent.

Note that under an interpretation in which every type has at most one element, every well formed equation is valid. By convention, such trivial interpretations are ruled out in the context of equational reasoning, so a *model* is required to have at least one type with more than one element. Now it is easy to see that in the polymorphic calculus, *True* = *False* if and only if every type has at most one element. Indeed, from the equation *True* = *False*, one can derive any well formed equation using standard inference rules. Hence, we say a set of equations is *inconsistent* if and only if the equation *True* = *False* follows from them. This is then equivalent to saying the set of equations has no model.

Proposition 1.2
In any model of polymorphic lambda calculus with all types nonempty, Equation (3) is not valid. In particular, there must be more than two elements of type *polybool* in such a model.

Proof Suppose f: $\forall t.\, t$ and (3) holds. Let $b ::= (\lambda t.\, \lambda x{:}\, t.\, \lambda y{:}\, t.\, (ft))$. Note that b: *polybool*. Now by definition of b, we have b *polybool* $y\,y = (f$ *polybool*$)$, so by definition of *Cond* and Equation (3), we have $y = (f$ *polybool*$)$; i.e., all elements y of type *polybool* are equal to $(f$ *polybool*$)$. In particular, *True* = *False*. □

So empty types are necessary if *polybool* is to model Booleans exactly. Of course, *polybool* is simply one example of a type where one would like and expect the only elements to be the definable ones. For example, a variation of the proof of Proposition 1.2 applies to the type *polyint* $::= \forall t.\, (t \to t) \to t \to t$ of Church's "polymorphic integers", so that without empty types, one must accept additional "nonstandard" polymorphic integers besides those definable by the familiar Church numerals.

It is an interesting open problem to explain how these propositions generalize to other types.

Conjecture 1.1

Propositions 1.1 and 1.2 generalize to arbitrary "universal" types u of the form $\forall t_1 \ldots \forall t_n.\, \sigma$ where σ is an expression built from type variables $t_1, \ldots, t_n$ using $\to$. Namely, there can be a model in which the elements of u are precisely those definable by the pure closed terms of type u (and moreover, no two such terms have the same value) if and only if models may have empty types.[2]

Propositions 1.1 and 1.2 make it clear that

- empty types force themselves into consideration in the context of polymorphism, and
- having them significantly changes the theory of various familiar types such as polymorphic Booleans and integers.

2 *Problems with Empty Types*

Empty types complicate the relationship between models and lambda-calculus theories. The set of equations valid in a given collection of models is called a (semantic) *theory*. If we assume no type is empty, then every theory is actually the theory of a *single* "generic" model. This fact is significant in proving completeness (with respect to models with nonempty types) of the familiar equational reasoning (cf. [4, 10, 17]). It fails to hold when we allow empty types.

2. This conjecture has recently been verified by Breazu-Tannen and Coquand based on their model construction in [2].

Proposition 2.1

Let b_0 and b_1 be constants denoting types. The theory of the collection of all models satisfying the equation

$$\lambda x{:}\, b_0.\, \lambda y{:}\, b_1.\, \mathit{True} = \lambda x{:}\, b_0.\, \lambda y{:}\, b_1.\, \mathit{False} \tag{4}$$

is not equal to the theory of any single model of the polymorphic lambda calculus.

Proof If types b_0 and b_1 are both nonempty, then by applying the functions on either side of the equation to arguments of these respective types, we can derive the inconsistency *True* = *False*. Therefore, in every model in the collection, either b_0 must be empty or b_1 must be empty. But it is not hard to find models in which only one of these types is empty. So the equation

$$\lambda x{:}\, b_0.\, \mathit{True} = \lambda x{:}\, b_0.\, \mathit{False}\,, \tag{5}$$

which says that b_0 is empty, is not in the theory of the collection, nor is the corresponding equation about b_1,

$$\lambda x{:}\, b_1.\, \mathit{True} = \lambda x{:}\, b_1.\, \mathit{False}. \tag{6}$$

But in any *single* model in the collection at least one of b_0, b_1 must be empty, so at least one of Equations (5) and (6) must be in the theory of that model. □

In fact, with suitable added axioms for a base-type *Bool*, the above argument applies to the simply typed lambda calculus as well.

A related model-theoretic contrast between the situations with and without empty types seems to arise from minimal models. For simple types constructed from only a *single* base type there is a *minimum* model, which is a "final" object in the space of models, i.e., it is a "homomorphic image of a submodel" of every model. Consequently, its theory is maximum, namely, contains all equations between pure closed lambda terms which are individually consistent [24], [1, A.1.23]. With two base types (with or without empty types), there are equations which assert that each of the base types has at most one element. These equations are separately consistent, but together are inconsistent, so no maximal theory or minimal model exists.

Theorem 2.1

There is a maximum pure theory with empty types of polymorphic lambda-calculus.

Open Problem 2.1

Is there a maximum pure theory *without* empty types of polymorphic lambda calculus?

3 *Typed Terms and Equations*

We now define precisely the two calculi in this paper: simply typed [1, Appendix A] and polymorphic [11, 22] lambda calculus. The types of simply typed lambda calculus are given by

$$\tau ::= \mathbf{a} \mid \tau \to \tau,$$

where **a** is a constant denoting a type. (There may be more than one type constant.)

Typed lambda terms are usually defined by assuming that there are infinitely many variables $x_1^\tau, x_2^\tau, \ldots$ for each type τ. However, when we assume there is a variable x^τ of type τ, we are in fact assuming that τ is nonempty. This leads us to present the syntax of terms in another form.

The terms, and their types, are defined using the subsidiary notion of type assignment. A *type assignment* A is a finite set of formulas $x: \tau$, with no x occurring twice in A. We write $A[x: \sigma]$ for the type assignment

$$A[x: \sigma] = \{y: \tau \in A \mid y \text{ different from } x\} \cup \{x: \sigma\}.$$

Terms will be written in the form $A \vdash M: \tau$, which may be read, "under type assignment A, the term M has type τ." The well typed terms are defined as follows.

$$A \vdash x: \tau \text{ for } x: \tau \in A,$$

$$\frac{A \vdash M: \sigma \to \tau, \ A \vdash N: \sigma}{A \vdash MN: \tau},$$

$$\frac{A[x: \sigma] \vdash M: \tau}{A \vdash \lambda x: \sigma.M: \sigma \to \tau}.$$

The types of polymorphic lambda calculus are defined by adding two more clauses to the rules for simple types:

$$\tau ::= \mathbf{a} \mid \tau \to \tau \mid t \mid \forall t.\tau .$$

Additional term formation rules for these new types are

$$\frac{A \vdash M: \forall t.\tau}{A \vdash M\sigma: [\sigma/t]\tau},$$

where $[\sigma/t]\tau$ is the result of substituting σ for t in τ, and

$$\frac{A \vdash M{:}\,\tau}{A \vdash \lambda t.M{:}\,\forall t.\tau},$$

where we assume t is not free in any type occurring in A.

Given this formulation of terms, it is natural to write equations in the form

$$A \vdash M = N{:}\,\tau, \tag{7}$$

where it is required that $A \vdash M{:}\,\tau$ and $A \vdash N{:}\,\tau$.

To facilitate reasoning about empty types, it is convenient to add assumptions of the form *empty*(σ) to type assignments. Therefore, an *equation* will be a formula of the form (7) where A is now to be the union of a type assignment A_1 and a set A_2 of formulas *empty*(σ), and also $A_1 \vdash M{:}\,\tau$ and $A_1 \vdash N{:}\,\tau$.

Note that the emptiness assertions in A are not used to determine the types of terms.

4 *Unsoundness of Variable Elimination*

There are no types which are empty in all models. Consequently, no type is provably empty in the pure lambda theory. More generally, we have the following theorem.

Theorem 4.1

An equation is valid in all models without empty types if and only if it is valid in all models with empty types.

This will follow from Corollary A.1 below. Thus, it might seem that admitting models with empty types should not have much affect on equational logic of terms.

However, when we reason from equational *hypotheses*, the valid consequences are very different depending on whether empty types are allowed. Specifically, an equation between terms which follows under some type assignment, does *not* necessarily follow under an assignment involving *only* the free variables of the terms.

For example, we have remarked that Equation (5), taken with the empty type assignment, is true in a model if and only if the type b_0 is empty. In particular, from (5), we can certainly conclude

$$x{:}\,b_0 \vdash (\lambda x{:}\,b_0.\, \mathit{True})x = (\lambda x{:}\,b_0.\, \mathit{False})x{:}\,(b_0 \rightarrow \mathit{polybool}),$$

so by β-reduction, we have

$$x{:}\,b_0 \vdash \mathit{True} = \mathit{False}{:}\,\mathit{polybool}. \tag{8}$$

Now if every type is nonempty, then the rule

$$\frac{A \cup \{x{:}\,\sigma\} \vdash M = N{:}\,\tau}{A \vdash M = N{:}\,\tau}, \quad x \text{ not free in } M, N, \qquad (\textit{nonempty})$$

is sound, since assuming something about the type of an irrelevant variable x has no effect on the validity of an equation. (This rule is usually not stated in proof systems for typed lambda calculus, since it is implicit in the usual formulation for terms over models without empty types.) Then from (8) and (*nonempty*), we deduce the inconsistency

$$\varnothing \vdash \mathit{True} = \mathit{False}{:}\ \mathit{polybool}. \qquad (9)$$

This is the formal confirmation of the obvious fact that the assertion that type b_0 is empty is inconsistent with the assumption that all types are nonempty. However, Equation (5) is not inconsistent if we allow models with b_0 interpreted as empty.

The problem is that a type assignment $x{:}\,\sigma$ implies σ is nonempty, and such an assumption cannot be discharged without justification when empty types are possible. In short, rule *nonempty* is *not sound* when empty types are allowed. (A similar kind of unsoundness was already observed for many-sorted algebras in [12].)

So extra care will be needed in manipulating type assignments when empty types occur.

5 *Completeness*

Our proof systems will differ from the usual ones (for models without empty types) in two respects: we carefully specify the rules for variable elimination, and we add an axiom scheme and inference rule for reasoning about empty types.

The rule for empty types is needed because even when the technical problem of variable discharge noted above is repaired to yield a sound lambda theory for empty types, the remaining standard systems are still not complete.

Theorem 5.1

The standard axioms and equational inference rules, which are complete for simply typed [10] or polymorphic [4] lambda calculus when all types are nonempty, are *not complete* for proving semantic consequences of equations over models with empty types.

The proof is by a proof-theoretic analysis, which we omit in this summary. For example, let $\pi_1 ::= \lambda x{:}\,b_0.\,\lambda y{:}\,b_0.\,x$, $\pi_2 ::= \lambda x{:}\,b_0.\,\lambda y{:}\,b_0.\,y$, and $\mathbf{f}$ be a constant of suitable type. Then the equation

$$\lambda x{:}\, b_0.(\mathbf{f}\pi_1) = \lambda x{:}\, b_0.(\mathbf{f}\pi_2)$$

implies

$$(\mathbf{f}\pi_1) = (\mathbf{f}\pi_2).$$

This follows by the same reasoning which led to (9) if b_0 is not empty, and if b_0 is empty, then $\pi_1 = \pi_2$, and again it follows trivially.

However, argument by cases like this cannot be formalized without new inference rules. This is what distinguishes the proof systems we describe below from previous proof systems for equality in models without empty types [4]. In particular as noted above, our equations use the additional formulas *empty*(σ) in type assignments.

In the appendix we give a complete proof system for equations with empty types (Theorem A.2). The proof, which we omit in this preliminary report, follows the usual proof of equational completeness by construction of term models, with an added twist resembling "model completion" in a Henkin-style completeness proof for predicate logic. The twist is brought on by the nonexistence of generic models noted in Proposition 2.1.

Acknowledgment

Albert R. Meyer's contribution to the research reported here was supported by NSF Grant No. 8511190–DCR and by ONR grant No. N00014–83–K–0125.

Appendix: Proof Rules

A.1 Without Empty Types

For ordinary typed lambda terms, we have the usual axioms:

$$A \vdash \lambda x{:}\, \sigma.M = \lambda y{:}\, \sigma[y/x]M{:}\, \sigma \to \tau, \quad \text{provided } y \notin FV(M), \tag{α_1}$$

$$A \vdash (\lambda x{:}\, \sigma.M)N = [N/x]M{:}\, \tau, \tag{β_1}$$

$$A \vdash \lambda x{:}\, \sigma.Mx = M{:}\, \sigma \to \tau, \quad \text{provided } x \notin FV(M). \tag{η_1}$$

For polymorphic lambda calculus, we need additional versions of each of these rules:

$$A \vdash \lambda t.M = \lambda s.[s/t]M{:}\, \forall t.\sigma, \quad \text{provided } s \notin FV(A \vdash M{:}\, \sigma), \tag{α_2}$$

$$A \vdash (\lambda t.M)\sigma = [\sigma/t]M{:}\, \tau, \tag{β_2}$$

$$A \vdash \lambda t.Mt = M{:}\, \forall t.\sigma, \quad \text{provided } t \notin FV(M). \tag{η_2}$$

The inference rules that are sound for all models are symmetry and transitivity,

$$\frac{A \vdash M = N: \sigma}{A \vdash N = M: \sigma}, \qquad (sym)$$

$$\frac{A \vdash M = N: \sigma, A \vdash N = P: \sigma}{A \vdash M = P: \sigma}, \qquad (trans)$$

congruence rules, and a rule for adding additional hypotheses to type assignments. The congruence rules for ordinary typed lambda calculus are

$$\frac{A \vdash M_1 = M_2: \sigma \rightarrow \tau, \ A \vdash N_1 = N_2: \sigma}{A \vdash M_1 N_1 = M_2 N_2: \tau}, \qquad (cong_1)$$

$$\frac{A[x: \sigma] \vdash M = N: \tau}{A \vdash \lambda x: \sigma.M = \lambda x: \sigma.N: \sigma \rightarrow \tau}. \qquad (\xi_1)$$

The additional rules for polymorphic terms are

$$\frac{A \vdash M_1 = M_2: \forall t.\sigma, \ \tau_1 = \tau_2}{A \vdash M_1 \tau_1 = M_2 \tau_2: [\tau_1/t]\sigma}, \qquad (cong_2)$$

$$\frac{A \vdash M = N: \sigma}{A \vdash \lambda t.M = \lambda t.N: \forall t.\sigma}, \quad t \text{ not free in } A. \qquad (\xi_2)$$

Since type assignments are explicitly included in equations, we also need the rule

$$\frac{A \vdash M = N: \sigma}{B \vdash M = N: \sigma}, \quad A \subseteq B \qquad (add\ hyp)$$

for adding additional typing hypotheses.

We write $\vdash_1$ for provability using the axiom schemes (α_1), (β_1), (η_1), and the inference rules (*sym*), (*trans*), $(cong_1)$, (ξ_1), and (*add hyp*), and we write $\vdash_1^{nonempty}$ for provability using *(nonempty)* in addition. We write $\vdash_2$ and $\vdash_2^{nonempty}$ for the corresponding proof systems for polymorphic lambda calculus. We omit subscripts to refer ambiguously to either (or both) proof systems.

Lemma A.1

Without equational hypotheses, rule (nonempty) is a derived rule, i.e., for any equation E,

$$\vdash E \quad \text{iff} \quad \vdash^{nonempty} E.$$

Theorem A.1 [4]

The rules for $\vdash^{nonempty}$ are sound and complete for deducing semantic consequences of equations over the class of models in which every type is nonempty.

Corollary A.1

The rules for $\vdash$ are sound and complete for deducing the equations that hold in all models.

A.2 *With Empty Types*

The proof system for reasoning about empty types makes use of the formulas $empty(\sigma)$ in equations. We have an axiom scheme for introducing equations that use emptiness assertions,

$$empty(\sigma), x{:}\,\sigma \vdash True = False{:}\ polybool,$$

and an inference rule which lets us use emptiness assertions to reason by cases,

$$\frac{A \cup \{x{:}\,\sigma\} \vdash M = N{:}\,\tau, \ A \cup \{empty(\sigma)\} \vdash M = N{:}\,\tau}{A \vdash M = N{:}\,\tau}, \quad x \text{ not free in } M, N.$$

We write $\vdash^{empty}$ for provability using $\vdash$ and the axiom and inference rule for empty types.

The semantics of polymorphic models, in particular the meaning of satisfaction, $\models$, follows [4], except of course that types may be empty. Our main result is that $\vdash^{empty}$ is a sound and complete proof system for deducing semantic consequences of equations.

Theorem A.2

Let Γ be a set of equations and E be any equation. Then

$$\Gamma \vdash^{empty} E \quad \text{iff} \quad \Gamma \models^{empty} E.$$

References

[1] Barendregt, H. *The Lambda Calculus: Its Syntax and Semantics.* Volume 103 of *Studies in Logic.* North-Holland, Amsterdam, 1981. Revised Edition, 1984.

[2] Breazu-Tannen, V. and Coquand, T. "Extensional models for polymorphism". *TAPSOFT'87—Colloquium on Functional and Logic Programming and Specifications,* pp. 291–307. Springer-Verlag, Berlin, 1987.

[3] Breazu-Tannen, V. and Meyer, A. "Computable values can be classical". *Proceedings of the 14th Symposium on Principles of Programming Languages,* pp. 238–245. ACM, New York, 1987. Reprinted in this volume (Chapter 12).

[4] Bruce, K. and Meyer, A. "The semantics of second-order polymorphic lambda calculus". *Semantics of Data Types,* G. Kahn, D. MacQueen, and G. Plotkin, eds., pp. 131–144. Springer-Verlag, Berlin, 1984. See also this volume, Chapter 10.

[5] Cardelli, L. "A polymorphic calculus with type:type". Technical Report, DEC System Research Center, 1985.

[6] Cardelli, L. and Wegner, P. "On understanding types, data abstraction, and polymorphism". *ACM Computing Surveys 17,* 4 (December 1985), pp. 471–522.

[7] Coquand, T. Communication in the TYPES electronic forum[3].

[8] Coquand, T. and Huet, G. "Constructions: A Higher Order Proof System for Mechanizing Mathematics". Rapport de Recherche 401, INRIA, Domaine de Voluceau, 78150 Rocquencourt, France, May 1985. Presented at EUROCAL 85, Linz, Austria.

[9] Fortune, S., Leivant, D., and O'Donnell, M. "The expressiveness of simple and second-order type structures". *J. ACM 30*, 1 (January 1983), pp. 151–185.

[10] Friedman, H. "Equality between functionals". *Logic Colloqium '73*, R. Parikh, ed., pp. 22–37. Springer-Verlag, Berlin, 1975.

[11] Girard, J.-Y. "Interprétation fonctionelle et élimination des coupures dans l'arithmétique d'ordre supérieure". PhD thesis, Université Paris VII, 1972.

[12] Goguen, J. and Meseguer, J. "Completeness of many-sorted equational logic". *SIGPLAN Notices 17* (1972), pp. 9–17.

[13] MacQueen, D. "Using dependent types to express modular structure". *Proceedings of the 13th Symposium on Principles of Programming Languages*, pp. 277–286. ACM, New York, 1986.

[14] Martin-Löf, P. "An intuitionistic theory of types: predicative part". *Logic Colloquium III*, F. Rose and J. Sheperdson, eds., pp. 73–118. North-Holland, Amsterdam, 1973.

[15] McCracken, N. "Investigation of a programming language with a polymorphic type structure". PhD thesis, Syracuse University, Syracuse, New York, June 1979.

[16] Meyer, A. and Reinhold, M. "'Type' is not a type: Preliminary report". *Proceedings of the 13th Symp. Principles of Programming Languages*, pp. 287–295. ACM, New York, 1986.

[17] Meyer, A. "What is a model of the lambda calculus?" *Information and Control 52* (1982), pp. 87–122.

[18] Mitchell, J. "Lambda calculus models of typed programming languages". PhD thesis, Massachusetts Institute of Technology, Cambridge, Massachusetts, August 1984.

[19] Moggi, E. Communication in the TYPES electronic forum[3], February 10, 1986.

[20] Mohring, C. "Algorithm development in the theory of constructions". *Symposium on Logic in Computer Science*, pp. 84–91. IEEE, New York, 1986.

[21] Reynolds, J. "Three approaches to type structure". *TAPSOFT Advanced Seminar on the Role of Semantics in Software Development.* Springer-Verlag, Berlin, 1985.

[22] Reynolds, J. "Towards a theory of type structure". *Coll. sur la programmation*, pp. 408–423. Springer-Verlag, Berlin, 1974.

[23] Scott, D. "Data types as lattices". *SIAM J. Computing 5* (1976), pp. 522–587.

[24] Statman, R. "Completeness, invariance and lambda-definability". *J. Symbolic Logic 47* (1982), pp. 17–26.

3. **types@xx.lcs.mit.edu**

Computable Values Can Be Classical

Preliminary Report[1]

12

Val Breazu-Tannen[2]
Albert R. Meyer
MIT

Abstract

In programming languages of universal power, the computational integers must be distinguished from the classical integers because of the "divergent" integer. Even the equational theory corresponding to evaluation of integer expressions is distinct from the theory of classical integers, and classical reasoning about computational integers yields inconsistencies. We show that there exist "programming languages", actually extensions of the polymorphic

1. This is a slightly revised version of a paper presented at the 14th Annual ACM Symposium on Principles of Programming Languages, Munich, January 21–23, 1987, and which appeared in the symposium's proceedings.
2. Currently with the Department of Computer and Information Science, University of Pennsylvania.

lambda calculus, that have tremendous computing power and yet whose computational integers, or any other algebraically specified abstract data type, *coincide* with their classical counterpart. In particular, the equational theory of the programming language is a *conservative extension* of the theory of the underlying base types as given by algebraic data type specifications.

---

1 Recursion is Not Conservative

The concerns of this paper are illustrated by the following simple data type specification (a variation of one given in [16]):

There is one sort *int*, function symbols,

$$\begin{aligned} cond &: int^3 \longrightarrow int\,, \\ - &: int^2 \longrightarrow int\,, \\ succ &: int \longrightarrow int\,, \\ 0, 1 &: int\,, \end{aligned}$$

and axioms,

$$cond(0, x, y) = x\,, \tag{1}$$

$$cond(1, x, y) = y\,, \tag{2}$$

$$x - x = 0\,, \tag{3}$$

$$succ(x) - x = 1\,. \tag{4}$$

Clearly the standard integers satisfy this specification, so it follows that equational reasoning from this specification cannot deduce, say, $0 = 1$. Now, consider the following program:

$$P \stackrel{\text{def}}{=} \textbf{letrec}\ f(x) = succ(f(x))\ \textbf{in}\ cond(f(0) - f(0), 0, 1)$$

Applying the axioms (3) and (1) to the conditional we get $P = 0$. On the other hand, expanding the first $f(0)$ to $succ(f(0))$ by the copy rule, and then using axioms (4) and (2) we get $P = 1$. Hence $0 = 1$!

What is going on here? We have started from a simple functional language—that of arithmetical expressions. Associated with this language there is an equational theory—the one given by the specification above. Then, we have extended the language to allow recursion, adding the copy rule to our computation rules. Again we have an equational theory, one that extends (contains) the theory of the basic data type. But this extension is not *conservative* since it allows us to prove an equation between purely arithmetical expressions, namely $1 = 0$, that was not derivable from the data type specification.[3]

This failure of conservative extension springs from a familiar source: a recursively defined function whose evaluation diverges. In the usual denotational semantics of functional programs, the copy rule for recursion is sound, but the classical axiom (3), $x - x = 0$, is not sound since $\perp - \perp = \perp \neq 0$, where $\perp$ is the "divergent" integer value. In order to reason about the underlying data types in such semantics, we need a logic that takes nontermination into account. LCF [11] is a well-developed programming environment supporting such logic, but problems of reasoning about divergent values remain apparent [21]. In another recently proposed logic of partial computable functions based on partial lambda calculus [18, 22], divergent values are eliminated but well-formed expressions with undefined meaning must be considered.

Potentially divergent constructs like recursion are ubiquitous in programming languages because they are essential for universal computing power. Both LCF and the logic of partial lambda calculus take recursion as a must and try to reason about the resulting data domains. In this paper, we take a different course: we aim to preserve classical reasoning about the data by achieving the kind of conservative extension that fails above. We do so by eliminating unrestricted recursion and consequently sacrificing universal computing power. We suggest that from a theoretical viewpoint, and possibly from a pragmatic one as well, the sacrifice need not be great.

2 *Conservative Extension ...*

Following familiar tradition [13], we take lambda calculi with reduction rules as models of programming languages and their evaluation. For reasons soon to become clear, our choice here is the Girard-Reynolds polymorphic lambda calculus [9, 24], cf. [8]. We will symbolize this calculus by $\lambda^{\forall}$. We expect the reader to be familiar with $\lambda^{\forall}$. The following example may help to bring us on common ground.

One way to compute "polymorphically" with integers is as follows. The numerals are taken to be the closed terms of type

$$polyint \stackrel{\text{def}}{=} \forall t.\,(t \rightarrow t) \rightarrow t \rightarrow t\,.$$

The numeral corresponding to the integer n is

$$\tilde{n} \stackrel{\text{def}}{=} \lambda t.\,\lambda f\!:\!t \rightarrow t.\,\lambda x\!:\!t.\,f^n x\,.$$

3. Indeed, in this case the extension is not only not conservative, it is equationally *inconsistent*, viz., one can prove *any* arithmetic equation from $1 = 0$ and axioms (1) and (2).

One can define, for example,

$$Add : polyint \rightarrow polyint \rightarrow polyint$$

by

$$Add \stackrel{\text{def}}{=} \lambda u{:}\,polyint.\ \lambda v{:}\,polyint.\ \lambda t.\ \lambda f{:}\,t \rightarrow t.\ \lambda x{:}\,t.\ utf(vtfx)$$

and prove in $\lambda^\forall$ that

$$Add\,\tilde{m}\,\tilde{n} = \widetilde{m+n}\,.$$

Note, however, that $\lambda^\forall$ cannot prove

$$Add\,u\,v = Add\,v\,u$$

with arbitrary u and v of type *polyint*.

We will take the position that, from a programming perspective, one would like a more general and flexible method of representing data types. In fact, we want to be able to add *separate* and *arbitrary* data type specifications to $\lambda^\forall$.

As we have seen, attempting to combine arbitrary data type specifications with unrestricted recursion leads to failure of conservative extension. However, the polymorphic type discipline is *strongly normalizing*, i.e., inherently "terminating"; therefore counterexamples in the spirit of the one we presented in Section 1 cannot be devised within it. And, indeed, the following initial technical result indicates that, in contrast to the situation with general recursion, it is *safe*, viz., conservative, to reason or compute polymorphically over a classical algebra.

In particular, as an illustrative model of data type specifications, we consider *many-sorted algebraic theories* [10, 12]. For α an (many-sorted) algebraic theory, let $\lambda^\forall\alpha$ be the extension of $\lambda^\forall$ in which the sorts of α are added as type constants, the function symbols of α are added as constants (of suitably curried type), and the equations specifying α are added to the axioms of $\lambda^\forall$.

Theorem 1

For any algebraic theory α, the extension $\lambda^\forall\alpha$ is conservative over α. That is, for any α-terms s and t,

$$\lambda^\forall\alpha \vdash s = t \Longleftrightarrow \alpha \vdash s = t\,.$$

3 ... *And Computing Power*

Theorem 1 tells us that we will not lose the ability to reason according to the data type specification, but it does not say anything about what can be *gained* when we enrich the algebraic setting to a polymorphic one. In fact, in $\lambda^{\forall}\alpha$ there is *no* gain in the computing power over the elements of α: any function of such elements that is definable in $\lambda^{\forall}\alpha$ has also a purely algebraic expression (an α-polynomial).

This is too bad, because we had chosen the polymorphic lambda calculus precisely for its computational power. This calculus is strongly normalizing and hence incapable of representing *all* computable functions. Nevertheless, it has an enormous built-in computational power, springing from its impredicative type discipline. The arithmetic functions that are numeralwise representable in the calculus (in the way addition was represented above) are exactly the partial recursive functions that are provably total in second-order Peano arithmetic [8, 9, 26]. No uncontrived example of a total recursive function that is not in this class is known. (In fact, until recently, no natural example of a total recursive function that was not provably so in *first*-order Peano arithmetic was known [20].) The limits on such computational power are hard to perceive, and one can argue that it is adequate for most purposes [14, 23]. [4]

However, there is a way to strengthen Theorem 1 that *does* guarantee a gain in computing with the algebraically specified data types. We will show that there exist languages that offer a "have your cake and eat it too" option—both conservative extension and tremendous computational power.

The gain can be explained in terms of computable functions over an arbitrary algebraic specification. Assume that among the objects specified there exists a set of *observables*—say character strings or lists or trees—and we care only about computational behavior on the observables. (Of course there may be many other unobservable objects that are definable in the programming language, but these are significant only because of their role as parts of programs which yield observable outputs.) Moreover, assume there is some standard way of enumerating the distinct observables. This is true for all the familiar data type examples. The enumeration of observables yields a correspondence with nonnegative integers and hence a correspondence between functions on observables and functions on integers.

Theorem 2

Let α be an algebraic theory. Let $c_0, c_1, c_2, \ldots$ be a sequence of distinct closed α-terms, called *observables*, of some sort *obs*, such that no two distinct observables are provably equal in α. Then, there is a uniform way of extending

4. Another strongly normalizing calculus, even more powerful than the polymorphic lambda calculus, is the calculus of constructions [6]. We believe that the conservative extension results of this paper can be carried over to it as well.

α to a larger theory, $\lambda^{\forall}\alpha IO$, such that

1. $\lambda^{\forall}\alpha IO$ is a conservative extension of α, and
2. every function on observables which is provably total recursive in second-order Peano arithmetic is representable by a closed $\lambda^{\forall}\alpha IO$-term.

Proof hint As suggested by the notation, we start with $\lambda^{\forall}\alpha$. The idea is to ensure that the computing power of $\lambda^{\forall}$ on its integer numerals connects properly with computability on user-specified observables.

The *IO* (for Input-Output) extension involves two typed function constants,

$$In \;:\; obs \rightarrow polyint\,,$$
$$Out \;:\; polyint \rightarrow obs\,,$$

and additional axioms,

$$In \circ Out \;=\; id_{polyint}\,,$$
$$Out\;\tilde{n} \;=\; c_n\,, \qquad n = 0, 1, \ldots .$$

The proof's method for achieving computational power on user defined observables is essentially via Gödel numbering and certainly does not suggest an attractive programming style. However, the case has been made elsewhere that programming in polymorphic style can be attractive [7, 6, 19, 23]. Theorem 2 thus provides an explanation for some of the theoretical benefits of adopting this style.[5]

4 *Starting from Higher-Order Specifications*

We take the opportunity here to announce further improvements to the results in Sections 2 and 3. The detailed development of these improvements will appear in a future paper.

Instead of algebraic specifications, we now consider higher-order specifications, specifically *simply typed lambda theories*. Such a theory consists of ground types out of which one builds simple (finite) types using the $\rightarrow$ operator, of a signature of constant symbols of arbitrary simple types and of axioms which are (*wlog* closed) equations between simply typed lambda terms built from the given signature. Algebraic theories are particular cases, but the "expressive power" of such higher-order specifications is much bigger.[6] We thus have Theorem 3.

5. There are others, e.g., guaranteed termination, and decidable type-checking and equivalence, cf. [16].
6. Actually, even unrestricted recursion (via higher-order fixed point operators) and the untyped lambda calculus (as in [25]) can be modeled as simply typed lambda theories! This may seem

Theorem 3
The addition of the polymorphic constructs to *any* simply typed lambda theory is conservative.

Theorem 2 and Theorem 3 both improve Theorem 1, but in different directions. Namely, Theorem 3 says that addition of polymorphism to a "large" system of higher functional types is safe, but it does not calibrate the gain of making the addition. On the other hand, Theorem 2 says that addition of polymorphism to a "small" system of first-order data types is not only safe but also guarantees substantial computational power over the small data type. One naturally asks whether both improvements can be achieved simultaneously.[7]

Conjecture
Let $\sigma\tau$ be a simply typed lambda theory. Let $c_0, c_1, c_2, \ldots$ be a sequence of distinct closed $\sigma\tau$-terms, called *observables*, of some ground type *obs*, such that no two distinct observables are provably equal in $\sigma\tau$. Then, there is a uniform way of extending $\sigma\tau$ to a larger theory, $\lambda^{\forall}\sigma\tau IO$, such that

1. $\lambda^{\forall}\sigma\tau IO$ is a conservative extension of $\sigma\tau$, and
2. every function on observables which is provably total recursive in second-order Peano arithmetic is representable by a closed $\lambda^{\forall}\sigma\tau IO$-term.

5 *About the Proofs*

By now, the reader has realized that we are more concerned with explaining the significance of our results than with spelling out all the technical details. We believe that the proofs are too long and too technical to develop adequately here; therefore we confine ourselves to providing some outlines, some comments, and a reference to a technical companion paper [2] which develops the model theory we have used.

Let us start from a conservative extension result that has a straightforward model-theoretic proof.

Proposition 1 [16]
For any algebraic theory α, the addition of α to the simply typed λ-calculus is a conservative extension of α.

puzzling in view of our counterexample in Section 1, but recall that conservative extension theorems ensure only that the extension does not get worse than the original theory, not that it gets better.

7. At the time when the first version of this paper was published in the proceedings of POPL'87, we thought we had a positive answer. We later realized this is not so. To the best of our knowledge, as of October 1989, this remains a conjecture.

That is to say, any algebra can serve as a base type for a classical frame of higher-order functions, i.e., where the type $A \rightarrow B$ is interpreted as *all* functions from A to B. The rules of the simply typed lambda calculus are certainly sound for this classical interpretation. (We say that any algebra can be *fully* and *faithfully* embedded in a model of the simply typed lambda calculus.) Since the original specified data type sits unchanged at the bottom of the type frame, no sound rules can prove anything that is not already true of it.

Unfortunately, models of the polymorphic lambda calculus are not as easy to come by as the above construction. This is why, initially, we looked for and found a reduction-theoretical approach to proving Proposition 1. This approach turned out to extend to Theorem 1 and actually yield an *effective* proof, i.e., one that indicates a procedure for transforming any proof of $s = t$ in $\lambda^{\forall}\alpha$ into a proof of $s = t$ in α. The argument hinges crucially on the strong normalization and the Church-Rosser properties of $\lambda^{\forall}$. The main lemma is as follows.

Lemma 1

Let M and N be $\lambda^{\forall}\alpha$-terms of a constant type corresponding to a sort of α. If M and N can be transformed into each other using an instance of some axiom of α, then the $\beta\eta$-normal forms of M and N can be transformed into each other by repeated application of the same axiom.

By taking all the terms that appear in the $\lambda^{\forall}\alpha$-proof of $s = t$ to $\beta\eta$-normal form we get, almost, the desired α-proof of $s = t$. Almost because, due to the possible presence of "noise"—free variables of nonconstant type—these terms are not necessarily α-terms. One needs the additional observation that by replacing the maximal subterms of constant type that have at head such "noise" variables with, say, some fixed variables of constant type, one gets α-terms that moreover give an α-proof of $s = t$.

An interesting byproduct of this method is the following result obtained by the first author.

Theorem 4

Let α be an algebraic *rewrite system*. If α has the Church-Rosser property then $\lambda^{\forall}\alpha$ has the Church-Rosser property too.

The proof uses a version of Lemma 1 in which "axiom" is replaced with "rewrite rule" followed by a more intricate combinatorial analysis of the resulting normalized terms. A detailed development will appear in a future paper.

We still don't know how to extend this method to obtain a purely syntactic proof of Theorem 2. Meanwhile, however, some new ideas for constructing more flexible models for $\lambda^{\forall}$ have been developed [5, 17]. Both constructions interpret types using partial equivalence relations. Using a generalization of the construction in [5], the first author and Thierry Coquand have obtained the following theorem.

Theorem 5 [2]
Any many-sorted algebra can be fully and faithfully embedded in a model of the polymorphic lambda calculus.

This leads directly to a model-theoretic proof of Theorem 1 paralleling the proof sketched for Proposition 1. Subsequently, the method was refined by the first author to yield Theorem 6.

Theorem 6 [2]
Let $\mathcal{A}$ be a many-sorted algebra. Let $c_0, c_1, c_2, \ldots$ be a sequence of distinct elements of some sort *obs* of $\mathcal{A}$, called *observables.* Then there exists a model $\mathcal{E}$ of the polymorphic lambda calculus such that

1. $\mathcal{A}$ is fully and faithfully embedded in $\mathcal{E}$, and
2. every function on observables which is provably total recursive in second-order Peano arithmetic is in $\mathcal{E}$.

Part 2 is obtained by establishing the same one-to-one correspondence between the observables and the polymorphic integers as in the proof hint for Theorem 2. Thus, Theorem 2 follows as a corollary of the proof of this model-theoretic version since the open term algebra of α can be fully and faithfully embedded into a model of $\lambda^{\forall}$ in which we also find a sound interpretation for the *IO* axioms. Call this model $\mathcal{E}$. As it turns out, $\mathcal{E}$ has empty types. Thus, Theorem 2 holds for any equational proof system whose axioms and rules are *sound* in models that can have empty types, in particular the standard, traditional, one (see for example [2] or [15]), or the new, complete for all models, one, introduced in [15].

In fact, $\mathcal{E}$ has a property that plays a crucial role in finding a sound interpretation for the *IO* axioms, namely, that its elements of type *polyint* are in one-to-one correspondence with the numerals. As indicated in [15], this property implies that $\mathcal{E}$ *must* have empty types. This argues against the possibility of a model theoretic proof of Theorem 2, as above, for the case of the proof system that is complete for all models with all types nonempty [4] (or see, for example, [2]).

Detailed proofs of all the results mentioned here also appear in [1].

Acknowledgments

We are grateful to John Mitchell and Eugenio Moggi for a very useful discussion. The research reported here was supported in part by the first author's IBM Graduate Fellowship, in part by NSF Grant DCR–8511190, and in part by ONR Grant N00014–83–K–0125.

References

[1] Breazu-Tannen, V. "Conservative extensions of type theories". PhD thesis, Massachusetts Institute of Technology, February 1987. Supervised by A. R. Meyer.

[2] Breazu-Tannen, V. and Coquand, T. "Extensional models for polymorphism". *Proceedings of TAPSOFT—Colloquium on Functional and Logic Programming and Specifications* (Pisa, March), pp. 291–307. Lecture Notes in Computer Science, vol. 250. Springer-Verlag, Berlin, 1987.

[3] Breazu-Tannen, V. and Meyer, A. "Polymorphism is conservative over simple types". *Proceedings of the Symposium on Logic in Computer Science*, pp. 7–17. IEEE, New York, 1987. Reprinted in revised form in this volume (Chapter 13).

[4] Bruce, K., Meyer, A., and Mitchell, J. "The semantics of second-order lambda calculus". *Information and Computation*, to appear. Included in this volume (Chapter 10).

[5] Coquand, T. Communication in the TYPES electronic forum,[8] April 14, 1986.

[6] Coquand, T. and Huet, G. "The calculus of constructions". *Information and Computation 76*, 2/3 (February/March 1988), pp. 95–120.

[7] Coquand, T. and Huet, G. "Constructions: A higher order proof system for mechanizing mathematics". Rapport de Recherche 401. INRIA, Domaine de Voluceau, 78150 Rocquencourt, France, May 1985. Presented at EUROCAL 85, Linz, Austria.

[8] Fortune, S., Leivant, D., and O'Donnell, M. "The expressiveness of simple and second-order type structures". *J. ACM 30*, 1 (January 1983), pp. 151–185.

[9] Girard, J.-Y. "Interprétation fonctionelle et élimination des coupures dans l'arithmétique d'ordre supérieure". PhD thesis, Université Paris VII, 1972.

[10] Goguen, J., Thatcher, J., and Wagner, E. "An initial algebra approach to the specification, correctness, and implementation of abstract data types". *Current Trends in Programming Methodology*, R.T. Yeh, ed. Prentice-Hall, 1978.

[11] Gordon, M., Milner, R., and Wadsworth, C. *Edinburgh LCF*. Lecture Notes in Computer Science, vol. 78. Springer-Verlag, Berlin, 1979.

8. **types@theory.lcs.mit.edu**

[12] Guttag, J., Horowitz, E., and Musser, D. "Abstract data types and software validation". *Communications of the ACM 21* (1978), pp. 1048–1064.

[13] Landin, P. "A correspondence between ALGOL 60 and Church's lambda notation". *Communications of the ACM 8* (1965), pp. 89–101 and 158–165.

[14] Leivant, D. "Reasoning about functional programs and complexity classes associated with type disciplines". *24th Symposium on Foundations of Computer Science*, pp. 460–469. IEEE, New York, 1983.

[15] Meyer, A., Mitchell, J., Moggi, E., and Statman, R. "Empty types in polymorphic λ-calculus". *Proceedings of the 14th Symposium on Principles of Programming Languages* (January), pp. 253–262. ACM, New York, 1987. Reprinted in revised form in this volume (Chapter 11).

[16] Meyer, A. and Reinhold, M. "'Type' is not a type: preliminary report". *Proceedings of the 13th Symposium on Principles of Programming Languages* (January), pp. 287–295. ACM, New York, 1986.

[17] Moggi, E. Communication in the TYPES electronic forum,[9] February 10, 1986.

[18] Moggi, E. Ph.D. thesis, University of Edinburgh, 1988.

[19] Mohring, C. "Algorithm development in the theory of constructions". *Symposium on Logic in Computer Science*, pp. 84–91. IEEE, New York, 1986.

[20] Paris, J. and Harrington, L. "A mathematical incompleteness in Peano arithmetic". *Handbook of Mathematical Logic*, J. Barwise, ed., pp. 1133–1142. North-Holland, Amsterdam, 1977.

[21] Paulson, L. "Deriving structural induction in LCF". *Semantics of Data Types*, G. Kahn, D. B. MacQueen, and G. Plotkin, eds., pp. 197–214. Springer-Verlag, Berlin, June 1984.

[22] Plotkin, G. "Denotational semantics with partial functions". Lecture at C. S. L. I. Summer School, 1985.

[23] Reynolds, J. "Three approaches to type structure". *Mathematical Foundations of Software Development*, pp. 97–138. Lecture Notes in Computer Science, vol. 185, Springer-Verlag, Berlin, 1985.

[24] Reynolds, J. "Towards a theory of type structure". *Programming Symposium*, B. Robinet, ed., pp. 408–425. Lecture Notes in Computer Science, vol. 19. Springer-Verlag, Berlin, 1974.

[25] Scott, D. "Relating theories of the lambda calculus". *To H. B. Curry: Essays on Combinatory Logic, Lambda Calculus and Formalism*, pp. 403–450. Academic Press, New York, 1980.

[26] Statman, R. "Number theoretic functions computable by polymorphic programs". *22nd Symposium on Foundations of Computer Science*, pp. 279–282. IEEE, New York, 1981.

9. **types@theory.lcs.mit.edu**

Polymorphism is Conservative over Simple Types

***Preliminary Report*[1]**

13

Val Breazu-Tannen[2]
Albert R. Meyer
MIT

Abstract

We prove that the addition of the Girard-Reynolds polymorphic constructs to arbitrary simply typed equational lambda theories is *conservative*. This implies that polymorphism can be superimposed on familiar programming languages without changing their behavior.

Using a purely syntactic method, we give an effective proof of conservative extension in the case of equational reasoning that is complete when all types are assumed nonempty. When polymorphic types may be empty, we prove the stronger result that any model of the simply typed lambda calculus can be *fully and faithfully embedded* in a model of the polymorphic lambda calculus.

1. This paper was presented at the 2nd IEEE Symposium on Logic in Computer Science, Cornell University, June 1987, and appeared in the symposium's proceedings.
2. Currently with the Department of Computer and Information Science, University of Pennsylvania.

1 *Introduction*

This paper is a sequel to a previous one [3] where the main result presented here was briefly announced. We will not, however, assume that the reader is familiar with [3]; we now recapitulate some of our motivation.

In programming languages of universal power, the *computational* data type domains must be distinguished from the *classical* data types because of the "divergent" element. This is illustrated in [3, 14] by a typical example in which one starts with a straightforward algebraic specification (for an integer data type with a conditional operator) and adds to it the ability to have recursive function declarations. Using the "copy rule" (on recursive calls) and the axioms of the specification, one can then prove equations between (algebraic) data type terms that the specification alone cannot prove.[3] Thus, the equational theory of the programming language with recursion is *not* a *conservative extension* of the data type specification.

In order to reason about the underlying data types in a semantics that accommodates recursion, we need a logic that takes nontermination into account. LCF [10] or the partial lambda calculus [19, 20] are such logics that take recursion as a must and try to reason about the resulting data domains. In both logics, however, when reasoning about expressions of data element type one needs to worry about *more* than the data type specification, namely, about whether certain subexpressions terminate or whether they are defined.

In [3], we took a different course: we aimed to preserve classical reasoning about the data by achieving the kind of conservative extension that fails above. Instead of recursion, we added to the data type the constructions made possible by procedural and polymorphic abstraction.

Following familiar tradition [12], we take lambda calculi with reduction rules as models of programming languages and their evaluation, and in particular the Girard-Reynolds polymorphic lambda calculus, denoted by $\lambda^{\forall}$, [8, 21], cf. [6] or [18] as a formal model of polymorphic programming.[4] Its syntax is reviewed in Section 2. First, we modeled data type specifications by algebraic theories [9]. Let $\alpha(\Sigma, E)$ be a many-sorted algebraic theory, where Σ is a many-sorted signature and E is a set of algebraic axioms. Let $\lambda^{\forall}(\Sigma, E)$ be the polymorphic lambda theory (an extension of $\lambda^{\forall}$) in which the sorts of Σ are added as type constants, the function symbols of Σ are added as constants (of suitably curried type), and the equations in E are added to the axioms of $\lambda^{\forall}$.

3. In fact, in the example in [3, 14] such reasoning is *inconsistent*; i.e., *any* equation is provable.
4. The version we consider here has *universal* types but it does not have *existential* types.

In [3], we proved that the addition of the polymorphic constructs to any algebraic data type specifications is conservative; i.e., $\lambda^{\forall}(\Sigma, E)$ is a *conservative extension* of $\alpha(\Sigma, E)$.

We now go further and enrich our model for specifications from many-sorted algebras to certain higher-order theories, specifically *simply (finitely) typed lambda theories.* We will denote the (pure) simply typed lambda calculus [1, 7] with $\lambda^{\rightarrow}$. A simply typed theory $\lambda^{\rightarrow}(\Sigma, E)$ consists of base (ground) types out of which one builds simple (finite) types using the $\rightarrow$ operator, of a signature Σ of constant symbols of arbitrary simple type out of which one builds simply typed lambda terms, and of a set E of arbitrary equational axioms between simply typed lambda terms which are added to the axioms of $\lambda^{\rightarrow}$. Let $\lambda^{\forall}(\Sigma, E)$ be the polymorphic lambda theory in which the base types, the constants in Σ, and the additional axioms in E are added to $\lambda^{\forall}$ ($\lambda^{\rightarrow}$ is already contained in $\lambda^{\forall}$). The main result of this paper is the following theorem.

Theorem 1
For any simply typed theory $\lambda^{\rightarrow}(\Sigma, E)$, the extension $\lambda^{\forall}(\Sigma, E)$ is conservative over $\lambda^{\rightarrow}(\Sigma, E)$. That is, for any $\lambda^{\rightarrow}(\Sigma)$-terms M and N,

$$E \vdash^{\lambda^{\forall}} M = N \quad \Longleftrightarrow \quad E \vdash^{\lambda^{\rightarrow}} M = N .$$

We remark that since adding $\lambda^{\rightarrow}$ to arbitrary algebraic theories is conservative [14], Theorem 1 implies the earlier result of [3].

In our view, what makes Theorem 1 considerably more interesting than the earlier result is the fact that more features, such as function and data type declarations, can be better and more naturally modeled by simply typed lambda theories than by algebraic theories. Indeed, while the pure simply typed lambda calculus does not get very far, the capability of having extra constants and extra equations to govern their behavior is quite powerful. For example, simply typed theories can be used to model full-fledged programming languages [24] by modeling unrestricted recursion via higher-order fixed point operators. Even arbitrary recursively defined types can be modeled, by axioms asserting isomorphism between types. For example, the untyped lambda calculus can be captured by declaring a type u together with constants $rep : (u \rightarrow u) \rightarrow u$ and $abs : u \rightarrow (u \rightarrow u)$ and axioms asserting that *rep* and *abs* are inverse to each other (cf. [10] or [22]).

Polymorphic type disciplines have recently enjoyed increased attention as the naturalness and usefulness of the types-as-values paradigm they embody have been recognized. As a result, the design of programming languages has witnessed the widespread adoption of polymorphic type systems. A number of examples and a survey of this field can be found in [5]. Theorem 1 shows that polymorphic constructs and reasoning can be added to any programming language features that can be described within the simple type discipline without changing the familiar behavior of these features. From this perspective, the adoption polymorphic type systems is *safe.*

There are two technical variants of the main theorem because there are two related proof systems for polymorphic lambda calculus which in general yield set-theoretically incomparable theories from the same axioms. The systems differ in the assumption of whether polymorphic types may be empty. The original polymorphic proof system is sound and complete for deriving semantic consequences over all models with all types nonempty [4]. But this system is *not sound* in models with empty types. After arguing that such models are of interest, [13] gives a new proof system that is sound and complete for deriving semantic consequences over *all* models.

The bulk of this paper (Section 3) focuses on establishing conservative extension for the older, proof system of [4] for nonempty types. Using purely syntactic methods, we give an *effective* proof of conservative extension; i.e., we describe a procedure that transforms any proof of $M = N$ from E in $\lambda^{\forall}$ into a proof of the same in $\lambda^{\rightarrow}$.

For the new proof system of [13] for empty types we give a quite different, *semantic*, proof of conservative extension (Section 4) by showing that any model of the simply typed lambda calculus can be *fully and faithfully embedded* in a model of the polymorphic lambda calculus. The desired models are constructed using a general method, the *extensional collapse*, developed in [2]. (Familiarity with [2] is desirable for understanding Section 4.)

In [3] we showed that adding the constructs of the Girard-Reynolds polymorphic lambda calculus to algebraic theories was not only safe but also that this could be done in a manner that guarantees substantial additional computing power on the original *algebraic* data types. It remains open whether conservative extension of *simply typed theories* by polymorphism *with transfer of computing power* is true. We examine this conjecture in Section 5.

2 *Basic Syntax*

Let K be a set of *(ground* or *base) type constants.* The *K-polymorphic type expressions* are defined by

$$\tau ::= k \mid t \mid \sigma \rightarrow \tau \mid \forall t.\, \sigma\,,$$

where k ranges over K and t ranges over an infinite set of *type variables.* The set of free type variables of σ will be denoted $fv(\sigma)$.

Let C be a set of *constants.* By definition, each constant $c \in C$ comes equipped with its type, $Type(c)$, which must be a *closed* K-type expression.

The (K, C)-*raw terms* are defined by

$$M ::= c \mid x \mid MN \mid \lambda x{:}\, \sigma.\, M \mid M\sigma \mid \lambda t.\, M\,,$$

where c ranges over C and x ranges over a separate infinite set of *variables*. The set of free variables of M will be denoted $FV(M)$ while the set of free *type* variables of M will be denoted $fv(M)$. We identify the expressions or terms that differ only in the names of bound variables.

A *type assignment*, Δ, is a partial function that maps variables to type expressions such that $dom\Delta$ is *finite*. We write $\Delta, x{:}\,\sigma$ for $\Delta \cup \{x{:}\,\sigma\}$ and, by convention, the use of this notation implies that $x \notin dom\Delta$. *Typing judgments* have the form

$$\Delta \vdash M : \sigma\,.$$

The rules for deriving typing judgments (the *type-checking* rules) are

$$\Delta \vdash c : Type(c)\,, \qquad c \in C\,, \qquad \textit{(constants)}$$

$$\Delta \vdash x : \Delta(x)\,, \qquad x \in dom\Delta\,, \qquad \textit{(projection)}$$

$$\frac{\Delta \vdash M : \sigma \to \tau \quad \Delta \vdash N : \sigma}{\Delta \vdash MN : \tau}\,, \qquad (\to \textit{elimination})$$

$$\frac{\Delta, x{:}\,\sigma \vdash M : \tau}{\Delta \vdash \lambda x{:}\,\sigma.\, M : \sigma \to \tau}\,, \qquad (\to \textit{introduction})$$

$$\frac{\Delta \vdash M : \forall t.\, \sigma}{\Delta \vdash M\tau : \sigma[t := \tau]}\,, \qquad (\forall \textit{ elimination})$$

$$\frac{\Delta \vdash M : \sigma}{\Delta \vdash \lambda t.\, M : \forall t.\, \sigma}\,, \quad t \notin fv(ran\Delta)\,. \qquad (\forall \textit{ introduction})$$

When $\Delta \vdash M : \sigma$ is derivable by these rules, we say that M *type-checks under* Δ *with type* σ. In this case, σ is *uniquely* determined by M and Δ. Moreover, only the restriction of Δ to the variables that occur (free) in M matters. By convention, the *empty* type assignment is omitted.

The *polymorphic integers* and *booleans* are

$$\tilde{n} \stackrel{\text{def}}{=} \lambda t.\, \lambda f{:}\, t \to t.\, \lambda x{:}\, t.\, f^n x$$

of type

$$polyint \stackrel{\text{def}}{=} \forall t.\, (t \to t) \to t \to t$$

and

$$True \stackrel{\text{def}}{=} \lambda t.\, \lambda x{:}\, t.\, \lambda y{:}\, t.\, x\,,$$

$$False \stackrel{\text{def}}{=} \lambda t.\, \lambda x{:}\, t.\, \lambda y{:}\, t.\, y\,,$$

of type

$$polybool \stackrel{\text{def}}{=} \forall t.\, t \to t \to t\,.$$

Equations have the form

$$\Delta\,;\, M = N\,,$$

and thus they are tagged with a type assignment whose role is to keep the equational reasoning type-correct. By convention, empty type assignments are again omitted.

As noted in Section 1, we are interested in two proof systems for deriving equations, which we will call $\neg\varnothing$ and *all*. We begin by presenting the rules that are common to the two systems. These rules form a proof system of independent technical interest, which we will call *core*.

The proof system *core* consists of

$$\frac{\Delta\,;\, M = N}{\Delta, x{:}\,\tau\,;\, M = N}\,,\quad x \notin dom\Delta\,, \qquad (extension)$$

reflexivity, symmetry, transitivity, congruence with respect to application,

$$\frac{\Delta, x{:}\,\sigma\,;\, M = N}{\Delta\,;\, \lambda x{:}\,\sigma.\, M = \lambda x{:}\,\sigma.\, N}\,, \qquad (\xi)$$

β, η, congruence with respect to polymorphic application, *type* ξ, *type* η, and

$$\Delta\,;\, (\lambda t.\, M)\tau = M[t := \tau]\,,\quad \text{where } \Delta \vdash M\,,\ t \notin fv(ran\Delta)\,. \qquad (type\ \beta)$$

The proof system $\neg\varnothing$ has the additional rule

$$\frac{\Delta, x{:}\,\sigma\,;\, M = N}{\Delta\,;\, M = N}\,,\quad \text{where } x \notin FV(M) \cup FV(N)\,. \qquad (discharging)$$

This presentation of $\neg\varnothing$ is equivalent to that in [4].

The proof system "*all*" uses a more complicated syntax [13]. The *extended* equations have the form

$$L\,;\, \Delta\,;\, M = N\,,$$

where L is a finite set of assertions of the form $empty(\tau)$. The proof rules are those of the *core* system, adapted to the extended equations (by ignoring L), plus

$$\frac{L\,;\, \Delta\,;\, M = N}{L'\,;\, \Delta\,;\, M = N}\,,\quad L \subseteq L'\,, \qquad (empty-extension)$$

$$empty(\sigma)\ ;\ x{:}\,\sigma\ ;\ True = False\,, \qquad (empty-trivial)$$

$$\frac{L, empty(\sigma)\ ;\ \Delta\ ;\ M = N \quad L\ ;\ \Delta, x{:}\,\sigma\ ;\ M = N}{L\ ;\ \Delta\ ;\ M = N}\,, \qquad (empty-discharging)$$

where $x \notin FV(M) \cup FV(N)$,

If E is a set of (extended) equations and e is an (extended) equation, we write $E \vdash_p^{\lambda^\forall} e$ when e is derivable in p using additional premises from E, where p is one of $\neg\varnothing$, *all*, or *core*. An (extended) equation

$$(L\ ;\ )\Delta\ ;\ M = N$$

is *type-correct* if M and N both type-check under Δ with the same type. It is easy to see that for each p, $\vdash_p^{\lambda^\forall}$ preserves type-correctness.

Models are like those in [4], and empty types are allowed. Note that (*discharging*) is not sound, in general, in models with empty types.

Since models are needed only in Section 4 we omit the definition here and refer the reader to [2]. Nonetheless, we recapitulate the basic completeness results.

Theorem 2 [4]
Let E, e be equations. $E \vdash_{\neg\varnothing}^{\lambda^\forall} e$ if and only if e is valid in all models of E that have all types nonempty.

Theorem 3 [13]
Let E, e be extended equations. $E \vdash_{all}^{\lambda^\forall} e$ if and only if e is valid in all models of E.

In contrast, the system *core* is *not* complete for deriving semantic consequences either over all models with all types nonempty (obvious) or over all models [13].

The *K-simple type expressions* (also known as simple types) are all closed:

$$\tau ::= k \mid \sigma \to \tau\,.$$

By definition, the constants have simple type. The (K, C)*-simple raw terms* are defined by

$$M ::= c \mid x \mid MN \mid \lambda x{:}\,\sigma.\, M\,.$$

From what we described for the polymorphic calculus, it is straightforward to define simple type-checking and simple equational reasoning (we use $\lambda^{\to}$ instead of $\lambda^{\forall}$) just by keeping those axioms and rules that deal only with the simply typed constructions *except* that the axiom (*empty-trivial*) is to be *replaced* with (*empty-trivial-simple*):

$$empty(\sigma)\ ;\ x\colon\sigma\ ;\ (\lambda y\colon\tau.\,\lambda z\colon\tau.\,y = \lambda y\colon\tau.\,\lambda z\colon\tau.\,z)\,.$$

Simply typed models are like those in [7] where the analog of Theorem 2 is shown. The analog of Theorem 3 also holds. The system *core*, while incomplete for simply typed models with or without empty types [13], is complete for deriving semantic consequences over simply typed Kripke-style models [17].

3 An Effective Proof

Theorem 4 (Conservative Extension)
If E, e are simple equations then

$$E \vdash^{\lambda^{\forall}}_{\neg\emptyset} e \iff E \vdash^{\lambda^{\to}}_{\neg\emptyset} e\,.$$

Moreover, any derivation of e from E in the polymorphic proof system can be effectively transformed into a derivation of the same in the simple proof system and conversely.

One direction is trivial because the simple proof system is contained in the polymorphic one. For the other direction, we need to review some facts about proofs.

Equational reasoning in $\neg\emptyset$ without additional premises can be analyzed with the *reduction* system that we denote by $\lambda^{\forall}$ and that consists of the union of the four *pure* notions of reduction: β, η, *type* β, and *type* η. $\lambda^{\forall}$-reduction preserves type-checking and is strongly normalizing and Church-Rosser on terms that type-check [8]. Our notation for reduction follows [1].

For proofs with additional premises in $\neg\emptyset$, we have an alternative characterization of the derivable equations by means of chains of "replacements of equals by equals". Without loss of generality, we will assume that any additional premise, e, is a *type-correct* equation of the form

$$;\ Left(e) = Right(e)$$

(thus $Left(e)$ and $Right(e)$ are *closed*).

We define on raw terms the relation of $\lambda^{\forall}$*-replacement* by $M \overset{\lambda^{\forall}}{\longleftrightarrow} N$ iff $M \overset{\lambda^{\forall}}{\longrightarrow} N$ or $N \overset{\lambda^{\forall}}{\longrightarrow} M$. For any additional premise e, we define, again on raw terms, e-*replacement* by $M \overset{e}{\longleftrightarrow} N$ if and only if there exists a term P and a variable z occurring *exactly once* in P such that $M \equiv P[z := Left(e)]$ and $N \equiv P[z := Right(e)]$ or the other way around.

Let E be a set of additional premises. A *proof by replacements from E* is a vector

$$(\Delta, P_0, r_1, P_1, \dots r_n, P_n)$$

such that $P_0, \dots, P_n$ type-check under Δ all with the same type, each r_j is either $\lambda^\forall$ or in E and, for $j = 1, \dots, n$,

$$P_{j-1} \overset{r_j}{\longleftrightarrow} P_j\,.$$

Instead of the tuple notation, we will use, for proofs by replacements, the following, more suggestive, notation:

$$\Delta\ ;\ P_0 \overset{r_1}{\longleftrightarrow} \cdots \overset{r_n}{\longleftrightarrow} P_n\,.$$

Proposition 1

$$E \vdash^{\lambda^\forall}_{\neg\emptyset} \Delta\ ;\ M = N$$

if and only if $\Delta\ ;\ M = N$ is type-correct and there exists a proof by replacements from E

$$\Delta'\ ;\ P_0 \leftrightarrow \cdots \leftrightarrow P_n$$

such that $P_0 \equiv M$, $P_n \equiv N$, and $\Delta \subseteq \Delta'$. Moreover, the proof by replacements can be *effectively* obtained from the derivation and conversely.

The proof consists of an induction on derivations and an induction on the length of proofs by replacements, both routine.

An analog alternative characterization of provability holds for $\lambda^{\to}$.

Proof of Theorem 4. In view of Proposition 1, we will work with proofs by replacements instead of derivations. Fix a polymorphic proof by replacements from E for $e \equiv \Delta\ ;\ M = N$,

$$\Delta'\ ;\ M \leftrightarrow \cdots \leftrightarrow N \quad (\Delta \subseteq \Delta')\,.$$

We will deal only with terms that type-check under Δ' or with their *subterms*. These subterms type-check under well-determined extensions of Δ' that add the type declarations of the bound variables in whose scope the subterm lies. To simplify notation, when we will talk about *the* type of these terms or subterms, we will mean their type under Δ' or the appropriate extension of Δ'.

The general strategy will be to "normalize" the terms of this proof hoping to get rid of the polymorphic constructions and steps. This is complicated by the fact that Δ' may declare additional free variables of nonsimple type which can then occur in the intermediate terms of the proof. (The normal form of a polymorphic term of simple type with free variables of simple type is a simple term, but this is not necessarily so if there are free variables of nonsimple type.) Hence the following definition.

A term Q is *quasi-simple* if it is of simple type, if it contains no *type* β-redexes, and if any β-redexes $(\lambda x{:}\sigma.\,X)Y$ that occur in Q are such that σ is simple and X is of simple type. The name is justified by the following lemma.

Lemma 1

Any quasi-simple term Q can be uniquely described as $Q \equiv C[Z_1, \ldots, Z_m]$ where $C[\ ,\ldots,\ ]$ is a simply typed *context* (see [1]) with m holes of simple type, each hole occurring exactly once, and each of $Z_1, \ldots, Z_m$ is of the form $z\,\alpha_1 \ldots \alpha_k$ where z is a variable that is free in Q and is of nonsimple type, $k \geq 1$, and α_k is either a type expression or, if it is a term, then it has nonsimple type.

The proof is by induction on the *length* of Q and is omitted here.

Clearly, simple terms are quasi-simple and any normal form of simple type is quasi-simple. It is not hard to see that the class of quasi-simple terms is closed under application, abstraction by a variable of simple type, substitution of quasi-simple terms, e-replacement ($e \in E$), and $\lambda^{\forall}$-reduction.

Lemma 2

Any polymorphic proof by replacements from E,

$$\Delta' ;\ X \leftrightarrow \cdots \leftrightarrow Y,$$

can be effectively transformed into a (still polymorphic) proof by replacements from E,

$$\Delta' ;\ U \leftrightarrow \cdots \leftrightarrow V,$$

such that $X \xrightarrow{\lambda^{\forall}} U$, $Y \xrightarrow{\lambda^{\forall}} V$, and all the terms in the second proof are *quasi-simple.*

Proof of Lemma 2. By induction on proofs by replacements.

Proofs of length 0. Take $U \stackrel{\text{def}}{=} V \stackrel{\text{def}}{=} nf(X)$ and notice that normalization is effective.

Proofs of length 1. Let $\Delta' ;\ X \stackrel{r}{\longleftrightarrow} Y$ be the proof. There are two cases:

1. $r = \lambda^{\forall}$. Take $U \stackrel{\text{def}}{=} nf(X) \equiv nf(Y) \stackrel{\text{def}}{=} V$.

2. $r = e \in E$. Then there exists a term P and a fresh variable z occurring *exactly once* in P such that $X \equiv P[z := Left(e)]$ and $Y \equiv P[z := Right(e)]$ (or the other way around). P can be effectively found from X, Y, and e (up to renaming z). Let $Q \stackrel{\text{def}}{=} nf(P)$. Take $U \stackrel{\text{def}}{=} Q[z := Left(e)]$ and $V \stackrel{\text{def}}{=} Q[z := Right(e)]$ (or the other way around). U and V are quasi-simple and one can transform U into V by as many successive e-replacements as there are occurrences of z in Q (maybe none). This gives the desired proof by replacements built of quasi-simple terms.

Concatenation of proofs. We will assume that the claim holds for Δ' ; $X \leftrightarrow \cdots \leftrightarrow Y$ and Δ' ; $Y \leftrightarrow \cdots \leftrightarrow Z$ and show that it holds for their concatenation Δ' ; $X \leftrightarrow \cdots \leftrightarrow Y \leftrightarrow \cdots \leftrightarrow Z$. Let Δ ; $U \leftrightarrow \cdots \leftrightarrow V$ and Δ ; $V' \leftrightarrow \cdots \leftrightarrow W$ be the corresponding proofs by quasi-simple terms. Since $V' \stackrel{\lambda^{\forall}}{\twoheadleftarrow} Y \stackrel{\lambda^{\forall}}{\twoheadrightarrow} V$, there exists, by the Church-Rosser property, a V'' such that $V \stackrel{\lambda^{\forall}}{\twoheadrightarrow} V'' \stackrel{\lambda^{\forall}}{\twoheadleftarrow} V'$. Once we know that such a V'' exists, we can effectively find one by, say, systematically trying all reduction paths (certain proofs of the Church-Rosser property probably yield better algorithms). Since V and V' are quasi-simple, all the terms that occur in the two reduction chains $V \stackrel{\lambda^{\forall}}{\twoheadrightarrow} V''$ and $V' \stackrel{\lambda^{\forall}}{\twoheadrightarrow} V''$ are also quasi-simple. The desired proof is then

$$\Delta \,;\, U \leftrightarrow \cdots \leftrightarrow V \stackrel{\lambda^{\forall}}{\longrightarrow} \cdots \stackrel{\lambda^{\forall}}{\longrightarrow} V'' \stackrel{\lambda^{\forall}}{\longleftarrow} \cdots \stackrel{\lambda^{\forall}}{\longleftarrow} V' \leftrightarrow \cdots \leftrightarrow W. \quad \square$$

Applying this lemma to the original proof Δ' ; $M \leftrightarrow \cdots \leftrightarrow N$, we can construct a proof by quasi-simple terms Δ' ; $U \leftrightarrow \cdots \leftrightarrow V$ such that $M \stackrel{\lambda^{\forall}}{\twoheadrightarrow} U$ and $N \stackrel{\lambda^{\forall}}{\twoheadrightarrow} V$. But M and N are simple, so all the terms that occur in the two reduction chains $M \stackrel{\lambda^{\forall}}{\twoheadrightarrow} U$ and $N \stackrel{\lambda^{\forall}}{\twoheadrightarrow} V$ are quasi-simple. We get a proof by replacements from E that contains only quasi-simple terms:

$$\Delta' \,;\, M \stackrel{\lambda^{\forall}}{\longrightarrow} \cdots \stackrel{\lambda^{\forall}}{\longrightarrow} U \leftrightarrow \cdots \leftrightarrow V \stackrel{\lambda^{\forall}}{\longleftarrow} \cdots \stackrel{\lambda^{\forall}}{\longleftarrow} N.$$

The point of all this is that quasi-simple terms can be "simplified". Let us fix, for each simple type σ, a *fresh* variable w_σ. If $Q \equiv C[Z_1, \ldots, Z_m]$ is a quasi-simple term, then we construct a *simple* term out of it: $s(Q) \stackrel{\text{def}}{=} C[w_{\sigma_1}, \ldots, w_{\sigma_m}]$. Let $s(\Delta')$ be obtained from Δ' by restriction to the variables to which Δ' gives simple type. Then, $s(Q)$ type-checks under

$$s(\Delta'), w_{\sigma_1}\!:\sigma_1, \ldots, w_{\sigma_m}\!:\sigma_m$$

with same type that Q has under Δ'.

Clearly, if Q is already simple then $s(Q) \equiv Q$. It is easy to see that $s(MN) \equiv s(M)s(N)$, $s(\lambda x\!:\sigma.\, M) \equiv \lambda x\!:\sigma.\, s(M)$, and $s(M[x := N]) \equiv s(M)[x := s(N)]$.

Lemma 3
Let P and Q be quasi-simple.

1. If $P \stackrel{e}{\longleftrightarrow} Q$ then $s(P) \stackrel{e}{\longleftrightarrow} s(Q)$ or $s(P) \equiv s(Q)$.

2. If $P \stackrel{\lambda^{\forall}}{\longleftrightarrow} Q$ then $s(P) \stackrel{\lambda^{\rightarrow}}{\longleftrightarrow} s(Q)$ or $s(P) \equiv s(Q)$.

Now, recall that we had obtained a proof,

$$\Delta' ;\, M \leftrightarrow \cdots \leftrightarrow N\,,$$

which contained only quasi-simple terms. By applying s to all the terms of this proof we get a *simple* proof by replacements from $\mathcal{E}$,

$$\Delta'' ;\, M \leftrightarrow \cdots \leftrightarrow N\,,$$

where Δ'' is obtained by adding to $s(\Delta')$ the type assumptions $w_\sigma : \sigma$ about the fresh variables that are introduced throughout the proof. □

4 *Full and Faithful Embedding*

Let $\mathcal{E}$ be a *polymorphic* model. There is a "canonical" way to extract a *simply typed* model, $s(\mathcal{E})$, out of $\mathcal{E}$ by selecting only the domains (of the meanings) of the simple types. Given a simply typed model $\mathcal{D}$ and a polymorphic model $\mathcal{E}$ we say that $\mathcal{D}$ is *fully and faithfully embedded* in $\mathcal{E}$ if $\mathcal{D}$ is isomorphic to $s(\mathcal{E})$. (Here, an *isomorphism* is a bijection that preserves types and meaning; hence, in particular, it will preserve also application and the interpretation of constants.) The crucial property of full and faithful embeddings is that for any simple extended equation e, $\mathcal{D} \models e$ iff $\mathcal{E} \models e$.

This section will be devoted to proving the following theorem.

Theorem 5
Any simply typed model can be fully and faithfully embedded in a polymorphic model.

This, together with the completeness result for $\vdash_{all}^{\lambda^{\rightarrow}} e$, immediately implies the following.

Corollary (Conservative Extension)
If E, e are simple extended equations, then

$$E \vdash_{all}^{\lambda^{\forall}} e \iff E \vdash_{all}^{\lambda^{\rightarrow}} e\,.$$

Proof of Theorem 5. Fix a set K of base types and a set C of constants of *simple* type. Let $\mathcal{D}$ be a (K, C)-simply typed model. For each element d of $\mathcal{D}$ we introduce a new constant q_d of the same type. Let $C' \stackrel{\text{def}}{=} C \cup \{q_d \mid d \in \mathcal{D}\}$. For each closed (K, C')-simply typed term M of type σ that is *not* a q_d, we introduce an equation,

$$M = q_{[\![M]\!]} \,.$$

We will denote by H the set formed by these equations.

The first step is to construct the closed type/closed term (K, C')-*polymorphic lambda interpretation* (p.l.i.) [2], I, associated with the theory determined by H. The type expressions are interpreted in the structure formed by the closed type expressions. The rest of the definition follows the usual "term model" technique; i.e., the domains consist of congruence classes of closed (K, C')-polymorphic terms modulo [5]

$$M \cong_\omega N \quad \text{iff} \quad H \vdash^{\lambda^\forall}_{core} M = N \,.$$

We claim that, as a (K, C')-interpretation, $\mathcal{D}$ is fully and faithfully embedded in I via the map that takes d to the congruence class of q_d. In particular, at simple types, functional application in I is *extensional* (because application in $\mathcal{D}$ is extensional).

Indeed, first note that for any closed (K, C')-polymorphic term M of simple type, $nf(M)$ is simple, and hence M is provably equal to $q_{[\![nf(M)]\!]}$.

Then, consider the reduction system $\lambda^\forall H$ consisting of the usual reductions of $\lambda^\forall$ plus the notion of reduction H defined as the union of all the equations in H oriented from left to right.

Lemma 4

$\lambda^\forall H$ is Church-Rosser on terms that type-check.

The proof uses the Hindley-Rosen lemma [1].

Since H-reduction also preserves type-checking, provability in $\lambda^\forall$ from H can be characterized by $\lambda^\forall H$-reduction. Thus, if

$$H \vdash^{\lambda^\forall}_{core} q_d = q_{d'} \,,$$

then $d \equiv d'$ since q_d and $q_d\,'$ are both $\lambda^\forall H$-normal forms.

While it is true that $\mathcal{D}$ is fully and faithfully embedded in I, I is not extensional and hence is not a model. We will therefore continue with what is called in [2] an *extensional collapse* and show that the full and faithful embedding "survives" it.

5. We chose *core* for simplicity, but, using Lemma 4 and Theorems 2 and 3, it can be shown that it does not matter which of the three proof systems we use.

There are two ideas to the extensional collapse construction. The first idea is that if we have a second-order logical relation [16] on a p.l.i. which is the identity on types and which is a partial equivalence relation (p.e.r.) on the domain of each type, then the *quotient* p.l.i. whose elements are the p.e.r. classes is actually extensional and thus is a *model.* The second idea is how to construct such a logical p.e.r. on any given p.l.i.; we will illustrate it with our I.

We construct from I a new p.l.i., I^{per}, which has as types the set of pairs $<\omega, R>$, where ω is a type of I and R is a p.e.r. on the domain of ω. The rest of I^{per} is defined from I by "taking the first projection". To make I^{per} into a (K, C')-p.l.i., we need an interpretation for the base types, and we will assign to each base type k the p.e.r. that is the *identity* on the domain of k. Now, we have a collection $\mathcal{R}^{per}$ of p.e.r.'s, one at each type, namely R at type $<\omega, R>$ which is a logical p.e.r. on I^{per}. The extensional collapse of I is the quotient $\mathcal{E} \stackrel{\text{def}}{=} I^{per}/\mathcal{R}^{per}$.

Lemma 5

$R^{per}_{[\![\sigma]\!]}$ is the identity for *any* simple type σ.

This follows by induction on simple types from the fact that functional application in I is extensional at simple types.

One consequence of the lemma is that $\mathcal{R}^{per}$ relates the constants in C' since they are all of simple type. Thus, $\mathcal{E}$ is a (K, C')-model. Another consequence is that the extensional collapse leaves the domains of (the meanings of) simple types unchanged, which was exactly the part of I onto which $\mathcal{D}$ was fully and faithfully embedded. Thus, $\mathcal{D}$ is fully and faithfully embedded in $\mathcal{E}$. The desired (K, C)-model is obtained by "forgetting" about the interpretation of the q_d's.

Our full and faithful embedding construction always produces polymorphic models that have some empty types, even if the embedded simple model had all types nonempty [2]. Thus, we cannot use Theorem 5 to prove our other conservative extension formulation, Theorem 4.

John Mitchell and Eugenio Moggi have discovered how to do full and faithful embeddings of many-sorted *algebras* with all sorts nonempty into polymorphic models that have all types nonempty [15]. [6] One direction for further investigation is to see if their idea could be used to embed simply typed models, thus providing a semantic proof for Theorem 4 also.

6. Full and faithful embeddings of algebras into polymorphic models with empty types had already been obtained, see [2].

5 *Transferring Computing Power*

As we said in Section 1, we argue in favor of eliminating all potentially divergent constructs such as unrestricted recursion. Clearly, this restriction commits us to programming in a language of less than universal power.

Nevertheless, it is known that an enormous class of total computable functions is programmable in the polymorphic lambda calculus, and the loss of universal power may not be noticeable. This calculus is strongly normalizing and hence incapable of representing *all* computable functions. However, if we use the polymorphic integers as numerals, $\lambda^{\forall}$ can represent all the recursive functions that are provably total in second-order Peano arithmetic [8]; see also [6, 23].

Unfortunately, the setting of Theorem 1 and that of its analog for algebraic theories [3] do not take advantage of this built-in computational power: the addition of just the polymorphic constructions does not cause any gain at all in the computing power over the specified data types. Indeed, all closed polymorphic terms of simple type can be "normalized" to simply typed terms.

As we have shown in [3], for the case of algebraic theories, there is a way to strengthen the results that *does* guarantee a gain in computing with the algebraically specified data types. The corresponding result for simply typed theories remains open; we proceed to state it precisely.

The gain in computing power that we hope to achieve can be explained in terms of computable functions over an arbitrary simply typed specification. Assume that among the objects (of some ground type) specified there exists a set of *observables*—say character strings, lists, or trees—and we care only about computational behavior on the observables. Moreover, assume there is some standard way of enumerating the distinct observables. This is true for all the familiar data type examples. The enumeration of observables yields a correspondence with nonnegative integers and hence a correspondence between functions on observables and functions on integers.

Conjecture 1

Let $\lambda^{\rightarrow}(\Sigma, E)$ be a simply typed lambda theory. Let $c_0, c_1, c_2, \ldots$ be a sequence of distinct closed $\lambda^{\rightarrow}(\Sigma)$-terms, called *observables*, of some base type *obs*, such that no two distinct observables are provably equal in $\lambda^{\rightarrow}(\Sigma, E)$. Then there is a uniform way of extending $\lambda^{\rightarrow}(\Sigma, E)$ to a larger theory, $\lambda^{\forall}IO(\Sigma, E)$, which is also an extension of $\lambda^{\forall}(\Sigma, E)$ such that

1. $\lambda^{\forall}IO(\Sigma, E)$ is a conservative extension of $\lambda^{\rightarrow}(\Sigma, E)$, and
2. every computable function on observables which is provably total in second-order Peano arithmetic is representable by a closed $\lambda^{\forall}IO(\Sigma)$-term.

What we have in mind for for the *IO* (for input–output) extension are two typed function constants, $In : obs \rightarrow polyint$ and $Out : polyint \rightarrow obs$ and the axiom schemes $In\, c_n = \tilde{n}$ and $Out\, \tilde{n} = c_n$.

The corresponding result for algebraic theories [3] is proved via semantic methods (full and faithful embedding) developed in [2]. Specifically, it is shown there that any algebra with distinct observables can be fully and faithfully embedded into a model of the polymorphic lambda calculus in which we also find a sound interpretation for the *IO* part.

However, such an embedding is *not possible* for simply typed models. Indeed, if the *IO* part is sound then the model will contain, say at type $obs \rightarrow obs$, all the computable functions that are provably total in second-order Peano arithmetic. These functions may not be in the simply typed model to be embedded. Hence, the embedding cannot be *full*.

Nevertheless, there is an easy way to prove the conjecture for a large class of simply typed theories. This is the case when the additional axioms E can be made into rewrite rules which, together with the $\lambda^{\forall}$-reduction rules and the *IO* axioms (oriented from left to right), form a *Church-Rosser reduction system*. For example, this is true when the rules E are *delta rules* [1, 11], since this is already the case for the *IO* axioms. Note that the rules must preserve type-checking, and therefore the reduction system characterizes provability in $\lambda^{\forall}IO(\Sigma, E)$. That is, a type-correct equation is provable iff its two terms reduce to some common reduct. Now, if these terms are simply typed then they contain neither polymorphic constructs nor *In* and *Out*, and thus the two reduction chains provide a simply typed proof.

While the Church-Rosser assumption gives such an easy proof, it also excessively undercuts the generality of the result. As seen in Section 3, a considerably more complicated argument, which also makes use of normalization, proves conservative extension for arbitrary additional axioms E but, of course, without the *IO* part. Thus, the obvious direction for further investigation is to try to extend the methods of Section 3 toward a proof of Conjecture 1.

Acknowledgments

The work reported here was supported in part by NSF Grant DCR–8511190 and in part by ONR Grant N00014–83–K–0125. The first author was also partially supported by an IBM Graduate Fellowship.

References

[1] Barendregt, H. *The Lambda Calculus: Its Syntax and Semantics*. Studies in Logic

and the Foundations of Mathematics, vol. 103. North-Holland, Amsterdam, second edition, 1984.

[2] Breazu-Tannen, V. and Coquand, T. "Extensional models for polymorphism". *Proceedings of TAPSOFT—Colloquium on Functional and Logic Programming and Specifications* (Pisa, March), pp. 291–307. Lecture Notes in Computer Science, vol. 250. Springer-Verlag, Berlin, 1987.

[3] Breazu-Tannen, V. and Meyer, A. "Computable values can be classical". *Proceedings of the 14th Symposium on Principles of Programming Languages* (January), pp. 238–245. ACM, New York, 1987. Reprinted, in revised form, in this volume (Chapter 12).

[4] Bruce, K., Meyer, A., and Mitchell, J. "The semantics of second order lambda calculus". *Information and Computation*, to appear. Included in this volume (Chapter 10).

[5] Cardelli, L. and Wegner, P. "On understanding types, data abstraction and polymorphism". *Computing Surveys 17*, 4 (1985), pp. 471–522.

[6] Fortune, S., Leivant, D., and O'Donnell, M. "The expressiveness of simple and second-order type structures". *J. ACM 30*, 1 (January 1983), pp. 151–185.

[7] Friedman, H. "Equality between functionals". *Proceedings of the Logic Colloqium '73*, R. Parikh, ed., pp. 22–37. Lecture Notes in Mathematics, vol. 453, Springer-Verlag, Berlin, 1975.

[8] Girard, J.-Y. "Interprétation fonctionelle et élimination des coupures dans l'arithmétique d'ordre supérieure". PhD thesis, Université Paris VII, 1972.

[9] Goguen, J., Thatcher, J., and Wagner, E. "An initial algebra approach to the specification, correctness, and implementation of abstract data types". In *Current Trends in Programming Methodology*, R.T. Yeh, ed. Prentice-Hall, 1978.

[10] Gordon, M., Milner, R., and Wadsworth, C. *Edinburgh LCF*. Lecture Notes in Computer Science, vol. 78. Springer-Verlag, Berlin, 1979.

[11] Klop, J. *Combinatory reduction systems*. Tract 129, Mathematical Center, Amsterdam, 1980.

[12] Landin, P. "A correspondence between ALGOL 60 and Church's lambda notation". *Communications of the ACM 8* (1965), pp. 89–101 and 158–165.

[13] Meyer, A., Mitchell, J., Moggi, E., and Statman, R. "Empty types in polymorphic lambda calculus". *Proceedings of the 14th Symposium on Principles of Programming Languages* (January), pp. 253–262. ACM, New York, 1987. Reprinted, in revised form, in this volume (Chapter 11).

[14] Meyer, A. and Reinhold, M. "'Type' is not a type: Preliminary report". *Proceedings of the 13th Symposium on Principles of Programming Languages* (January), pp. 287–295. ACM, New York, 1986.

[15] Mitchell, J. Personal communication, August 1986.

[16] Mitchell, J. and Meyer, A. "Second-order logical relations (extended abstract)". *Proceedings of the Conference on Logics of Programs* (Brooklyn, June), R. Parikh, ed., pp. 225–236. Lecture Notes in Computer Science, vol. 193. Springer-Verlag, Berlin, 1985.

[17] Mitchell, J. and Moggi, E. "Kripke-style models for typed lambda calculus". *Proceedings of the Symposium on Logic in Computer Science* (June), pp. 303–314. IEEE, New York, 1987.

[18] Mitchell, J. "Lambda Calculus Models of Typed Programming Languages". Ph.D thesis, Massachusetts Institute of Technology, Cambridge, Mass., August 1984.

[19] Moggi, E. Ph.D. thesis, University of Edinburgh, 1988.

[20] Plotkin, G. "Denotational semantics with partial functions". Lecture at C. S. L. I. Summer School, 1985.

[21] Reynolds, J. "Towards a theory of type structure". *Programming Symposium*, B. Robinet, ed., pp. 408–425. Lecture Notes in Computer Science, vol. 19. Springer-Verlag, Berlin, 1974.

[22] Scott, D. "Relating theories of the lambda calculus". *To H.B. Curry: Essays on Combinatory Logic, Lambda Calculus and Formalism*, pp. 403–450. Academic Press, New York, 1980.

[23] Statman, R. "Number theoretic functions computable by polymorphic programs". *22nd Symposium on Foundations of Computer Science*, pp. 279–282. IEEE, New York, 1981.

[24] Trakhtenbrot, B., Halpern, J., and Meyer, A. "From denotational to operational and axiomatic semantics for ALGOL-like languages: an overview". *Logic of Programs, Proceedings 1983*, pp. 474–500. Springer-Verlag, Berlin, 1984.

Functorial Polymorphism

Preliminary Report

14

E. S. Bainbridge
University of Ottawa

P. J. Freyd
University of Pennsylvania

A. Scedrov
University of Pennsylvania

P. J. Scott
University of Ottawa

Abstract

We introduce a functorial calculus for types and terms in polymorphic languages that accounts for natural uniformity conditions related to parametricity. In particular, this framework leaves intact the basic feature of the function-type constructor $A \Rightarrow B$, i.e., contravariance in A and covariance in B. This calculus also emphasizes structural aspects of type abstraction required by parametricity, namely, those related to the uniformity of type instantiations under term substitutions.

Introduction

The concept of polymorphism in typed programming languages was first introduced by Strachey. Various notions of polymorphism were delineated, e.g., in [20], the most influential among them being the notion of *parametric* polymorphism. Intuitively, a parametric polymorphic function is one that has a uniformly given algorithm for all types.

A formal language designed to capture parametric polymorphism was proposed by Reynolds in [15] and previously by Girard in [5] as an extension of Curry's propositions-as-types paradigm in logic. This language, second-order lambda calculus, reflects the capability of specifying parametrized abstract data types now available in Ada, CLU, ML-like languages, and in many other typed languages.

A semantic criterion necessary for parametricity was proposed by Reynolds in [16, Section 8], as a kind of invariance under relations between type values. Reynolds's criterion may be illustrated on the example of "polymorphic numerals", i.e., entities of the type $\forall p\ ((p \Rightarrow p) \Rightarrow (p \Rightarrow p))$. A *parametric* function t of this type should be invariant *at least* under isomorphisms between values of type parameter p; i.e., given type values A and B and an isomorphism $\xi\colon B \longrightarrow A$, t should send related maps to related maps. More precisely, denoting composition by " ; " (in order of execution), the instances $t_A\colon (A \Rightarrow A) \Rightarrow (A \Rightarrow A)$ and $t_B\colon (B \Rightarrow B) \Rightarrow (B \Rightarrow B)$ should satisfy the following condition: given $f\colon A \longrightarrow A$ and $g\colon B \longrightarrow B$ such that $\xi;f = g;\xi$, it must be the case that $\xi;\ t_A(f) = t_B(g);\ \xi$. (This example is further discussed at the end of Section 1.)

This strongly suggests that in order to capture parametricity semantically, the value of a type abstraction should not be an entire product, but only that part consisting of parametric polymorphic functions. In the language of category theory, this says that type abstraction should not be considered *a priori* as a product, but rather as a limit over a diagram that is not discrete.

Issues related to the above problems of parametricity also arise in the mathematical areas of tensor algebra and algebraic topology. A functorial calculus was developed by Yoneda, Eilenberg, Kelly, Dubuc, and Street in the late 1960's to deal partially with these issues [11, pp. 214–228]. It is a remarkable fact that this functorial calculus and its stronger formulations are actually satisfied in an extensive class of models of the Girard-Reynolds lambda calculus. Indeed, we show below that HEO-like models (see, e.g., [1]) naturally have rich closure properties needed for the strong versions of the functorial calculus.

Reynolds's criterion for parametricity was further studied by Mitchell and Meyer in [12] and in [13], but in terms of second-order logical relations based on the notion of environment model proposed in [2]. In particular, Mitchell and Meyer show that in the term model, all elements are invariant under logical relations.

In comparison, we give an intrinsic treatment not so tied to syntax and second-order definability. On the one hand, we deal with aspects of parametricity for arbitrary functorial type constructors, so the type discipline is richer than that of second-order lambda calculus. On the other hand, the natural uniformity conditions we consider (including invariance under isomorphisms illustrated above) are less restrictive than a full extension of Reynolds's criterion to our type discipline (see the remarks at the end of Section 2).

The full paper based on this report will appear in *Theoretical Computer Science.*

1 *A Functorial Calculus of Types*

The main feature of our approach is already inherent in the simple typed lambda calculus. For example, consider term application. Because the type constructor $\Rightarrow$ is contravariant in its first argument and covariant in its second, term application naturally satisfies the following uniformity condition (almost always overlooked in standard treatments).

Let $a : A$ denote that term a is of type A. We write $[x := a]f$ for the substitution of a for variable x in f. Application of p to q will be written as $(q)p$. If $u : A \Rightarrow A'$, $v : A' \Rightarrow B$, and $x : A$ is not free in u or in v, then let $(u; v)$ denote the "composition term" $\lambda x{:}\, A.\ ((x)u)v$.

The term application has the uniformity property that for a fixed type B and arbitrary types A, A', if $f{:}\, A'$ and the free variables of f are at most $x : A$, then

$$(a)(\lambda x{:}\, A.\, f\,;\ v) \ = \ ([x := a]f)v. \qquad (*)$$

We think of this family of equations (parametrized by f) as a uniformity condition on the A-indexed family of application terms $(q)p$, where $q : A$ and $p : A \Rightarrow B$ (B is arbitrary but fixed).

In the category of *SETS* (indeed in any cartesian closed category [9]) the condition (*) says that for each fixed B, the A-indexed family of evaluation maps $ev_A : (A \Rightarrow B) \times A \longrightarrow B$ has the property that for each map $f{:}\, A \longrightarrow A'$ the following diagram commutes:

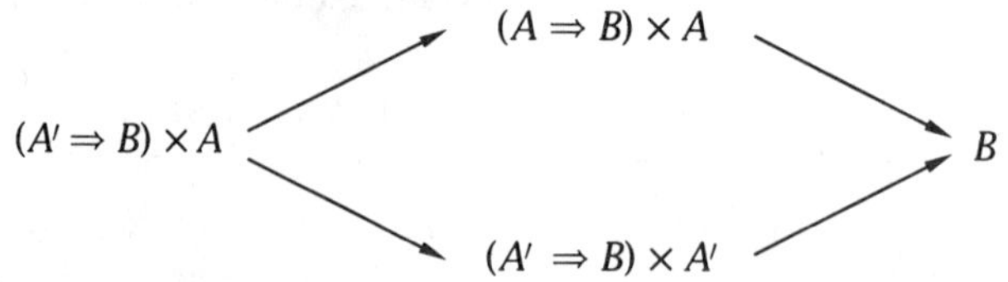

(Henceforth all diagrams commute unless specified otherwise.)

For another example in the same vein, consider the Church numerals: For each fixed natural number n consider the A-indexed family of maps n_A : $A{\Rightarrow}A \longrightarrow A{\Rightarrow}A$ each given by sending g to the nth iterate g^n. The following uniformity condition holds for every $f\colon A \longrightarrow A'$:

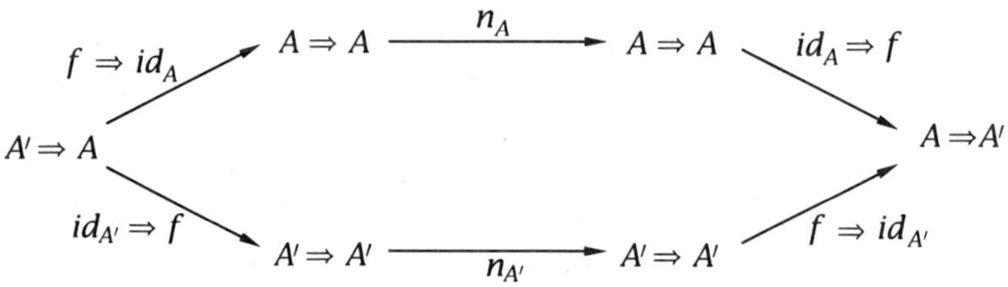

i.e., $(f;\, g)^n;\, f = f;\, (g;\, f)^n$ (an instance of associativity of composition).

In general, let $\mathbf{C}$ be a cartesian closed category (= *ccc*). Let w be a finite word in the alphabet $\{+,-\}$. We will consider functors from $\mathbf{C}^w$ to $\mathbf{C}$ for any w, where $+$ indicates a covariant argument and $-$ a contravariant argument ("multivariate endofunctors"). We may make our presentation follow the discussion by Mac Lane in [11, p. 214], by disguising these functors as $-+$ary functors from a power of $\mathbf{C}$ to $\mathbf{C}$ by using dummy arguments if necessary. So, without loss of generality, we may assume that all multivariate endofunctors are $-+$ary. We shall say that a word w in the alphabet $\{+,-\}$ is balanced if it has the same number of each sign.

Given two $-+$ary functors F, G, a diagonally natural (= *dinatural*) transformation from F to G is a family θ of morphisms in $\mathbf{C}$ indexed by the objects of $\mathbf{C}$, $\theta_A\colon FAA \longrightarrow GAA$, satisfying the following condition: for any arrow $f\colon A \longrightarrow A'$,

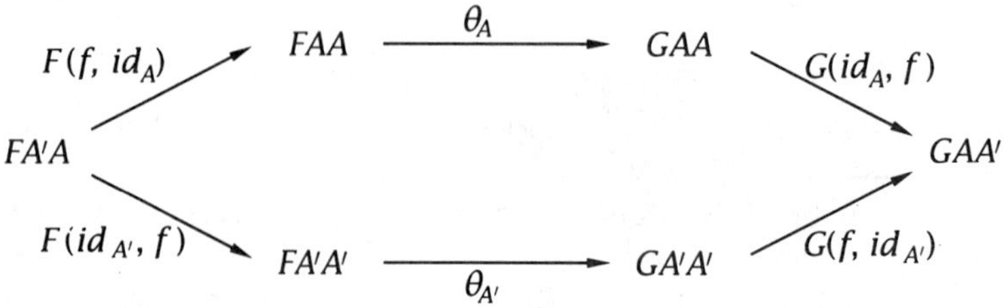

We use Mac Lane's notation $\theta\colon F \overset{..}{\longrightarrow} G$ for a dinatural transformation θ from F to G.

The crucial obstacle to having a *calculus* of multivariate functors and dinatural transformations is the lack of a well-defined notion of composition of dinatural transformations. In particular, if one attempts to compose two dinatural transformations $\theta\colon F \overset{..}{\longrightarrow} G$ and $\xi\colon G \overset{..}{\longrightarrow} H$, one encounters the following difficulty for each $f\colon A \longrightarrow A'$. While both given hexagons commute, there is no reason why the merged hexagon should commute (even though the middle diamond does in fact commute):

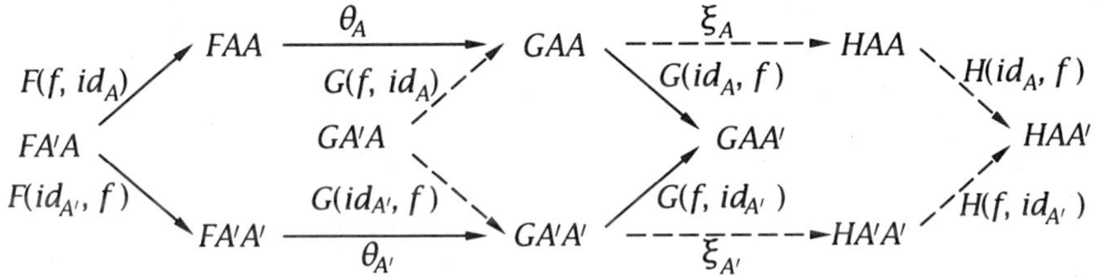

This obstacle will be resolved below for HEO-like models [1] for the endofunctors and dinatural transformations intrinsic to those models, including at least the endofunctors and dinatural transformations definable in second-order lambda calculus. So for the moment let us assume we may compose dinatural transformations by horizontal merging to form a category.

Even in this generality, there are some functor "constructors" worth mentioning: projections, products, tensor products, and two notions of exponentiation. Given two w ary functors F and G, where, say, w is $-+$, define their product to be the w ary functor $F \times G$, where $(F \times G)(C, D) = F(C, D) \times G(C, D)$, and their exponential $F \Longrightarrow G$, where $(F \Longrightarrow G)(C, D) = F(D, C) \Rightarrow G(C, D)$. Here $\Rightarrow$ is the exponential in the *ccc* $\mathbf{C}$. Also note the twist in the exponent. For each fixed balanced w, this yields a *ccc*. In addition, if F is w ary and G is w' ary, define their tensor product $F \otimes G$ to be the ww' ary functor where $(F \otimes G)(C, D, C', D') = F(C, D) \times G(C', D')$ and define the $(-w)w'$ ary functor $F \Longrightarrow\!\!\!> G$ by $(F \Longrightarrow\!\!\!> G)(C, D, C', D') = F(D, C) \Rightarrow G(C', D')$. (Here $(-w)$ is the word obtained from w by switching signs and keeping the same order.) (We note for the specialists in category theory that the operations $\otimes$ and $\Longrightarrow\!\!\!>$ define a monoidal closed structure on the multivariate endofunctors and suitably generalized dinatural transformations.) The operations of product and tensor product resemble the connectives & and $\otimes$ in linear logic discussed in [7].

For the purposes of discussing polymorphism, we shall also need to assume that *ccc* $\mathbf{C}$ has certain categorical limits called "ends" by Mac Lane in [11, pp. 218–224]. Let A be an object of $\mathbf{C}$. The constant functor $K_A\colon \mathbf{C}^{-+} \longrightarrow \mathbf{C}$ is given on objects by $K_A(C) = A$ and on morphisms by $K_A(f) = id_A$. Let F be a $-+$ary endofunctor on $\mathbf{C}$. An *end* of F is a dinatural transformation $\omega\colon K_B \overset{..}{\longrightarrow} F$

such that any dinatural transformation $\theta\colon K_C \xrightarrow{\cdot\cdot} F$ factors uniquely as:

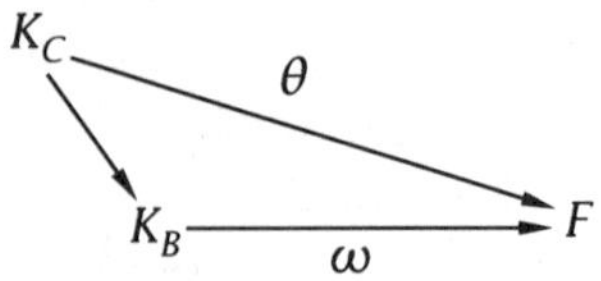

(By abuse of language, we sometimes call the object B the "end", written $\int_A FAA$.)

Returning to the example of polymorphic Church numerals discussed in the introduction, we may describe the type $\forall p((p \Rightarrow p) \Rightarrow (p \Rightarrow p))$ as an end. Consider the $-+$ary functor $F(A,B) = A \Rightarrow B$. Then the type of the polymorphic numerals is the end $N = \int_A (F \Longrightarrow F)(A,A)$. This means in particular there is a distinguished dinatural transformation $\omega\colon K_N \xrightarrow{\cdot\cdot} (F \Longrightarrow F)$, with components $\omega_A\colon N \longrightarrow ((A \Rightarrow A) \Rightarrow (A \Rightarrow A))$, where if $t\colon N$, ω_A applied to t corresponds to t_A in the example of polymorphic numerals in the introduction. This satisfies: for any $f\colon B \longrightarrow A$,

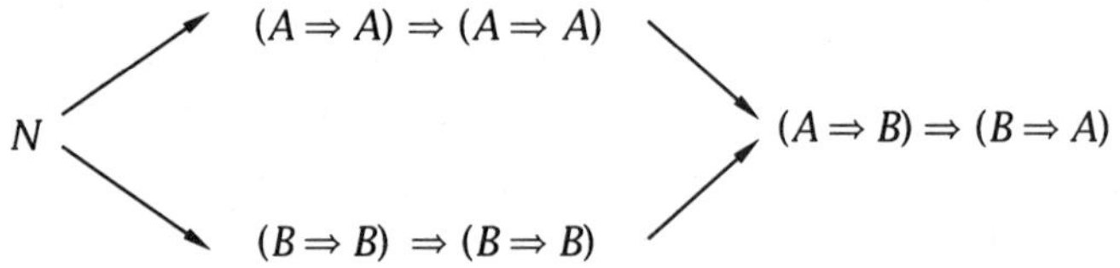

where the right-hand arrows are induced by functoriality. For example, the upper arrow sends t_A to $\lambda g\colon (A \Rightarrow B).\ (f;\ (g;\ f)t_A)$. In particular f may be an isomorphism ξ as discussed in the introduction. Observe, however, that ω must also satisfy the universal property given in the definition of ends.

2 *Realizable Endofunctors on Partial Equivalence Relations*

A partial equivalence relation on a set is a symmetric transitive relation on that set. Let PER be the category whose objects are partial equivalence relations (in short, *pers*) on natural numbers and whose morphisms $E \longrightarrow E'$ are named by partial recursive functions f such that for any n, m:

$$\text{if } n\,E\,m, \text{ then } f(n) \text{and } f(m) \text{ are defined and } f(n)\,E'\,f(m).$$

Two morphisms named by $f, f'\colon E \longrightarrow E'$ will be considered equal if and only if for the restrictions of f and f' to the field of E, if $n\,E\,m$ then $f(n)\,E'\,f'(m)$.

PER is a *ccc*. (A partial equivalence relation whose field is a one-element set is a terminal object in PER. A product $E \times E'$ may be described by means of a binary recursive pairing function $(\ ,\ )$: $(n,m)\,E \times E'(i,j)$ if and only if $n\,E\,i$

and $m\ E'\ j$. Finally, let $n\ E \Rightarrow E'\ m$ if and only if n and m are Gödel numbers of morphisms from E to E' and for all i, j, if $i\ E\ j$ then $\{n\}(i)\ E'\ \{m\}(j)$.)

We consider dinatural transformations between multivariate endofunctors on PER. We now begin a proof of a startling fact that in this case there exist many dinatural transformations that do compose (see Theorem 1). Our argument will apply to any (partial) combinatory algebra, not only to the case of partial recursive functions.

Let I be the subcategory of PER with the same objects, but whose morphisms are only those named by the identity function on the natural numbers. They are ordinary inclusions of *pers* as sets. They are *not* monomorphisms in PER.

Proposition 1

Every morphism in PER may be decomposed into an isomorphism followed by an I-map followed by an isomorphism.

Proof Let $f\colon E \longrightarrow E'$ be a morphism of *pers*. Let D be the *per*: $(n,k)\ D\ (n',k')$ if and only if $n\ E\ n'$, $f(n)\ E'\ k$, and $f(n')\ E'\ k'$. Let D' be the *per*: $(n,k)\ D'\ (n',k')$ if and only if $k\ E'\ k'$. Note that f factors into an isomorphism between E and D, the inclusion of D in D', and an isomorphism between D' and E'. □

A *realizable* functor $F\colon$ PER $\longrightarrow$ PER is one which takes I-maps to I-maps and for which there exists a mapping Φ from the set of partial recursive functions to itself such that for any morphism of *pers* $f\colon E \longrightarrow E'$, $F(f)$ is named by $\Phi(f)$. (A reader familiar with the realizability universe, i.e., the effective topos [3, 4, 8, 10], may check that among the realizable endofunctors on PER are those endofunctors on the full subcategory of double negation closed *pers* on the natural number object of the realizability universe that are given internally in the realizability universe.) We wish to point out that the class of realizable endofunctors is quite extensive; it includes all those endofunctors on double negation closed *pers* on the natural numbers that are definable using intuitionistic set theory (because intuitionistic set theory may be interpreted in the realizability universe).

We shall say that the dinaturality condition is satisfied for a morphism $f\colon A \longrightarrow A'$ if and only if the hexagon given in the second figure on p. 318 commutes for that particular morphism f.

Proposition 2

Let F and G be realizable functors from PER^{-+} to PER and let φ be a partial recursive function such that for any *per* A, φ names a morphism of *pers*

$FAA \longrightarrow GAA$. Then the following are equivalent:

1. the assignment $\theta_A = \varphi \restriction FAA$ is a dinatural transformation from F to G;
2. the assignment $\theta_A = \varphi \restriction FAA$ satisfies the dinaturality condition for any isomorphism of *pers* $f\colon A \longrightarrow A'$.

If $F, G\colon \mathrm{PER}^{-+} \longrightarrow \mathrm{PER}$ are realizable, a dinatural transformation $\theta\colon F \longrightarrow G$ is *realizable* if and only if it is defined as in Proposition 2. (A reader familiar with the realizability universe may verify that the class of realizable dinatural transformations includes those dinatural transformations between realizable $-+$ary endofunctors on PER that are given internally in the realizability universe.)

Beside relying on the decomposition property stated in Proposition 1, the proof of the nontrivial direction in Proposition 2 uses a general argument about "vertical merging" of hexagons described in the second figure on p. 318.

Lemma 1

Let **C** be any category and let F and G be $-+$ary endofunctors on **C**. Let θ be an assignment of morphisms $\theta_A\colon FAA \longrightarrow GAA$ in **C** to the objects in **C**. Then the collection of morphisms $f\colon A \longrightarrow A'$ in **C** for which θ satisfies the dinaturality condition is a subcategory of **C**.

Proof θ trivially satisfies the dinaturality condition for the identities. Suppose that θ satisfies the dinaturality condition for $f\colon A \longrightarrow A'$ and for $f'\colon A' \longrightarrow A''$. Then we have:

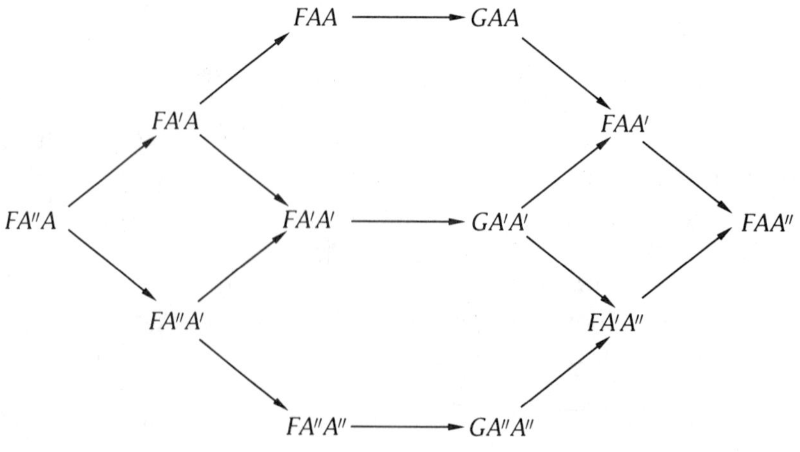

And hence θ satisfies the dinaturality condition for $f; f'$. □

We are particularly interested in the instances of the dinaturality condition for hexagons obtained by horizontal merging (see the figure on p. 319). It is important to observe that when $f\colon A \longrightarrow A'$ is an isomorphism, the middle diamond in the figure on p. 319 is a pullback and hence the outer hexagon does commute.

Lemma 2

Under the assumptions of Lemma 1, let H be a $-+$ary endofunctor on $\mathbf{C}$ and let ξ be an assignment of $\mathbf{C}$-morphisms $\xi_A\colon GAA \longrightarrow HAA$ to the objects of $\mathbf{C}$. Let $(\theta;\ \xi)_A = \theta_A;\ \xi_A$. Then whenever θ and ξ satisfy the dinaturality condition for all isomorphisms in $\mathbf{C}$, so does $\theta;\ \xi$.

We conclude this section by describing "realizable" ends of realizable multivariate endofunctors. The *per* $\int_A FAA$ is obtained by first taking the intersection of all FAA's, and then relating only those elements n and m such that for any morphism $f\colon A \longrightarrow A'$, the morphisms $F(id_A, f)\colon FAA \longrightarrow FAA'$ and $F(f, id_{A'})\colon FA'A' \longrightarrow FAA'$ given by the functoriality of F satisfy the condition that $F(id_A, f)(n)$ and $F(f, id_{A'})(m)$ are related in FAA'. The universal realizable dinatural transformation ω required in the figure at the top of p. 319 is given by I-maps from the *per* $\int_A FAA$ to the *per*s FAA's (all these maps are restrictions of the identity function on natural numbers; hence this dinatural transformation is realizable). Note that, of course, only *realizable* dinatural transformations $K_C \stackrel{\cdot\cdot}{\longrightarrow} F$ factor through ω, hence we speak of a realizable end $\int_A FAA$.

Example It is a remarkable fact that the polymorphic numerals are the only morphisms from the terminal *per* $\mathbf{1}$ to the realizable end

$$\int_A ((A \Rightarrow A) \Rightarrow (A \Rightarrow A)).$$

It is even more remarkable that the statement still holds if the end is replaced by the intersection.

Theorem 1

Realizable dinatural transformations do compose. For every balanced word w on $-+$, the category of realizable w ary endofunctors on PER and realizable dinatural transformations between them is a cartesian closed category. Furthermore, every realizable multivariate endofunctor on PER has a realizable end.

Open Problem

Is it true that for any realizable endofunctor F, the product of all FAA's is a realizable end of F? Alternatively, do the conditions in Proposition 2 always hold?

Remarks In light of the discussion after Proposition 1, observe that the collection of multivariate realizable endofunctors is much more extensive than the collection of multivariate endofunctors on PER obtainable from covariant projections by finitely many exponentiations, realizable ends, and identifications of arguments of the same sign. In short, the class of realizable multivariate endofunctors includes those definable in intuitionistic set theory, not just those definable in second-order lambda calculus.

Reynolds's criterion for parametricity is formulated in terms of set-theoretic models [16]. It is shown by Reynolds in [17] that there are no such models. However, it is possible to consider Reynolds's criterion as formulated in an intuitionistic set theory. Hence this criterion makes sense in *any* topos model of polymorphic lambda calculus, in particular in the realizability universe. We discuss this point in the full paper based on this report, to appear in *Theoretical Computer Science.*

The results and arguments of this section may be generalized to realizability models over any partial combinatory algebra, and hence they hold for all HEO-like models. (See [1] for the definition of HEO-like models.)

3 *Second-Order Definable Endofunctors and Dinatural Transformations*

A typed lambda theory may be considered as a *ccc* [9]. The objects are types, and morphisms are (equivalence classes of) terms. More precisely, a morphism $t\colon A \longrightarrow B$ is named by a term of type B with at most one free variable, where the type of that variable is A (it is convenient to assume product types in the language).

Here we consider the second-order typed lambda theory obtained from second-order lambda calculus with product types and with possibly empty types by imposing the alpha, beta, and eta conversions (both first and second order), surjective pairing equations, as well as certain additional equations that are discussed below and that hold in the setting described in Section 2 (if one interprets universal quantification as an end). Let **C** be the associated *ccc*.

A "type shape" is a type with mutually distinct type variables. Type shapes induce multivariate endofunctors on **C** roughly by substitution of types for the type variables. This is made prėcise by indicating the arity w and a correlation among distinguished slots, together with giving a type shape. For example, the type $(A \Rightarrow B)\times B$ may be considered as a functor of arity $+--+-+$, of shape $(A \Rightarrow B) \times C$ where A is in the second contravariant slot, B is in the second and third covariant slots, and the other slots are dummy. The action of this functor on terms is the obvious one: contravariant in A and covariant in B. Note that according to the convention introduced in Section 1, this functor may be considered as a functor from $(\mathbf{C}^3)^{-+}$ to $\mathbf{C}$. Note, on the other hand, that $A \Rightarrow A$ is not functorial unless all slots are considered to be dummy; that is, it is a constant functor.

The full definition is given by induction. For example, $F \Longrightarrow G$ is defined by the "twisted exponential" $(F \Longrightarrow G)(A, B) = F(B, A) \Rightarrow G(A, B)$. Here it is assumed that F and G have the same specified arity, which is then the arity of $F \Longrightarrow G$. The following example may illuminate the case of universal quantification. $\forall_A((A \Rightarrow A) \Rightarrow A)$ is obtained from $(B \Rightarrow A) \Rightarrow B$ by "quantifying out the opposing pair (A, B) of sign $-+$". In fact, one has to consider (A, A) versus (B, B), where the second A is dummy. The arity of $\forall_C FCC$ is the same as that of F, but functor $\forall_C FCC$ is required to be constant in the slots indicated by C. Let us call the functors thus induced "definable functors".

Terms should induce dinatural transformations between such functors. For example, recall the dinaturality of application and of polymorphic Church numerals discussed in Section 1. We *impose* the dinaturality conditions and these are our additional equations mentioned at the beginning of this section. For example, consider $\forall_A(A \Rightarrow A)$ as a constant functor and consider the $-+$ary functor $F(A, B) = A \Rightarrow B$. We ensure that second-order application is a dinatural transformation from $\forall_A(A \Rightarrow A)$ to F by requiring that for a variable y of type $\forall_A(A \Rightarrow A)$ and any $f\colon B \longrightarrow C$ in $\mathbf{C}$, $y[B]$ composed with $id_B \Rightarrow f$ equals $y[C]$ composed with $f \Rightarrow id_C$. Dinatural transformations uniformly given by a term are called "definable dinatural transformations" (definition by induction, relying on our additional equations). Composition of these by horizontal merging is ensured by composition of terms.

Theorem 2

For every balanced word w on $\{-, +\}$, the category of w ary definable endofunctors and definable dinatural tansformations between them is a cartesian closed category. Moreover, universal quantification has the universal property of the end with respect to definable dinatural transformations. The second-order lambda theory of definable endofunctors and definable dinatural transformations is consistent.

Is every dinatural transformation between definable endofunctors definable? (This question is similar in spirit to the questions raised in [14].)

Remark An alternative approach is to give a simultaneous inductive definition of type shapes and the related endofunctors, of term shapes and the related dinatural transformations, and of type and term instances that form the *ccc* **C**. Then one must show that all types and terms of second-order lambda calculus appear as type instances and, respectively, term instances. Second-order types may also be considered as definable endofunctors given together with identifications of slots, but that approach requires a more elaborate categorical setting.

Acknowledgments

We would like to thank John Reynolds, Albert Meyer, Dana Scott, and John Mitchell for discussions about parametricity, and Thomas Streicher for detailed comments on realizable functors. P. J. Freyd and A. Scedrov are partially supported by grants from the U.S. National Science Foundation and from the U.S. Office of Naval Research. P. J. Scott is partially supported by a grant from the Natural Sciences and Engineering Research Council of Canada.

References

[1] Breazu-Tannen, V. and Coquand, T. "Extensional polymorphism". In *Proceedings of TAPSOFT '87 — CFLP* (Pisa, 1987). *Theoretical Computer Science 59* (1988), pp. 85–114.

[2] Bruce, K., Meyer, A., and Mitchell, J. "The semantics of second-order lambda calculus". To appear in *Information & Computation*; included in this volume (Chapter 10).

[3] Carboni, A., Freyd, P., and Scedrov, A. "A categorical approach to realizability and polymorphic types". *Proceedings of the 3rd ACM Workshop on Mathematical Foundations of Programming Language Semantics*, M. Main et al., eds., pp. 23–42. Lecture Notes in Computer Science, vol. 298. Springer-Verlag, New York, 1988.

[4] Freyd, P. and Scedrov, A. "Some semantic aspects of polymorphic lambda calculus". *Proceedings of the 2nd IEEE Symposium on Logic in Computer Science* (Ithaca, N.Y.), pp. 315–319. IEEE, New York, 1987.

[5] Girard, J-Y. "Une extension de l'interprétation fonctionelle...". In *Proceedings of the 2nd Scandinavian Logic Symposium*, J. Fenstad, ed. North-Holland, Amsterdam, 1971.

[6] Girard, J-Y. "The system *F* of variable types, fifteen years later". *Theoretical Computer Science 45* (1986), pp. 159–192. Reprinted in this volume (Chapter 6).

[7] Girard, J-Y. "Linear logic". *Theoretical Computer Science 50* (1987), pp. 1–102.

[8] Hyland, J. M. E. "A small complete category". *Annals Pure Appl. Logic 40* (1988), pp. 135–165.

[9] Lambek, J. and Scott, P. *Introduction to Higher-Order Categorical Logic*. Cambridge University Press, 1986.

[10] Longo, G. and Moggi, E. "Constructive natural deduction and its 'modest' interpretation". In *Proceedings of Semantics of Natural and Computer Languages* (Stanford, March 1987), J. Meseguer et al., eds. MIT Press, to appear.

[11] Mac Lane, S. *Categories for the Working Mathematician*. Graduate Texts in Mathematics. Springer-Verlag, New York, 1971.

[12] Mitchell, J. "Representation independence and data abstraction". *Proceedings of the 13th ACM Symposium on Principles of Programming Languages*, pp. 263–276. ACM, New York, 1986.

[13] Mitchell, J. and Meyer, A. "Second-order logical relations". Extended Abstract. *Logics of Programs*, R. Parikh, ed., pp. 225–236. Lecture Notes in Computer Science, vol. 193. Springer-Verlag, New York, 1985.

[14] Plotkin, G. "Lambda-definability in the full type hierarchy". *To H. B. Curry: Essays on Combinatory Logic, Lambda Calculus and Formalism*, J. P. Seldin and J. R. Hindley, eds., pp. 363–373. Academic Press, New York, 1980.

[15] Reynolds, J. "Towards a theory of type structure". *Programming Symposium*, B. Robinet, ed., pp. 408–425. Lecture Notes in Computer Science, vol. 19. Springer-Verlag, New York, 1974.

[16] Reynolds, J. "Types, abstraction, and parametric polymorphism". *Information Processing 83*, R. E. A. Mason, ed., pp. 513–523. North-Holland, Amsterdam, 1983.

[17] Reynolds, J. "Polymorphism is not set-theoretic". In *Semantics of Data Types*, Proceedings, G. Kahn, D. B. MacQueen, and G. Plotkin, eds. Lecture Notes in Computer Science, vol. 173. Springer-Verlag, New York, 1984.

[18] Scott, D. "Constructive validity". *Symposium on Automatic Demonstration*, pp. 237–275. Lecture Notes in Mathematics, vol. 125. Springer-Verlag, New York, 1970.

[19] Scott, D. "Relating theories of the λ-calculus". *To H. B. Curry: Essays on Combinatory Logic, Lambda Calculus, and Formalism*, J. P. Seldin and J. R. Hindley, eds., pp. 403–450. Academic Press, New York, 1980.

[20] Strachey, C. "Fundamental concepts in programming languages". Lecture Notes, International Summer School in Computer Programming, Copenhagen, August 1967.

Part III

Topics in Constructive Type Theory

Introduction to Part III

15

Gérard Huet
INRIA

The recent interest in type theory and constructive mathematics in computer science has its roots in foundational studies and in proof theory. Let us give a short historical perspective on these topics and their general relevance for computer science.

1 *Prehistory: Prewar Research on Foundations*

Traditionally mathematicians used to distinguish between arithmetic, the science of numbers, and geometry, the science of figures. Logic, the science of reasoning, belonged to philosophy. One computed with numbers, whereas one reasoned with Euclid's laws and Aristotle's rules. Extending the notion of numbers from counters to measurements forced a progressive identification of calculus and geometry, through extensions of the number notion corresponding to successive crises of mathematics: The square brought the irrationals, the circle brought the transcendentals. One could compute geometrical truths with analytical geometry, and soon the achievements of analysis and its applications to physics established mathematics as the definite basis for technical achievements. Arithmetic, reduced to the study of whole numbers, became a pure refuge.

Meanwhile, logic slowly incorporated itself into mathematics. After the discovery of the laws of propositional calculus by Boole, Frege invented predicate calculus together with a universal calculus of proof figures. A complete unification of mathematics appeared possible at the turn of the century: Hilbert proposed as a program the "bootstrap" of mathematics, which should be able to prove its own consistency, and Cantor presented the notion of set as unifying semantic object. But the construction of a paradox in naive set theory by Burali-Forti, and in Frege's system by Russell, cast some doubt on the foundations of mathematics. This led Russell to refine Frege's system into a stratified language of typed objects, and to propose the development of formalized mathematics in the Principia Mathematica system.

The program of Hilbert was still very much relevant: A consistency proof was needed for the Principia. But now it was clear that logic reasoning could be expressed by mathematical computations amenable themselves to logical axiomatization. This "arithmetization of syntax" led Gödel to refute Hilbert's program definitively, by showing that consistency was not provable in consistent systems. This crisis led to the disinterest of most mathematicians in foundational problems, whereas it prompted the logicians to investigate the notion of "computable function".

Not all mathematicians agreed with the view that completed infinite objects were meaningful mathematical objects. Brouwer founded the doctrine of "intuitionism", which rejected the excluded middle principle, at least for propositions concerning infinite objects, and insisted that a mathematical proof of existence should somehow exhibit a mathematical object with the required property, in a constructive manner. This doctrine was made more precise by Heyting, who formulated laws for well-understood fragments of intuitionism.

By 1935 all the ingredients existed to connect the mathematical notion of integer function computable mechanically (recursive and partial recursive functions), with the intuitionism requirement (due to Kolmogorov) of interpreting mathematical propositions as problem statements requiring effectively computable solutions. This was achieved first by Kleene, who gave various "realizability interpretations" of Heyting's axiomatizations of intuitionistic calculi.

At about the same time, Church invented λ-calculus, one of the many equivalent ways of presenting effective algorithms. The mathematical elegance of this calculus prompted Church to formulate an axiomatic system using the calculus to express the terms, propositions, schemas, etc. of higher-order logic. Alas, Rosser showed that Russell's paradox applied again, and Curry's independent analyses of Shönfinkel's combinatory algebra showed clearly that logical soundness was not compatible with computational completeness without some kind of distinction between logical propositions and computational algorithms. Church went on to simplify the Principia system into what is now known as the simple theory of types, based on the simply typed λ-calculus.

The failure of Hilbert's program in an absolute way still left open the possibility of relative consistency proofs, leading to a mathematical analysis of the relative strength of various logical systems. This was developed by Gentzen, who pioneered the new field of *proof theory*. Gentzen showed that deductions could be transformed into normal forms (so-called *cut-free* proofs) which were obviously consistent. This reduced the consistency proof to a single trouble spot, namely, the induction schema necessary to prove the termination of the normalization process; that is, consistency could be characterized by an arithmetic truth. Furthermore, the intuitionistic systems led to canonical forms of proof; i.e., the normal forms were unique.

The normalization process could be seen as some kind of computation on proof objects. Actually, the *natural deduction* systems of Gentzen corresponded to a λ-calculus formalization of proof structures. This correspondence between proofs and programs (and thus between propositions and types of functional systems) was ignored for a long time, however, and thus the theory of λ-calculus and combinatory algebra developed largely independently from proof theory. This correspondence is now called the Curry-Howard isomorphism, and it is discussed in Coquand's contribution (Chapter 17).

2 *Modern History*

Proof theory is now one of the most active areas of mathematical logic. The *predicative*, or first-order, systems are contrasted to the *nonpredicative* systems, which use in an essential way some second-order quantification (i.e., quantification over possibly infinite sets) and thus do not correspond immediately to systems of iterated inductive definitions. The normalization theorem of Gentzen, now well understood by Tait's method as an inductive termination proof in λ-calculus in the predicative case, posed a delicate problem for nonpredicative systems such as second-order arithmetic, also called "analysis" by the logicians. This was solved in 1970 by Girard through his proof of normalization of second-order λ-calculus with the method of *candidats de réductibilité.* This story, and its continuation, has been amply told in the preceding chapter of this volume.

The predicative versus nonpredicative controversy is still very active. Prompted by Bishop's development of constructive analysis on predicative grounds, Martin-Löf is attempting a reconstruction of the foundations of mathematics formalized in his *intuitionistic type theory* framework. This line of development attracts the interest of computer scientists such as Constable, who proposes with his NUPRL system a systematic development methodology for provably correct programs. This line of research was not represented in the YoP Institute, and thus no paper in the present volume is relevant to this approach. The interested reader is referred to the bibliographic entries of Constable and Martin-Löf in Chapter 16.

Studies in λ-calculus were very much reactivated with the development of computer science, since this formalism may be seen as a clean mathematical basis for computer programming languages. The influence of λ-calculus on programming languages was implicit in Algol 60 and to a lesser extend in LISP, and more explicit in Landin's papers on the semantics of Algol 60 and on his ISWIM proposal. ISWIM, equipped by Milner with polymorphic types, became ML, a programming language discussed at length in Chapter 1. A more general view of parametricity in programming languages was proposed by Reynolds in 1974, but it was only recently realized that this polymorphic λ-calculus was basically Girard's second-order system F, while McCracken's generalization corresponded to the higher-order system $F\omega$.

The model theory of pure λ-calculus was actually prompted by computer science research. The pioneering work of Scott and Plotkin led to the field of *denotational semantics*, an active research area that is outside the scope of the present volume. Typed λ-calculus, on the other hand, can be interpreted very naturally in categorical models. This story, which leads to a very interesting interaction between pure categoricians, proof theorists, and computer scientists, pervades this whole volume.

Computer scientists are also interested in logic for its application to mechanical theorem-proving, in order to automate the design and verification of computer programs developed consistently with logical specifications. Besides the NUPRL effort already mentioned, let us list the Boyer-Moore theorem-prover, based on an extension of primitive recursive arithmetic, and the LCF proof assistant developed by Milner and his colleagues at Edinburgh and Cambridge Universities, which implements variants of Scott's domain theory. Such proof assistants obviously benefit from research in type and proof theory, and the design of general systems manipulating *logical frameworks* is a very active recent research topic.

One of the earliest logical frameworks is the Automath family of calculi. It originated with de Bruijn's endeavor to describe and mechanically verify mathematics formalized in a typed λ-calculus language. This very promising framework has not received all the attention it deserves, and we need more metamathematical studies of calculi with such complicated dependences between types and objects. We must cite in this connection the ELF (Edinburgh Logical Framework), as well as similar studies around Martin-Löf's type-theory languages.

It is possible to extend the Automath language with higher-order quantification. Thus Coquand presented in his 1985 thesis the first *calculus of constructions* system, an extension of Girard's $F\omega$ with dependent types. This calculus is an active topic of current research, since its great expressive power makes it a good candidate for logically founded program development systems. In Chapter 18, Scedrov gives a realizability interpretation for this calculus.

One of the problems in this area is to understand how to embed a possibly nonterminating programming language, possessing computational completeness (i.e., a general recursion operator), within a proof development system for a consistent logic. One current line of research, due to Feferman and Beeson, proposes logics of *partial terms*, where terms of the logic may not always denote semantic values. This is to be contrasted with the logics of *partial values* of Scott domains, where the syntax is total but the semantic objects partially defined.

Another problem is to understand how to relate classical logic and intuitionistic logic in a program development system. It is clear that the proofs of consistency of logical specifications are too redundant to be used as actual programs: We want to be able to write an integer program using the knowledge that its argument is positive, without actually demanding a run-time extra argument containing the actual justification for this fact. Since no constructive contents should be assigned to this part of the specification, it is clear that we may use all the power of classical logic for the part of the proof that deals with this information. The article by Hayashi, Chapter 19, which concludes this volume, presents a program-extracting algorithm **PX**, based on a logic of partial terms, which extracts computationally meaningful parts of proofs in the form of actual LISP programs.

This field of computational type theory is very much in its infancy. Without pretending to give a complete picture of a fast developing field, the third part of this volume presents a few specific recent research articles. Its first chapter —Chapter 16— is a survey on type systems, presented systematically according to the formal underlying structures.

A Uniform Approach to Type Theory[1]

16

Gérard Huet
INRIA Roquencourt

Abstract

We present in a unified framework the basic syntactic structures used to model deductive and computational notions. The guiding principle is "propositions as types".

A preliminary version of these course notes was presented at the "Advanced Course in Artificial Intelligence" held in Vignieu (France) in July 1985, and appeared under the title "Deduction and Computation" in *Fundamentals in Artificial Intelligence*, edited by W. Bibel and Ph. Jorrand and published by Springer-Verlag as Lecture Notes in Computer Science, vol. 232. An expanded version was prepared during my sabbatical year at Carnegie-Mellon University, as course notes for my course on "Formal Structures for Computation

1. An earlier version of this chapter appeared as "Deduction and Computation" in Manfred Broy (ed.), *Logic of Programming and Calculi of Discrete Design* (NATO ASI F36), Springer-Verlag, Berlin, 1987. Used with permission.

and Deduction", in May 1986. These notes were also presented at the Marktoberdorf International Summer School on Logic of Programming and Calculi of Discrete Design in August 1986. The current augmented version was prepared for the Institute on Logical Foundations of Functional Programming organized by The University of Texas at Austin in June 1987.

---

1 *Terms and Types*

1.1 *General Notations*

We assume known elementary set theory and algebra. $\mathcal{N}$ is the set $\{0, 1, \ldots\}$ of natural numbers, $\mathcal{N}_+$ the set of positive natural numbers. We shall identify the natural n with the set $\{0, \ldots, n-1\}$, and thus 0 is also the empty set $\emptyset$. Every finite set S is isomorphic to n, with n the cardinal of S, denoted $n = |S|$. If A and B are sets, we write $A \to B$, or sometimes B^A, for the set of functions with domain A and codomain B.

1.2 *Languages, Concrete Syntax*

Let Σ be a finite alphabet. A *string* u of *length* n is a function in $n \to \Sigma$. The set of all strings over Σ is

$$\Sigma^* = \bigcup_{n \in \mathcal{N}} \Sigma^n.$$

We write $|u|$ for the length n of u. We write u_i for $u(i-1)$, when $i \leq n$. The null string, unique element of Σ^0, is denoted Λ. The unit string mapping 1 to $a \in \Sigma$ is denoted "a". The concatenation of strings u and v, defined in the usual fashion, is denoted $u \wedge v$; and when there is no ambiguity we write, e.g., "abc" for "a" $\wedge$ "b" $\wedge$ "c". When $u \in \Sigma^*$ and $a \in \Sigma$, we write $u \cdot a$ for $u \wedge$ "a". We define an ordering $\leq$ on Σ^*, called the *prefix* ordering, by

$$u \leq v \Leftrightarrow \exists w \quad v = u \wedge w.$$

If $u \leq v$, the residual w is unique, and we write $w = v/u$. We say that strings u and v are *disjoint*, and we write $u|v$, iff u and v are unrelated by the partial ordering $\leq$. Finally, we let $u < v$ iff $u \leq v$ with $u \neq v$.

The set Σ^* has the structure of a monoïd, that is:

$$Ass: \ (u \wedge v) \wedge w = u \wedge (v \wedge w)\,,$$

$$IdL: \ \Lambda \wedge u = u\,,$$

$$IdR: \ u \wedge \Lambda = u\,.$$

Actually, Σ^* is the *free* monoïd generated by Σ.

Examples

1. $\Sigma = 0$. We get $\Sigma^* = 1$.
2. $\Sigma = 1$. We get $\Sigma^* = \mathcal{N}$. Here, strings are natural numbers in unary notation, and concatenation corresponds to addition.
3. $\Sigma = 2 = \{0, 1\}$ (the Booleans). The set Σ^* is the set of all binary words.
4. $\Sigma = \mathcal{N}_+$. We call the elements of Σ^* *occurrences*. When $u = w \cdot m$ and $v = w \cdot n$, with $m < n$, we say that u is *left* of v, and write $u <_L v$.

1.3 *Terms: Abstract Syntax*

We first define a *tree domain* as a subset D of $\mathcal{N}_+^*$ closed under $<$ and $<_L$:

$$u \in D \wedge v < u \Rightarrow v \in D,$$

$$u \in D \wedge v <_L u \Rightarrow v \in D.$$

We say that M is a Σ-tree iff $M \in D \to \Sigma$, for some tree domain D. We define $D(M)$ as D, and we say that $D(M)$ is the *set of occurrences* in M. M is said to be *finite* whenever $D(M)$ is, which we shall assume in the following.

We shall now use occurrences to designate nodes of a tree and the subtree starting at that node. If $u \in D(M)$, we define the Σ-tree M/u as mapping occurrence v to $M(u \,\hat{}\, v)$. We say that M/u is the sl subtree of M at occurrence u. If N is also a Σ-tree, we define the *graft* $M[u \leftarrow N]$ as the Σ-tree mapping v to $N(w)$ whenever $v = u \,\hat{}\, w$ with $w \in D(N)$, and to $M(v)$ if $v \in D(M)$ and not $u \leq v$.

We need one auxiliary notion, that of *width* of a tree. If $M \in \Sigma^*$, we define the (top) width of M as

$$||M|| = \max\{n \mid \text{“}n\text{”} \in D(M)\}.$$

We shall now consider Σ a *graded* alphabet, that is given with an *arity* function α in $\Sigma \to \mathcal{N}$. We then say that M is a Σ-*term* iff M is a Σ-tree verifying the supplementary consistency condition:

$$\forall u \in D(M) \;\; ||M/u|| = \alpha(M(u)).$$

That is, every subtree of M is of the form $F(M_1, M_2, \ldots, M_n)$, with $n = \alpha(F)$. We write $T(\Sigma)$ for the set of Σ-terms. If $M_1, M_2, \ldots, M_n \in T(\Sigma)$ and $F \in \Sigma$, with $\alpha(F) = n$, then $M = F(M_1, M_2, \ldots, M_n)$ is easily defined as a Σ-term. This gives $T(\Sigma)$ the structure of a Σ-algebra. Since, conversely, the decomposition of M is uniquely determined, we call $T(\Sigma)$ the *completely free* Σ-algebra.

Example With $\Sigma = \{+, S, 0\}$, $\alpha(+) = 2$, $\alpha(S) = 1$, $\alpha(0) = 0$, the following structure represents a Σ-term:

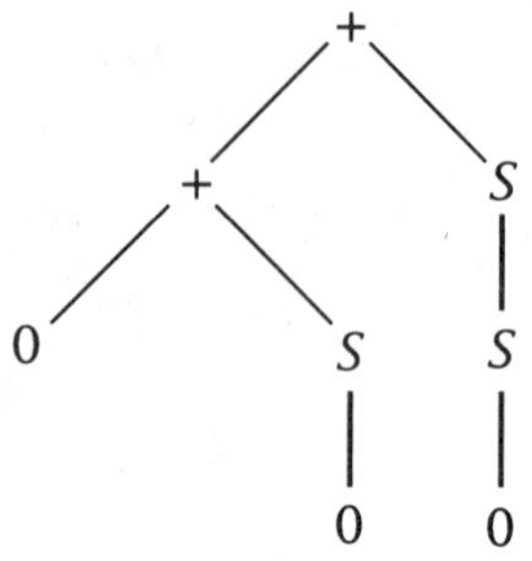

The following proposition is easy to prove by induction. All occurrences are supposed to be universally quantified in the relevant tree domain.

Proposition 1

Embedding : $M[u \leftarrow N]/(u \wedge v) = N/v$,

Associativity : $M[u \leftarrow N][u \wedge v \leftarrow P] = M[u \leftarrow N[v \leftarrow P]]$,

Persistence : $M[u \leftarrow N]/v = M/v \quad (u|v)$,

Commutativity : $M[u \leftarrow N][v \leftarrow P] = M[v \leftarrow P][u \leftarrow N] \quad (u|v)$,

Distributivity : $M[u \leftarrow N]/v = (M/v)[u/v \leftarrow N] \quad (v \leq u)$,

Dominance : $M[u \leftarrow N][v \leftarrow P] = M[v \leftarrow P] \quad (v \leq u)$.

We define the *length* $|M|$ of a (finite) term M recursively by:

$$|F(M_1, \ldots, M_2)| = 1 + \Sigma_{i=1}^{n} |M_i|.$$

1.4 *Parsing*

It is well known that the term in the example above can be represented unambiguously as a Σ-string, for instance in *prefix polish notation*, which is here $++0S0SS0$. This result is not very interesting: Such strings are neither good notations for humans nor good representations for computers, since the graft operation necessitates unnecessary copying. We shall discuss better machine representations later, using binary graphs. As far as human readibility is concerned, we assume known parsing techniques. This permits us to represent terms on an extended alphabet with parentheses and commas, which is closer to standard mathematical practice. Also, infix notation and indentation permit us to keep some of the string's tree structure more apparent. We shall not make explicit the exact representation grammar, and we shall allow ourselves to write freely, for instance, $(0+S(0))+S(S(0))$. Note that we avoid explicit quotes as well, which permits us to mix freely meta-variables with object structures, as in $S(M)$, where M is a meta-variable denoting a Σ-term.

1.5 *Terms with Variables, Substitution*

The idea is to internalize the notation $S(M)$ above as a term $S(x)$ over an extended alphabet containing special symbols of arity 0 called *variables*. Such terms with variables are thus polynomial expressions, in the case of completely free operators.

Let V be a denumerable set disjoint from Σ. We define the set of terms with variables, $T(\Sigma, V)$, in exactly the same way as $T(\Sigma \cup V)$, extending the arity function so that $\alpha(x) = 0$ for every x in V. The only difference between the variables and the constants (symbol of arity 0) is that a constant has an existential import: it denotes a value in the domain we are modeling with our term language, whereas a variable denotes a term. The difference is important only when there are no constants in Σ, since then $T(\Sigma)$ is empty.

All of the notions defined for terms extend to terms with variables. We define the set $V(M)$ of *variables* occurring in M as:

$$V(M) \;=\; \{x \in V \mid \exists u \in D(M) \quad M(u) = x\},$$

and we define the number of distinct variables in M as $\nu(M) \;=\; |V(M)|$.

We shall now formalize the notion of substitution of terms for variables in a term containing variables. From now on, the sets Σ and V are fixed, and we use T to denote $T(\Sigma, V)$. A *substitution* σ is a function in $V \to T$, identity almost everywhere. That is, the set $D(\sigma) \;=\; \{x \in V \mid \sigma(x) \neq x\}$ is finite. We call it the *domain* of σ. Substitutions are extended to Σ-morphisms over T by

$$\sigma(F(M_1, \ldots, M_n)) \;=\; F(\sigma(M_1), \ldots, \sigma(M_n)).$$

Bijective substitutions are called *permutations*. When $U \subseteq V$, we write σ_U for the restriction of substitution σ to U. It is easy to show that, for all σ, M, and U:

$$V(M) \subseteq U \;\Rightarrow\; \sigma(M) = \sigma_U(M).$$

Alternatively, we can define the replacement $M[x \leftarrow N]$ as

$$M[u_1 \leftarrow N] \ldots [u_n \leftarrow N],$$

where $\{u_1, \ldots, u_n\} = \{u \mid M(u) = x\}$ and then

$$\sigma(M) = M[x \leftarrow \sigma(x) \mid x \in V(M)]$$

with an obvious notation.

We now define the quasi-ordering $\leq$ of *matching* in T by:

$$M \leq N \Leftrightarrow \exists\sigma \quad N = \sigma(M).$$

It is easy to show that if such a σ exists, $\sigma_{V(M)}$ is unique. We shall call it the *match of N by M*, and denote it by N/M.

We define $M \equiv N \Leftrightarrow M \leq N \wedge N \leq M$. When $M \equiv N$, we say that M and N are *isomorphic*. This is equivalent to saying that $M = \sigma(N)$ for some permutation σ. Note that $M \equiv N$ implies $|M| = |N|$. Finally, we define

$$M > N \Leftrightarrow N \leq M \wedge \neg M \leq N.$$

Proposition

$>$ is a well-ordering on T.

Proof We show that $M > N$ implies $\mu(M) > \mu(N)$, with $\mu(M) = |M| - \nu(M)$.

Let φ be any bijection between $T \times T$ and V. We define a binary operation $\cap$ in T by:

$$F(M_1, \ldots, M_n) \cap F(N_1, \ldots, N_n) = F(M_1 \cap N_1, \ldots, M_n \cap N_n)$$

$$M \cap N = \varphi(M, N) \quad \text{in all other cases.}$$

$M \cap N$ is uniquely determined from φ and, for distinct φ's, is unique up to $\equiv$.
□

Proposition

$M \cap N$ is a g.l.b. of M and N under the match quasi-ordering.

Let **T** be the quotient poset $T/\equiv$, completed with a maximum element $\top$. From the propositions above we conclude the following.

Theorem

T is a complete lattice.

Corollary

If two terms M and N have an upper bound, i.e., a common instance $\sigma(M) = \sigma'(N)$, they have a least upper bound $M \cup N$, which is a most general such instance; that is, $\sigma = \sigma_0 \circ \tau$, and $\sigma' = \sigma'_0 \circ \tau$, for some substitution τ called the *principal unifier* of M and N. The term $M \cup N$ is unique modulo $\equiv$ and may be found by the *unification* algorithm [159].

Proposition

$$D(\sigma(M)) = D(M) \cup \bigcup_{\{u \mid M(u) \in V\}} \{u \wedge v \mid v \in D(\sigma(M(u)))\},$$

$$\forall u \in D(M) \;\; M(u) = x \in V \Rightarrow \forall v \in D(\sigma(x)) \;\; \sigma(M)/(u \wedge v) = \sigma(x)/v,$$

$$\forall u \in D(M) \;\; \sigma(M)/u = \sigma(M/u),$$

$$\forall u \in D(M) \;\; \sigma(M)[u \leftarrow \sigma(N)] = \sigma(M[u \leftarrow N]).$$

1.6 *Graph Representations, Dags*

It is usual to represent trees in computers by binary graphs implemented as pairs of machine words. In the simplest scheme, a word is partitioned into one tag bit, and one field interpreted either as an address in the graph memory or as a natural number, according to the value of the tag. In this last case, some natural (say 0) is reserved for *nil*, the empty list of trees. Symbols from Σ are then coded up as positive naturals. If tree M is represented by the word W and the list L is represented by the word W', then the list $M \cdot L$ is represented by the address of a graph node implemented as the pair (W, W'). Similarly, if symbol F is coded up as the word W and the list L is represented by the word W', then the tree $F(L)$ is represented by the address of a graph node implemented as the pair (W, W').

Thus every tree is mapped into a graph, and this representation allows sharing of common subtrees. Assignment to fields may implement grafting without copying, but this method is not usually compatible with sharing. This is the standard way of representing trees and lists in symbol-manipulation languages such as LISP [124]. The principal problem to be solved in such languages is to keep track dynamically of which areas of the storage are used to represent actively used subtrees. Garbage-collection algorithms have been proposed to solve this problem, but this method is becoming problematic with the current technology of very large virtual memories. A precise description of such memory allocation issues is beyond the scope of these notes.

Terms are of course represented as trees. A global table holds the arity function. There are several possibilities for the representation of variables. They may be represented as symbols. But then the scope structure must be computed by an algorithm, rather than being implicit in the structure. Also, a global scanning of the term is necessary to determine its set of variables, and substitution involves copying of the substituted term. For these reasons, variables are often represented rather as integer offsets in stacks of bindings. Such "structure sharing" representations are now standard for PROLOG implementations.

A precise account of the various representation schemes for term structures, and of the accompanying algorithms, is out of the scope of these notes. It should be borne in mind that the crucial problem is memory utilization: the trade-off between copying and sharing is often the deciding factor for an implementation. Languages with garbage-collected structures, such as LISP, are ideal for programming "quick and dirty" prototypes. But serious implementation efforts should aim at good algorithmic performance on applications of realistic size.

The crucial algorithms in formula and proof manipulation are matching, unification, substitution, and grafting. First-order unification has been specially well studied. A linear algorithm is known [142, 28], but in practice quasi-linear algorithms based on operations on congruence classes are preferred [115, 116]. Furthermore, these algorithms extend without modification to unification of infinite rational terms represented by finite graphs [79].

Implementation methods may be partitioned into two families. Some depend on logical properties (e.g., sharing subterms in dags arising from substitution to a term containing several occurrences of the same variable). Some are purely statistical (e.g., sharing structures globally through hash-coding techniques). Particular applications require a careful analysis of the optimal trade-off between logical and statistical techniques.

There is no comprehensive survey on implementation issues. Some partial aspects are described in [9, 160, 117, 115, 189, 184, 135, 54, 1, 45, 56, 20, 59, 168, 185].

2 *Inference Rules*

We shall now study *inference systems*, defined by inference rules. The general form of an inference rule is:

$$IR : \frac{P_1 \; P_2 \; \ldots \; P_n}{Q},$$

where the P_i's and Q are *propositions* belonging to some formal language. We shall here regard these propositions as *types*, and the inference rule as the description of the signature of IR considered as a typed operator. More precisely, IR has arity n, P_i is the type of its ith argument, and Q is the type of its result. Well-typed terms composed of inference operators are called the *proofs* defined by the inference system. Let us now examine a few familiar inference systems.

2.1 *The Trivial Homogeneous Case: Arities*

A graded alphabet Σ may be considered as the simplest inference system, where types are reduced to arities. That is, the set of propositions is 1, and an operator F of arity n is an inference rule

$$F: \ \frac{0\,0\ \ldots\ 0}{0}$$

(with n zero's in the numerator). A Σ-proof corresponds to our Σ-terms above.

2.2 *Finite Systems of Types: Sorts*

The next level of inference systems consists in choosing a finite set S of elementary propositions, usually called *sorts*. For instance, let $S = \{int, bool\}$, and let Σ be defined by:

$$\begin{aligned}
&0 : \ int\,, && S: \ int \to int\,,\\
&true : \ bool\,, && false : \ bool\,,\\
&if : \ bool, int, int \to int,
\end{aligned}$$

where we use the alternative syntax $P_1, \ldots, P_n \to Q$ for an inference rule. The term $if(true, 0, S(0))$ is of sort *int*; i.e., it is a proof of proposition *int*.

As another example, consider the puzzle "missionaries and cannibals". We call any triple $\langle b, m, c\rangle \in 2 \times 4 \times 4$ a *configuration*. The boolean b indicates the position of the boat, m (resp. c) is the number of missionaries (resp. cannibals) on the left bank. The set of states S is the set of *legal* configurations, i.e., those that obey the condition

$$P(m, c) \ \equiv \ m = c \ or \ m = 0 \ or \ m = 3\,.$$

There are thus ten distinct states or sorts. The rules of inference comprise first a constant denoting the starting configuration,

$$s_0 : \ \langle 0, 3, 3\rangle\,,$$

then the transitions carrying p missionaries and q cannibals from left to right,

$$\begin{aligned}
L_{m,c,p,q} : \ &\langle 0, m, c\rangle \to \langle 1, m-p, c-q\rangle\\
&(m \geq p, c \geq q, P(m, c), P(m-p, c-q), 1 \leq p+q \leq 2)\,,
\end{aligned}$$

and finally the transitions $R_{m,c,p,q}$, which are inverses of $L_{m,c,p,q}$. The game consists in finding a proof of $\langle 1, 0, 0\rangle$.

This simple example of a finite group of transformations applies to more complex tasks, such as Rubik's cube. All state transition systems can be described in a similar fashion. Examples of such proofs are parse-trees of regular grammars, where the inference rules' signatures correspond to a finite automaton transition graph. Slightly more complicated formalisms allow subsorts, i.e., containment relationships between the sorts. That is, we postulate primitive implications between the elementary propositions. These systems reduce to simple sorts by considering dummy transitions corresponding to the implicit coercions.

2.3 *Types as Terms: Standard Proof Trees*

We shall here describe our types as terms formed over an alphabet Φ of type operators, which we shall call *functors*. For the moment, we shall assume that we have just one category of such propositions; i.e., the functors have just an arity. The alphabet Σ of inference rules determines the legal proof trees.

Example: Combinatory logic We take as functors a set Φ of constants Φ_0, plus a binary operator $\Rightarrow$, which we shall write in infix notation. We call *functionality* a term in $T(\Phi)$. We have three families of rules in Σ. In the following, the meta-variables A, B, C denote arbitrary functionalities. The operators of the K and S families are of arity 0, the operators of the App family are binary.

$$K_{A,B} : A \Rightarrow (B \Rightarrow A)\,,$$

$$S_{A,B,C} : (A \Rightarrow (B \Rightarrow C)) \Rightarrow ((A \Rightarrow B) \Rightarrow (A \Rightarrow C))\,,$$

$$App_{A,B} : \frac{A \Rightarrow B \quad A}{B}\,.$$

Here is an example of a proof. Let A and B be any functionalities, $C = B \Rightarrow A$, $D = A \Rightarrow C$, $E = A \Rightarrow A$, $F = A \Rightarrow (C \Rightarrow A)$, $G = D \Rightarrow E$. The term

$$App_{D,E}(App_{F,G}(S_{A,C,A}, K_{A,C}), K_{A,B})$$

has type E; i.e., it gives a proof of the proposition $A \Rightarrow A$.

We express formally that proof M proves proposition P in the inference system Σ as:

$$\Sigma \vdash M : P\,.$$

That is, we think of a theorem as the type of its proof tree. Proof-checking is identified with type-checking. Here this is a simple consistency check; that is, if operator F is declared in Σ as: $F : P_1, \ldots, P_n \to Q$ and if $\Sigma \vdash M_i : P_i$ for $1 \leq i \leq n$, then $\Sigma \vdash F(M_1, \ldots, M_n) : Q$.

2.4 *Polymorphism: Rule Schemas*

This next level of generality consists in allowing variables in the propositional terms. This is very natural, since it internalizes the meta-variables used to index families of inference rules as propositional variables. The rules of inference become thus *polymorphic* operators, whose types are expressions containing free variables. This is the traditional notion of schematic inference rule from mathematical logic: each rule is a schema, denoting a family of operators, whose types are all instances of the clause.

Example The example from the previous section is more naturally expressed in this polymorphic formalism. We replace the set Φ_0 by a set of variables V, and now we have just three rules of inference: K, S, and App.

Type-checking is now explained in terms of instantiation. Let Σ be the current signature of polymorphic operators. We define what it means for a tree T to be *consistently typed* of type τ in theory Σ, which we write $\Sigma \vdash T : \tau$. The definition is by induction on the size of T. Assume that $F : Q_1; Q_2; \ldots; Q_n \to P$ is in Σ, and that for some substitution σ we have $\Sigma \vdash T_i : \sigma(Q_i)$ for all $1 \leq i \leq n$. Then we get $\Sigma \vdash F(T_1, \ldots, T_n) : \sigma(P)$.

The types can actually be completely dispensed with, since a well typed term possesses a most general type, called its *principal type*. For instance, in the example above, the proof $App(App(S, K), K)$ has the principal type $A \Rightarrow A$, with $A \in V$. This term is usually written $I = SKK$ in combinatory logic, where the concrete syntax convention is to write combinator strings to represent sequences of applications associated to the left.

The notion of principal type, first discovered by Hindley in the combinatory logic context, and independently by Milner for ML type-checking [129], is actually completely general.

Theorem (The Principal Type Theorem)
Let Σ be any signature of polymorphic operators over a functor signature Φ. Let M be a legal proof term. Then M possesses a principal type $\tau \in T(\Phi, V)$. That is, $\Sigma \vdash M : \tau$, and for all $\tau' \in T(\Phi, V)$, $\Sigma \vdash M : \tau'$ implies $\tau \leq \tau'$.

Proof Simple induction, using the properties of the principal unifier. Let $T = F(T_1, \ldots, T_n)$, with $\Sigma \vdash T : M$. This means that $F : Q_1; Q_2; \ldots; Q_n \to P$ is in Σ, and that $M = \sigma(P)$, with $\Sigma \vdash T_i : \sigma(Q_i)$. By the induction hypothesis, $\Sigma \vdash T_i : \tau_i$, with τ_i principal. Thus for some ρ_i we have $\sigma(Q_i) = \rho_i(\tau_i)$. We may assume without loss of generality that the τ_i are renamed so that they have no variable in common, and no variable in common with the defining clause for F. Thus the tuples $< \ldots, Q_i, \ldots >$ and $< \ldots, \tau_i, \ldots >$ are simultaneously unifiable, and their principal unifier θ gives a tuple $< \ldots, N_i, \ldots >$ such that $N_i = \theta(Q_i) = \theta(\tau_i)$. The construction defines $\tau = \theta(P)$ having the required properties. $\square$

By now we have developed enough formalism to make sense out of our "propositions as types" paradigm. Actually, the example we have discussed above is the fragment of propositional logic known as "minimal logic". When regarding the functor $\Rightarrow$ as (intuitionistic) implication, and *App* as the usual inference rule of Modus ponens, K and S are the two axioms of minimal logic presented as a Hilbert calculus. Combinatory logic is thus the calculus of proofs in minimal logic [50, 103].

Actually combinators don't just have a type, they have a value. They can be *defined* with definition equations in terms of application. Using the concrete syntax mentioned above, we get, for instance, K and S defined by the following equations:

$$Def_K : \; K\,x\,y = x\,,$$

$$Def_S : \; S\,x\,y\,z = x\,z\,(y\,z)\,.$$

Exercise Verify that the two equations above, when seen as unification constraints, define the expected principal types for K and S.

This point of view of considering equality axiomatizations of the proof structures corresponds to what the proof-theorists call *cut elimination.* That is, the two equations above can be used as rewrite rules in order to eliminate redundancies corresponding to useless detours in the proofs. We shall develop more completely this point of view of *computation as proof normalization* below.

The current formalism of inference rules typed by terms with variables corresponds to intuitionistic sequents in proof theory and to Horn clauses in automated reasoning. For instance, a PROLOG [33] interpreter may be seen in this framework as a proof synthesis method. Given an alphabet Σ of polymorphic inference rules (usually called definite clauses), and a proposition τ over functor alphabet Φ, it returns (when possible) a proof term M such that M is a legal Σ-proof term consistently typed with type τ' instance of τ:

$$\Sigma \vdash M : \tau' \geq \tau.$$

With σ the principal unifier of τ and the principal type of M, we say that σ is a PROLOG *answer* to the *query* τ. Of course this explanation is incomplete; we have to explain that PROLOG finds all such instances by a backtrack procedure constructing proofs in a top-down, left-to-right fashion, using operators from Σ in a specific order (the order in which clauses are declared);

this last requirement leads to incompleteness, since PROLOG may loop with recursively composable operators, whereas a different order might lead to termination of the procedure. Also, PROLOG may be presented several goals together, and they may share certain variables, but this may be explained by a simple extension of the above proof-synthesis explanation.

We claim that this explanation of PROLOG is more faithful to reality than the usual one with Horn clauses. In particular, our explanation is completely constructive, and we do not have to explain the processes of conjunctive normalization and Skolemization. Furthermore, there is no distinction in Φ between predicate and function symbols, consistently with most PROLOG implementations. Actually, we even allow polymorphic signatures that would not be accepted as definite clauses, since some of the types may be reduced to single variables, like for *App* above.

2.5 *Allowing Lemmas*

The next convenience in a general formalism for manipulating proofs consists in providing the user with a facility to derive and use lemmas.

Let us use the notation $\pi_\Sigma(M)$ to denote the principal type of the (legal) Σ-term M. Thus we have

$$\Sigma \vdash M : \pi_\Sigma(M).$$

It is now possible to use M as a lemma, choosing to name it with a symbol *name* not in Σ, using the new term constructor: *let name* $=$ *M in N*. The term N is a proof term constructed in Σ, enriched with the new (nullary operator) constant *name*. More precisely, the legal proofs using lemmas are defined using the rule:

$$\Sigma \vdash let\ name\ =\ M\ in\ N : \tau \Longleftrightarrow \Sigma \cup \{name :\ \pi_\Sigma(M)\} \vdash N : \tau.$$

Example Using the minimal logic combinators above, i.e., $\Sigma = \{K, S, App\}$, derive:

$$\Sigma \vdash let\ I\ =\ S\ K\ K\ \ in\ \ I\ I\ \ :\ A \Rightarrow A.$$

This shows that constant I is used in a polymorphic way, similarly to the basic combinators from Σ, since its two occurrences in $App(I, I)$ above are typed with two distinct instances of its principal type $\pi_\Sigma(S\ K\ K)\ =\ (A \Rightarrow A)$.

Remark 1 The complexity of ML's type computation algorithm has been recently analysed by Kanellakis and Mitchell [92]. Rather surprisingly, the problem was shown to be PSPACE hard. This stands in contrast to the linear time algorithm, which may be used to compute principal types in the principal type theorem above. This may be explained intuitively as follows. Lambda expressions typable in the simple type discipline possess a principal type which is computable in linear time, like for combinatory logic above. ML's polymorphism, and typing complexity, arises from the *let* construct. Intuitively, *let* expressions are marked redexes whose parallel reduction is simulated by ML's typing algorithm. The exponential factor comes from a possible blow-up in the size of the corresponding reduced term, due to embeddings of *let*'s. This potential exponential blow-up does not seem to be practically problematical, since programmers do not usually write expressions with a high level of *let* nesting.

Remark 2 We might more generally expect a facility to use derived inference rules. But here we have a notational difficulty, in order to explain how the free variables from the principal types of the argument proofs are shared, since in the *let* constant declaration mechanism above we kept the type of M implicit. In standard mathematical practice we think of lemmas as names of propositions (i.e., types) than proofs. Thus instead of derived inference rules we tend to use proofs modulo hypotheses. This level of term description corresponds to λ-calculus, which we shall now study.

3 *Combinatory Algebra and λ-Calculus*

3.1 *Proofs with Variables: Sequents*

We first come back to the general theory of proof structures. We assume the alphabet Σ of rules of inference to be fixed, and thus we abbreviate $\Sigma \vdash M : N$ as $\vdash_\Sigma M : N$ or even $\vdash M : N$ when Σ is clear from the context.

We saw earlier that the Hilbert presentation of minimal logic was not very natural, in that the trivial theorem $A \Rightarrow A$ necessitated a complex proof $S\ K\ K$. The problem is that in practice one does not use just proof terms, but *deductions* of the form

$$\Gamma \vdash A,$$

where Γ is a set of (hypothetic) propositions.

Deductions are exactly proof terms *with variables*. Naming these hypothesis variables and the proof term, we write:

$$\{\ldots [x_i : A_i] \ldots \mid i \leq n\} \vdash M : A,$$

with $V(M) \subseteq \{x_1, \ldots, x_n\}$. Such formulas are called *sequents*. Since this point of view is not very well known, let us emphasize this observation:

Sequents represent proof terms with variables.

Note that so far our notion of proof construction has not changed: $\Gamma \vdash_\Sigma M : A$ iff $\vdash_{\Sigma \cup \Gamma} M : A$; i.e., the hypotheses from Γ are used as supplementary axioms, in the same way that in the very beginning we have defined $T(\Sigma, V)$ as $T(\Sigma \cup V)$.

In the next section, we assume fixed the combinatory algebra proof system: $\Sigma = \{K, S, App\}$.

3.2 *The Deduction Theorem*

This theorem, fundamental for doing proofs in practice, gives an equivalence between proof terms with variables and functional proof terms:

$$\Gamma \cup \{A\} \vdash B \;\Leftrightarrow\; \Gamma \vdash A \Rightarrow B\,.$$

That is, in our notations:

a) $\Gamma \vdash M : A \Rightarrow B \;\Rightarrow\; \Gamma \cup \{x : A\} \vdash (M\ x) : B$. This direction is immediate, using App, i.e., Modus Ponens.

b) $\Gamma \cup \{x : A\} \vdash M : B \;\Rightarrow\; \Gamma \vdash [x]M : A \Rightarrow B$ where the term $[x]M$ is given by the following algorithm.

Schönfinkel's Abstraction Algorithm

$$
\begin{aligned}
[x]x &= I, && (= S\,K\,K), \\
[x]M &= K\,M, && \text{if } M \text{ atom (variable or constant)} \neq x, \\
[x](M\,N) &= S\ [x]M\ [x]N.
\end{aligned}
$$

Note that this algorithm motivates the choice of combinators S and K (and optionally I). Again we stress a basic observation:

Schönfinkel's algorithm is the essence
of the proof of the deduction theorem.

Now let us consider the rewriting system R defined by the rules:

$$Def_K : \ K\,x\,y = x,$$

$$Def_S : \ S\,x\,y\,z = ((x\ z)\ (y\ z)),$$

optionally supplemented by:

$$Def_I : I\,x = x\,,$$

and let us write $\triangleright$ for the corresponding reduction relation.

Fact $([x]M\ N) \ \triangleright^* \ M[x \leftarrow N]$.

We leave the proof of this very important property to the reader. The important point is that the abstraction operation, together with the application operator and the reduction $\triangleright$, define a *substitution* machinery. We shall now use this idea more generally, in order to internalize the deduction theorem in a basic calculus of functionality. That is, we forget the specific combinators S and K, in favor of abstraction seen now as a new term constructor.

Remark 1 Other abstraction operations may be defined. For instance, the *strong* abstraction algorithm is more economical:

$$\begin{array}{ll} [x]x = I\,, & \\ [x]M = K\,M\,, & \text{if } x \text{ does not occur in } M\,, \\ [x](M\,x) = M\,, & \text{if } x \text{ does not occur in } M\,, \\ [x](M\,N) = S\ [x]M\ [x]N\,, & \text{otherwise}\,. \end{array}$$

Remark 2 The computation relation $\triangleright$ of combinatory algebra is confluent. Actually, it is defined by a particularly simple case of necessarily sequential rewrite rules. It is compatible with the term structure of combinatory algebra, and in particular with application. But it is not compatible with the derived operation of abstraction, and thus the ξ rule of λ-conversion is not valid. That is, combinatory computation simulates only weak β-reduction.

As in λ-calculus, there are typed and untyped versions of combinatory algebra.

Combinators other than K, S, and I have been considered. A general combinator is defined by a rewrite rule:

$$C\,x_1\,x_2\,\ldots\,x_n := M,$$

where the left-hand side stands for the pattern $App(\cdots App(C, x_1)\cdots, x_n)$, and the right-hand side is an arbitrary term constructed from the x_i's, App, and previously defined combinators.

A set of combinators is said to form a *basis* if it is sufficient to derive an abstraction algorithm (equivalently, if S and K are definable from the set). The state of the art about combinatory completeness is described in Statman [174].

3.3 *Typed λ-Calculus*

We now abandon the first-order term structures of combinatory algebra and turn to λ-calculi. We first consider *typed* λ-calculus, where the set of types $\mathcal{T}$ is defined as the set of terms constructed over some functor alphabet Φ containing the binary functor $\Rightarrow$. We write $\mathcal{T}^*$ for the set of finite sequences of types, with 1 the empty sequence and $\Gamma \times A$ the sequence obtained from sequence Γ by adding one more type A.

We define recursively a relation $\Gamma \vdash M : A$, read "M is a *term* of *type* A in *context* Γ", where $A \in \mathcal{T}$ and $\Gamma \in \mathcal{T}^*$, as follows:

Variable : If $1 \le n \le |\Gamma|$ then $\Gamma \vdash n : \Gamma_n$.
Abstraction : If $\Gamma \times A \vdash M : B$ then $\Gamma \vdash [A]M : A \Rightarrow B$.
Application : If $\Gamma \vdash M : A \Rightarrow B$ and $\Gamma \vdash N : A$ then $\Gamma \vdash (M\ N) : B$.

Thus a term may be a natural number, or may be of the form $[A]M$ with A a type and M a term, or may be of the form $(M\ N)$ with M, N two terms.

We thus obtain typed λ-terms with variables coded as de Bruijn's indexes [16], i.e., as integers denoting their reference depth (distance in the tree to their binder). This representation avoids all the renaming problems associated with actual names (α conversion), but we shall use such names whenever we give examples of terms. For instance, the term $[A](1\ [B](1\ 2))$ shall be presented under a concrete representation such as $[x : A](x\ [y : B](y\ x))$. In Church's original notation, the left bracket was a λ and the right bracket a dot, typing being indicated by superscripting, like: $\lambda x^A \cdot (x\ \lambda y^B \cdot (y\ x))$.

Note that the relation $\Gamma \vdash M : A$ is functional, in that A is uniquely determined from Γ and M. Thus the definition above may be interpreted as the recursive definition of a function $A = \tau_\Gamma(M)$.

The set $\mathcal{T}$ of types used in the λ-terms has been defined as all terms constructed from Φ containing $\Rightarrow$. The ordinary Curry-Church λ-calculus is obtained when $\Phi = \{\Rightarrow\} \cup \mathcal{T}_0$, where $\mathcal{T}_0$ is a finite set of atomic types, for instance, $\{bool, int\}$. But we may include other functors in Φ. The proofs of the intuitionistic version *NK* of Gentzen's natural deduction system may be represented by typed λ-terms, over the alphabet of functors defined by the propositional connectives.

3.4 *Computation*

We are now ready to define the *computation* relation $\triangleright$ as follows:

$$([A]M\ N) \triangleright M\{N\}\,, \qquad (\beta)$$

$$M \triangleright M' \Longrightarrow [A]M \triangleright [A]M'\,, \qquad (\xi)$$

$$M \rhd M' \Longrightarrow (M\ N) \rhd (M'\ N)\,,$$

$$M \rhd M' \Longrightarrow (N\ M) \rhd (N\ M')\,.$$

It is clear that computation preserves the types of terms. The computation relation presented above is traditionally called (strong) β-reduction. It is confluent and nœtherian (because of the types!), and thus every term possesses a canonical form, obtainable by iterating computation nondeterministically. Another valid conversion rule is η-conversion:

$$[x : A](M\ x) \ = \ M \qquad (\eta)$$

whenever x does not appear in M.

3.5 *Weak Reduction*

There are many variations on λ-calculus. What we have just presented is typed λ-calculus, with Curry-Church types. The notion of computation $\rhd$ is strong β reduction. It is also interesting to consider a weak reduction, obtained by not allowing rule ξ above. Thus, weak reduction is not compatible with the abstraction operator [ ]. As we have already seen, λ-calculus may be translated into combinatory algebra, but the natural computation rule associated with the set of combinator definitions seen as term rewriting system corresponds then to weak reduction, *not* strong reduction.

3.6 *Pure λ-Calculus*

If we remove the types, we get the theory of pure λ-calculus. The set of pure lambda terms is defined as:

$$\lambda = \bigcup_{n \geq 0} \lambda_n$$

where the set λ_n of λ-terms with n potential free variables is defined inductively by:

$$i \in \lambda_n \qquad \text{if } 1 \leq i \leq n\,,$$

$$[\,]M \in \lambda_n \qquad \text{if } M \in \lambda_{n+1}\,,$$

$$(M\ N) \in \lambda_n \qquad \text{if } M, N \in \lambda_n\,.$$

As we did previously, we get readable concrete syntax by sticking variable names in the brackets, as in $[x]\,x$. The terms in λ_0 are the *closed* pure λ-terms. Analogous untyped versions of the rules above define analogous computation rules. Sometimes syntactic properties are easier to prove in pure λ-calculus. For instance, the confluence property in typed calculi is an easy consequence of the corresponding property in the pure calculus, if we remark that computation preserves typing. The classical method, due to Tait and Martin-Löf [4], consists in proving that the relation $\trianglerighteq$ is strongly confluent, with $\trianglerighteq$ defined as the reflexive and compatible closure of:

$$\frac{M \trianglerighteq M' \quad N \trianglerighteq N'}{([\,]M\ N) \trianglerighteq M'\{N'\}}.$$

It is easy to check that indeed $\trianglerighteq$ and $\triangleright$ have the same reflexive-transitive closure, whence the result. As we saw for regular term rewriting system, such a "parallel moves" theorem is actually much stronger than strong confluence, since it corresponds to the existence of pushouts in an appropriate category of computations. The theory of λ-calculus derivations is worked out in detail in J.J. Lévy's thesis [108, 109]. Note that contrarily to the theory of regular term rewriting systems, the parallel reduction $\trianglerighteq$ is not limited to parallel disjoint redexes, since in λ-calculus residuals of a redex may not be disjoint. For instance, consider $([u](u\ u)\ \ [v]([x]v\ y))$.

The theory of β-η-reduction is rather complicated. Actually, note that there is a critical pair between the two rules, since $([x](M\ x)\ N)$ contains conflicting redexes for the two rules. Fortunately, the two rules reduce to the same term $(M\ N)$. However, the two rules are usually dealt with separately, since it can be shown that η conversions can be postponed after β reductions. In the following, we write $\triangleright$ for the β-reduction rule, and $\equiv$ for its associated congruence. The theory of β-reduction is similar to the theory of regular term rewriting systems. Certain results are simpler. For instance, the standardization theorem has a simpler form, since the standard derivation always reduces the leftmost needed redex. Others are more complicated, due to the residual embedding noted earlier.

Certain theorems are identical for the pure calculus and for the typed case. Other aspects of pure λ-calculus differ from the typed version. In the pure calculus, some terms do not always admit normal forms. For instance, with $\Delta = [u](u\ u)$ and $\bot = (\Delta\ \Delta)$, we get $\bot \triangleright \bot \triangleright \ldots$. A more interesting example is given by

$$Y = [f]([u](f\ (u\ u))\ \ [u](f\ (u\ u)))$$

since $(Y\ M) \equiv (M\ (Y\ M))$ shows that Y defines a general fixpoint operator. Y is called the *Curry* fixpoint operator. Other fixpoint operators are known. For instance, the *Turing* fixpoint operator is defined as:

$$\Theta = ([x]\,[y](y\ (x\ x\ y))\ \ [x]\,[y](y\ (x\ x\ y))),$$

and it verifies the stronger property that for every M we have

$$(\Theta\ M)\ \trianglerighteq^*\ (M\ (\Theta\ M))\,.$$

Exercise Show that $\Phi = [\varphi]\,[f]\,(f\ (\varphi\ f))$ is a generator of fixpoints, in that M is a fixpoint combinator iff $\Phi(M) \equiv M$.

The existence of fixpoint operators, and the easy encoding of arithmetic notions in pure λ-calculus, make it a computationally complete formalism: all partial recursive functions are definable. We shall not develop further this aspect of λ-calculus, but we just remark that it entails the undecidability of most syntactic properties. Thus ≡ is an undecidable relation, and it is generally undecidable whether a given term is normalizable or not.

We are mostly concerned here with the application of λ-calculus to logic. And one may worry about the interpretation of fixpoints of propositional connectives such as negation. The next section shows that indeed pure λ-calculus is logically problematic.

3.7 *Curry's Version of Russell's Paradox*

Our framework is minimal logic, with propositions represented as pure λ-expressions. That is, we assume that ⇒ is a constant of the calculus. We assume that we have as rules of inference:

$$A \Rightarrow B\,,\ A \vdash B\,, \qquad (App)$$

$$\vdash A \Rightarrow A\,, \qquad (I)$$

$$\vdash (A \Rightarrow (A \Rightarrow B)) \Rightarrow (A \Rightarrow B)\,. \qquad (W)$$

It is easy to see that (W) is valid in minimal logic (consider $[u : A \Rightarrow (A \Rightarrow B)]\,[v : A]\,(u\ v\ v)$). Now consider an arbitrary proposition X. Let us define $N = [A]A \Rightarrow X$, and let $M = (Y\ N)$. N is in a way the minimal meaning for negation, and M is a fixpoint of it. That is:

$$M \equiv (M \Rightarrow X)\,. \qquad (*)$$

Now we get $M \Rightarrow M$ from I_M, and thus $M \Rightarrow (M \Rightarrow X)$ by $(*)$ used as an equality. Using *App* and W we infer $M \Rightarrow X$, and thus M using $(*)$ in the reverse direction. A final use of *App* yields X, which is an arbitrary proposition, and thus the logic is inconsistent [50].

Thus combinatory completeness of the pure λ-calculus at the level of propositions is not compatible with the logical completeness issued from the typed λ-calculus at the level of proofs.

Halfway between the typed and the pure calculus we find typed calculi where additional constants and reduction rules have been added. For instance, it is possible to add typed recursion operators in order to develop recursive arithmetic in a sound way [175].

3.8 *ML's Polymorphism*

We saw that formal systems could be pleasantly presented using polymorphic operators (inference rules) at the meta level. This possibility could be pushed at the user level, by allowing the user to extend the system with derived polymorphic constants. We also saw that λ-calculus allowed the user to do proofs modulo a set of hypotheses Γ. There is a fundamental difference, however, despite the apparent similarity, between the notations $\Sigma \vdash \ldots$ and $\Gamma \vdash \ldots$. That is, when a constant declaration $C : \tau$ is in Σ we allow it to be polymorphic, whereas when a variable declaration $x : \tau$ is in Γ we request its type τ to be a constant term.

There is no immediate possible extension of polymorphism to variables, because the implicit universal quantification of type variables does not commute well with abstraction, because $\Rightarrow$ is contravariant on the left. We need to face up to this problem by introducing some explicit quantification for type variables. A weak form of such polymorphism is implemented in ML and explained below. A more general form will be explained in the section on polymorphic λ-calculus below.

This idea of type quantification corresponds to allowing proposition quantifiers in our propositional logic. First we allow a universal quantifier in prenex position. That is, with $T_0 = T(\Phi, V)$, we now introduce *type schemas* in $T_1 = T_0 \cup \forall\alpha \cdot T_1,\ \alpha \in V$. A (type) term in T_1 has thus both free and bound variables, and we write $FV(M)$ and $BV(M)$ for the sets of free (respectively bound) variables. We shall use systematically in the following the meta variables τ, τ', etc. for type schemes in T_1, whereas unquantified types from T_0 are denoted $\tau_0, \tau_0{}'$, etc.

We now define *generic instantiation.* Let $\tau = \forall\alpha_1 \ldots \alpha_m \cdot \tau_0 \in T_1$ and $\tau' = \forall\beta_1 \ldots \beta_n \cdot \tau'_0 \in T_1$. We define $\tau' \geq_G \tau$ iff $\tau'_0 = \sigma(\tau_0)$ with $D(\sigma) \subseteq \{\alpha_1, \ldots, \alpha_m\}$ and $\beta_i \notin FV(\tau)\ \ (1 \leq i \leq n)$. Note that $\geq$ acts on FV, whereas $\geq_G$ acts on BV. Also note

$$\tau' \geq_G \tau \ \Rightarrow\ \sigma(\tau') \geq_G \sigma(\tau)\,.$$

We now present the Damas-Milner inference system for polymorphic λ-calculus [52]. In what follows, a sequent hypothesis Γ is assumed to be a list of specifications $x_i : \tau_i$, with $\tau_i \in T_1$, and we write $FV(\Gamma) = \bigcup_i FV(\tau_i)$.

$$TAUT\ :\ \Gamma \vdash x : \tau, \quad (x : \tau \in \Gamma),$$

$$INST : \frac{\Gamma \vdash M : \tau}{\Gamma \vdash M : \tau'}, \quad (\tau \leq_G \tau'),$$

$$GEN : \frac{\Gamma \vdash M : \tau}{\Gamma \vdash M : \forall \alpha \cdot \tau}, \quad (\alpha \notin FV(\Gamma)),$$

$$APP : \frac{\Gamma \vdash M : \tau_0{}' \rightarrow \tau_0 \quad \Gamma \vdash N : \tau_0{}'}{\Gamma \vdash (M\ N) : \tau_0},$$

$$ABS : \frac{\Gamma \cup \{x : \tau_0{}'\} \vdash M : \tau_0}{\Gamma \vdash [x]M : \tau_0{}' \rightarrow \tau_0},$$

$$LET : \frac{\Gamma \vdash M : \tau' \quad \Gamma \cup \{x : \tau'\} \vdash N : \tau}{\Gamma \vdash let\ x = M\ in\ N : \tau}.$$

Note that here the context Γ stores both the variables (introduced with *ABS*) and the constants (introduced with *LET*). However, constants are allowed to be polymorphic, whereas variables are limited to ordinary types from T_0.

Example We get, for instance,

$$\vdash let\ i = [x]x\ in\ (i\ i) : \alpha \rightarrow \alpha,$$

whereas the term $[x](x\ x)$ cannot be typed in the system.

The above system may be extended without difficulty by other functors such as product, and by other ML constructions such as conditional, equality, and recursion:

$$PROD : \frac{\Gamma \vdash M : \tau \quad \Gamma \vdash N : \tau'}{\Gamma \vdash (M, N) : \tau \times \tau'},$$

$$FST : \Gamma \vdash fst : \forall \alpha\beta \cdot (\alpha \times \beta) \rightarrow \alpha,$$

$$SND : \Gamma \vdash snd : \forall \alpha\beta \cdot (\alpha \times \beta) \rightarrow \beta,$$

$$IF : \frac{\Gamma \vdash P : bool \quad \Gamma \vdash M : \alpha \quad \Gamma \vdash N : \alpha}{\Gamma \vdash if\ P\ then\ M\ else\ N : \alpha},$$

$$EQ : \Gamma \vdash = : \forall \alpha \cdot (\alpha \times \alpha) \rightarrow bool,$$

$$REC : \Gamma \vdash Y : \forall \alpha \cdot (\alpha \rightarrow \alpha) \rightarrow \alpha,$$

and we define $let\ rec\ x = M\ in\ N$ as an abbreviation for $let\ x = Y([x]M)\ in\ N$.

Every ML compiler contains a type checker implementing implicitly the above inference system. For instance, with the unary functor *list* and the following ML primitives: $[\,] : (list\ \alpha)$, $cons : \alpha \times (list\ \alpha)$ (written infix as a dot), $hd : (list\ \alpha) \rightarrow \alpha$, and $tl : (list\ \alpha) \rightarrow (list\ \alpha)$, we may define recursively the *map* functional as:

$$let\ rec\ map\ f\ l\ =\ if\ l = [\,]\ then\ [\,]\ else\ (f\ (hd\ l))\ \cdot\ map\ f\ (tl\ l),$$

and we get as its type:

$$\vdash\ map : (\alpha \to \beta) \to (list\ \alpha) \to (list\ \beta).$$

Of course the ML compiler is not implemented directly from the inference system above, which is nondeterministic because of rules *INST* and *GEN*. It uses unification instead and thus computes deterministically a principal type, which is minimum with respect to $\leq_G$.

Theorem (Milner)
Every typable expression of the polymorphic λ-calculus possesses a principal type, minimum with respect to generic instantiation [129].

ML is a strongly typed programming language, where type inference is possible because of the above theorem: the user need not write type specifications. The compiler of the language does more than type-checking, since it actually performs a proof synthesis. Types disappear at run time, but because of the type analysis no dynamic checks are needed to enforce the consistency of data operations, and this allows fast execution of ML programs. ML is actually a generic name for languages of the ML family. For instance, by adding exceptions, abstract data types (permitting, in particular, user-defined functors), and references, one gets approximately the meta-language of the LCF proof assistant [68]. By adding record type declarations (i.e., labeled sums and products) one gets L. Cardelli's ML [22]. By adding constructor types, pattern-matching, and concrete syntax, we get the ML presented in Chapter 1. A more complete language, including modules, is under design as Standard ML [130]. Current research topics on the design of ML -like languages are the incorporation of object-oriented features allowing subtypes, remanent data structures and bitmap operations [23], and "lazy evaluation" permitting streams and ZF expressions [187, 138].

As to the relationship between ML and λ-calculus, first, ML uses so-called call by value implementation of procedure call, corresponding to innermost reduction, as opposed to the outermost regime of the standard reduction. Next, lazy evaluation permits standard reductions, but closures (i.e., objects of a functional type $\alpha \to \beta$) are *not* evaluated. Finally, types in ML serve for ensuring the integrity of data operations but still allow infinite computations by nonterminating recursions.

Remark The typing rule for recursion is not as general as one might wish, since the bound recursive variable may not be used polymorphically inside the body. We may rather define *let rec x = M in N* as an abbreviation for *let x* $= \mu x \cdot M$ *in N*, where the μ binding operator obeys the typing rule:

$$MU : \frac{\Gamma \cup \{x : \tau\} \vdash M : \tau}{\Gamma \vdash \mu x \cdot M : \tau}.$$

With this new convention, we may now type-check terms such as:

$$let\ K = [x]\,[y]x \ \ in\ \ let\ rec\ F = [x](F\ (K\ x)).$$

However, it is not known whether such an extended system admits a principal typing algorithm[132] (and even whether type-checking stays indeed decidable).

3.9 *The Limits of ML's Polymorphism*

Consider the following ML definition:

$$let\ rec\ power\ n\ f\ u \ = \ if\ n = 0\ then\ u\ else\ f\ (power\ (n-1)\ f\ u)$$

of type $nat \rightarrow (\alpha \rightarrow \alpha) \rightarrow (\alpha \rightarrow \alpha)$. This function, which associates to natural n the polymorphic iterator mapping function f to the nth power of f, may be considered a coercion operator between ML 's internal naturals and Church's representation of naturals in pure λ-calculus [30]. Let us recall briefly this representation. Integer 0 is represented as the projection term $[f]\,[u]u$. Integer 1 is $[f]\,[u](f\ u)$. More generally, n is represented as the functional $\bar{n}$ iterating a function f to its nth power:

$$\bar{n} = [f]\,[u](f\,(f\ \ldots(f\ u)\ldots)),$$

and the arithmetic operators may be coded respectively as:

$$n + m = [f]\,[u](n\ f\ (m\ f\ u)),$$

$$n \times m = [f](n\ (m\ f)),$$

$$n^m = (m\ n).$$

For instance, with $\bar{2} = [f]\,[u](f\ (f\ u))$, we check that $\bar{2} \times \bar{2}$ converts to its normal form $\bar{4}$.

We would like to consider a type

$$NAT = \forall\alpha \cdot (\alpha \rightarrow \alpha) \rightarrow (\alpha \rightarrow \alpha)$$

and be able to type the operations above as functions of type $NAT \rightarrow NAT \rightarrow NAT$. However the notion of polymorphism found in ML does not support such a type; it allows only the weaker

$$\forall\alpha \cdot ((\alpha \rightarrow \alpha) \rightarrow (\alpha \rightarrow \alpha)) \rightarrow ((\alpha \rightarrow \alpha) \rightarrow (\alpha \rightarrow \alpha)) \rightarrow ((\alpha \rightarrow \alpha) \rightarrow (\alpha \rightarrow \alpha)),$$

which is inadequate, since it forces the *same* generic instantiation of NAT in the two arguments.

4 Polymorphic λ-Calculus

The example above suggests using the universal type quantifier *inside* type formulas. We thus consider a functor alphabet based on one binary → constructor and one quantifier ∀. We shall now consider a λ-calculus with such types, which we shall call *second-order* or *polymorphic λ-calculus*, owing to the fact that the type language is now a second-order propositional logic, with propositional variables explicitly quantified. In order to emphasize this connection, we actually write ⇒ instead of →. In this calculus, we shall be able to form types (propositions) such as:

$$(\forall A \cdot A \Rightarrow A) \Rightarrow (\forall A \cdot A \Rightarrow A).$$

Such a calculus was proposed by J. Y. Girard [63, 64] and independently discovered by J. Reynolds [155].

4.1 The Inference System

We now have two kinds of variables, the variables bound by λ-abstraction and the propositional variables. Each kind will have its own de Bruijn indexing scheme, but we put both kinds of bindings in one context sequence, in order to ensure that in a λ-binding $[x : P]$ the free propositional variables of P are correctly scoped. A *context* Γ is thus a sequence of bindings $[x : P]$ and of bindings $[A : Prop]$. We use de Bruijn indexes $V(n)$ and $P(n)$ to reference respectively the two kinds of variables. However, there is a slight difficulty if one tries to adhere too strictly to de Bruijn's notation. Consider the context $\Gamma = [A : Prop]\,[x : A]\,[B : Prop]$. In concrete syntax, we write $\Gamma \vdash x : A$. But if we use de Bruijn's indexes for propositional names, we get in the abstract syntax $\Gamma \vdash V(1) : P(2)$; i.e., the propositions have to be relocated.

In order to remedy this notational difficulty, we shall assume a mixed naming scheme, allowing concrete names for free variables of expressions as well as integers for bound variables. The binding operation $[x : P]M$ denotes now the abstract $[P]M'$, where M' is M where every occurrence of x is replaced by the correct de Bruijn's index. Similarly we provide a binding operation $\forall A \cdot P$

for propositional variables. Finally an operation $\Lambda A \cdot M$ binds a propositional variable in a term.

A context Γ is said to be *valid* if it binds variables with well-formed propositions. Thus the empty context is valid; if Γ is valid and does not bind A, then $\Gamma[A : Prop]$ is valid; and finally if Γ is valid and does not bind x, then $\Gamma[x : P]$ is valid provided $\Gamma \vdash P : Prop$. This last judgement (propositional formation) is defined recursively as follows:

$$\frac{[A : Prop] \in \Gamma}{\Gamma \vdash A : Prop},$$

$$\frac{\Gamma \vdash P : Prop \qquad \Gamma \vdash Q : Prop}{\Gamma \vdash P \Rightarrow Q : Prop},$$

$$\frac{\Gamma[A : Prop] \vdash P : Prop}{\Gamma \vdash \forall A \cdot P : Prop}.$$

Let us now give the term-formation rules. We have two more constructors: $\Lambda A \cdot M$, which makes a term polymorphic by $\forall$-introduction, and $< M\ P >$, which instantiates the polymorphic term M over the type corresponding to proposition P, by $\forall$-elimination.

$$Var \ : \ \frac{[x : P] \in \Gamma}{\Gamma \vdash x : P},$$

$$Abstr \ : \ \frac{\Gamma \vdash P : Prop \qquad \Gamma[x : P] \vdash M : Q}{\Gamma \vdash [x : P]M : P \Rightarrow Q},$$

$$Appl \ : \ \frac{\Gamma \vdash M : P \Rightarrow Q \qquad \Gamma \vdash N : P}{\Gamma \vdash (M\ N) : Q},$$

$$Gen \ : \ \frac{\Gamma[A : Prop] \vdash M : P}{\Gamma \vdash \Lambda A \cdot M : \forall A \cdot P},$$

$$Inst \ : \ \frac{\Gamma \vdash M : \forall A \cdot P \qquad \Gamma \vdash Q : Prop}{\Gamma \vdash < M\ Q > : P\{Q\}_P}.$$

We do not make explicit the propositional substitution operation $P\{Q\}_P$, which is defined similarly to the λ-calculus substitution $M\{N\}$ seen previously. The latter will be denoted here by $M\{N\}_V$.

Proposition 1

If Γ is valid, then $\Gamma \vdash M : P$ implies $\Gamma \vdash P : Prop$.

We leave the proof of such easy (but tedious) lemmas to the patient reader.

Let us now give an example of a derivation. Let $Id := \Lambda A \cdot [x : A]x$. Id is the polymorphic identity algorithm, and we check easily that $\vdash Id : One$, where

$One := \forall A \cdot A \Rightarrow A$. Note that indeed *One* is well formed in the empty context. Now we may instantiate *Id* over its own type *One*, yielding: $\vdash <Id\ One>: One \Rightarrow One$. The resulting term may thus be applied to *Id*, yielding: $\vdash (<Id\ One>\ Id) : One$.

Similarly, we can define a composition operator for proofs, whose type is the analogue of the cut, or detachment rule:
$[P : Prop]\ [Q : Prop]\ [R : Prop] \vdash [f : P \Rightarrow Q]\ [g : Q \Rightarrow R]\ [x : P]\,(g\ (f\ x)) : ((P \Rightarrow Q) \Rightarrow (Q \Rightarrow R) \Rightarrow (P \Rightarrow R))$.
We shall use the notation $f;g$ as a shorthand for the too cumbersome $(< Compose\ P\ Q\ R>\ f\ g)$, since the type arguments P, Q, and R can be retrieved as subparts of the types of f and g.

4.2 *The Conversion Rules*

The calculus admits two conversion rules. The first one is just β:

$$\beta \ : \ \frac{}{\Gamma \vdash ([x : P]M\ N) \rhd M\{N\}_V}\ .$$

The second one eliminates the cut formed by introducing and eliminating a quantification:

$$\beta' \ : \ \frac{}{\Gamma \vdash <\Lambda A \cdot M\ P> \rhd M\{P\}_P}\ .$$

Of course, we assume all other rules extending $\rhd$ as a term congruence, as usual. We may also consider analogues of the η rule.

Proposition 2

If Γ is valid, $\Gamma \vdash M : P$ and $\Gamma \vdash M \rhd N$ then $\Gamma \vdash N : P$.

4.3 *The Syntactic Interpretation*

We proceed as in the preceding section. Here, however, there are no primitive types. In order to have a nontrivial interpretation, we introduce a supplementary constant Ω to our untyped λ-terms. Let λ_Ω be the set of such terms, and let *SN* be the set of strongly normalizable terms of λ_Ω.

Definition A subset S of *SN* is said to be *saturated* if and only if

$$\forall N \in SN \quad (M\{N\}\ M_1\ \ldots\ M_n) \in S \Rightarrow ([\,]M\ N\ M_1\ \ldots\ M_n) \in S\,,$$

$$\Omega \in S\,,$$

$$N_1, \ldots, N_k \in SN \Rightarrow (\Omega\ N_1 \ldots N_k) \in S\,.$$

Note that in the first clause, we may limit ourselves to considering M and the M_i's in SN. We write Sat for the set of saturated subsets of SN.

We now define the interpretation I by defining for every term M its corresponding pure term $I(M) = \nu(M)$, where

$$\nu(V(n)) = n\,,$$

$$\nu([x : P]\,M) = [\,]\,\nu(M)\,,$$

$$\nu((M\ N)) = (\nu(M)\ \nu(N))\,,$$

$$\nu(\Lambda A \cdot M) = \nu(M)\,,$$

$$\nu(<M\ P>) = \nu(M)\,.$$

Note that $\nu(M)$ is a pure λ-term constructed over the list of free variables $\{x \mid [x : P] \in \Gamma\}$.

Finally, to every A such that $[A : Prop] \in \Gamma$ we associate an arbitrary saturated set $I(A)$. Let $I(\Gamma)$ be the product of all such $I(A)$'s. We define recursively the interpretation $I_{I(\Gamma)}(P)$ of a proposition P, such that $\Gamma \vdash P : Prop$, as follows:

$$I_G(P \Rightarrow Q) = \{M \mid \forall N \in I_G(P) \quad (M\ N) \in I_G(Q)\}\,,$$

$$I_G(\forall A \cdot P) = \bigcap_{S \in Sat} I_{G \times S}(P)\,,$$

$$I_G(A) = G_A\,.$$

Example $I(Id) = [\,]\,1$. $I(One)$ contains all strongly normalizable terms whose canonical form is $[\,]\,1$, plus strongly normalizable terms whose canonical form has head variable Ω.

4.4 *Basic Meta-Mathematical Properties*

The main use of the interpretation above is to prove the follwing theorem.

Theorem (Girard)
If Γ is valid and $\Gamma \vdash M : P$, then $I(M) \in I(P) \in Sat$.

Corollary 1
$\nu(M) \in SN$.

Corollary 2 (Strong Normalization)
The conversion $\triangleright$ on typed terms is nœtherian.
(Note that β' alone is nœtherian.)

Definition Let Γ be a valid context, with $\Gamma \vdash P : Prop$. We say that P is *inhabited* in Γ if and only if $I_{\mathcal{I}(\Gamma)}(P)$ contains a term without Ω's.

Note that if $\Gamma \vdash M : P$, then P is inhabited (by $\mathcal{I}(M)$). We now obtain the consistency of the logical system as follows.

Theorem (Soundness)
The type $\nabla = \forall A \cdot A$ is not inhabited.

Corollary
There is no term M which proves ∇.

Theorem (Undecidability (Löb))
The following problem is recursively unsolvable: Given a valid context Γ and a proposition P, with $\Gamma \vdash P : Prop$, find whether or not there exists an M such that $\Gamma \vdash M : P$.

The second-order λ-calculus does not admit principal types. For instance, we shall show below that the combinator K may be typed in several incompatible manners. We may still wonder whether it is decidable whether an arbitrary pure λ-term is typable in the system or not. This is an important open problem.

Problem Give a procedure which, given a pure λ-term T, decides whether or not there exist M and P such that $\vdash M : P$, with $T = \nu(M)$. Alternatively, show that the problem is undecidable.

4.5 *Examples of Polymorphic Proofs*

In this section, we demonstrate the power of expression of the second-order calculus by way of examples.

Intuitionistic Connectives We first show that the other propositional connectives are definable in the calculus. It is well known that the intuitionistic connectives are definable in the second-order propositional calculus. The encoding of conjunction was already proposed by Russell, as explained in Prawitz [150].

Let P and Q be two propositions. We define $P \wedge Q$ as the proposition:

$$P \wedge Q \;:=\; \forall A \cdot (P \Rightarrow Q \Rightarrow A) \Rightarrow A\,.$$

As usual, we associate implications to the right and applications to the left.

The definition above is a correct encoding of $\wedge$, as can be seen from the derivation of the standard rules of conjunction:

$$[P : Prop]\ [Q : Prop]\ [x : P]\ [y : Q] \vdash \Lambda A \cdot\ [h : P \Rightarrow Q \Rightarrow A](h\ x\ y) : P \wedge Q\,,$$

$$[P : Prop]\ [Q : Prop]\ [x : P \wedge Q] \vdash (< x\ P >\ \ [u : P]\ [v : Q]\, u) : P\,,$$

$$[P : Prop]\ [Q : Prop]\ [x : P \wedge Q] \vdash (< x\ Q >\ \ [u : P]\ [v : Q]\, v) : Q\,.$$

In order to understand this sort of definition, it is best to wonder what is the *operational* use of the concept one is trying to define. Once this is clear, the concept can be easily *programmed.* This *procedural interpretation* is faithful to the intuitionistic semantics. For instance, $P \wedge Q$ is a method for proving any proposition A, provided one has a proof that A follows from P and Q. Note that the proof of $\wedge$-introduction above is a pairing algorithm, the two projections being the proofs of $\wedge$-elimination on the left and on the right.

We may similarly "program" the (intuitionistic) sum $P+Q$ of two propositions P and Q:

$$P+Q\ := \ \forall A \cdot (P \Rightarrow A) \Rightarrow (Q \Rightarrow A) \Rightarrow A\,.$$

Sum elimination is proved by the conditional, or *case* expression:

$$[P : Prop]\ [Q : Prop] \vdash \Lambda A \cdot\ [u : P \Rightarrow A]\ [v : Q \Rightarrow A]\ [x : P+Q](< x\ A >\ \ u\ v)$$

$$: \forall A \cdot (P \Rightarrow A) \Rightarrow (Q \Rightarrow A) \Rightarrow (P+Q) \Rightarrow A.$$

The two sum introductions correspond to the two injections:

$$[P : Prop]\ [Q : Prop] \vdash$$
$$[x : P] \Lambda A \cdot\ [u : P \Rightarrow A]\ [v : Q \Rightarrow A](u\ x) : P \Rightarrow (P+Q)\,,$$

$$[P : Prop]\ [Q : Prop] \vdash$$
$$[y : Q] \Lambda A \cdot\ [u : P \Rightarrow A]\ [v : Q \Rightarrow A](v\ y) : Q \Rightarrow (P+Q)\,.$$

Classical Logic Classical reasoning is reasoning by contradiction. The contradiction, or absurd proposition, proves every proposition A by mere application:

$$\nabla\ :=\ \forall A \cdot A\,.$$

∇ has no proof, and may thus play the role of the truth-value *False.* Negating a proposition amounts to asserting that it implies ∇, whence the concept of negation:

$$\neg\ [A : Prop] \ := \ A \Rightarrow \nabla\,.$$

The Sheffer's stroke $A \mid B$ (read "A contradictory with B") may be defined as:

$$[A : Prop] \mid [B : Prop] \ := \ A \Rightarrow B \Rightarrow \nabla.$$

It is easy to show $\forall A \cdot \forall B \cdot (A \mid B) \Longleftrightarrow \neg(A \wedge B)$. The other classical connectives may be simply expressed in term of $\mid$:

$$[A : Prop] \supset [B : Prop] \ := \ A \mid \neg B\,,$$

$$[A : Prop] \vee [B : Prop] \ := \ (\neg A) \mid (\neg B)\,,$$

$$[A : Prop] \equiv [B : Prop] \ := \ (A \supset B)\,.$$

Let us call *classical closure* of proposition A its double negation:

$$C([A : Prop]) \ := \ \neg(\neg A)\,.$$

Every proposition denies its negation:

$$[A : Prop] \vdash [p : A]\ [q : \neg A]\,(q\ p) : A \Rightarrow C(A).$$

The reverse implication holds only of classical propositions:

$$Classical([A : Prop]) \ := \ C(A) \Rightarrow A\,.$$

We can show that $\nabla, \neg\,, \mid$ construct only classical propositions, and thus so do $\vee$ and $\supset$. Finally, $\wedge$ preserves the property of being classical, and thus $\equiv$ constructs also classical propositions.

Actually, classical reasoning consists in general in showing that a set of propositions $\{A_1, \ldots, A_n\}$ is contradictory. The connectives $\nabla, \neg\,, \mid$ express this notion for $n = 0, 1, 2$, respectively.

Let us remark that it is easy to prove the principle of the excluded middle:

$$[A : Prop] \vdash <Id\ C(A)> : \neg A \vee A\,.$$

Remark Many other encodings of the propositional connectives may be used. Let us give two alternate definitions for classical disjunction:

$$[A : Prop] \vee '\, [B : Prop] \ := \ C(A + B)\,,$$

$$[A : Prop] \vee ''\, [B : Prop] \ := \ \forall C \cdot Classical(C) \Rightarrow (A \Rightarrow C) \Rightarrow (B \Rightarrow C) \Rightarrow C\,.$$

We now turn to axiomatizing universal algebra and abstract data types.

Initial Algebras We first show how to formalize the elementary notions from algebra, in particular the notion of free algebra over a given signature. We start with the homogeneous case; that is, we assume in the following that contexts start with a proposition letter taken as unique sort: $[A : Prop]$.

For every $n \geq 0$, we define the *A-cardinal* $\overline{n}$ associated to n by induction:

$$\overline{0} = A\,,$$

$$\overline{n+1} = A \Rightarrow \overline{n}\,.$$

We define now the *functionality* $\varphi(\Sigma)$ associated to a signature Σ represented as a list of operators given with their arity, by:

$$\varphi(\varnothing) = A\,,$$

$$\varphi([F : n]\ \Sigma) = \overline{n} \Rightarrow \varphi(\Sigma)\,.$$

Such definitions are easily programmable in the meta-language.

We now obtain the *weakly initial algebra* associated to signature Σ by abstracting over the type given as carrier of the algebra:

$$I(\Sigma) = \forall A \cdot \varphi(\Sigma)\,.$$

Let us now consider an arbitrary Σ-algebra. That is, we assume we place ourselves in context Γ :

$$\Gamma = [A : Prop]\ [F_1 : \overline{n_1}]\ \cdots\ [F_s : \overline{n_s}]\,.$$

If $M : I(\Sigma)$ is an arbitrary construction of an element of the initial Σ-algebra, we call *image* of M in the Σ-algebra Γ the term $M^\Gamma = (<M\ A>\ \ F_1\ \cdots\ F_s)$. We remark that this term is well formed, with type A. This notion of image corresponds, classically, to taking the image of M by the unique Σ-morphism from $I(\Sigma)$ to Γ. For instance, when $M_1 : I(\Sigma)$, $M_2 : I(\Sigma)$, ... , $M_{n_k} : I(\Sigma)$, we get $(F_k\ M_1^\Gamma\ \cdots\ M_{n_k}^\Gamma) : A$. We define thus a F_k operator of arity n_k over $I(\Sigma)$, that we call the F_k-constructor, obtained in discharging Γ, and a list of n_k variables of type $I(\Sigma)$.

Definition Let Σ be an arbitrary signature of length s:

$$\Sigma = [F_1 : \overline{n_1}]\ \cdots\ [F_s : \overline{n_s}].$$

We define the set $Dat(\Sigma)$ of *data elements* of Σ as the set:

$$\{v(M) \mid M = \Lambda A \cdot [F_1 : \overline{n_1}]\ \cdots\ [F_s : \overline{n_s}]N \text{ with } N \text{ canonical}\}.$$

Remark The set of canonical elements in $\mathcal{I}(\Sigma)$ has too much redundancy if we do not assume the η rule of conversion. The data elements restrict consideration to the λ-terms in η-expanded normal form.

Theorem (Representation)
$Dat(\Sigma)$, structured with the constructors, is isomorphic to the initial algebra in the class of all Σ-algebras.

Exercise Prove the theorem above.

Examples of Data Types Let us now give a few examples. When $\Sigma = \emptyset$, we get $I(\Sigma) = \nabla$, the empty algebra. When $\Sigma = [i : 0]$, we get $I(\Sigma) = One := \forall A \cdot A \Rightarrow A$, and the i-constructor is $Id = \Lambda A \cdot [i : A]\, i$.

With $\Sigma = [t : 0]\, [f : 0]$, we get: $I(\Sigma) = Bool := \forall A \cdot A \Rightarrow A \Rightarrow A$, and the two constructors are the booleans of Church [30]:

$$True := \Lambda A \cdot [t : A]\, [f : A]\ t\,,$$

$$False := \Lambda A \cdot [t : A]\, [f : A]\ f\,.$$

When $\Sigma = [s : 1]\, [z : 0]$, we get $I(\Sigma) = Nat$, Church's naturals :

$$Nat := \forall A \cdot (A \Rightarrow A) \Rightarrow A \Rightarrow A\,,$$

$$S := [n : Nat]\Lambda A \cdot [s : A \Rightarrow A]\, [z : A]\ (s\ (<n\ A>\ \ s\ z))\,,$$

$$0 := \Lambda A \cdot [s : A \Rightarrow A]\, [z : A]\ z\,.$$

When $\Sigma = [c : 2]\, [n : 0]$, we get $I(\Sigma) = Bin$, the binary trees:

$$Bin := \forall A \cdot (A \Rightarrow A \Rightarrow A) \Rightarrow A \Rightarrow A\,,$$

$$Cons := [a_1 : Bin]\, [a_2 : Bin]\Lambda A \cdot [c : A \Rightarrow A \Rightarrow A]\, [n : A]$$
$$(c\ (<a_1\ A>\ \ c\ n)\ (<a_2\ A>\ \ c\ n))\,,$$

$$Nil := [A : Prop]\, [c : A \Rightarrow A \Rightarrow A]\, [n : A]\ n\,.$$

Generalization to Nonhomogeneous Algebras It is straightforward to generalize these notions to the nonhomogeneous case, introducing as many sorts as necessary. For instance, the list structure is axiomatized on two sorts A and B as follows:

$$List := \forall A, B \cdot (A \Rightarrow B \Rightarrow B) \Rightarrow B \Rightarrow B\,.$$

The operation of adding an element to a list is polymorphic. Let us consider the list schema, over proposition A:

$$List\ A\ := \forall B \cdot (A \Rightarrow B \Rightarrow B) \Rightarrow B \Rightarrow B\,.$$

We now define, in context $\Gamma = [A : Prop]$,

$$\begin{aligned} Add\ :=\ & [x : A]\,[L : (List\ A)]\Lambda B \cdot [c : A \Rightarrow B \Rightarrow B]\,[e : B] \\ & (c\ x\ (<L\ B>\ \ c\ e)) \\ & : \forall A \cdot A \Rightarrow (List\ A) \Rightarrow (List\ A)\,. \end{aligned}$$

We note the analogy with ML 's list constructor. Here the empty list is doubly polymorphic:

$$Empty\ := \Lambda A \cdot \Lambda B \cdot [c : A \Rightarrow B \Rightarrow B]\,[e : B]e\ \ : List\,.$$

More generally, we may define all the data structures corresponding to free algebras. We remark that the corresponding propositions are restricted to degree 2, with the degree δ defined as:

$$\delta(A) = 0\,, \qquad (A\ variable)\,,$$

$$\delta(\forall A \cdot M) = \delta(M)\,,$$

$$\delta(P \Rightarrow Q) = max\{1 + \delta(P), \delta(Q)\}\,.$$

Problem Generalize the representation theorem above to the nonhomogeneous case.

Second-Order Arithmetic Let us give a few examples of programs over naturals. Addition is obtained by iterating successor:

$$Plus\ := [m : Nat]\,[n : Nat](<n\ Nat>\ \ S\ m)\,.$$

Other definitions are possible. Multiplication is similarly obtained by iterating addition:

$$Times\ := [m : Nat]\,[n : Nat](<n\ Nat>\ \ (Plus\ m)\ 0)\,.$$

We may also "see" our naturals as polymorphic iterators. Another possible definition of multiplication of m and n would thus be the composition $m; n$.

Exponentiation is obtained by iterating multiplication:

$$Exp\ := [m : Nat]\,[n : Nat](<n\ Nat>\ \ (Times\ m)\ (S\ 0))\,.$$

Iterating a natural on a functional type may produce nonprimitive recursive functions; for instance we get Ackermann's function by diagonalization:

$$
\begin{aligned}
Ack \;:=\; & [n : Nat](<n\ (Nat \Rightarrow Nat)> \\
& \qquad ([f : Nat \Rightarrow Nat]\ [m : Nat]\ (<m\ Nat>\ f\ m)) \\
& \qquad S).
\end{aligned}
$$

Indeed, most (total) recursive functions are definable as proofs in this formal system.

Theorem (Girard [64]. See also [173])
Every recursive function provably total in second-order arithmetic is definable as a proof of type $Nat \Rightarrow Nat$ in the polymorphic λ-calculus.

Algebraic Programming We may consider the polymorphic λ-calculus a powerful applicative programming language. It is both poorer than ML, in that no universal recursion operator is available, and richer, in that it provides a more complicated type structure. The price to pay is that there is no algorithm for synthesizing a principal type.

This language is revolutionary, in that it confuses *data structures* and *control structures*. Here, a data structure is but an unfulfilled control structure, waiting for more arguments to be able to "compute itself out". Thus to each of the data types seen above corresponds naturally a control structure. For *One* it is just the identity algorithm. For *Bool* it is the notion of conditional; that is, if $b : Bool$ and $M : A$, $N : A$ are the two branches of the conditional, the expression *If b Then M Else N* may be implemented as $(< b\ A >\ M\ N) : A$. For *Nat*, the polymorphic natural $n : Nat$ may be thought of as the construction **`for i:= 1 to n do`**. Compare this with **`iterate n`**, as defined in 1.1.1. Note that equality to zero is easily defined as:

$$EqZero \;:=\; [n : Nat](<n\ Bool>\ \ [b : Bool]False\ True).$$

As remarked above, the conjunction connective builds in product. Writing alternatively $A \times B$ for $A \wedge B$ as defined above, we get the pairing and projection algorithms as proofs of $\wedge$-intro and $\wedge$-elim, respectively:

$$Pair \;:=\; \Lambda A, B \cdot [x : A]\ [y : B] \Lambda C \cdot [h : A \Rightarrow B \Rightarrow C](h\ x\ y),$$

$$Fst \;:=\; \Lambda A, B \cdot [x : A \times B](<x\ A>\ \ [u : A]\ [v : B]\ u),$$

$$Snd \;:=\; \Lambda A, B \cdot [x : A \times B](<x\ B>\ \ [u : A]\ [v : B]\ v).$$

Thus, for instance, for any types A and B, $<Fst\ A\ B>: A \times B \Rightarrow A$, just as in ML.

However, the sum constructor is different: there is no analogue of the operators **outl** and **outr** here, since all the functions we may define are total:

$$Case := \Lambda A,B \cdot [x : A+B]\Lambda C \cdot [u : A \Rightarrow C]\ [v : B \Rightarrow C](<x\ C>\ u\ v),$$

$$Inl := \Lambda A,B \cdot [x : A]\Lambda C \cdot [u : A \Rightarrow C]\ [v : B \Rightarrow C](u\ x),$$

$$Inr := \Lambda A,B \cdot [x : B]\Lambda C \cdot [u : A \Rightarrow C]\ [v : B \Rightarrow C](v\ x).$$

Primitive Recursion It is possible to represent standard program schemas by combinators. For instance, it is shown in [41] how to define simple primitive recursive schemes.

Ordinals All the propositions (types) considered above are very simple, since they are restricted to degree 2.

With more complex types, we may define richer data structures. For instance, Th. Coquand [38] has shown how to define ordinal notations, as an extension of the naturals above. We just enrich *Nat* with a limit operation, which associates an ordinal to a sequence of ordinals, represented as a function of domain *Nat*. We define thus:

$$Ord := \forall A \cdot ((Nat \Rightarrow A) \Rightarrow A) \Rightarrow (A \Rightarrow A) \Rightarrow A \Rightarrow A,$$

$$Olim := [\sigma{:}Nat{\Rightarrow}Ord]\Lambda A \cdot [li{:}(Nat{\Rightarrow}A){\Rightarrow}A]\ [s{:}A{\Rightarrow}A]$$
$$[z{:}A](li\ [n{:}Nat](<(\sigma\ n)\ A>\ li\ s\ z)),$$

$$Osucc := [\alpha : Ord]\Lambda A \cdot [li : (Nat \Rightarrow A) \Rightarrow A]\ [s : A \Rightarrow A]$$
$$[z : A]\ (s\ (<\alpha\ A>\ s\ z)),$$

$$Ozero := \Lambda A \cdot [li : (Nat \Rightarrow A) \Rightarrow A]\ [s : A \Rightarrow A]\ [z : A]\ z.$$

It is straightforward to coerce a natural into the corresponding ordinal, which defines the sequence of finite ordinals:

$$Finite := [n : Nat]\ (<n\ Ord>\ Osucc\ Ozero).$$

Note that we instantiate the polymorphic natural n over type *Ord*. Thus the meaning of type quantification is to quantify over an arbitrary proposition definable in the calculus, and not simply over some totality circumscribed to the construction at hand. In other words, the calculus is inherently *non-predicative*, and we are using this feature in an essential way.

The first transfinite ordinal, ω, may be simply obtained as limit of finite ordinals:

$$\omega := (Olim\ Finite)\,.$$

We may program over ordinals the same way we do with naturals:

$$Oplus := [\alpha : Ord]\,[\beta : Ord](<\beta\ Ord>\ Olim\ Osucc\ \alpha)\,,$$

$$Otimes := [\alpha : Ord]\,[\beta : Ord](<\beta\ Ord>\ Olim\ (Oplus\ \alpha)\ Ozero)\,,$$

$$Oexp := [\alpha : Ord]\,[\beta : Ord]\ (<\beta\ Ord>\ Olim\ (Otimes\ \alpha)\ (Osucc\ Ozero))\,.$$

Our ordinals are in fact *ordinal notations*, i.e., ordinals presented by fundamental sequences. In particular, (*Oplus* (*Osucc Ozero*) ω) and ω are two distinct constructions.

We may get the ordinal ϵ_0 as the iteration (*Oexp* ω (*Oexp* $\omega \cdots$)):

$$\epsilon_0 := (<\omega\ Ord>\ Olim\ (Oexp\ \omega)\ Ozero)\,.$$

We may now use ordinals to define functional hierarchies. First, we give preliminary definitions concerning integer functions:

$$Incr := [f : Nat \Rightarrow Nat]\ [n : Nat]\ (S\ (f\ n))\,,$$

$$Iter := [f : Nat \Rightarrow Nat]\ [n : Nat]\ (<n\ Nat>\ f\ n)\,,$$

$$Diag := [\sigma : Nat \Rightarrow Nat \Rightarrow Nat]\ [n : Nat]\ (\sigma\ n\ n)\,.$$

Schwichtenberg's fast hierarchy may be defined as:

$$Fast := [\alpha : Ord](<\alpha\ (Nat \Rightarrow Nat)>\ Diag\ Iter\ Osucc)\,,$$

and the slow hierarchy is defined similarly (note that we just change the successor argument):

$$Slow := [\alpha : Ord](<\alpha\ (Nat \Rightarrow Nat)>\ Diag\ Incr\ Osucc)\,.$$

It is to be noted that (*Fast* ϵ_0) is a total recursive function, but this fact is independent (i.e., undecidable) from Peano's arithmetic [60, 100].

5 *The Calculus of Constructions*

5.1 *Designing a Higher-Order System*

The first step consists in extending the polymorphic λ-calculus in order to allow the binding of proposition *schemas*. This permits the definition of propositional connectives within the formalism. For instance, in polymorphic λ-calculus, we defined $\wedge$ at the level of the meta-notation: $\wedge$ was just a macro of the meta-language expanding into a proposition of the formal system. Now we want to be able to write $\wedge$ as a combinator internally.

Next we abstract on such propositional connectives, leading to a higher-order propositional calculus. The first problem we encounter is a notational one. We shall have to distinguish between the proposition schemas, where some variable is functionally abstracted, and the propositions where the same variable is universally quantified.

Convention We shall keep the square brackets for functional abstraction and use parentheses for universal quantification, using the traditional notation $(x : A)M$.

The second extension consists in adding a first-order part, allowing quantification and abstraction on "elements". The natural question to investigate is: what are we going to choose as the types of the elements? The simplest decision is to follow once more the Curry-Howard paradigm: We already have the proofs, as elements of the types of the propositions. This gives us not only first-order logic, but higher-order logic as well, since an implication will play the role of a functional type, and thus we encompass Church's theory of types just because we shall have intuitionistic propositional calculus as a subsystem of the propositions. We may wonder why it is legitimate to use the proofs as elements: Aren't we presupposing some structure of our domains? Actually not, since the proofs are the bare bones of a functional type system: they are nothing more and nothing less than the λ-expressions of the right type.

Let us thus assume that we have propositions closed under quantification $(x : P)Q$ and abstraction $[x : P]\,Q$. The first remark is that implication becomes a derived notion: $P \Rightarrow Q$ is just a notational variant for $(x : P)Q$ in the special case when x does not occur in Q. What we shall now get is an intuitionistic version of Church's theory of types with dependent products.

5.2 The Calculus of Constructions, First Version

The Inference System Let us now introduce explicitly a constant *Prop* for the type of propositions. At the level of proofs $[P : Prop]M$ gives us what we wrote previously, $\Lambda P \cdot M$. Similarly, quantifying a proposition over *Prop*, as in $(P : Prop)Q$, gives us what we wrote previously, $\forall P \cdot Q$. This suggests unifying also the notation $<M\ P>$ with $(M\ N)$. We thus arrive at a very simple calculus.

The types of proposition schemas are formed by quantification over the constant *Prop*. Let us use the constant *Type* for denoting all such types. We thus have two "kinds" of types: the types in the sense of Church's type theory, which here are all the terms of type *Type*, and the types in the sense of the propositions as types principle, which are here all the terms of type *Prop*. In the following, we use the meta-variable K (for an arbitrary *kind*) to stand for either of the constants *Type* and *Prop*.

In all the following rules, Γ is assumed to be a valid context, where the rules for valid contexts are as follows.

The *empty context* {} is valid.

If Γ is a valid context which does not bind variable x and $\Gamma \vdash T : K$, then $\Gamma[x : T]$ is a valid context.

If Γ is a valid context which does not bind variable t, then $\Gamma[t : Type]$ is a valid context.

The first rule concerns accessing variables in a context:

$$Var : \frac{[x : T] \in \Gamma}{\Gamma \vdash x : T}.$$

The above rule is shorthand for $\Gamma \vdash Var(k) : T^{+(k-1)}$ when $\Gamma_k = [x : T]$.

We state that *Prop* is the only predefined atomic type:

$$Prop : \Gamma \vdash Prop : Type\,.$$

More types are obtained by quantification, seen as generalized product:

$$Product : \frac{\Gamma \vdash P : K \quad \Gamma[A : P] \vdash M : Type}{\Gamma \vdash (A : P)M : Type}.$$

Similarly, quantification on propositions gives more propositions:

$$Quant : \frac{\Gamma \vdash P : K \quad \Gamma[A : P] \vdash M : Prop}{\Gamma \vdash (A : P)M : Prop}.$$

Finally, we have term formation rules:

$$Abstr : \frac{\Gamma \vdash T : K \quad \Gamma[x : T] \vdash P : K' \quad \Gamma[x : T] \vdash M : P}{\Gamma \vdash [x : T]M : (x : T)P},$$

$$Appl: \frac{\Gamma \vdash M : (x:T)P \quad \Gamma \vdash N : T}{\Gamma \vdash (M\ N) : P\{N\}}.$$

Remark The constant *Type* is a "type of all types". However, it is not itself of type *Type*.

Definitions Let $\Gamma \vdash M : N$, with Γ a valid context. When $N = Type$, we say that M is a valid *Γ-type*. When $N = Prop$, we say that M is a valid *Γ-proposition*. Finally, when $\Gamma \vdash M : N$, with N a valid Γ-proposition, we say that M is a *Γ-element*. The *pure* system of constructions is obtained by deleting the third rule of context formation, which allows the introduction of *Type* variables. In the pure system, the only primitive type is *Prop*, and thus the only valid types are the products of the form $(A_1 : P_1)(A_2 : P_2) \cdots (A_n : P_n)Prop$.

We shall use a number of abbreviations. First, we write $\vdash M : P$ for $\{\} \vdash M : P$. Then, we give notations for the nondependent products, that is, for terms $(u : P)Q$ in the case where u does not occur in Q. When both P and Q are propositions, we write $P \Rightarrow Q$. In other cases we write rather $P \rightarrow Q$. Finally, we abbreviate $(A : Prop)M$ into $\forall A \cdot M$ and $[A : Prop]M$ into $\Lambda A \cdot M$.

Adding Type Conversion In the polymorphic λ-calculus seen in the last chapter, we defined propositional connectives as abbreviations. Thus for propositions P and Q, the notation $P \wedge Q$ was just a meta-linguistic notation for the appropriate proposition. In the new calculus under consideration, connectives are indeed definable as expressions, and propositions are formed using the general rules of λ-calculus. We should therefore expect to need internal reduction rules for playing the role of macro-expansion.

It is indeed the case that such rules are necessary for type-checking. For instance, let us assume we define conjunction along the ideas of the previous chapter:

$$\wedge := [P : Prop]\,[Q : Prop](R : Prop)(P \Rightarrow Q \Rightarrow R) \Rightarrow R.$$

Now if we try to define the first projection, in a context

$$\Gamma = [P : Prop]\,[Q : Prop]\,[x : (\wedge\ P\ Q)],$$

we shall be unable to form the term $(x\ P)$, unless we are able to recognize that the type $(\wedge\ P\ Q)$ is equal (by β-conversion) to $(R : Prop) \cdots$.

The above discussion shows that some amount of type equality rules must be provided in a higher-order calculus. To what extent such rules should be explicit (from the point of view of a user checking a derivation using inference rules) is unclear. For instance, we may profit from meta-theoretical results (confluence, strong normalization) and convert all types to normal form using λ-calculus reduction rules. Now type equality is just identity of such canonical forms. But there is an obvious drawback here: we may spend useless time converting to normal form some types which could be recognized as different immediately by inspection of their head normal form. Thus $[u : A]\,[v : A](u \cdots)$ and $[u : A]\,[v : A](v \cdots)$ need not be reduced any further. This problem is aggravated by the fact that the higher-order nature of the calculus makes it possible to have subparts of types which are elements. For instance, if P is a predicate over a propositional type A, then for any element $p : A$ we may have to convert p to q in order to apply $x : (P\ p)$ as argument to a proof of some lemma of type $(P\ q) \Rightarrow \cdots$.

We now present various rules of conversion which may be used to axiomatize type equality ≡. Various subcalculi are obtainable by taking a subset of these rules, together with the rule of type conversion:

$$\textit{Type Equality}: \quad \frac{\Gamma \vdash M : P \quad \Gamma \vdash P \equiv Q}{\Gamma \vdash M : Q},$$

$$\textit{Refl}: \quad \frac{\Gamma \vdash M : N}{\Gamma \vdash M \equiv M},$$

$$\textit{Sym}: \quad \frac{\Gamma \vdash M \equiv N}{\Gamma \vdash N \equiv M},$$

$$\textit{Trans}: \quad \frac{\Gamma \vdash M \equiv N \quad \Gamma \vdash N \equiv P}{\Gamma \vdash M \equiv P},$$

$$\textit{Abseq}: \quad \frac{\Gamma \vdash P_1 \equiv P_2 \qquad \Gamma[x : P_1] \vdash M_1 \equiv M_2}{\Gamma \vdash [x : P_1]M_1 \equiv [x : P_2]M_2},$$

$$\textit{Quanteq}: \quad \frac{\Gamma \vdash P_1 \equiv P_2 \qquad \Gamma[x : P_1] \vdash M_1 \equiv M_2}{\Gamma \vdash (x : P_1)M_1 \equiv (x : P_2)M_2},$$

$$\textit{Appleq}: \quad \frac{\Gamma \vdash (M\ N) : P \qquad \Gamma \vdash M \equiv M_1 \qquad \Gamma \vdash N \equiv N_1}{\Gamma \vdash (M\ N) \equiv (M_1\ N_1)},$$

$$\textit{Beta}: \quad \frac{\Gamma[x : A] \vdash M : P \qquad \Gamma \vdash N : A}{\Gamma \vdash ([x : A]M\ N) \equiv M\{N\}},$$

$$\textit{Eta}: \quad \frac{\Gamma \vdash M : P}{\Gamma \vdash [x : A](M^{+}\ x) \equiv M}.$$

Various subsystems can now be discussed. First, the rule *Eta* may be omitted. Then the rule *Abseq* (corresponding to the ξ rule of λ-calculus) may be deleted, yielding a weak conversion system corresponding to combinatory conversion.

Finally, when the conversions at the level of the elements (i.e., the terms of a propositional type) are omitted, we get the *restricted* calculus of constructions.

The calculus of constructions presented above was defined in Th. Coquand's thesis [38], where he proved the main meta-theoretic properties. Variations on the basic calculus are presented in [42, 44].

Example We want to define the intersection of a class of classes on a given type A. A natural attempt is to take

$$\begin{aligned} Inter \;:=\; & [C : (A \to Prop) \to Prop]\,[x : A] \\ & (P : A \to Prop)(C\,P) \to (P\,x)\,. \end{aligned}$$

Let us place ourselves in the context

$$\Gamma = [C_0 : (A \to Prop) \to Prop]\,[P_0 : A \to Prop]\,[p_0 : (C_0\,P_0)]\,.$$

We shall build a proof of the inclusion of the predicate $(Inter\ C_0)$ in the predicate P_0. Let us consider

$$\Delta = \Gamma[x : A]\,[h : (Inter\ C_0\ x)]\,.$$

We want to build with p_0, x, h, P_0, C_0 a term of type $(P_0\ x)$.

Intuitively, h, which is of type $(Inter\ C_0\ x)$, is also (by logical conversion using the definition of $Inter$) of type $(P : A \to Prop)(C_0\ P) \Rightarrow (P\ x)$, and thus we may construct the term $(h\ P_0\ p_0)$. Now, taking:

$$\begin{aligned} Subset \;:=\; & [P : A \to Prop]\,[Q : A \to Prop]\,(x : A)P(x) \Rightarrow Q(x)\ : \\ & (P : A \to Prop)(Q : A \to Prop)Prop, \end{aligned}$$

we get

$$\Gamma \vdash [x : A]\,[h : (Inter\ C_0\ x)]\,(h\ P_0\ p_0) : (Subset\ (Inter\ C_0)\ P_0).$$

This example shows that the conversion of types rules are absolutely needed as soon as one wants to develop mathematical proofs (note that this example can be developed in the restricted calculus as well as in the full calculus). The need for conversion rules is equally emphasized in [121] and [166].

Consistency

Definition A proposition $\vdash P : Prop$ is *inhabited* if and only if there is an element term M such that $\vdash M : P$.

Theorem (Consistency)
The calculus of constructions is consistent, in the sense that there exists a proposition that is not inhabited.

The intuitive meaning of this statement is that the calculus does not prove all its well-formed propositions. Indeed, the term $\bot \;:=\; \forall A \cdot A$ is such a proposition.

5.3 *Examples of Constructions*

All the examples discussed in polymorphic λ-calculus can be developed without modification in this new calculus, which extends it in a natural way. Let us now show how quantifiers can be expressed in the calculus.

Universal Quantification Universal quantification, or general product, is implicit from the notation:

$$\Pi \;:=\; \Lambda A \cdot [P : A \to Prop]\;(x : A)(P\;x)\,.$$

Π-introduction, i.e., universal generalization, is proved by abstraction:

$$\begin{aligned} Gen \;:=\; & \Lambda A \cdot [P : A \to Prop]\Lambda B \cdot [f : (x : A)\;B \Rightarrow (P\;x)]\;[y : B]\;[x : A](f\;x\;y) \\ & : \forall A \cdot (P : A \to Prop)\forall B \cdot ((x : A)\;B \Rightarrow (P\;x)) \Rightarrow (B \Rightarrow (\Pi\;A\;P))\,. \end{aligned}$$

Similarly, Π-elimination is proved by instantiation, i.e., application:

$$\begin{aligned} Inst \;:=\; & \Lambda A \cdot [P : A \to Prop]\;[x : A]\;[p : (\Pi\;A\;P)]\,(p\;x) \\ & : \forall A \cdot (P : A \to Prop)(x : A)(\Pi\;A\;P) \Rightarrow (P\;x)\,. \end{aligned}$$

Existential Quantification Existential quantification, or general sum, can be defined by a generalization of the binary sum:

$$\Sigma \;:=\; \Lambda A \cdot [P : A \to Prop]\;\forall B \cdot ((x : A)\;(P\;x) \Rightarrow B) \Rightarrow B.$$

We leave it as an exercise for the reader to prove existential introduction and elimination:

$$Exist \;:=\; \forall A \cdot (P : A \to Prop)(x : A)\;(P\;x) \Rightarrow (\Sigma\;A\;P)\,,$$

$$Witness := \forall A \cdot (P : A \to Prop)\, (\Sigma\ A\ P) \Rightarrow A\,.$$

Note that in a certain sense existential quantification is an abstraction mechanism: from $(\Sigma\ A\ P)$ it is possible to get some $a : A$ such that $(P\ a)$, but *not* the proof $p : (P\ a)$ that it indeed satisfies predicate P. Thus the existential quantification of the calculus of constructions is fundamentally different from the sum in Martin-Löf's calculus [122].

Equality Leibniz' equality is definable in the calculus:

$$Equal := \Lambda A \cdot [x : A]\,[y : A]\,(P : A \to Prop)(P\ x) \Rightarrow (P\ y).$$

Exercise Define the properties for a polymorphic relation to be reflexive, symmetric, and transitive. Give the three proofs that *Equal* verifies these properties.

Tarski's Theorem Let us now present a simple example of a higher-order proof. The goal is to prove Tarski's theorem [186].

Theorem (Tarski)
A function monotonous over a complete partial ordering admits a fixpoint.

The first difficulty in formalizing Tarski's theorem is to give it in as abstract a setting as possible, in order to get the most direct proof. Let us try the following. Let A be a set, R a transitive relation over A which is complete, in the sense that every subset of A has a least upper bound. Let $f : A \to A$ be monotonously increasing. Then f admits a fixpoint.

We must now formalize the notions of set, subset, and fixpoint. A simple attempt at axiomatizing sets consists in assuming some type A given with an equality relation $=$, and to represent sets in the "universe" A by their characteristic predicate, i.e., as elements of type $A \to Prop$. As for fixpoint, it turns out that all we need to require is that for some X we have $(R\ (f\ X)\ X)$ and $(R\ X\ (f\ X))$. That is, the only property of equality that is needed here is the fact that R is antisymmetric.

We thus assume that we are in a context Γ, containing the following hypotheses:

$$[A : Type]\,,$$

$$[\,= : A \to A \to Prop]\,,$$

$$[R : A \to A \to Prop]\,,$$

$$[Rtrans : (x : A)(y : A)(z : A)(R\ x\ y) \Rightarrow (R\ y\ z) \Rightarrow (R\ x\ z)]\ ,$$

$$[Rantisym : (x : A)(y : A)(R\ x\ y) \Rightarrow (R\ y\ x) \Rightarrow (=\ x\ y)]\ ,$$

$$[lim : (A \rightarrow Prop) \rightarrow A]\ ,$$

$$[Upperb : (P : A \rightarrow Prop)(y : A)(P\ y) \Rightarrow (R\ y\ (lim\ P))]\ ,$$

$$[Least : (P : A \rightarrow Prop)(y : A)((z : A)(P\ z) \Rightarrow (R\ z\ y)) \Rightarrow (R\ (lim\ P)\ y)]\ ,$$

$$[f : A \rightarrow A]\ ,$$

$$[Incr : (x : A)(y : A)(R\ x\ y) \Rightarrow (R\ (f\ x)\ (f\ y))]\ .$$

Now we consider the predicate Q defined as:

$$Q\ :=\ [u : A](R\ u\ (f\ u))$$

(that is, Q is the set of pre-fixpoints of f) and the element $X : A$ defined as:

$$X\ :=\ (lim\ Q).$$

The first part of the proof consists in showing a proof of $(R\ X\ (f\ X))$ in context Γ. Let us first consider $\Delta = \Gamma[y : A]\ [h : (Q\ y)]$, and terms $M = (Upperb\ Q\ y)$ and $N = (Incr\ y\ X)$. We get:

$$\Delta \vdash M : (R\ y\ (f\ y)) \Rightarrow (R\ y\ X), \text{ and}$$

$$\Delta \vdash N : (R\ y\ X) \Rightarrow (R\ (f\ y)\ (f\ X)).$$

Composing the two proofs we get:

$$\Delta \vdash M; N : (R\ y\ (f\ y)) \Rightarrow (R\ (f\ y)\ (f\ X))\ .$$

Thus, taking $p = (M; N\ h)$, we obtain:

$$\Delta \vdash (Rtrans\ y\ (f\ y)\ (f\ X)\ h\ p) : (R\ y\ (f\ X))\ .$$

Discharging the hypotheses h and y, we get

$$T = [y : A]\ [h : (Q\ y)]\ (Rtrans\ y\ (f\ y)\ (f\ X)\ h\ p)\ ,$$

such that

$$\Gamma \vdash T : \forall y \in Q \cdot (R\ y\ (f\ X))\ .$$

The proof is completed by constructing $U = (Least\ Q\ (f\ X)\ T)$, since

$$\Gamma \vdash U : (R\ X\ (f\ X))\ .$$

The second part of the proof is the converse. Taking $Z = (Incr\ X\ (f\ X)\ U)$, we get

$$\Gamma \vdash Z : (R\ (f\ X)\ (f\ (f\ X)))\,,$$

but since this last proposition converts to $(Q\ (f\ X))$, we get

$$\Gamma \vdash (Upperb\ Q\ (f\ X)\ Z) : (R\ (f\ X)\ X)\,.$$

The proof of Tarski's theorem is thus obtained as

$$\Gamma \vdash (Rantisym\ (f\ X)\ X\ (Upperb\ Q\ (f\ X)\ Z)\ U) : (=\ (f\ X)\ X)\,.$$

Exercise Use the above argument and the quantifier manipulation combinators above to prove Tarski's theorem as a fully quantified statement.

Numerous examples of proofs verified on machine are presented in [41]. A general discussion on the formalization of mathematical arguments in higher order intuitionistic logic is given in [164].

6 A Constructive Theory of Types

Let us now augment the calculus of constructions with rules allowing for the abstraction over all types. The first natural attempt is to allow *Type* : *Type*. We would thus get a system of rules very close to the one considered by Martin-Löf in [118]. However, this was shown to be inconsistent by Girard, who showed that it was possible to encode the paradox of Burali-Forti in such a system. An abstract analysis of such paradoxes is given by Coquand in [39]. Coquand showed that it was possible to quantify propositions over all types, but *not* other types such as product types. Such a system is presented below.

6.1 A System for Uniform Proofs

First, two rules provide for abstraction over all types:

$$TypeQuant : \frac{\Gamma[t : Type] \vdash P : Prop}{\Gamma \vdash (t : Type)P : Prop}\,,$$

$$TypeAbstr : \frac{\Gamma[t : Type] \vdash P : Prop \quad \Gamma[t : Type] \vdash M : P}{\Gamma \vdash [t : Type]M : (t : Type)P}\,.$$

Finally, we give one more type conversion rule:

$$TypeEq : \frac{\Gamma[t : Type] \vdash P : Prop \qquad \Gamma[t : Type] \vdash P \equiv Q}{\Gamma \vdash (t : Type)P \equiv (t : Type)Q}\,.$$

In such a system, we may now abstract the above proof of Tarski's theorem.

6.2 A System with a Hierarchy of Universes

It is even possible to iterate the idea of a type gathering all the types obtained so far. One thus gets a system with a hierarchy of universes like in Martin-Löf's system [122]. Let us present along those lines Coquand's generalized calculus of constructions [39].

Terms

1. $Type(i)$, for i a nonnegative integer, and $Prop$ are terms;
2. a variable x is a term;
3. if M and N are terms, then $(M\ N)$ is a term (application);
4. if M and N are terms, then $[x : M]N$ is a term (abstraction);
5. if M and N are terms, then $(x : M)N$ is a term (product).

As previously, we denote by $\equiv$ the relation of $\lambda\beta$-conversion between terms.

Contexts Contexts are ordered lists of *bindings* of the form $x : M$, where x is a variable and M is a term. Not every context is valid. The following rules define the valid contexts.

The empty context is valid,

$$\frac{\Gamma \text{ is valid} \quad \Gamma \vdash M : Prop \quad x \text{ is not bound in } \Gamma}{\Gamma, x : M \text{ is valid}},$$

$$\frac{\Gamma \text{ is valid} \quad \Gamma \vdash M : Type(i) \quad x \text{ is not bound in } \Gamma}{\Gamma, x : M \text{ is valid}}.$$

These rules are defined mutually recursively with the following type inference rules, which define the judgements $\Gamma \vdash M : N$, to be read "the term M is of type N in context Γ".

Type Inference Rules

$$\frac{\Gamma \text{ is valid}}{\Gamma \vdash Prop : Type(0)},$$

$$\frac{\Gamma \text{ is valid}}{\Gamma \vdash Type(i) : Type(i+1)}, \qquad (*)$$

$$\frac{\Gamma \vdash M : Type(i)}{\Gamma \vdash M : Type(i+1)}, \qquad \text{(coerce)}$$

$$\frac{\Gamma \text{ is valid} \quad x : M \in \Gamma}{\Gamma \vdash x : M},$$

$$\frac{\Gamma, x : M \vdash N : P}{\Gamma \vdash [x : M]N : (x : M)P},$$

$$\frac{\Gamma, x : M \vdash N : Prop}{\Gamma \vdash (x : M)N : Prop},$$

$$\frac{\Gamma \vdash M : Type(j) \quad \Gamma, x : M \vdash N : Type(i)}{\Gamma \vdash (x : M)N : Type(max(i, j))},$$

$$\frac{\Gamma \vdash M : Prop \quad \Gamma, x : M \vdash N : Type(i)}{\Gamma \vdash (x : M)N : Type(i)}, \qquad (**)$$

$$\frac{\Gamma \vdash M : (x : Q)P \quad \Gamma \vdash N : R \quad Q \equiv R}{\Gamma \vdash (M\ N) : [N/x]P}.$$

The only serious departure from [39] is the addition of rule $(*)$, which was inadvertently omitted, and of rule $(**)$, which is needed to prove the following lemma.

Lemma

If $\Gamma \vdash M : N$ is derivable, then either $\Gamma \vdash N : Prop$ is derivable, in which case we say that M is a *proof* of *proposition* N in context Γ, or else $\Gamma \vdash N : Type(i)$ is derivable for some $i \geq 0$, in which case we say that M is a *realization* of *specification* N in context Γ.

This lemma shows that there are two distinct kinds of types in the system, in the sense of terms appearing to the right of a colon in a derivable sequent.

A Digression on Types, Specifications, and Propositions We say that term T is a *type* (in a given context) if it is either a specification or a proposition. We remark that the rules for context formation are that variables may be bound only to types, not to arbitrary terms. Since these are the two kinds of bindings, we shall speak of the constants *Prop* and *Type(i)* of the system as the *kinds*, following the MacQueen-Sethi terminology[112]. Specifications are the natural generalization of the notion of types in the sense of Church's theory of types. They are more general in that the product formation operator is *dependent*, like in Martin-Löf's theory of types [122]. When x does not occur in N, the specification $(x : M)N$ may be abbreviated in the more traditional $M \rightarrow N$. For instance, the specification of a predicate over type T would be $T \rightarrow Prop$. Similarly, when P is a proposition and Q is a proposition in which x does not occur, we may abbreviate $(x : P)Q$ in $P \Rightarrow Q$. Also, we use $\forall x : M \cdot P$ for $(x : M)P$ when M is a specification and P is a proposition. When P is a proposition and M

is a specification, the specification $(x : P)M$ has realizations depending on the proof of P. It is not usual to consider such types in ordinary logic. However, they are needed to formalize constructive mathematics in Bishop's sense, where evidence of properties is taken as computationally meaningful. Here evidence (of properties) is internalized as proofs (of propositions). This is in contrast to the formalism LF (logical framework) developed at the University of Edinburgh [71], where judgements (as opposed to propositions) are types. We refer to [123] for a philosophical discussion of the issues involved.

Note that the only specifications P which are typable of type $Type(0)$ in the empty context are (convertible to) the terms of the form:

$$(x_1 : M_1)(x_1 : M_1)\dots(x_1 : M_1)Prop\,.$$

The types of the system are more general than just specifications, since we use the paradigm of propositions as types [74]. More precisely, the formulation of the logical part of the system in natural deduction style allows the use of λ-abstraction for the dual purpose of building functional realizations as well as building proofs under hypotheses.

The inference system is completed by type equality rules, as follows.

Type Equality Rules

$$\frac{\Gamma \vdash M : N \quad \Gamma \vdash P : Prop \quad N \equiv P}{\Gamma \vdash M : P}\,,$$

$$\frac{\Gamma \vdash M : N \quad \Gamma \vdash P : Type(i) \quad N \equiv P}{\Gamma \vdash M : P}\,.$$

Note that we allow λ-conversion only for types, not for other terms.

Remark 1 It might seem that the previous lemma allows us to simplify the two rules in one simpler rule:

$$\frac{\Gamma \vdash M : N \quad N \equiv P}{\Gamma \vdash M : P}\,.$$

However, we are careful to specify that P must be itself well typed, since otherwise we might introduce nontypable terms as types of other terms. Indeed, we need this restriction in order to preserve the validity of the lemma above.

Remark 2 The types equality rules allow us to replace the rule of application by the simpler:

$$\frac{\Gamma \vdash M : (x : Q)P \quad \Gamma \vdash N : Q}{\Gamma \vdash (M\,N) : [N/x]P}\,.$$

Indeed, this is the way it was formulated originally [39]. However, our formulation is more consistent from the point of view of the meaning of the meta-variables in the rules, since several occurrences of the same meta-variable should mean that the corresponding term or context is *shared*, and this is not the case for Q above.

The system GCC is quite powerful. It extends Girard's higher-order system F^{ω} strictly. It permits complete formalization of the Principia's, including the so-called "typical ambiguity" feature. However, it is not very convenient to use, since we have to manipulate the universe hierarchy explicitly. Furthermore, there is no unicity of types (even modulo lambda-conversion), because of rule (*coerce*). This difficulty can be solved by manipulating the integer arguments to the *Type* constant as symbolic expressions (as explained in [85]).

References

[1] Aho, A., Hopcroft, J., and Ullman, J. *The Design and Analysis of Computer Algorithms.* Addison-Wesley, Reading, Mass., 1974.

[2] Andrews, P. "Resolution in type theory". *J. Symbolic Logic 36*,3 (1971), pp. 414–432.

[3] Andrews, P., Miller, D., Cohen, E., and Pfenning, F. "Automating higher-order logic". Dept. of Mathematics, Carnegie-Mellon University, January 1983.

[4] Barendregt, H. *The Lambda-Calculus: Its Syntax and Semantics.* North-Holland, Amsterdam, 1980.

[5] Barendregt, H. and Rezus, A. "Semantics for classical AUTOMATH and related systems". *Information and Control 59* (1983), pp. 127–147.

[6] Bishop, E. *Foundations of Constructive Analysis.* McGraw-Hill, New York, 1967.

[7] Bishop, E. "Mathematics as a numerical language". *Intuitionism and Proof Theory*, J. Myhill, A. Kino and R.E. Vesley, eds., pp. 53–71. North-Holland, Amsterdam, 1970.

[8] Böhm, C. and Berarducci, A. "Automatic synthesis of typed lambda-programs on term algebras". Unpublished manuscript, June 1984.

[9] Boyer, R. and Moore, J. "The sharing of structure in theorem proving programs". *Machine Intelligence 7* (1972), pp. 101–116.

[10] Boyer, R. and Moore, J. "A lemma driven automatic theorem prover for recursive function theory". *Proc. 5th International Joint Conference on Artificial Intelligence* (1977), pp. 511–519.

[11] Boyer, R. and Moore, J. *A Computational Logic.* Academic Press, New York, 1979.

[12] Boyer, R. and Moore, J. "A mechanical proof of the unsolvability of the halting problem". Report ICSCA–CMP–28, Institute for Computing Science, The University

of Texas at Austin, July 1982.

[13] Boyer, R. and Moore, J. "Proof checking the RSA public key encryption algorithm". Report ICSCA–CMP–33, Institute for Computing Science, The University of Texas at Austin, September 1982.

[14] Boyer, R. and Moore, J. "Proof checking theorem proving and program verification". Report ICSCA–CMP–35, Institute for Computing Science, The University of Texas at Austin, January 1983.

[15] de Bruijn, N. "The mathematical language AUTOMATH, its usage and some of its extensions". *Proc. Symposium on Automatic Demonstration* (IRIA, Versailles, 1968), pp. 29–61. Lecture Notes in Mathematics, vol. 125. Springer-Verlag, Berlin, 1970.

[16] de Bruijn, N. "Lambda-calculus notation with nameless dummies, a tool for automatic formula manipulation, with application to the Church-Rosser theorem". *Indag. Math. 34*, 5 (1972), pp. 381–392.

[17] de Bruijn, N. *Automath: A Language for Mathematics.* Les Presses de l'Université de Montréal, Montréal, 1973.

[18] de Bruijn, N. "Some extensions of Automath: The AUT–4 family". Internal Automath memo M10, January 1974.

[19] de Bruijn, N. "A survey of the project Automath". In *To H. B. Curry: Essays on Combinatory Logic, Lambda Calculus and Formalism*, J. P Seldin and J. R. Hindley, eds. Academic Press, New York, 1980.

[20] Bruynooghe, M. "The memory management of PROLOG implementations". Logic Programming Workshop, S. A. Tarnlund, ed., July 1980.

[21] Burstall, R. and Lampson, B. "A kernel language for modules and abstract data types". *Proc. International Symposium on Semantics of Data Types* (Sophia-Antipolis), G. Kahn, D. B. MacQueen, and G. Plotkin, eds., pp. 1–50. Lecture Notes in Computer Science, vol. 173. Springer-Verlag, Berlin, 1984.

[22] Cardelli, L. "ML under UNIX". Bell Laboratories, Murray Hill, N.J., 1982.

[23] Cardelli, L. "Amber". Technical Memorandum TM 11271–840924–10. Bell Laboratories, Murray Hill, N.J., 1984.

[24] Cardelli, L. "The Amber machine". Bell Laboratories, Murray Hill, N.J., 1985.

[25] Cardelli, L. "Basic polymorphism type-checking". *Polymorphism*, January 1985.

[26] Cardelli, L. "A polymorphic λ-calculus with type:Type". Systems Research Center Report 10, Digital Equipment Corporation, May 1986.

[27] Cardelli, L. and Wegner, P. "On understanding types, data abstraction, and polymorphism". *ACM Computing Surveys 17*, 4 (Dec. 1985), pp. 471–522.

[28] de Champeaux, D. "About the Paterson-Wegman linear unification algorithm". *J. Computer and System Sciences 32* (1986), pp. 79–90.

[29] Church, A. "A formulation of the simple theory of types". *J. Symbolic Logic 5*, 1 (1940), pp. 56–68.

[30] Church, A. *The Calculi of Lambda-Conversion.* Princeton University Press, Princeton, N.J., 1941.

[31] Clément, D., Despeyroux, J., Despeyroux, T., and Kahn, G. "Natural semantics on the computer". Research Report 416, INRIA, June 1985.

[32] Clément, D., Despeyroux, J., Despeyroux, T., and Kahn, G. "A simple applicative language: Mini-ML". Research Report (to appear), INRIA, 1986.

[33] Colmerauer, A., Kanoui, A., Pasero, R., and Roussel, Ph. "Un système de communication homme-machine en francais". Rapport de recherche, Groupe Intelligence Artificielle, Faculté des Sciences de Luminy, Marseille, 1973.

[34] Constable, R. and Bates, J. "Proofs as programs". Dept. of Computer Science, Cornell University, February 1983.

[35] Constable, R. and Bates, J. "The nearly ultimate Pearl". Dept. of Computer Science, Cornell University, December 1983.

[36] Constable, R. and Mendler, N. "Recursive definitions in type theory". Private Communication, 1985.

[37] Constable, R. et al. *Implementing Mathematics in the NuPrl System.* Prentice-Hall, Englewood Cliffs, N.J., 1986.

[38] Coquand, Th. "Une théorie des constructions". Thèse de troisième cycle, Université Paris VII, January 1985.

[39] Coquand, Th. "An analysis of Girard's paradox". Proc. First Conference on Logic in Computer Science, Boston, June 1986.

[40] Coquand, Th. and Huet, G. "A theory of constructions". Preliminary version, presented at the International Symposium on Semantics of Data Types, Sophia-Antipolis, June 1984.

[41] Coquand, Th. and Huet, G. "Constructions: A higher order proof system for mechanizing mathematics". *Proc. EUROCAL'85* (Linz). Lecture Notes in Computer Science, vol. 203. Springer-Verlag, Berlin, 1985.

[42] Coquand, Th. and Huet, G. "Concepts mathématiques et informatiques formalisés dans le calcul des constructions". Colloque de Logique, Orsay, July 1985.

[43] Coquand, Th. and Huet, G. "A selected bibliography on constructive mathematics, intuitionistic type theory and higher order deduction". *J. Symbolic Computation 1* (1985), pp. 323–328.

[44] Coquand, Th. and Huet, G. "The calculus of constructions". *Information and Computation 76*, 2/3 (February/March 1988), pp. 95–120.

[45] Corbin, J. and Bidoit, M. "A rehabilitation of Robinson's unification algorithm". *IFIP 83*, pp. 909–914. Elsevier Science, New York, 1983.

[46] Cousineau, G., Curien, P-L., and Mauny, M. "The Categorical Abstract Machine". *Functional Programming Languages and Computer Architecture*, J.P. Jouannaud, ed., pp. 50–64. Lecture Notes in Computer Science, vol. 201. Springer-Verlag, Berlin, 1985.

[47] Curien, P-L. "Combinateurs catégoriques, algorithmes séquentiels et programmation applicative". Thèse de Doctorat d'Etat, Université Paris VII, December 1983.

[48] Curien, P-L. "Categorical combinatory logic". In *Proc. ICALP 85* (Nafplion). Lecture Notes in Computer Science, vol. 194. Springer-Verlag, Berlin, 1985.

[49] Curien, P-L. *Categorical Combinators, Sequential Algorithms and Functional Programming.* Pitman, 1986.

[50] Curry, H. and Feys, R. *Combinatory Logic*, Vol. I. North-Holland, Amsterdam, 1958.

[51] Van Daalen, D. "The language theory of Automath". Ph.D. Dissertation, Technological Univ. Eindhoven, 1980.

[52] Damas, L. and Milner, R. "Principal type-schemas for functional programs". Edinburgh University, 1982.

[53] Demers, A. and Donahue, J. "Datatypes, parameters and type checking". *Proc. 7th ACM Symposium on Principles of Programming Languages* (Las Vegas), pp. 12–23. ACM, New York, 1980.

[54] Downey, P., Sethi, R., and Tarjan, R. "Variations on the common subexpression problem". *J. ACM 27*, 4 (1980), pp. 758–771.

[55] Dummett, M. *Elements of Intuitionism.* Clarendon Press, Oxford, 1977.

[56] Fages, F. "Formes canoniques dans les algèbres booléennes et application à la démonstration automatique en logique de premier ordre". Thèse de troisème cycle, Université Paris VI, June 1983.

[57] Fages, F. "Associative-commutative unification". Submitted for publication, 1985.

[58] Fages, F. and Huet, G. "Unification and matching in equational theories". In *Proc. CAAP 83* (l'Aquila, Italy). Lecture Notes in Computer Science, vol. 159. Springer-Verlag, Berlin, 1983.

[59] Flajolet, P. and Steyaert, J. "On the analysis of tree-matching algorithms". *Proc. 7th International Colloquium on Automata, Languages and Programming*, pp. 208–219. Lecture Notes in Computer Science, vol. 85. Springer-Verlag, Berlin, 1980.

[60] Fortune, S., Leivant, D., and O'Donnell, M. "The expressiveness of simple and second-order type structures". *J. ACM 30*, 1 (Jan. 1983), pp. 151–185.

[61] G. Frege. "Begriffschrift, a formula language, modeled upon that of arithmetic, for pure thought". (1879). Reprinted in *From Frege to Gödel*, J. van Heijenoort, ed. Harvard University Press, 1967.

[62] Gentzen, G. *The Collected Papers of Gerhard Gentzen.* E. Szabo, ed. North-Holland, Amsterdam, 1969.

[63] Girard, J-Y. "Une extension de l'interprétation de Gödel à l'analyse, et son application à l'élimination des coupures dans l'analyse et la théorie des types". *Proc. Second Scandinavian Logic Symposium*, J.E. Fenstad, ed., pp. 63–92. North Holland, Amsterdam, 1970.

[64] Girard, J-Y. "Interprétation fonctionnelle et élimination des coupures dans l'arithmétique d'ordre supérieure". Thèse d'Etat, Université Paris VII, 1972.

[65] Gödel, K. "Uber eine bisher noch nicht benutze Erweitrung des finiten Standpunktes". *Dialectica 12* (1958).

[66] Goldfarb, W. "The undecidability of the second-order unification problem". *Theoretical Computer Science 13* (1981), pp. 225–230.

[67] Gordon, M., Milner, R., and Wadsworth, C. "A metalanguage for interactive proof in LCF". Internal Report CSR-16-77, Department of Computer Science, University of Edinburgh, September 1977.

[68] Gordon, M., Milner, R., and Wadsworth, C. *Edinburgh LCF.* Lecture Notes in Computer Science, vol. 78. Springer-Verlag, Berlin, 1979.

[69] Gould, W. "A matching procedure for Omega order logic". Scientific Report 1, AFCRL 66-781, Contract AF19 (628)-3250, 1966.

[70] Guard, J. "Automated logic for semi-automated mathematics". Scientific Report 1, AFCRL, 1964.

[71] Harper, R., Honsell, F., and Plotkin, G. "The Edinburgh Logical Framework". Private communication, October 1986.

[72] Herbrand, J. "Recherches sur la théorie de la démonstration". Thèse, U. de Paris (1930). In *Ecrits logiques de Jacques Herbrand*, PUF Paris, 1968.

[73] Hoffmann, C. and O'Donnell, M. "Programming with equations". *ACM Trans. Programming Languages and Systems 4*, 1 (1982), pp. 83–112.

[74] Howard, W. "The formulæ-as-types notion of construction". Unpublished manuscript (1969). Reprinted in *To H. B. Curry: Essays on Combinatory Logic, Lambda Calculus and Formalism*, J. P. Seldin and J. R. Hindley, eds. Academic Press, New York, 1980.

[75] Huet, G. "Constrained resolution: A complete method for type theory". Ph.D. Thesis, Jennings Computing Center Report 1117, Case Western Reserve University, 1972.

[76] Huet, G. "A mechanization of type theory". In *Proc. 3rd International Joint Conference on Artificial Intelligence* (Stanford, August). 1973.

[77] Huet, G. "The undecidability of unification in third order logic". *Information and Control 22* (1973), pp. 257–267.

[78] Huet, G. "A unification algorithm for typed lambda calculus". *Theoretical Computer Science 1*, 1 (1975), pp. 27–57.

[79] Huet, G. "Résolution d'équations dans des langages d'ordre 1,2, ..., ω". Thèse

d'Etat, Université Paris VII, 1976.

[80] Huet, G. "Confluent reductions: Abstract properties and applications to term rewriting systems". *J. ACM 27*, 4 (1980), pp. 797–821.

[81] Huet, G. "A complete proof of correctness of the Knuth-Bendix completion algorithm". *J. Computer and System Sciences 23*, 1 (1981), pp. 11–21.

[82] Huet, G. "Initiation à la théorie des catégories". Polycopié de cours de DEA, Université Paris VII, November 1985.

[83] Huet, G. "Cartesian closed categories and lambda-calculus". Category Theory Seminar, Carnegie-Mellon University, December 1985.

[84] Huet, G. "Formal structures for computation and deduction". Course Notes, Carnegie-Mellon University, May 1986.

[85] Huet, G. "Extending the calculus of constructions with type:Type". In preparation.

[86] Huet, G. and Hullot, J. "Proofs by induction in equational theories with constructors". *J. Computer and System Sciences 25*, 2 (1982), pp. 239–266.

[87] Huet, G. and Lévy, J. "Call by need computations in non-ambiguous linear term rewriting systems". Rapport Laboria 359, IRIA, August 1979.

[88] Huet, G. and Oppen, D. "Equations and rewrite rules: A survey". In *Formal Languages: Perspectives and Open Problems*, R. Book, ed. Academic Press, New York, 1980.

[89] Jutting, L. "A translation of Landau's 'Grundlagen' in AUTOMATH". Eindhoven University of Technology, Dept. of Mathematics, October 1976.

[90] Jutting, L. "The language theory of Λ_∞, a typed λ-calculus where terms are types". Unpublished manuscript, 1984.

[91] Kahn, G. and Plotkin, G. "Domaines concrets". Rapport Laboria 336, IRIA, December 1978.

[92] Kanellakis, P. and Mitchell, J. "Polymorphic unification and ML typing". Proceedings, 16th Annual ACM Symposium on Principles of Programming Languages (Jan. 1989), pp. 105–113.

[93] Ketonen, J. and Weening, J. "The language of an interactive proof checker". Stanford University, 1984.

[94] Ketonen, J. "EKL—a mathematically oriented proof checker". In *Proc. 7th International Conference on Automated Deduction* (Napa, California, May). Lecture Notes in Computer Science, vol. 170. Springer-Verlag, Berlin, 1984.

[95] Ketonen, J. "A mechanical proof of the Ramsey theorem". Stanford University, 1983.

[96] Kleene, S. "On the interpretation of intuitionistic number theory". *J. Symbolic Logic 10* (1945).

[97] Kleene, S. *Introduction to Meta-mathematics.* North-Holland, Amsterdam, 1952.

[98] Klop, J. "Combinatory reduction systems". Ph. D. Thesis, Mathematisch Centrum Amsterdam, 1980.

[99] Knuth, D., Morris, J., and Pratt, V. "Fast pattern matching in strings". *SIAM J. Computing 6*, 2 (1977), pp. 323–350.

[100] Kreisel, G. "On the interpretation of nonfinitist proofs", Parts I, II. *J. Symbolic Logic 16,17* (1952, 1953).

[101] Lambek, J. "From λ-calculus to Cartesian closed categories". In *To H. B. Curry: Essays on Combinatory Logic, Lambda Calculus and Formalism*, J. P. Seldin and J. R. Hindley, eds. Academic Press, New York, 1980.

[102] Lambek, J. and Scott, P. "Aspects of higher order categorical logic". *Contemporary Mathematics 30* (1984), pp. 145–174.

[103] Lambek, J. and Scott, P. *Introduction to Higher Order Categorical Logic.* Cambridge University Press, 1986.

[104] Landin, P. "The next 700 programming languages". *Communications of the ACM 9*, 3 (1966), pp. 157–166.

[105] Le Chenadec, P. "Formes canoniques dans les algèbres finiment présentées". Thèse de troisème cycle, Université d'Orsay, June 1983.

[106] Leivant, D. "Polymorphic type inference". In *Proc. 10th ACM Symposium on Principles of Programming Languages.* ACM, New York, 1983.

[107] Leivant, D "Structural semantics for polymorphic data types". In *Proc. 10th ACM Symposium on Principles of Programming Languages.* ACM, New York, 1983.

[108] Lévy, J. "Réductions correctes et optimales dans le λ-calcul". Thèse d'Etat, Univ. Paris VII, 1978.

[109] Lévy, J. "Optimal reductions in the λ-calculus". In *To H. B. Curry: Essays on Combinatory Logic, Lambda Calculus and Formalism*, J. P. Seldin and J. R. Hindley, eds. Academic Press, New York, 1980.

[110] Mac Lane, S. *Categories for the Working Mathematician.* Springer-Verlag, Berlin, 1971.

[111] MacQueen, D., Plotkin, G., and Sethi, R. "An ideal model for recursive polymorphic types". *Proc. Symposium on Principles of Programming Languages* (January), pp. 165–174. ACM, New York, 1984.

[112] MacQueen, D. and Sethi, R. "A semantic model of types for applicative languages". In *Proc. ACM Symposium on Lisp and Functional Programming* (August). ACM, New York, 1982.

[113] Manes, E. *Algebraic Theories.* Springer-Verlag, Berlin, 1976.

[114] Mann, C. "The connection between equivalence of proofs and Cartesian closed categories". *Proc. London Mathematical Society 31* (1975), pp. 289–310.

[115] Martelli, A. and Montanari, U. "Theorem proving with structure sharing and effi-

cient unification". *Proc. 5th International Joint Conference on Artificial Intelligence* (Boston), p. 543. 1977.

[116] Martelli, A. and Montanari, U. "An efficient unification algorithm". *ACM Trans. Programming Languages and Systems 4*, 2 (1982), pp. 258–282.

[117] Martin, W. "Determining the equivalence of algebraic expressions by hash coding". *J. ACM 18*, 4 (1971), pp. 549–558.

[118] Martin-Löf, P. "A theory of types". Report 71–3, Dept. of Mathematics, University of Stockholm, February 1971. Revised October 1971.

[119] Martin-Löf, P. "About models for intuitionistic type theories and the notion of definitional equality". Paper read at the Orléans Logic Conference, 1972.

[120] Martin-Löf, P. "An intuitionistic theory of types: Predicative part". *Logic Colloquium 73*, H. Rose and J. Shepherdson, eds., pp. 73–118. North-Holland, Amsterdam, 1974.

[121] Martin-Löf, P. "Constructive mathematics and computer programming". *Logic, Methodology and Philosophy of Science 6* (1980), pp. 153–175.

[122] Martin-Löf, P. *Intuitionistic Type Theory.* Studies in Proof Theory. Bibliopolis, 1984.

[123] Martin-Löf, P. "Truth of a proposition, evidence of a judgment, validity of a proof". Transcript of talk at the workshop "Theories of Meaning", Centro Fiorentino di Storia e Filosofia della Scienza, Villa di Mondeggi, Florence, June 1985.

[124] McCarthy, J. "Recursive functions of symbolic expressions and their computation by machine". *Communications of the ACM 3*, 4 (1960), pp. 184–195.

[125] McCracken, N. "An investigation of a programming language with a polymorphic type structure". Ph.D. Dissertation, Syracuse University (1979).

[126] Meyer, A. and Reinhold, M. "Type is not a type: Preliminary report". *Proc. 13th Annual ACM Symposium on Principles of Programming Languages* (St. Petersburg, Florida, January), pp. 287–295. ACM, New York, 1986.

[127] Miller, D. "Proofs in higher-order logic". Ph.D. Dissertation, Carnegie-Mellon University, August 1983.

[128] Miller, D. "Expansion tree proofs and their conversion to natural deduction proofs". Technical report MS–CIS–84–6, University of Pennsylvania, February 1984.

[129] Milner, R. "A theory of type polymorphism in programming". *J. Computer and System Sciences 17* (1978), pp. 348–375.

[130] Milner, R. "A proposal for Standard ML". Report CSR–157–83, Computer Science Dept., University of Edinburgh, 1983.

[131] Mohring, C. "Algorithm development in the calculus of constructions". In *Proc. IEEE Symposium on Logic in Computer Science* (Cambridge, Mass., June). IEEE, New York, 1986.

[132] Mycroft, A. "Polymorphic type schemes and recursive definitions". *Proc. 6th International Symposium on Programming*, pp. 217–228. Lecture Notes in Computer Science, vol. 167. Springer-Verlag, Berlin, 1984.

[133] Nederpelt, R. "Strong normalization in a typed λ calculus with λ structured types". Ph.D. Thesis, Eindhoven University of Technology, 1973.

[134] Nederpelt, R. "An approach to theorem proving on the basis of a typed λ-calculus". In *Proc. 5th Conference on Automated Deduction* (Les Arcs, France). Lecture Notes in Computer Science, vol. 87. Springer-Verlag, Berlin, 1980.

[135] Nelson, G. and Oppen, D. "Fast decision procedures based on congruence closure". *J. ACM 27*, 2 (1980), pp. 356–364.

[136] Newman, M. "On theories with a combinatorial definition of 'equivalence' ". *Annals of Mathematics 43*, 2 (1942), pp. 223–243.

[137] Nordström, B. "Programming in constructive set theory: Some examples". *Proc. ACM Conference on Functional Programming Languages and Computer Architecture* (Portsmouth, New Hampshire, October), pp. 141–154. ACM, New York, 1981.

[138] Nordström, B. "Description of a simple programming language". Report 1, Programming Methodology Group, University of Göteborg, April 1984.

[139] Nordström, B. and Petersson, K. "Types and specifications". *Information Processing 83*, R. Mason, ed., pp. 915–920. North-Holland, Amsterdam, 1983.

[140] Nordström, B. and Smith, J. "Propositions and specifications of programs in Martin-Löf's type theory". *BIT 24* (1984), pp. 288–301.

[141] Obtulowicz, A. "The logic of categories of partial functions and its applications". *Dissertationes Mathematicae 241*, 1982.

[142] Paterson, M. and Wegman, M. "Linear unification". *J. Computer and Systems Sciences 16* (1978), pp. 158–167.

[143] Paulson, L. "Recent Developments in LCF: Examples of structural induction". Technical Report No. 34, Computer Laboratory, University of Cambridge, January 1983.

[144] Paulson, L. "Tactics and tacticals in Cambridge LCF". Technical Report No. 39, Computer Laboratory, University of Cambridge, July 1983.

[145] Paulson, L. "Verifying the unification algorithm in LCF". Technical Report No. 50, Computer Laboratory, University of Cambridge, March 1984.

[146] Paulson, L. "Constructing recursion operators in intuitionistic type theory". Technical Report No. 57, Computer Laboratory, University of Cambridge, October 1984.

[147] Peterson, G. and Stickel, M. "Complete sets of reduction for equational theories with complete unification algorithms". *J. ACM 28*, 2 (1981), pp. 233–264.

[148] Pietrzykowski, T. and Jensen, D. "A complete mechanization of ω-order type theory". *Proc. ACM Annual Conference.* ACM, New York, 1972.

[149] Pietrzykowski, T. "A complete mechanization of second-order type theory". *J. ACM 20* (1973), pp. 333–364.

[150] Prawitz, D. *Natural Deduction.* Almqist and Wiskell, Stockholm, 1965.

[151] Prawitz, D. "Ideas and results in proof theory". *Proc. Second Scandinavian Logic Symposium*, 1971.

[152] Quine, W. "The problem of simplifying truth functions". *American Math. Monthly 59*, 8 (1952), pp. 521–531.

[153] Rasiowa, H. and Sikorski, R. "The mathematics of metamathematics". *Monografie Matematyczne 41*, PWN, Polish Scientific Publishers, Warsaw, 1963.

[154] Reynolds, J. "Definitional interpreters for higher order programming languages". *Proc. ACM National Conference* (Boston, August), pp. 717–740. ACM, New York, 1972.

[155] Reynolds, J. "Towards a theory of type structure". *Programming Symposium* (Paris), pp. 408–425. Lecture Notes in Computer Science, vol. 19. Springer-Verlag, Berlin, 1974.

[156] Reynolds, J. "Types, abstraction, and parametric polymorphism". *Proc. IFIP Congress'83* (Paris, September). 1983.

[157] Reynolds, J. "Polymorphism is not set-theoretic". In *Proc. International Symposium on Semantics of Data Types* (Sophia-Antipolis, France, June). Lecture Notes in Computer Science, vol. 173. Springer-Verlag, Berlin, 1984.

[158] Reynolds, J. "Three approaches to type structure". In *Proc. TAPSOFT Advanced Seminar on the Role of Semantics in Software Development* (Berlin, March). 1985.

[159] Robinson, J. "A machine-oriented logic based on the resolution principle". *J. ACM 12* (1965), pp. 32–41.

[160] Robinson, J. "Computational logic: The unification computation". In *Machine Intelligence 6*, B. Meltzer and D. Michie, eds. American Elsevier, New York, 1971.

[161] Russell, B. and Whitehead, A. *Principia Mathematica,* vols. 1,2,3. Cambridge University Press, 1912.

[162] Schütte, K. *Proof Theory.* Springer-Verlag, Berlin, 1977.

[163] Scott, D. "Constructive validity". In *Proc. Symposium on Automatic Demonstration.* Lecture Notes in Mathematics, vol. 125. Springer-Verlag, Berlin, 1970.

[164] Scott, D. "Identity and existence in intuitionistic logic". *Proc. Research Symposium on Applications of Sheaf Theory to Logic, Algebra and Analysis* (Durham, July 1977), M. P. Fourman, C. J. Mulvey, and D. S. Scott, eds., pp. 660–696. Lecture Notes in Mathematics, vol. 753. Springer-Verlag, Berlin, 1979.

[165] Scott, D. "Relating theories of the lambda-calculus". In *To H. B. Curry: Essays on Combinatory Logic, Lambda-calculus and Formalism,* J. P. Seldin and J. R. Hindley, eds. Academic Press, New York, 1980.

[166] Seldin, J. "Progress report on generalized functionality". In *Annals of Mathematical Logic 17* (1979).

[167] Shoenfield, J. *Mathematical Logic.* Addison-Wesley, Reading, Mass., 1967.

[168] Shostak, R. "Deciding combinations of theories". *J. ACM 31*, 1 (1985), pp. 1–12.

[169] Smith, J. "Course-of-values recursion on lists in intuitionistic type theory". Unpublished notes, Göteborg University, September 1981.

[170] Smith, J. "The identification of propositions and types in Martin-Löf's type theory: A programming example". In *Proc. International Conference on Foundations of Computation Theory* (Borgholm, Sweden, August). Lecture Notes in Computer Science, vol. 158. Springer-Verlag, Berlin, 1983.

[171] Statman, R. "Intuitionistic propositional logic is polynomial-space complete". *Theoretical Computer Science 9* (1979), pp. 67–72.

[172] Statman, R. "The typed lambda-calculus is not elementary recursive". *Theoretical Computer Science 9* (1979), pp. 73–81.

[173] Statman, R. "Number theoretic functions computable by polymorphic programs". *Proc. 22nd IEE Symposium on Foundations of Computer Science*, pp. 279–282. IEEE, New York, 1981.

[174] Statman, R. "On translating λ-terms into combinators; the basis problem". In *Proc. IEEE Conference on Logic in Computer Science* (Boston, June). IEEE, New York, 1986.

[175] Stenlund, S. *Combinators, λ-terms, and Proof Theory.* Reidel, 1972.

[176] Stickel, M. "A complete unification algorithm for associative-commutative functions". *J. ACM 28*, 3 (1981), pp. 423–434.

[177] Szabo, M. *Algebra of Proofs.* North-Holland, Amsterdam, 1978.

[178] Tait, W. "A nonconstructive proof of Gentzen's Hauptsatz for second order predicate logic". In *Bull. Amer. Math. Soc. 72* (1966).

[179] Tait, W. "Intensional interpretations of functionals of finite type I". *J. Symbolic Logic 32* (1967), pp. 198–212.

[180] Tait, W. "A realizability interpretation of the theory of species". In *Logic Colloquium*, R. Parikh, ed. Lecture Notes in Mathematics, vol. 453. Springer-Verlag, Berlin, 1975.

[181] Takahashi, M. "A proof of cut-elimination theorem in simple type theory". In *J. Math. Society of Japan 19* (1967).

[182] Takeuti, G. "On a generalized logic calculus". *Japan J. Mathematics 23* (1953).

[183] Takeuti, G. *Proof Theory.* Studies in Logic, vol. 81. North-Holland, Amsterdam, 1975.

[184] Tarjan, R. "Efficiency of a good but nonlinear set union algorithm". *J. ACM 22*, 2 (1975), pp. 215–225.

[185] Tarjan, R. and van Leeuwen, J. "Worst-case analysis of set union algorithms". *J. ACM 31*, 2 (1985), pp. 245–281.

[186] Tarski, A. "A lattice-theoretical fixpoint theorem and its applications". *Pacific J. Mathematics 5* (1955), pp. 285–309.

[187] Turner, D. "Miranda: A non-strict functional language with polymorphic types". *Functional Programming Languages and Computer Architecture*, J.P. Jouannaud, ed., pp. 1–16. Lecture Notes in Computer Science, vol. 201. Springer-Verlag, Berlin, 1985.

[188] de Vrijer, R. "Big trees in a λ-calculus with λ-expressions as types". *Proc. Conference on λ-calculus and Computer Science Theory* (Rome), pp. 252–271. Lecture Notes in Computer Science, vol. 37. Springer-Verlag, Berlin, 1975.

[189] Warren, D. "Applied logic — its use and implementation as a programming tool". Ph.D. Thesis, University of Edinburgh, 1977.

On the Analogy Between Propositions and Types[1]

17

Thierry Coquand
CMU and INRIA

Introduction

The purpose of this paper is to analyze the analogy between propositions (in logic) and types (in a programming language). This analogy was observed by Curry [13], developed by Howard [19], and exploited in a systematic manner by de Bruijn [6] for the Automath project.

This analogy may be made precise in the form of an isomorphism between certain natural deduction systems and certain functional systems. In the first part, we develop this isomorphism in detail for the simplest possible logical system, minimal logic, which is the intuitionistic calculus of implication.

1. Originally appeared in French as "Sur l'analogie entre les propositions et les types" in *Combinators and Functional Programming Languages*, G. Cousineau, P-L. Curien, and B. Robinet, eds.; Lecture Notes in Computer Science, vol. 242. Springer-Verlag, Berlin, 1986. Translation by Walt Hill (Hewlett-Packard Laboratories).

Then we indicate how to extend this isomorphism to more complex logics (first to propositional logic and then to first-order logic) and we show how the classical results on realizability [20] enter naturally in this context. Then we present some concrete examples of this analogy in computer science. A final part treats problems raised by second-order calculi in [15] and [30] in regard to this analogy between propositions and types. It is indeed evident that on such a vast subject, our treatment doesn't pretend to be complete. Our aim is only to indicate certain landmarks, some of which are suggested by an implementation (in the language ML) of a type-checker used as a proof-checker.

1 *Natural Deduction Systems and Functional Systems*

1.1 *Minimal Propositional Logic*

Natural Deduction The set F of formulas of this calculus is defined inductively as follows: one is given a set At of base propositions; if A and B are formulas, then $A \Rightarrow B$ is also a formula. The aim of this section is to make precise in a formal way what is a "true" formula in this calculus (the route described for arriving at this definition generalizes to richer calculi).

Historically, the first solution to this problem was the development of what one calls Hilbert systems. One starts with certain axiom schemes: here, if x, y, and z are meta-variables over the set of formulas F, the axiom schemes are $x \Rightarrow (y \Rightarrow x)$ and $(x \Rightarrow (y \Rightarrow z)) \Rightarrow ((x \Rightarrow y) \Rightarrow (x \Rightarrow z))$. Then one defines the notion of a derivation: a sequence $A_1, \ldots, A_n$ of formulas is a derivation if and only if, for each i between 1 and n, A_i is an instance of an axiom scheme or there exist $j, k < i$ such that A_k is the formula $A_j \Rightarrow A_i$. A formula A will then be called "true" if and only if there is a derivation ending in A.

This definition of "truth" isn't very satisfactory, however, essentially because intuitively "trivial" formulas turn out to be relatively complicated to prove (for example, the formula $A \Rightarrow A$ if A is a formula) and this definition doesn't provide a way of deciding the truth of a formula (for example, Peirce's axiom $((A \Rightarrow B) \Rightarrow A) \Rightarrow A$ is not "true", but it is very difficult to see this with the definition of truth given above). In practice, it turns out to be essential to introduce the notion of truth "modulo hypotheses": if H is a subset of the set of formulas F and if A is a formula, we will say that the formula is true modulo the hypotheses H, and write $H \vdash A$ if and only if there exists a sequence of formulas $A_1, \ldots, A_n$ such that A_n is A, and for each i between 1 and n, either A_i is an instance of an axiom scheme, or A_i is an element of H, or there exist $j, k < i$ such that A_k is $A_j \Rightarrow A_i$. If H is a subset of F and A is a formula, we will write H, A for the union of H with the singleton set formed by the formula A.

This notion of relative truth contains the previous notion (it suffices to take for H the empty set) but is much more tractable than this last notion. This is expressed formally by the following theorem.

Theorem (Deduction Theorem)
Let H be a subset of F, and A and B two formulas. Then $H, A \vdash B$ if and only if $H \vdash A \Rightarrow B$ [20].

This theorem permits one to show that formulas are true without having to exhibit a proof explicitly. For example, if A is a formula, then $A \Rightarrow A$ is true since we have $A \vdash A$ (still, this theorem is not sufficient for the decidability of our notion of truth).

We deduce the following proposition.

Proposition
The relation $\vdash$ between subsets of F and elements of F is the smallest relation such that

1. $H \vdash A$ if A belongs to H,

2. $H \vdash A \Rightarrow B$ if $H, A \vdash B$, and

3. if $H \vdash A \Rightarrow B$ and $H \vdash A$, then $H \vdash B$.

This proposition permits a direct axiomatization of the relation $\vdash$ as the smallest relation satisfying the above conditions. Once the relation $\vdash$ is defined, one can redefine the notion of truth. We will say that the formula A is true if and only if A is related to the empty set by $\vdash$ (this will be denoted by $\vdash A$).

This last definition is much more satisfactory: First of all, it doesn't depend on an arbitrary system of axioms; hence it permits formulas to be shown in a manner that is "natural" and much more concise (for example, $A \Rightarrow A$ is true since $A \vdash A$). This mode of presentation of the notion of "truth" is essentially what one calls natural deduction (in contrast to a Hilbert system) which was originally developed by Gentzen.

The following point is thus the study of this relation $\vdash$, for example, in order to show that this relation is decidable. For this, one needs a notation that denotes the act of recognizing that one has $H \vdash A$. For that, one idea is to mark the hypotheses explicitly and to introduce terms that translate the operations one has performed to convince oneself of $H \vdash A$. We remark that this idea of "marking" proofs and hypotheses to refer to them is suggested by practice when one develops effectively long proofs in symbolic form [31].

It happens that the system of notation for these operations already exists in the form of the λ-calculus. In what follows, I will assume known the basic notions of the λ-calculus [3]. To fix the notation, I recall simply that this calculus is defined by the rules:

1. identifiers and natural numbers (de Bruijn indices) are λ-terms,

2. (abstraction) if N is a λ-term, then $\lambda(N)$ is a λ-term, and

3. (application) if M and N are λ-terms, then (MN) is a λ-term.

I will also assume known the notation of de Bruijn [5], adopting the following notational convention. If x is an identifier and M is a λ-term, then $\lambda x.M$ designates the λ-term obtained by the following operations: first replace each occurrence of x in M by the appropriate integer (as in [5]), then make the abstraction. Thus the identifier x does not appear in $\lambda x.M$. For example, if M is the term $(x\ \lambda y.(y\ x\ z))$ (which denotes $(x\ \lambda(1\ x\ z))$), then $\lambda x.M$ will be $\lambda(1\ \lambda y.(y\ 2\ z))$ (which denotes $\lambda(1\ \lambda(1\ 2\ z))$). This allows us to avoid the difficulties bound up with the notion of bound variables.

One can then develop a calculus of derivations: the following rules construct "sequents", that is to say objects of the form $\Gamma \vdash t : A$ where A is a formula, t a λ-term, and Γ a list of marked hypotheses $x_1 : A_1, \ldots, x_n : A_n$, where the x_i are pairwise distinct identifiers and the A_i are formulas.

1. $\Gamma \vdash x : A$ if x appears in Γ as a "marking" for the formula A.

2. If $\Gamma, x : A \vdash M : B$, then $\Gamma \vdash \lambda x.M : A \Rightarrow B$.

3. If $\Gamma \vdash M : A \Rightarrow B$ and $\Gamma \vdash N : A$, then $\Gamma \vdash (MN) : B$.

Note the "overloading" of the symbol $\vdash$, which is not a problem in light of the following proposition in which $g(\Gamma)$ denotes the set of formulas that appear in the list Γ of hypotheses.

Proposition

If A is a formula then $g(\Gamma) \vdash A$ if and only if there is a λ-term M such that $\Gamma \vdash M : A$.

One can view the λ-terms as the justifications of formulas: one is no longer satisfied with demonstrating the truth of this or that formula; one exhibits at the same time the reason (in the form of a λ-term) for which the formula is true. For example, if A is a formula, one has $\vdash \lambda x.x : A \Rightarrow A$ and can consider that the λ-term $\lambda x.x$ represents the reasoning one does to convince oneself of the truth of $A \Rightarrow A$. This interpretation is compatible with β-conversion in light of the following property.

Property If $\Gamma \vdash M : A$ and M β-reduces to N, then $\Gamma \vdash N : A$.

We remark that the Hilbert formalism corresponds to the point of view of combinatory logic. Instead of considering all λ-expressions, one restricts oneself to those that are terms constructed by means of certain constants (which are analogous to the axiom schemes). From this point of view, the deduction theorem corresponds to the theorem of functional completeness [23].

Explicit consideration of the justification of a formula permits a finer study of our notion of truth. For example, to prove the decidability of our notion of truth, it suffices to show that if $\Gamma \vdash M : A$, then M is normalizable. For example, the axiom scheme (of Peirce) $((x \Rightarrow y) \Rightarrow x) \Rightarrow x$ is not "true" with respect to our definition since simple combinatorial reasoning shows that there is no λ-term in normal form which justifies it. We will demonstrate this property as an illustration of the isomorphism between this system of natural deduction and a functional system constructed from monomorphic types. We remark that the decidability of the minimal calculus does not result from that of Boolean propositional logic since the example of Peirce's axiom shows that the notions of truth for formulas constructed from implication are distinct, Peirce's axiom being true in the Boolean calculus.

The Monomorphic Calculus We consider the following type system: we assume given a set of base types B and define the set of monomorphic types over B as the smallest set T containing B such that if A and B are in T then $A \rightarrow B$ is in T. Intuitively, B is the set of primitive types of a programming language, and this language is functional: one can consider the types of arbitrary functions on the base types.

We will now consider the programs one can construct on these types in a purely functional manner, that is, without using recursion or the primitive functions of a programming language. For this, we introduce the notion of a type environment, which is a list $x_1 : A_1, \ldots, x_n : A_n$ of type declarations for pairwise distinct identifiers $x_1, \ldots, x_n$, and the notion of sequents of type $\Gamma \vdash M : A$, which can be read as "the λ-term M has type A in the type environment Γ." The derivation rules in this calculus are exactly similar to those of the preceding logical calculus:

1. $\Gamma \vdash x : A$ if the type environment Γ assigns the type A to the identifier x.

2. If $\Gamma, x : A \vdash M : B$, then $\Gamma \vdash \lambda x.M : A \rightarrow B$.

3. If $\Gamma \vdash M : A \rightarrow B$ and $\Gamma \vdash N : A$, then $\Gamma \vdash (MN) : B$.

Let f be an arbitrary function between the "base" set At for propositions and the "base" set B for types. This function extends to a function f from F

and T by putting $f(A \Rightarrow B) = f(A) \rightarrow f(B)$, and if Γ is a list of hypotheses of the minimal calculus, we denote again by $f(\Gamma)$ the type environment obtained by substituting all formulas in Γ with their corresponding types. If f is injective, we have the following propositon.

Proposition

If Γ is a list of hypotheses and A is a formula, then $\Gamma \vdash A$ if and only if $f(\Gamma) \vdash f(A)$.

This is an illustration (for the simplest possible logic) of what one calls the Curry-Howard isomorphism between propositions (here, propositions of the minimal calculus) and types of a functional system (here, the monomorphic calculus). We see that there is a perfect correspondence between the functions and the justifications of formulas.

For the special correspondence where a formula becomes a type in a programming language which is the type of the justifications of the formula, a justification of the formula $A \rightarrow B$ becomes an algorithm that to each justification of the formula A associates a justification of the formula B. Thus we recognize (for a very simple logic) Heyting's interpretation of intuitionistic truth where a formula is interpreted as the type of its proofs.

1.2 *Adding Propositional Connectives*

It is remarkable that the isomorphism above extends when one enriches the logic by adding the usual connectives of conjunction and disjunction. However, it holds at the level of proofs only for intuitionistic logic. One adds to the type constructors of formulas the binary operators $\wedge$ and $\vee$, and to the constructors of the lambda-calculus the unary constructors $p1, p2, i1, i2$, the binary constructor $<,>$, and the ternary constructor *case*. The type rules are extended by the rules:

1. if $\Gamma \vdash t : A$ and $\Gamma \vdash u : B$, then $\Gamma \vdash < t, u >: A \wedge B$;

2. if $\Gamma \vdash t : A \wedge B$, then $\Gamma \vdash p1(t) : A$ and $\Gamma \vdash p2(t) : B$;

3. if $\Gamma \vdash t : A$, then $\Gamma \vdash i1(t) : A \vee B$ and $\Gamma \vdash i2(t) : B \vee A$
for every formula B;

4. if $\Gamma \vdash t : A \vee B$, $\Gamma \vdash u : A \Rightarrow C$ and $\Gamma \vdash v : B \Rightarrow C$,
then $\Gamma \vdash case(t, u, v) : C$.

The functional interpretation is standard: $\wedge$ corresponds to product and $\vee$ to disjoint sum. There is again a correspondence between "proofs" and "programs": $p1$ and $p2$ are analogous to the projections, $<,>$ to the pairing operation, $i1$ and $i2$ are the injections, and finally *case* corresponds to the notion of a conditional in a programming language. We remark that there is not (as in the language ML) a type function $A \vee B \rightarrow A$ that would correspond to a partial function, while all the functions considered here are total.

This interpretation motivates the following reduction rules:

1. $p1(< t, u >)$ reduces to t, and $p2(< t, u >)$ reduces to u;

2. $case(i1(t), u, v)$ reduces to $u(t)$, and $case(i2(t), u, v)$ reduces to $v(t)$.

An algorithm for calculating these functions is given by the following theorem.

Theorem

If $\Gamma \vdash t : A$, then the λ-term t is strongly normalizable.

The proof of this theorem can be found in, for example, [33]. It follows that the minimal calculus, and its extension with conjunction and disjunction, are decidable (note the unusual character of this decidability proof, which brings in explicit consideration of proofs instead of considering only the notion of truth). An example of an application of this theorem is the following theorem.

Theorem

Let A be a formula. If $\vdash A \vee B$, then $\vdash A$ or $\vdash B$.

We note that this theorem does not relativize in general (if $\Gamma \vdash A \vee B$, in general one doesn't have $\Gamma \vdash A$ or $\Gamma \vdash B$, for example, if Γ is reduced to $A \vee B$). The hypotheses must be "Harrop formulas". These are the formulas described by the rules: every atomic formula is a Harrop formula, if A and B are Harrop formulas then $A \wedge B$ is a Harrop formula, and if A is a Harrop formula and B is an arbitrary formula then $B \Rightarrow A$ is a Harrop formula. See [17, 18].

There is a "Hilbert" presentation of this extension with conjunction and disjunction. One adds the following axiom schemes:

1. $A \Rightarrow (B \Rightarrow A \wedge B)$,

2. $A \wedge B \Rightarrow A$ and $A \wedge B \Rightarrow B$,

3. $A \Rightarrow A \vee B$ and $A \Rightarrow B \vee A$,

4. $(A \vee B) \Rightarrow ((A \Rightarrow C) \Rightarrow ((B \Rightarrow C) \Rightarrow C))$.

The deduction theorem remains true for this calculus. It allows one to show the equivalence with the calculus of natural deduction, and it corresponds again to a completely functional theorem for the corresponding functional calculus.

One could also extend the previous calculus, for example, by introducing the absurd proposition $\bot$, which would correspond to the empty type (dually, one can introduce the true proposition T). It would be possible then to interpret intuitionistic negation in terms of types in a programming language. The extension of the isomorphism between natural deduction and functional systems by introducing the law of the excluded middle (in the form $(\neg(\neg A)) \Rightarrow A$) doesn't seem to have been studied. In the case of a set-theoretic interpretation one must have a function of type $((A \to \bot) \to \bot) \to A$, and one can interpret such a function as a general choice function: if A is empty then $(A \to \bot) \to \bot$ is empty, and if A is nonempty, then $(A \to \bot) \to \bot$ has exactly one element. Therefore, to extend the isomorphism in the case of a set-theoretic functional calculus, it suffices to add a choice function.

All the laws of the usual intuitionistic logic have "functional" counterparts. In what follows, we examine the extension to first-order logics and then to second-order logics.

2 *Extension to First-Order Logic*

It is natural to try to extend the preceding isomorphism to first-order logic. First of all, it is necessary to generalize the formalism of natural deduction to have a satisfying presentation of the notion of an n-ary predicate and of an n-ary function symbol. I limit myself here to the treatment of Heyting arithmetic [19]. The generalization to the case of an arbitrary first-order theory poses no problems [17]. We will extend the logical system based on implication, conjunction, disjunction, and the absurd proposition (this is roughly the class of types definable without recursion in the language ML).

We extend the class of formulas by introducing a universal quantifier $\forall$ and an existential quantifier $\exists$. We will adopt the same notational conventions for variables bound with respect to this quantifier as for λ-calculus. For example, $\forall x.x = x$ is the concrete syntax for $\forall 1 = 1$. Since the theory considered here treats natural numbers, it is necessary to pay attention to the confusion between de Bruijn indices and formal symbols. Here $O, S(O), \ldots$ are chosen to represent natural numbers, but we always use concrete syntax so there is no possibility of confusion.

We need to extend the class of "justifications" in two distinct ways: for the notion of natural numbers and for the notion of (Peano) axioms.

First of all, we describe the terms corresponding to natural numbers.

1. Identifiers are terms.

2. O is a term.

3. If x and y are terms, then $S(x), x + y$, and $x.y$ are terms.

Then we enlarge the class of formulas by the clause: If t and u are terms, then $t = u$ is a formula.

Then we introduce justifications that correspond to the Peano axioms *axi*, for i from 1 to 8, and *red* (the significance of these constants is explained below), and new rules for quantifiers in the natural deduction system (they correspond to the formal system of [20]) where we must introduce a new binary operator *inst* for the case of an existential quantifier.

1. If $\Gamma \vdash t : A$ and the identifier x doesn't appear in Γ, then $\Gamma \vdash \lambda x.t : \forall x.A$.
2. If $\Gamma \vdash t : \forall x.A$ and n is a term, then $\Gamma \vdash (t\ n) : A[1/n]$.
3. If If $\Gamma \vdash t : A[1/n]$, then $\Gamma \vdash < n, t >: \exists A$.
4. If $\Gamma \vdash t : \exists x.A$ and $\Gamma \vdash u : \forall x.A \Rightarrow B$ where 1 doesn't appear in B, then $\Gamma \vdash inst(t, u) : B$.
5. $\Gamma \vdash ax1 : x = y \Rightarrow (x = z \Rightarrow y = z)$ and $\Gamma \vdash ax2 : S(x) = O \Rightarrow \bot$.
6. $\Gamma \vdash ax3 : x = y \Rightarrow S(x) = S(y)$ and $\Gamma \vdash ax4 : S(x) = S(y) \Rightarrow x = y$.
7. $\Gamma \vdash ax5 : x + O = x$ and $\Gamma \vdash ax6 : x + S(y) = S(x + y)$.
8. $\Gamma \vdash ax7 : x.O = O$ and $\Gamma \vdash ax8 : x.S(y) = x.y + y$.
9. If $\Gamma \vdash t : A[x/O]$ and $\Gamma \vdash u : \forall x.(A \Rightarrow A[x/S(x)])$, then $\Gamma \vdash rec(u, t) : \forall x.A$.

The first four rules have a quite general status. The others correspond to the particular first-order theory chosen here.

Again it is possible to give a "Hilbert" presentation of this calculus (cf. [20] where such a system is called "Heyting arithmetic") for which the deduction theorem remains valid. This theorem shows the equivalence of the presentation of [20] with this presentation. This equivalence implies the "realizability theorem" [20], but our treatment has the advantage of avoiding the notion of the Gödel number of a recursive function (these are replaced here by λ-terms).

Theorem

If A is a formula, then A is true for Heyting arithmetic (that is, a consequence of the previous axioms by the rules of intuitionistic deduction) if and only if there is a term t such that $\vdash t : A$.

This shows that our notion of deduction coincides with the usual notion, being still more explicit since one keeps a copy of the proof.

We note that the notion of realizability may be seen as an illustration of the Curry-Howard isomorphism. Kleene's principal motivation was to establish a link between two disciplines that both treat the notion of effective procedures: the theory of recursive functions and the notion of proofs in intuitionism (cf. [21], where Kleene makes precise the relation between the notion of realizability and the notion of the Heyting interpretation of propositions). The functional system associated with this calculus is obtained by adding a type constant *Nat* for the type of the natural numbers as well as the types dependent on this type (of which the type of tables is an example). In particular, the equality predicate is interpreted as a dependent type. If n and m are two integers, then $n = m$ is interpreted as the type $\perp$ if n and m are distinct and as the type T if n and m are equal. The symbol S (resp. $+, -$) is interpreted by the successor algorithm (resp. addition, multiplication). The other formulas and terms then have the standard interpretation: in particular, $\forall x.A$ will be interpreted as the product of interpretations $A[x/S^n(O)]$, n a natural number, and $\exists x.A$ as the disjoint sum if the interpretations $A[x/S^n(O)]$, n a natural number. This interpretation is described completely (but in a little different way) in [19].

It is worthwhile to note the remarkable character of this functional system: the natural numbers are put at the same level as the objects corresponding to proofs! This fact, which is an illustration of the Curry-Howard isomorphism, will be discussed later in the context of Martin-Löf's system.

To calculate these functions, one extends the reduction rules by requiring that $(rec(t, u)\ O)$ reduce to t, $(rec(t, u)\ S(n))$ reduce to $((u\ n)\ (rec(t, u)\ n))$, and $inst(< n, t >, u)$ reduce to $((u\ n)\ t)$. One can then state the following proposition.

Proposition

If $\Gamma \vdash t : A$ and t reduces to u, then $\Gamma \vdash u : A$.

Theorem

If $\Gamma \vdash t : A$, then the λ-term t is strongly normalizable.

This theorem has several remarkable logical consequences for Heyting arithmetic (a very concise proof of this statement may be found in [32] in a slightly different context).

Corollary 1

Let A be a formula with a free variable x. If $\exists x.A$ is true in Heyting arithmetic, then there is (and it is possible to find explicitly from a proof of $\exists x.A$) a natural number n such that $A[S^n(O)/x]$ is true in Heyting arithmetic.

Corollary 2

Let A be a formula with two free variables x and y. If $\forall x.\exists y.A$ is true in Heyting arithmetic, then there exists (and it is possible to find effectively from a proof of $\forall x.\exists y.A$) a (recursive) function f such that for all natural numbers n,

$A[S^n(O)/x, S^{f(n)}(O)/y]$ is true in Heyting arithmetic.

To understand why these statements are not obvious, see [22]. The proof amounts simply to normalizing the terms corresponding to the given proofs. These corollaries do not remain true in general for Peano arithmetic, which is the classical or "Boolean" version of Heyting arithmetic. On the other hand, they remain valid if the formula A is quantifier-free. This is usually proved by another method for extracting a function from a proof, called the Dialectica interpretation, due to Gödel [22, 32]. As Mints [27] has shown, one obtains the same function by the two methods in the case of Corollary 2 for a quantifier-free formula. It would be interesting to study the pertinence of the Dialectica interpretation vis-à-vis the Curry-Howard isomorphism; however, we will not do this here. See [17] for a discussion of this interpretation. We note simply that the normalization theorems continue to hold in classical logic. Kreisel [22] gives a characterization in terms of a "functional hierarchy" of the class of functions, which one may obtain in Corollary 2 in the case of a quantifier-free formula.

The algorithmic interest of Corollary 2 is clear. The aim of what follows is to examine more generally what the pertinence of the Curry-Howard isomorphism may be for computer science.

3 *Using the Analogy Between Propositions and Types*

We will try to show the degree to which the isomorphisms discussed above between natural deduction systems and functional systems can be utilized in programming. The general idea is to use the preceding Corollary 2 to extract programs from proofs in intuitionistic logic. This point of view has been generalized extensively by Martin-Löf, who uses the Curry-Howard isomorphism to develop a system that is at the same time a programming language and the analogue for constructive mathematics of what the Zermelo-Fraenkel system is for classical mathematics, that is to say, a system powerful enough for the development of intuitionistic mathematics. We will only indicate here how this system relates the preceding considerations. We will then attempt to present analogies between existential formulas and the notion of "abstract type".

3.1 *Martin-Löf's System*

As Martin-Löf's system is still being developed, I should specify that I will be referring in what follows to the system presented in [24]. The originality of this system from a "foundational" point of view is, I think, to show that it is possible to develop a predicative type theory (in other words, one without the axiom of reducibility [31], which makes it possible to quantify over propositions, predicates, ...), however rich enough to be able to develop, among other things, the theory of real numbers (which was an insurmountable problem in [31] without the axiom of reducibility). This is due to an extension of the notion of types in comparison with [31] since the types can be types of a programming language and no longer just types of propositions, predicates, relations,...as in [31]. However, it is not this aspect of Martin-Löf's theory which will concern us here, but rather the use of this system as a programming language.

Martin-Löf's system may be seen as a generalization of Heyting arithmetic as it was presented above. One again adds type constructors, for example, for lists or finite types. But the most important difference is in the treatment of the quantifier $\exists$.

In effect, it is possible to axiomatize such a quantifier in a "stronger" way. For this, we remark that the interpretation of $\exists x.A$ as a type is the set of pairs $< n, p >$ such that p proves $A[x/n]$. One can give (thus generalizing the notion of product) the following projection rules:

1. if $\Gamma \vdash t : \exists x.A$, then $\Gamma \vdash p1(t) : Nat$;

2. if $\Gamma \vdash t : \exists x.A$, then $\Gamma \vdash p2(t) : A[x/p1(t)]$.

While the previous system still kept the distinction between formulas and the type *Nat*, this distinction is completely lost here. For example, we have $\lambda t.p1(t) : (\exists x.x = x) \Rightarrow Nat$, where the formula $\exists x.x = x$ and the type *Nat* are put "on the same level". This is certainly one of the most surprising aspects of Martin-Löf's system. He doesn't consider the relation between propositions and types as an analogy, but as an identity.

More generally, Martin-Löf's system contains the notion of a sum $\exists x : B.A$ for an arbitrary type B and a type A dependent on the type B, and two projection rules that allow one to extract from an element of type $\exists x : B.A$ at the same time its first and second components. We note that a defect of these rules is that one loses the idea of an existential type as a "package" (the "program" $p2(t) : A[x/p1(t)]$ becomes visible to the user), which we discuss below. With this rule, one can show that the axiom of choice (or more precisely, the interpretation of this axiom in this system) holds.

The language one obtains can then be viewed as an extremely general functional language in which there is an identity between the notion of types and the notion of specification. This language seems especially suited for using constructive mathematics, as it is presented in [4] for example, as a programming language.

While the notion of types is very much broader than in usual functional languages, in that every formula is a type, one should note the absence of a general recursion operator in this language. This is replaced by a "recursion primitive" for each given structure (for example, for natural numbers, we have the operator *rec*), and the class of programs obtained is, despite the absence of general recursion, extremely important [2] for the examples of program development in this language. The question of making precise what would be the analogue in terms of proofs of general recursion used in programming languages is nevertheless very interesting in view of the analogy between propositions and types. For an example application, see [17].

Martin-Löf's system thus proposes a view of programming where the notion of types is identified with the (intuitionistic) notion of set, and with the notion of specification, of a logical proposition, which may be seen as a "problem". The solution of the problem is an algorithm if the type is the type defined by, and here identified with, this "problem". The algorithm itself may be viewed again as an element of the set represented by this "problem". It is based entirely on the Curry-Howard isomorphism and offers a spectacular interrelation between constructive mathematics and programming. A system similar to Martin-Löf's may be found in [8].

3.2 *Existential Types and the Notion of an "Abstract Type"*

We will show here how the analogy between propositions and types permits one to make precise the notion of a "package" by analyzing the relation between the existential quantifier and abstract types. In what follows, in the spirit of the Curry-Howard isomorphism (and Martin-Löf's system), I will consider the notions of propositions and of types to be identical, and I will present just a single calculus for the calculus of natural deduction and for the functional calculus.

First of all, we generalize the preceding first-order system by permitting an existential variable to vary over the set of types of the language. We distinguish this quantification from the former with the explicit notation $\exists x : Type.A$ (adopting the same notational conventions as for the bound variable of a λ-abstraction). Then we generalize the class of terms: If T is a type (such as $Nat, Nat \rightarrow Nat$) and t is a term, then $< T, t >$ is a term; and if t and u are terms, then $rep(t, u)$ is a term.

1. If $\Gamma \vdash p : A[x/T]$ where T is a type, then $\Gamma \vdash < T, t >: (\exists x : Type).A$.
2. If $\Gamma \vdash t : (\exists x : Type).A$ and $\Gamma, h : A \vdash u : B$, and if x doesn't appear in B, then $\Gamma \vdash rep(t, u) : B$.

The analogy with the existence rules for natural numbers is clear. The difference in the formulation comes from not having a universal quantifier over types. The following example shows why this formalization of an existential quantifier over types gives an account of the notion of abstract types.

We consider the following ML declaration:

abstype $complex = real \times real$

with $create\ x\ y = (x, y)$

and $plus\ z\ w = (fst(z) + fst(w),\ snd(z) + snd(w))$

and $reel\ z = fst(z);;$

This corresponds exactly to defining "complex" by the "proposition"

$$(\exists x : Type).(real \to real \to x) \wedge (x \to x \to x) \wedge (x \to real)$$

and noting that one then has

$$\begin{aligned} \vdash < real \wedge real, (&\lambda x.\lambda y. < x, y >, \\ &\lambda z.\lambda w.(fst(z) + fst(w), snd(z) + snd(w)), \\ &\lambda z.fst(z) \\ &) >: complex\ . \end{aligned}$$

The existential quantifier has the effect of "hiding" more explicit information. According to Kleene [20], one can view the confirmation of $\exists t.A$ as incomplete information for giving a term T and a proof of $A[t/T]$. This is exactly analogous to the notion of a "package", where one can conceal the complete implementation from the user and only give him partial information about it. This is an illustration of the analogy between propositions and types, which allows us to give a precise treatment of the notion of "package" [28].

It is very natural to "dualize" this notion of existential quantifier over types and consider universal quantification. We note that for this kind of quantification, the logical system is no longer predicative in the sense of [31]. The object of what follows is to make precise the system one obtains with a universal quantifier over types and the problems raised by this impredicativity for the analogy between propositions and types.

4 *The Second-Order Calculus*

We consider the first-order system of the previous chapter, but now we permit universal type quantification, which we will write $(\forall x : Type)A$ (adopting the same notational conventions as for other bound variables). We generalize the notion of terms as follows: if t is a term and T is a type, then $(t\ T)$ is a term. The added rules are:

1. if $\Gamma \vdash t : A$ and x doesn't appear in Γ, then $\Gamma \vdash \lambda x.t : (\forall x : Type)A$;

2. if $\Gamma \vdash t : (\forall x : Type)A$ and T is a type, then $\Gamma \vdash (t\ T) : A[x/T]$.

Again we note the analogy with the rules for first-order quantifiers (we've simply replaced *Nat* by *Type*).

The calculus obtained in this way is very expressive. For example, it is possible to code, uniquely for universal quantifiers, the existential quantifier (in a way so that the associated rules still hold) [11, 15, 16]. Moreover, this calculus is, as is the previous existential quantifier calculus, impredicative in the sense of [31]. For example, one can define the generic identity function $Id = \lambda T.\lambda x.x$ of type $(\forall T : Type)(T \to T)$ and it is possible to apply this function to its own type. The term obtained $(Id(\forall T : Type)(T \to T))$ is simply of type $((\forall T : Type)(T \to T)) \to ((\forall T : Type)(T \to T))$. As the notion of impredicativity is associated with classic paradoxes [31], one may ask whether this logic is consistent (in other words, whether there is no proof of the absurd proposition $\bot$).

Curiously enough, it is very easy to show consistency for this calculus: the method of truth tables suffices to show that all provable formulas are true (in other words, that their truth tables only contain 1), and thus that one can't prove $\bot$. It is much more difficult to show that this calculus, viewed as a functional system, satisfies the normalization property (this is not amazing given the remark that this property implies the consistency of the axiom of infinity [1]). This property is proved in [15].

The functional calculus thus obtained may be viewed as a very general functional language, and it is shown in [9] that one can extend this calculus by adding dependent types without losing the normalization property. This calculus generalizes the notion of generic types of the functional language ML, and it provides the programmer with a very wide class of functions without using recursion [11, 15, 29]. However, in contrast to the preceding calculi (except the calculus with an existential quantifier), it seems difficult to have a "semantics" for the programs one constructs. In effect, if one interprets the types as sets, then the product operation on types presents problems of interpretation (it would be necessary to define a "product over all sets"). This is formalized in [30], where it is shown that, for a very general definition of set-theoretic model of a functional calculus, there are no set-theoretic models of the second-order calculus.

This result shows in a certain way that it is dangerous to identify the notion of proof (of a proposition) with the notion of element (of a set). This is made precise by a result of Girard [15], [10], which shows that it isn't possible to extend in a consistent way Church's calculus of types [7] by adding second-order types (this result is the syntactic counterpart of the result of [30]). This means that in this extended calculus, all formulas (in Church's notation, the terms of type o) are provable (the definition of inconsistency for intuitionistic calculi). We note that the notion of generic type in the language ML is appropriately the good notion of universal quantification to avoid this inconsistency result [10, 14, 26]. A consequence of this result is that if one adds to a typed programming language a type of all types (including itself!), one can construct a typed program that loops, without using a recursion operator (it is no longer possible to consider this language as a logical calculus).

5 *Conclusions*

The preceding shows that the relation between propositions and types, and between proofs and programs, is a great deal more than a simple analogy. There are precise connections, and in some cases one can establish the existence of an isomorphism, between logical calculi and functional systems. One is then led to appreciate that there are no essential differences between the notion of type (in a programming language) and the notion of a proposition (in intuitionistic logic). An very representative example of this is the similarity between the intuitionistic existential quantifier and the notion of an abstract type [28]. We are thus witnessing a fusion between the notion of programs and that of constructive proofs. As this domain is relatively recent, many points remain to be clarified, for example, the question of knowing whether the enormous combinatorial complexity of mathematical proofs (which ultimately are just certain λ-terms) has a counterpart in programming.

In the last paragraph, we have seen that there is a structural difference between the "functionality" of sets and that of proofs: the calculus of proofs admits impredicativity, while sets do not. The "level" at which one must view programs isn't really very clear yet. This may be formulated as the question of knowing whether the analogy between types and propositions can be viewed as an identity (as Martin-Löf seems to do) or not. Be that as it may, this analogy plays a certain heuristic role in providing unexpected connections between deduction and computation.

References

[1] Andrews, P. "Resolution in type theory". *J. Symbolic Logic 36*, 3 (1971), pp. 414–432.

[2] Backhouse, R. "Algorithm development in Martin-Löf's type theory". University of Essex, July 1984.

[3] Barendregt, H. *The Lambda Calculus: Its Syntax and Semantics.* North-Holland, Amsterdam, 1980.

[4] Bishop, E. *Foundations of Constructive Analysis.* McGraw-Hill, New York, 1967.

[5] de Bruijn, N. "Lambda-calculus notation with nameless dummies, a tool for automatic formula manipulation, with application to the Church-Rosser theorem". *Indag. Math. 34*, 5 (1972), pp. 381–392.

[6] de Bruijn, N. "A survey of the project Automath". In *To H. B. Curry: Essays on Combinatory Logic, Lambda Calculus and Formalism*, J. P Seldin and J. R. Hindley, eds. Academic Press, New York, 1980.

[7] Church, A. "A formulation of the simple theory of types". *J. Symbolic Logic 5*, 1 (1940), pp. 56–68.

[8] Constable, R. and Bates, J. "The nearly ultimate Pearl". Dept. of Computer Science, Cornell University, December 1983.

[9] Coquand, Th. "Une théorie des constructions". Thèse de troisième cycle, Université Paris VII, January 1985.

[10] Coquand, Th. "An analysis of Girard's paradox". Submitted to the Symposium on Logic and Computer Science, 1986.

[11] Coquand, Th. and Huet, G. "Constructions: A higher order proof system for mechanizing mathematics". *Proc. EUROCAL 85* (Linz). Lecture Notes in Computer Science, vol. 203. Springer-Verlag, Berlin, 1985.

[12] Coquand, Th. and Huet, G. "Concepts mathematiques et informatiques formalisés dans le calcul des constructions". Paper presented at the Colloque de Logique d'Orsay (1985).

[13] Curry, H. and Feys, R. *Combinatory Logic*, vol. I. North-Holland, Amsterdam, 1958.

[14] Damas, L. and Milner, R. "Principal type-schemas for functional programs". Edinburgh University, 1982.

[15] Girard, J-Y. "Interprétation fonctionnelle et élimination des coupures de l'arithmetique d'ordre supérieur". These d'Etat, Paris VII, 1972.

[16] Fortune, S., Leivant, D., and O'Donnell, M. "The expressiveness of simple and second-order type structures". *J. ACM 30*, 1 (January 1983), pp. 151–185.

[17] Goad, Ch. "Computational uses of the manipulation of formal proofs". Ph.D thesis, Stanford University, 1980.

[18] Harrop, R. "Concerning formulas of the type $A \Rightarrow A \vee B, A \Rightarrow \exists x.B(x)$ in intuitionistic formal systems". *J. Symbolic Logic 25* (1960), pp. 27–32.

[19] Howard, W. "The formulæ-as-types notion of construction". Unpublished manuscript (1969). Reprinted in *To H. B. Curry: Essays on Combinatory Logic, Lambda Calculus and Formalism*, J. P. Seldin and J. R. Hindley, eds. Academic Press, New York, 1980.

[20] Kleene, S. *Introduction to Metamathematics.* Van Nostrand, New York, 1952.

[21] Kleene, S. "Realizability: A retrospective survey". L.N. 337, Cambridge Summer School in Mathematical Logic, 1971.

[22] Kreisel, G. "On the interpretation of nonfinitist proofs", parts I, II. *J. Symbolic Logic 16,17* (1952, 1953).

[23] Lambek, J. "From λ-calculus to Cartesian closed categories". In *To H. B. Curry: Essays on Combinatory Logic, Lambda Calculus and Formalism*, J. P. Seldin and J. R. Hindley, eds. Academic Press, New York, 1980.

[24] Martin-Löf, P. *Intuitionistic Type Theory.* Studies in Proof Theory. Bibliopolis, 1980.

[25] Meyer, A. and Mitchell, J. "Second-order logical relations". Extended abstract, 1985.

[26] Milner, R. "A theory of type polymorphism in programming". *J. Computer and System Sciences 17*, 3 (1978), pp. 348–375 .

[27] Mints, G. "E-theorems". *J. Soviet Math. 8* (1978), pp. 323–329.

[28] Mitchell, J. "Lambda calculus models of typed programming languages". Ph.D. thesis, Massachusetts Institute of Technology, 1984.

[29] Mohring, C. "Exemples de developpement de programmes dans la théorie des constructions". Report of the DEA, Université d'Orsay, September 1985.

[30] Reynolds, J. "Polymorphism is not set-theoretic". In *Semantics of Data Types* (Proceedings). Lecture Notes in Computer Science, vol. 173. Springer-Verlag, Berlin, 1984.

[31] Russell, B. and Whitehead, A. *Principia Mathematica,* vols. 1,2,3. Cambridge University Press, Cambridge, UK, 1912.

[32] Schoenfeld, J. *Mathematical Logic.* Addison-Wesley, Reading, Mass., 1967.

[33] Tait, W. "Intensional interpretations of functionals of finite type I". *J. Symbolic Logic 32* (1967), pp. 198–212.

[34] Werner, G. "Méthodes et problemes de la synthèse de programmes dans un univers typé". Université de Lille I, 1984.

Author's Note

Since this paper was written, some progress has been made in understanding the question of existential types and abstraction, but the issue is not clear yet. A good reference is D. MacQueen's paper, "Using dependent types to express modular structure".[2] It is argued in this paper that the strong notion of sums, as it appeared in Martin-Löf type theory, is better suited for representing the idea of modules than second-order existential quantification. Particularly interesting also is the idea that ML polymorphism corresponds

2. In *Proc. Symposium on Principles of Programming Languages*, ACM, New York, 1986.

rather to a "predicative" product over types (polymorphic types have a different status than ordinary types) than a second-order product. Another important reference is the paper of J. Mitchell and G. Plotkin, "Abstract data types have existential types",[3] which represents, so to speak, the "opposite" point of view, i.e., the view that a correct representation of abstract data type is second-order existential quantification.

Notice that the form in which the strong notion of sums is expressed is not the ordinary one. The ordinary form (as it appears in Martin-Löf's book [24]) is a kind of "induction principle" on the sum type and expresses the isomorphism between $(\Pi u : (\Sigma x : A)B(x))C(u)$ and $(\Pi x : A)(\Pi y : B(x))C((x, y))$. This implies the rules given in the paper, but the converse is not true (one needs furthermore the η-rule for pairing, or surjective pairing).

The computational behavior of Girard's paradox (cited in page 387) has been completely analyzed by D. Howe, using the NuPrl system.[4] By using ideas from Meyer and Reinholdt,[5] this analysis shows that it is possible to program any computable function in a type system with a type of all types, without using recursion.

An intriguing, but unexplored and perhaps only superficial, relation between propositions and types may be found in calculi with fixed-point operators on formulae (the greatest and the least fixed-point), like the one of K. Larsen,[6] which are similar to the ones used to define recursive and infinite types (see for instance "Infinite objects in type theory" of N. Mendler et al.[7]).

3. In *Proc. Symposium on Principles of Programming Languages*, ACM, New York, 1985.
4. Symposium on Logic in Computer Science, 1987.
5. "Type is not a type: preliminary report". *Proc. Thirteenth Annual ACM Symposium on Principles of Programming Languages* (St. Petersburg, Florida, January), pp. 287–295. ACM, New York, 1986.
6. "Proof systems for Hennessy-Milner logic with recursion", T. R. Aalborg Universitetscenter.
7. Symposium on Logic in Computer Science, 1986.

Recursive Realizability Semantics for Calculus of Constructions[1]

Preliminary Report

18

Andre Scedrov
University of Pennsylvania

1 *Introduction*

Types have become an important component of programming language design. They provide ways of incorporating a powerful, flexible syntax of a logic of program specifications into a programming language itself. Thus types provide both a context for an organized, logical development of programs according to given specifications and a framework for a partial verification mechanism. These features are instrumental in enhancing software reliability and maintainability.

One of the most important aspects of recently developed programming languages such as ML, Ada, Miranda, and CLU is that they feature polymorphic

1. This is a modified version of a technical report written in January 1987 for Odyssey Research Associates, Inc., sponsored by the U.S. Air Force Systems Command, Rome Air Development Center, Griffiss AFB, New York 13441-5700, under contract No. F30602-85-C-0098.

or generic data types that allow the programmer a new form of flexibility and abstraction in programming. The study of of these aspects of programming languages has led in recent years to the investigation of various rich type systems, mainly in the framework of typed lambda-calculi. These systems allow types which are dependent on other types and possibly on ordinary values. A formal calculus of such variable types was developed by Girard [10] as a higher-order extension of the Curry-Howard propositions-as-types paradigm in pure mathematical logic. A second-order fragment of this calculus was independently proposed by Reynolds [15] as a framework for programming languages that feature polymorphic types.

Calculus of constructions is an extension of the Girard-Reynolds calculus that combines higher-order polymorphic types with dependent products. In calculus of constructions the expressions for *proofs* and *assertions* (or, synonymously, for *programs* and *specifications*) may be given uniformly in all higher orders and types. Several versions of this kind of lambda formalism have been studied and implemented by T. Coquand and G. Huet [5, 6, 8, 11, 13].

Here we outline a semantics for calculus of constructions in which typing of terms is interpreted as set membership. More precisely, typings "term M has type A in context Γ" are interpreted by assigning a set $ext(\Gamma)$ to Γ and certain maps $\| M \|$ and $\| A \|$ to M and A so that for each c in $ext(\Gamma)$, $\| M \| (c)$ belongs to $\|A\| (c)$. On the one hand, this interpretation is related to the HEO_n semantics for finite higher-order lambda-calculi (cf. Girard [10]). On the other hand, our interpretation may be viewed as an interpretation of calculus of constructions in the realizability universe (a setting for intuitionistic theory of sets, e.g. [2, 12]).

2 *Terms and Inference Rules*

We mostly follow the presentation in [11]. Here we briefly review the main points. The terms are defined inductively:

$$\mathbf{Prop} \mid \mathbf{Type} \mid x \mid [x\colon A]B \mid (x\colon A)B \mid (AB)\,.$$

Abstraction over A is denoted by square brackets $[x\colon A]$. Product and quantification over A are denoted by parentheses $(x\colon A)$. We often write κ for either **Prop** or **Type**. As in [11], we think of variables and terms as presented by de Bruijn indices, and thus we are not concerned with alpha conversion.

Contexts are finite lists of bindings of variables: either empty or the expressions of the form $[x_1 : A_1] \ldots [x_n : A_n]$, where x_k is a variable and A_k is a term for each $1 \leq k \leq n$. If Γ is such a nonempty context, we write Γ_k for the term A_k.

Judgments are expressions of the form:

$$\Gamma \vdash A : B,$$

or

$$\Gamma \vdash A = B,$$

where Γ is a context and A and B are terms.

Derived judgments and *valid contexts* are defined simultaneously by the following rules of inference, in all of which Γ is assumed to be a valid context. In addition, in the second rule, variable x may not occur in Γ; in the third rule, Γ must be nonempty. In the rule *Appl*, $B\{N/x\}$ is the result of substituting N for x in B; similarly in the rule *Beta*.

The empty context is valid,

$$\frac{\Gamma \vdash A : \kappa}{\Gamma[X : A] \quad \text{valid}},$$

Var $\quad \Gamma \vdash x_k : \Gamma_k,$

Prop $\quad \Gamma \vdash \mathbf{Prop} : \mathbf{Type},$

Prod $$\frac{\Gamma \vdash A : \kappa \qquad \Gamma[x : A] \vdash B : \mathbf{Type}}{\Gamma \vdash (x : A)B : \mathbf{Type}},$$

Quant $$\frac{\Gamma \vdash A : \kappa \qquad \Gamma[x : A] \vdash B : \mathbf{Prop}}{\Gamma \vdash (x : A)B : \mathbf{Prop}},$$

Abstr $$\frac{\Gamma \vdash A : \kappa \qquad \Gamma[x : A] \vdash B : \kappa' \qquad \Gamma[x : A] \vdash M : B}{\Gamma \vdash [x : A]M : (x : A)B},$$

Appl $$\frac{\Gamma \vdash (x : A)B : \kappa \qquad \Gamma \vdash L : (x : A)B \qquad \Gamma \vdash N : A}{\Gamma \vdash (LN) : B\{N/x\}},$$

Equal $$\frac{\Gamma \vdash M : A \qquad \Gamma \vdash B : \kappa \qquad \Gamma \vdash A = B}{\Gamma \vdash M : B},$$

Refl $$\frac{\Gamma \vdash M : A}{\Gamma \vdash M = M},$$

Sym $$\frac{\Gamma \vdash M = N}{\Gamma \vdash N = M},$$

Trans $$\frac{\Gamma \vdash L = M \qquad \Gamma \vdash M = N}{\Gamma \vdash L = N},$$

AbsEq $$\frac{\Gamma \vdash A = A' \qquad \Gamma[x : A] \vdash M = M'}{\Gamma \vdash [x : A]M = [x : A']M'},$$

QuantEq $$\frac{\Gamma \vdash A = A' \qquad \Gamma[x : A] \vdash B = B'}{\Gamma \vdash (x : A)B = (x : A')B'},$$

ApplEq $$\frac{\Gamma \vdash (LN) : A \qquad \Gamma \vdash L = L' \qquad \Gamma \vdash N = N'}{\Gamma \vdash (LN) = (L'N')},$$

$$\textit{Beta} \qquad \frac{\Gamma[x:A] \vdash M:B \qquad \Gamma \vdash N:A}{\Gamma \vdash ([x:A]MN) = M\{N/x\}}.$$

Constructions consist of finitely many successive applications of the inference rules. From now on we assume that all exhibited judgments are derivable and that Γ denotes a valid context.

Lemma

If $\Gamma \vdash M: A$, then either $\Gamma \vdash A =$ **Type**, or $\Gamma \vdash A$: **Type**, or $\Gamma \vdash A$: **Prop.**

Referring to the three cases given by the lemma, we say that M is a *Γ-type*, a *Γ-proposition*, or a *Γ-proof*. We often omit the prefix Γ when discussing the cases in a single construction.

Given a valid context Γ of the form $[x_1 : A_1] \dots [x_n : A_n]$, $n \geq 0$, we count the number $\#\Gamma$ of nontypes among $A_1, \dots, A_n$ and define a canonical injection $j_\Gamma : \{1, \dots, \#\Gamma\} \to \{1, \dots, n\}$ as follows: $\#_{-} = 0$, $j_{-} = 0$; if Γ' is $[x_1 : A_1] \dots [x_{n-1} : A_{n-1}]$ and A_n is a type, then $\#\Gamma = \#\Gamma'$ and $j_\Gamma(k) = j_{\Gamma'}(k) + 1$, else $\#\Gamma = (\#\Gamma') + 1$, $j_\Gamma(1) = 1$, and $j_\Gamma(k + 1) = j_{\Gamma'}(k) + 1$. We will often confuse Γ with a derived judgment $\Gamma \vdash$ **Prop: Type** and thus with a derived judgment $\vdash (x_1 : A_1) \dots (x_n : A_n)$ **Prop: Type**. Every type is derivably equal to one of this form.

3 *An Interpretation of Constructions*

Given any derived judgment $\Gamma \vdash M: A$, we specify a set $ext(\Gamma)$ (the *extent* of Γ) and a mapping $\|M\|$ defined on $ext(\Gamma)$ (the value of M). This will be done in such a way that whenever $\Gamma \vdash M: A$ and $\Gamma \vdash A: \kappa$ (recall the three cases in the lemma above), it will be the case that for any $c \in ext(\Gamma)$, $\|M\|(c) \in \|A\|(c)$. Moreover, derivable equality of terms will be interpreted as ordinary equality of their values.

Let $\|$**Prop**$\|$ be the collection of all quotients of equivalence relations on sets of natural numbers. We proceed by induction on the definition of constructions and valid contexts. Simultaneously, we show that a value of a Γ-proof M is uniquely determined by a partial recursive function ϕ_M of $\#\Gamma$ arguments that preserves the relevant symmetric transitive relations. Of course, ϕ_M depends on the construction. We shall say that ϕ_M *realizes* M.

A few words about notation: for A/R in $\|$**Prop**$\|$, let $dom(A/R) = A$, $rel(A/R) = R$. Given Q in $\|$**Prop**$\|$ and a map $F : Q \to \|$**Prop**$\|$, we write $\tilde{n}$ for the equivalence class of n in Q. Let $\Pi rec_{a \in Q} F(a)$ be the quotient in $\|$**Prop**$\|$ given as follows: First consider the set of numerical codes of partial recursive functions f such that if $n\ rel(Q)m$, then $f(n)$ and $f(m)$ are defined, and $f(n)$ and $f(m)$ are related in $F(\tilde{n})$. Note that if $n\ rel(Q)m$, $F(\tilde{n}) = F(\tilde{m})$. We consider two such codes e, e' equivalent if $\{e\}(n)$ and $\{e'\}(m)$ are related in $F(\tilde{n})$

whenever $n\ rel(Q)m$.

In the following definition, c is assumed to be in $ext(\Gamma)$.

Rules for valid contexts: Let the extent of a blank context be a one-element set. Let $ext(\Gamma[x : A])$ consist of all ordered pairs $\langle c, a\rangle$ such that $c \in ext(\Gamma)$ and $a \in \|A\|(c)$.

Var: Since $ext(\Gamma)$ is the set of n-tuples $\langle a_1, \ldots, a_n\rangle$ such that $a_{m+1} \in \|A_m\|(a_1, \ldots, a_m)$ for $1 \le m \le n$, let $\|x_k\|(a_1, \ldots, a_n) = a_k$. If Γ_k is a proposition in the context $[x_1 : A_1] \ldots [x_{k-1} : A_{k-1}]$, then let the required partial recursive function of several arguments be the projection of $\#\Gamma$ arguments to the relevant coordinate, the one which is the inverse image of k under j_Γ.

Prod: Let $\|(x : A)B\|(c) = \Pi_{a \in \|A\|(c)} \|B\|(c, a)$, an ordinary product of sets. (Note that if $\|A\|(c)$ is empty, then $\|(x : A)B\|(c)$ is the singleton consisting of the empty function.)

Quant: *Case 1*: κ is **Type**. Let $dom(\|(x : A)B\|(c))$ be the intersection of $dom(\|B\|(c, a))$ for all $a \in \|A\|(c)$. Let $rel(\|(x : A)B\|(c))$ be the intersection of $rel(\|B\|(c, a))$ for all $a \in \|A\|(c)$. *Case 2*: κ is **Prop.** Let $\|(x : A)B\|(c) = \Pi rec_{a \in \|A\|(c)} \|B\|(c, a)$.

Abstr: *Case 1*: κ' is **Type**. Let $\|[x : A]M\|(c)$ be the assignment defined by $\|[x : A]M\|(c)(a) = \|M\|(c, a)$ for all $a \in \|A\|(c)$. *Case 2*: κ' is **Prop**, κ is **Type**. Then $\#\Gamma[x : A] = \#\Gamma$. We know that $\|M\|(c, a) =$ the equivalence class of $\phi_M(n_1, \ldots, n_{\#\Gamma})$. Now simply let $\phi_{[xA]M} = \phi_M$. *Case 3*: κ' and κ are both **Prop**. Then $\#\Gamma[x : A] = \#\Gamma + 1$. We define $\phi_{[xA]M}$ by the s-m-n theorem from recursion theory. For each fixed $n_1, \ldots, n_{\#\Gamma}$, let $\phi_{[x:A]M}(n_1, \ldots, n_{\#\Gamma})$ be the numerical code (given by the s-m-n theorem) of the unary partial recursive function that maps k to $\phi_M(n_1, \ldots, n_{\#\Gamma}, k)$. $\phi_{[xA]M}$ preserves the required relations because, according to *Quant, Case 2*, $\|(x : A)B\|$ is of the form Πrec.

Appl: *Case 1*: κ is **Type**. Let $\|LN\|$ be given by evaluation, that is: $\|LN\|(c) = \|L\|(c)(\|N\|(c))$. *Case 2*: κ is **Prop** and $\Gamma \vdash A :$ **Type**. Let $\phi_{LN} = \phi_L$. *Case 3*: κ is **Prop** and $\Gamma \vdash A :$ **Prop**. Then let $\phi_{LN}(n_1, \ldots, n_{\#\Gamma})$ be obtained by computing the value of the partial recursive function with numerical code $\phi_L(n_1, \ldots, n_{\#\Gamma})$ on input $\phi_N(n_1, \ldots, n_{\#\Gamma})$ (when all data are defined). In recursion-theoretic notation,

$$\phi_{LN}(n_1, \ldots, n_{\#\Gamma}) \simeq \{\phi_L(n_1, \ldots, n_{\#\Gamma})\}(\phi_N(n_1, \ldots, n_{\#\Gamma})) .$$

One verifies the following theorem by induction on constructions.

Theorem (Soundness Theorem)
Let $\Gamma \vdash M : A$ and $\Gamma \vdash A : \kappa$. Then for any $c \in ext(\Gamma)$, $\|M\|(c) \in \|A\|(c)$. Furthermore, if $\Gamma \vdash A = B$, then for any $c \in ext(\Gamma)$, $\|A\|(c) = \|B\|(c)$.

The consistency follows because $\|(x :$ **Prop**$)x\|$ is empty.

Corollary

There is no term M such that $\vdash M : (x\colon \mathbf{Prop})x$.

Example 1 Consider the following construction:

1.		$\vdash \mathbf{Prop} : \mathbf{Type}$,	
2.	$[x\colon \mathbf{Prop}]$	valid,	
3.	$[x\colon \mathbf{Prop}]$	$\vdash x\colon \mathbf{Prop}$,	
4.	$[x\colon \mathbf{Prop}]\ [y\colon x]$	valid,	
5.	$[x\colon \mathbf{Prop}]\ [y\colon x]$	$\vdash y\colon x$,	
6.	$[x\colon \mathbf{Prop}]\ [y\colon x]$	$\vdash x\colon \mathbf{Prop}$,	
7.	$[x\colon \mathbf{Prop}]$	$\vdash [y\colon x]y : (y\colon x)x$	(*Abstr* on 6, 6, 5),
8.	$[x\colon \mathbf{Prop}]$	$\vdash (y\colon x)x : \mathbf{Prop}$	(*Quant* on 3,6),
9.		$\vdash (x\colon \mathbf{Prop})(y\colon x)x : \mathbf{Prop}$	(*Quant* on 1, 8),
10.		$\vdash [x\,\mathbf{Prop}][y\colon x]y : (x : \mathbf{Prop})(y\colon x)x$	(*Abstr*).

We may interpret this construction "as it unfolds". Recall that $\|\mathbf{Prop}\|$ is the set of all quotients of equivalence relations on subsets of natural numbers. Also recall that the extent of the empty context is a one-element set. We proceed along the construction:

2. $ext([x\colon \mathbf{Prop}]) = \|\mathbf{Prop}\|$,

3. $\|x\|$ is the identity function on $\|\mathbf{Prop}\|$,

4. $ext([x : \mathbf{Prop}][y : x])$ consists of all ordered pairs $\langle Q, a\rangle$ where $Q \in \|\mathbf{Prop}\|$ and $a \in Q$,

5. $\#[x : \mathbf{Prop}][y : x] = 1, \|y\|(Q, a) = a,\ \phi_y$ is the identity function on the natural numbers,

6. $\|x\|(Q, a) = \|x\|(Q) = Q$,

7. $\#[x : \mathbf{Prop}] = 0, \|[y : x]y\|(Q) =$ the s-m-n numerical code of the identity function,

8. $\|(y : x)x\|(Q) = \Pi rec_{a\in Q}Q$, that is: the set I_Q of numerical codes of partial recursive functions that map $dom(Q)$ to itself and preserve $rel(Q)$; modulo the equivalence relation R_Q on I_Q : $e\ R_Q\ e'$ iff $n\ relQ)m$ implies $\{e\}(n)\ rel(Q)\ \{e'\}(m)$,

9. $\|(x\colon \mathbf{Prop})(y\colon x)x\|$ is the quotient I/R, where I is the intersection of all I_Q's and R is the intersection of all R_Q's,

10. $\|[x\colon \mathbf{Prop}][y\colon x]y\|$ is the code of the identity used in 7.

In the discussion below we use the following abbreviations for $(x : A)B$ if x does not occur in B : When both A and B are propositions we write $A \Rightarrow B$, else $A \rightarrow B$. We associate to the right.

Example 2 We discuss the recursive realizability interpretation of example 5.2.3 in [11]. The example is a good illustration of the importance of equality of judgments. Given a type A in a valid context Γ', we will construct a proof of the proposition that the intersection of a class of predicates on A is included in any predicate of the class. Let us begin by defining the inclusion of predicates on A. Let *Subset* be the term:

$$[P : A \rightarrow \textbf{Prop}][Q : A \rightarrow \textbf{Prop}](x : A)(Px) \Rightarrow (Qx).$$

We first show that:

$$\Gamma' \vdash \mathit{Subset} : (A \rightarrow \textbf{Prop}) \rightarrow (A \rightarrow \textbf{Prop}) \rightarrow \textbf{Prop}.$$

Indeed, let Γ'' be the context:

$$\Gamma'[P : A \rightarrow \textbf{Prop}][Q : A \rightarrow \textbf{Prop}][x : A].$$

Continuing from $\Gamma' \vdash A : \textbf{Type}$, it is readily shown that Γ'' is valid, hence:

i)	Γ''	$\vdash x : A$,
ii)	Γ''	$\vdash P : A \rightarrow \textbf{Prop}$,
iii)	Γ''	$\vdash Px : \textbf{Prop}$,
iv)	$\Gamma''[y : Px]$	is valid,
v)	$\Gamma''[y : Px]$	$\vdash x : A$,
vi)	$\Gamma''[y : Px]$	$\vdash Q : A \rightarrow \textbf{Prop}$,
vii)	$\Gamma''[y : Px]$	$\vdash Qx : \textbf{Prop}$,
viii)	Γ''	$\vdash (Px) \Rightarrow (Qx) : \textbf{Prop}$,

and thus the desired typing judgment for *Subset* follows by a quantification and two abstractions.

Let us pause to realize what we have constructed so far. Fix an arbitrary $c \in \mathit{ext}(\Gamma')$. All values will depend on c (except $\|\textbf{Prop}\|$, which is always the collection of quotients of equivalence relations on subsets of natural numbers). We shall often suppress c for the sake of brevity.

First note that $\|A \rightarrow \textbf{Prop}\|$ is simply the set of all functions from $\|A\|$ to $\|\textbf{Prop}\|$. Thus $\mathit{ext}(\Gamma'')$ consists of all tuples of the form $\langle c, f, g, a\rangle$, where $a \in \|A\|$

and f and g are functions from $\|A\|$ to $\|\mathbf{Prop}\|$. Thus:

i) $\|x\|\,(c, f, g, a) = a,$

ii) $\|P\|\,(c, f, g, a) = f,$

iii) $\|Px\|\,(c, f, g, a) = f(a),$

iv) $ext(\Gamma''[y\colon Px])$ consists of all tuples $\langle c, f, g, a, \tilde{n}\rangle$ where $\langle c, f, g, a\rangle \in ext(\Gamma'')$ and the equivalence class $\tilde{n}$ belongs to $f(a)$,

v) $\|x\|\,(c, f, g, a, \tilde{n}) = a,$

vi) $\|Q\|\,(c, f, g, a, \tilde{n}) = g,$

vii) $\|Qx\|\,(c, f, g, a, \tilde{n}) = g(a),$

viii) $\|(Px) \Rightarrow (Qx)\|\,(c, f, g, a) = \Pi rec_{b \in f(a)}\, g(a)$
(that is: the set of numerical codes of partial recursive functions that map $f(a)$ to $g(a)$; modulo the required equivalence relation.)

Thus $\|(x\colon A)\,(Px) \Rightarrow (Qx)\|\,(c, f, g)$ is obtained from $\Pi rec_{b \in f(a)}\, g(a)$ by intersection over all $a \in \|A\|$, and hence $\|Subset\|(c)$ is given as the assignment:

$$\|Subset\|(c)(f)(g) = \|(x\colon A)(Px) \Rightarrow (Qx)\|(c, f, g)$$

for any $f,\ g\colon \|A\| \to \|\mathbf{Prop}\|$. (The notation in calculus of constructions here nicely coincides with the ordinary mathematical notation for functions from a given domain to a given codomain.)

Now we continue with the construction by defining the intersection of a class of predicates on A. Let *Inter* be the term:

$$[C : (A \to \mathbf{Prop}) \to \mathbf{Prop}][x : A](P : A \to \mathbf{Prop})(CP) \Rightarrow (Px).$$

The reader will easily check that:

$$\Gamma' \vdash Inter : ((A \to \mathbf{Prop}) \to \mathbf{Prop}) \to A \to \mathbf{Prop}.$$

The value of the type is again obtained simply by reading the arrows as "the set of all functions from ... to ...". Thus given a mapping F that takes functions from $\|A\|$ to $\|\mathbf{Prop}\|$ to the quotients in $\|\mathbf{Prop}\|$, and given a in $\|A\|$, we may obtain $\|Inter\|(c)(F)(a)$ as the quotient of the set of numerical codes of partial recursive functions that map $F(f)$ to $f(a)$ for every $f\colon \|A\| \to \|\mathbf{Prop}\|$. Two such codes e and e' are equivalent iff for every $f\colon \|A\| \to \|\mathbf{Prop}\|$, if n and m are equivalent in $F(f)$, then $\{e\}(n)$ and $\{e'\}(m)$ are equivalent in $f(a)$.

The reader will have noticed that the logical structure of this definition is exactly the one expressed in the syntax, namely, the universal quantification of an implication. In fact, realizability interpretation provides a way of reading the syntax of the calculus of constructions in the ordinary mathematical way, except that proofs are read as codes of partial recursive functions. (The equivalence relations are there to account for the rules *AbsEq* and *ApplEq*.) Square brackets are read "let ... be in ...".

We continue with the construction. Let Γ be the valid context:

$$\Gamma'[C_0 : (A \to \mathbf{Prop}) \to \mathbf{Prop}][P_0 : A \to \mathbf{Prop}][p_0 : (C_0 P_0)]\,.$$

In this context, we shall construct a proof of the proposition that the predicate $(\mathit{Inter}\ C_0)$ is included in the predicate P_0. Let Δ be the valid context

$$\Gamma[x : A][h : ((\mathit{Inter}\ C_0)x)].$$

The inference rule *Beta* yields

$$\Gamma[x : A] \vdash ((\mathit{Inter}\ C_0)x) = (P : A \to \mathbf{Prop})\ (C_0 P) \Rightarrow (Px).$$

Because this is an equality of propositions, we may use the inference rule *Equal* to obtain

$$\Delta \vdash h : (P : A \to \mathbf{Prop})(C_0\ P) \Rightarrow (Px)\ ;$$

hence:

$$\Delta \vdash ((h\ P_0)p_0) : (P_0\ x)\,.$$

Using *Beta* again, we obtain:

$$\Gamma \vdash ((\mathit{Subset}\ (\mathit{Inter}\ C_0))P_0) = (x : A)((\mathit{Inter}\ C_0)x) \Rightarrow (P_0\ x)\,.$$

This is also an equality of propositions; hence the rule *Equal* yields:

$$\Gamma \vdash [x : A][h : ((\mathit{Inter}\ C_0)x)]((h\ P_0)p_0) : ((\mathit{Subset}(\mathit{Inter}\ C_0))P_0).$$

We conclude the discussion of this example by describing the partial recursive function that realizes the Γ-proof just constructed. This function must depend only on the construction, not on $c \in ext(\Gamma')$. Let $k = \#\Gamma'$; hence $\#\Gamma = k+1$ and $\#\Delta = k + 2$. $\|((h\ P_0)p_0)\|$ is given by the partial recursive function ϕ that computes $\{e\}(n)$ from input$\langle i_1, \ldots, i_k, n, e\rangle$. Our Γ-proof is then realized by the partial recursive function that computes the s-m-n code of ϕ for any given $i_1, \ldots, i_k$, and n.

4 Concluding Remarks

We have interpreted constructions by certain meaning maps. A similar approach to semantics of second-order lambda calculus is discussed by Breazu-Tannen and Coquand in [1]. This approach is also taken by Coquand and Huet in [7] in interpreting a weaker version of calculus of constructions by a realizability based on application in Scott domains. Our interpretation, which has also been outlined by Dana Scott and by Martin Hyland, is based on the partial recursive function application.

The calculus interpreted here is basically the *pure* calculus of constructions considered by Huet in [11], but our interpretation also extends to various stronger calculi considered there. Such extensions are facilitated by considering the interpretation described here as an interpretation in a fragment of the (recursive) realizability universe rather than in the universe of ordinary sets. The realizability universe, i.e., the effective topos, is a setting for intuitionistic theory of sets [2, 9, 12]. We have in fact interpreted $(x : A)B$ as products given intrinsically in the realizability universe. This point of view makes it plausible to consider notions of valid contexts that are much more extensive than in the pure calculus. (The price is a more involved definition of meaning maps, obtained by considering the intrinsic maps in the realizability universe.)

We also observe that the realizability interpretation itself may be formalized in an appropriate fragment of intuitionistic set theory (depending on a particular version of the calculus), and thus it may be used in obtaining information about the logical power of calculus of constructions. This kind of information is often presented in terms of numerical functions representable in the calculus. A convenient way to deal with the natural numbers in the calculus is by stating arithmetic via constants and axioms (similarly to [3]). Let **Nat**, **0**, names of some basic numerical functions, *recursor*, and *inductor* be constants in the language. Postulate some typing judgments, e.g.,

$$\Gamma \vdash \mathbf{Nat} : \mathbf{Prop},$$

$$\Gamma \vdash \mathbf{0} : \mathbf{Nat},$$

$$\Gamma \vdash \mathbf{s} : \mathbf{Nat} \to \mathbf{Nat},$$

$$\Gamma \vdash \mathbf{Peano} \;:\; (x{:}\,\mathbf{Nat})(P{:}\,\mathbf{Nat} \to \mathbf{Prop})P\mathbf{0} \Rightarrow ((y{:}\,\mathbf{Nat})(Py \Rightarrow P(\mathbf{s}y))) \Rightarrow Px,$$

$$\Gamma \vdash + : \mathbf{Nat} \to \mathbf{Nat} \to \mathbf{Nat},$$

etc.,

as well as the equalities for the base functions and recursion. The soundness theorem for the recursive realizability semantics for the amended calculus holds if $\|\mathbf{Nat}\|$ is defined as the set of natural numbers with the equality as the equivalence relations, if **0** and the basic numerical functions are interpreted as such, and if recursion on partial recursive functions is used to interpret *recursor* and *inductor*. (It has been shown by Hyland and by Freyd that this is still the case if **Nat** is *defined* as $(A : \mathbf{Prop})((A \Rightarrow A) \Rightarrow A \Rightarrow A)$.) Formalizing the recursive realizability interpretation of this version of the pure calculus of constructions in higher-order arithmetic yields the result that the numerical functions representable in this calculus (as proofs of the proposition **Nat** → **Nat**) are exactly the numerical functions representable in Girard's higher-order polymorphic lambda calculus F^{ω}, to wit, the recursive functions provably total in higher-order arithmetic. Stronger versions of the calculus correspond in this manner to stronger systems of set theory.

Acknowledgments

The author's research is partially supported by N.S.F. We would like to thank Bob Constable, Thierry Coquand, Jean-Yves Girard, Gérard Huet, Anil Nerode, Richard Platek, Garrel Pottinger, Dana Scott, and Jon Seldin for stimulating and helpful conversations, personal or electronic.

References

[1] Breazu-Tannen, V. and Coquand, T. "Extensional models for polymorphism". *Proc. TAPSOFT '87—CFLP* (Pisa). To appear in *Theoretical Computer Science.*

[2] Carboni, A., Freyd, P., and Scedrov, A. "A categorical approach to realizability and polymorphic types". *Proc. Third ACM Workshop on the Mathematical Foundations of Programming Language Semantics* (New Orleans, April 1987), pp. 23–42. Lecture Notes in Computer Science, vol. 298. Springer-Verlag, Berlin, 1988.

[3] Constable, R. L., et al. *Implementing Mathematics in the NUPRL Proof Development System.* Prentice-Hall, Englewood Cliffs, N.J., 1986.

[4] Coquand, T. "Une théorie des constructions." Thèse de troisème cycle, Université Paris VII, 1985.

[5] Coquand, T. "An analysis of Girard's paradox". *Proc. First IEEE Symposium on Logic in Computer Science* (Cambridge, Mass.), pp. 227–236. IEEE Press, New York, 1986.

[6] Coquand, T. and Huet, G. "Constructions: A higher-order proof system for mechanizing mathematics". *Proc. EUROCAL'85*, pp. 151–184. Lecture Notes in Computer Science, vol. 203. Springer-Verlag, Berlin, 1985.

[7] Coquand, T. and Huet, G. "A calculus of constructions". Preprint, June 1985.

[8] Coquand, T. and Huet, G. "Concepts mathématiques et informatiques formalisés dans le calcul des constructions". In *Logic Colloquium 85.* The Paris Logic Group, ed. North-Holland, Amsterdam, 1987.

[9] Freyd, P. and Scedrov, A. "Some semantic aspects of polymorphic lambda calculus". *Proc. Second IEEE Symposium on Logic in Computer Science* (Ithaca, N.Y.), pp. 315-

319. IEEE Press, New York, 1987.

[10] Girard, J-Y. "Interprétation fonctionelle et élimination des coupures de l'arithmétique d'ordre supérieur". Thèse de Doctorat d'Etat, Université Paris VII, 1972.

[11] Huet, G. "A uniform approach to type theory". This volume, Chapter 16.

[12] Longo, G. and Moggi, E. "Constructive natural deduction and its 'modest' interpretation". In *Semantics of Natural and Computer Languages* (Proceedings, Stanford, March 1987), J. Meseguer et al., eds. MIT Press, Cambridge, Mass., to appear.

[13] Mohring, C. "Algorithm development in the calculus of constructions". *Proc. First IEEE Symposium on Logic in Computer Science* (Cambridge, Mass.), pp. 84–91. IEEE Press, New York, 1986.

[14] Pottinger, G. "Strong normalization for terms of the theory of constructions". Preprint, February 1987.

[15] Reynolds, J. "Towards a theory of type structure". *Programming Symposium*, B. Robinet, ed., pp. 408–425. Lecture Notes in Computer Science, vol. 19. Springer-Verlag, Berlin, 1974.

[16] Seldin, J. "Theory of MATHESIS". Technical Report, Odyssey Research Associates, Inc., Ithaca, N.Y., March 1987.

An Introduction to PX

19

Susumu Hayashi[1]
Kyoto University

Introduction

This paper gives an introduction to a system, **PX**, which realizes the paradigm of "proofs as programs". The aim of **PX** is to check constructive proofs and to extract programs from the proofs. We will give a brief description of the underlying logic of **PX** and its implementation. Some techniques for extracting programs from proofs are also presented.

This paper was written for the Proceedings of the UT Year of Programming's Institute on Logical Foundations of Functional Programming, collecting materials from my paper, "**PX**: a system extracting programs from constructive proofs", and from my monograph with Nakano, "**PX**: a computational logic". For further information, see the monograph.

1. Now at Ryukoku University.

The aim of the **PX** project is to build a computer system extracting LISP programs from verified constructive proofs via the so-called Curry-Howard isomorphism, which was one of the main subjects of the Institute on Logical Foundations of Functional Programming.

Type theories are known as *good* logical foundations for developing correct functional programs. Types in Martin-Löf's type theory and Coquand-Huet's type theory (Calculus of constructions, see Huet's paper in this volume) can represent specifications describing a detailed relation between inputs and outputs. All programs with legal types terminate and are correct with respect to such specifications, so they are *totally* correct. This implies that in program development through type theories, one has to verify termination of one's programs. But each type theory is a finite formal system, so it is impossible to cover all of computable functions by a single type theory, and hence one may miss functions. It is known that the Coquand-Huet type theory can cover a very wide class of computable functions, which appears sufficient to cover eventually all computable functions in actual use. Even the weakest version of their calculus can cover all number-theoretic functions computable in the second-order arithmetic.

But this is correct only from a theoretical point of view. Even if a function has a very high complexity of computation, a program using such a function may be necessary, since such a program may be run only on a few inputs. Then it is hopeless to code functions with high complexity of computation effectively. But still programmers program them, and such programs can be useful. For example, it is known that the satisfiability problem of propositional logic is *NP*-complete.

Nevertheless, a program deciding satisfiability is efficient and useful in proof-checkers. Why? Because we do not test huge formulas of propositional logic. All formulas we can write are relatively small. We cannot rely on the theory of computational complexity to measure efficiency of a program used only for relatively small inputs, for complexity theory measures the efficiency of an algorithm with respect to *all* possible inputs.

Furthermore, sometimes a program runs only once. For example, a program that computes the smallest unknown prime number need not be run twice, if the program is correct. Consider a function f whose computational complexity is so high that it is impossible to program it in an existing type theory, but suppose the aim is to compute a number $f(0)$. How can we compute it in the type theory? One may say that the value of $f(0)$ is a number n, so the program is n itself. Of course, this argument is meaningless, for n is the number we wish to compute by f. So we cannot say we do not miss a function even if it has a very high complexity of computation. (These arguments were inspired by a discussion with G. Huet.)

Furthermore, even if we ignore functions not available in a type theory, we may miss "algorithms". Type theories have only very limited numbers of control structures for recursion, so even if one can program a function by means of a type theory, it may be very slow, for it must employ the control structures available only in the type theory. Furthermore, even if one can write efficient programs by a type theory, one must verify that they are *totally* correct through type-checking—that is, one must check that the program terminates before one runs it. This is a heavy burden. Checking termination is normally the hardest part of program verification. We wish to distinguish it from others.

PX gives a solution to these problems. It can extract all computable functions over "concrete" data types, such as an initial algebra of a finitely presented algebraic theory, from constructive proofs. It can distinguish termination problems and lemmata on data types that are not relevant to computation from the parts of constructive proofs which are relevant to computation (control structures). Termination conditions can be explicitly expressed in the language of **PX**, even if they cannot be proved in the proof-checker of **PX**, and **PX** has a wide variety of recursions (called CIG-recursions).

The mathematical tools behind these techniques were already known, so there are no brand new mathematical observations in this paper. The point was how to organize the known mathematical theories. The Nuprl group uses very similar techniques and solves these problems in a very similar way in the framework of the type theory of Nuprl. The point is to use a logic (in **PX**) or a type theory (in Nuprl) allowing terms that may fail to denote a value, and to use an inductive (recursive) definition of classes (in **PX**) or types (in Nuprl).

The price we have to pay to solve these problems is that such an extended logic or extended type theory is more complicated than the usual logic or type theory, and (at least in the case of **PX**) a proof that respects efficiency and the separation of termination condition of the extracted program is not a "good proof" from the mathematicians' point of view. Normally, a proof that is simple from a mathematical point of view represents a very simple-minded and slow program. Another problem is that neither **PX** nor Nuprl can program all computable higher-order functions. So the solutions of the problems of (i) extracting efficient programs from mathematically good proofs and (ii) extracting all higher-order computable functions from constructive proofs, or programming all higher order computable functions in a single type theory, are still unknown. It seems that the second problem has a negative solution from a theoretical point of view.

This paper consists of four sections. Section 1 describes the formal theory of **PX**. Section 2 describes the logical foundation for the extraction of programs from proofs via **PX**. Section 3 describes a methodology by which we can separate the termination problem from others and extract all recursive functions over natural numbers. Section 4 describes an implementation of **PX**.

1 *Formal Theory*

We will give a brief explanation of the formal theory of **PX**. The underlying logic of **PX** is a variant of Feferman's theory of T_0. It is an *untyped* theory of computations and data types. Data types are represented as codes which are called *classes*, so data types are objects in **PX**. The logic of **PX** allows partial terms, i.e., terms that may fail to denote a value.

1.1 *Expressions*

In this section, we will define the expressions (terms) and functions of **PX**. The objects (values) that expressions describe are *S-expressions*, i.e., the objects generated from atoms by successive applications of dotted-pair operations.

The expressions and functions of **PX** are defined by the following:

$$\begin{aligned} e \quad &::= \quad x \mid c \mid fn(e_1, \ldots, e_n) \mid cond(e_1, d_1; \ldots; e_n, d_n) \\ &\quad\;\; \mid \Lambda(x_1 = e_1, \ldots, x_n = e_n)(fn) \mid let\ p_1 = e_1, \ldots, p_n = e_n\ in\ e\,, \\ fn \quad &::= \quad f \mid \lambda(x_1, \ldots, x_n)(e)\,. \end{aligned}$$

Here $e, e_1, d_1, \ldots$ and fn range over expressions and a function, respectively, x ranges over variables, c ranges over constants, and f ranges over function identifiers. Besides these official expressions, we use *case expression* defined by

$$case(e, e_1, \ldots, e_n) \equiv_{\mathrm{def}} cond(equal(e, 1), e_1; \ldots; equal(e, n), e_n).$$

These are mathematically refined M-expressions of a class of well-formed LISP programs, so **PX** may be thought of as a system based on LISP. The semantics of the expressions are given by a LISP interpreter. To that end we translate the above M-expressions to S-expressions as usual. Applications, conditional forms, **let** forms, and λ-notations are translated as usual. The patterns $p_1, \ldots, p_n$ of the **let** form are patterns in the sense of Franz LISP ([8]), but they may include constants, e.g., (1 . x), which is not a pattern of Franz LISP.

The Λ-notation $\Lambda(x_1 = e_1, \ldots, x_n = e_n)(fn)$ is translated into an expression whose value is the function closure of *fn* with the local environment $\{x_1 = [\![e_1]\!], \ldots, x_n = [\![e_n]\!]\}$, where $[\![e]\!]$ stands for the value of e. The point is that *all of the free variables of the function fn, FV(fn) in symbol, must be included in* $x_1, \ldots, x_n$. Otherwise it is an illegal expression. Besides, two Λ-expressions are α-convertible only when their functions are *literally* equal.

The translation of Λ-notation is arbitrary as far as translated Λ-notations satisfy the axioms given in 1.3.1. One possibility is to translate, e.g., $\Lambda(x = e)(\lambda(y)(pair(x, y)))$ to an expression whose value is the expression

```
(lambda (y) (let ((x (quote ⟦e⟧))) (pair x y))).
```

Since e is evaluated when the translated Λ-form is evaluated, the Λ-notation has a value only when e has a value.

Λ-notation corresponds to S_n^m function or Λ-notation of [15]. A similar mechanism was used in CAM to represent a functional value. (See Cousineau's paper in this volume.)

We may introduce functions by recursive definitions as is usual in LISP. The scoping is lexical so that a function cannot be declared unless its arguments include all of the free variables of its body of definition.

We assume that at least the following functions are included in the basic (built-in) functions of **PX**:

app, app∗, list, atom, fst, snd, pair, equal, suc, prd.

These ten function identifiers are intended to be the following LISP functions, respectively:

*apply, funcall, list, atom, car, cdr, cons, equal, add*1*, sub*1.

In our theory, neither a variable nor a constant need have a value. This is unusual but quite convenient for describing a programming language. The constants (variables) are divided into two groups. One is the *total* constants (variables), which are supposed to have values. The other is the *partial* constants (variables), which need not have values.

Total variables are further divided into two groups. One is the *individual* variables, which range over all of the objects (S-expressions) and the other is the *class* variables, which range over classes. Total constants are also divided in the same manner.

1.2 *Formulas*

Formulas of **PX** are defined by the following grammar:

$$\begin{aligned} F ::= & E(e) \mid Class(e) \mid [e_1, \ldots, e_n] : e \mid e_1 = e_2 \mid \top \mid \bot \\ & \mid F_1 \wedge \ldots \wedge F_n \mid F_1 \vee \ldots \vee F_n \mid F_1 \supset F_2 \mid e_1 \to F_1; \ldots; e_n \to F_n \mid \neg F \mid \Diamond F \\ & \mid \forall \vec{x}_1 : e_1, \ldots, \vec{x}_n : e_n.F \mid \exists \vec{x}_1 : e_1, \ldots, \vec{x}_n : e_n.F \mid \nabla p_1 = e_1, \ldots, x_n = e_n.F, \end{aligned}$$

where $F, F_1, \ldots$ are formulas and $e, e_1, \ldots$ are expressions. We will explain the meaning of formulas informally. $E(e)$ means e has a value; i.e., the execution of e under the current environment terminates.

Class(e) means that e has a value that is a description of a class. Classes are particular sets of objects. Since classes are considered as data types, **PX** is a system of the discipline of "types are first class objects".

The equality $e_1 = e_2$ is Kleene's equality; i.e., if e_1 has a value then e_2 has the same value and vice versa. The expression $[e_1, \ldots, e_n] : e$ means $e_1, \ldots, e_n, e$ have values, say $v_1, \ldots, v_n, v$, respectively, and v is a description of a class to which the tuple $[v_1, \ldots, v_n]$ belongs. (The meaning of the tuple notation $[\alpha_1, \ldots, \alpha_n]$ is as follows: if $n = 1$, then $[\alpha_1]$ means α_1 and if $n \neq 1$, then $[\alpha_1, \ldots, \alpha_n]$ means $list(\alpha_1 \ldots \alpha_n)$.) $\top$ and $\bot$ mean *true* and *false*, respectively.

The logical connectives except $\to$, $\Diamond$ have their usual definitions. The modal operator $\Diamond$ is just double negation. The expression $e_1 \to A_1; \ldots, e_n \to A_n$ means there is m such that $e_1 = \cdots = e_{m-1} = nil$, e_m has a non-nil value, and A_m holds. Note that if all of $e_1, \ldots, e_n$ have the value *nil* then the formula is false. Since this semantics resembles McCarthy's conditional form, we call this formula a *conditional formula*. As in the case of the conditional form we can define "serial or" and "case formula":

$$\begin{aligned} Sor(e_1, \ldots, e_n) &\equiv e_1 \to \top; \ldots; e_n \to \top, \\ Case(a, A_1, \ldots, A_n) &\equiv equal(a, 1) \to A_1; \ldots; equal(a, n) \to A_n. \end{aligned}$$

The universal quantifier and existential quantifier are defined as usual except that we may use *tuple variables* (i.e., tuples of variables) as bound variables. For example $\forall [x, y] : C.R(x, y)$ means that $R(x, y)$ holds for all x, y such that $[x, y] : C$. We will denote tuple variables by vector notations such as $\forall \vec{x} : e.A$ (strictly speaking, it should be $\forall [\vec{x}] : e.A$, but we omit the square brackets for simplicity.) Since we identify a tuple variable $[x]$ with x, we write $\forall x : e.A$ instead of $\forall [x] : e.A$. We abbreviate $\forall \ldots, x : V, \ldots$ as $\forall \ldots, x, \ldots$, where V is the class of all objects. Bound variables must be total variables.

The ∇-quantifier resembles *let* of LISP. $\nabla p = e.A$ means e has a value that matches the pattern p, and under the matching A holds. We use tuple notations as patterns; e.g., $\nabla[x, y] = a.A$ is $\nabla(x\ y) = a.A$, and $\nabla[x] = a.A$ is $\nabla x = a.A$. Bound variables of ∇-quantifiers must also be total variables.

Note that we can define ∇ by universal quantification and also by existential quantification. For example, $\nabla x = e.A$ is defined by $E(e) \wedge \forall x.(x = e \supset A)$ and also by $\exists x.(x = e \wedge A)$. But our realizability interpretation of $\nabla x = e.A$ is different from the realizability interpretations of these two formulas. This is one of the reasons that ∇ is a primitive logical sign. The reason that $\rightarrow$ is a primitive logical connective is the same.

With each formula A, we associate a nonnegative integer called the type of A, which we will write as $type(A)$. Types of formulas will be used for defining **px**-realizability interpretation.

Definition 1 (Type of Formula)

1. The type of atomic formulas and formulas of the forms $\neg A$ or $\diamond A$ is 0.

2. A is $A_1 \wedge \ldots \wedge A_n$. If all of $A_1, \ldots, A_n$ are of type 0, then so is A. Otherwise, set

$$type(A) = \#\{i | type(A_i) > 0\},$$

where $\#x$ means the cardinality of x.

3. A is $A_1 \vee \ldots \vee A_n$. If all of $A_1, \ldots, A_n$ are of type 0, then $type(A)$ is 1. Otherwise, $type(A)$ is 2.

4. A is $B \supset C$. If C is of type 0, then so is A. Otherwise, $type(A)$ is 1.

5. A is $\forall \vec{v}_1 : e_1, \ldots, \vec{v}_n : e_n.B$. If B is of type 0, then so is A. Otherwise, $type(A)$ is 1.

6. A is $\exists \vec{v}_1 : e_1, \ldots, \vec{v}_n : e_n.B$. Then $type(A)$ is $m+type(B)$, where m is the number of variables in $\vec{v}_1, \ldots, \vec{v}_n$.

7. A is $e_1 \rightarrow A_1; \ldots; e_n \rightarrow A_n$. If all of $A_1, \ldots, A_n$ are of type 0, then so is $type(A)$. Otherwise, $type(A)$ is 1.

8. A is $\nabla p_1 = e_1, \ldots, p_n = e_n.B$. Then $type(A)$ is $type(B)$.

1.3 *Axiom System*

We will give a full presentation of the axiom system of **PX** below. The axiom system has two parts. One is the logic of partial terms (expressions). The other is the axioms on classes.

A Logic of Partial Terms The logic of partial terms (LPT) is a logic that allows terms not denoting values. LPT has been used in recursion theory informally. Formalizations of LPT have been introduced in [3, 4, 10, 11, 19, 20].

If all recursions can be used to define functions, then a term may fail to terminate. Then usual logic, which assumes that every term has a value, implies a contradiction. For example, $f() = pair(f(), f())$ is a legal function definition in **PX**. Then it follows that $cond(equal(f(), pair(f(), f())), 1; t, 2) = 1$. But then $x \neq pair(x, x)$, so it follows that $cond(equal(f(), pair(f(), f())), 1; t, 2) = 2$, from which $1 = 2$ (this example is essentially due to Meyer and Reinhold).

To avoid this, one must use LPT instead of ordinary logic. In LPT, $f()$ is not defined from this contradiction, for we substitute $f()$ for the variable x only when $f()$ is defined ($E(f())$ in our notation).

Axioms for Primitives

$$E(e) \quad (e \text{ is a total constant or a total variable}),$$

$$Class(e) \quad (e \text{ is a class constant or a class variable}),$$

$$[e_1, \ldots, e_n] : e \supset Class(e), \quad Class(e) \supset E(e), \quad [e_1, \ldots, e_n] : e \supset E(e_i),$$

$$E(fn(e_1, \ldots, e_n)) \supset E(e_i), \quad E(\Lambda(v_1 = a_1, \ldots, v_n = a_n)(fn)),$$

$$e = e, \quad e_1 = e_2 \supset e_2 = e_1, \quad (E(e_1) \vee E(e_2) \supset e_1 = e_2) \supset e_1 = e_2,$$

$$a = b \vee \neg a = b, \quad \frac{\Gamma \Rightarrow P[e_1/a] \qquad \Pi \Rightarrow e_1 = e_2}{\Gamma \cup \Pi \Rightarrow P[e_2/a]},$$

$$app(\Lambda(v_1 = a_1, \ldots, v_n = a_n)(fn), list(e_1, \ldots, e_n)) = (fn\sigma)(e_1, \ldots, e_n),$$

$$app{*}(\Lambda(v_1 = a_1, \ldots, v_n = a_n)(fn), e_1, \ldots, e_n) = (fn\sigma)(e_1, \ldots, e_n),$$

$$(\lambda(v_1, \ldots, v_n)(e))(a_1, \ldots, a_n) = e[a_1/v_1, \ldots, a_n/v_n],$$

$$cond(e_1, d_1; \ldots; e_n, d_n) = a \;\supset\subset\; e_1 \to a = d_1; \ldots; e_n \to a = d_n; t \to a = nil,$$

$$(let\ p_1 = e_1, \ldots, p_n = e_n\ in\ e) = a \;\supset\subset\; \nabla p_1 = e_1, \ldots, p_n = e_n(e = a),$$

where $a, b, a_1, \ldots, a_n$ are total variables and σ is $[a_1/v_1, \ldots, a_n/v_n]$.

Structural Rules

$$\{A\} \Rightarrow A\,, \qquad \text{(assume)}$$

$$\Gamma \Rightarrow \top\,, \qquad (\top)$$

$$\frac{\Gamma \Rightarrow \bot}{\Gamma \Rightarrow A}\,, \qquad (\bot)$$

$$\frac{\Gamma \Rightarrow A}{\Gamma \cup \Pi \Rightarrow A}, \qquad \text{(thin)}$$

$$\frac{\Gamma \Rightarrow A \quad \Pi \Rightarrow B}{\Gamma \cup (\Pi - \{A\}) \Rightarrow B}, \qquad \text{(cut)}$$

$$\frac{\Gamma \Rightarrow A \quad \Pi \Rightarrow SC(\sigma)}{\Gamma\sigma \cup \Pi \Rightarrow A\sigma}, \qquad \text{(inst)}$$

$$\frac{\Gamma \Rightarrow A}{\Pi \Rightarrow B}, \qquad \text{(alpha)}$$

$$\left.\begin{array}{c} \dfrac{\Gamma \Rightarrow A[B]_+ \quad \Pi \Rightarrow Env_{A[*]}[B \supset C]}{\Gamma \cup \Pi \Rightarrow A[C]_+} \\ \dfrac{\Gamma \Rightarrow A[C]_- \quad \Pi \Rightarrow Env_{A[*]}[B \supset C]}{\Gamma \cup \Pi \Rightarrow A[B]_-} \end{array}\right\}, \qquad \text{(replacement)}$$

where $SC(\sigma)$ of (*inst*) is the *substitution condition* of σ; e.g., if σ is $[e/a]$ and a is a total variable, then it is $E(e)$. The upper and lower sequents of (*alpha*) must be α-convertible. $A[*]$ of (*replacement*) is a *context*, which is a formula with *just one* "hole" $*$. Subscripts $+, -$ indicate whether the hole appears positively or negatively. B, C of (*replacement*) must be type 0 formulas. $Env_A[*]$ is a context representing the local environment of the hole; e.g., if A is $\forall x : e_1.\exists y : e_2.\nabla p = e_3.(* \wedge F)$, then Env_A is $\forall x : e_1.\forall y : e_2.\nabla p = e_3.(* \wedge F)$. In particular, $Env_A[*]$ is obtained from $A[*]$ by replacing every existential quantifier with a universal quantifier as far as the hole $*$ is in its scope.

Rules for Ordinary Logical Constructs The logical rules for ordinary logical constructs are more or less standard except that some substitution conditions are required when an expression is substituted for a total variable:

$$\frac{\Gamma_1 \Rightarrow A_1, \ldots, \Gamma_n \Rightarrow A_n}{\Gamma_1 \cup \ldots \cup \Gamma_n \Rightarrow A_1 \wedge \ldots \wedge A_n}, \qquad (\wedge I)$$

$$\frac{\Gamma \Rightarrow A_1 \wedge \ldots \wedge A_n}{\Gamma \Rightarrow A_{i_1} \wedge \ldots \wedge A_{i_m}}, \qquad (\wedge E)$$

$$\frac{\Gamma \Rightarrow A_i}{\Gamma \Rightarrow A_1 \vee \ldots \vee A_i \vee \ldots \vee A_n}, \qquad (\vee I)$$

$$\frac{\Gamma_1 \Rightarrow A_1 \vee \ldots \vee A_n \quad \Pi_1 \Rightarrow C, \ldots, \Pi_n \Rightarrow C}{\Gamma \cup \Pi_1 - \{A_1\} \cup \ldots \cup \Pi_n - \{A_n\} \Rightarrow C}, \qquad (\vee E)$$

$$\frac{\Gamma \Rightarrow B}{\Gamma - \{A\} \Rightarrow A \supset B}, \qquad (\supset I)$$

$$\frac{\Gamma \Rightarrow A \supset B \quad \Pi \Rightarrow A}{\Gamma \cup \Pi \Rightarrow B}, \qquad (\supset E)$$

$$\frac{\Gamma \Rightarrow \bot}{\Gamma - \{A\} \Rightarrow \neg A}, \qquad (\neg I)$$

$$\frac{\Gamma \Rightarrow \neg A \quad \Pi \Rightarrow A}{\Gamma \cup \Pi \Rightarrow \bot}, \qquad (\neg E)$$

$$\frac{\Gamma \Rightarrow A}{\Gamma - S \Rightarrow \forall \vec{v}_1 : e_1, \ldots, \vec{v}_n : e_n.A}, \qquad (\forall I)$$

$$\frac{\Gamma \Rightarrow \forall \vec{v}_1 : e_1, \ldots, \vec{v}_n : e_n.A \quad \Pi \Rightarrow SC(\sigma)}{\Gamma \cup \Pi \Rightarrow A\sigma}, \qquad (\forall E)$$

$$\frac{\Gamma \Rightarrow A\sigma \quad \Pi \Rightarrow SC(\sigma)}{\Gamma \cup \Pi \Rightarrow \exists \vec{v}_1 : e_1, \ldots, \vec{v}_n : e_n.A}, \qquad (\exists I)$$

$$\frac{\Gamma \Rightarrow \exists \vec{v}_1 : e_1, \ldots, \vec{v}_n : e_n.A \quad \Pi \Rightarrow C}{\Gamma \cup \Pi - \{A, \vec{v}_1 : e_1, \ldots, \vec{v}_n : e_n\} \Rightarrow C}. \qquad (\exists E)$$

S of $(\forall I)$ is $\{\vec{v}_1 : e_1, \ldots, \vec{v}_n : e_n\}$. $SC(\sigma)$ of $(\exists I)$ and $(\forall E)$ is the substitution condition. The subscripts $\{i_1, \ldots, i_m\}$ of $(\wedge E)$ are a subset of $\{1, \ldots, n\}$.

Rules for ∇ and $\to$ The logical meanings of $e_1 \to A_1; \ldots; e_n \to A_n$ and $\nabla p_1 = e_1, \ldots, p_n = e_n.A$ are:

$$(e_1 : T \wedge A_1) \vee (e_2 : T \wedge e_1 = nil \wedge A_2)$$
$$\vee \ldots \vee (e_n : T \wedge e_{n-1} = nil \wedge \ldots \wedge e_1 = nil \wedge A_n)$$

$$\exists \vec{x}.(exp(p_1) = e_1 \wedge \ldots \wedge exp(p_n) = e_n \wedge A).$$

Here $exp(p)$ is the *expansion* of a pattern p, which is defined as $exp(v) = v$ and $exp((p_1 \, . \, p_2)) = pair(exp(p_1), exp(p_2))$, etc. T is the class of non-nil objects. These validate the following rules. Each rule for ∇ ($\to$) has a counter rule for $\forall$ and $\exists$ ($\wedge$ and $\vee$) as indicated by the names of rules:

$$\frac{\Gamma \Rightarrow A_i \quad \Pi \Rightarrow \bigwedge S_i}{\Gamma \cup \Pi \Rightarrow e_1 \to A_1; \ldots; e_n \to A_n}, \qquad (\to \vee I)$$

$$\frac{\Gamma \Rightarrow e_1 \to A_1; \ldots; e_n \to A_n \quad \Pi_1 \Rightarrow C, \ldots, \Pi_n \Rightarrow C}{\Gamma \cup \bigcup_{i=1}^{n} (\Pi_i - \{A_i\} - S_i) \Rightarrow C}, \qquad (\to \vee E)$$

$$\frac{\Gamma_1 \Rightarrow A_1, \ldots, \Gamma_n \Rightarrow A_n \quad \Pi \Rightarrow Sor(e_1, \ldots, e_n)}{\Pi \cup \bigcup_{i=1}^{n} \Gamma_i - S_i \Rightarrow e_1 \to A_1; \ldots; e_n \to A_n}, \qquad (\to \wedge I)$$

$$\frac{\Gamma \Rightarrow e_1 \to A_1; \ldots; e_n \to A_n \quad \Pi \Rightarrow \bigwedge S_i}{\Gamma \cup \Pi \Rightarrow A_i}, \qquad (\to \wedge E)$$

$$\frac{\Gamma \Rightarrow A\sigma \quad \Pi \Rightarrow \bigwedge R}{\Gamma \cup \Pi \Rightarrow \nabla p_1{=}e_1, \ldots, p_n{=}e_n.A}, \qquad (\nabla \exists I)$$

$$\frac{\Gamma \Rightarrow \nabla p_1{=}e_1, \ldots, p_n{=}e_n.A \quad \Pi \Rightarrow C}{\Gamma \cup (\Pi - \{A\} - Q_1) \Rightarrow C}, \qquad (\nabla\exists E)$$

$$\frac{\Gamma \Rightarrow A \quad \Pi \Rightarrow \bigwedge R}{(\Gamma{-}Q_1) \cup \Pi \Rightarrow \nabla p_1{=}e_1, \ldots, p_n{=}e_n.A} \qquad \frac{\Gamma \Rightarrow \nabla p_1{=}e_1, \ldots, p_n{=}e_n.A}{\Gamma \cup Q_2 \Rightarrow A}, \qquad (\nabla\forall I)$$

where

$$S_i = \{e_1 = nil, \ldots, e_{i-1} = nil, e_i : T\},$$

$$R = \{exp(p_1)\sigma = e_1, E(e_1), \ldots, exp(p_n)\sigma = e_n, E(e_n)\},$$

$$Q_1 = \{exp(p_1) = e_1, E(e_1), \ldots, exp(p_n) = e_n, E(e_n)\},$$

$$Q_2 = \{exp(p_1) = e_1, \ldots, exp(p_n) = e_n\}.$$

Miscellaneous Axioms In the following, $\alpha,\beta,\gamma,\ldots$ are metavariables for objects, and $a,a_1,\ldots,b,b_1,\ldots$ are *total* individual variables:

$$quote(\alpha) = quote(\beta) \qquad (\alpha = \beta),$$

$$\neg quote(\alpha) = quote(\beta) \qquad (\alpha \neq \beta),$$

$$t = quote(t), \qquad nil = quote(nil), \qquad 0 = quote(0),$$

$$quote(\alpha) : Atm \qquad (\alpha \in Atom),$$

$$quote((\alpha\ .\ \beta)) = pair(quote(\alpha), quote(\beta)),$$

$$quote(\nu + 1) = suc(quote(\nu)) \quad (\nu \in N).$$

For each function definition $f_1(\vec{v}_1) = e_1, \ldots, f_n(\vec{v}_n) = e_n$, the following are axioms:

$$f_1(\vec{v}_1) = e_1, \ldots, f_n(\vec{v}_n) = e_n\,,$$

$$E(atom(a)),\ E(equal(a,b)),\ E(pair(a,b)),\ E(list(a_1, \ldots, a_n))\,,$$

$$atom(a) = t \supset\subset a : Atm,\ equal(a,b) = t \supset\subset a = b,\ a : T \supset\subset \neg a = nil\,,$$

$$E(e) \supset e : V, \quad 0 : N, \quad \forall a : N.suc(a) : N\,,$$

$$\forall a : N.prd(suc(a)) = a, \quad \forall a : N.(\neg a = 0 \supset\subset suc(prd(a)) = a)\,,$$

$$\forall X.(0 : X \wedge \forall a : X.suc(a) : X \supset \forall a : N.a : X)\,,$$

$$fst(pair(a,b)) = a, \quad snd(pair(a,b)) = b\,,$$

$$\neg a : Atm \supset\subset pair(fst(a), snd(a)) = a\,,$$

$$\forall X.(\forall a : Atm.a : X \wedge \forall a : X, b : X.pair(a, b) : X \supset \forall a : V.a : X)\,.$$

Rules and Axioms for $\diamond$ The modal symbol $\diamond$ is just double negation. We may consider that the formula $\diamond A$ stands for "A holds classically"; i.e., the logic in the scope of $\diamond$ is the ordinary classical logic. The axiom ($\diamond$2) is the principle of "double negation shift" of constructive logic.

$$\neg\neg A \supset\subset \diamond A, \tag{$\diamond$1}$$

$$\forall \vec{x}_1 : e_1, \ldots, \vec{x}_n : e_n.\diamond F \supset \diamond\forall \vec{x}_1 : e_1, \ldots, \vec{x}_n : e_n.F, \tag{$\diamond$2}$$

$$A \supset\subset \diamond A \quad (A \text{ is a type 0 formula}). \tag{$\diamond$3}$$

By virtue of these axioms we can prove the following proposition, which shows that type 0 formulas obey classical logic.

Proposition 1

A type 0 formula is provable in **PX** if and only if it is provable in **PX**+(classical logic).

Classes: Data Types as Objects A class is a *name* of a set of objects. Classes and axioms on them play very important roles in **PX** in two ways. For one thing we can define various kinds of data types, including the dependent types of Martin-Löf. Since a class is merely a code of a set, we can program various operations on types in the usual way of programming. So data types are first-class objects, and the type discipline of **PX** is close to those of the typed languages Russell and Pebble, although it does not have the type of all types. (The type of all types can be accommodated in **PX**, provided the axioms of *join* and *product* are absent.) For another, the induction principle is quite useful for representations of recursions called CIG-recursions, and their domains of termination are also representable by classes.

The axioms on classes are divided into two groups. One is the axioms of conditional inductive generations (CIG), which maintain the existence of a particular kind of inductively defined sets; it is an extension of the principle of inductive generation of [7]. The other is the axioms of dependent types, which maintain that the dependent types in the sense of Martin-Löf exist.

Let's explain CIG-inductive definitions. In the following, variables $\vec{X} = X_0, \ldots, X_n$ are always class variables. Formulas called *CIG-templates with re-*

spect to $\vec{X}$ and n_0, $CIG_{n_0}(\vec{X})$ for short, are generated by the following grammar:

$$\begin{aligned} H ::= & E(e) \mid [e_1, \ldots, e_{n_0}] : X_0 \mid [e_1, \ldots, e_n] : X_{i+1} \mid e_1 = e_2 \mid \top \mid \bot \\ & \mid H_1 \wedge \ldots \wedge H_n \mid e_1 \to H_1; \ldots; e_n \to H_n \mid \Diamond P \mid K \supset H \mid \neg K \\ & \mid \forall \vec{x}_1 : e_1, \ldots, \vec{x}_n : e_n.H \mid \nabla p_1 = e_1, \ldots, p_n = e_n.H, \end{aligned}$$

$$\begin{aligned} P ::= & H \mid P_1 \wedge \ldots \wedge P_n \mid e_1 \to P_1; \ldots; e_n \to P_n \mid K \supset P \mid P_1 \vee \ldots \vee P_n \\ & \mid \forall \vec{x}_1 : e_1, \ldots, \vec{x}_n : e_n.P \mid \exists \vec{x}_1 : e_1, \ldots, \vec{x}_n : e_n.P \mid \nabla p_1 = e_1, \ldots, p_n = e_n.P, \end{aligned}$$

$$\begin{aligned} K ::= & E(e) \mid [e_1, \ldots, e_n] : X_{i+1} \mid e_1 = e_2 \mid \top \mid \bot \\ & \mid K_1 \wedge \ldots \wedge K_n \mid K_1 \vee \ldots \vee K_n \mid e_1 \to K_1; \ldots; e_n \to K_n \mid \Diamond K \mid P \supset K \mid \neg P \\ & \mid \forall \vec{x}_1 : e_1, \ldots, \vec{x}_n : e_n.K \mid \exists \vec{x}_1 : e_1, \ldots, \vec{x}_n : e_n.K \mid \nabla p_1 = e_1, \ldots, p_n = e_n.K, \end{aligned}$$

where $H, H_1, \ldots$ range over $CIG_{n_0}(\vec{X})$, $e, e_1, \ldots$ range over expressions which contain neither elements of $\vec{X}$ nor any free partial variables, and all of the variables of $\vec{x}_1, \ldots, \vec{x}_n$ are individual variables. $P, P_1, \ldots$ $(K, K_1, \ldots)$ are formulas in which X_0 appears positively (negatively). Note that the length of the argument tuple of X_0 *must* be n_0. For each $A \in CIG_n(\vec{X})$ and variables $\vec{a} = a_1, \ldots, a_n$, there is an expression $\mu X_0\{\vec{a}|A\}$, whose free variables are just $FV(A) - \{X_0, a_1, \ldots, a_n\}$. It is the smallest fixed point of the monotone map "$X_0 \mapsto \{\vec{a}|A\}$" so that the following are axioms:

$$Class(\mu X_0\{\vec{a}|A\}), \quad \nabla[a_1, \ldots, a_n] = x.A[\mu X_0\{\vec{a}|A\}/X_0] \supset\subset x : \mu X_0\{\vec{a}|A\}. \quad \text{(CIG def)}$$

If X_0 does not appear in A, we write $\{\vec{a}|A\}$ in the usual set notation. The induction rule for $\mu X_0\{\vec{a}|A\}$, called CIG-induction, is as follows:

$$\frac{\Gamma \Rightarrow F(\vec{a})}{\{[\vec{a}] : \mu X_0\{\vec{a}|A\}\} \cup \Gamma - \{A[F(\vec{a})/X_0], A[\mu X_0\{\vec{a}|A\}/X_0]\} \Rightarrow F(\vec{a}).} \quad \text{(CIG ind)}$$

We substitute a *formula* $F(\vec{a})$ for a class variable X_0. This means replacing all of the subformula of the form $[e_0, \ldots, e_n] : X_0$ by $F[e_0/a_1, \ldots, e_n/a_n]$.

The actual CIG is more flexible than the version of CIG presented here, in the following respects:

0. Simultaneous definitions of classes are possible.

1. If e is an expression whose class variables belong to $X_1, \ldots, X_n$ (X_0 not allowed) and confirmed to be a class by a specific algorithm, then not only $[e_1, \ldots, e_n] : X_{i+1}$ but also $[e_1, \ldots, e_n] : e$ is allowed as H and K in the grammar of CIG-templates.

2. For a class whose body of definition is a conditional formula, a more convenient form of CIG-induction is available.
3. A class may be specified as a superset of the class to be defined.

To illustrate (1)–(3) we define the class of nonempty lists:

$$a : Dp = \{a \mid \nabla(x\,.\,y) = a.\mathrm{T}\},$$

$$\textbf{deCIG}\ a : List_1(X) \equiv_{Dp} snd(a) \rightarrow fst(a) : X, snd(a) : List_1(X),$$

$$t \rightarrow fst(a) : X.$$

The arrow sign $\rightarrow$ in the definition is not the logical sign, so the right-hand side of the definition is not a formula. The class defined by this is

$$\mu X_0\{a \mid a : Dp \wedge (snd(a) \rightarrow fst(a) : X \wedge snd(a) : X_0; t \rightarrow fst(a) : X)\}. \tag{A}$$

Dp is the class of dotted pairs, and it is to be a superset of $List_1(X)$ so that all lists of the class are non-nil. After defining these, $[e_1, \ldots, e_n] : List_1(X)$ is allowed as a CIG-template, for it is a class whenever X is a class. So the class of lists of lists is defined by

$$\textbf{deCIG}\ a : List_2(X) \equiv a : List_1(List_1(X)).$$

The induction principle (*CIG ind*) associated with $List_1(X)$:

$$\frac{\Gamma \Rightarrow A(a) \qquad \Pi \Rightarrow A(a)}{\begin{array}{l}\{\, a : List_1(X)\,\} \\ \cup\left(\Gamma - \left\{\begin{array}{l} a : Dp,\ snd(a) : T,\ fst(a) : X, \\ snd(a) : List_1(X),\ A(snd(a)) \end{array}\right\}\right) \\ \cup(\Pi - \{\, a : Dp,\ snd(a) = nil,\ fst(a) : X\,\})\end{array} \Rightarrow A(a)}. \tag{B}$$

By virtue of this form of CIG-induction we may avoid cumbersome applications of the rules ($\rightarrow \vee E$), ($\wedge E$), and (*cut*), which are necessary to derive (B) from (*CIG ind*) for (A). The following is called the *generalized CIG-template with superclass Dp* of $List_1(X)$:

$$(snd(a); fst(a) : X, snd(a) : X_0), (t; fst(a) : X). \tag{C}$$

The class variable X_0 is used for the variable representing the class that is defined by this template. The (*CIG def*) associated with $List_1$ is just the (*CIG def*) of (A).

The following are more examples of definitions of data types by means of CIG:

1. *Function space*: The space of functions (programs) from X to Y is given by

$$X \rightarrow Y = \{f \mid \forall a : X.app*(f, a) : Y\}.$$

This is a space of unary functions; function spaces with more arguments are defined similarly. Note that the functions of this space are *intensional.* Even if X and Y are equipped with equivalence relations R_X and R_Y, functions of the space need not preserve them. If $\{a, b | a : X \wedge b : X \wedge R_X(a, b)\}$ and $\{a, b | a : Y \wedge b : Y \wedge R_Y(a, b)\}$ are classes, say E_X and E_Y, respectively, then the extensional function space can be defined by the following:

$$X \to Y = \{f | \forall [a, b] : E_X.[app{*}(f, a), app{*}(f, b)] : E_Y\}.$$

Then the extensional equality on the space is defined in the obvious way, and it again defines a class. Hence we can construct higher-order extensional function spaces over it.

2. *Finite set*: The enumeration type of Pascal, or finite set, is easily defined through "serial or" as follows:

$$\{x_1, \ldots, x_n\} = \{a | Sor(equal(x_1, a), \ldots, equal(x_n, a))\}.$$

For example, **Bool** is defined by $\{t, nil\}$. Note that $Sor()$ is $\perp$ by definition, so $\{\} = \{a | \perp\}$ is an empty class.

3. *Cartesian product*: The Cartesian product of two classes is defined by

$$X \times Y = \{a_1, a_2 | a_1 : X \wedge a_2 : Y\}.$$

Similarly, we can define n-times products. 0-times product is $\{[] | \top\}$, i.e., the class $\{nil\}$.

4. *Disjoint sum*: The disjoint sum, or coproduct, of two classes is defined by the following:

$$X + Y = \{x | \nabla(a\ .\ b) = x.(equal(a, t) \to b : X; equal(a, nil) \to b : Y)\}.$$

The *fst*-part of the dotted pair specifies the class to which the *snd*-part belongs. Finite disjoint sums of any numbers of classes are defined similarly. The infinite disjoint sum will be introduced by the *Join* operator below.

5. *Propositional equality*: The following is an implementation of the type of propositional equality of [17]. Its extension is empty when $a = b : X$, and equals the extension of the 0-times product $\{nil\}$ otherwise (Martin-Löf uses a constant **r** instead of *nil*):

$$I(X, a, b) = \{x | x = nil \wedge a = b\}.$$

In almost all cases, CIG-definitions are enough to implement useful data types as classes, but **PX** has another kind of class formation method. We assume **PX** has a basic function Σ whose arity is two, and the following is an axiom:

$$\forall a : A.Class(app{*}(f, a)) \supset Class(\Sigma(A, f)) \qquad \text{(Join)}$$

$$\wedge \forall x.(x : \Sigma(A, f) \supset\subset \nabla(a\ .\ b) = x.(a : A \wedge b : app{*}(f, a)))).$$

This corresponds to Martin-Löf's dependent sum. By the aid of this axiom and CIG, we can derive the existence of dependent products (see [3]). For symmetry, however, we introduce the axiom of the dependent products:

$$\forall a : A.Class(app{*}(f,a)) \supset Class(\Pi(A,f)) \qquad \text{(Product)}$$
$$\land \forall x.(x : \Pi(A,f) \supset\subset \forall a : A.app{*}(x,a) : app{*}(f,a)).$$

By these two dependent types and the types introduced in the previous section, we can interpret an *intensional* version of Martin-Löf's type theory $\mathbf{ML}_0$ without the type of well-orderings.

2 *Giving Computational Meanings to Logic*

There are many ways of giving computational meanings to constructive proofs. We use **px**-realizability interpretation, which is a variant of Robin Grayson's **g**-realizability interpretation. The advantage of **px**-realizability interpretation is that if a theorem is **px**-realized, then it is also valid in the sense of classical logic. So we need not change our intended semantics to interpret a theorem as a specification of extracted algorithms.

2.1 px-*Realizability*

For each formula A, we assign a formula $a\,\mathbf{x}\,A$, $A^{\mathbf{x}}$ for short, whose type is 0, and we call it the **px**-realizability interpretation, or **px**-realization, of A. When $a\,\mathbf{x}\,A$ holds, we say "a is a realizer of A". An important point is that a is a total individual variable not occurring in A, so a realizer must be a value (object). The variable a will be called a *realizing variable* of A.

We assume that if two formulas are α-convertible then their realizing variables are the same. We denote the set $\{A^{\mathbf{x}} | A \in \Gamma\}$ by $\Gamma^{\mathbf{x}}$.

Grayson's **px**-realizability interpretation reads as follows in our setting:

1. A is an atomic formula. Then $a\,\mathbf{x}\,A$ is $A \land a = nil$.

2. $a\,\mathbf{x}\,A_1 \land \ldots \land A_n$ is $\nabla(a_1 \ldots a_n) = a.((a_1\,\mathbf{x}\,A_1) \land \ldots \land (a_n\,\mathbf{x}\,A_n))$.

3. $a\,\mathbf{x}\,A \supset B$ is $E(a) \land A \supset B \land \forall b.((b\,\mathbf{x}\,A) \supset \nabla c = app{*}(a,b).c\,\mathbf{x}\,B)$.

4. $a\,\mathbf{x}\,A_1 \lor \ldots \lor A_n$ is $\nabla(b\,.\,c) = a.Case(b, c\,\mathbf{x}\,A_1, \ldots, c\,\mathbf{x}\,A_n)$.

5. $a\,\mathbf{x}\,\forall \vec{x}_1 : e_1, \ldots, \mathbf{x}_n : e_n.A$ is

$$E(a) \land \forall \vec{x}_1 : e_1, \ldots, \vec{x}_n : e_n.\nabla y = app{*}(a, a_1, \ldots, a_m).y\,\mathbf{x}\,A.$$

6. $a\,\mathbf{x}\,\exists \vec{x}_1 : e_1, \ldots, \vec{x}_n : e_n.A$ is

$$\nabla(a_1 \ldots a_m\ b) = a.(\vec{x}_1 : e_1 \land \ldots \land \vec{x}_n : e_n \land (b\,\mathbf{x}\,A)).$$

7. $a \mathbf{x} \nabla p_1 = e_1, \ldots, p_n = e_n.A$ is $\nabla p_1 = e_1, \ldots, p_n = e_n.a \mathbf{x} A$.

8. $a \mathbf{x} e_1 \to A_1; \ldots; e_n \to A_n$ is $e_1 \to a \mathbf{x} A_1; \ldots; e_n \to a \mathbf{x} A_n$.

In 5 and 6, $a_1, \ldots, a_m$ is the concatenation of $FV(\vec{x}_1), \ldots, FV(\vec{x}_n)$. ($FV(\vec{x})$ is the variables appearing in the tuple of variables $\vec{x}$; e.g., $FV([x, y])$ is x, y.) From the definition we see that if $a \mathbf{x} A$ holds, then A holds.

This **px**-realizability interpretation is satisfactory for mathematical use, but for computational use it has some redundancies, so we adapt it to computational use in the next section.

The following gives the logical foundation of program extraction via **PX**. A detailed proof of this theorem is given in [13].

Theorem 1 (Soundness of **px**-Realizability)
If $\Gamma \Rightarrow A$ is a provable sequent of **PX** without free partial variables, then we can effectively find an expression e from its proof so that $\Gamma^{\mathbf{x}} \Rightarrow e \mathbf{x} A$ is also provable in **PX**. Furthermore, we may assume that $FV(e)$ is a subset of $FV(\Gamma^{\mathbf{x}} \cup \{A\})$.

An algorithm based on this theorem, for extracting optimized programs, is presented in Section 2.2. The condition on the variables is necessary to validate the **px**-realizability interpretations of ($\forall I$) and ($\supset I$), etc. Any sequent without partial variables, if it is provable, can be proved without partial variables; partial constants may occur, so this is not a serious restriction. From the definition of **px**-realizability interpretation, we can easily conclude the following corollary.

Corollary

If $\forall [x_1, \ldots, x_n] : e.\exists y.F(x_1, \ldots, x_n, y)$ is a provable sentence in **PX**, then we can find a closed function fn such that the following is provable:

$$\forall [x_1, \ldots, x_n] : e.\nabla y = fn(x_1, \ldots, x_n).F(x_1, \ldots, x_n, y).$$

PX uses this corollary as a way of introducing new functions. In the terminology of constructive logic, it reads as a derived rule of choice:

$$\frac{\Gamma \Rightarrow \exists x_1, \ldots, x_n.A}{\Gamma \Rightarrow \nabla(x_1 \ldots x_n) = f(a_1, \ldots, a_m).A}, \qquad \text{(choice)}$$

where f is a *new* function with arity n, and Γ is a set of type 0 formulas. This means whenever you can *prove* the upper sequent you may define a new function f that satisfies the lower sequent. Note that we do not consider this an official inference rule of **PX**, since it contradicts classical logic when we read it as "if the upper sequent is *valid* then there is a computable function f such that the lower sequent is valid".

2.2 A *Refined* px-*Realizability Interpretation*

The **px**-realizability interpretation of the previous section is mathematically simple, but the mathematical simplicity often causes redundancies in actual practice. Therefore we introduce a more elaborated realizability interpretation that extracts more natural programs.

Definition 2 (Refined **px**-Realizability Interpretation)

1. Suppose A is of type 0. Then $a \mathbf{x} A$ is $A \wedge a = nil$.
2. Suppose $A = A_1 \wedge \ldots \wedge A_n$. Set A_i^* is the formula A_i if $type(A) = 0$, and is $a_i \mathbf{x} A_i$ otherwise. Let $i_1 < \cdots < i_m$ be the list of the indices i such that $type(A_i) \neq 0$. Then $a \mathbf{x} A$ is

$$\nabla[a_{i_1}, \ldots, a_{i_m}] = a.(A_1^* \wedge \ldots \wedge A_n^*).$$

3. $a \mathbf{x} A \supset B$ is

$$E(a) \wedge A \supset B \wedge \forall b.(b \mathbf{x} A \supset \nabla c = fn(a, b).c \mathbf{x} B),$$

   where fn is $app*$ if $type(A) = 1$, and is app otherwise.
4. Suppose A is $A_1 \vee \ldots \vee A_n$. If $type(A_1) = \cdots = type(A_n) = 0$, then

$$a \mathbf{x} A \equiv Case(a, A_1, \ldots, A_n),$$

   else

$$a \mathbf{x} A \equiv \nabla(b\ c) = a.Case(b, c \mathbf{x} A_1, \ldots, c \mathbf{x} A_n).$$

5. $a \mathbf{x} \forall \vec{x}_1 : e_1, \ldots, \vec{x}_n : e_n.A$ is

$$E(a) \wedge \forall \vec{x}_1 : e_1, \ldots, \vec{x}_n : e_n.\nabla y = app*(a, a_1, \ldots, a_m).y \mathbf{x} A,$$

   where $a_1, \ldots, a_m$ is the concatenation of $FV(\vec{x}_1), \ldots, FV(\vec{x}_n)$.
6. Suppose A is $\exists \vec{x}_1 : e_1, \ldots, \vec{x}_n : e_n.A_0$. Let $a_1, \ldots, a_m$ be the concatenation of the variables $FV(\vec{x}_1), \ldots, FV(\vec{x}_n)$. If $type(A_0) = 0$ then

$$a \mathbf{x} A \equiv \nabla[a_1, \ldots, a_m] = a.(\vec{x}_1 : e_1 \wedge \ldots \wedge \vec{x}_n : e_n \wedge A_0),$$

   else

$$a \mathbf{x} A \equiv \nabla p = a.(\vec{x}_1 : e_1 \wedge \ldots \wedge \vec{x}_n : e_n \wedge b \mathbf{x} A_0),$$

   where p is $(a_1 \ldots a_m\ b)$ if $type(A_0) = 1$, and $(a_1 \ldots a_m\ .\ b)$ otherwise. The last dot of the latter pattern is an actual dot.
7. $a \mathbf{x} \nabla p_1 = e_1, \ldots, p_n = e_n.A$ is $\nabla p_1 = e_1, \ldots, p_n = e_n.a \mathbf{x} A$.
8. $a \mathbf{x}\, e_1 \rightarrow A_1; \ldots; e_n \rightarrow A_n$ is $e_1 \rightarrow a \mathbf{x} A_1; \ldots; e_n \rightarrow a \mathbf{x} A_n$.

We present a detailed description of the actual extraction algorithm below. The algorithm associates with each assumption as its realizing variable a *tuple variable*, instead of a single variable, whose length is the type of the assumption. The tuple is the realizing variable, if it is considered a tuple variable. Recall that when the type of an assumption is one, then it is a single variable; otherwise it is a list of variables. This is for optimizations of the extracted programs.

We have to introduce some auxiliary functions to describe the extractor.

Auxiliary Functions

If A is a formula, then $rvars(A)$ is a sequence of mutually distinct variables of length $type(A)$. It is considered as a tuple variable that realizes A. We call it the realizing variable of A. We assume $rvars(A)$ and $rvars(B)$ are identical if and only if A and B are α-convertible.

$rpattern(A)$ is the pattern $[a_1, \ldots, a_n]$, where $a_1, \ldots, a_n = rvars(A)$.

$rpatterns(A_1, \ldots, A_n)$ is the sequence $rpattern(A_1), \ldots, rpattern(A_n)$.

$newfunc()$ is a new function name.

$new(n)$ is a sequence of n new variables.

$dummy(n)$ is a list of n atoms.

$upseqs(P)$ is the upper sequents of a proof P.

$rule(P)$ is the last rule of the proof P.

$con(P)$ is the conclusion of the proof P.

$asp(P)$ is the assumptions of the proof P.

When $rule(P)$ is $(\vee E)$, $disch_{\vee E}(P)$ is the sequence of the discharged formulas. Similarly, $disch_{\supset I}(P)$ is the discharged formula of $(\supset I)$.

When $rule(P)$ is $(inst)$, $subst(P)$ is the substitution σ of the rule of $(inst)$.

$delete0(P_1, \ldots, P_n)$ is the subsequence of $P_1, \ldots, P_n$ obtained by deleting proofs whose conclusions are of type 0.

$tuple[e_1, \ldots, e_n]$ is another notation for the tuple $[e_1, \ldots, e_n]$.

If $rule(P)$ is $(\wedge E)$, then $indices\wedge E(P)$ stands for the indices of the sequence of indexed formulas obtained by deleting all type 0 formulas from the sequence of indexed formulas $A_{i_1}, \ldots, A_{i_m}$ of $(\wedge E)$.

If $rule(P)$ is $(\vee I)$, then $index_{\vee I}(P)$ is the index i in the rule of $(\vee I)$.

$eigenvars_{\forall I}$, etc., denote the sequence of eigenvariables of the rule $(\forall I)$, etc.

Let *rule*(*P*) be $(\forall E)$ and $[e_1/a_1, \ldots, e_m/a_m]$ be the substitution σ of $(\forall E)$. Then $instances_{\forall E}(P)$ are the expressions $e_1, \ldots, e_m$. $instances_{\exists I}$ is defined similarly.

$body_{\exists}(A)$ is the immediate subformula of an existential formula $A.body_{\forall}(A)$ and $bodys_{\rightarrow}(A)$ are defined similarly.

conditions(*A*) is the sequence of conditions of a conditional formula.

Let ϕ be $\nabla p_1 = e_1, \ldots, p_n = e_n.A$. Then *patterns*($\phi$) is $p_1, \ldots, p_n$ and *bindings*(ϕ) is $e_1, \ldots, e_n$.

$disch_{CIG}(P_i)$ is the sequence of discharged formulas of the subproof P_i.

We associate a realizer with the generalized CIG-induction rule instead of the plain CIG-induction rule (CIG *ind*), but we consider only nonsimultaneous cases for simplicity, i.e.,

$$\begin{aligned} \textbf{deCIG}\ \vec{x} : C \equiv_D\ & e_1 \rightarrow \phi_{1,1}, \ldots, \phi_{1,q_1}, \\ & \ldots \\ & e_n \rightarrow \phi_{n,1}, \ldots, \phi_{n,q_n}. \end{aligned} \qquad \text{(CIG } dec_1\text{)}$$

$$\frac{\Gamma_1 \Rightarrow F, \ldots, \Gamma_n \Rightarrow F}{\bigcup_{i=1}^{n} \tilde{\Gamma}_i \Rightarrow x : C \supset F,} \qquad \text{(CIG } ind_1^*\text{)}$$

where $\tilde{\Gamma}_i$ is the set

$$\begin{aligned} \Gamma_j^i - (\{\vec{x} : D\} & \\ & \cup \{e_1 = nil, \ldots, e_i = nil, e_i : T\} \\ & \cup \{\phi_{i,1}[F/C], \ldots, \phi_{i,q_i}[F/C]\} \\ & \cup \{\phi_{i,1}, \ldots, \phi_{i,q_i}\}). \end{aligned}$$

We associate an expression called *CIG-predecessor*, denoted by $pred(A; f; \vec{b})$, with each triple of CIG-template A, function name *f*, and finite sequence of variables *b*. We will simply write *pred*(*A*) or *pred*(*A*; *f*) instead of $pred(A; f; \vec{b})$, whenever *f* and $\vec{b}$ are clear from contexts. We call *pred*(*A*) the *CIG-predecessor* of *A*.

1. *A* is a template of type 0 with respect to X_0. Then *pred*(*A*) is *nil*,
2. $pred([e_1, \ldots, e_n] : X_0; f; \vec{b}) = f(e_1, \ldots, e_n, \vec{b})$,
3. $pred(A \supset B) = \Lambda(\lambda().pred(B))$,
4. $pred(A_1 \wedge \ldots \wedge A_n) = list(pred(A_{i_1}), \ldots, pred(A_{i_m}))$, where the $i_1, \ldots, i_m$ are defined as in clause 2 of Definition 2.

5. $pred(\forall \vec{v}_1 : e_1, \ldots, \vec{v}_n : e_n.A) = \Lambda(\lambda(\vec{x}).pred(A))$, where $\vec{x}$ is the concatenation of the sequences of variables $\vec{v}_1, \ldots, \vec{v}_n$,
6. $pred(e_1 \to A_1; \ldots; e_n \to A_n) = cond(e_1, pred(A_1); \ldots; e_n, pred(A_n))$,
7. $pred(\nabla p_1 = e_1, \ldots, p_n = e_n.A) = let\ p_1 = e_1, \ldots, p_n = e_n\ in\ pred(A)$.

For a proof P such that $rule(P)$ is ($CIG\ ind_1^*$), we introduce the following auxiliary functions:

> $template(P)$ is $(e_1; \phi_{1,1}, \ldots, \phi_{1,q_1}), \ldots, (e_n; \phi_{n,1}, \ldots, \phi_{n,q_n})$.
>
> $pred(A_1, \ldots, A_n)$ is $pred(A_1), \ldots, pred(A_n)$.
>
> $disch_{CIG}(P_i)$ is the discharged formulas $\phi_{i,1}[F/C], \ldots, \phi_{i,q_i}[F/C]$ of the proof of $\Gamma_i \Rightarrow F$.

We use three functions for optimizations— $Optimize_{case}$, $Optimize_\beta$, and $Optimize_\eta$— and a construct **subst**, which does some substitution and/or builds a *let* form in an optimized way. $Optimize_\beta$, $Optimize_\eta$ do β-reduction and η-reduction, respectively. $Optimize_{case}$ does an optimization such as

$$case(cond(e, 1; t, 2), e_1, e_2) \quad \longmapsto \quad case(e, e_1, e_2).$$

What **subst** does is rather complicated, but essentially it is a *let* form. The value of the expression **subst** $p \leftarrow e$ **in** e_1 is always equivalent to the value of $let\ p = e\ in\ e_1$ as far as they both have values. If the pattern p (exactly $exp(p)$) occurs only once in e_1, however, then **subst** does a partial evaluation by replacing p by e; for example, **subst** $(a\,.\,b) \leftarrow e$ **in** $pair(a, b)$ is just the expression e. Furthermore, if p is the empty pattern () (or *nil*), then **subst** neglects the substitution for p; e.g., **subst** $() = e_1$ **in** e_2 is just e_2. For the purposes of this monograph, it suffices to assume that **subst** does only these optimizations; see [13, Appendix C] for a full description.

In the following description of the extraction algorithm, the above auxiliary functions, which are *meta-level* functions in the sense that they deal with syntactic entities of **PX**, will be printed in `this typewriter-like font`. Metavariables for such entities are also printed in that font. On the other hand, the program constructs of **PX** are printed in the font of mathematical formulas. Meta-level program constructs, e.g., **def, let, case**, are in bold-face letters.

The Extraction Algorithm

```
def extr(P) =
  let type=type(con(P)), P1,...,Pn=upseqs(P)
  in if type=0 then nil else
```

```
case rule(P) of
(= 5): cond(equal(a, b), 1; t, 2) ;
        (= 5) is the axiom a = b ∨ ¬a = b
(assume): rvars(con(P))
(⊥): dummy(type(con(P)))
(inst): let A1,...,An=asp(P1), σ=subst(P)
        in extr(P1)σ[rvars(A1σ)/rvars(A1),...,
                     rvars(Anσ)/rvars(An)]
(cut): substrpattern(con(P1))← extr(P1)in extr(P2)
(∧I): let Q1,...,Qm=delete0(P1,...,Pn)
      in tuple[extr(Q1),...,extr(Qm)]
(∧E): let a1,...,an=new(n), j1,...,jp=indices∧E(P)
      in subst[a1,...,an]← extr(P1)
        in tuple[aj1,...,ajp]
(∨I): if type(con(P))=1
      then index∨I(P)
      else pair(index∨I(P),extr(P1))
(∨E): if type(con(P1))=1
      then Optimizecase
           (case(extr(P1),extr(P2),..., extr(Pn)))
      else
        let c,r=new(2),
            p1,...,pn-1 = rpatterns(disch∨E(P))
        in Optimizecase
           (subst(c . r)← extr(P1)
            in case(c, substp1← r in extr(P2),
                        ...,
                        substpn-1← r in extr(Pn)))
(⊃I): let a1,...,am=rvars(disch⊃I(P))
      in Optimizeη(Λ(λ(a1,...,am).extr(P1)))
(⊃E): let f = if type(con(P2))=1 then app* else app
      in Optimizeβ(f(extr(P1),extr(P2)))
(∀I): let a1,...,am=eigenvars∀I(P)
      in Optimizeη(Λ(λ(a1,...,am).extr(P1)))
(∀E): let e1,...,em=instances∀E(P)
      in Optimizeβ(app*(extr(P1),e1,..., em))
(∃I): let e1,...,em=instances∃I(P),
          u=type(body∃(con(P1)))
```

```
        in if u=0 then list(e1,...,em)
           else if u=1 then list(e1,...,em, extr(P1))
           else pair(e1, pair(e2,..., pair(em,extr(P1)) ···))
(∃E): let a1,...,am = eigenvars∃E(P),
          b1,...,bu = rvars(body(con(P1)))
      in if u=0 then subst[a1,...,am]← extr(P1)
                     in extr(P2)
         else if u=1
              then subst(a1...am b1) ← extr(P1)
                   in extr(P2)
         else let b=new(1)
              in subst(a1...am . b) ← extr(P1)
                 in subst(b1...bu) ← b in extr(P2)
(→ ∨E): let c1,...,cn=conditions(con(P1))
            p1,...,pn-1= rpatterns(bodys→(con(P1)))
            e=extr(P1),
            e1=extr(P2),
                ...,
            en-1=extr(Pn),
        in cond(c1,subst p1← e in e1;
                   ...;
                cn,subst pn← e in en)
(→ ∧I): let c1,...,cn=conditions(con(P))
        in cond(c1,extr(P1);...;cn,extr(Pn))
(∇∀I): let p1,...,pm=patterns(con(P1)),
           e1,...,em=bindings(con(P1))
       in let p1=e1,...,pm=em in extr(P1)
(∇∃E): let p=rpattern(body∇(con(P1))),
           p1,...,pm=patterns(con(P1)),
           e1,...,em=bindings(con(P1))
       in substp1=e1,...,pn=em,p ←extr(P1)
          in extr(P2)
(CIG ind*1): let a⃗=eigenvarsCIG(P),
                 f=newfunc(),
                 (e1;A⃗1),...,(en;A⃗n) = template(P),
                 pred1⃗=pred(A⃗1),
                   ...
                 predn⃗=pred(A⃗n),
                 r⃗1=rpatterns(dischCIG(P1)),
```

```
                 ...
                 r⃗n=rpatterns(dischCIG(Pn))
             in
             begin
               def f(a⃗,b⃗) = cond(e1, substr⃗1← pred⃗1
                                         in extr(P1);
                                         ...
                                     en, substr⃗n← pred⃗n
                                         in extr(Pn))
             end
             f(a⃗,b⃗)
   default: extr(P1)
   end.
```

Besides the above, the extraction algorithm realizes the rule of (*choice*) of Section 2.1. As described in Section 6.2, if you construct a proof of an existential theorem, say $\exists y : C.A$, with assumptions, say Γ, which are of type 0, then you can declare a function, say f, for which $\Gamma \Rightarrow \nabla y = f(a_1, \ldots, a_n).(y : C \wedge A)$ is an axiom, where $a_1, \ldots, a_n$ are free variables of Γ and $\exists y.A$. Then the extraction algorithm computes a realizer of the proof of the existential theorem, say **e**; it associates a realizer $\mathbf{e_1}$ with the axiom, and attaches an expression $\mathbf{e_2}$ as its definition as follows: $\mathbf{e_1}$ is *nil* and $\mathbf{e_2}$ is **e**, if A is of type 0, and $\mathbf{e_1}$ is **subst**pp ←**e in b** and $\mathbf{e_2}$ is **subst**pp ←**e in y** otherwise, where pp is **(y b)** if $type(A) = 1$, and is **(y . b)** otherwise.

We have explained only the case where the number of the bound variables of the existential quantifier is one. The general case is treated similarly.

3 *Writing Programs Via Proofs*

In this section, we present a methodology for solving the problems described in the introduction. The methodology is based on LPT, CIG-recursion, and the fact that a type 0 formula is realized by *nil* if and only if it holds.

3.1 *CIG-Recursion*

A recursion generated by the extraction algorithm from (*CIG ind*), which is called a *CIG-recursion*, has the following form:

$$\begin{aligned} f(\vec{a}, \vec{b}) = cond(&e_1, let\ \vec{r}_1 = \overrightarrow{pred}_1(\vec{A}_1)\ in\ e'_1; \\ &\ldots; \\ &e_n, let\ \vec{r}_n = \overrightarrow{pred}_n(\vec{A}_n)\ in\ e'_n). \end{aligned} \qquad (*)$$

CIG-recursion is not a full form of recursion, but it is complete in a sense. The aim of this section is to explore it.

CIG-predecessors are defined by the following grammar without the help of CIG-templates. CIG-recursion is therefore a logic-free concept except that $e'_1, \ldots, e'_n$ of $(*)$ must be derived from proofs.

$$\begin{aligned} \alpha ::= & f(e_1, \ldots, e_n) \mid list(e_1, \ldots, e_n) \\ & \mid cond(e_1, \alpha_1; \ldots; e_n, \alpha_n) \mid \Lambda(\lambda(x_1, \ldots, x_n)\alpha) \\ & \mid let\ p_1 = e_1, \ldots, p_n = e_n\ in\ \alpha, \end{aligned}$$

where $e_1, \ldots, e_n$ are arbitrary expressions in which f does not appear. The point is that $f(\alpha_1, \ldots, \alpha_n)$ is not a CIG-template, although $f(e_1, \ldots, e_n)$ is. Consequently CIG-recursions tend not to be nested. By the aid of higher-order programming, however, some nested recursions can be programmed by CIG-recursions; later we show how the Ackerman function is programmable in **PX**.

To illustrate CIG-recursions we give some examples. The first example is the quotient-remainder algorithm:

$$\{a : N,\ b : N^+\} \Rightarrow \exists q : N, r : N.(a = b * q + r \wedge r < b). \tag{I}$$

N^+ is the class of positive integers. For readability, we use infix operators like $+$, and some functions like $<$ will be used as both functions and predicates. Assume that $e(a, b)$ realizes (I). Then it returns a list $(q\ r)$ in which q and r are the quotient and the remainder of the division of a by b provided that $a : N$ and $b : N^+$. Set

$$\textbf{deCIG}\ a : D(b) \equiv_N a < b \to \mathrm{T}, t \to a - b : D(b).$$

A natural number a belongs to $D(b)$ iff a eventually becomes smaller than b by successive subtractions of b. In other words, $D(b)$ is the domain on which the Euclidian division algorithm with divisor b terminates (note that $D(0)$ is the empty set). We abbreviate $a = b * q + r \wedge r < b$ by $\phi(a, b, q, r)$. We assume the following type 0 sequents (sequents with type 0 conclusions) are known:

$$\{a : N, b : N, a < b\} \Rightarrow \phi(a, b, 0, a), \tag{A1}$$

$$\{a : N, b : N, q : N, r : N, \phi(a - b, b, q, r), \neg a < b\} \Rightarrow \phi(a, b, q + 1, r). \tag{A2}$$

By applying $(\exists I)$ to (A1) and by applying $(\exists I)$ and $(\exists E)$ to $(A2)$ we prove

$$\{a : N, b : N, a < b\} \Rightarrow \exists q : N, r : N.\phi(a, b, q, r), \tag{A3}$$

$$\begin{aligned} &\{a : N, b : N, \neg a < b, \exists q : N, r : N.\phi(a - b, b, q, r)\} \Rightarrow \\ &\quad \exists q : N, r : N.\phi(a, b, q, r). \end{aligned} \tag{A4}$$

Let a_1, a_2 be the realizing variables of the formula $\exists q : N, r : N.\phi(a - b, b, q, r)$. Then $list(a_1 + 1, a_2)$ is extracted from $(A4)$ thanks to the optimization done by **subst**. Applying CIG-induction to $a : D(b)$ with $\exists q : N, r : N.\phi(a, b, q, r)$ we prove the following sequent from $(A3)$ and $(A4)$:

$$\{a : D(b), b : N\} \Rightarrow \exists q : N, r : N.\phi(a, b, q, r). \tag{A5}$$

From the proof is extracted $f(a, b)$, where f is a function defined by

$$f(a, b) = cond(a < b, list(0, a);$$
$$t, let\ (a_1\ a_2) = f(a - b, b)\ in\ list(a_1 + 1, a_2)).$$

This recursion has the form of iteration in the sense of [2]. So far, we have established only *partial* correctness of f, since $\{(a\ b) \mid a : D(b) \wedge b : N\}$ is a domain on which f terminates. To show that $f(a, b)$ realizes (I) it is sufficient to prove

$$\begin{aligned} &\{a : N, b : N^{+}\} \Rightarrow b : N\,, \\ &\{a : N, b : N^{+}\} \Rightarrow a : D(b)\,. \end{aligned} \tag{A6}$$

These sequents, which maintain the termination of f on the domain $\{a, b | a : N \wedge b : N^{+}\}$, are of type 0 and are easily proved. By applications of (*cut*) we finally prove the total correctness statement (I) from the partial correctness statement (A5) and the termination statement (A6). Since the sequents of (A6) are of type 0, the applications of (*cut*) do not change the realizer; i.e., $f(a, b)$ is again extracted from the proof of (I).

This example shows how to separate "termination" and "partial correctness" in the framework of "proofs as programs". No formal systems are complete for the termination problem. Since the "proofs as programs" discipline involves total correctness, it appears that there is no way to program all computable functions by proofs of a single formal system. The above example shows, however, that we can overcome this difficulty by "cutting out termination problems" with the aid of CIG-induction. In fact we can prove the following theorem.

Theorem 2 (Extensional Completeness of **PX**)
For each partial recursive function $\phi(x_1, \ldots, x_n)$, in the sense of [15], there are classes D_ϕ and G_ϕ which represent the domain and graph of ϕ, respectively. Furthermore, there is a proof Π_ϕ of

$$\forall [x_1, \ldots, x_n] : D_\phi \exists y.[x_1, \ldots, x_n, y] : G_\phi\,,$$

such that $extr(\Pi_\phi)(x_1, \ldots, x_n)$ equals to $\phi(x_1, \ldots, x_n)$ provided that $[x_1, \ldots, x_n] : D_\phi$.

We do not give a proof of this theorem, but we will give a detailed proof of a more refined result —Theorem 3— in the next section. In fact their proofs are essentially the same.

Let us explain how to use this theorem for verification problems. If one wants to verify that a function ϕ, which is extracted from the proof Π_ϕ, has a property, say,

$$\forall x_1, \ldots, x_n.(Input(x_1, \ldots, x_n) \supset Output(x_1, \ldots, x_n, \phi(x_1, \ldots, x_n))), \qquad (**)$$

then it is sufficient to verify the following two conditions:

$$Input(x_1, \ldots, x_n) \supset [x_1, \ldots, x_n] : D_\phi,$$

$$Input(x_1, \ldots, x_n) \wedge [x_1, \ldots, x_n, y] : G_\phi \supset Output(x_1, \ldots, x_n, y)$$

The first condition says that as far as the input $x_1, \ldots, x_n$ satisfies the input condition, ϕ terminates on the input. The second condition says that if ϕ terminates on the input with an output y, then it satisfies the output condition. These are just the conditions of termination and partial correctness of the statement of $(**)$. Note that the input and output conditions may be considered type 0, since they are merely statements on data; i.e., they embody no computational (or constructive) meaning. Since the above two conditions are of type 0, we may prove them by virtue of classical logic.

We may even verify them by a semantic consideration. This resembles the fact that in Hoare logic, formulas that are valid in the intended interpretation of an assertion language are used as axioms in the consequence rule. The point is that we can write down those verification conditions naturally in the language of **PX**. Later we will see a closer relationship of **PX** to Hoare logic.

We derive the Ackerman function as another example of this programming methodology (it is also an example of nested CIG-recursion). First we define the Ackerman function's graph:

$$\textbf{deCIG}\ [x, y, z] : Ack \equiv_{N \times N \times N}$$
$$equal(x, 0) \rightarrow suc(y) = z,$$
$$equal(y, 0) \rightarrow [prd(x), 1, z] : Ack,$$
$$t \rightarrow \Diamond(\exists z_1 : N.([x, prd(y), z_1] : Ack \wedge [prd(x), z_1, z] : Ack)).$$

Next we define a class whose CIG-induction is just the double induction:

$$\textbf{deCIG}\ [x,y] : Db \equiv_{N\times N} equal(x,0) \rightarrow \top,$$
$$equal(y,0) \rightarrow [prd(x),1] : Db,$$
$$t \Rightarrow [x, prd(y)] : Db, \forall y : N.[prd(x), y] : Db.$$

By CIG-induction for *Db* with $(\exists I)$, $(\exists E)$, and $(\forall E)$, we can prove

$$\{[x,y] : Db\} \Rightarrow \exists z : N.[x,y,z] : Ack.$$

Its realizer is $f(x,y)$ where f is defined by

$$f(x,y) = cond(equal(x,0), suc(y);$$
$$equal(y,0), f(prd(x),1);$$
$$t, f(prd(x), f(x, prd(y)))).$$

Without the optimization by $Optimize_\beta$, the third clause of the above function definition would be

$$app{*}(\Lambda()(\lambda(y).f(prd(x),y)), f(x, prd(y))).$$

We prove the termination statement $\{x : N, y : N\} \Rightarrow [x,y] : Db$ by nested applications of mathematical induction, and by (cut) we finally prove

$$\{x : N, y : N\} \Rightarrow \exists z : N.[x,y,z] : Ack\,, \tag{II}$$

and the realizer is the same as the above. The clauses of the definition of the class *Ack* may be thought of as a Prolog program of the Ackerman function. What we did is to compile it to a deterministic functional program and verify the compiled code's total correctness.

As another example, we derive a function that computes the maximal element of a list of natural numbers. The theorem we prove is

$$\{a : List_1(N)\} \Rightarrow \exists m : N.(m \in a \wedge \forall x : N.(x \in a \supset x \leq m))\,. \tag{III}$$

The formula $m \in a$ means m is an element of the list a, and we suppose it is expressed in a type 0 formula. We define a class

$$\textbf{deCIG}\ [n,a] : M \equiv_{N\times List(N)}$$
$$equal(a, nil) \rightarrow \top,$$
$$n < fst(a) \rightarrow [fst(a), snd(a)] : M,$$
$$t \rightarrow [n, snd(a)] : M\,,$$

where $List(N)$ is the class of lists (possibly empty) of natural numbers. Set

$$\phi(m, a) = m \in a \wedge \forall x : N.(x \in a \supset x \leq m),$$

$$\psi(m, n, a) = \Diamond(m = n \vee m \in a) \wedge \forall x : N.((x = n \vee x \in a) \supset x \leq m).$$

Suppose the following three valid type 0 sequents:

$$\{equal(a, nil) : T, [n, a] : N \times List(N)\} \Rightarrow \psi(n, n, a), \quad \text{(B1)}$$

$$\Gamma \cup \{\psi(m, fst(a), snd(a)), n < fst(a)\} \Rightarrow \psi(m, n, a), \quad \text{(B2)}$$

$$\Gamma \cup \{\psi(m, n, snd(a)), n \geq fst(a)\} \Rightarrow \psi(m, n, a), \quad \text{(B3)}$$

where Γ is $\{equal(a, nil) = nil, [n, a] : N \times List(N)\}$. Applying ($\exists I$), ($\exists E$), and CIG-induction to these sequents we can prove

$$\{[n, a] : M\} \Rightarrow \exists m : N.\psi(m, n, a). \quad \text{(B4)}$$

Its realizer is $f(n, a)$ where f is defined by

$$\begin{aligned} f(n, a) = cond(&equal(a, nil), n; \\ &n < fst(a), f(fst(a), snd(a)); \\ &t, f(n, snd(a))). \end{aligned}$$

This definition is tail-recursive, and $f(n, a)$ computes the maximum element of the list $pair(n, a)$. By CIG induction for $List_1(N)$ we can prove

$$\{a : List_1(N)\} \Rightarrow [fst(a), snd(a)] : M, \quad \text{(B5)}$$

$$\{a : List_1(N)\} \Rightarrow \forall m : N(\psi(m, fst(a), snd(a)) \supset \phi(m, a)). \quad \text{(B6)}$$

Substituting $fst(a)$ and $snd(a)$ for n and a of (B4), and applying (*cut*) with (B5), we obtain

$$\{a : List_1(N)\} \Rightarrow \exists m : N.\psi(m, fst(a), snd(a)).$$

By (*replacement*) with (B6) we can finally prove (III). Its realizer is $f(fst(a), snd(a))$. This example suggests the possibility of programming all "iterative programs" as tail recursions in **PX**, which is the subject of the next section.

3.2 *Simulating Hoare Logic*

In this section we present a method by which we can "simulate" Hoare logic in **PX**. In light of the technique of developing programs with proofs of correctness, e.g., of [1], a derivation in Hoare logic may be thought of not only as a verification of a program but also as a "trace" or "history" of the program's development. In Hoare logic of Pascal-like regular programming languages, each program construct has exactly one logical inference rule by which the construct is introduced. Morally, a verified program is determined by the structure of its correctness proof. Hence we can extract or reconstruct a program from a derivation in Hoare logic whose programs are eliminated. This observation is a key to relating the notion of "propositions as types" and Hoare logic.

Consider the following skeleton of a proof in Hoare logic:

$$\dfrac{\dfrac{\dfrac{\Pi_1}{\{x \geq y\} \Rightarrow F_1} \quad \dfrac{}{\{F_1\}S_1\{G\}}\,{\scriptstyle(AA)}}{\{x \geq y\}S_3\{G\}}\,{\scriptstyle(CR)} \qquad \dfrac{\dfrac{\Pi_2}{\{\neg x \geq y\} \Rightarrow F_2} \quad \dfrac{}{\{F_2\}S_2\{G\}}\,{\scriptstyle(AA)}}{\{\neg x \geq y\}S_4\{G\}}\,{\scriptstyle(CR)}}{\{\ \}S_5\{G\}}\,{\scriptstyle(\mathit{if}R)} \qquad \text{(A)}$$

where

$$F_1 = x \geq x \wedge x \geq y \wedge x \in \{x, y\},$$

$$F_2 = y \geq x \wedge y \geq y \wedge y \in \{x, y\},$$

$$G = z \geq x \wedge z \geq y \wedge z \in \{x, y\},$$

and (AA), (CR), (*if*R) mean assignment axiom, consequence rule, and conditional rule, respectively. The matching of G and F_1 is $z = x$, so, ignoring identical assignment, S_1 must be $z := x$. Similarly we see S_2 is $z := y$. Since consequent rules do not change programs, S_3, S_4 must be S_1, S_2. Similar considerations reveal that S_5 is *if* $x \geq y$ *then* $z := x$ *else* $z := y$. Hence the program S_5 is uniquely determined by the structure of the logical inferences of the proof (A).

On the other hand, replacing G by $\exists z.G$, further replacing $\{P\}A\{Q\}$ by $\{P\} \Rightarrow Q$, and adding some trivial sequents, (A) turns into a proof in **PX**:

$$\dfrac{\dfrac{}{Sor(x \geq y, \neg x \geq y)} \quad \dfrac{\dfrac{\Pi_1}{\{x \geq y\} \Rightarrow F_1} \quad \dfrac{\overline{\{F_1\} \Rightarrow F_1}}{\{F_1\} \Rightarrow \exists z.G}}{\{x \geq y\} \Rightarrow \exists z.G} \quad \dfrac{\dfrac{\Pi_2}{\{\neg x \geq y\} \Rightarrow F_2} \quad \dfrac{\overline{\{F_2\} \Rightarrow F_2}}{\{F_2\} \Rightarrow \exists z.G}}{\{\neg x \geq y\} \Rightarrow \exists z.G}}{\{\ \} \Rightarrow \exists z.G} \qquad \text{(B)}$$

where the last inference is regarded as $(\rightarrow \vee E)$.

Furthermore we can reconstruct (A) from (B), and the realizer of (B) is equivalent to a function that returns the value of z of S_5. Morally, deriving proof

(B) is equivalent to developing the program S_5 with the correctness proof (A). A system based on this idea has been implemented by Takasu and Nakahara [21]. Their system constructs a Pascal program through an interactive development of a proof of an existence theorem. They used logical inference rules tailored to their specific purpose. In essence, their inference rules are rules of Hoare logic hiding programs. We will show that the inference rules of **PX** can be used for the same purpose, although they were designed for other general purposes.

We formulate our technique for the simulation as the following mathematical theorem.

Theorem 3

Let **HL** be the Hoare logic given below with an assertion language L. If $\{Q\}B\{R\}$ is provable in **HL** with all true statements of the assertion language as axioms, then there is a proof, say Π, of **PX**, with all true type 0 sequents as axioms, that satisfies the following conditions:

(a) $extr(\Pi)$ is an iterative program that is equivalent to B under Q.

(b) The assumption of Π is Q under the interpretation of L in **PX**.

(c) The conclusion of Π is $\exists\vec{x}.R$ under the interpretation of L in **PX**, where $\vec{x}$ is the sequence of variables to which B assigns values.

PX does not have imperative programming features, so we have to represent them by state transition functions. A functional program is called an iterative program if its recursions involve only tail-recursion; a compiler or an optimizer can transform such programs *directly* to actual Pascal-like imperative programs. In the notation of Backus' FP, the set of iterative programs, say S, is defined by

1. Let $e_1, \ldots, e_n$ be expressions such that $FV(e_i) \subseteq \{x_1, \ldots, x_n\}$. Then the function

$$\langle x_1, \ldots, x_n \rangle \longmapsto \langle e_1, \ldots, e_n \rangle.$$

belongs to S.

2. If $f_1, f_2 \in$ S, then $f_1 \circ f_2 \in$ S.

3. If e is an expression and $f_1, f_2 \in$ S, then $e \to f_1; f_2 \in$ S.

4. If e is an expression and $f_1 \in$ S, then the function f defined by the tail-recursion

$$f = e \to id; f \circ f_1.$$

(This definition is not quite complete; in reality, lengths of tuples must sometimes be adjusted.) Clauses (1)–(4) are counterparts of the statements of assignment, composition, conditional, and **while**-iteration, respectively.

A program e of **PX** is said to be equivalent to an imperative program P under Q iff $FV(e)$ is a subset of $Var(P)$, the set of *all* variables appearing in P, and under the function declaration

$$\textbf{function}\ foo(x_1,\ldots,x_n,y_1,\ldots,y_m)\ \textbf{begin}\ P;\ foo := [x_1,\ldots,x_n]\ \textbf{end}$$

e equals to $foo(x_1,\ldots,x_n,y_1,\ldots,y_m)$ under the condition Q, where $x_1,\ldots,x_n$ are the variables to which the program P assigns values and $y_1,\ldots,y_n$ are the rest of the variables appearing in P. We call $x_1,\ldots,x_n$ the *program variables* of P and write it as $PV(P)$.

We assume that there is an interpretation of L in **PX**. The interpretations of expressions of L in **PX** must have values; in particular, *true* and *false* must be interpreted as t and *nil*, respectively. We assume that L does not have logical symbols $\exists$ and $\vee$; since the logic of L is classical, this is not a restriction. Furthermore, we assume that $\{\vec{x}|P\}$ is a class in **PX** for any formula P of L. This mild assumption is not actually necessary but simplifies the proof. The rules and axiom of **HL** are as follows:

Assignment axiom : $\{P(\vec{t})\}\ \vec{x} := \vec{t}\ \{P(\vec{x})\}$,

Composition rule : $\dfrac{\{P\}A\{Q\}\quad \{Q\}B\{R\}}{\{P\}A;B\{R\}}$,

Conditional rule : $\dfrac{\{P \wedge e = true\}B_1\{Q\}\quad \{P \wedge e = false\}B_2\{Q\}}{\{P\}\ \textbf{if}\ e\ \textbf{then}\ B_1\ \textbf{else}\ B_2\ \{Q\}}$,

while rule : $\dfrac{\{P \wedge e = true \wedge \vec{x} = \overline{snap}\}B\{P \wedge \overline{snap} \succ \vec{x}\}}{\{P\}\textbf{while}\ e\ \textbf{do}\ B\ \textbf{od}\{P \wedge e = false\}}$,
where $\overline{snap}$ is a sequence of "snapshot variables" appearing neither in the program B nor in the formula P, $\vec{x}$ is $PV(B)$, e is a boolean expression, and the binary relation $\succ$ is well founded,

Consequence rule : $\dfrac{P' \supset P\quad \{P\}A\{Q\}\quad Q \supset Q'}{\{P'\}A\{Q'\}}$.

Proof We prove Theorem 3 by induction on the structure of proofs of Hoare logic. For simplicity we assume that the domain of the assertion language is the domain of **PX**.

With the assignment axiom we associate

$$\Pi = \frac{\{P(t_1,\ldots,t_n)\} \Rightarrow P(t_1,\ldots,t_n)}{\{P(t_1,\ldots,t_n)\} \Rightarrow \exists x_1,\ldots,x_n.P(x_1,\ldots,x_n)}(\exists I)\,.$$

Then $extr(\Pi)$ is $[t_1, \ldots, t_n]$, and it may be regarded as an assignment statement of S, i.e., $\langle t_1, \ldots, t_n \rangle$, satisfying the conditions of the theorem.

Assume

$$\Pi_1 \vdash \{P\} \Rightarrow \exists \vec{x}\,'.Q \quad \text{and} \quad \Pi_2 \vdash \{Q\} \Rightarrow \exists \vec{x}.R$$

are associated with the premises of the composition rule. Then Π is

$$\frac{\Pi_1 \quad \Pi_2}{\{P\} \Rightarrow \exists \vec{x}.R}\,(\exists E)\,,$$

and

$$extr(\Pi) = \textbf{subst}\ \vec{x}\,' \leftarrow extr(\Pi_1)\ \textbf{in}\ extr(\Pi_2).$$

This may be regarded as a composition statement for iterative programs S.

Let Π_1 and Π_2 be assigned to the premises of the conditional rule. Since P is a type 0 formula, by the aid of $(\wedge I)$ and (cut) there are $\Pi_1\,'$ and $\Pi_2\,'$ such that

$$\Pi_1\,' \vdash \{e : T, P\} \Rightarrow \exists \vec{x}\,'.Q, \quad extr(\Pi_1\,') \equiv extr(\Pi_1),$$

$$\Pi_2\,' \vdash \{e = nil, P\} \Rightarrow \exists \vec{x}\,''.Q, \quad extr(\Pi_2\,') \equiv extr(\Pi_2).$$

Then Π is

$$\frac{\dfrac{\Pi_0}{Sor(e,t)} \quad \dfrac{\Sigma_1}{\{P, e : T\} \Rightarrow \exists \vec{x}.Q} \quad \dfrac{\Sigma_2}{\{P, e = nil\} \Rightarrow \exists \vec{x}.Q}}{\{P\} \Rightarrow \exists \vec{x}.Q}\,(\to\vee E)\,,$$

where $\vec{x}$ is the union of $\vec{x}\,'$ and $\vec{x}\,''$, and

$$\Sigma_1 = \frac{\dfrac{\Pi_1\,'}{\{e : T, P\} \Rightarrow \exists \vec{x}\,'.Q} \quad \dfrac{\{Q\} \Rightarrow Q}{\{Q\} \Rightarrow \exists \vec{x}.Q}}{\{P, e : T\} \Rightarrow \exists \vec{x}.Q}\,(\exists E)\,,$$

$$\Sigma_2 = \frac{\dfrac{\Pi_2\,'}{\{e : T, P\} \Rightarrow \exists \vec{x}\,''.Q} \quad \dfrac{\{Q\} \Rightarrow Q}{\{Q\} \Rightarrow \exists \vec{x}.Q}}{\{P, e = nil\} \Rightarrow \exists \vec{x}.Q}\,(\exists E)\,.$$

Then its realizer is

$$\textit{if e then } \textbf{subst}\ \vec{x}\,' \leftarrow extr(\Pi_1)\ \textit{in}\ \vec{x}\ \textit{else}\ \textbf{subst}\ \vec{x}\,'' \leftarrow extr(\Pi_2)\ \textit{in}\ \vec{x}\,.$$

Except for the adjustment of the length of the tuple variables $\vec{x}\,'$ and $\vec{x}\,''$, this may be thought of as a conditional statement of iterative programs S.

Suppose

$$\Sigma \vdash \{P \wedge e = true \wedge \vec{x} = \overrightarrow{snap}\} \Rightarrow \exists \vec{x}.(P \wedge \overrightarrow{snap} \succ \vec{x})$$

is associated to the premise of the **while** rule. Let $\vec{x}$ be $x_1, \ldots, x_n$ and let $extr(\Sigma)$ be b. Set

$$b_i = nth(i, b), \quad \vec{b} = b_1, \ldots, b_n\,,$$

where $nth(i, b)$ is the function that returns the ith element of the list b. By (*choice*) we may regard $\vec{b}$ as a sequence of expressions defined in **PX**. Hence we can declare a class $W(\vec{s})$, where $\vec{s} = (FV(\vec{b}) \cup FV(e)) - \{\vec{x}\}$, such that

$$\textbf{deCIG}\ \vec{x} : W(\vec{s}) \equiv e \rightarrow \vec{b} : W(\vec{s}), t \rightarrow \top\,.$$

Set

$$F(\vec{x}) = \exists \vec{x}\,'.\vec{x} : R(\vec{x}\,', \vec{s})\,,$$

$$\textbf{deCIG}\ \vec{x} : R(\vec{x}\,', \vec{s}) \equiv_{\{\vec{x}|P\}} e \rightarrow \vec{b} : R(\vec{x}\,', \vec{s}), t \rightarrow \vec{x} = \vec{x}\,'\,.$$

Clearly $\{P, e = nil\} \Rightarrow \vec{x} : R(\vec{x}, \vec{s})$ is provable. Let $\Sigma_1{}'$ be its proof. Set

$$\Sigma_1 = \cfrac{\begin{array}{c}\Sigma_1{}'\\ \{P, e = nil\} \Rightarrow \vec{x} : R(\vec{x})\end{array}}{\{P, e = nil\} \Rightarrow F(\vec{x})}\,(\exists I). \tag{1}$$

Then $extr(\Sigma_1)$ is $\vec{x}$. By (*CIG def*)

$$\{e : T, P\} \Rightarrow \forall \vec{x}\,'.(\vec{b} : R(\vec{x}\,', \vec{s}) \supset \vec{x} : R(\vec{x}\,', \vec{s})) \tag{2}$$

is provable. Set

$$\Sigma_0 = \frac{\{F(\vec{b})\} \Rightarrow F(\vec{b}) \quad (2)}{\{e : T, P, F(\vec{b})\} \Rightarrow F(\vec{x})}\,(replacement)\,.$$

Then $extr(\Sigma_0)$ is just the realizing variables of $F(\vec{b})$. By (*CIG ind*) we derive a proof Σ such that

$$\Sigma = \cfrac{\begin{array}{c}\Sigma_0\\ \{e : T, P, F(\vec{b})\} \Rightarrow F(\vec{x})\end{array} \quad \begin{array}{c}\Sigma_1\\ \{e = nil, P\} \Rightarrow F(\vec{x})\end{array}}{\{\vec{x} : W(\vec{s}), P\} \Rightarrow F(\vec{x})}\,.$$

Then its realizer is $f(\vec{x}, \vec{s})$, and f is defined by

$$f(\vec{x}, \vec{s}) = cond(e, f(\vec{b}, \vec{s}); t, [\vec{x}]).$$

This is the **while** statement of iterative programs S. This is not the end of the proof, however; we have to adapt Σ so as to satisfy the conditions (a), (b) of the theorem. By the definition of W we see from the validity of the premise of the **while** rule that

$$\{P\} \Rightarrow \vec{x} : W(\vec{s}) \tag{3}$$

is a true type 0 sequent, so that we may use it as an axiom. (This is the assumption that we may have to assume without a formal proof of **PX**.) On the other hand, there is a proof Σ_3 such that

$$\Sigma_3 \vdash \{\,\} \Rightarrow \forall \vec{x}'.(\vec{x} : R(\vec{x}', \vec{s}) \supset (P \wedge e = nil)[\vec{x}'/\vec{x}])\,.$$

Set

$$\Pi = \cfrac{\cfrac{(3)\quad \Sigma}{\{P\} \Rightarrow F(\vec{x})}(cut) \qquad \Sigma_3}{\{P\} \Rightarrow \exists \vec{x}.(P \wedge e = nil)}(replacement)\&(alpha)\,.$$

Then $extr(\Pi) = extr(\Sigma)$, and Π satisfies the conditions of the theorem.

The counterpart of the consequence rule is just (*replacement*); it does not change the program (realizer). This ends the proof of Theorem 3. □

What we have proved can be summarized by the following diagram:

$$\begin{array}{ccc} \Sigma \vdash_{\mathbf{HL}} \{P\}A\{Q\} & \longrightarrow & \Pi \vdash_{\mathbf{PX}} \{P\} \Rightarrow \exists \vec{x}.Q \\ \downarrow & & \downarrow \\ A & \cong & extr(\Pi) \end{array}$$

The important point is that $extr(\Pi)$ is not only extensionally equivalent to A but also *essentially intensionally equivalent* to A; i.e., the imperative program A is directly reconstructible from the functional program $extr(\Pi)$. The correspondence between **HL** and **PX** used in the above proof are summarized in the following table:

HL	**PX**
Assertion formula	Type 0 formula
$\vdash \{P\}\ A\ \{Q\}$	$\Pi \vdash \{P\} \Rightarrow \exists \vec{x}.Q$
Assignment	$(\exists I)$
Composition	$(\exists E)$
Conditional	$(\rightarrow \vee E)$
While	$(CIG\ ind)$
Consequence	(*replacement*)

As an example of the above method we derive a program which computes the quotient and remainder of division a by b. Set

$$D(a,b) = \{q, r | q : N \wedge r : N \wedge a = b * q + r\}$$

and

$$\mathbf{deCIG}\ [x,y] : W(a,b) \equiv_{D(a,b)}\ y \geq b \rightarrow [x+1, y-b] : W(a,b), t \rightarrow \mathrm{T}.$$

$$\textbf{deCIG } [x, y] : R(q, r, a, b) \equiv_{D(a,b)} y \geq b \rightarrow [x+1, y-b] : R(q, r, a, b),$$
$$t \rightarrow x = q, y = r.$$

In the symbols of the proof of Theorem 3, $\vec{x}$ is q, r, $\vec{x}'$ is q_1, r_1, and $\vec{s}$ is a, b. As in the proof we can derive a program Σ such that

$$\Sigma \vdash \{a : N, b : N^+, [x, y] : W(a, b)\} \Rightarrow \exists q : N, r : N.[x, y] : R(q, r, a, b) \tag{1}$$

and $extr(\Sigma)$ is $f(x, y, a, b)$ whose f is defined by

$$f(x, y, a, b) = cond(y \geq b, f(x+1, y-b, a, b); t, list(x, y)).$$

We substitute $0, a$ for x, y in (1); since $[0, a] : W(a, b)$ holds provided $a : N, b : N^+$, we can eliminate this from the assumption of (1). Since R is inductively defined, if $R(q, r, a, b)$ is nonempty, then there is a value $[x_0, y_0]$ of $[x, y]$ satisfying the conditions of the base case:

$$[x_0, y_0] : D(a, b),\ y_0 < b, x_0 = q,\ y_0 = r.$$

Consequently, $a = b * q + r \wedge r < b$ holds. Formalizing this consideration, we can derive

$$\forall q : N, r : N.([0, a] : R(q, r, a, b) \supset a = b * q + r \wedge r < b).$$

So the sequent (I) of 3.1 is derived by (*replacement*), and its realizer is $f(0, a, a, b)$. This is just a tail-recursive version of the usual Euclidean division algorithm.

4 *Implementing* PX

In this section, we describe an implementation of **PX**. The implementation is based on the formal theory described in earlier sections, but the actual implementation has more extended features. Because the extensions are more or less inessential, the actual implementation is interpretable in the formal theory of **PX**. The features of **PX** that are not described in this paper are *(i)* proving hypotheses by another proof checker (EKL [14]), and *(ii)* printing proofs written by inference macros in a natural-language-like format using TEX[16]. See [13] for descriptions of these features and also for an example of actual program extraction using **PX**.

In Section 4.1 we introduce the concept of "hypothesis" extending the basic logic. It is an inessential extension but provides a way of "top-down" proof developments. The actual implementation of **PX** is described in Sections 4.2 and 4.3.

4.1 *Hypotheses*

As was explained in Section 3, it is not necessary to fill in all of a proof's details to extract its executable program. Giving the full details of a proof in the course of its development, one often loses the proof's main idea; to avoid this, a programmer often wants to leave certain lemmas unproved as trivial "hypotheses" (as in mathematical texts). We therefore desire a mechanism by which some "trivial" facts can be left as unproved hypotheses during a proof's development, to be retrieved and certified later when all the details of the proof are filled in.

PX has such a feature, called *hypothesis*. A *hypothesis* is merely a sequent whose conclusion is a type 0 formula, and any proof may have any finite number of hypotheses. This idea is similar to Martin-Löf's *nested* hypothetical judgment (see [18]), but we do not admit hypotheses with hypotheses, as are allowed by his nested hypothetical judgment. Our much restricted and simpler notion is enough for our purposes.

To formalize the notion of proofs with hypotheses, it is enough to introduce the following two inference rules:

$$\Gamma \Rightarrow F \quad (F \text{ is of type } 0) \qquad (hypI)$$

$$\frac{\Gamma_1 \Rightarrow F_1 \quad \Gamma_2 \Rightarrow F_2}{\Gamma_1 \Rightarrow F_1}. \qquad (hypE)$$

The rule (*hypI*) allows any hypothesis to be used as an axiom. We define the *hypotheses* of a proof.

Definition 3 Let P be a hypothetical proof that ends with a rule r. Then the hypotheses of P, say $hyp(P)$, are defined as follows:

1. In the case r is (*hypI*). Then $hyp(P)$ is $\{\Gamma \Rightarrow F\}$.
2. In the case r is (*hypE*). Let P_1 and P_2 be the left and right immediate subproofs of P. Then we set

$$hyp(P) = (hyp(P_1) - \{\Gamma_2 \Rightarrow F_2\}) \cup hyp(P_2).$$

If a proof P has hypotheses, i.e., $hyp(P) \neq \emptyset$, then P is called a *hypothetical proof* or an *incomplete proof*; otherwise, it is called a *complete proof*. A sequent is a theorem iff there is a complete proof that ends with it.

A proof of the form $S_1/S_2/S_3$ may be considered to be constructed in two ways: $(S_1/S_2)/S_3$ and $S_1/(S_2/S_3)$. The former is a proof by forward reasoning, and the latter is by backward reasoning. But the official inductive definition of proof trees does not allow an "incomplete" proof like (S_2/S_3). In this sense, backward reasoning is forbidden in the traditional formal systems. Regarding

S_2 as a hypothesis, i.e., a proof of S_2 created by (*hypI*), we consider (S_2/S_3) a hypothetical proof, and we get a complete proof $S_1/(S_2/S_3)$ by applying (*hypE*). Morally, (*hypI*) reserves a point (leaf) of a proof tree, and another proof tree is grafted on the tree at that point by (*hypE*).

Backward reasoning builds a proof tree from root to leaves; in this sense (*hypI*) and (*hypE*) provide a way to do backward reasoning. Note that to do "one-step backward inference" we have to make a proof from new goals created by (*hypI*) by the corresponding forward inference rule, and then apply (*hypE*). This takes many steps, so if a proof is built mainly by backward reasoning our mechanism is not useful.

In mathematics, however, actual proof writing proceeds mainly in a forward direction. Although one-step backward reasoning may be useful when used with meta-languages like ML [9] as a tool for proof *development* (cf. [5]), it seems not quite useful for natural proof *writing*.

By attaching the realizer of the left upper sequent to the lower sequent, we can realize the rule (*hypE*). Obviously the following holds.

Proposition 1

Let P be a hypothetical proof of $\Gamma \Rightarrow F$ and r be a program extracted from P. Then r is a realizer of $\Gamma \Rightarrow F$, if all of the hypotheses of P are valid.

Furthermore, the realizer extracted from a proof P_1 obtained by eliminating hypotheses of a proof P by successive applications of (*hypE*) is identical to the realizer extracted from P. So a proof-program development in **PX** may proceed in any of the following ways, and the results are completely identical.

Approach A

0. Give a specification as a sequent.

1. Make an incomplete proof of the specification.

2. Extract a realizer of the specification from the proof.

3. Prove the hypotheses of the proof.

Approach B

0. Give a specification as a sequent.

1. Make an incomplete proof of the specification.

2. Complete the proof, eliminating hypotheses by (*hypE*).

3. Extract a realizer of the specification from the completed proof.

A termination condition can be stated as a hypothesis, as we saw in Section 3, and it is the hardest part of verification. So we normally put it in as hypotheses and take approach A, for we can see the program before we finish the cumbersome verification of the termination condition. Since hypotheses are type 0 sequents, we are free to prove them even by another proof checker, provided that it is coherent with the semantics of **PX**.

In particular, step 3 of approach A may be done by another proof-checker. To do so we have to make a translator from languages and theories of **PX**, in which the proof is developed, to those of the servant proof-checker. (In a proof development, a theory is built up on plain **PX** by declaring functions and so on; see the next section.) Given such a conversion method, the approach A is modified as follows.

Approach C

0. Give a specification as a sequent.

1. Make an incomplete proof of the specification.

2. Extract a realizer of the specification from the proof.

3. Translate the theory and hypotheses into the servant proof-checker.

4. Prove the translated hypotheses in the theory of the servant proof-checker.

We have implemented a translator that translates a theory and hypotheses of **PX** into the powerful proof-checker EKL [13, Section 4.4]. An actual program-proof development by approach C with **PX**-EKL translator will be given in [13, Appendix B].

4.2 *Proof Checker*

In this section we briefly describe the proof checker of **PX**. We will not give accounts of all functions supported by **PX**; such references are available in the **PX** manual [12].

Formulas First we will give the concrete syntax of formulas. Table 1 shows the correspondence between the abstract syntax and the concrete syntax. For readability, any formula may be surrounded by parentheses, but the print routine of **PX** always deletes a repeated grouping of parentheses. If you type in ((**COND**...)), therefore, **PX** prints it as (**COND**...).

When the length of a tuple variable is just one, it is treated as a single variable. Moreover, the restriction by V may be omitted, so you may type in (**UN x**)(F) instead of (**UN** (**x**) : **V**)(F). Furthermore, (**UN x** : **C y** : **C**)(F) may

Table 1. Correspondence between abstract syntax and concrete syntax.

Abstract syntax	Concrete syntax
app, app∗	**apply, funcall**
pair, fst, snd, list	**cons, car, cdr, list**
atom, equal	**atom, equal**
suc, prd	**add1, sub1**
0, *t, nil, V, N, Atm, T, quote*(α)	**0, t, nil, V, N, Atm, T, (quote** α**)**
$f(e_1, \ldots, e_n)$	$(f\ e_1\ \ldots\ e_n)$
$cond(e_1, d_1; \ldots, e_n; d_n)$	**(cond** $(e_1\ d_1)\ldots(e_n\ d_n)$**)**
$\lambda(x_1, \ldots, x_n)(e)$	**(lambda** $(x_1\ \ldots\ x_n)\ e$**)**
$\Lambda(x_1 = e_1, \ldots, x_n = e_n)(e)$	**(Lambda** $((x_1\ e_1)\ldots(x_n\ e_n))\ e$**)**
$let\ p_1 = e_1, \ldots, p_n = e_n\ in\ e$	**(let!** $((p_1\ e_1)\ldots(p_n\ e_n))\ e$**)**
$\top, \bot$	**TRUE, FALSE**
$[e_1, \ldots, e_n] : e$	$e_1\ \ldots\ e_n : e$
$e_1 = e_2$	$e_1 = e_2$
$E(e)$	**E** e
$Class(e)$	**CL** e
$F_1 \wedge \ldots \wedge F_n$	F_1 **&** ... **&** F_n
$F_1 \vee \ldots \vee F_n$	F_1 **+** ... **+** F_n
$F_1 \supset F_2$	F_1 **->** F_2
$F_1 \supset\subset F_2$	F_1 **<->** F_2
$\neg F$	**-** F
$\diamond F$	**$** F
$e_1 \to F_1; \ldots; e_n \to F_n$	**(COND** $(e_1\ F_1)\ldots(e_n\ F_n)$**)**
$\nabla p_1 = e_1, \ldots, p_n = e_n.F$	**(LET** $(p_1\ e_1)\ldots(p_n\ e_n))(F)$
$\forall[x_1, \ldots, x_l] : e_1, \ldots, [y_1, \ldots, y_m] : e_n.F$	**(UN** $(x_1\ \ldots\ x_l) : e_1 \ldots (y_1\ \ldots\ y_m) : e_n)(F)$
$\exists[x_1, \ldots, x_l] : e_1, \ldots, [y_1, \ldots, y_m] : e_n.F$	**(EX** $(x_1\ \ldots\ x_l) : e_1 \ldots (y_1\ \ldots\ y_m) : e_n)(F)$

be abbreviated as (**UN x y** : **C**)(F). In addition, **PX** allows you to use defined predicates and predicate variables; these are explained in Section 4.2.3.

The concrete syntax defines formulas' external forms. Within the system, they have internal forms. Every internal form is just an S-expression; e.g., $x = y$ is represented by (**%= x y**). formula by pretty printing it.

To cause **PX** to recognize an input sequence as a formula, you surround it by braces, such as **{x=y}**. The left brace is a one-character macro that reads the input sequence up to the next right brace and returns the formula's internal form. So the internal form of $x = y$ is input by typing in **' {x=y}**.

Variables and constants in the concrete syntax are as follows:

⟨individual variable⟩ := ⟨**a–z**⟩ | ⟨**a–z**⟩ ⟨numeral⟩
| $⟨an alphanumeric except **A–Z**⟩ ⟨symbol⟩
| ⟨individualvariable⟩∗

⟨class variable⟩ := $⟨**A–Z**⟩ ⟨**symbol**⟩ | ⟨**A–Z**⟩ | ⟨**A–Z**⟩ ⟨**numeral**⟩ except ⟨**N**|**V**⟩
| < class variables⟩∗

⟨partial variable⟩ := ?⟨symbol⟩

⟨individual identifier⟩ := ⟨**a–z**⟩ ⟨**a–z**|**A–Z**⟩ ⟨symbol⟩ | **t** | ⟨numeral⟩
| (**quote** ⟨S–expression⟩)

⟨class identifier⟩ := ⟨**A–Z**⟩ ⟨**a–z** | **A–Z**⟩ ⟨symbol⟩ | **N** | **V** | **T**

⟨alpha numeric⟩ := **0**|**1**| . . . |**9**|**A**|**B**| . . . |**y**|**z**
| < alphanumeral⟩ ⟨alphanumeral⟩

⟨numeral⟩ := **0**|**1**| . . . |**9**| ⟨numeral⟩ ⟨numeral⟩

An individual identifier may be either an individual constant or a function identifier; it belongs to one of the two groups exclusively, according to its declaration (without declaring it, you cannot use it as either). To show which group an individual identifier belongs to, a command **syncat**, which returns the syntax category of each atom, is available.

Similarly, a class identifier may be eithera class constant or a function identifier. When a class identifier is declared as a function identifier, the function always returns a class as its value. The arity of a defined function is determined by its declaration. Declaration is done only through **deCONST**, **deFUN**, **deEXFUN**, **deCIG**, and **deECA** (see Section 4.2.6). Some function identifiers and constants are predeclared, however; for example, **car** is a function identifier, **t** is an individual constant and **N** is a class constant. Note that variables need not be declared.

In addition to these, **PX** creates some individual variables and individual identifiers during extraction. When renaming of bound variables is necessary for substitution of expressions, **PX** adds sufficiently many instances of "*" to the end of variables.

Proofs Just as a formula in **PX** is an S-expression, a *proof* is also an S-expression. A proof is a list beginning with the atom `%%proof%%`. A list beginning with `%%proof%%` is called a *pseudo-proof*; as far as you use **PX** legally, any pseudo-proof has the same structure as a proof. The second and third items of a proof are the conclusion and the list of assumptions.

In **PX** mode, the default mode of **PX**, any illegal input is detected by the top level and is not executed, so pseudo-proofs are always proofs. In LISP mode, however, you may execute any LISP commands, so it is child's play to make an S-expression which is a pseudo-proof but not a proof. For example the value of `(list '%%proof%% '%FALSE nil)` is a pseudo-proof of **FALSE** with no assumptions. **PX** does not provide any way to check whether an S-expression is an actual proof, so the only way to assure you have not built pseudo-proofs that are not proofs is to use **PX** only in **PX** mode. The form of the prompt shows whether you have ever got into LISP mode.

Top Level and Commands The top level of **PX** is a modification of the CMU top level of Franz LISP. So you may omit the outermost parentheses at the top level, and the top level keeps the events and you can redo them (see [8].) Although the read and print routines of **PX** are almost the same as ones of the CMU top level of Franz LISP, the brace macro "{" for reading external formulas is supported as mentioned above, and read-eval routines support a checking mechanism for legal commands.

A command is any program of LISP. **PX** checks whether it may create an illegal pseudo-proof, and executes it as a LISP program only when it is safe. Such a safe program is called a *legal command.* A legal command is a command whose execution does not violate the condition: Every object created in **PX** represents a proof as far as it is a **cons** cell and its **car** part is `%%proof%%`. For example a destructor, e.g., **car**, is safe, for it does not create new cells. On the contrary, **cons** is dangerous, so a command that uses **cons** is illegal. But list constructors are essential if we are to use LISP as a meta-language in the sense of ML (of Edinburgh LCF), so **PX** supports safe constructors **pcons**, **plist**, etc., which check that the actual arguments, which may be the **car** part of a cell to be created, is not `%%proof%%`, and then create such cells.

Other functions besides constructors that may violate the condition are the loading function, for only the top-level read routine checks if a program is legal, and functions that assign a value or a function definition to atoms. For the former, a legal function **pload** is available. It checks each input from a file if it is legal. Its actual use is shown in Section 4.2.6. The latter will be discussed in Section 4.2.6, too.

The print routine supports pretty-printing of formulas and proofs. If an S-expression is a formula, the print routine prints it as an external formula surrounded by braces. If an S-expression is a proof, the print routine prints a sequence of dots representing it and a yield sign "]-" followed by the conclusion (as Edinburgh LCF does). A printed proof is also surrounded by braces, and if it is a hypothetical proof, then an asterisk follows the left brace. The following shows how these work:

```
1:assume {(add1 x) = (sub1 x)}
{.]- (add1 x) = (sub1 x)}                ; A proof with an assumption.
2:(deprf prf1 it)                         ; Assign it to the atom prf1.
{.]- (add1 x) = (sub1 x)}
3:showseq prf1                      ; Display the sequent of the proof.
prf1.
  {(add1 x) = (sub1 x)}
    from
  [1] {(add1 x) = (sub1 x)}

t
4:(deprf prf2 (hypI '{x = (cons x x)}  ; Introduce a hypothesis.
        '{(car x) = x}
        '{(cdr x) = x}))
{*..]- x = (cons x x)}                       ; An asterisk is observed.
5:showseq it  ; The value of the last event is assigned to the atom it.
it.
  {x = (cons x x)}
    from
  [1] {(car x) = x}
  [2] {(cdr x) = x}

  with 1 hypotheses    ; showseq tells there is a hypothesis.

t
6:(deprf prf3 (conjI prf1 prf2))  ; Conjunction introduction.
{*...]- (add1 x) = (sub1 x) & x = (cons x x)}
7:(showseq prf3)
prf3.
  {(add1 x) = (sub1 x) & x = (cons x x)}
    from
  [1] {(add1 x) = (sub1 x)}
  [2] {(car x) = x}
  [3] {(cdr x) = x}
```

```
   with 1 hypotheses

t
9:(showhyp prf3)        ; Display the hypotheses of prf3.

  Hypothesis
   {x = (cons x x)}
     from
   [1] {(car x) = x}
   [2] {(cdr x) = x}

t
```

In **PX** mode, the prompt is an event number followed by ":", so the first thing you see when **PX** is loaded is "1:" as above. In LISP mode, the prompt is an event number followed by "." as in the CMU top level. When you enter LISP mode, the prompt of **PX** mode turns to an event number followed by ";". The function **mode** changes the mode.

The following shows the changes of modes:

```
1:mode                                  ; Mode is PX.
PX
2:assume {FALSE}                        ; Create a proof of {⊥} ⇒ ⊥.
{.]- FALSE}
3:showseq it                            ; Display the sequent of it.
it.
   {FALSE}
     from
   [1] {FALSE}

t
4:vl 2                                  ; Get the value of the event 2.
{.]- FALSE}
5:pp it                             ; Print it to see the internal form.
(setq it '(%%proof%% (%FALSE) ((%FALSE))
                              (%assume (0 (%FALSE)))))

t
6:'(%%proof%% (%FALSE) ())              ; Make an illegal proof.
'(%%proof%% (%FALSE) nil)
Illegal input for PX                    ; The attempt failed.
nil
7:mode lisp                             ; Change to LISP mode.
```

```
LISP
8.'(%%proof%% (%FALSE) ())             ; Make an illegal proof.
{]- FALSE}                             ; It succeeded, this time.
9.showseq it                           ; Display it.
it.
  {FALSE}


t
10.(setq fff (vl 8))                   ; Keep the illegal proof.
{]- FALSE}
11.mode px                             ; Again PX mode.
PX
12;'(%%proof%% (%FALSE) ())            ; So you can't remake
                                       ; the illegal one.
'(%%proof%% (%FALSE) nil)
Illegal input for PX
nil
13;fff                                 ; But the old one is still kept.
{]- FALSE}
```

Observe that after entering LISP mode once, you may have a bad proof, even if you returned to **PX** mode again.

The function **con** returns a proof's conclusion, the function **asp** returns a proof's list of the assumptions, and the function **get_hyp** returns a proof's list of the hypotheses. A hypothesis $\{A_1, \ldots, A_n\} \Rightarrow F$ is represented as a list $(F\ (A_1\ \ldots\ A_n))$. To display hypotheses, a function **showhyp** is available as above. pretty-prints conclusion

Inference Rules Since a proof is an S-expression, any inference rule is a LISP function that returns a proof. For example, (*assume*) is implemented as a function **assume** such that

$$(\textbf{assume}\ F) = \{F\} \Rightarrow F \quad (F \text{ is a formula}),$$

and the conjunction introduction ($\wedge I$) is a function **conjI** such that

$$(\textbf{conjI}\ P_1\ \ldots\ P_n) = \frac{P_1, \ldots, P_n}{F_1 \wedge \ldots \wedge F_n}\ (\wedge I).$$

Hence the value of **(conjI (assume '{x=*y*}) (assume '{y=z}))** is a proof of the sequent

$$\{\mathbf{x} = \mathbf{y},\ \mathbf{y} = \mathbf{z}\} \Rightarrow \mathbf{x} = \mathbf{y}\ \&\ \mathbf{y} = \mathbf{z}.$$

The **PX** manual [12] will provide detailed accounts of inference functions.

Almost all inference rules are implemented as functions as described above, respecting their abstract description, but there are some exceptions. One is that the axioms about the modal operator are implemented not separately, but as a part of a tautology checker. **PX** has a tautology checker which returns a proof of a *type 0 formula* if the following procedures succeed: Regarding the modal operator as double negation, eliminate all double negations; regarding any quantified formula as a propositional variable, and any two quantified formulas as the same propositional formula when they are α-convertible, check if it is a tautology. The following shows a use of the tautology checker **TAUT**.

```
1:deGP ^Prd 1 0                ; Declare ^Prd as a type 0 predicate.
^Prd
2:TAUT $ ^Prd(x) <-> ^Prd(x)      ; Axiom (◇3).
]- $ ^Prd (x) <-> ^Prd (x)
3:TAUT $ ^Prd(x) <-> - - ^Prd(x)     ; Axiom (◇1).
]- $ ^Prd (x) <-> - - ^Prd (x)
4:TAUT $(UN x)(^Prd(x)) <-> (UN x) ^?($ ^Prd(x))
                                                ; Axiom (◇2).
]- $ (UN x) (^Prd (x)) <-> (UN x) ($ ^Prd (x))
5:TAUT - (EX x)(- ^Prd(x)) <-> (UN x)(^Prd(x))
nil         ; TAUT doesn't know predicate calculus.
```

Another exception is schemas for miscellaneous axioms. There is a table of axiom schemas, and you can ask **PX** if a formula is an instance of its axiom schema by a query function **axiom?** as follows:

```
1:axiom? E x    ; axiom? knows a total variable has a value.
]- E x
2:axiom? E ?1  ; axiom? doesn't know about this.
Error in axiom?: I don't know E ?1
3:axiom? (cons ?1 ?2) : Dp ! (assume 'E ?1)
      ! (assume 'E ?2) ..]- (cons ?1 ?2) : Dp
4:showseq it
it.
  (cons ?1 ?2) : Dp ; (cons ?1 ?2) is a dotted pair,
    from                ; under the assumptions.
  [1] E ?1
  [2] E ?2
t
5:axiom? (car (cons x y)) = x
]- (car (cons x y)) = x
```

```
6:axiom? E ?1 ! (assume 'E (cons ?1 0))
.]- E ?1
7:showseq it
it.
  E ?1
    from
  [1] E (cons ?1 0)
t
8:(deprf th (axiom? '?1 = ?1))
]- ?1 = ?1
9:(exI '(EX x)(x = x) th (assume 'E (cons ?1 x)))
.]- (EX x) (x = x)     ; axiom? is called in (∃I)(exI).
10:showseq it
it.
  (EX x) (x = x)
    from
  [1] E (cons ?1 x)
t
```

Inference Macros **PX** provides macros by which you can naturally write programs by building proofs up. They are expanded to programs written by the inference rules described above, so we call them inference macros. In this subsection, we will give an overview of them.

Let e be a program whose value is a list of proofs. Then **(We_see** A e**)** is expanded to an appropriate inference rule about propositional connectives. For example, if the values of e_1 and e_2 are proofs whose conclusions are A and B, then **(We_see** $\{A$ **&** $B\}$ **(plist** e_1 e_2**))** is expanded to **(conjI** e_1 e_2**)**. When you wish to specify what rule is used, you can say, e.g., **(We_see** A **by conjI** e**)**.

The output of function **plist** does not look natural. **PX** provides some *connectives* such as **since**, **for**, **by**, **in_the_following**, etc., which are aliases of **plist**. Using them, the above example may be restated as **(We_see** $\{A$ **&** $B\}$ **(for** e_1 e_2**))**. The connectives starting with upper-case letters, such as **By**, **Since**, **In_the_following**, etc., provide a way to change the order of sentences in proofs. For example, **(By** e **(we_see** A**))** is expanded to **(we_see** A **(by** e**))**. (Note that **we_see** is an alias of **We_see**; all macros except certain connectives have such aliases.)

The macro **proofs** is similar to **prog** of LISP. The expression **(proofs** $e1$ ... e_n**)** is equivalent to **(prog** $e1$ ... e_n**)**, but in e_{n+1} the value of e_n can be referred to as **the_previous_fact**. On the other hand, **the_previous_facts** stands for the list of the values of the previous expressions.

Let and **Set** are aliases of **psetq**. When **(We_prove (A)** F e**)** is evaluated, the formula F is bound to the atom **A** and then e is evaluated; subsequently you can refer to F by the label **A**. Furthermore, the rule of (*alpha*) is applied to F and the value of e. Thus, if the value of e is a proof whose conclusion is α-convertible to F, then the value of the program is a proof of F. The label **(A)** may be omitted; then only the adjustment by (*alpha*) is done.

In mathematical texts, elimination rules such as existential elimination introduce *local assumptions*. When we prove $\exists x.A \Rightarrow C$ by existential elimination, we introduce a local assumption A and prove C; then the proof is finished. But the official rule ($\exists E$) does not allow such an inference. We must build proofs of $\{\exists x.A\} \Rightarrow \exists x.A$ and $\{A\} \Rightarrow C$ and then apply the rule.

This is not quite a natural way of proving theorems. The above proof can be written as follows by a macro **We_assume**:

(We_assume there_exists x such_that (Asp1) A e**)** .

When this expression is evaluated, a proof of {**A**} ⇒ **A** is bound to **Asp1**, and then e is evaluated. Hence you can refer to the local assumption **A** by **Asp1** in e.

These are not the macro's only features, however. **PX** has an *assumption stack* in which local assumptions are kept. The macro also pushes the local assumption on the stack; when you say **(Obviously** B G_1 ... G_m**)** in e, it is expanded to **(hypI** B F_1 ...,F_n G_1 ... G_m**)**, where $F_1, \ldots, F_n$ is the content of the assumption stack. After evaluating e, the local assumption pushed by the macro is popped up. The macro **Obviously_there_there_exists** is a combination of **Obviously** and ($\exists I$).

When the major premise of ($\exists E$) is not an assumption but a proved fact, then you may say

(We_may_assume there_exists x such_that (A) A e_1 e_2**)**

Then the value of e_2 is used as the major premise of ($\exists E$). By combining this with connectives such as **By**, etc., you can say, e.g., **(By** e_2 **(we_may_assume** ... e_1**))**.

The macros for the elimination rule for ∇ are also **We_may_assume** and **We_assume**. The macros understand the rule should be ($\exists E$) if the keyword **there_exists** is present. If it is absent and a declaration such as **(Asp1)** p **matches** e is present, then ($\nabla\exists E$) is used.

The macros for ($\vee E$) and ($\rightarrow \vee E$) are **By_cases**. The keywords by which the macro decides which rule should be used are **or** for ($\vee E$) and **otherwise** for ($\rightarrow \vee E$).

To push assumptions onto the assumption stack, you may say **(Suppose (A)** *F e*). Then *F* is pushed onto the stack, the assumption is bound to the label **A**, and *e* is evaluated. The expression **(We_assume (A)** *F e*) has the same effect, since **We_assume** turns out to be an alias of **Suppose** if the keywords mentioned above are absent.

There are some other macros; they are described in the **PX** manual [12] and in [13, Appendix B].

Declarations Conceptually, **PX** is considered to be based on a regular DEF-system. A regular DEF-system consists of an infinite number of function definitions, but a DEF-system created by the actual **PX** always has only a *finite* number of function definitions. We may therefore regard any environment created with the proof checker of **PX** as a finite subsystem of a regular DEF-system.

The environment created by **PX** is called a *theory*, and it consists of a finite number of declarations. A declaration is classified to a *constant declaration*, a *function declaration*, or a *predicate declaration*. Declarations are exclusive; i.e., an identifier once declared cannot be redeclared. Furthermore, declarations cannot be modified. This restriction preserves the consistency of proofs and an environment built by declarations.

A declaration is created via one of the following functions: **deCONST**, **deFUN**, **deEXFUN**, **deCIG**, **deECA**, **deDP**, **deGP**. The function **deCONST** declares an individual or class identifier as a individual or class constant, respectively, so declarations created via **deCONST** are always constant declarations.

Invoking **(deCONST xx 1)** declares the individual identifier **xx** as an individual constant with the value 1 (if **xx** were not an individual identifier, the declaration would be aborted). After the declaration, the axiom **xx** = **1** is added to the theory. Invoking **(axiom 'xx)** yields a proof of this axiom. When the identifier is an individual identifier, the body of **deCONST** may be replaced by any *closed* expression. When it is a class identifier, only closed class expressions, in the sense of Section 1.4.1, are allowed as the body of the declaration. It is *illegal* to use the identifier being declared in the body of its declaration.

The constant is a total constant if the body has a value and is a partial constant otherwise. If the body of **deCONST** is empty, e.g., **(deCONST xx)**, then it is declared to be a constant, but no axioms are added to the theory. When an option **&total** is placed after the identifier, then it is declared as a total constant. So after the declaration **(deCONST xx &total)**, **(axiom? '{E xx})** returns a proof of **E xx**. If **XX** is declared with the option, then the axiom is **CL XX**. (You may use "hypotheses" to add new axioms for such constants. Then consistency of the theory you develop depends on the hypotheses.) It is possible to declare several constants without bodies together. The declaration **(deCOST xx yy)** will declare both **xx** and **yy**. The option **&total** may be used in such multideclarations.

If an individual or class identifier is used as a global variable by LISP or **PX**, then you are not allowed declare it as a constant of **PX**. For example, **PX** uses **it** as the value of the last event, so you cannot declare it as an individual constant. You are free, however, to declare it as a function identifier.

The function **deFUN** declares functions. For example, **append** is declared as

```
(deFUN append
       (x y)
       (cond(x (cons (car x) (append (cdr x) y)))
              (t y)))
```

A function declaration must be lexical; i.e., all free variables of the function body must appear in the arguments list. Incremental programming is *not* available in **PX**; i.e., all functions in the body of **deFUN** must have been declared. Simultaneous function declaration is available; e.g., **even** and **odd** can be declared as follows:

```
(deFUN
  (even (x) (cond ((equal x 0) t) (t (odd (sub1 x)))))
  (odd (x) (cond ((equal x 1) t) (t (even (sub1 x))))))
```

The axioms added by a function declaration are definition equations of the declared functions. For example, after the above declaration, you will get a proof of

```
(odd x)=(cond ((equal x 1) t) (t (even (sub1 x))))
```

by invoking **(axiom 'odd)**.

The derived rule of (*choice*) of Section 2.1 is implemented as a function declaration. If *P* is a proof of an existential formula whose assumptions are type 0 formulas, then its choice function is declared as

(deEXFUN foo (x1 ... xn) '*P*).

Invoking **(axiom foo)**, you will get a proof of the lower sequent of the rule of (*choice*). The realizer for the existential quantifier is attached to **foo**, so you may execute it, but no axiom that shows the definition (implementation) of the realizer is added to the theory.

A CIG-definition is done by **deCIG** or **deECA**. **(deECA** x y_1 ... y_n**)** is just a macro for **(deCIG** x **(t** x y_1 ... y_n**))**. The concrete syntax of (*CIG* dec_1) of 2.2 is as follows:

$$\textbf{(deCIG } \{\textbf{xx} : \textbf{C}\} \textbf{ (in D)}\ (e_1\ \phi_{1,1}\ \dots\ \phi_{1,q_1})\ \dots\ (e_n\ \phi_{n,1}\ \dots\ \phi_{n,q_n})\textbf{)}.$$

The class notation C may be a class identifier or an expression of the form $(f\ \vec{x})$, where f is a class notation and $\vec{x}$ is a sequence of total variables. In the former case, the declaration is a class declaration, and in the latter it is a function declaration. The axiom that maintains that **C** is the fixed point of the inductive definition is available by **(axiom C)**. The axiom that maintains that **C** is a class is available by the function **axiom?**. When you declare **C** by CIG, **(axiom? '{CL C})** will return a proof of **CL C**. The following shows these functions in actual use:

```
1.(deCIG {x : (Tree X)}       ; Declare the class of binary trees.
         ((atom x) {x : (Tree X)})
         (t {(car x) : (Tree X)} {(cdr x) : (Tree X)}))
(Tree X)
2.axiom Tree                   ; The axiom (CIG def) for (Tree X).
{]- (COND ((atom x) x : (Tree X))
         (t (car x) : (Tree X) & (cdr x) : (Tree X)))
       <-> x : (Tree X)}
3.axiom? {CL (Tree X)}                   ; (Tree X) is a class.
{]- CL (Tree X)}
4.(deCIG              ; Simultaneous definition of Even and Odd.
     ({x : Even} (in N) ((equal x 0) {TRUE})
                        (t {(sub1 x) : Odd}))
     ({x : Odd}  (in N) ((equal x 0) {TRUE})
                        (t {(sub1 x) : Even})))
(Even Odd)
9.axiom Even                   ; The axiom (CIG def) for Even.
{]- x : N & (COND ((equal x 0) TRUE) (t (sub1 x) : Odd))
   <-> x : Even}
10.axiom Odd                   ; The axiom (CIG def) for Odd.
{]- x : N & (COND ((equal x 0) TRUE) (t (sub1 x) : Even))
   <-> x : Odd}
```

The function implementing the inference of (*CIG ind*) is **cigIND**. The following shows a part of an actual session that creates a hypothetical proof of (A5) of Section 3.1. It also shows an example of usage of **pload**.

Programs that create hypothetical proofs of (A1) and (A2) of Section 3.1 and assign them to **BASIS** and **STEP** are in a file named **divitr.px**, whose first few lines look as follows:

```
; These are proofs of (A1) and (A2) of 3.1.

(deCIG {a : (DD b)} (in N)
  ((lessp a b) {TRUE}) (t {(diff a b) : (DD b)}))

(psetq Goal
 '{(EX q r : N)
    (a = (plus (times b q) r) & (lessp r b) : T)})

(deprf BASIS
  (exI Goal
        (deprf Lemma1

                              :
```

So first we **pload** them and create a proof of (A5) by the CIG-induction rule **cigIND**.

```
1:pload divitr                           ; Load the file of the proof.
[loading divitr.px in PX mode]
t
2:showseq BASIS STEP       ; Display basis and induction step.
BASIS.
  {(EX q r : N)
    (a = (plus (times b q) r) & (lessp r b) : T)}
    from
  [1] {(lessp a b) : T}
  [2] {a : N}
  [3] {b : N}

  with 1 hypotheses

STEP.
  {(EX q r : N)
    (a = (plus (times b q) r) & (lessp r b) : T)}
    from
 [1] {(EX q r : N)
      ((diff a b) =
```

```
        (plus (times b q) r) & (lessp r b) : T)}
   [2] {(lessp a b) = nil}
   [3] {a : N}
   [4] {b : N}

   with 1 hypotheses


t
3:(cigIND '{a : (DD b)} BASIS STEP})
                                   ; Apply CIG induction of DD.
{*..]- (EX q r : N)
        (a = (plus (times b q) r) & (lessp r b) : T)}
4:showseq it
it.
   {(EX q r : N)
    (a = (plus (times b q) r) & (lessp r b) : T)}
     from
   [1] {a : (DD b)}
   [2] {b : N}

   with 2 hypotheses


t
```

The function **deDP** declares a user-defined predicate. A predicate identifier must be a symbol whose first character is "*" and whose second character is an upper-case letter. For example, invoking the command **(deDP *A (x y) {y = x})** declares ***A(0 1)** as a formula that is equivalent to **1 = 0**.

There are two rules for predicate declaration. The rule **dpI** does folding, and **dpE** does unfolding, of defined predicates for the conclusion of a proof. The variable list of the declaration must contain all of the free variables of the definition body.

The function **deGP** declares a predicate variable. Such a variable is called a *generic variable* and is always free; i.e., we do not have quantifiers over generic variables. A generic variable is a symbol whose first character is "^" and whose second is an upper-case letter. For example, invoking **(deGP ^A 2)** declares **^A** as a variable for formulas whose type is 2. Since the extraction algorithm needs type information of any formula, such a declaration is necessary. The only inference rule for generic variables is the instantiation rule **gpE**, which substitutes a generic predicate for any formula with the same type.

LISP is adopted as the meta-language for **PX**. To define a new function using LISP, a function **pdefun** is available for declaring LISP functions. It is the same as the ordinary **defun** of Franz LISP except that

(i) the function name must not be in use by another function or macro, although a definition of a function declared by **pdefun** may be redefined, and

(ii) the definition body must be a legal command of **PX**.

This restriction assures that such function declarations do not break **PX**.

Similarly, **pdefmacro** is a counterpart of **defmacro**. Values are assigned by **psetq**, which is the same as ordinary **setq** of Franz LISP except

(i) an atom to which a value is assigned must not be a special global variable of either **PX** or LISP, and

(ii) an expression whose value is assigned must be a legal command of **PX**.

The atom **it** is in use as a global variable, but it is free to be assigned a legal value, for it does not violate **PX**. A function **freep** is available to check if an atom is free to be assigned a value. All function names surrounded by $\langle$ and $\rangle$ are reserved for function names created by the extractor.

4.3 *Extractor*

The implemented extraction algorithm is more or less the same as the algorithm presented in Section 2.2. The name of the extraction algorithm in **PX** is **Extract**. The essential differences are the following:

1. The extractor extracts a program even from a proof that does not satisfy the condition on partial variables of Theorem 1. Free partial variables are regarded by the extractor as partial constants.
2. The extractor includes a trick that avoids unnecessary usage of stacks by functions created by CIG-recursion.

The first difference amounts to applying the same extraction algorithm to a proof that may have partial variables, and later substituting arbitrary constants for partial variables in the extracted program. The only difficulty in applying the extraction algorithm to a proof that has partial variables is that in the extracted code a partial variable may occur in the body of Λ-expression which may not be an expression of **PX**. But treatinging it as a partial constant overcomes the difficulty; what the extractor actually does is (i) to check that the sequent of the given proof has no partial variables, (ii) to extract a code from it, and (iii) to substitute a partial constant **partial***n* for each of partial variables **?***n* remaining in the code to ensure that the extracted code is actually a **PX** expression. The following shows an example:

```
6.prf1
{]- E (cond (t 1) (t ?1))}
7.(exI (quote {(EX x) (E x)}) it)
{]- (EX x) (E x)}
8.(Extract it)          ; Extract the code.
(cond (t 1) (t partial1))
```

The following example is a program extraction from the proof shown in a session example in Section 4.2.5.

```
5:(Extract (vl 3))
Function definitions are as follows:

(defrec <DD-0>
        (a)
        (b)
        (cond ((lessp a b) (list 0 a))
              (t
               (let! (((@1:1 @1:2) (<DD-0> (diff a b) b)))
                     (list (add1 @1:1) @1:2))))))

The extracted realizer is

(<DD-0> a b)
```

The function **<DD-0>** with two arguments *a* and *b* is defined by CIG-recursion extracted from the CIG-inductive definition of **DD**; it is certain that the value of **b** is constant in the course of computation of **(<DD-0> a b)**. Declaring the function **<DD-0>** by **defrec** as above, it can be executed without consuming stacks by pushing the name and values of **b**.

References

[1] Alagić, S. and Arbib, M. *The Design of Well-Structured and Correct Programs.* Springer-Verlag, New York, 1978.

[2] Backus, J. "Can programming be liberated from the von Neumann style?" *Communications of ACM 21*, 8 (August 1978), pp. 613–641.

[3] Beeson, M. *The Foundations of Constructive Mathematics.* Springer-Verlag, Berlin, 1985.

[4] Beeson, M. "Proving programs and programming proofs". *Logic, Methodology, and Philosophy of Sciences VII*, R. Barcan Marcus, G. J. W. Dorn, and P. Weingartner, eds., pp. 51–82. North-Holland, Amsterdam, 1986.

[5] Constable, R. et al. *Implementing Mathematics in the NuPrl System.* Prentice-Hall, Englewood Cliffs, N.J., 1986.

[6] Coquand, T. and Huet G. "The calculus of constructions". Rapports de Recherche No. 530, INRIA. *Information and Computation 76* (1988), 2/3, pp. 95–120.

[7] Feferman, S. "Constructive theories of functions and classes". *Logic Colloquium '78*, pp. 159–224. North-Holland, Amsterdam, 1979.

[8] Foderaro, J., Sklower, K., and Layer, K. *The Franz Lisp Manual.* 1984.

[9] Gordon, M., Milner, R., and Wadsworth, C. *Edinburgh LCF.* Lecture Notes in Computer Science, vol. 78. Springer-Verlag, Berlin, 1979.

[10] Hayashi, S. "Extracting LISP programs from constructive proofs: A formal theory of constructive mathematics based on LISP". *Publications of the Research Institute for Mathematical Sciences 19* (1983), pp. 169–191.

[11] Hayashi, S. "**PX**: A system extracting programs from proofs". In *Formal Description of Programming Concepts-III*, M. Wirsing, ed. North-Holland, Amsterdam, 1987.

[12] Hayashi, S. "**PX** manual". In preparation.

[13] Hayashi, S. and Nakano, H. "**PX**: A computational logic". Preprint RIMS-573, Research Institute for Mathematical Sciences, Kyoto University; MIT Press, Cambridge, Mass., 1988.

[14] Ketonen, J. and Weening, J. S. "The language of an interactive proof checker". Report STAN–CS–83–992, Stanford University, 1983.

[15] Kleene, S. *Introduction to Metamathematics.* Van Nostrand, Princeton, N.J., 1952.

[16] Knuth, D. *The TEXbook.* Addison-Wesley, Reading, Mass., 1984.

[17] Martin-Löf, P. "Constructive mathematics and computer programming". *Logic, Methodology, and Philosophy of Science VI*, L. J. Cohen et al., eds., pp. 153–179. North-Holland, Amsterdam, 1982.

[18] Martin-Löf, P. "On the meanings of the logical constants and the justifications of the logical laws". Lectures given at Siena, April 1983. Included in *Proc. Third Japanese-Swedish Workshop*, Institute of New Generation Computing Technology, 1985.

[19] Plotkin, G. Lectures given at ASL Stanford meeting, July 1985.

[20] Scott, D. "Identity and existence in intuitionistic logic". *Applications of Sheaves*, M. P. Fourman, C. J. Mulvey, and D. S. Scott, eds., pp. 660–696. Lecture Notes in Mathematics, vol. 753. Springer-Verlag, Berlin, 1979.

[21] Takasu, S. and Nakahara, T. "Programming with mathematical thinking". *Proc. IFIP 83*, pp. 419–424. North-Holland, Amsterdam, 1983.

The Authors

GUY COUSINEAU was born in 1949. He obtained his Thèse d'Etat in Computer Science at the University of Paris 7 in 1977. He has been Maitre-Assistant at the University Pierre-et-Marie Curie in Paris and then Professor at the University of Paris 7 from 1981 to 1987. He is now Professor at the Ecole Normale Supérieure where he is the head of a research group that participates in the Formel Project. His research activities are in theoretical computer science and programming languages. Address: Prof. Guy Cousineau, Ecole Normale Supérieure, 45 rue d'Ulm, Paris, 75005–France.

JEAN-YVES GIRARD was born in 1947 in Lyon (France). His studies in mathematics and research in logic led to System F (polymorphic λ-calculus) in 1970; his Thèse d'Etat in 1972 was on the same subject. Later (1975–1985) he took up geometrical studies of ordinals (theory of dilators). His recent interests in theoretical computer science include linear logic and the geometry of interaction. He has published two books: *Proof Theory and Logical Complexity*, Bibliopolis, Napoli, 1987, and *Proof and Types* (with Y. Lafont and P. Taylor), Cambridge Tracts in Computer Science, 1983. He is currently working at

CNRS; his address: Prof. Jean-Yves Girard, Équipe de Logique Mathématique, UA 753 du CNRS, 75251 Paris Cedex 05, France.

SUSUMU HAYASHI is an associate professor of computer science in the Department of Applied Mathematics and Informatics of Ryukoku University. He received bachelor's and master's degrees from Rikkyo University, and the Ph.D. from the University of Tsukuba. His main research activities have been in logic, category theory, and computer science. His current interests are constructive mathematics, category theory, and type theory, for computer science. He developed the **PX** system and is the author, with H. Nakano, of it PX: A Computational Logic. Address: Prof. Susumu Hayashi, Ryukoku University, Dept. of Applied Math and Informatics, 1-5 Yokotani, Oe-cho Seta, Otsu-shi 520-21, Japan.

GERARD HUET is currently Research Director at the Rocquencourt branch of the French Institut National de Recherche en Informatique et Automatique (INRIA), where he heads the Formel research project. He has worked in automated deduction, equational logic and rewriting theory, programming language design, structured programming environments, and type theory. His current interest is the design and implementation of a proof support environment for constructive logic based on higher-order natural deduction type theory, in which programs consistent with their formal specifications can be extracted mechanically. Address: Dr. Gérard Huet, Groupe "FORMEL", INRIA, Domaine de Voluceau – Rocquencourt, 78153 Le Chesnay CEDEX, FRANCE.

ALBERT MEYER was a graduate student at Harvard in 1963–67, working on automata and complexity theory. While at CMU during 1967–69 he developed some of the basic results in machine-independent complexity theory. He has been at MIT since 1969.

Prof. Meyer discovered the first provably hard (exponential or more) decidable problems, and the first PSPACE-complete problem (regular expression inequivalence) as well as the Polynomial-Time Hierarchy in 1972. He developed metamathematics of Dynamic Logic in 1977–82, and gave a general formulation of models of the untyped lambda calculus in 1982. Recently he has been working on foundations of polymorphic type theory, denotational and operational semantics, logic of higher-order procedures, and semantics of concurrent processes. he is Editor-in-Chief of *Information and Computation* and editor of several other journals and scholarly handbooks. He supervised the Ph.D's of numerous active researchers in theoretical computer science. Address: Prof. Albert R. Meyer, M.I.T. Lab. for Computer Science, NE43–315, Cambridge, MA 02139.

JOHN C. MITCHELL is currently Assistant Professor in the Department of Computer Science at Stanford University. He received his B.S. in mathematics (with distinction) from Stanford in 1978, worked on numerical computation for the University of Wisconsin Solar Energy Laboratory from 1978-80, and received S.M. and Ph.D. degrees from MIT in 1982 and 1984. Prior to joining the Stanford faculty in 1988, he was Member of Technical Staff in the Computing Science Research Center at AT&T Bell Laboratories.

Prof. Mitchell's primary research interests are mathematical analysis of programming languages and applications of logic to computer science. Among his publications are studies of polymorphism and data abstraction, object-oriented languages, and algorithms for automatically inferring static properties of programs. He has also made contributions to database theory, program verification, relevance logic, and the complexity of various unification problems. In 1988, Mitchell received a Presidential Young Investigator Award from the National Science Foundation. Address: Prof. John C. Mitchell, Department of Computer Science, Stanford University, Stanford, CA 94305.

JOHN C. REYNOLDS received his Ph.D., in theoretical physics, from Harvard University in 1961. He worked at Argonne National Laboratory until 1970, and at Syracuse University until 1986. Presently, he is Professor of Computer Science at Carnegie Mellon University.

The general area of his research is the design and definition of programming langauges and languages for program specification. Specific topics include type theory and Algol-like languages. Address: Prof. John Reynolds, Computer Science Department, Carnegie–Mellon University, Schenley Park, Pittsburgh, PA 15213.

ANDRE SCEDROV is an Associate Professor of Mathematics and Computer Science at the University of Pennsylvania, where he recently received the Young Faculty Award of the Natural Sciences Association. His contributions are in logic, category theory, type theory, and the semantics of programming languages.

Born in Zagreb, Yugoslavia in 1955, he came to the United States in 1977 and received his Ph.D. in Mathematics from the State University of New York at Buffalo in 1981. He was a T. H. Hildebrandt Research Assistant Professor of Mathematics at the University of Michigan, Ann Arbor before coming to University of Pennsylvania. He has held several visiting positions and has lectured at many universities in North America, Europe, and Australia. Address: Prof. Andre Scedrov, University of Pennsylvania, Department of Mathematics, 33rd & Walnut Streets, Philadelphia, PA 19104.

The following contributors to this volume, who were not speakers at the Year of Programming institute, did not supply biographies.

Dr. Thierry Coquand, INRIA, Domaine de Voluceau – Rocquencourt, 78153 Le Chesnay CEDEX, FRANCE.

Dr. Ascander Suarez, Paris Research Laboratory, Digital Equipment Corporation, 83-85 avenue Victor Hugo, 92500 Rueil-Malmaison, Paris, FRANCE.

The Year of Programming on Videotape

All six of the Programming Institutes were recorded on videotape, and edited versions of these tapes have been prepared by MPA Productions, Inc., under the auspices of the Computer Sciences Department of The University of Texas at Austin. They are available for purchase in various combinations from individual lectures to the complete set. Tapes can be provided in all formats and standards; for most sessions, photocopies of the speakers' overhead-projector transparencies are also available.

For a complete listing of the tapes, including prices, please write to

Year of Programming (Tapes)
3103 Bee Caves Road, Suite 235
Austin, TX 78746
U.S.A

or call (512) 328–9800.